ISBN 978-1-5279-9513-0
PIBN 11010168

STATE OF NEW YORK

DEPARTMENT

OF

PUBLIC INSTRUCTION

FORTY-FOURTH ANNUAL REPORT

OF THE

STATE SUPERINTENDENT

For the School Year Ending July 31, 1897

VOL. II.

TRANSMITTED TO THE LEGISLATURE MARCH 28, 1898.

EXHIBIT No. 12

STATE CERTIFICATES

1. Questions Submitted at Examinations, 1897
2. Tabulated Statement of Examinations, 1897
3. List of Successful Candidates, 1897
4. Statistical Table, 1875 to 1897
5. Circular, Regulations and Program for 1898

82403

DEPARTMENT OF EDUCATION
LELAND STANFORD JUNIOR UNIVERSITY

I.

STATE CERTIFICATES

1. QUESTIONS SUBMITTED AT THE EXAMINATION FOR STATE CERTIFICATES

August 23-27, 1897

Every correct answer will receive 10 credits, and a proportionate number as the answer approximates correctness.

ALGEBRA

1. (a) What sum of money at b per cent. interest will produce c dollars interest in d years? (b) How many rods of fence are required to enclose a square field containing r acres? (c) If a pipe can empty $\frac{1}{m}$ of a tank in one minute, how many hours will it require to empty the entire tank? (d) What is the value per pound of a mixture of c pounds of tea at d cents and of b pounds at a cents?
2. Simplify the expression—$[-2x-\{3y-(2x-3y)+(3x-2y)\}+2x]$.
3. Find the prime factors of the following:
   (a) x^2-x-6
   (b) $a^2-b^2-c^2-2bc$
   (c) $a^{2m}+2a^mb+b^2$
   (d) x^3-y^3
4. (a) Reduce to its simplest form the complex fraction $\dfrac{1+\dfrac{a}{1-a}}{\dfrac{1+a}{1-a}}$
   (b) $\frac{x^2+3}{x-3}\times\frac{1}{x+3}-\frac{x-3}{x+3}=?$
5. Solve, (a) $\frac{a-bx}{b}-\frac{b-ax}{a}=ax+bx$.
   (b) $x^2+ax-x=a$.
6. Show that the equation $\frac{4x}{x+3}-\frac{x-3}{2x+5}=2$ is satisfied when x equals either 3 or $2\frac{1}{3}$
   (b) If $\sqrt{x+9}=6$, by what axiom may it be proved that $x+9=36$? (c) Prove, giving the fundamental principles of fractions applying, that the expression $\frac{m}{a-b}+\frac{n}{b-a}$ is equal to the expression $\frac{m}{a-b}-\frac{n}{a-b}$.
7. Solve for the values of x and y:
   $$\begin{cases}5x-y=13\\3xy-2y^2=10\end{cases}$$
8. Three towns are at the three angles of a triangle. From the first to the second through the third is 82 miles; from the first to the third through the second is 97 miles; from the second to the third through the first is 89 miles; find the direct distances between the towns.

7. A bond and mortgage for $800 given for 3 years at 6 per cent. per annum was sold the day it was made for such a sum as would net the purchaser 5 per cent. per annum on his investment. For how much was it sold?
8. If equal sums be put at interest for 1 yr. 8 mo. 12 da. at 5½ per cent. and 7 per cent. per annum, the difference in interest received on the two principals will be $7.65. Find the sum invested in each case.
9. The specific gravity of copper is 8.9, of silver 10.5, and in an alloy of these metals the weight of the copper is to the weight of the silver as 5:6. Find the ratio of the bulk of copper in the alloy to that of the silver.
10. The diagonal of a square field is 40 rods. How many acres does the field contain?

ASTRONOMY

1. For what is astronomy indebted to (a) Ptolemy; (b) to Kepler; (c) Thales, (d) Galileo; (e) Copernicus?
2. Name the classes of subordinate circles in the equinoctial system, and state the use of each.
3. What is the zodiac?
4. Give the commonly accepted theory to account for the heat of the sun.
5. Define the following terms: Conjunction, transit, occultation.
6. Represent by figure the effect of refraction of light on the apparent position of a heavenly body.
7. Draw a diagram to represent the relative position of the earth and sun in (a) winter; (b) summer.
8. Describe meteors as to (a) appearance; (b) supposed origin.
9. Mention some important discoveries that have been made concerning the sun by means of the spectroscope.
10. Name and locate by constellations three stars of the first magnitude.

BOOKKEEPING

Memoranda.—February 1, 1897, Elmer K. Jones, of Watertown, N. Y., begins business as a dealer in furniture, with a stock of goods and fixtures valued at $4,580 and $750 cash on hand in bank. He transacts business as follows: February 2d, sold E. G. Howard, for cash, one parlor set, 6 pieces, for $80, one bedroom set for $35, and 6 chairs at $1.85 each; sold Ezra Keyes, on account, one dining-room table for $26, 2 rockers at $6.50 each, and a sideboard for $42; bought of Gould & Stover, on account, one dozen commodes at $3.25 each, 2 dozen bedsteads at $4.75 each and 3 bedroom sets at $22.50 each. February 4th, sold Edward Titus, on account, one bedroom set for $33, one bedroom set for $27, 8 chairs at $2 each, and 1 couch for $16; paid freight and cartage $13.15; bought of R. G. Bostwick, for cash, 24 dozen unfinished chairs at $9. February 6th, paid clerk's salary $20; sold Elliott Graves 2 rockers at $10.50 each, 1 couch for $20, one writing desk for $21, one bookcase for $55, one hat rack for $25, one center table for $18, receiving in part payment $75 in cash, the balance being charged to account; sold C. L. Black, on his note for 60 days, 1 parlor set, 7 pieces, for $95. February 16th, Received of Elliott Graves his check on the First National Bank of Watertown to balance account; paid rent of store for February $75; sold Robert Beebe, for cash, 1 bureau for $16, and 1 table for $8.25. February 21st, discounted the note of C. L. Black (transaction of February 6th), at bank; paid clerk's salary $20. February 28th, received of Edward Titus, on account, $50; bought of Elbert Drake & Co., on account, 6 unfinished bedroom sets at $19 each; paid Gould & Stover account in full by check on the First National Bank of Watertown, deducting from their bill a discount of 5 per cent. (Stock and fixtures were this day inventoried at $5,803.50.)

Journalize (books of Elmer K. Jones), using proper abbreviations and conventions:

1. The investment.
2. The transaction of February 2d and 4th.
3. The transactions of February 6th and 16th.
4. The transactions of February 21st and 28th.

2. (a) Who, according to the Constitution, are citizens of the United States? (b) What law with reference to citizens of the United States is each state forbidden by the Constitution to make?
3. What has been the uniform method of adopting amendments to the national Constitution?
4. In general, a majority of the members chosen to each house of the state Legislature constitutes a quorum to do business. State an exception to this rule.
5. Name two officers with whom certificates of election returns are deposited by inspectors of election.
6. A body politic which makes laws for its own control is said to possess governmental power. Name two divisions of a state which have no governmental power.
7. Distinguish between concurrent action and joint action of the Senate and Assembly.
8. Give reasons for and against educational qualification for suffrage.
9. Name two officers having judicial power in school district matters. (b) Name two officers having executive power in school district matters. (c) In whom is the legislative power of a school district vested?
10. State the provisions of the compulsory attendance law in regard to children (a) between the ages of 8 and 12; (b) between the ages of 12 and 14; (c) between the ages of 14 and 16.

COMPOSITION AND RHETORIC

1. Explain the difference between grammar and rhetoric. Write a sentence which is grammatically correct but rhetorically faulty.
2. State some distinction in use between the following pairs of words, and illustrate with sentences: Thankful and grateful, right and privilege, interfere and interpose, irony and sarcasm. Select for answer three pairs of synonyms only.
3. Write a letter to the state Superintendent of Public Instruction, asking for a pamphlet copy of the consolidated school act. Give attention to the general form and punctuation of the letter, as well as to its contents. Give the direction of the envelope.
4. Name the figure found in each of the following sentences:
   (a) Hope, enchanted smiled, and waved her golden hair.
   (b) I see before me the gladiator lie.
   (c) The coat does not make the man.
   (d) His reasons are as two grains of wheat hid in two bushels of chaff.
   (e) It was written at white heat.
5. Define (a) alliteration, (b) harmony, (c) climax, (d) allegory.
6. Correct each of the following sentences and state what law or principle of rhetoric is violated:
   (a) An equestrian statue of General Grant on a horse stands in the park.
   (b) A torrent of superstition consumed the land.
   (c) He gave himself away.
   (d) When David came into the presence of Saul, he threw a javilin at him.
7. (a) William has made a great effort to succeed.
   (b) That was a heroic deed.
   (c) Macaulay said that Lord Byron was the most celebrated man of the nineteenth century.
   (d) He heard that we had left town.

   Vary the above sentences as specified in each case: In (a) deny the negative of the assertion; (b) emphasize by the use of the exclamatory or interrogative form; (c) change to the direct form of quotation; (d) abridge the clause to a phrase.
8. Mark the scansion of the following selections:

(a)

It was many and many a year ago,
  In a kingdom by the sea,
That a maiden lived whom you may know,
  By the name of Annabel Lee.

EXHIBIT No. 12

STATE CERTIFICATES

1. Questions Submitted at Examinations, 1897
2. Tabulated Statement of Examinations, 1897
3. List of Successful Candidates, 1897
4. Statistical Table, 1875 to 1897
5. Circular, Regulations and Program for 1898

82403

9. Draw the pattern of object given. Diameter of equilateral triangle pocket 1⅛ inches.

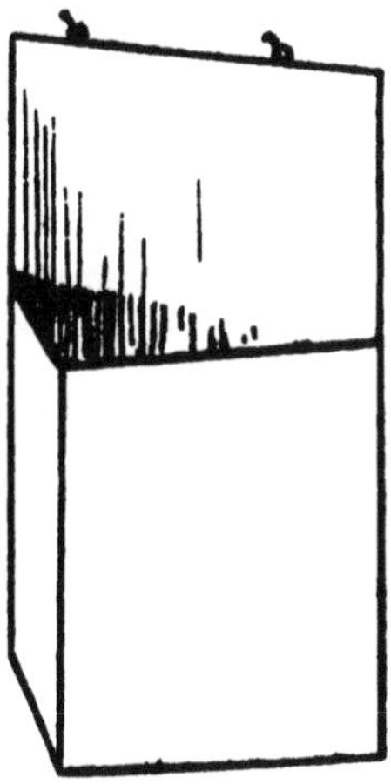

10. Draw to illustrate and indicate sharply, the difference between linear and mass drawing, using the half-tone given.

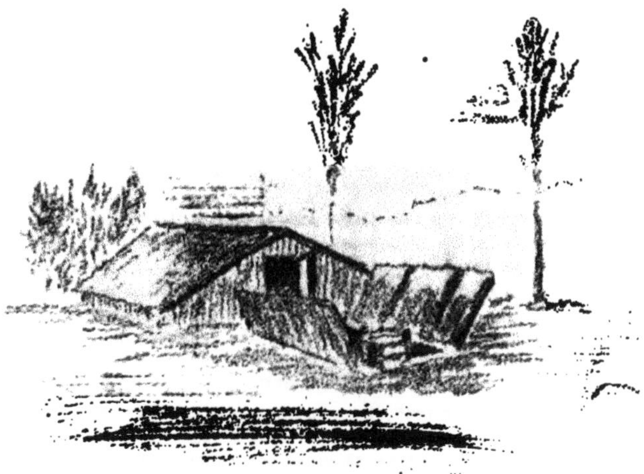

FRENCH

NAPOLÉON A SAINTE-HÉLÈNE

TRANSLATE:

A mesure que, l'ennui et l'inaction détruisant sa santé, il voyait la mort s'approcher, il s'entretenait plus fréquemment de philosophie et de religion. "Dieu, disait-il, est partout visible dans l'univers, et bien aveugles ou bien faibles sont les yeux qui ne l'aperçoivent pas. Pour moi, je le vois dans le nature entiére, je me sens sous sa main toutepuissante, et je ne cherche pas à douter de son existence, car je n'en ai pas peur. Je crois qui'il est aussi indulgent qu' il est grand, et je suis convaincu que revenus dans son vaste sein nous y trouverons confirmés tous les pressentiments de la conscience humaine, et que là sera bien ou sera mal, ce que les esprits vraiment éclairés ont déclaré bien ou mal sur la terre. Je mets dè côté les erreurs des peuples, qu'on peut reconnaitre

9. Two persons, A and B, can do a piece of work in 16 days. They work together 4 days; after which B finishes the work in 36 days more. In what time can each do it separately?

10. (a) Simplify the expression $4^{-\frac{5}{2}}$. (b) Divide $8\sqrt{7}$ by $2\sqrt{8}$ and express the result in its simplest form. (c) Simplify the expression $\left(\frac{a^{\frac{1}{m+1}}}{b^m}\right)^{m^2-1}$

AMERICAN HISTORY

1. Give a short account of the struggle between the early settlers of St. Augustine and those of Port Royal, South Carolina.
2. The English army in 1778 left Philadelphia to concentrate on the city of New York. What battle, with what results, was fought on the march?
3. Mention some respect in which the treaty of 1783 was not carried out satisfactorily by (a) England, (b) the United States.
4. What were the reasons which influenced the selection of the site of the capital of the United States?
5. What was the condition of the commercial interests of the United States during the last term of Jefferson's administration and the first term of Madison's administration, 1805-1813? What was the cause of that condition?
6. Name the political party which advocated, at the presidential election specified, the following measures: the re-establishment of the United States bank, in 1840; the extension of slavery in the territories, in 1860; the reduction of the existing tariff in 1888?
7. Wendell Philips wrote in the presidential campaign of 1864, "The administration I regard as a civil and military failure." Mention some of the facts used in support of such statements and as arguments against the re-election of Lincoln.
8. (a) What was the object of Sheridan's raid in the Shenandoah valley? (b) Locate that valley.
9. Mention an important historical fact connected with each of the following governors of this colony or state: Peter Stuyvesant, Thomas Dongan, George Clinton. Answer two only.
10. (a) Why was it considered essential to the success of the present form of government that New York should adopt the Constitution, although nine states had already ratified the federal compact? (b) What were some of the special objections urged in this state against the adoption of the Constitution? (c) Mention some important prerogative, exercised by the state under the confederation, but delegated to the general government under the Constitution.

ARITHMETIC

1. Express by signs of per cent., by a decimal, and by a common fraction in its lowest terms, each of the following: (a) 3-16 per cent.; (b) 4 2-7 per cent.; (c) five sixty-fourths; (d) three thousand one hundred fifteen thousandths.
2. Give a full classification of each of the following numbers: (a) 264; (b) 3-7 lb.; (c) 11 horses.
3. A cubic foot of water weighs 1,000 ounces avoirdupois, and the specific gravity of gold is 19.34 (i, e., gold weighs 19.34 times as much as water). Find the weight of a piece of gold 8 in. by 4 in. by 2 in.
4. The difference in time between New York (74 degree W.) and Constantinople is 6 hr. 51 min. 12 sec. Find the longitude of Constantinople.
5. After diminishing a certain number by 2-3 of itself, and the remainder by 2-11 of itself, the remainder is 45. Find the number.
6. I insured my house and furniture at an expense of $33.60, paying 3-5 of 1 per cent. premium for insuring the house and 1 1-5 per cent. for the furniture. The amount of insurance on the house was one ane one-half times that on the furniture. Required the amount of insurance on both.

7. A bond and mortgage for $800 given for 3 years at 6 per cent. per annum was sold the day it was made for such a sum as would net the purchaser 5 per cent. per annum on his investment. For how much was it sold?
8. If equal sums be put at interest for 1 yr. 8 mo. 12 da. at 5½ per cent. and 7 per cent. per annum, the difference in interest received on the two principals will be $7.65. Find the sum invested in each case.
9. The specific gravity of copper is 8.9, of silver 10.5, and in an alloy of these metals the weight of the copper is to the weight of the silver as 5:6. Find the ratio of the bulk of copper in the alloy to that of the silver.
10. The diagonal of a square field is 40 rods. How many acres does the field contain?

ASTRONOMY

1. For what is astronomy indebted to (a) Ptolemy; (b) to Kepler; (c) Thales; (d) Galileo; (e) Copernicus?
2. Name the classes of subordinate circles in the equinoctial system, and state the use of each.
3. What is the zodiac?
4. Give the commonly accepted theory to account for the heat of the sun.
5. Define the following terms: Conjunction, transit, occultation.
6. Represent by figure the effect of refraction of light on the apparent position of a heavenly body.
7. Draw a diagram to represent the relative position of the earth and sun in (a) winter; (b) summer.
8. Describe meteors as to (a) appearance; (b) supposed origin.
9. Mention some important discoveries that have been made concerning the sun by means of the spectroscope.
10. Name and locate by constellations three stars of the first magnitude.

BOOKKEEPING

Memoranda.—February 1, 1897, Elmer K. Jones, of Watertown, N. Y., begins business as a dealer in furniture, with a stock of goods and fixtures valued at $4,580 and $750 cash on hand in bank. He transacts business as follows: February 2d, sold E. G. Howard, for cash, one parlor set, 6 pieces, for $80, one bedroom set for $35, and 6 chairs at $1.85 each; sold Ezra Keyes, on account, one dining-room table for $26, 2 rockers at $6.50 each, and a sideboard for $42; bought of Gould & Stover, on account, one dozen commodes at $3.25 each, 2 dozen bedsteads at $4.75 each and 3 bedroom sets at $22.50 each. February 4th, sold Edward Titus, on account, one bedroom set for $33, one bedroom set for $27, 8 chairs at $2 each, and 1 couch for $16; paid freight and cartage $13.15; bought of R. G. Bostwick, for cash, 24 dozen unfinished chairs at $9. February 6th, paid clerk's salary $20; sold Elliott Graves 2 rockers at $10.50 each, 1 couch for $20, one writing desk for $21, one bookcase for $55, one hat rack for $25, one center table for $18, receiving in part payment $75 in cash, the balance being charged to account; sold C. L. Black, on his note for 60 days, 1 parlor set, 7 pieces, for $95. February 16th, Received of Elliott Graves his check on the First National Bank of Watertown to balance account; paid rent of store for February $75; sold Robert Beebe, for cash, 1 bureau for $16, and 1 table for $8.25. February 21st, discounted the note of C. L. Black (transaction of February 6th), at bank; paid clerk's salary $20. February 28th, received of Edward Titus, on account, $50; bought of Elbert Drake & Co., on account, 6 unfinished bedroom sets at $19 each; paid Gould & Stover account in full by check on the First National Bank of Watertown, deducting from their bill a discount of 5 per cent. (Stock and fixtures were this day inventoried at $5,803.50.)

Journalize (books of Elmer K. Jones), using proper abbreviations and conventions:
1. The investment.
2. The transaction of February 2d and 4th.
3. The transactions of February 6th and 16th.
4. The transactions of February 21st and 28th.

5. Post the several journal entries.
6. Write (a) the note mentioned in transaction of February 6th, and (b) the endorsement thereon necessary when discounted.
7. Make an itemized bill of the transaction with Elliott Graves February 6th.
8. Write (a) the check mentioned in transaction of February 28th with Gould & Stover, and (b) the endorsement necessary when presented for payment.
9. Make trial balances of ledger footings and differences.
10. Make statement showing the condition of the business February 28th (setting forth resources and liabilities, gain or loss, and net present worth).

BOTANY

1. (a) What name is applied to each of the two great divisions of plants? (b) Give three distinguishing characteristics of each.
2. Distinguish between (a) stem; (b) root; (c) root stock; (d) tuber; (e) name a plant that has root stocks and one that has tubers.
3. Name a plant whose flowers is (a) a raceme; (b) an umbel; (c) a spike; (d) a spadis; (e) a catkin.
4. In the processes of nature what ends are subserved (a) by fruits; (b) by the colors of flowers; (c) by the nectar of flowers?
5. (a) In what part of a plant is mineral matter found most abundantly? (b) Through what process of nature is it there deposited?
6. Flowers may be (a) staminate; (b) pistilate; (c) perfect; (d) complete; (e) regular. What is meant by each of these terms?
7. Name two natural means of propagation of (a) plum; (b) dahlia; (c) strawberry; (d) quack grass; (e) raspberry.
8. What is the botanical term for (a) the silk and (b) the tassel of Indian corn; (c) the turnip; (d) the cabbage; (e) celery? In the last three the question refers to the edible portion.
9. (a) Explain the adaptation of plants to their habitat in dry countries. (b) Give an example of such adaptation.
10. Name a plant whose flowers are adapted to (a) close fertilization; (b) cross fertilization.

CHEMISTRY

1. Give an example of a chemical change effected (a) by light; (b) by heat; (c) by electricity; (d) by affinity alone.
2. (a) Give a method of preparing chlorine from common salt. (b) Give two physical and two chemical properties of chlorine.
3. What is the law of (a) definite (constant) proportions; (b) multiple proportions?
4. Distinguish between the nomenclature of (a) acids; (b) bases; (c) salts.
5. (a) Give two reasons for believing that the air is only a mixture of its component parts. (b) Name four substances which are always found in the air, and which may be said to compose it.
6. Select two of the following groups, and name two elements of each: (a) Chlorine group; (b) sulphur group; (c) nitrogen group.
7. Name (a) a metal which at ordinary temperatures will decompose water by uniting with its oxygen; (b) a metal which will so unite when heated to redness.
8. Give (a) three allotropic forms of carbon; (b) two of sulphur.
9. Give the symbols and the commercial names of (a) two salts; (b) two acids.
10. (a) Why is carbon called a reducing agent? (b) Describe an experiment in which it acts as such agent.

CIVIL GOVERNMENT AND SCHOOL LAW

1. (a) What was the purpose of the framers of the Constitution in providing that the President should be chosen by electors rather than by popular vote? (b) Has their purpose been realized in this matter? (c) Give reason for your answer.

Gras wuchert zwischen den breiten Fliesen, und in der Morgendämmerung flattern Tausende von Tauben um den freistehenden, hohen Turm herum. Auf drei Seiten bist du von Bogengängen umgeben. Unter ihnen sitzt still der Türke mit seiner langen Pfeife, der schöne Griechenknabe lehnt sich an die Säule und betrachtet die aufgerichteten Trophäen, die hohen Masten, Andenken an die verschwundene Macht. Die Flaggen hängen gleich Trauerflor herab. Ein Mädchen ruht dort aus, die schweren Eimer, mit Wasser gefüllt, hat sie hingesetzt, das Joch, an welchem sie dieselben getragen hat, ruht auf einer ihrer Schultern, sie lehnt sich an den Siegesmast. Es ist kein Feenschloss, sondern eine Kirche die du vor dir erblickst, die vergoldeten Kuppeln, die glänzenden Kugeln ringsum glänzen in meinem Lichte; die prächtigen ehernen Rosse dort oben haben Reisen gemacht, wie das eherne Pferd im Märchen, sie sind erst hierher, dann fort von hier und wieder hierher gereist. Siehst du die bunte Pracht der Mauern und der Fenster? Es hat das Ansehen, als ob das Genie den Launen eines Kindes nachgegeben hätte, indem es diesen seltsamen Tempel schmückte. Siehst du auf der Säule den geflügelten Löwen? Das Gold glänzt noch, die Flügel aber sind gebunden, der Löwe ist todt, denn der König des Meeres ist todt, die grossen Hallen stehen verödet, und wo früher die herrlichsten Gemälde prangten, scheint jetzt die nackte Mauer durch. Der Lazzarone schläft unter dem Bogengange, dessen Fussboden früher nur der vornehmste Adel betreten durfte. Aus dem tiefen Brunnen oder auch vielleicht aus den Gefängnissen bei der Seufzerbrücke tönt Jammer, wie zu der Zeit, als das Tambourin aus den bunten Gondeln erscholl, als der Brautring von dem glänzenden Bucentoro zur Adria hinunterflog, zur Adria, der Königin der Meere. Adria! Hülle dich in Nebel! Lass den Witwenschleier deinen Busen verhüllen, hänge ihn über das Mausoleum deines Bräutigams: das marmorne gespenstige Venedig!"

Hans Christian Andersen.

GRAMMAR

EACH AND ALL

Little thinks, in the field, yon red-cloaked clown
Of thee from the hill-top looking down;
The heifer that lows in the upland farm,
Far-heard, lows not thine ear to charm;
The sexton, tolling his bell at noon,
Deems not that great Napoleon
Stops his horse, and lists with delight,
While his files sweep round yon Alpine height,
Nor knowest thou what argument
Thy life to thy neighbor's creed has lent.
All are needed by each one;
Nothing is fair or good alone.

The first six questions refer to the above selection.

In order to secure some degree of uniformity in answer papers, it is recommended that candidates observe the following suggestions:

1. Clauses are principal or subordinate. Subordinate clauses include (a) subject clauses; (b) objective clauses; (c) adjective clauses; (d) adverbial clauses.

2. In naming a clause, include only its unmodified subject and unmodified predicate.

3. In giving modifiers, if words, name the parts of speech to which they belong. In like manner state the character of modifying phrases and clauses, as adjective, adverbial, etc.

4. An object of a transitive verb is classed as a modifier of that verb.

5. In parsing a noun or pronoun, observe the following order: Class, person, number, gender, case. Give the reason for case. In parsing a relative pronoun, state the agreement with its antecedent.

6. In giving the syntax of a noun or pronoun, give only the case and the reason for it.

7. Verbs are divided into two classes, viz., transitive and intransitive. A transitive verb may be used in the active or the passive voice.

(b) This is the forest primeval. The murmuring pines and the hemlocks,
Bearded with moss, and in garments green, indistinct in the twilight,—

(c) A mighty fortress is our God,
A bulwark never failing;
Our helper He amid the flood
Of mortal ills prevailing.

9-10. Write an article of from 100 to 150 words, giving an account of a real or imaginary school meeting.

DRAWING

1. (a) Sketch a unit of design, and by shading indicate three tones in analogous harmony. Letter the same.
(b) What process is necessary to produce the color known as blue-green?
(c) Name the warm hues found in the spectrum of 18 colors.

2. Sketch to represent a group of five poplar trees; show perspective in position, and in the shading.

3. (a) What is the peculiarity of all the recesses in Egyptian arthitecture?
(b) The egg and dart moulding belongs to what class of ornament?

4. (a) Copy sketch given. (b) Conventionalize the full front within a pentagon, and the buds within a triangle. (c) Start a pattern which will repeat, and produce a design.

5. The triangular space given is to be filled with main lines based upon the laws of growth, the lines must balance (while filling necessary space), in such manner that the support for the horizontal bar shall be ornamental.

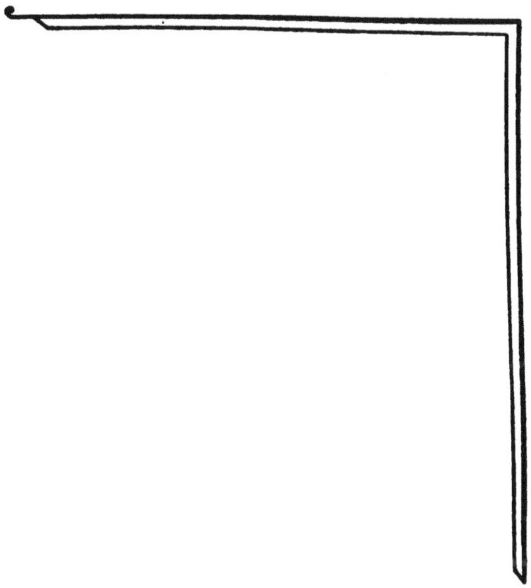

6. Copy sketch and draw the pole shown, as lying on the ground line.

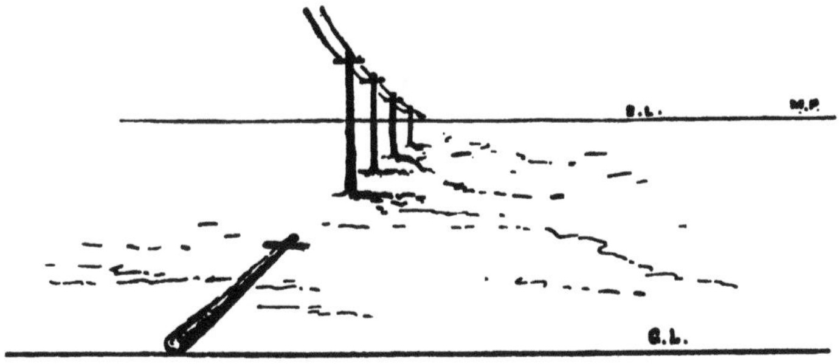

7. Read the working drawing given, and sketch the object thus described.

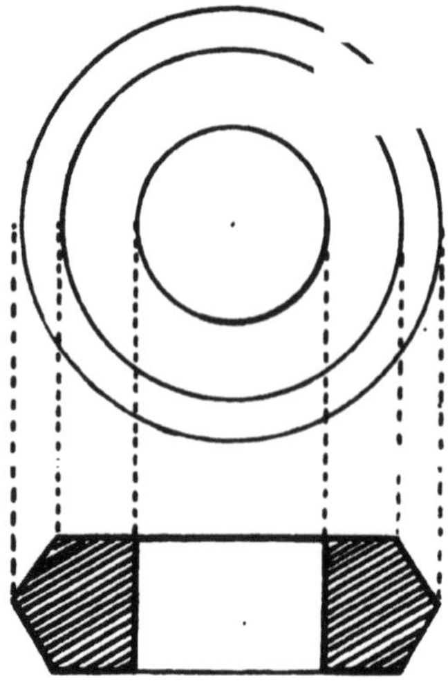

8. Within lines given inscribe two circles tangent to each other.

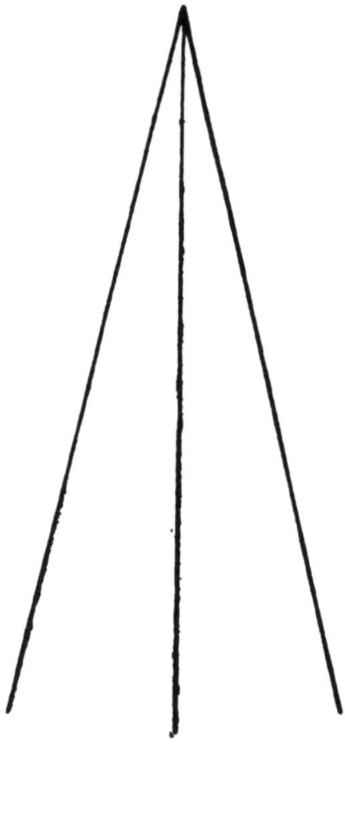

9. Draw the pattern of object given. Diameter of equilateral triangle pocket 1½ inches.

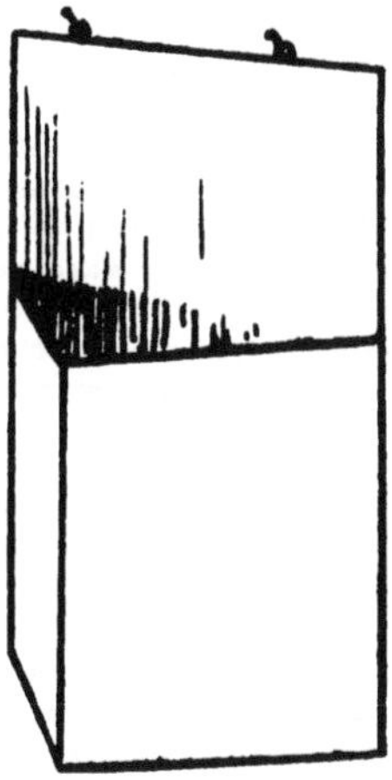

10. Draw to illustrate and indicate sharply, the difference between linear and mass drawing, using the half-tone given.

FRENCH

NAPOLÉON A SAINTE-HÉLÈNE

TRANSLATE:

A mesure que, l'ennui et l'inaction détruisant sa santé, il voyait la mort s'approcher, il s'entretenait plus fréquemment de philosophie et de religion. " Dieu, disait-il, est partout visible dans l'univers, et bien aveugles ou bien faibles sont les yeux qui ne l'aperçoivent pas. Pour moi, je le vois dans le nature entière, je me sens sous sa main toutepuissante, et je ne cherche pas à douter de son existence, car je n'en ai pas peur. Je crois qui'il est aussi indulgent qu' il est grand, et je suis convaincu que revenus dans son vaste sein nous y trouverons confirmés tous les pressentiments de la conscience humaine, et que là sera bien ou sera mal, ce que les esprits vraiment éclairés ont déclaré bien ou mal sur la terre. Je mets dè côté les erreurs des peuples, qu'on peut reconnaitre à ce trait que l'erreur de l'un n'est jamais celle de l'autre; mais ce que les grands esprits de toutes les nations auront déclaré bon ou mauvais, restera dans le sein de Dieu. . . ."

Conduit par ces sujets sublimes à occuper de certaines questions morales, Napoléon s'entretenait de ce qu'on avait appelé son fatalisme. "Sur ce sujet, disait-il, comme sur tous les autres, la calomnie a tracé de mes opinions de vraies caricatures. On a voulu me représenter comme une espèce de musulman stupide, qui voyait tout écrit là-haut, et qui ne se serait détourné ni devant un précipice, ni devant un cheval lancé au galop, par cette idée que notre vie, notre mort, ne dépendent pas de nous, mais d'un destin implacable et impossible à fléchir. S'il en était ainsi, l'homme devrait se mettre dans son lit à sa naissance, et n'en plus sortir, attendant que Dieu fit arriver les aliments à sa bouche. L'homme deviendrait stupidement inerte. Ce n'est pas moi, qui pendant le cours des plus longues guerres ai tant déployé d'efforts, hélas! sans y réussir toujours, pour faire prédominer l'intelligence humaine sur le hasard, ce n'est pas moi puis penser de la sorte! Ma croyance, et celle de tout être raisonable, c'est que l'homme est ici-bas chargé de son sort, qu'il a le droit et le devoir de le rendre par son industrie le meilleur possible. . . ."

"A la guerre on a beau faire, le péril est presque partous égal. J'ai vu des hommes quitter une place comme dangereuse, et être frappés juste à celle qu'ils venaient de prendre comme plus sûre. On s'agite donc vainement à la guerre, on perd en s'agitant son sang-froid, son courage, sans éviter le danger, et le mieux évidemment est de se résigner aux chances de son état, de ne pas plus penser aux projectiles qui traversent l'air qu'au vent qui souffle dans vos cheveux.

"Alors on a tout son courage, tout son sang-froid, tout son esprit, et on recouvre avec le calme la clairvoyance. Voilà mon fatalisme, voilà celui que je prêchais à mes soldats, en y employant les formes qui leur convenaient, en cherchant à leur persuader que leur destin était arrêté là-haut, qu'ils n'y pouvaient rien changer par la lâcheté, que dès lors le mieux était de se donner les honneurs du courage, et au précepte j'aujoutais l'example on affichant sur mon front que tous regardaient, une insouciance qui avait fini par être sincère.—*Thiers.*

GENERAL HISTORY

1. Give a brief account of any two of the following events of Roman history: The proscriptions of Sulla, the conspiracy of Cataline, the battle of Cannae, the civil war of Caesar and Pompey.
2. What was the effect of the Crusades (a) on the wealth and power of the papacy; (b) on the intellectual development of Europe; (c) To what extent was the object of the Crusades attained?
3. (a) What was the cause of the thirty years' war? (b) What was its effect on the German nation? (c) Mention one of the important events of the war.
4. (a) What was the cause of the Crimean War? (b) What nations were allied against Russia in that war? (c) About what stronghold were the principal operations of the war?
5. Give a brief account of England under the Commonwealth, stating (a) the form of government; (b) approximate duration; (c) its executive head; (d) the manner of its termination.

HISTORY OF GREECE.

6. Mention some important fact connected with each of the following persons: Phidias, Sappho, Solon, Xerxes, Aristides.
7. Compare the Spartans and Athenians as to (a) the cultivation of the fine arts, (b) commercial enterprise, (c)aristocratic tendencies, (d) military spirit.
8. What was the cause and the result of the Peloponnesian War?
9. What was the object of the confederacy of Delos? Locate Delos.
10. (a) What "was the retreat of the ten thousand?" (b) Of what service to the Greeks were the facts learned during this remarkable march?

GENERAL LITERATURE

1. Relate briefly the incidents of the play Macbeth.
2. State Macbeth's motives for the murder of Duncan and Banquo, and for his intention to destroy Macduff.
3. Describe fully the character which Shakespeare illustrates in Lady Macbeth.
4. What historical setting has the Scarlet Letter in time, place and character?
5. Mention an important foreign office which Hawthorne held, and give the title of a work which is the result of this sojourn or other foreign visits.
6. Discuss briefly the sentiment and the lesson of Thanatopsis.
7. (a) For what besides his purely literary work is the name of Bryant famous? (b) Discuss his rank among American poets.
8. Discuss Tennyson's poetry as to (a) its scope, (b) its form, and (c) its place in modern literature.
9. (a) Give a brief historical account of the palace and fortress Alhambra. (b) What circumstances led to the writing of the book Alhambra?
10. Relate briefly the story told in "The Pilgrim of Love."

GEOGRAPHY

1. (a) Show that on the 22d of June the sun's rays are more nearly vertical at the latitude of New York than at the equator. (b) Why then is it warmer at that time at the equator than at New York?
2. What climate is necessary for raising (a) coffee; (b) cotton; (c) oats? Under what conditions might all these products be raised in the same latitude?
3. (a) What places on the earth have the days and nights equal throughout the year? (b) What places have six months of day and six months of night?
4. Mention four great rivers which have their sources in the melting snows of the Himalaya mountains.
5. What is the most valuable product of (a) Alaska; (b) Brazil; (c) New Foundland; (d) Florida; (e) Cuba?
6. Mention and locate a great delta formation of (a) North America; (b) Asia; (c) Africa; (d) South America. What is the character of the soil deposited at these formations?
7. What city is the chief educational center of (a) Scotland; (b) Prussia; (c) Ireland; (d) France?
8. What waters would be traversed on a direct voyage from the mouth of the Danube to the mouth of the Thames?
9. (a) How do the mountain and desert districts of Asia affect the climate of Egypt? (b) How does the Sahara desert affect the climate of southern Europe?
10. Mention a great seaport of each of the following countries, connected with New York by steamship lines: (a) Scotland; (b) Denmark; (c) Germany; (d) Holland; (e) France.

GEOLOGY

1. Give the accepted theory for the formation of limestones.
2. What is meant by the following terms as applied to rock formations: (a) stratified; (b) metamorphic; (c) igneous.
3. Define (a) erosion; (b) folds; (c) fault; (d) drift; (e) outcrop.
4. Under what conditions are glaciers formed?
5. Give the names of the main divisions of paleozoic time.
6. (a) What is the name of the primitive rock? (b) Where in this state is it principally found? (c) How do all rocks of later formation differ from the primitive rock structure?
7. Why is it highly improbable that coal will ever be found in quantities in this state?
8. Arrange the following names of rocks in the order of their deposition, beginning with the oldest: Niagara, corniferous, Trenton, carboniferous, glacial.
9. (a) What are the constituents of granite? (b) How does gneiss differ from granite? (c) What deposit contains large quantities of aluminum?
10. Name five natural agencies which have caused changes in rock formations.

GEOMETRY

1. Prove: Two triangles are equal when the three sides of the one equal respectively the three sides of the other.
2. Prove: The angle formed by two secants meeting without the circumference is measured by one-half the difference of the intercepted arcs.
3. In the quadrilateral ABCD, let E, F, G and H be the middle points of the sides. Prove: EFGH is a parallelogram.

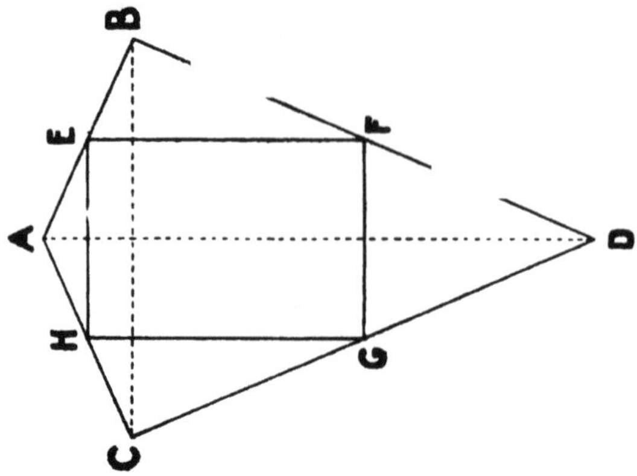

4. Construct a mean proportional between two given straight lines, and give proof.

Note.—In question 5 construct the figure accurately, using instruments; indicate resultant lines clearly; leave all auxiliary lines on paper; do not give proof.

5. Let AB be a given line and C and D any two points without that line. Construct a circle whose center shall be in the line AB, and whose circumference shall pass through the points C and D.
6. Define: (a) equal polygons, (b) similar polygons, (c) equivalent polygons, (d) regular polygons.
7. State and prove the proposition concerning the area of a trapezoid.

Note.—In the following problems, indicate the operations:

8. (a) Find, to three decimal places the area of a triangle having equal sides each 5 inches in length. (b) If the radius of a circle is 6 inches, find the area of a sector of 10 degrees.
9. (a) The diagonal of a square is d; what is its area? (b) The radii of two circles are m and n respectively. What is the ratio of their areas?
10. The base of a triangle is m, its altitude is n. The base of an equivalent rectangle is b; find its altitude.

GERMAN

Fünfzehnter Abend.

TRANSLATE:

„Ich habe," sagte der Mond, „dir von Pompeji dieser Leiche einer Stadt, in der Reihe der lebendigen Städte ausgestellt, erzählt; ich kenne eine andere noch seltsamere, sie ist keine Leiche, aber das Gespenst einer Stadt. Ueberall, wo die Strahlen der Springbrunnen in Marmorbecken plätschern, kommt es mir vor, als hörte ich das Märchen von der schwimmenden Stadt. Ja, der Strahl des Wassers mag von ihr erzählen, die Wellen des Strandes mögen von hr singen! Ueber die Fläche des Meeres ruht oft ein Nebel, das ist ihr Witwenschleier; der Bräutigam des Meeres ist todt, sein Schloss und seine Stadt ist sein Mausoleum! Kennst du diese Stadt? Nie hörte sie das Rollen der Räder oder den Hufschlag des Pferdes in ihren Strassen, dort schwimmt nur der Fisch herum, und gespensterhaft fliegt die schwarze Gondel über das grüne Wasser. Ich will," sagte der Mond, „dir das Forum der Stadt, den grössten Platz derselben, zeigen, und du wirst dich in die Stadt der Märchen versetzt glauben. Das

The examination in General Literature for 1898 will be limited to Shakespeare's "King Lear," Thackeray's "Henry Esmond," George Eliot's "Romola," Whittier's "Snow Bound" and "Tent on the Beach," and Thoreau's "Walden," together with the literary and personal character of their respective authors.

In the Natural Sciences, Bookkeeping, Composition and Rhetoric, the ordinary text-books will furnish all needed information.

In Civil Government, special attention will be given to the Constitution of the United States and of the state of New York.

In School Law, give attention to the rules and regulations of the Department of Public Instruction in addition to the provisions of the consolidated school law of 1894, and amendments thereto.

Candidates are required to fill out a copy of the following statement before entering upon an examination:

Statement of Candidate

Candidates who have received Partial Certificates for previous examinations (within two years), will submit them with this statement to be transmitted to the State Superintendent. They will be returned with the New Partial Certificate, or with the State Certificate, if issued.

Examination held at..August 22 to 26, 1898.
Full name.................................... Residence..................................
P. O. Address............, Age......years. Successful experience in teaching......years.
Give three references as to experience, with names and post-office addresses.
Is this your first examination for a State Certificate?..
If not, when and where yere you present at previous examinations?....................
Give three references as to moral character, with name and post-office addresses.
If you are not a resident of the state of New York, do you intend to teach in this state?..

I hereby certify that the foregoing statement is correct in every particular.

Signature of Candidate......................................

Copies of the above statement will be supplied at the examinations.

General Regulations

1. The printed questions will be sent to the examiners in sealed envelopes, and these will be first opened in the presence of the class at the time indicated in the accompanying program for the examination in each subject.

2. For evidence as to good character and successful experience, reference may be made to school commissioners, city superintendents, principals of academies, and high schools.

3. All applicants entering the examination for the first time must be present Monday afternoon, August 22, and must register their names and give such other information as the examiners may require, before taking a question paper. Candidates who have passed in a part of the subjects at a previous examination, need be present on the half-days only on which examinations occur in those subjects which they intend to take at this examination; but they must be present at the beginning of such half-day session, and should bring with them all partial certificates obtained at previous examinations.

4. The examination in each subject is restricted to the half-day designated in the accompanying program.

5. Penmanship will be judged from the papers on Geography.

6. In the solution of all problems, process should be indicated. The simple answer, without the process by which it was obtained, will not be accepted.

Candidates will be informed of the results of the examination as early as practicable.

7. Candidates will not be permitted to take to the examination room books or papers of any description.

8. In parsing a verb, observe the following order: Principal parts, regular or irregular, transitive or intransitive, voice, mode, tense, person, number, agreement; give the special use of an infinitive or a participle after tense.

1. Select and classify three subordinate clauses.
2. Give (a) three modifiers of clown (line 1) and (b) three modifiers of heifer (line 3).
3. State what each infinitive and participle modifies.
4. Select and classify as parts of speech the words which connect clauses.
5. Give syntax of (a) lows (line 3); (b) ear (line 4); (c) argument (line 9).
6. (a) Rewrite the eleventh line, changir· the voice of the verb; (d) describe the changes made.

> Like the tiger, that seldom desists from pursuing man after having once preyed upon human flesh, the reader, who has once gratified his appetite with calumny, makes ever after the most agreeable feast upon murdered reputation.
>
> OLIVER GOLDSMITH.

7-8. (a) Give the subject and predicate of the principal clause of the above sentence. (b) Give the modifiers of such subject, and (c) of such predicate. (d) Do the same with each subordinate clause. (e) Give the modifiers, if any, of all other words.

9. Give the syntax of me and opinion, in the sentence: He asked me my opinion. (b) Recast the sentence, using the passive voice of the verb, and give syntax of the same words.

10. Illustrate the use of (a) an infinitive as the object of a transitive verb; (b) a clause as an appositive.

LATIN

Caesar, quod memoria tenebat Lucium Cassium consulem occisum, exercitumque ejus ab Helvetiis pulsum et sub jugum missum, concedendum non putabat, neque homines inimico animo, data facultate per provinciam itineris faciendi, temperaturos ab injuria et maleficio existimabat.

Caesar primo et propter multitudinem hostium et propter eximiam opinionem virtutis, proelio supersedere statuit; quotidie tamen equestribus proeliis, quid hostis virtute posset et quid nostri auderent, periclitabatur.

Huic magnis praemiis pollicitationibusque persuadet, uti ad hostes transeat, et, quid fieri velit edocet.

1-4. Translate:

5. Give the principal parts and the voice, mode, and tense of the following verbs: (a) pulsum (line 2); (b) supersedere (line 7); (c) auderent (line 8); (d) fieri (line 11); (e) edocet (line 12).
6. Give the syntax of (a) Cassium (line 1); (b) consulem (line 1); (c) itineris (line 4); (d) huic (line 10); (e) quid (line 11).
7. Select (a) a gerundive and account for its case; (b) a passive infinitive and give its subject.
8. Select a verb (a) in the active periphrastic conjugation; (b) in the passive periphrastic conjugation, and give the subject of each; (c) select a deponent verb and give its mode and tense.
9. Account for the mode and tense of (a) posset (line 8); (b) transeat (line 11); (c) change the clause, quid fieri velit, (line 11) to direct discourse.
10. Give a synopsis of volo in the first person singular of the indicative and subjunctive.

METHODS AND SCHOOL ECONOMY

1. Show why pupils generally acquire a better knowledge of English grammar, when taught by a teacher who has a knowledge of the grammar of some other language, especially Latin.
2. In teaching physiology to children of the lower grades, what should be the chief aim?
3. What is the maximum number of pupils that should be seated in a room 20 x 30?
4. (a) State the essential conditions of the proper ventilation of a schoolroom. (b) Describe some mechanical device to facilitate the removal of impure air.

5. Mention three proper incentives to study and compare their relative value.
6. State what considerations should guide the teacher in making a program as to (a) relative length and frequency of a recitation; (b) order of recitations.
7. Give a method for explaining the rule for pointing off the product in the multiplication of decimals.
8. Outline a year's work in reading for an eighth grade class as to (a) character of books; (b) number of books; (c) method of conducting the work.
9. Arrange a topical plan for teaching the geography of South America and give reason for the order followed.
10. Outline the first lesson in civics for a grammar grade.

ORTHOGRAPHY

Each of the following words has two credits assigned to it.

1. peaceable,
2. laity,
3. financier,
4. pneumonia,
5. pavilion,
6. fascination,
7. diphtheria,
8. condescension,
9. auxiliary,
10. Susquehanna,
11. benefited,
12. architect,
13. believer,
14. luscious,
15. miracle,
16. velocity,
17. precocious,
18. sequel,
19. felicity,
20. corridor,
21. piercing,
22. proposal,
23. luncheon,
24. control,
25. Venezuela,
26. seizing,
27. bureau,
28. chaos,
29. extravagant,
30. autocratic,
31. cholera,
32. scaling,
33. miscellaneous,
34. preferred,
35. acquittal,
36. idiom,
37. balance,
38. valise,
39. inflammable,
40. unique,
41. Poughkeepsie,
42. partiality,
43. ascertain,
44. Oklahoma,
45. tactics,
46. internal,
47. grisly,
48. muscular,
49. monkeys,
50. inferring.

PHYSICS

1. State the law of equilibrium between time and power, involved in the use of machinery.
2. (a) How does a change of temperature affect the running of a clock having an ordinary pendulum? (b) Describe some self-regulating device for preventing the irregular running of pendulum clocks.
3. (a) What is energy? (b) Water held in a mill-dam is an example of what kind of energy? Water turning a water-wheel?
4. Define (a) center of gravity; (b) line of direction; (c) specific gravity.
5. State the law of the vibration of pendulums of different lengths.
6. At Laredo, Tex., July 17, 1896, a Centigrade thermometer registered 47 degrees in the shade. What would have been the reading on a Fahrenheit scale?
7. What is the effect on sound caused by a vibrating cord (a) if the cord be shortened ; (b) if its tension be diminished; (c) if a heavier cord be used?
8. (a) Distinguish between a real and a virtual image. (b) What is the appearance of an object seen through a concave lens? A convex lens?
9. Define (a) volt; (b) ohm; (c) ampere.
10. During the winter the ground was frozen, but the sidewalks were free from snow and were dry; after the south wind had been blowing for several days, while the ground was still frozen, the stone walks became very wet while the plank walks remained dry. Account for this difference.

PHYSIOLOGY AND HYGIENE

1. What two long bones articulate with (a) the ulna; (b) the tibia?
2. Describe the means by which the nutrient elements of food are enabled to reach every tissue of the body.
3. What is the function of (a) the olfactory nerve; (b) the radial artery; (c) the pericardium?
4. Explain how an inflamed or sore throat may sometimes result in temporary deafness.
5. The cavity between the lungs and the walls of the chest is air-tight. Why is this essential to respiration?
6. The lining of the intestines is arranged in folds, affording an extensive surface. Explain the wisdom of this provision.
7. What is the effect of respiration upon (a) the blood; (b) the air breathed?
8. Explain how the mind is relieved of much responsibility by "reflex action."
9. Man is omniverous. What characteristics of the teeth show this?
10. Athletes in training are generally required to abstain totally from the use of tobacco and coffee. Explain.

ZOOLOGY

1. Describe an amoeba as to (a) method of receiving and digesting food; (b) reproduction.
2. Some insects have three stages of development; others, four. Name and describe these stages and give an example of each of the two kinds.
3. By what means is respiration effected in (a) insects; (b) fishes; (c) amphibia; (d) mammals?
4. How many cavities are there in the heart of (a) reptiles; (b) birds; (c) fishes?
5. What are the four grand divisions of the animal kingdom? Name one characteristic member of each.
6. What is meant by the following terms: (a) hibernation; (b) crustacean; (c) ruminant; (d) quadrumana; (e) plantigrade.
7. The terms vertebrate, mammal, and rodent are applied to a squirrel. What characteristics of that animal make these terms applicable?
8. Define (a) oviparous; (b) carnivorous; (c) raptores; (d) bovidae. Give the name of an animal to which each of these terms may be properly applied.
9. Show adaptation of structure to use in the case (a) of the ears of the rabbit; (b) the claws of the cat; (c) the eyes of the owl.
10. Compare the nervous system of a bird with that of a lobster.

2. TABULATED STATEMENT OF STATE EXAMINATIONS, 1897

Place	NAME OF EXAMINERS	Number of candidates who appeared at examination for first time	Number of candidates who had previously appeared	Total number examined	Number to whom certificates were granted
Albany	John J. Gannon	34	29	63	11
Buffalo	James M. Cassety	23	12	35	3
Chautauqua	P. M. Hull	6	8	14	5
Elmira	Hiram C. Case	18	11	29	3
Newburgh	R. V. K. Montfort	14	7	21	0
New York	James B. Sanford	22	27	49	8
Ogdensburg	Barney Whitney	7	6	13	2
Oneonta	Elizabeth W. Blackall	13	10	23	4
Plattsburgh	E. N. Jones	2	2	4	1
Rochester	John G. Allen	19	28	47	6
Syracuse	Willis D. Graves	20	28	48	12
Utica	S. W. Maxson	21	25	46	9
Watertown	Wm. G. Williams	8	10	18	6
		207	203	410	70

3. LIST OF SUCCESSFUL COMPETITORS FOR STATE CERTIFICATES, 1897

Following is a list of the persons to whom state certificates were issued for the year 1897

NAME	County	Post-office address
Glavin, James Edward	Albany	West Albany.
Jacobia, Spencer P.	Albany	1191 Broadway, Albany.
Hurlburt, J. Edward	Broome	Brook Vale.
Rutherford, Edith	Cattaraugus	Cattaraugus.
Appleby, Alton H.	Chautauqua	Lakewood.
Blaisdell, William B.	Chautauqua	Cherry Creek.
Persell, Charles Bowen	Chautauqua	Frewsburg.
Persell, George A.	Chautauqua	Frewsburg.
Soule, Le France F	Chautauqua	Fredonia.
Tubbs, Levi R	Chemung	Big Flats.
Butts, Herbert W.	Chenango	Smyrna.
Grotke, Charles J. M	Erie	Lancaster.
Hoag, Ada H.	Essex	Lake Placid.
Hardy, Mary D	Fulton	9 Fosdick street, Gloversville.
Taylor, James F.	Greene	Result.
Wilcox, Glenn Avery	Herkimer	North Litchfield.
Smith, De Vere Eugene	Herkimer	104 Burwell street, Little Falls.
Knapp, Harriet	Jefferson	Chaumont.
Lewis, Arthur C	Jefferson	Pillar Point.
Slate, Philip Sheridan	Jefferson	Black River.
Bull, Bertha F.	Jefferson	4 Massey avenue, Watertown.
Doggett, William E.	Kings	Flatbush.
Gilligan, Peter E	Lewis	Harrisville.
Beecher, Martha A	Livingston	Livonia.
Main, Mattie L.	Madison	Leonardsville.
White, Jane Elizabeth,	Madison	Eaton.
Sheip, Mary E.	Montgomery	Fultonville.
Barkley, William H.	Montgomery	Fort Hunter.
Collier, Edward L.	New York	New York.
Shellington, A Mary	Niagara	Niagara Falls.
Bortle, Amelia	Oneida	Madison.
Hay, Della M	Oneida	830 Bleecker street, Utica.
Cavanagh, Catharine E.	Oneida	Boonville.
Putnam, Sara E	Oneida	Boonville.
Chapman, Gertrude	Onondaga	Skaneateles.
Van Valkenburg, Ethel	Onondaga	Solvay.
Avery, Floyd Bentley	Onondaga	Lysander.
Brush, Rose M.	Onondaga	Baldwinsville.
Helfer, Philetus Martin	Onondaga	Ninoa.
Woodford, Harriet M	Onondaga	Fayetteville.
Ellis, Ada E.	Ontario	Canandaigua.
Bartlett, Harry D.	Orleans	Holley.
Hollis, Harriet Seymour	Oswego	Pulaski.
Raggs, Martha	Oswego	Fulton.
Gifford, Arthur Warner	Oswego	Hannibal.
Lewis, Grace M	Oswego	Oswego Falls
Spurr, Lillian H	Otsego	S. Edmeston.
Spangler, Arthur	Otsego	S. Worcester.
Sheehan, Kate	Queens	Woodhaven.
Godley, Eleanor L.	Queens	Whitestone.
Bryant, Frances C.	Queens	Seaford.
Cole, Annie E.	Richmond	Tottenville.
Denton, Lewis H.	Richmond	Linoleumville.
Miller, George W	Rockland	Spring Valley.
Nisbeth, Clyde M	St. Lawrence	Hammond.
Van Ness, Myron James	St. Lawrence	20 Cottage street, Potsdam.
Chamberlin, Lottie A.	Saratoga	Jonesville.
Billings, Erwin B	Schenectady	Delanson.
Kingsley, Julius Stanton	Tioga	Newark Valley.
Muldoon, Mary Warren	Tioga	491 Cayuta street, Waverly.
Boyd, Alice Mercy	Warren	Glens Falls.
Clapp, Juliett A.	Washington	North Argyle.
Flood, Rose E.	Washington	Sandy Hill.
Baldwin, George Ensign	Washington	W. Hebron.
Tolman, Howard N.	Wayne	Savannah.
Cullings, George H	Wayne	Macedon.
Webster, Frederick P.	Wyoming	Wyoming.
Niver, Harmon Bay		Orange, N. J.
Gleason, Mrs. Charles W		77 W. 33d street, Bayonne, N. J.

4. STATISTICAL TABLE—STATE CERTIFICATES

The following table shows the number of persons examined, and the number who have passed the examinations since the law was enacted, June 9, 1875, whereby state certificates are granted only upon examination, instead of upon recommendation, as formerly:

YEARS	Number examined	Number passed
1875	9	4
1876	47	21
1877	25*	11
1878	27	14
1879	45	30
1880	47	20
1881	34	12
1882	30	7
1883	63	19
1884	71	22
1885	111	21
1886	126	34
1887	150	40
1888	376	64
1889	350	71
1890	250	27
1891	224	36
1892	182	29
1893	167	25
1894	199	32
1895	255	30
1896	347	54
1897	410	70
Total	3,485	693

* Estimated.

5. EXAMINATIONS FOR STATE CERTIFICATES, 1898. CIRCULAR, REGULATIONS, AND PROGRAM

STATE OF NEW YORK

DEPARTMENT OF PUBLIC INSTRUCTION,
SUPERINTENDENT'S OFFICE,
ALBANY, *August* 23, 1897

Under the authority of chapter 556 of the Laws of 1894, which provides that state certificates may be granted by the State Superintendent of Public Instruction "only upon examination," and which authorizes the State Superintendent to "appoint times and places for holding such examinations at least once in each year," I have directed that examinations of applicants for state certificates be held on Monday, Tuesday, Wednesday, Thursday and Friday, August 22, 23, 24, 25 and 26, 1898, at the following places:

Albany.—At High School Building.
Buffalo.—At Normal School Building.
Elmira.—At the Academy.
Newburgh.—At the Newburgh Academy.
New York.—Grammar School No. 69, No. 125 Fifty-fourth street, between Sixth and Seventh avenues.
Ogdensburgh.—At the Academy.
Oneonta.—At Normal School Building.
Plattsburgh.—At Normal School Building.
Rochester.—At High School Building.
Syracuse.—At High School Building.
Utica.—At High School Building.
Watertown.—At High School Building.

At the conclusion of the examinations, all papers submitted will be forwarded to this Department. These papers will be carefully examined, and such of the candidates as shall have given satisfactory evidence of their learning, ability, experience, and good character, will receive certificates entitling them to teach for life in any of the public schools of the state.

In order to be admitted to the examinations, candidates must have had two years' successful experience in teaching, and must be present at the beginning of the examination.

Subjects for Examination:

GROUP I

Algebra, Arithmetic, American History, Geography, Grammar and Analysis, Orthography, Penmanship, Physiology and Hygiene.

GROUP II

Astronomy, Bookkeeping, Botany, Chemistry, Civil Government, Composition and Rhetoric, Drawing, General History, General Literature, Geology, Methods and School Economy and Philosophy of Education, Plane Geometry, Physics, School Law, Zoölogy.

Note.—Latin through the first three books of Caesar's Commentaries, or the ability to read at sight French or German, written in a plain style, will be accepted in place of Zoölogy or Astronomy.

A standing of at least 75 per cent. is required in each of the subjects of Group I, and an average standing of at least 75 per cent. in the subjects of Group II, but no paper showing a standing of less than 50 per cent. will be considered in this average.

All candidates who attain the required percentage in five or more of the designated subjects, exclusive of Orthography and Penmanship, but not in all, will be credited at this Department for those studies in which they shall have passed, and a partial certificate to that effect will be mailed to each candidate. On passing the required percentage in the remaining designated subjects at any subsequent examinations, held not later than the second year thereafter, they will be entitled to receive State Certificates. This gives to candidates opportunity for three distinct yearly trials.

Candidates who have had three trials but have failed to obtain a certificate will forfeit the standing earned on the first trial only. The standing earned on the last two trials will be credited to such candidates, and by completing the work required at the next examination they may receive certificates.

In the uniform examinations. school commissioners will recognize "partial certificates," issued not more than five years previously, in all subjects in which candidates have attained 75 per cent.

The examinations will be open to candidates residing in any part of the state, and to such residents of other states as shall declare it to be their intention to teach in this state.

Attention is directed to the following extract from section 10 of title I of the consolidated school law of 1894, relating to the powers of the State Superintendent of Public Instruction touching this subject: "He may grant under his hand and seal of office a certificate of qualification to teach, and may revoke the same. While unrevoked, such certificate shall be conclusive evidence that the person to whom it was granted is qualified by moral character, learning and ability, to teach any common school in the state. Such certificate may be granted by him only upon examination. Every such certificate so granted shall be deemed and considered a legal license and authority to teach in any of the public schools of this state without further examination, * * * any provision of law in conflict with this provision to the contrary notwithstanding." There can be no evasion of this law, and no certificate will be granted in any case except in conformity with its provisions.

It is the intention of this Department to make these examinations a thorough test of merit. No "catch questions" will be introduced, but the examinations will be sufficiently rigid to prove the ability of the applicant, to the end that a State Certificate when granted shall be the most signal honor that is bestowed upon the progressive teachers of the commonwealth.

Commissioners, city superintendents, academic principals, and institute conductors are requested to give all possible publicity to this circular among teachers of their acquaintance who may desire to take this examination, and to invite the co-operation of the press in calling the attention of the public to the dates of the examinations, and to the plans and regulations adopted.

Special Information to Candidates

Candidates should aim to acquire not merely certain facts, but well-digested knowledge and analytic power that will fit them to guide, criticise, and instruct their pupils successfully.

When explanations are required they should be given with the same clearness, system and thoroughness that a competent teacher would use in instructing a class. All work should be of the best quality. The papers will be criticised as the work of teachers—not as that of mere pupils.

The scope of the examination will correspond to the subject-matter of the ordinary text-books. The following special suggestions are given to emphasize certain points, and to indicate the work required:

Candidates should examine each question with great care and fully answer it, but should write no more than is necessary. Quantity will not be allowed as a substitute for quality.

In Arithmetic, the candidate should be familiar with the analysis of problems and deduction of rules, particularly in the elementary operations, common and decimal fractions, percentage and its applications, ratio and proportion, and mensuration, and should give strict attention to arithmetical theory as well as practice. The composition of problems to illustrate rules or principles may be required.

In Algebra, pay special attention to the laws of signs and exponents, the transformations of equations, factoring, the derivation of rules in the various operations, quadratic equations, radical quantities, proportion, square and cube roots, and the expansion of binomials, with or without numeral or literal, positive or negative coefficients and exponents, by the binomial theorem.

In Geometry, note especially,—(a) general propositions; (b) the solution of arithmetical and algebraic problems involving geometrical principles, particularly in relation to the right-angle triangle, squares, rectangles, circles, areas of similar figures compared, and proportional lines; (c) actual and accurate constructions with dividers and ruler will be required.

In Grammar and Analysis the definition of terms, parts of speech and their modifications, inflections, rules of syntax, the analysis of sentences, including principal and subordinate clauses and the modifiers of the different parts composing the same, and constructive work illustrating any of the foregoing.

In Drawing, attention should be given to the study as considered from an educational point of view, together with its application to the practical uses of life. In the mechanical department, accuracy and correct methods should be studied; while in free-hand work from the object, relative proportion of parts should be carefully observed. Note well that geometric form is the basis of all industrial drawing. In design give special attention to the principles of decoration. A knowledge of the prismatic colors and their elementary combinations will be required. Sketching from familiar and convenient objects may form a portion of the examination in this subject.

In Geography, include all important facts and discoveries up to the present time, giving special attention to the state of New York.

In History, note important events, their causes and results. In American History, part of the questions will refer to the history of the state of New York.

In General History for 1898, one-half the questions will be upon the "Thirty Years' War."

English. It is believed that the power of translating at sight ordinary nineteenth century prose can be acquired by reading not less than four hundred duodecimo pages from the works of at least three different authors. Not more than one-half of this amount ought to be from works of fiction. This number of pages is to include not only prepared work, but all sight reading done in class. (b) The translation from English into French of sentences or of a short connected passage to test the candidate's familiarity with elementary grammar. Elementary grammar is understood to include the conjugations of regular verbs, of the more frequent irregular verbs, such as aller, envoyer, tenir, pouvoir, voir, vouloir, dire, savoir, faire, and those belonging to the classes represented by ouvrir, dormir, connaître, conduire, and craindre; the forms and positions of personal pronouns, the uses of other pronouns and of possessive, demonstrative, and interrogative adjectives; the inflection of nouns and adjectives for gender and number, except rare cases; the uses of articles, and the partitive constructions.

Pronunciation should be carefully taught and pupils be trained to some extent to hear and understand spoken French. The writing of French from dictation is recommended as a useful exercise.

Elementary German: (a) the rudiments of grammar, and especially these topics: The declension of articles, adjectives, pronouns, and such nouns as are readily classified; the conjugation of weak and of the more usual strong verbs; the commoner prepositions; the simpler uses of the modal auxiliaries; the elementary rules of syntax and word order. The proficiency of the applicant may be tested by questions on the above topics and by the translation into German of simple English sentences. (b) Translation at sight of a passage of easy prose containing no rare words. It is believed that the requisite facility can be acquired by reading not less than two hundred duodecimo pages of simple German.

Practice in pronunciation, in writing German from dictation, and in the use of simple German phrases in the classroom is recommended.

Method of Conducting the Examinations

It is suggested that the manner of procedure be as follows:

Upon calling the class to order, have each member fill out with ink, in his own handwriting, the blank statement of name, residence, post-office address, etc. Collect the same and dismiss any candidate whose statement does not indicate his eligibility to the scholarship under the provisions of the statute and return these statements with your report.

Next, submit the question papers on History and Algebra. Continue the sitting upon the two subjects named without interruption from 9 to 12 o'clock, unless candidates finish prior to that time. Close the sitting at 12 o'clock in any event, having notified the class at the opening that this will be done.

Direct that the candidates write their answers in ink upon uniform paper supplied by this Department. You will supply to applicants ink and pens, forwarding your bill for the same, together with the bills for publishing the notices of the examinations, to the board of supervisors of your county, which is required by law to audit and pay these necessary expenses. Keep the answers in each subject upon a sheet of paper by themselves.

Let the afternoon sitting for the examination in English, Plane Geometry and Latin, French, or German begin at 1.30 and end at 5 o'clock, unless candidates finish their work earlier.

Each answer will be marked upon a scale having a maximum of 10. Each absolutely correct answer will receive 10 credits, and a correspondingly less number as it approximates correctness; an absolutely erroneous answer will be marked zero. There are thirty-five questions in all. The paper in English will be given 100 credits, 50 credits being assigned to each part (A and B). Each of the History papers will be given 50 credits. The papers in Algebra, Plane Geometry, Latin, French or German will also be given 50 credits each. If all are correctly answered the candidate will

8. Collusion or communication between candidates during the examinations or willful misrepresentation in statements furnished will wholly vitiate their examination.

9. All statements and answers must be written with ink.

Uniform paper, pens, pencils, and memorandum pads will be supplied by the Department.

Candidates should make themselves thoroughly familiar with the above regulations.

Program of Examination, 1898

Monday, August 22, 2 to 5 p. m.—Registering, Grammar, Civil Government, School Law.

Tuesday, August 23, 9 a. m. to 12 m.—Arithmetic, American History; 2 to 5 p. m.—Composition and Rhetoric, Geology, Chemistry.

Wednesday, August 24, 9 a. m. to 12 m.—Algebra, General Literature; 2 to 5 p. m.—Geography, Methods and School Economy, Orthography.

Thursday, August 25, 9 a. m. to 12 m.—Geometry, Physics; 2 to 5 p. m.—Drawing, Botany.

Friday, August 26, 9 a. m. to 12 m.—Physiology and Hygiene, Bookkeeping; 2 to 5 p m.—General History, Zoölogy, Astronomy, Latin, French or German, as a substitute for Zoölogy or Astronomy.

CHAS. R. SKINNER,
State Superintendent.

state scholarships must also register, each term, before the close of registration day, and a failure to do so, without assigning a valid reason, forfeits the scholarship.

Very respectfully yours,

CHARLES R. SKINNER,
State Superintendent.

Note.—It will be well to read the essential portions of this circular to the class before the examination begins.

Form of Notice

(Form of notice to be published in two newspapers in each county, once a week, for three weeks prior to the examination)

CORNELL UNIVERSITY

State Scholarships

(Notice Pursuant to Title XII, Chapter 556, Laws of 1894)

A competitive examination of candidates for the state scholarships in Cornell University, falling to the county of.........................will be held at the (name the building)...................in the city (or village) of.......................on Saturday, the 4th day of June, 1898, commencing at 9 a. m.

Candidates must be at least sixteen years of age and of six months' standing in the common schools or academies of the state during the year immediately preceding this examination, and actual residents of this state.

No person should enter an examination unless prepared to accept a scholarship, should one be awarded.

The examination will be upon the following subjects, viz.: English, History, Plane Geometry, Algebra, through quadratic equations, and either Latin, French, or German, at the option of the candidate.

There will be as many candidates appointed from this county as there are Assembly districts in this county. Candidates will become entitled to the scholarships in the order of merit.

Dated at ...., this .... day of May, 1898.

....
Superintendent of Schools, City of.....................

....
School Commissioner.....................

....
School Commissioner.....................

---

2. QUESTIONS SUBMITTED AT EXAMINATIONS JUNE 5, 1897

A. M.

ARITHMETIC

1. Multiply five hundred and four thousandths by five hundred thousandths and divide the product by eight ten-thousandths.
2. (a) How many cords in a pile of wood 10.3 M. long, 3 M. high and 6.25 M. wide? (b) What will it cost at $1.50 a ster?
3. A box is 5 ft. long, 3 ft. wide and 2.4 ft. high on the inside. What is the length of the longest iron rod pointed at each end that can be placed in the box and the lid be closed?
4. If the interest on $3,750 for 8 mo. at 6 per cent. is $150, on what sum placed at interest at 5 per cent. for 2 yr. 4 mo. is the interest $280? (Solve by proportion.)

	Credits
1. Translate the above selection.	25
2. Give the principal parts of fecerct, arbitratus, jubet, perlata, perspexissct.	5
3. Give the reason for the mood of fecerat, erat, polliceantur.	5
4. Give the case and the reason for the case of cognoscenda, huic domum, quem, facultatis.	
5. Write in Latin: Although Caesar knew nothing about Britain except that auxiliaries were furnished to his enemies from that island, still he decided to proceed there in order to examine into the character of the people and to reconnoitre the harbors and approaches.	10

FRENCH

CHRISTOPHE COLOMB.

Agissant avec la prudence que demandait un pareil danger, Colomb *allait* de l'un à l'autre de ses matelots; il encourageait ceux-ci, promettait à ceux-là que le voyage touchait à sa fin, et menaçait les plus obstinés de l'autorité du roi. Dans la journée on vit plusieurs *oiseaux*, et l'on prit des crabes de mer dans les herbes flottant à la surface des eaux. L'amiral *crut pouvoir* profiter de ces circonstances, et il ordonna aux matelots de continuer la route vers l'ouest; alors l'orage èclata d'une maniére terrible. Se formant en groupes sur le pont, les matelots firent succéder les menaces aux murmures. "C'est un fou," disait l'un en désignant la chambre où l'amiral ètait occupé à écrire les détails de son voyage, "un fou qui veut devenir grand à nos dépens — "Aux dépens de notre vie," ajoutait un second.—"Quelle idée de croire découvrir des terres inconnues," disait un troisième, qui s'appelait Toreo; "d'abord, mes amis, vous êtes témoins que je n'ai jamis cru à cette bêtise là."—"Ni moi non plus," répliquait un quatrième; "aussi vrai que je m'appelle Fernandès, j'ai toujours *dit* que nous avions tort d'aller si loin."—Oui; mais comment retourner?" observa Toreo. "C'est facile," dit son voisin, un grand et gros homme, d'une *voix* sombre.— "Eh bien! puisque c'rest *facile*," dit Toreo, "décide-le, toi."—"Je le jetterai à la mer le soir quand il se promène su rle pont," reprit l'autre. "Ce sera un accident."— "Tais-toi, c'est lui," dirent sourdement quelques-uns.

En effet, l'amiral passa devant les groupes qui complotaient sa mort; les avaitil entendus? c'était ce que chacun se demandait, et ce que personne ne pouvait affirmer, car l'amiral était calme et froid. Cela se passait le 25 septembre, au coucher du soleil. Colomb donna quelques ordres en passant, puis, s' approchant d'Yanez Pincon, il se mit à causer avec lui. Au même instant un jeune mousse, très attachè l'amiral et auquel celui-ci avait dit quelques mots à l'oreille en passant, monta sur un mât, et tout à coup s'écria, "Terre, terre!"

	Credits
1. Translate the above selection.	30
2. Give the principal parts of *allait, pouvoir, dit, crut, est.*	5
3. Give a synopsis of *avoir* in the indicative mood, first person singular.	5
4. Compare *facile;* give the singular of *oiseaux* and the plural of *voix.*	5
5. Translate into French: The sailors were obstinate and plotted his death, but Columbus continued his course toward the west.	

GERMAN

UNKEL UND NICHTE

In einem schönen Thale, an einem kleinen See, war ein Dorf von geschichtlicher Bedeutung. In diesem Dorfe war ein Greis von 60 Jahren, ein Veteran aus napoleonischen Zeiten, der in Ruhestand versetzt worden war und den Rang eines Majors bekleidete. Die vielseitigen Erfaurungen und Erlebnisse des Herrn Major von Gablenz, so hies der Veteran, erregten grosses Interesse in den Kreisen mit denen er Umgang

shall, in the order of their excellence become entitled to the scholarships belonging to their respective counties.

5. In case any candidate who may become entitled to a scholarship shall fail to claim the same, or shall fail to pass the entrance examination at such University, or shall die, resign or absent himself without leave, be expelled, or for any other reason shall abandon his right to or vacate such scholarship either before or after entering thereupon, then the candidate certified to be next entitled in the same county shall become entitled to the same. In case any scholarship belonging to any county shall not be claimed by any candidate resident in that county, the State Superintendent may fill the same by appointing thereto some candidate first entitled to a vacancy in some other county, after notice has been served on the superintendent or commissioners of schools of said county. In any such case the president of the university shall at once notify the Superintendent of Public Instruction, and that officer shall immediately notify the candidate next entitled to the vacant scholarship of his right to the same.

6. Any state student who shall make it appear to the satisfaction of the president of the university that he requires leave of absence for the purpose of earning funds with which to defray his living expenses while in attendance, may, in the discretion of the president be granted such leave of absence, and may be allowed a period not exceeding six years from the commencement thereof for the completion of his course at said university.

7. In certifying the qualifications of the candidates preference shall be given (where other qualifications are equal) to the children of those who have died in the military or naval service of the United States.

8. Notices of the time and place of the examinations shall be given in all the schools having pupils eligible thereto, prior to the first day of January in each year, and shall be published once a week for three weeks in at least two newspapers in each county immediately prior to the holding of such examinations. The cost of publishing such notices and the necessary expenses of such examinations shall be a charge upon each county respectively, and shall be audited and paid by the board of supervisors thereof. The State Superintendent of Public Instruction shall attend to the giving and publishing of the notices hereinbefore provided for. He may, in his discretion, direct that the examination in any county be held at some other time and place than that above specified, in which case it shall be held as directed by him. He shall keep full records in his department of the reports of the different examiners, showing the age, post-office address and standing of each candidate, and shall notify candidates of their rights under this act. He shall determine any controversies which may arise under the provisions of this act. He is hereby charged with the general supervision and direction of all matters in connection with the filling of such scholarships. Students enjoying the privileges of free scholarships shall, in common with the other students of said university, be subject to all of the examinations, rules and requirements of the board of trustees or faculty of said university, except as herein provided.

Notice of Examination

Notice of this examination is to be published once a week, for three weeks prior thereto, in two newspapers in each county. At the proper time you will advise with the other officers, who with you are to have charge of the examination in your county, and will jointly prepare, sign and publish the required notice. A form of notice for publication which may be used will be found on the last page of this communication. You will instruct publishers of newspapers to forward their bill for such publication to the board of supervisors of your county, as the law makes the cost of publication a county charge.

Where Examinations May be Held

While the law provides that the examination shall be held in the county court-house in each county, it, at the same time, permits it to be held elsewhere by the direction of the Superintendent of Public Instruction. It is the evident purpose of the law to provide at least one place where the examination may of right be held, hence the court-house is designated. It would undoubtedly be better to hold the examination in a school building in all cases where the local school officers will consent thereto, which they will probably do in most instances. Where such consent is obtained, you may insert such place in the notice without communicating with the Department for direction in the matter. No expense must be incurred on this account. Unless school buildings are offered free of cost, the examination will be held at the county court-house.

How Question Papers Will be Sent

In all counties having but one school commissioner, printed question papers, blank forms for reports, blank statements of candidates, etc., will be forwarded to him on the first day of June next. In counties having two or more school commissioners, or one or more city superintendents, they will confer together and advise me promptly to whom the question papers, etc., should be sent.

Special Attention

Examiners will call the attention of all interested to the following:

1. Candidates must be actual residents of this state.

2. Candidats must be at least sixteen years of age.

3. Candidates must show that they have attended a common school or academy of this state for at least six months during the year immediately preceding the date of the examination. Teaching cannot be considered equivalent to attendance. Attendance at private schools or in normal departments of normal schools does not comply with the provisions of the law.

4. Candidates should, in all cases, attend the examinations in the counties in which they actually reside.

5. No person should enter an examination unless prepared to accept a scholarship, should one be awarded.

6. No person can receive a Cornell state scholarship who does not enter an examination.

7. Any person appointed to a scholarship and afterwards declining the same, forfeits it absolutely, and the vacancy is filled from the list of other eligible candidates. The candidate is eligible, however, to enter a succeeding examination by meeting the conditions required.

8. It is advisable for candidates who fail to obtain scholarships to take the entrance examination at the University in September, as all vacancies will be filled by appointments from candidates on the eligible lists who have passed the entrance examination and registered in the University. No direct assurance can be given that a scholarship can be awarded, as there may be no vacancies.

9. To be entitled to be placed upon the eligible list from which appointments to scholarships in counties having no claimants will be made, candidates must attain at least an average standing of $66\frac{2}{3}$ per cent. Candidates who fail to attain such standing cannot receive consideration by the Department in making appointments to these vacant scholarships until the eligible list is exhausted.

Subjects for Examination

The president of Cornell University has designated the following subjects for the examination of 1898, viz.: English, History, Algebra, Plane Geometry, and either Latin, French, or German, at the option of the candidates.

Scope of Examination

English: questions upon the books marked A; a short English composition—correct in spelling, punctuation, grammar, division by paragraphs, and expression—upon a subject taken from the books marked B. For 1898: A. Milton, Paradise Lost, Books i and ii; Pope, Iliad, Books i and xxii; The Sir Roger de Coverley Papers in the Spectator; Goldsmith, The Vicar of Wakefield; Coleridge, The Ancient Mariner; Southey, Life of Nelson; Carlyle, Essay on Burns; Lowell, The Vision of Sir Launfal; Hawthorne, The House of the Seven Gables. B. Shakespeare, Macbeth; Burke, Conciliation with America; De Quincey, Flight of a Tartar Tribe; Tennyson, The Princess.

History: two of the four following subjects:

(a) The History of Greece to the death of Alexander, with due reference to Greek life, literature and art.

(b) The History of Rome to the accession of Commodus, with due reference to literature and government.

(c) English History, with due reference to social and political development.

(d) American History, with the elements of civil government. It is expected that the study of American History will be such as to show the development and origin of the institutions of our own country; that it will, therefore, include the colonial beginnings; and that it will deal with the period of discovery and early settlement sufficiently to show the relations of peoples on the American continent, and the meaning of the struggle for mastery.

Algebra: factors, common divisors and multiples, fractions, equations of the first degree with one or more unknown quantities, involution including the binomial theorem for positive entire exponents, evolution, the doctrine of exponents, radicals and equations involving radicals, quadratic equations of one or two unknown quantities and equations solved like quadratics, ratio and proportion, and putting problems into equations, and including radicals; as much as is contained in the larger American and English text-books.

[In the fundamental operations of Algebra, such as multiplication and division, the management of brackets, the solving of numerical and literal equations, of the first and second degrees, the combining and simplifying of fractions and radicals, the interpretation and use of negative quantities and of 0 and ∞, the putting of problems into equations—the student should have distinct notions of the meaning and the reason of all that he does, and be able to state them clearly in his own language; he should also be able to perform all these operations, even when somewhat complex, with rapidity, accuracy, and neatness; and to solve practical problems readily and completely. In his preparatory study he is advised to solve a great many problems, and to state and explain the reasons for the steps taken.]

Plane Geometry: including the solution of simple original exercises, numerical problems, and questions on the metric system; as much as is contained in the larger American and English text-books.

[In Geometry the student should learn the definitions accurately, whether in the language of the text-book or not, and in proving a theorem or solving a problem he should be able to prove every statement made, going back step by step till he rests upon the primary definitions and axioms. He should be able to apply the principles of Geometry to practical and numerical examples, to construct his diagrams readily with rule and compass, and to find for himself the solutions of simple problems and the demonstrations of simple theorems. To cultivate this power of origination, he should always, before reading the solution or proof given in his text-book try to find out one for himself, making use, if necessary, of his author's diagram; and if successful, he should compare critically his own work with his author's, and see wherein either is the better. Besides oral recitation, he is advised to write out his demonstrations, having regard both to the matter and to the form of his statements; and when written he should carefully study them to make sure, first, that he has a complete chain of argument, and secondly, that it is so arranged that without defect or redundance one step follows as a logical consequence of another.]

Latin: four books of Caesar's Commentaries, or a corresponding number of pages of Nepos, or an equivalent, with a good knowledge of the grammar.

Elementary French: (a) the translation at sight of ordinary nineteenth century prose. It is important that the passages set be rendered into clear and idiomatic

English. It is believed that the power of translating at sight ordinary nineteenth century prose can be acquired by reading not less than four hundred duodecimo pages from the works of at least three different authors. Not more than one-half of this amount ought to be from works of fiction. This number of pages is to include not only prepared work, but all sight reading done in class. (b) The translation from English into French of sentences or of a short connected passage to test the candidate's familiarity with elementary grammar. Elementary grammar is understood to include the conjugations of regular verbs, of the more frequent irregular verbs, such as aller, envoyer, tenir, pouvoir, voir, vouloir, dire, savoir, faire, and those belonging to the classes represented by ouvrir, dormir, connaître, conduire, and craindre; the forms and positions of personal pronouns, the uses of other pronouns and of possessive, demonstrative, and interrogative adjectives; the inflection of nouns and adjectives for gender and number, except rare cases; the uses of articles, and the partitive constructions.

Pronunciation should be carefully taught and pupils be trained to some extent to hear and understand spoken French. The writing of French from dictation is recommended as a useful exercise.

Elementary German: (a) the rudiments of grammar, and especially these topics: The declension of articles, adjectives, pronouns, and such nouns as are readily classified; the conjugation of weak and of the more usual strong verbs; the commoner prepositions; the simpler uses of the modal auxiliaries; the elementary rules of syntax and word order. The proficiency of the applicant may be tested by questions on the above topics and by the translation into German of simple English sentences. (b) Translation at sight of a passage of easy prose containing no rare words. It is believed that the requisite facility can be acquired by reading not less than two hundred duodecimo pages of simple German.

Practice in pronunciation, in writing German from dictation, and in the use of simple German phrases in the classroom is recommended.

Method of Conducting the Examinations

It is suggested that the manner of procedure be as follows:

Upon calling the class to order, have each member fill out with ink, in his own handwriting, the blank statement of name, residence, post-office address, etc. Collect the same and dismiss any candidate whose statement does not indicate his eligibility to the scholarship under the provisions of the statute and return these statements with your report.

Next, submit the question papers on History and Algebra. Continue the sitting upon the two subjects named without interruption from 9 to 12 o'clock, unless candidates finish prior to that time. Close the sitting at 12 o'clock in any event, having notified the class at the opening that this will be done.

Direct that the candidates write their answers in ink upon uniform paper supplied by this Department. You will supply to applicants ink and pens, forwarding your bill for the same, together with the bills for publishing the notices of the examinations, to the board of supervisors of your county, which is required by law to audit and pay these necessary expenses. Keep the answers in each subject upon a sheet of paper by themselves.

Let the afternoon sitting for the examination in English, Plane Geometry and Latin, French, or German begin at 1.30 and end at 5 o'clock, unless candidates finish their work earlier.

Each answer will be marked upon a scale having a maximum of 10. Each absolutely correct answer will receive 10 credits, and a correspondingly less number as it approximates correctness; an absolutely erroneous answer will be marked zero. There are thirty-five questions in all. The paper in English will be given 100 credits, 50 credits being assigned to each part (A and B). Each of the History papers will be given 50 credits. The papers in Algebra, Plane Geometry, Latin, French or German will also be given 50 credits each. If all are correctly answered the candidate will receive 350 credits, and a correspondingly less number as he approaches correctness. The aggregate number of credits received will determine the relative standing of the candidates.

Examiners, immediately upon the close of the examination, will forward by express to the state Superintendent, at Albany, all papers submitted by candidates.

As soon as may be, and certainly within four days after the examination, examiners will forward the report, signed by all city superintendents and school commissioners in the county to the state Superintendent, giving the names in full of all persons examined, and showing in what subjects each candidate submitted papers. All statements of candidates must be forwarded with the report of the examiners to the Superintendent.

How Vacancies will be Filled

The law now authorizes the state Superintendent to fill vacancies arising in any county, by appointing some candidate standing highest on the list of candidates selected from other counties after the quota of scholarships belonging to such other counties has been filled. In exercising this power the following system will be followed, of which it may be well to advise the class. The examination papers of the candidates standing highest upon the list in each county (after the appointments have been made from that county) will be classified and arranged in the order of merit, and appointments will be made from this list in the order in which the names stand. If this list should be exhausted, the same course would be pursued as to candidates coming next upon the list selected in like manner. In this way all candidates will secure such rights as their merits entitle them, the state Superintendent will be relieved from the disagreeable duty of discrimination, and the scholarships will be equitably distributed over the territory of the state.

Examinations must not be Omitted

There may be cases in which the number of candidates who present themselves will be smaller than the number of scholarships belonging to the county, and in such cases it may be thought unnecessary to go through the examination. To take that course would be a mistake. Candidates will become entitled to their scholarships only after the steps indicated by the statute shall have been taken. The law must be fully complied with. Therefore, it is advised that all the proceedings be taken regularly, and that the examination papers be filed in the Department, even though the number should be so small in any county as to remove the necessity for competition between candidates.

Entrance Examinations

The entrance examinations at the University will be held June 10-15 inclusive, and September 13-17 inclusive. Successful candidates must appear at the opening of one or the other of these examinations, but as the time which will elapse between the date of the competitive examination and the June entrance examination at the University is only six days, it will be impossible for this Department to notify candidates of the result of examinations sufficiently early for them to appear at the June entrance examination.

All appointments will be awarded at the earliest date possible and certainly before July 1st. This Department will notify all candidates of the standing which they attained in the examinations and their rights in the premises.

Registration of State Scholars

Examiners should inform all candidates that holders of state scholarships whose appointment takes effect at the beginning of the university year 1898, must be registered before 6 p. m., on registration day, September 21, 1898; a failure to thus register without furnishing a valid excuse will forfeit all rights to scholarships. Holders of

EXHIBIT No. 14

College Graduates' Certificates

Indorsement of Normal Diplomas and State Certificates Issued in Other States

1. Law of 1888
2. Circular of Information
3. List of College Graduates' Certificates Granted 189
4. List of Normal Diplomas Indorsed 1897
5. List of State Certificates Indorsed 1897

5. A sold a horse to B for $160, thereby gaining 25 per cent. B sells the horse to C at a gain of 10 per cent. What was the per cent advance paid by C over what the horse cost A?

ALGEBRA

1. Resolve into prime factors the following quantities:

   (1) $a^4 - b^4$; (2) $a - b)^2 - c$; (3) $a^2 - 2ab + b^2 - 9c^2$.

2. Simplify the following radical expressions:

   (1) $2\sqrt[3]{320} - 3\sqrt[3]{40}$; (2) $\sqrt{\frac{a^4c}{b^3}}$ — $\sqrt{\frac{a^2c^3}{bd^2}}$ — $\sqrt{\frac{a^2cd^2}{bm^2}}$

3. $\sqrt{x+3} + \sqrt{x+8} = 5\sqrt{x}$. Find value of x.
4. $x - y - 2 = 0$

   $15(x^2 - y^2) = 16xy$. Find values of x and y.
5. Every affected quadraic can be reduced to the form $ax^2 + bx + c = 0$. (a) Derive from this form an expression representing the roots of the equation; (b) applying the formula derived determine without solving the character of the roots of the following equation: $3x^2 - 4x = 4$; (c) suppose the square of the coefficient of x, in the above general equation, minus four times the product of a and c is less than zero, what is true of the roots?

P. M.

ENGLISH

Write a short English composition, correct in spelling, punctuation, grammar, division by paragraphs and expression, upon one of the following subjects: Scott's Marmion, Hawthorne's Twice Told Tales, Shakespeare's As You Like It.

PLANE GEOMETRY

1. If two sides of a triangle are unequal, what is true of the angles opposite? Demonstrate your answer.
2. To what is the sum of the interior angles of a polygon equal? Prove.
3. When a secant and tangent are drawn from a point without a circle, show that the tangent is a mean proportional between the whole secant and its external segment.
4. Develop a formula for computing the altitude of a triangle in terms of its sides.
5. To what is the area of a trapezoid equal? Demonstrate.

LATIN

Ad haec cognoscenda, priusquam periculum faceret, idoneum esse arbitratus Gaium Volusenum cum navi longa praemittit. Huic mandat, ut, exploratis omnibus rebus, ad se quam primum revertatur. Ipse cum omnibus copiis in Morinos proficiscitur, quod inde erat brevissimus in Britanniam trajectus. Huc naves undique ex finitimis regionibus et quam superiore aestate ad Veneticum bellum effecerat classem, jubet convenire. Interim, consilio ejus cognito, et per mercatoris perlato ad Britannos, a compluribus insulae civitatibus ad eum legati veniunt, qui polliceantur obsides dare atque imperio populi Romani obtemperare. Quibus auditis, liberaliter pollicitus hortatusque, ut in ea sententia permanerent, eos domum remittit; et cum iis una Commium, quem ipse, Atrebatibus superatis, regem ibi constituerat, cujus et virtutem et consilium probabat, et quem sibi fidelem esse arbitrabatur, cujusque auctoritas in his regionibus magni habebatur, mittit. Huic imperat, quas possit, adeat civitates; horteturque, ut populi Romani fidem sequantur, seque celeriter eo venturum nuntiet. Volusenus, perspectis regionibus omnibus, quantum ei facultatis dari potuit, qui navi egredi ac se barbaris committere non auderet, quinto die ad Caesarem revertitur, quaque ibi perspexisset, renuntiat.

Credits

1. Translate the above selection. 25
2. Give the principal parts of fecerct, arbitratus, jubet, perlata, perspexisset. 5
3. Give the reason for the mood of fecerat, erat, polliceantur. 5
4. Give the case and the reason for the case of cognoscenda, huic domum, quem, facultatis.
5. Write in Latin: Although Caesar knew nothing about Britain except that auxiliaries were furnished to his enemies from that island, still he decided to proceed there in order to examine into the character of the people and to reconnoitre the harbors and approaches. 10

FRENCH

CHRISTOPHE COLOMB.

Agissant avec la prudence que demandait un pareil danger, Colomb *allait* de l'un à l'autre de ses matelots; il encourageait ceux-ci, promettait à ceux-là que le voyage touchait à sa fin, et menaçait les plus obstinés de l'autorité du roi. Dans la journée on vit plusieurs *oiseaux*, et l'on prit des crabes de mer dans les herbes flottant à la surface des eaux. L'amiral *crut pouvoir* profiter de ces circonstances, et il ordonna aux matelots de continuer la route vers l'ouest; alors l'orage èclata d'une maniére terrible. Se formant en groupes sur le pont, les matelots firent succéder les menaces aux murmures. " C'est un fou," disait l'un en désignant la chambre où l'amiral ètait occupé à écrire les détails de son voyage, " un fou qui veut devenir grand à nos dépens — " Aux dépens de notre vie," ajoutait un second.—" Quelle idée de croire découvrir des terres inconnues," disait un troisième, qui s'appelait Toreo; " d'abord, mes amis, vous êtes témoins que je n'ai jamis cru à cette bêtise là."—" Ni moi non plus," répliquait un quatrième; " aussi vrai que je m'appelle Fernandès, j'ai toujours *dit* que nous avions tort d'aller si loin."—Oui; mais comment retourner? " observa Toreo. " C'est facile," dit son voisin, un grand et gros homme, d'une *voix* sombre.— " Eh bien! puisque c'rest *facile*," dit Toreo, " décide-le, toi."—" Je le jetterai à la mer le soir quand il se promène su rle pont," reprit l'autre. " Ce sera un accident."— " Tais-toi, c'est lui," dirent sourdement quelques-uns.

En effet, l'amiral passa devant les groupes qui complotaient sa mort; les avaitil entendus? c'était ce que chacun se demandait, et ce que personne ne pouvait affirmer, car l'amiral était calme et froid. Cela se passait le 25 septembre, au coucher du soleil. Colomb donna quelques ordres en passant, puis, s' approchant d'Yanez Pincon, il se mit à causer avec lui. Au même instant un jeune mousse, très attachè l'amiral et auquel celui-ci avait dit quelques mots à l'oreille en passant, monta sur un mât, et tout à coup s'écria, " Terre, terre! "

Credits

1. Translate the above selection. 30
2. Give the principal parts of *allait, pouvoir, dit, crut, est.* 5
3. Give a synopsis of *avoir* in the indicative mood, first person singular. 5
4. Compare *facile;* give the singular of *oiseaux* and the plural of *voix.* 5
5. Translate into French: The sailors were obstinate and plotted his death, but Columbus continued his course toward the west.

GERMAN

ONKEL UND NICHTE

In einem schönen Thale, an einem kleinen See, war ein Dorf von geschichtlicher Bedeutung. In diesem Dorfe war ein Greis von 60 Jahren, ein Veteran aus napoleonischen Zeiten, der in Ruhestand versetzt worden war und den Rang eines Majors bekleidete. Die vielseitigen Erfahrungen und Erlebnisse des Herrn Major von Gablenz, so hies der Veteran, erregten grosses Interesse in den Kreisen mit denen er Umgang pflegte, umsomehr, da seine Erzählungen aus dem Leben gegriffen waren und wahrheitsgetreu geschildert wurden. Sein Vater war in preussischen Staatsdiensten, hatte eine zahlreiche Familie und musste sich, um standesgemäss zu leben, sehr einschränken im Kreise der Seinigen. Major von Gablenz war der zweite Sohn.

Schon in seinen Knabenjahren legte er eine Vorliebe zur Technik an den Tag. Bei Gelegenheit einer Parade die er zum ersten Male besichtigte als elfjähriger Knabe, *sagte* er zu seinem Vater: "Wenn ich einmal Soldat werde, so scheue ich keine Mühe und keine Anstrengung, und wäre sie noch so gross, meiner Pflicht auf das Pünktlichste nachzukommen: denn mein Grossvater sagte mir, dass ich bei getreuer Pünktlicher Erfüllung durch Tapferkeit, Mut und Ausdauer es vielleicht zum Offizier *bringen* komme, und wenn ich einmal Offizier bin, dann werde ich am Ende noch General."

Der junge Gablenz hatte ein gutes Gedächtniss, einen regen Sinn für alles Gute und Schöne. Seine Zeugnisse bekundeten Fleiss, Aufmerksamkeit und Ausdauer. Auf dem Turnplatze, in der Schwimmerschule und bei allen körperlichen Uebungen galt er unter seinen Kameraden als Vormann und Leiter. Ein alter Gerichtsdiener, ein ausgedienter Soldat, wurde von den Stadtbehörden beauftragt, mit den Knaben des Gymnasiums militarische Uebungen zu *machen;* in dem Schlosshofe einer alten Burg, welche sich dort befand, wurde zweimal wöchentlich exerziert, und hölzerne Gewehre wurden zu diesem Zwecke angeschafft.

HOFFNUNG

Es reden und traumen die Menschen viel
  Von bessern künftigen Tagen;
Nach einem glücklichen, goldenen Ziel
  Sieht man sie *rennen* und jagen.
  Die Welt wird alt und wieder jung,
Doch der Mensch hofft immer Verbesserung!

Die Hoffnung führt ihn ins Leben ein,
  Sie umpflattert den fröhlichen Knaben,
Den Jungling locket ihr Zauberschein,
  Sie wird mit dem Greis nicht begraben.
Denn beschliesst er im Grade den müden Lauf,
  Noch am Grabe pflanzt er—die Hoffnung auf.

Es ist kein leerer, schmeichelnder Wahn,
  Erzeugt im Gehirne des Thoren,
Im Herzen kündet es laut sich an:
  Zu was Besserm sind wir geboren;
Und was die innere Stimme *spricht*,
Das täuscht die hoffende Seele nicht.

SCHILLER.

	Credits
1. Translate the above passages.	30
2. Give the principal parts of *sagte, bringen, machen, rennen, spricht.*	5
3. Give a synopsis in the indicative mood, third person singular of *machen.*	5
4. Compare schön. Decline the personal pronoun of the second person.	5
5. Translate into German: My father was a general and when I am a man I shall be a soldier and at last, I hope, an officer.	

3. COMPLETE LIST OF STATE SCHOLARS AT CORNELL UNIVERSITY, APPOINTED UPON EXAMINATION HELD JUNE 5, 1897

NAME	County appointed for	County of residence
Brown, Frazer	Albany	Albany.
McGovern, John P.	Albany	Albany.
Ashby, Chester	Albany	Albany.
Kelsey, Charles A.	Albany	Albany.
Wyvell, Manton Marble	Allegany	Allegany.
Walter, Richard Oliver	Broome	Broome.
Whitney, George Stoddard	Broome	Broome.
Newton, Thomas Lee	Cattaraugus	Cattaraugus.
Wilson, William Edwards	Cattaraugus	Oneida.
Allen, Louis Edward	Cayuga	Cayuga.
Treat, Lillian A.	Cayuga	Cayuga.
Price, Albert S.	Chautauqua	Chautauqua.
Keyes, Marion A., Jr.	Chautauqua	Chautauqua.
Canfield, Amos	Chemung	Chemung.
Hansen, Anthony H.	Chenango	Chenango.
Hagerty, James Andrew	Clinton	Clinton.
De Lamater Wm. Jonas	Columbia	Columbia.
Mack, Harry E.	Cortland	Cortland.
Voegelin, Carl Oswald	Delaware	Delaware.
Butchers, Earl Burdett	Dutchess	Madison.
Hausner, Frank H.	Dutchess	Ontario.
Weidner, Paul Gustavus	Erie	Erie.
Carrier, Willis Haviland	Erie	Erie.
Massie, James H.	Erie	Erie.
Wilgus, Herbert Sedgwick	Erie	Erie.
Dunham, Frederick Gibbons	Erie	Erie.
O'Malley, James	Erie	Erie.
Slocum, Alexander M	Erie	Erie.
Smith, Don E.	Erie	Erie.
Beers, Charles Emerson	Essex	Essex.
Gray, Edward Townsend	Franklin	Oswego.
Geer, Hdwaro Earl	Fulton and Hamilton	Fulton.
Page, Sophy Ellen	Genesee	Genesee.
Dobbins, Elizabeth Calden	Greene	Monroe.
Armstrong, Alexander Floyd	Herkimer	Herkimer.
Haas, Sherwin Ward	Jefferson	Jefferson.
Penney, Albert Silas	Jefferson	Jefferson.
Johnston, Richard Harry	Kings	Kings.
Crouch, Frank Monroe	Kings	Kings.
Dresser, John Olmstead	Kings	Kings.
Folk, Frederick Jackson	Kings	Kings.
Caruth, William Alexander	Kings	Kings.
Phelps, Walter Edwin	Kings	Kings.
Redfield, Harry Westfall	Kings	Kings.
Blakeslee, J. Roy	Kings	Washington.
Mills, Frederic Alden	Kings	Kings.
Puig, Louise Margarita	Kings	Kings.
Searing, Benj. Haff	Kings	Kings.
Bliss, Theodore	Kings	Albany.
Williams, Howard Shay	Kings	Kings.
Henry, Florence F.	Kings	Cortland.
Cobleigh, Henry Rice	Kings	Kings.
Fiero, Harry Hunt	Kings	Yates.
Ackerman, Ira Jason	Kings	Kings.
Kerlin, Ward Dix	Kings	Kings.
Newbury, Frank Davies	Kings	Kings.
Dodge, Robert Irving	Kings	Kings.
Healy, Thomas David Joseph	Kings	Kings.
Wormuth, Romeyn	Lewis	Lewis.
Stanton, John M.	Livingston	Livingston
Root, Samuel Charles	Madison	Madison.
Ferguson, George Alexander	Monroe	Monroe.
May, Alice Ruth	Monroe	Monroe.
Carr, E Wheeler Jr.	Monroe	Monroe.
Lowenthall, Sidney S.	Monroe	Monroe.
Sanders, Frederick Morton	Montgomery	Montgomery.
Harris, Lena	New York	Tompkins.
Hayes, Rud. Bryant	New York	Tioga.
Mider, Carrol A.	New York	Lewis.
Gay, John Sedgwick	New York	Seneca.
Tryon, Clarence A.	New York	Genesee.
Skinner, John A.	New York	Chautauqua.

LIST OF STATE SCHOLARS — (*Concluded*)

NAME	County appointed for	County of residence
Harris, John B.	New York	Jefferson.
Wickham, Robert Sloane	New York	Broome.
Curtiss, Clarence James	New York	Saratoga.
Seymour, Claire	New York	Fulton.
Brand, Walter Nathan	New York	Herkimer.
Lauren, Edness Chester	New York	Cayuga.
Griswold, Jonas W	New York	Chemung.
Crandell, Walter S.	New York	Columbia.
Griffith, James Harvey, Jr	New York	Queens.
Ellis, Williard Waldo	New York	Allegany.
Gray, Leon W.	Niagara	Niagara.
Day, George W.	Niagara	Niagara.
Parry, Elizabeth	Oneida	Oneida.
Rose, Harry	Oneida	Oneida.
Sweet, Arthur Jeremiah	Oneida	Oneida.
Shea, Mabel M	Onondaga	Onondaga.
Lawrence, Morton R.	Onondaga	Onondaga.
Pratt, Marion	Onondaga	Onondaga.
Donohue, Robert Daniel	Onondaga	Onondaga.
Morrison, Archibald Bostwick	Ontario	Ontario.
Senior, John L.	Orange	Orange.
Sayer, Harry A.	Orange.	Orange.
Skinner, Mary Pendexter	Orleans	Orleans.
Phillips, Mary Antoinette	Oswego	Oswego.
Wilcox, Clark Luzerne	Oswego	Oswego.
Ackerman, Fred Lee	Otsego	Otsego.
Edgerton, Chauncey T	Queens	Queens.
Pettit, Irving Coles	Queens	Queens.
Doerffling, Arrey	Queens	Queens.
Stone, Charles Lucius	Rensselaer	Rensselaer.
Kemp, William James	Rensselaer	Rensselaer.
Tompkins, Sidney	Rensselaer	Rensselaer.
Heath, Daisy Winifred	Richmond	Richmond.
Cohen, Herbert D	Rockland	Rockland.
Hartley, Seward W.	St. Lawrence	St. Lawrence.
Austin, Jessie P.	St. Lawrence	St. Lawrence.
Bailey, Frederic William	Saratoga	Saratoga.
Borst, Victor Dow	Schoharie	Schoharie
Sears, Keith	Schuyler	Schuyler.
Smith, Leroy Burns	Seneca	Seneca.
Stevens, Charles Edmund	Steuben	Steuben.
Fay, Clarence Huntington	Steuben	Steuben.
Downs, Irving Garfield	Suffolk	Suffolk.
Jetter, Clifford Hawkins	Suffolk	Suffolk.
Kilbourne, Byron Albert	Sullivan	Sullivan.
Clauson, Robert	Tioga	Tioga.
Blair, John Hamilton	Tompkins	Tompkins
Sherwood, Arthur Henry	Ulster	Ulster.
Ryon, Arthur Clark	Ulster	Ulster.
Scoville, Addison Beecher	Warren	Warren.
Tooley, William Benjamin	Washington	Washington.
Albright, Johnson Stanley	Wayne	Wayne
Wakeman, Samuel S.	Westchester	Westchester.
Gunn, Spencer C.	Westchester	Clinton.
Conable, Barber B., Jr.	Wyoming	Wyoming.
Smith, Helen Florence	Yates	Yates.

4. TABLE SHOWING BY COUNTIES THE NUMBER OF CANDIDATES FOR STATE SCHOLARSHIPS AT CORNELL UNIVERSITY, EXAMINED JUNE 5, 1897, AND NUMBER APPOINTED FROM EACH COUNTY

	Whole No. examined	Number appointed		Whole No. examined	Number appointed
Albany	10	5	Ontario	6	2
Allegany	6	2	Orange	6	2
Broome	7	3	Orleans	2	1
Cattaraugus	2	1	Oswego	9	3
Cayuga	5	3	Otsego	3	1
Chautauqua	9	3	Putnam	0	0
Chemung	6	2	Queens	8	4
Chenango	2	1	Rensselaer	8	3
Clinton	2	2	Richmond	3	1
Columbia	4	2	Rockland	2	1
Cortland	5	2	St. Lawrence	4	2
Delaware	1	1	Saratoga	7	2
Dutchess	1	0	Schenectady	0	0
Erie	17	6	Schoharie	1	1
Essex	2	1	Schuyler	4	1
Franklin	0	0	Seneca	4	2
Fulton and Hamilton	2	2	Steuben	3	2
Genesee	5	2	Suffolk	7	2
Greene	1	0	Sullivan	2	1
Herkimer	5	2	Tioga	5	2
Jefferson	8	3	Tompkins	17	2
Kings	38	17	Ulster	12	2
Lewis	3	2	Warren	1	1
Livingston	7	1	Washington	4	2
Madison	3	2	Wayne	1	1
Monroe	7	5	Westchester	2	1
Montgomery	3	1	Wyoming	1	1
New York	1	0	Yates	6	2
Niagara	8	2			
Oneida	9	4	Total	309	128
Onondaga	7	4			

5. LIST OF PERSONS WHO RECEIVED CORNELL STATE SCHOLARSHIPS IN 1896, BUT WHO ARE NO LONGER STUDENTS IN THE UNIVERSITY

NAME	County appointed for	Person appointed to fill vacancy	County of residence
Willis, Rodney R.	Rensselaer	Giltner, Louis Curtis	Tompkins
Carr, Walter	Albany	Quigley, James Patrick	Cattaraugus
Coe, Glen Earle	Jefferson	McMenany, Helen E	Greene

EXHIBIT No. 14

College Graduates' Certificates

Indorsement of Normal Diplomas and State Certificates Issued in Other States

1. Law of 1888
2. Circular of Information
3. List of College Graduates' Certificates Granted 189
4. List of Normal Diplomas Indorsed 1897
5. List of State Certificates Indorsed 1897

COLLEGE GRADUATES' CERTIFICATES

INDORSEMENT OF NORMAL DIPLOMAS AND STATE CERTIFICATES ISSUED IN OTHER STATES

1. THE LAW OF 1888

The Legislature of 1888, amended by chapter 331, section 15 of title 1, of the "Consolidated School Act" so as to read as follows (amendments in italics):

§ 15. He (the State Superintendent) may grant, under his hand and seal of office a certificate of qualification to teach, and may revoke the same. While unrevoked, such certificate shall be conclusive evidence that the person to whom it was granted is qualified by moral character, learning and ability to teach any common school in the State. Such certificate may be granted by him only upon examination He shall determine the manner in which such examination shall be conducted, and may designate proper persons to conduct the same and report the result to him. He may also appoint times and places for holding such examinations, at least once in each year, and cause due notice thereof to be given. *He may also, in his discretion, issue a certificate without examination, to any graduate of a college or university who has had three years experience as a teacher. Such last-mentioned certificate shall be known as the "college graduate's certificate," and may be revoked at any time for cause. He may also, in his discretion, indorse a diploma issued by a State normal school or a certificate issued by a State Superintendent or State Board of Education in any other State, which indorsement shall confer upon the holder thereof the same privileges conferred by law upon the holders of diplomas or certificates issued by State normal schools or by the State Superintendent in this State.* He may also issue temporary licenses to teach, limited to any school commissioner district or school district, and for a period not exceeding six months, whenever, in his judgment, it may be necessary or expedient for him to do so.

2. CIRCULAR OF INFORMATION

The following information concerning college graduates' certificates is furnished for the benefit of those interested:

The Law

(From section 10 of title I, Consolidated School Law.)

§ 10. He (the State Superintendent) * * * * may also, in his discretion, issue a certificate, without examination, to any graduate of a college or university who has had three years' experience as a teacher. Such last-mentioned certificate shall be known as the "college graduate's certificate," and may be revoked at any time for cause. He may also, in his discretion, indorse a diploma issued by a State normal school or a certificate issued by a State Superintendent or State board of education in any other State which indorsement shall confer upon the holder thereof the same privileges conferred by law upon the holders of diplomas or certificates issued by State normal schools or by the State Superintendent in this State.

The Purpose

The purpose of the college graduate's certificate is to relieve persons entitled to receive it from the necessity of taking examinations which would otherwise be required. It is in no sense a test of scholastic merit, but a privilege which the Superintendent *may confer* upon those deemed worthy. It is issued *in the discretion* of the Superintendent.

It is intended for the benefit and convenience of teachers actually employed in New York state, and of such as propose to follow the profession of teaching in the state. It is not intended for use of teachers who leave the state, nor for the purpose of securing advantage or position in this or other states.

Requirements

All applicants are informed that as these certificates may be made good for life in this state, they will not be issued until the Superintendent is in possession of the most conclusive evidence of the good character and ability of applicants, and is satisfied that they have taught successfully for at least three years *since graduation.* A reasonable portion of this experience must have been gained in the public schools of this state. On these points the most satisfactory proof must be submitted. The names of at least three persons must be furnished as references who are known in educational work in the state, and at the Department, who are personally acquainted with the applicant and are familiar with the applicant's work as a teacher.

Applicants must show that they have taken a full course in, and have been graduated from a college or university of good standing. They must also show that they are actually teaching, or that they are under engagement to teach in New York state.

Ample time will be taken by the Superintendent for investigation in all cases. Haste must not be expected, and applicants are cautioned against making engagements which are contingent upon the issue of certificates, or upon the expectation that they will be issued within a fixed time.

It should be borne in mind that teachers employed in private schools and academies do not require certificates, and college graduates' certificates are not intended for such teachers. They are of no value to teachers in city schools, unless the boards of education in such cities accept a state certificate without further examinations. They are for the *relief* of persons entitled to receive them— for *use* and not for *ornament*.

Blank forms of application will be sent upon request.

State Certificates and Normal School Diplomas from other States

Application for the indorsement of state certificates and normal school diplomas issued in other states will not be approved, unless the state superintendents of such states extend a like courtesy to holders of state certificates and normal school diplomas issued in this state.

Efforts have been made for concert of action in legislation among all the states, but thus far little has been accomplished.

The following states, so far as known, recognize state certificates and normal school diplomas issued in New York state: Alabama, New Jersey, Maryland (limited in time and renewable except in Baltimore), Michigan, Florida, Oregon and Wisconsin.

CHARLES R. SKINNER,
State Superintendent.

3. LIST OF COLLEGE GRADUATES' CERTIFICATES GRANTED, 1897

Number	NAME	Residence	Graduated at	Year of [illegible]	Date of [illegible], 1897
481	Ezra [illegible] Benedict	Salem	Middlebury College	1891	February 4
482	Mary Dianthe Allis	Syracuse	Syracuse University	1887	February 4
483	Byron H. Heath	[illegible]	Cornell University	1891	February 4
484	Laura [illegible] Smith	Moravia	Vassar College	1893	February 4
485	John Leroy Hurlbert	Dunkirk	Yale University	1893	February 4
486	[illegible] Louise Saxton	Clyde	Syracuse [illegible]	1893	February 4
487	[illegible] Estabrook [illegible]	Brooklyn	Amherst College	1889	February 4
488	[illegible] Emily Wakeman	Watertown	Vassar College	1892	April 9
489	Arthur Cecil Perry, Jr.	[illegible]	New York University	[illegible]	[illegible] 9
490	John W. Rafferty	Brooklyn	St. Lawrence University	1887	April 9
491	Anna Frances [illegible]	Albion	Cornell University	1893	April 9
492	John [illegible]	New York	[illegible] College	1893	April 9
493	Oscar D. Robinson	Albany	Dartmouth College	1869	April 9
494	[illegible] Grace Fisher	[illegible]	Vassar College	1891	April 9
495	F. May West Herrick	Canajoharie	Wellesley College	1891	April 9
496	John Russell Olin	Watertown	Hobart College	1893	June 16
497	Frances Clara Nearing	Matteawan	St. Lawrence University	1894	June 16
498	Laura Elizabeth Shurtliff	Warsaw	Oberlin College	1893	June 16
499	[illegible] C. Pierce	Rochester	Rochester [illegible]	1860	June 16
500	Schuyler Fox Herron	Elizabethtown	Syracuse University	1894	June 16
501	Frederick B. Van Ornum	Whitesboro	St. Lawrence University	1894	June 16
502	Christine Karslake	Lockport	Wellesley College	1890	June 16
503	[illegible] E. Lindsey	Lockport	Cornell [illegible]	1894	June 30
504	Fred Hermance [illegible]	Marlboro	Hamilton College	1890	June 30
505	Calvin Patterson	Brooklyn	Rochester University	1877	July 13
506	Katherine E. Youmans	Elmira	Elmira [illegible]	1891	August 9
507	M. Louise Godfrey	Elmira	Elmira College	1886	August 9
508	Wm. Dodge Lewis	Syracuse	Syracuse University	1892	August 9
509	Bridget Mahoney	Canton	St. Lawrence University	1893	A[illegible]gust 9
510	J. Schuyler Fox	Three Mile Bay	Brown University	1894	August 9
511	Milicent A. Hinkley	Syracuse	Syracuse University	1894	August 9
512	Rose May [illegible]	[illegible]	St. Lawrence [illegible]	1890	August 9
513	Walter T. Cowper	Clinton	Hamilton College	1892	August 9
514	Clara E. Schouton	Brockport	Cornell [illegible]	1891	August 9
515	John J. Chickering	F[illegible]	Amherst College	1879	August 9
516	Mary B. D. Poland	Brooklyn	University of the City of N. Y.	1891	August 9
517	L. [illegible] Henderson	Pulaski	Vassar College	1893	[illegible] 25
518	John Payson Slocum	Angelica	Yale University	[illegible]	September 21

519	Rose Adele Baird	Dunkirk	Syracuse University	1891	September 21
520	Wm. M. Marvin	Middleburg	Williams College	1886	October 6
521	Jessie A. E. Whyborn	Syracuse	Syracuse University	1893	October 6
522	Wm. J. Deans	Chateaugay	St. Lawrence University	1894	October 6
523	Agnes Arbuckle	Delhi	Vassar College	1892	October 26
524	Elizabeth Ostrander	Belmont	Alfred University	1892	November 1
525	Howard Conant	Waverly	Union University	1892	November 1
526	Sarah Pratt	Watertown	Smith College	1894	November 1
527	Harry J. Walter	Wolcott	Cornell University	1892	November 1
528	Media K. Carrier	Batavia	Wellesley College	1892	November 1

4. LIST OF NORMAL SCHOOL DIPLOMAS INDORSED, 1897

No.	NAME	Residence	Graduated at	Date of indorsement
76	Charles W Waring .	Fayette	Michigan State Normal School....	June 15, 1897

1 year limited certificate

5. STATE CERTIFICATES INDORSED, 1897

None

EXHIBIT No. 15

TEACHERS' INSTITUTES

1. Report of Supervisor of Institutes
2. Reports of Institute Conductors
3. Reports of Drawing and Primary Work
4. The Institute Law Regulating Attendance
5. Statistical Tables

TEACHERS' INSTITUTES

SUPERVISOR OF INSTITUTES

Augustus S. Downing, A. M. .... Albany.

INSTITUTE CONDUCTORS

NAMES AND ADDRESSES

Henry R. Sanford, A. M., Ph. D. .... Penn Yan.
Isaac H. Stout, A. M. .... Geneva.
Welland Hendrick, A. M. .... Cortland.
Archibald C. McLachlan, A. M. .... Binghamton.
Percy I. Bugbee, A. M. .... Oneonta.

SPECIAL INSTRUCTORS

Drawing — Miss Gratia L. Rice, P. O. box 321, Buffalo; Miss Florence B. Himes, Albany.

Primary Work — Miss Anna K. Eggleston, 45 Wadsworth street, Buffalo.

INSTITUTE LECTURER

Hon. Charles E. Fitch, LL. D. .... Rochester.

---

1. REPORT OF SUPERVISOR OF TEACHERS' INSTITUTES

In accordance with the usual custom I submit my annual report as supervisor of teachers' institutes. The year has been one of continued success in institute work. The faculty of instructors has been unchanged, so that the unity of purpose in the work done has been more marked than ever before. The principal feature of the year's labor has been the growing demand for graded institutes. This has necessitated additional assistance and therefore it has been incumbent on me to be present at more than the usual number of institutes. This has afforded the opportunity of observing the work both of those connected directly with the corps of instructors and of those called upon to assist. It is my pleasure as the result of such observation to report that in no year has the effectiveness of institute work been more apparent than during the year just closed. The conductors have done their work with more ease and the control of the institute through the efficiency of the instruction has been more perfect.

The institute which is graded into three divisions requires forty-six hours of instruction. The conductor cannot to advantage take more than 12 of these hours. If assistants in primary work and in drawing had been assigned to the institute, each will take six of the hours. Thus the Department provides for 24 of the 46 hours of instruction, leaving 22 hours to be provided for from normal schools and by local teachers. The latter can not ordinarily, be depended upon for much assistance. The commissioner and teachers alike prefer to reserve their work for the district or county association. Hence, almost the entire assistance must come from the normal schools. These schools have responded most promptly to the requests of the conductors and commissioners. Moreover, the assistance afforded has been of the very best, inasmuch as it is quite a certainty that only a few in each normal school faculty are capable of doing institute work, however efficient the others may be in their respective classrooms and the efficient few have done most of the work. The demand on the normal schools has, therefore, been so great that I am fully satisfied that if continued the authorities in immediate control of these schools will rightfully demur. I think that the remedy lies in holding only four institutes per week, thus permitting the utilizing of the services of one conductor in two institutes and of one of the instructors in drawing in each institute. This would have the effect of distributing the institutes over a greater part of the year, and though at first the commissioners might object, I am sure in the end they would see the advantages which would accrue. It is clearly a mistake to think that the great good of an institute is to be found in its immediate effect. I am convinced there is a lasting influence which is of far more value than the first impression. Many of the commissioners who now have the institute in the fall, can equally well have the institute in January, February or March, so far as accommodating the teachers is concerned and can much better have it in one of these months when the availability of instructors is considered. I further believe that greater efficiency would be secured in the work by such an arrangement.

During the year the interest in drawing seems to have been increasing. This is due to a new spirit in the view taken of it. Formerly, teachers were interested in drawing largely because they must pass an examination in this subject. During this year I have observed that they are interested in the subject for its own sake, that is, they have discovered its educational value, and therefore want to know it. The growing appreciation of this special branch speaks well for the efficiency of the instructors therein.

It has been a most difficult task to meet the demand for a primary instructor for each institute. The special primary instructor has made this feature of institute work so popular that it is embarrassing to be unable to distribute her work over all the institutes each week. If possible to secure another regular primary instructor it would be of great assistance in relieving the pressure upon the normal schools for such work, and it would tend to satisfy the demands of commissioners and teachers for skilled primary instruction.

The conductors have been untiring in their efforts to increase the effectiveness of the institutes, and it must be a pleasure to you to see the happy results of their efforts. For support no one could desire a more earnest, faithful and loyal body of co-workers than you have in the institute conductors and instructors.

The following table shows the result of the year in comparison with those of other years:

	1894–5			1895–6			1896–7		
	Men	Women	Total	Men	Women	Total	Men	Women	Total
Teachers in attendance	3,473	12,869	16,342	3,474	12,748	16,222	3,484	12,789	16,273
Average attendance	3,299	12,639	15,938	3,411	12,584	15,995	3,431	12,620	16,051
Aggregate days' attendance	......	......	79,912	......	......	80,031	......	......	80,372
Local expenses	......	......	$4,259 97	......	......	$4,072 53	......	......	$3,674 99
Number of institutes	......	......	108	......	......	106	......	......	106

The following table shows the comparison for fifteen years:

Comparative Summary of Teachers' Institutes for Fifteen Years

YEAR	Number of counties	Number of institutes	Number of teachers in attendance	Average daily attendance	Per cent of average attendance to total number of teachers	Aggregate number of days' attendance	Days of attendance per teacher	Average number of teachers per institute	Amount paid by the state	Average expense per institute	Average expense per teacher
1883	58	73	14,477	10,231	70.67	50,015	3.50	198	$15,770 08	$216 03	$1 08
1884	58	71	14,770	10,272	69.54	51,303	3.48	208	16,998 81	228 11	1 14
1885	58	79	18,298	14,378	78.59	71,892	3.93	231	18,433 21	230 01	1 00
1886	58	77	17,739	14,925	84 13	71,639	4.21	230	18,980 98	240 00	1 07
1887	56	80	14,818	13,271	89.58	66,340	4 47	186	18,555 54	228 18	1 25
1888	58	110	16,214	15,138	93 36	75,031	4 63	147	21,097 81	200 95	1 30
1889	59	118	16,316	15,566	95.25	76,052	4.69	140	21,208 75	208 21	1 30
1890 (a)	55	98	12,600	12,105	95.90	60,119	4 70	137	19,873 84	210 17	1 53
1891 (b)	57	100	15,075	14,450	95.86	70,766	4 69	130	21,144 41	212 83	1 54
1892 (c)	47	70	9,329	9,018	96.66	41,049	4 82	133	13,917 00	197 80	1 48
1893 (d)	59	110	15,430	15,069	97.22	74,990	4 81	140	24,016 09	251 07	1 87
1894	59	111	15,607	15,200	97 45	75,879	4 50	141	24,919 71	217 39	2 31
1895	57	108	16,342	15,908	97.53	79,019	4 80	151	30,786 40	310 96	2 25
1896	57	106	16,238	15,905	98.00	80,011	4 03	153	35,071 30	330 86	2 16
1897	57	103	16,278	16,051	98.63	80,379	4.94	158	34,999 59	330 04	2 16

(a) For eleven months. (b) For year ending Dec. 1, 1891. (c) For eight months ending June 15, 1892. (d) For school year 1892-3.

Three summer institutes were held at Chautauqua, Glens Falls and Thousand Island Park, respectively. The regular institute work is by far the most exacting and hence wearing work done in connection with the educational system of the state, and I am convinced that it is not good economy to require the regular institute conductors to conduct the summer institutes. There is so short a time between the close of these institutes and the beginning of the Fall labors that there is between the two really no time either for recuperation or for preparation for the regular work. It seems to me to be feasible to train some one of the faculty in each summer institute so that he would be able to assume the management the year following. That the special primary and drawing instructors should be exempt from the summer institute work is thoroughly settled in my mind. The strain incident to the double amount of travel necessary for them to attend two institutes per week can only be endured by giving them perfect rest during the summer. I am fully conscious of the difficulties which are to be encountered in exempting the entire institute faculty from labor in the summer institutes, but I am just as fully convinced that these difficulties can be obviated and that greater good will result in the end.

SUMMER INSTITUTES

PLACE	Number of instructors	Registered Members		
		Men	Women	Total
Chautauqua	15	55	368	423
Glens Falls	19	13	178	191
Thousand Island Park	16	27	199	226
Total	50	95	743	840

The reports of the conductors of the several summer institutes follow, and show the plan of the work and the method of executing the plan.

ALBANY, N. Y., *August* 1, 1897.

CHAUTAUQUA

ISAAC H. STOUT, A. M., CONDUCTOR

The summer institute at Chautauqua showed a large increase in enrollment over that of 1896 and undiminished appreciation and enthusiasm on the part of those in attendance. Of the instructors and the instruction given I can speak only in terms of the highest commendation. The courtesy and consideration of the former, and the thorough, systematic character of the latter were matters of constant and favorable comment on the part of the members of the institute. Of the generous and courteous treatment accorded to the faculty and teachers in attendance, by the authorities at Chautauqua I feel that I cannot say too much in praise. At all times they gave the most careful attention to necessary details for the accommodation of the unexpectedly large number enrolled, and at all times were ready to grant more in the way of special privileges than from the terms of their contract the state or the individual had a right to demand or expect. The only drawback to the summer's work was that the term of the institute and the school of pedagogy began on different dates, but this has been satisfactorily arranged for the coming year, when both are to begin July 11th and close July 29th. The following comparative table and program of daily work are made part of this report

	1896	1897
Counties represented in membership	37	48
Cities represented in membership	20	24
Total registration	256	423
Men	35	55
Women	221	368
Enrolled in College Courses	8	97
Enrolled in School of Pedagogy	179	265
Enrolled in Drill and Review Department	147	232
Class enrollments—School of Pedagogy	362	584
Class enrollments—Drill and Review	235	465

In the Drill and Review Department the class enrollment in subjects was as follows:

Arithmetic	25	55
Algebra	19	46
American History	19	50
Astronomy	2	7
Bookkeeping	25	24
Chemistry	..	9
Civics	23	22
Drawing	57	115
English Grammar	24	47
English Composition	..	18
Geography	11	21
Geology	3	8
Physics	30	59
Physiology	..	15

NEW YORK STATE SUMMER INSTITUTE, 1897

Daily Program

[Drill and Review Classes]

	Normal Hall	Temple	Annex A-2	Annex B-1	Annex B-2	College 1	College 2	College 6	College 11	College 12
8:00 to 8:30										School Law
8:30 to 9:30					Geography		Algebra			Civics
9:30 to 10:20			Chemistry	Grammar						
10:20 to 11:10	(Laboratory) Nature Study		Astronomy		English Composition				American History	
11:10 to 12:00	Nature Study						Arithmetic			
2:00 to 3:00			Geology			Drawing				
3:00 to 4:00						Drawing		Physics		
4:00 to 5:00		Book-keeping				(Round Table) Drawing		Physics		
5:00 to 6:00								Physiology		

NEW YORK STATE SUMMER INSTITUTE, 1897 — (*Concluded*)

PEDAGOGICAL DEPARTMENT

	Normal Hall	Kellogg Hall	Annex A-1	Annex B-1	Annex B-2	College 7	Old Chapel			
8:30 to 9:30	Pedagogy		(Observation) Nature Study	English Literature	Story Telling					
9:30 to 10:20	Psychology and Child Study		(Methods) Nature Study		Story Telling	Teachers' Training Course in Latin				
10:20 to 11:10				English Composition						
11:10 to 12:00	Primary Methods		(Observation) Nature Study		Grammar School Methods					
12:00 to 1:00	Primary Teaching									
2:00 to 3:00	Physical Training	Theory of the Kindergarten								
3:00 to 4:00	Physical Training	Kindergarten Methods								
4:00 to 5:00							How to Teach Reading			

THOUSAND ISLAND PARK

WELLAND HENDRICK, A. M., CONDUCTOR

The Thousand Island Park Summer Institute was held from July 12th to the 30th, fourteen days being given to regular school work.

The accommodations for classes were improved over last year, but were still inadequate in many particulars. There was however, a ready good will on the part of instructors and pupils to make the best of crude conditions; and the park authorities were willing and efficient in improvising needed facilities. The new building erected by the park association is a pleasant cottage and is fairly well adapted to our work. A house of double the capacity is needed in addition.

The faculty of the school was as follows:

Professional Training Department.—Psychology and Pedagogy, Samuel H. Albro, Ph. D., State Normal School, Mansfield, Pa.; Primary Work and Methods, Gertrude M. Bacon, State Normal School, Buffalo, N. Y.; Methods in Mathematics, Caroline Coman, Hamilton, N. Y.; Kindergarten Methods, Helen L. Sewell, State Normal College, Albany, N. Y.; Methods in English, Henry R. Sanford, Ph. D., Penn Yan, N. Y.; Methods in Science, Darwin L. Bardwell, State Normal School, Cortland, N. Y.; Methods in Reading, Charles S. Davis, Superintendent of Schools, Amsterdam, N. Y.; History of Education and School Management.—Professor S. R. Shear, Superintendent of Schools, White Plains, N. Y.; Historial Lectures, Charles E. Fitch, State Institute Lecturer, Rochester, N. Y.; Music, Hollis E. Dann, Ithaca, N. Y.; Physical Culture, Mrs. Amy R. Blair, Pittsburg, Pa.; Elocution, Henry Ludlam, Philadelphia, Pa.

Drill and Review Department.—Natural Science, D. L. Bardwell, Cortland, N. Y.; P. F. Piper, Buffalo, N. Y.; Mathematics, S. R. Shear, White Plains, N. Y.; Caroline Coman, Hamilton, N. Y.; Bookkeeping, Penmanship and Commercial Arithmetic, Hollis E. Dann, Ithaca, N. Y.; American History, Civics and School Law, Charles A. Shaver, Watertown, N. Y.; English Language, Composition, Grammar, Rhetoric, Henry R. Sanford, Ph. D., Penn Yan, N. Y.; Drawing, Methods and Review, Florence B. Himes and Ida C. Greene.

The services rendered by these instructors are deserving of more than formal recognition. They devoted careful attention to their regular work; and their personal care for their pupils' needs and their extra labor in special cases were commendable features of the school.

The number of members of the school registered was 226, an increase over last year of forty-one. This increase is partly due to the fact that in the 1896 summer institute none were registered except teachers or those preparing to teach. There was an actual increase of membership however, in number, and a noticeable advance over last year in the character of the pupils. The number taking advanced subjects was nearly doubled. I regard this increase in quality the decided advancement of the summer; numbers are immaterial. The boast of a long roll comes with poor effect from a training school for teachers. There are certain limitations imposed by the nature of the accommodations, the character of the work done and the corps of instructors provided; and while I sympathize with those who predict a bright future for this summer school, I regard a membership of three hundred as large as can be profitably instructed.

The distribution of the members by counties was as follows: Jefferson, 49; St. Lawrence, 39; Oswego, 20; Monroe, 19, Onondaga, 19; Oneida, 13; Albany, 7; Cayuga, 6; Franklin, 4; Lewis, 4; Ontario, 4; Kings, 4; Otsego, 4; Queens, 3; Rensselaer, 3; Orange, 3; Montgomery, 2; Herkimer, 2; Orleans, 2; Rockland, 2; Chenango, 2; Broome, 1; Dutchess, 1; Putnam, 1; Richmond, 1; Chemung, 1; Niagara, 1; Cortland, 1; Allegany, 1; Tompkins, 1; Fulton, 1; Washington, 1; Madison, 1; Essex, 1. The number of counties represented is 34, as compared with twenty-five in 1896. The distribution in the different parts of the state is about as follows: Northern part, 50 per cent., central, 25 per cent., eastern, 15 per cent., western, 10 per cent., being a decided increase in the eastern part and a falling off in the northern counties.

Of the 226 members but 27, 12 per cent., were men.

The daily program of work was as follows:

	TABERNACLE	CHAPEL	SCHOOL HOUSE	INSTITUTE HOUSE	
8:15	Physical Culture	Primary Method *History of Education	Penmanship	Drawing, Review	Zoology
9:00	Kindergarten	Elocution *Psychology	Music	Algebra, Elementary	Physiology
9:45	Physical Culture	Primary Method *Psychology	Arithmetic, Review	Drawing, Pictorial	Physics
10:30	English	Elocution *History, U. S.	Book-keeping	Drawing, Mechanical	Astronomy
11:15	Kindergarten English	Civics	Geometry	Reading, Method	Chemistry
12:00		School Management *Geology	Algebra, Advanced	Drawing, Method	Nature Study Familiar Science

*Chapel Annex

In addition to the above program, work on the subject of nature study was given during the last week, two hours a day, by Mrs. Anna B. Comstock and Miss Mary F. Rogers, of Cornell University. Honorable Charles E. Fitch, State Lecturer, gave a course of three lectures on "The Making of the Nation," Alexander Hamilton, and General Grant. Bishop John H. Vincent delivered his lecture on "Tom and his Teachers." Miss Sewell, in connection with her work, conducted a kindergarten class of children gathered from the park. Round table conferences on "Correlation," and "The Township System" were held, and general sessions of the institute were called for special purposes.

The institute was visited by Superintendent Skinner, Deputy Superintendent Ainsworth and Supervisor Downing.

The rates charged for rooms and board were more satisfactory than last year. Many had good accommodations for five dollars a week, while those, who engaged cottages and arranged for their own cooking, obtained lower rates. The average rate paid for room and board was between five and a half and six dollars.

I renew my suggestion of last year to change the name of this branch of our work to "Summer School." The word "institute," carrying the idea of our regular institute work, is confusing and unsatisfactory.

On the whole the work at Thousand Island Park was a success, and, developed along conservative lines, can be made a more pronounced success.

GLENS FALLS

PERCY I. BUGBEE, A. M., CONDUCTOR

The institute consisted of two separate departments, the Drill and Review department and the department of Professional Training. These departments were under the instruction of the following faculties:

Drill and Review department: Algebra and Geometry, Wayland E. Stearns, Inspector of Teachers' Training Classes; Arithmetic and Book-keeping, Principal S. McK. Smith, Chatham, N. Y.; Physics, Astronomy, Zoology and Geology, Wm. M. Bennett, Canandaigua, N. Y.; Physiology, Botany and Chemistry, Principal W. D. Johnson, Cooperstown, N. Y.; Grammar, Composition and Rhetoric, Harriet B. Clapp, Fulton, N. Y.; History and Geography, Principal H. J. Walter, Wolcott, N. Y.; Civics and School Law, Frank H. Wood, Inspector of Teachers' Training Classes; History of Education and School Management, Principal Judson I. Wood, Ilion, N. Y.; Elocution and Physical Culture, Mrs. Helena Crummett Lee, Canton, N. Y.; Drawing, Gratia L. Rice, State Instructor in Drawing, and Laura E. McDowell, Teacher of Methods, Jamaica Normal School; Vocal Music, John B. Shirley, Lansingburgh, N. Y.

Department of Profesional Training: Psychology and Science of Education, Dr. Richard G. Boone, Ypsilanti, Michigan; Methods in Arithmetic, English and Literature, George T. Aldrich, Superintendent of Schools, Newton, Mass.; Methods in Geography, Charles F. King, Principal of Schools, Boston, Mass.; Methods in History, W. F. Gordy, Principal of Schools, Hartford, Conn.; General Pedagogy, Dr. Edgar D. Shimer, New York city; Reading and Elocution, Henry S. Southwick, Emerson College of Oratory, Boston, Mass.; Supplemental Reading and the Use of Libraries, Superintendent Sherman Williams, Glens Falls, N. Y.

The department of Professional Training did not open until July 20. I submit daily programs of both departments.

In addition to the regular work of the institute, there were two evening lectures, one by Charles E. Fitch, LL.D., and the other by Bishop Vincent of Chautauqua.

Though the attendance was not so large as last year, still the numbers were all that could be well accommodated; and the efficiency of the institute, as evidenced by the interest of teachers and their regularity of attendance, was all that could be desired.

PROGRAM STATE SUMMER INSTITUTE

ORDWAY HALL

Department of Professional Training

Second Week

2:00 p. m.—Principal Gordy on History.

2:40 p. m.—Professor Shimer on Fundamentals in Education.

3:20 p. m.—Principal Gordy on History.

4:00 p. m.—Professor Shimer on Fundamentals in Education.

4:40 p .m.—Professor Southwick on Reading and Elocution.

5:20 p. m.—Tuesday and Wednesday, Professor Russell on Elementary Science. Thursday, Friday and Saturday, Mr. King on Geography.

Third Week

2:00 p. m.—Mr. Aldrich on Arithmetic.

2:40 p. m.—Dr. Boone on Science of Education.

3:20 p. m.—Mr. Aldrich on Arithmetic.

4:00 p. m.—Dr. Boone on Science of Education.

4:40 p. m.—Mr. King on Geography.

STATE SUMMER INSTITUTE

Glen Street School

TIME	Mr. Stearns	Mr. Smith	Mr. Bennett	Mr. Johnson	Miss Clapp	Mr. Walter	Mr. Wood	Mr. Wood	Mrs. Lee	Miss Rice Miss McDowell	Mr. Shirley
8.00—8.30	Algebra Room 6		Astronomy Room 10			American History Room 7				Elementary Drawing Assembly	
8.30—9.00	Geometry Room 8	Book-keeping Room 6		Physiology Room 11		General History Room 7				Elementary Drawing Assembly	
9.00—9.30	Algebra Room 6		Zoology Room 10			Geography Room 7				Advanced Drawing Assembly	Music Room 12
9.30—10.00				Botany Room 11	Composition and Rhetoric Room 6	Geography Room 7	Civics Room 10			Advanced Drawing Assembly	
10.00—10.30		Arithmetic Room 7	Physics Room 10					School Management Room 11		Drawing Rooms 12 and 13	
10.30—11.00		Arithmetic Room 7		Chemistry Basement	Grammar Room 6		Civics Room 10		Physical Culture Room 13	Drawing Rooms 12 and 13	
11.00—11.30			Geology Room 10		Grammar Room 6	American History Room 7				Drawing Rooms 12 and 13	
11.30—12.00							School Law Room 10	History of Education Room 11	Elocution Assembly	Advanced Drawing Rooms 12 and 13	Music at 2.00 p. m. Room 12

A much larger percentage of those attending this year were experienced teachers.

---

2. REPORTS OF INSTITUTE CONDUCTORS

REPORT OF HENRY R. SANFORD, A. M., PH. D., INSTITUTE CONDUCTOR

During the past year the teachers' institutes have been marked by very full and regular attendance and deep interest; and the number of villages which voluntarily close their schools in order that their teachers may attend the institutes is increasing. The enthusiastic interest manifested by teachers of all grades, especially, principals and other teachers of the best education and the largest experience, has been very gratifying, and the teachers have entered with great heartiness into the discussion of important educational topics.

Many letters received from school commissioners, training class teachers, and others, attest the value of the notes of some of my institute lectures printed by the Department. The notes on teaching reading have now reached the seventh edition and the sixtieth thousand.

The disastrous effects of our district system are becoming more apparent as year after year the people are learning of the great advantages of the township system. Nearly all of the states have now made either the town or the county a school district. It is feared that the Empire state will be the last to abandon our system of small school districts which has outlived every advantage that it ever had.

The historical lectures delivered by Dr. Charles E. Fitch in connection with the institutes continue to maintain their high rank, are doing great good, and are appreciated. They give popular instruction in a much neglected field. The illustrated lectures still draw large audiences. I have given the lecture illustrating my trip to Mexico in twenty-six different places, and the total attendance has probably reached nearly twenty thousand.

The training class teachers give considerable assistance in the work of the institute, and I have been pleased to find them and the members of their classes in regular attendance.

In accordance with your desire to secure the co-operation of colleges in this work, I have from time to time secured valuable assistance from Union University, Cornell University, Syracuse University and Hamilton College.

Marked success has attended the presentation of nature study in the institutes by Mrs. Anna B. Comstock and Miss Mary F. Rogers of the Agricultural Department of Cornell University.

PENN YAN, *December* 18, 1897.

REPORT OF ISAAC H. STOUT, A. M., INSTITUTE CONDUCTOR

I have the honor to make the following report of institute work for the year ending July 31, 1897, done in twenty-three counties, for twenty-seven commissioner districts and one city, and in the summer institute held at Chautauqua, July 12th to 30th inclusive, a range wide enough to be fairly representative of the conditions existing throughout the state.

The attendance upon these institutes has been prompt and regular, the professional spirit and zeal of the teachers have been greater than ever before in my experience, the school commissioners have uniformly been loyal to the institute and interested in its work, and have given intelligent and efficient assistance to the conductor, while the public has more and more shown its appreciation of both teachers and teachers' institutes, their aims and their work.

The following comparative table relating to institutes under my charge for the past three years shows the rapid increase in efficiency of institutes, together with the change in organization that the times have demanded, better than I can state the facts in any other way—facts that reflect the highest credit on the broad and liberal policy of your administration as related to this line of educational activity:

YEAR	Counties	Commissioner districts	Cities	Ungraded institutes	Graded institutes	Aggregate attendance	Summer institute	Attendance
1895	21	24	....	22	2	3,595	....	....
1896	21	24	1	20	4	3,727	1	256
1897	23	27	1	13	12	4,106	1	423

The constantly growing demand for graded institutes by teachers and commissioners is indicative of their efficiency and their popularity; but their efficiency and consequently their popularity, can be maintained only by wise organization, an adequate supply of capable instructors and intelligent arrangement and balance of program. The present organization of the bureau of teachers' institutes, with a responsible supervisor in the Department of Public Instruction, provides for the organization, the institute conductor may be held responsible for the program, but a still greater proportion of graded institutes will necessitate an increase in the force of regular instructors, in order to keep the institute up to the standard which the teaching force has learned to expect and has a right to demand.

The work of the regular instructors in primary work and drawing seems to increase in popularity, usually drawing the largest numbers to the sections in which such work is given. This is particularly noticeable in view of the fact that a large majority of the teachers select from the program, with nice discrimination, that work which promises to be most helpful.

In some institutes school commissioners have secured a very general attendance of town and village truant officers to meet one of the state attendance officers, who has discussed with them and the teachers the problems constantly arising under the compulsory attendance law. It is entirely safe to say that in those commissioner districts the compulsory law is more intelligently and effectively enforced. I wish to commend this feature as desirable and as productive of results not obtainable unless teachers and truant officers have a common understanding of the workings of the law and the policy of the Department regarding its enforcement.

The growing recognition of the teaching force as a social factor by communities where institutes are held is well shown by the fact that in thirteen of the regular institutes under my charge during the past year receptions and entertainments have been given to the teachers by local organization. This recognition is the natural result of the substantial growth of culture and refinement among teachers, one of the most promising of upward educational tendencies.

GENEVA, N. Y., *November* 27, 1897.

REPORT OF WELLAND HENDRICK, A. M., INSTITUTE CONDUCTOR

Hon. CHARLES R. SKINNER, *State Superintendent of Public Instruction:*

Dear Sir.—During the past year I have conducted eighteen institutes and have assisted at five others. Of the institutes of which I have had charge nine have been graded and nine ungraded. The average number registered was 164. In addition to the help furnished by this Department, I was assisted by instructors from various sources as follows: Normal school teachers, 33 (times); members of institute, 13; city school superintendents, 4; academy and college teachers, 2; representatives of the regents, 2; commissioners, 1.

I have two suggestions to offer in view of the year's experience:

Instructors

The graded feature, which has been a slow evolution, has come to be a permanent feature of our work; it doubles the amount of help required. The normal school instructors, willing and efficient as they are, are overtaxed to assist us. I advise that two or three additional department instructors be furnished. One or two of these might well be specialists, taking up some branch that needs particular attention, or that schools are temporarily calling for. I might just now in this connection mention penmanship. After a year or two a change could be made and another special topic could be taken up. Such an instructor, if a man, could spend a day in a place and attend three institutes each week.

Session Rooms

I renew my suggestion of a year ago: The great drawback to good institute work remains the poor accommodations for the sessions. Of my institutes of the past year—as I have reported separately under the head of condition of room—33 1-3 per cent. were well adapted to the work, 50 per cent. were poorly ventilated, 28 per cent. were too small, and 22 per cent. were described as unfit in all respects. Teachers may be amused for a week in bad air and in opera houses and churches; but profitable instruction must be under favorable conditions. I believe that the firm principle of this Department should be that no town without a suitable schoolroom or rooms for an institute may be designated for such a purpose, in case there is a suitable schoolhouse in the commissioner district.

September 1, 1897.

REPORT OF A. C. McLACHLAN, A. M., INSTITUTE CONDUCTOR

The teachers' institutes of 1896-7 were, I believe, a means of helpfulness and inspiration to teachers. Although a few self-styled progressive teachers saw no good in them, yet I am confident that the fault was more in the attitude of these self-sufficient people toward the institutes than in the institutes themselves. Whatever good work was done by instructors was most appreciated by the best teachers.

One of the most enlightened superintendents in the state, who this year closed his schools for the first time to enable his teachers to attend the institute, declared with enthusiasm at the close of the session, that the institute had been of great profit to him and his teachers, both in work and in suggestiveness. "In the future," he said, "we shall welcome every opportunity for improvement afforded by the institute."

In the city institute held at Binghamton, Mr. Rogers, president of the school board, who was present at several sessions, said at the close, "This institute has been of inestimable value to our teachers. It has produced an awakening such as Binghamton has not experienced in years. We must have another next year." In view of these and similar expressions of approval, I believe there is a great work yet to be accomplished through the institutes.

It is true that every effort should be made to improve the work and to raise it to the highest degree of efficiency. The best instructors must be employed. Only people of scholarship, and broad and sound views should be invited to assist in the work. Teachers must not be chained to the past, neither should they be led to make a mad rush for things that are new. The old ways that have been proven to be good by enduring the test of time must be preserved, and new methods must be well considered before they are adopted.

There are few positions in educational work that afford larger opportunities for usefulness than that of an institute conductor. Thousands of teachers, instructors of tens of thousands of children come before him each year for aid and encouragement. If he is a man of culture, scholarship, magnanimity, of high ideals, and power to inspire, there is no measure to the good he may do.

Poor as were my efforts in attempting to perform the duties of this office, I was very reluctant to resign my position to accept another trust. Everywhere, I found teachers generous, charitable, helpful, and, with few exceptions, eager to learn. My associates in the institute faculty were men and women always courteous, cordial, and companionable; and the State Superintendent and his assistants in the Department were a source of never-failing aid and encouragement. Fortunate, indeed, is he whose lot is cast in such an environment. The memory of my work in the institutes will always be pleasant and my kindest wishes go with those who continue in the work.

REPORT OF PERCY I. BUGBEE, A. M., INSTITUTE CONDUCTOR

The teachers' institutes of the year 1896-'97 have, in my judgment, shown constant improvement in interest and efficiency. I believe there is a steady growth of professional pride in the teaching force and an increasing confidence in the value of special preparation. The raising of the requirements for teaching service as to age, scholarship and professional training has had marked effect on the institutes.

More than half of the institutes which I have conducted during the year have been graded, and added experience has confirmed and strengthened my opinion of the efficiency of the graded institute. The primary, the intermediate and the advanced sections meet the needs of teachers much more fully than the ungraded institute, while the increased opportunity for discussion and the greater personal element are marked features of improvement. I have, however, had considerable difficulty in arranging programs, as some of the normal schools, to which we look for expert assistants, complain of the drafts on them and refuse aid or grant it with reluctance. While the plan of the graded institute is much the better, an ungraded institute, with tried and competent assistants, is better than the graded with less efficient help.

In most places where institutes have been held, well-lighted and well-ventilated rooms have been provided, but it has occasionally happened that the work of the week has been hampered and much discomfort caused by rooms unfit for institute purposes.

I am continually impressed with the power and influence of the zealous and competent school commissioner. A commissioner who manifests a personal interest in the institute, who is present and participates in its exercises, and who shows, thus, his approval of and confidence in its work, inspires a ready following among his teachers which not only adds to the efficiency of the institute but must also strengthen his own leadership throughout the year.

REPORT OF GRATIA L. RICE, INSTRUCTOR IN DRAWING

During the past year the work has been, more than ever before, in line of regular institute work or methods. The immediate necessity for subject matter seems to have been passed, as the little pamphlet on drawing issued by the Department meets the demands and needs of the new comers. This little booklet, "Drawing for Training Classes and Teachers' Institutes," has been of special value, both to would-be-teachers, and to the instructors in drawing, helping in the first place and relieving the instructors of monotonous drill in the second place. There may be found within its covers all work necessary to meet the uniform examinations in drawing (to date at least), thus relieving the anxiety of the candidates as to what to study. The correspondence in one line has grown less, though it branches out and assumes tremendous proportions in other directions.

Many classes for private study have been formed throughout the state. These volunteers start their work with the first page of the drawing book and work through a certain number of lessons, their work is mailed to my address and the necessary criticisms and corrections are made, and the papers are then returned to the various classes. While I have, ordinarily, little faith in "Correspondence Schools" on a pay basis, I must acknowledge the success of this work, which is wholly gratis. The letters are so frank that they can be prompted only by the most earnest desire to do better work. The very earnestness indicates a thorough interest and a working spirit which calls for a strong effort on my part to help these teachers. The classes are more numerous than last year, and the cheering feature of the work *is*, that so many continue their work after necessary examinations have been successfully met. My first impression was that these classes were formed only to do work required to meet the demands of the uniform examinations; while this is true of some, it is not true of the majority. If the correspondence continues I would respectfully recommend that special blanks be printed, that we may in every way expedite the work. In consequence of the unavoidable delay caused by my almost constant absence during the institute season, such blanks would be invaluable.

The summer institutes now supply the necessary instruction for both classes of teachers—those working for examinations and the many who deny themselves everything to become better prepared for their work. The teacher pupils at the Glens Falls summer institute were always zealous, and frequently worked far into the night that they might be sure of every step and be ready for the following day's work. Not only this, but many devoted Saturday to the work, at the cost of the rest and the recreation they so much needed. At all hours, in the rooms devoted to the drawing, busy students could be found. These always received encouragement and help from Miss Laura E.

McDowell, who, during the three weeks, exhibited the keenest interest in the work, and whose valuable assistance it gives me pleasure to acknowledge.

The past year has been, in a way, marked, inasmuch as so many new features have been introduced in connection with the drawing. One line of work, not exactly drawing, but so closely allied to it as to be inseparable from it, the "blue print," has found a place in almost every school. This process gives a perfect record of objects varied in character, and affords a satisfactory reference throughout the year. Many schools have difficulty in procuring botanical and other specimens. Some schools are wholly without either specimens or means to procure them at the time needed in class. The blue prints supply every demand, and the simplicity of their production is such that any little child can make them. The process has been explained so many times that it seems unnecessary to incorporate it here. The value of the blue prints does not rest with simply furnishing records for class use. They do away entirely with the paper cutting and pasting in the primary grades. From the prints can be taught the principles of growth, which principles form the basis for work in design. Again, the blue print comes into play in connection with drawing, in connection with nature study, and, in fact, may be made helpful throughout the school curriculum.

These blue prints may be made to record the leaf, the plant, the blossom, the fruit, beetles, bugs, or butterflies. It will be seen that it furnishes a line of work, both interesting and profitable, as it brings about the closest and keenest observation on the part of the students. To this work we add drawing and "color washes." The process of Lavis work or "color washes" referred to, is simply that of covering the surface of the drawing paper where desired, by "floating in" the color. This method gives a perfect representation of any object which may be chosen. This "wash work," not necessarily "brush work" begins in the second year and continues through the high school, and in each grade every pupil has an equal chance to produce work of quality superior to that previously accomplished, and every school has an equal opportunity to do work on a par with other schools. Some of the high schools are at this time obviating many of their difficulties through this process. I presented the question of the Lavis work to the "Regents" and was given authority to state that the charts produced by this process, in the botanical work, would be accepted in lieu of an herbarium. This step by the "Regents" was particularly gratifying inasmuch as it gives an impetus to the drawing because every lesson in this work counts in the general preparation to meet the final requirements in drawing. This line of work has already exceeded my most sanguine expectations. I think it is quite original with us and therefore I am especially pleased to have it so generally accepted and approved.

I have not forgotten the value of art work, nor the power of freehand drawing, through my seeming enthusiasm for the later work. The regular work goes steadily on. It is my endeavor to keep before the teachers the one great aim, that of making and using drawing a means of expression—a language—keener, sharper, and more readily understood and carrying more power than words have ever achieved.

As the work grows and assumes more definite lines it is becoming much easier for the teachers to gain knowledge and skill, and as the subject broadens and deepens, the interest in it quickens, and I therefore have little anxiety for the complete success of the work where teachers have passed the first steps and are now reaping the fruits which the subject of drawing has to offer.

The greatest problem now is the work which may rightfully be expected from the ungraded district schools, where the teachers have many classes and the recitations are crowded into a very limited time. Yet under all the difficulties which could surround a teacher, good work has been done, in the district schools. There are some districts which have produced work which compares favorably with that from schools where every improvement and convenience is at hand.

In making comparison with a neighboring state (the only other I believe wherein organized work is carried on by the state authorities), I am satisfied that creditable work is being done in our schools, quite as good in many points as that in those of Massachusetts which have had the advantage of nearly thirty years training in drawing, and where at the present time there are employed three state instructors of drawing. When twenty-five years shall have been added to the work in the state of New York, I am sure that those who may see the results will acknowledge the wisdom of those who have been instrumental in laying the firm foundation of the present.

I shall feel satisfied with my work only when class teachers shall be able to freely and skillfully illustrate any point in the school work. To this end I am devoting my best energies.

BUFFALO, N. Y., *August* 1, 1897.

REPORT OF FLORENCE B. HIMES, INSTRUCTOR IN DRAWING

During the past year the work in subject matter has followed closely the manual on drawing published and issued by the Department to the various school districts of the state. This manual, together with the Revised Course of Study, has given the teachers a very definite line of work, so that I believe there has been more actual work in drawing done by them during this past year than in any previous year, and, from expressions heard on every side, these helps are fully appreciated. In addition to the subject matter above mentioned, methods in drawing have formed a part of the work of each institute, while in the graded institutes the work has been mainly along that line. Considerable attention has been paid also to such lines of the work as may be carried on with great benefit and with but little expense in the district schools, since it is our desire to have the drawing not only taught, but practically used in every school in the state.

The second year of the summer institute, in July last, found the drawing classes large and enthusiastic. Four classes were instructed, viz.: In drawing for the various examinations, in mechanical drawing, in pictorial drawing, and in methods, while the studio was open to students for extra work every day until six o'clock, and classes in out-of-door sketching were instructed as often as the weather permitted. The interest manifested and the results accomplished were in every way satisfactory, and I feel that these summer institutes give many teachers a highly appreciated opportunity for a serious and somewhat prolonged study of certain subjects in which they feel they need strengthening.

ALBANY, N. Y., *August* 1, 1897.

REPORT OF ANNA K. EGGLESTON, INSTRUCTOR IN PRIMARY WORK

This report covers the work done in forty-one institutes. Of this number fourteen institutes were with teachers with whom I had never worked, eighteen were in districts I had visited but once, while the remaining nine were in districts visited for the third time. The topics for these nine institutes were "Subjects Taught in Primary Grades," "Methods of Teaching Reading,"

"First Lessons in Reading," "Children's Hopes," and "How Gertrude Teaches Her Children." The last theme was selected because it embodied Pestalozzi's ideal of home and school life—a subject which, at the present time, is attracting much attention through its important bearing upon the education of children. As a separate report upon Child Study is submitted to you I will omit all remarks on that subject here.

The instructor who comes before the same institute for the third year has an opportunity for testing the true value of his past work, for in the first institute the teachers listen, at the second they begin to work, while at the third they bring their questions, and, better still, a willingness to relate their experiences. It is impossible to estimate how valuable or how profitless an exercise has been when teachers are silent. All instruction that is given without a clear knowledge of the actual needs of the teachers must ever be a waste of force, as well as disheartening to the instructor and discouraging to the listeners.

Grading institutes has served to put speakers and teachers into their proper relations more quickly than has any other agency, at least so far as I have observed its workings in the primary and the intermediate departments. Nothing has brought about such freedom in discussion as this classifying of teachers. In presenting subjects for primary teachers in the ungraded institute the speaker is always obliged to bear in mind that part of the audience is not especially interested in primary methods and, therefore, much of the detail which is helpful to teachers of elementary grades must be omitted in order to hold the attention of the entire institute. The grading into sections has made it possible to concentrate work to such a degree that not only is attention sustained, but teachers feel that some definite results have been accomplished. For instance, the twelve morning periods of the week in which primary teachers, assembled by themselves, listen to and discuss ways and means of teaching afford opportunities for practical work. It is possible under these conditions to continue one line of instruction until teachers have suggestions for further investigations that will enable them to do independent study. My observation on this point has been confirmed by the testimony of teachers, who say that more good has been derived when three of the twelve periods have been spent upon drawing, three upon reading or number, three upon nature lessons, and the remaining three possibly upon miscellaneous topics, than when ten or twelve subjects have been touched upon. It is not desirable to have a little of many things simply to make a program attractive for its variety, but it is essential to the growth of the institute idea to have a few things treated as thoroughly as possible.

It is often said that inspiration is the great thing in institute work, but a close study of those institutes where it has been made the only end, brings convincing proof that it is a source of evil if it is not firmly attached to the doing of something. He who has never been aroused to the possibilities of work may be awakened through inspiration, but if permanent good is to result the field of activity must be at hand and there must be definite knowledge of what is to be done. The afternoon lectures, which are usually upon some topic of general interest, are a means of creating a professional spirit and a desire for educational advancement, and when teachers bring that spirit and desire into the work of the morning, the highest province of the institute may be realized.

The most fruitful results doubtless come from the exercises of the graded institute, when teachers are brought into contact and labor hand in hand along the lines of their own work with the skilled instructor. These are the periods that most closely resemble school work, that may, indeed, be taken as model classroom teaching, and it would be difficult to estimate too highly their effect upon the teachers of our state. Whatever of refinement and gentle manners the instructor may possess is a force which creates higher ideals and those who have had but slight advantages become determined to make the necessary sacrifices to secure better training. A desire for higher education becomes a strong purpose in their lives as they feel the influence of the broader mind and deeper culture of the instructor. If the men and women who come from the various institutions of learning could realize how much they are affecting the educational progress of the State through the one day they spend at institutes, I am sure that whatever of sacrifice is necessary would be cheerfully borne. Those who have had the management of institutes must in a measure feel repaid for their untiring efforts to make them successful, as they hear the words of commendation uttered by teachers.

August 1, 1897.

---

4. LAW REGULATING ATTENDANCE AND CLOSING OF SCHOOLS

TITLE X OF CONSOLIDATED SCHOOL ACT

Section 1. It shall be the duty of the superintendent of public instruction to appoint a teachers' institute once in each year in each school commissioner district of the state, for the benefit and instruction of the teachers in the public schools, and of such as intend to become teachers, with special reference to the presentation of subjects relating to the principles of education and methods of instruction in the various branches of study pursued in the schools. After consultation with the school commissioners, the said superintendent shall have power to determine the duration of each institute and to designate the time and place of holding the same. He shall also have power to employ suitable persons, at a reasonable compensation, to supervise and conduct the institutes, and, in his discretion, to provide for such additional instruction as he may deem advisable and for the best interests of the schools. He may also, in his discretion appoint an institute for two or more commissioner districts. He shall establish such regulations for the government of institutes as he may deem best; and he may establish regulations in regard to certificates of qualification or recommendation which may be issued by school commissioners as will, in his judgment, furnish incentives and encouragement to teachers to attend the institutes. So far as consistent with other duties imposed upon him, the superintendent shall visit the institutes, or cause them to be visited by representatives of the department of public instruction, for the purpose of examining into the course and character of instruction given, and of rendering such assistance as he may find expedient.

§ 2. It shall be the duty of every school commissioner, subject always to the advice and direction of the superintendent of public instruction, and in such form and manner as may be deemed most effectual, to notify all teachers, trustees, boards of education and others known to him, who may desire to become teachers under his jurisdiction, of the time when and the place where the institute will be held. The school commissioner shall make all necessary arrangements for holding the institute when appointed; see that a suitable room is provided; attend to all necessary details connected therewith; assist the conductor in organization; keep a record of all teachers in attendance; and notify the trustees of the number of days attended by the teachers of the various districts, which shall be the basis of pay to such teacher for attendance as hereinafter provided. He shall also transmit to the superintendent of public instruction at the close of each institute, in such form, and within such time as the superintendent shall prescribe, a full report of the institute, including a list of all teachers in attendance, the number of days attended by each teacher. with such other statistical information as may be required. He shall present a full statement of all expenses incurred by him in carrying on the institute, with vouchers for all expenditures made, accompanying the same by an affidavit of the correctness of statements made and of accounts presented.

§ 3. The school commissioner shall have the right to hold an institute when appointed in any school building in any district under such commissioner's jurisdiction which receives public money from the state, without expense therefor to the state beyond a reasonable allowance to said district for lighting, heating and janitor service, provided always that due and proper care shall be maintained, and the school building left in the like condition as found as regards cleanliness and neatness.

§ 4. All schools in school districts and parts of school districts within any school commissioner district wherein an institute is held, not included within the boundaries of an incorporated city, or certain union free school districts hereinafter mentioned, shall be closed during the time such institute shall be in session. The closing of a school within the school commissioner district wherein an institute shall be held, at which a teacher has attended, shall not work a forfeiture of the contract under which such teacher was employed. In union free school districts having a population of more than five thousand, and employing a superintendent whose time is exclusively devoted to the supervision of the schools therein, the schools may be closed or not, at the option of the boards of education in such districts. The trustees of every school district are hereby directed to give the teacher or teachers employed by them, the whole of the time spent by them in attending at an institute or institutes held as hereinbefore stated, without deducting anything from the wages of such teacher or teachers for the time so spent. All teachers under a contract to teach in any school commissioner district shall attend such institute so held for that district, and shall receive wages for such attendance.

§ 5. In the apportionment of public school money, the schools thus closing in any school time shall be allowed the same average pupil attendance during such time, as was the average weekly aggregate during the week previous to such institute, and any school continuing its sessions, in violation of the above provision shall not be allowed any public money based upon the aggregate attendance for the period during which the institute was held. Trustees and boards of education in such school districts and parts of school districts shall report, in their annual reports to the school commissioners, the number of days and the dates thereof on which a teachers' institute was held in their districts during the school year, and whether schools under their charge were or were not closed during such days; and whenever the trustees' report shows a district school has been supported for the full time required by law, including the time spent by the teacher or teachers in their employ in attendance upon such institute, and that the trustees have given the teacher or teachers the time of such absence, and have not deducted anything from his or their wages on account thereof, the superintendent of public instruction may include the district in his apportionment of the state school moneys, and direct that it be included by the school commissioner or commissioners in their apportionment of school moneys; provided, always, that such school district be in all other respects entitled to be included in such apportionment.

§ 6. Willful failure on the part of a teacher to attend a teachers' institute as required, shall be considered sufficient cause for the revocation of such teacher's license, and a willful failure on the part of the trustees to close their schools during the holding of an institute as required, shall be considered sufficient cause for withholding the public moneys to which such districts would otherwise be entitled. Any person under contract to teach, for the term in which an institute is held, in a school in any commissioner district is required to attend an institute, if held for that district, even though at the time the school is not in session, and shall be entitled to receive wages for such attendance.

§ 7. The treasurer shall pay, on the warrant of the comptroller, to the order of any one or more of the school commissioners, such sum or sums of money as the superintendent of public instruction shall certify to be due to them for expenses in holding a teachers' institute; and, upon the like warrant and certificate, to pay to the order of any persons employed by the superintendent as additional instructors to conduct, instruct, teach or supervise any such teachers' institute.

§ 8. There shall be annually appropriated out of the free school fund the sum of thirty thousand dollars for the maintenance of teachers' institutes.

5. STATISTICAL TABLES

TEACHERS' INSTITUTES — *Attendance, Experience, Local Expenses, from August* 31, 1896, *to May* 31, 1897

COUNTIES	District	Place	Conductor	Date	Teachers in Attendance			Average Attendance			Aggregate days' attendance	Average Number of Terms Taught			Local expenses
					Males	Females	Total	Males	Females	Total		Males	Females	Total	
Ulster	3	Ellenville	Stout	1896 Aug. 31	26	88	114	25	85	110	551	10	9	10	$36 01
Ulster	1	Kingston	Holman and Sanford	Sept. 7	30	130	160	29	122	151	754	23	12	15	49 54
Rensselaer	2	Averill Park	McLachlan	14	30	100	130	29	98	127	687	16	14	14	22 50
Wayne	1	Wolcott	Stout	21	45	136	181	42	130	172	860	13	9	10	26 74
Wayne	2	Newark	Shaver	21	25	123	148	24	121	145	725	10	8	8	45 68
Albany	1-2	Altamont	Hendrick	21	52	117	169	52	113	165	823	11	10	11	53 42
Erie	1	Tonawanda	Sanford	21	29	92	121	28	91	119	597	9	9	9	88 35
Suffolk	2	Northport	Holman	21	31	153	184	30	150	180	896	15	10	11	37 48
Delaware	1	Walton	Bugbee	21	49	185	234	44	185	229	1,165	8	8	8	37 90
Putnam	....	Carmel	Sanford	28	19	54	73	19	54	73	365	27	13	17	25 49
Tompkins	1	Trumansburg	McLachlan	28	17	78	95	17	77	94	468	8	6	7	44 30
Lewis	1	Port Leyden	Bugbee	28	17	105	122	17	105	122	609	4	8	7	37 91
Columbia	1	Philmont	Stout	28	17	66	83	17	64	81	409	19	13	14	33 14
Monroe	1	Fairport	Hendrick	28	26	124	150	26	124	150	749	7	9	8	35 06
Ulster	2	Port Ewen	Hendrick	Oct. 5	32	78	110	32	77	109	543	25	11	15	46 39
Livingston	1	Geneseo	McLachlan	5	32	85	117	32	85	117	583	6	8	7	28 75
Greene	1-2	Catskill	Bugbee	5	66	140	206	64	140	204	1,020	12	8	9	25 00
Madison	1	Hamilton	Stout	5	41	135	176	40	135	175	875	5	8	7	66 06
Onondaga	2	Skaneateles	Sanford	5	35	137	172	35	136	171	855	9	8	8	42 88
Sullivan	2	Liberty	Stout	12	50	67	117	50	67	117	584	9	8	9	38 65
Chenango	2	Oxford	Hendrick	12	30	120	150	29	119	148	740	13	9	10	46 60
Madison	2	Canastota	Holman	12	31	147	178	31	146	177	885	16	9	10	40 84
Schoharie	1	Middleburg	Bugbee	12	46	67	113	45	67	112	560	11	8	8	27 16
Tompkins	2	Groton	Sanford	12	18	84	102	18	82	100	501	8	9	9	58 14
Chautauqua	3	Cherry Creek	Shaver	12	45	79	124	45	79	124	618	8	8	8	37 51
Rensselaer	1	Lansingburg	Bugbee	19	22	186	208	23	188	205	1,025	17	11	12	25 85
Livingston	2	Dansville	Shaver	19	17	106	123	17	104	121	606	10	10	10	31 60
Orleans	....	Albion	Sanford	19	46	160	206	46	158	204	1,020	9	9	9	33 75
Cattaraugus	2	Little Valley	Stout	19	68	193	261	58	197	255	1,279	8	9	8	54 01

[illegible]	1	Sherman	Hendrick	19	27	97	124	27	97	124	619	7	9	8	35 57
[illegible]	1	[illegible]	McLachlan	19	23	118	136	28	118	136	680	11	9	9	44 79
Washington	2	[illegible]ville	Stout	26	26	178	199	26	168	194	972	8	9	9	68 49
Allegany	2	Belmont	[illegible]	26	42	193	235	41	[illegible]	232	1,101	7	8	8	25 60
Wyoming	1-2	Warsaw	[illegible]	26	52	193	245	51	193	244	1,218	7	9	8	44 58
Schoharie	2	Cobleskill	[illegible]	26	47	74	121	46	73	119	509	12	9	10	41 84
Chenango	1	Sherburne	[illegible]	26	37	129	166	37	128	165	825	7	7	7	48 62
Niagara	2	Niagara Falls	Hendrick	Nov. 9	26	147	173	26	145	171	855	14	10	11	26 02
[illegible]		Batavia	[illegible]	9	45	154	199	45	153	198	990	11	8	9	33 51
Dutchess	2	[illegible]	[illegible]	9	25	68	93	24	68	92	461	14	14	14	36 96
Erie	2	[illegible] Aurora	[illegible]	9	37	98	135	37	98	135	673	7	8	8	36 14
Delaware	2	Delhi	Sanford	9	68	147	215	68	147	215	1,075	9	8	8	50 90
Monroe	2	[illegible]ville	Hendrick	16	32	112	144	32	111	143	714	12	8	9	40 46
[illegible]	1	[illegible]	Stout	16	31	142	173	29	142	171	855	9	8	8	45 64
[illegible]		Horseheads	McLachlan	16	21	157	178	21	155	176	880	14	6	8	66 00
[illegible]	2	[illegible]	Bugbee	16	45	158	203	45	158	203	1,015	9	13	2	42 17
Schenectady		[illegible]	Sanford	16	17	54	71	17	54	71	355	10	8	8	47 41
Allegany	1	Belfast	Stout	30	36	137	173	36	137	173	865	7	8	7	33 50
[illegible]	1	[illegible]	Bugbee	30	24	121	145	24	121	145	725	10	12	11	54 25
Saratoga	1	Ballston Spa	Hendrick	30	17	124	141	17	124	141	701	13	9	10	42 06
Queens	2	[illegible]	[illegible]	30	37	217	254	37	213	250	1,250	25	13	14	18 45
[illegible]	3	Camden	[illegible]	30	33	70	103	33	70	103	515	12	8	9	39 90
[illegible]	3	[illegible]	[illegible]	Dec. 7	48	120	168	48	120	168	839	9	7	8	32 50
Cayuga	2	[illegible]	[illegible]	7	35	124	159	35	123	158	791	7	6	6	42 08
[illegible]	3	Fayetteville	Bugbee	7	33	131	164	33	130	163	813	8	6	7	31 84
Steuben	2	Addison	Hendrick	7	37	109	146	37	109	146	728	9	10	9	38 49
Cayuga	1	[illegible]	[illegible]	14	28	107	135	28	106	134	668	12	8	9	39 30
[illegible]mery		Canajoharie	Stout and Sanford	14	60	116	176	60	115	175	877	10	10	10	44 35
[illegible]		[illegible]	[illegible]	14	38	100	138	38	99	137	686	9	9	9	39 34
				1897											
Sullivan	1	[illegible]ello	Stout	Feb. 1	31	73	108	31	71	102	512	12	9	10	42 00
Yates		Penn Yan	[illegible]	1	39	120	159	38	118	156	783	8	8	7	47 45
Niagara	1	Middleport	Hendrick	1	26	75	101	25	74	99	498	8	6	6	30 66
[illegible]	1	[illegible]	Stout	8	46	146	192	43	140	183	917	12	10	11	45 36
[illegible]	1	[illegible]	McLachlan and Bugbee	8	21	123	144	20	120	140	702	8	15	14	34 00
[illegible]		[illegible]	McLachlan	Mar. 29	32	154	186	32	150	182	908	25	15	18	32 81
[illegible]		Farmer	Stout	29	25	92	117	25	92	117	583	10	8	9	40 00
[illegible]	1	[illegible]	[illegible]	April 5	25	144	169	24	142	166	830	15	10	10	20 20
[illegible]	1-2-3	Peekskill	Stout and Sanford	5	44	216	260	44	213	257	1,288	24	12	14	44 00
[illegible]	2	Canandaigua	Bugbee	5	26	184	210	26	182	208	788	5	11	10	19 93
Oswego	3	Sandy Creek	McLachlan	5	41	149	190	40	147	187	934	9	7	7	46 44
[illegible]	1	Ful[illegible]	Hendrick	12	29	120	149	28	117	145	725	10	11	11	43 09
[illegible]	1	Riverhead	[illegible]	12	32	93	125	32	92	124	622	13	12	12	32 80
[illegible]	1	Whitesboro	Sanford	12	16	63	79	15	63	78	392	12	10	11	24 50
Broome	2	[illegible]	[illegible]	12	35	116	151	35	114	149	744	6	11	9	25 75
[illegible]	4	B[illegible]nville	Stout	12	37	114	151	37	111	148	741	9	9	9	21 54
Herkimer	2	Ilion	[illegible]	19	28	134	162	27	130	157	786	9	9	9	31 08
Herkimer	1	Herkimer	[illegible]	19	30	104	134	29	101	130	652	8	9	9	30 50
Tioga		Owego	[illegible]	19	27	211	238	25	204	229	1,143	8	9	9	52 14

TEACHERS' INSTITUTES—*Attendance, Experience, Local Expenses, Etc.*—(Concluded)

COUNTY	District	Place	Conductor	Date	Teachers in Attendance: Males	Teachers in Attendance: Females	Teachers in Attendance: Total	Average Attendance: Males	Average Attendance: Females	Average Attendance: Total	Aggregate days' attendance	Average Number of Days Taught: Males	Average Number of Days Taught: Females	Average Number of Days Taught: Total	Local expenses
				1897											
Saratoga	2	Saratoga Springs	Bugbee	April 19	81	165	196	30	163	193	967	10	12	11	$50 57
Lewis	2	Lowville	Hendrick	19	30	119	149	30	116	146	729	4	8	7	31 99
Cortland	1	Cortland	McLachlan	26	16	93	109	16	92	108	512	11	13	12	24 27
Cortland	2	Homer	[illegible]rd	26	18	69	87	18	69	87	434	12	9	9	28 90
Orange	1-2	Newburg	Stout	26	57	227	284	56	223	279	1,394	19	22	21	27 91
Rockland	....	Stony [illegible]int	Hendrick	26	28	81	109	28	79	107	536	20	13	15	23 78
Columbia	2	[illegible]atham	Bugbee	26	26	94	120	26	93	119	595	19	9	12	23 83
Fulton	....	Broadalbin	[illegible]St.	May 3	39	73	112	39	73	112	560	9	9	9	31 00
Jefferson	2	Redwood	[illegible]n	3	28	122	150	27	122	149	745	7	9	8	83 64
Broome	1	[illegible]r	[illegible]d	3	31	106	137	30	105	135	677	8	9	9	30 57
Otsego	1-2	[illegible]ta	Hendrick	3	116	286	402	116	286	402	2,009	8	8	8	59 76
Erie	3	Springville	Bugbee	3	19	87	106	18	85	103	514	9	9	9	30 15
Dutchess	1	Fishkill	Bugbee	10	36	153	189	35	152	187	937	16	13	13	32 73
St. Lawrence	3	Norwood	[illegible]t	10	43	153	196	43	151	194	970	7	7	7	01 77
St. Lawrence	1	[illegible]r	McLachlan	10	47	161	208	47	161	208	1,040	5	9	8	44 14
Essex	2	Port [illegible]y	Sanford	10	30	114	144	30	112	142	718	9	9	9	19 05
Jefferson	3	Dexter	[illegible]k	10	33	127	160	28	125	153	790	8	9	8	53 85
St. Lawrence	2	Canton	Hendrick	17	37	166	203	37	165	202	1,010	7	9	9	45 80
Clinton	2	West Chazy	Bugbee	17	21	97	118	21	95	116	582	10	10	10	31 85
Queens	1	Flushing	Stout	17	20	179	199	19	174	193	967	23	12	14	29 51
Oneida	2	[illegible]n	[illegible]d	17	33	115	148	33	114	147	736	12	9	10	21 80
Warren	1-2	Warrensburg	[illegible]t St.	24	28	124	152	28	123	151	759	11	12	12	37 50
Essex	1	Elizabethtown	Sanford	24	21	68	89	21	67	88	441	12	11	12	27 40
Jefferson	1	Adams	[illegible]n	24	32	104	136	32	103	135	674	7	11	10	36 45
Oswego	2	Phoenix	Bugbee	24	20	91	111	19	89	108	540	14	10	11	15 17
Franklin	1-2	Malone	McLachlan	31	41	210	251	40	197	237	1,187	9	9	9	45 08
					3,484	12,789	16,273	3,431	12,620	16,051	80,322	......	......	......	$3,873 99

EXHIBIT No. 16

TEACHERS' TRAINING CLASSES

1. Report of Supervisor of Training Classes
2. Reports of Inspectors
3. Regulations and Course of Study for the Training Classes in the Academies and Union Schools of the State
4. Regulations for Teachers' Training School and Classes in Cities
5. Statistical Tables
   a. List of Institutions which Organized Teachers' Training Classes for First and Second Terms, 1896-97, with Amount of Money Apportioned to Each Institution
   b. Statistics Showing Condition of Teachers' Training Classes for First Term of School Year 1896-97
   c. Statistics Showing Condition of Teachers' Training Classes for Second Term of School Year 1896-97
   d. Statistics Showing by Classes the Maximum Number of Students Reported Either Term, the Number of Candidates for Certificates, and the Number of Certificates Granted
   e. Teachers' Training Classes — General Summary From 1889-97

TEACHERS' TRAINING CLASSES

AUGUSTUS S. DOWNING, A. M., *Supervisor of Training Classes*

Inspectors

S. Whitford Maxson	Adams Centre
Frank H. Wood, A. M	Chatham
Wayland E. Stearns, A. M	Rome
Willis D. Graves	Delhi

1. REPORT OF SUPERVISOR OF TEACHERS' TRAINING CLASSES

It is with satisfaction that I submit my annual report of the Teachers' Training Schools and Classes. The year has been one of gratifying evidence of the policy which you inaugurated. The first year under this policy served to fix upon a firm basis the principles upon which the organization and maintenance of training schools and classes should depend. During this second year, therefore, the work has been carried on so understandingly that the value of these fixed principles could be fairly tested. The proof of their effectiveness is shown by the following results: First, the members of the classes are more mature; second, the scholarship of the classes is better; third, the members of the classes take fewer studies outside of the training-class course; fourth, the training-class instructors are not required to give so much time to classes other than the training class; fifth, more attention and better supervision is given to the observation and practice work; sixth, there is a livelier interest in the work on the part of pupils, instructors, principals, boards of education and school commissioners.

The conclusion of these proofs is manifest in the final test, namely, the number who completed the work and received certificates. There were in the classes in all, 1,438. Of these, 1,080 were eligible to receive certificates, having been in the class one year or more. Of this number, 766 received their certificates. This is 71 per cent., against 14 per cent. in 1894-95.

Another most gratifying feature of the year's work has been the earnest, enthusiastic support which has been manifested by the principals of the schools in which these classes are located; and no little degree of the success of the work has been due to their earnestness of purpose to make a training-class certificate mean something.

School commissioners have shown their interest not only by aiding the organization of the classes, but most effectively by giving to those who hold training-class certificates preference as teachers, and the estimate in which such teachers are held is steadily growing higher as a logical result.

The inspection of the schools has been more thorough than in the year previous, and the school authorities speak in the highest terms of praise of the helpfulness that comes from the inspectors.

I respectfully call your attention again to the consideration of devising some plan for paying for the tuition of pupils that shall be more equitable than that under the present law. If the law could be modified so that a school maintaining a training class of the minimum number for the full year should receive at least five hundred dollars, there would be more justice shown to those schools which must, from necessity, be limited in securing classes not exceeding twelve in number and a greater willingness to give to the class the entire time of the training-class instructor. The tables follow to show the different items of interest to the public.

The following table will show by comparison the attendance and cost of these classes since 1889-90:

TERM	Number of classes organized	Number of Pupils Registered			Number who had already taught	Number of scholars allowed	Amount paid schools for instruction of classes
		Men	Women	Total			
1889-90, first term	49	162	596	758	256	680	$7,932
1889-90, second term	59	225	844	1,069	327	928	19,863
1890-91, first term	61	221	758	979	304	873	14,759
1890-91, second term	56	236	726	962	291	808	13,037
1891-92, first term	82	262	1,012	1,274	461	1,053	17,612
1891-92, second term	77	292	964	1,256	390	1,070	16,774
1892-93, first term	95	304	1,120	1,424	456	1,153	19,530
1892-93, second term	100	339	1,179	1,518	518	1,370	21,740
1893-94, first term	109	396	1,276	1,672	558	1,317	21,998
1893-94, second term	118	464	1,517	1,981	702	1,709	26,842
1894-95, first term	127	531	1,621	2,152	681	1,655	27,189
1894-95, second term	140	642	1,840	2,482	799	2,212	36,063
1895-96, first term	74	190	875	1,065	212	851	15,846
1895-96, second term	72	203	886	1,089	237	1,050	19,723
1896-97, first term	83	161	1,211	1,372	257	1,242	18,726
1896-97, second term	83	169	1,201	1,370	216	1,268	29,372

The following table shows the result of the expenditure:

(D) Statistics showing by classes the maximum number of students reported either term, the number of candidates for certificates, and the number of certificates granted

County	Name of institution	Maximum number of students reported either term: Men	Women	Total	Number of candidates for certificates*	Number of certificates granted
Albany	Albany Training School	......	37	37	30	14
Allegany	Alfred University	3	14	17	16	14
	Cuba High School	3	16	19	17	8
	Friendship High School	3	10	13	12	3
	Genesee Valley Seminary	3	10	13	10	8
	Wellsville Union School	2	10	12	12	11
	Wilson Academy	2	9	11	11	8
Broome	Binghamton Training School	......	21	21	22	21
	Union Union School	4	9	13	11	3
	Whitney's Point Union School	......	12	12	12	6
	Windsor Union School	5	6	11	8	5
Cattaraugus	Chamberlain Institute	3	8	11	8	6
	Delavan Union School	2	9	11	9	8
Chautauqua	Forestville Free Academy	10	3	13	12	9
	Jamestown Training School	......	15	15	11	10
Chemung	Elmira Training School	......	24	24	23	21
Chenango	Norwich High School	3	10	13	13	10
Delaware	Margaretville High School	2	15	17	15	10
	Walton Union School	......	12	12	11	5
Dutchess	Poughkeepsie Training School	......	22	22	19	10
Erie	Buffalo Training School	2	46	48	41	26
Essex	Port Henry Union School	......	12	12	9	5
	Westport Union School	1	9	10	11	5
Franklin	Franklin Academy	1	10	11	10	8
Greene	Catskill High School	......	8	8	7	5
Herkimer	Ilion Union School	1	11	12	8	6
Jefferson	Watertown Training School	......	12	12	10	6
Kings	Brooklyn Training School	......	203	203	3	2
Lewis	Copenhagen Union School	6	5	11	8	7
	Lowville Academy	2	14	16	10	5
	Port Leyden Union School	1	10	11	8	3
Madison	De Ruyter Union School	6	12	18	18	14
	Oneida High School	2	18	20	18	17
Monroe	Fairport Classical Union School	......	10	10	11	11

(*D*) *Statistics showing by classes the maximum number of students reported either term, the number of candidates for certificates, and the number of certificates granted* — (Concluded)

County	NAME OF INSTITUTION	MAXIMUM NUMBER OF STUDENTS REPORTED EITHER TERM			Number of candidates for certificates*	Number of certificates granted
		Men	Women	Total		
Monroe	Rochester Training School	.....	24	25	24	21
Montgomery	Canajoharie Union School	8	3	11	11	4
	St. Johnsville Union School	5	11	16	16	13
Niagara	Lockport Training School	.....	16	16	15	11
	Middleport Union School	1	10	11	10	6
Oneida	Utica Training School	.....	16	16	12	9
Onondaga	Baldwinsville Free Academy	.....	12	12	12	2
	Fabius Union School	7	5	12	10	7
	Fayetteville Union School	.....	12	12	12	11
	Onondaga High School	7	18	25	18	11
	Syracuse Training School	.....	37	37	20	15
	Tully Union School	3	14	17	11	7
Ontario	Canandaigua Union School	1	10	11	9	6
	Geneva High School	.....	14	14	12	11
Orange	Port Jervis Union School	.....	15	15	12	8
Orleans	Albion Union School	6	11	17	12	7
Oswego	Fulton High School	4	11	15	15	10
	Mexico Union School	2	9	11	9	7
	Pulaski Academy and Union School	2	16	18	17	14
	Sandy Creek High School	2	11	13	13	9
Otsego	Cooperstown High School	3	13	16	14	10
	Morris High School	3	10	13	13	12
	Richfield Springs High School	4	10	14	12	9
	Unadilla Union School and Academy	6	4	10	9	6
Rensselaer	Hoosick Falls High School	1	9	10	10	7
	Lansingburg Academy	.....	14	14	13	5
	Troy Training School	.....	33	33	27	20
St. Lawrence	Gouverneur High School	1	13	14	14	13
	Ogdensburg Training School	1	10	11	9	7
Saratoga	Corinth Union School	4	13	17	17	9
Schuyler	Cook Academy	1	10	11	11	11
Steuben	[illegible] Academy	3	14	17	17	12
	North Cohocton Union School	4	8	12	12	7
Sullivan	Monticello Union School	6	8	14	13	8

Tioga	Owego Free [illegible]cady	1	12	13	12	11
	Waverly [illegible]h School	3	10	13	11	9
Tompkins	Trumansburg Union school	3	11	14	14	18
Ulster	Ellenville High School	1	17	18	18	16
	Kingston Training [illegible]al	......	12	12	9	5
Warren	[illegible] Union Free School	......	15	15	15	12
Washington	Sandy Hill High School	3	18	21	20	15
[illegible]e	Clyde High School	1	10	11	11	10
	Palmyra Classical Union School	1	13	14	13	10
Wyoming	Arcade Union School	3	15	18	12	11
	Warsaw Union School	5	10	25	10	5
Yates	[illegible] Union School	2	9	11	9	8
	Penn Yan Academy	1	10	11	10	9
Totals		176	1,261	1,438	1,060	766

* Candidates for a certificate must have been in attendance upon a training class for at least one year.

TRAINING SCHOOLS

Under the provisions of chapter 1031 of the laws of 1895, thirteen cities have organized training schools. These schools have followed the course of instruction outlined in the regulations which accompany this report. The pupils admitted to these schools had completed the required academic course in some school whose course of study had been approved by you; but in order to assure the city superintendents under whose direction pupils are admitted to training schools that candidates for admission had followed such course, it became necessary to inspect the schools applying to have their course of study approved. Your appointment, May 1st, of Willis D. Graves and Wayland E. Stearns as inspectors gave the opportunity to do this. There have been up to date sixty-five high schools and academies whose course of study has been approved, and these schools have been inspected to ascertain how fully the course is actually pursued. From the reports of inspection I am convinced that each pupil admitted to a training school should be furnished with a blank upon which to specify the school from which he graduated and the exact amount of time devoted to each study designated in the approved course. This would be a guarantee to city superintendents, would aid your inspectors and would insure a closer adherence to the studies prescribed. After another year's inspection I am certain that you will see the necessity for such a course. The work in the training schools is efficiently done in all the cities. You may well be gratified with the successful working of the law. For the cities these schools must eventually be the means for providing teachers specially trained for city work, and, as this becomes more apparent, the classes entering the schools will be proportionately larger.

Statistics showing the condition of Teachers' Training Schools for the school year 1896–97

City	NAME OF INSTITUTION	NUMBER OF STUDENTS REPORTED			Apportionment to each city
		Men	Women	Total	
Albany	Albany Training School	0	32	32	$1,140
Binghamton	Binghamton Training School	0	22	22	844
Brooklyn	Brooklyn Training School	0	203	203	7,355
Buffalo	Buffalo Training School	2	46	48	1,610
Jamestown	Jamestown Training School	0	15	15	545
Lockport	Lockport Training School	0	15	15	577
Ogdensburg	Ogdensburg Training School	1	10	11	418
Poughkeepsie	Poughkeepsie Training School	0	19	19	666
Rochester	Rochester Training School	0	25	25	888
Syracuse	Syracuse Training School	0	33	33	1,066
Troy	Troy Training School	0	33	33	1,194
Utica	Utica Training School	0	11	11	454
Watertown	Watertown Training School	0	12	12	377

ALBANY, *August* 1, 1897.

2. REPORTS OF INSPECTORS OF TEACHERS' TRAINING CLASSES

REPORT OF S. W. MAXSON

It has been my privilege to visit, at least once during the year, every training class organized in this state, and as I inspected the same schools during the previous school year, an opportunity for comparing the work of the two years, and noting the progress made in that time, has been given.

The evidence of increased efficiency is everywhere clearly apparent, and the undoubted advance along all lines of the work in these classes, with scarcely a single exception, is sufficient reason for a feeling of gratification on the part of the Department and all others interested.

There are many causes to which may be ascribed this satisfactory result. Among them may be noted that, as a rule, the members of the classes have been more mature in mind and body, and have had a higher educational standing at the time of entering upon the course. The members of the classes have a clearer understanding of the character and amount of training required, and consequently do not undertake to do so much outside of the regular training-class course.

The teachers in charge of the classes are better prepared, by the experience of the previous year, to lead the classes along those lines of investigation best adapted to secure the most satisfactory results. This is especially marked in regard to age, observation and practice. In this connection may be noted the changed attitude of the grade teachers in regard to this branch of training-class work. Many grade teachers did not cordially welcome the visits of the members of the class, but they are becoming more in sympathy with the object in view, and, consequently, are of great service in aiding and directing in the practice and observation training. Many of these teachers now welcome the visits for observation as a benefit to their grade and to themselves, as well as to the members of the training classes.

Boards of education are coming to a clearer understanding of the purposes and needs of the classes, and, consequently, are furnishing better accommodations and a more liberal supply of professional books, and are allowing the training-class instructors more time for this special work.

In some of the schools the teachers devote their entire time to the classes. This should be the situation in every instance, but such a condition cannot justly be required nor expected in the smaller classes while the compensation remains as at present.

In at least one school a model department has been organized, made up of pupils from the four lower grades, and it is entirely under the care of the teacher and the members of the class. The work of this department has been so satisfactory that other schools will doubtless adopt the same course during the coming school year. That an experiment of this kind may be successful, it is absolutely essential that the training-class teacher be excused from all work not directly connected with the training class and the model department.

In the schools having the smaller classes, boards of education feel that the compensation allowed does not warrant the employment of teachers to do training-class work only. It is to be hoped that the inequitable method of giving state aid for the support of these classes may soon be replaced by some plan whereby every class organized will be granted sufficient funds to warrant the employment of a teacher who will be required to devote her whole time to professional training.

Another very encouraging feature noticed is the large percentage of the graduates who immediately find employment in the public schools in the vicinity. Diligent inquiry during the year has failed to disclose a single instance in which a training-class graduate has failed to have offered her an opportunity to put her training to the final test of actual experience in the public schools, and the fact that school commissioners, trustees and patrons so generally agree as to the success of these teachers is valuable evidence regarding the efficiency of the training received and the thoroughness of the work done in the training classes.

All these gratifying evidences of progress should not lead to the conclusion that the work has reached perfection, but rather realizing that there is still very much to be accomplished, we should take new courage from the many indications of improvement and go forward with a fixed determination to do still better work in the years to come.

ADAMS CENTRE, *August* 1, 1897.

REPORT OF FRANK H. WOOD, A. M.

As a result of one or more visits to nearly all of the training classes and training schools of the state, it is gratifying to be able to report a year of unusual interest, increased efficiency, and marked progress. While the improved condition is not confined to any particular branch of the work, some features deserve special mention.

The students composing the classes were unusually mature in mind and in years, the average age being nearly nineteen. They were also more proficient in scholarship than heretofore, and hence better prepared to do the work and receive benefit therefrom. In only exceptional cases have the members pursued other than training class subjects.

The quality of instruction has manifestly improved. A year's experience under the new regulations served not only to make the instructors more familiar with the work, but also to emphasize its importance. More thorough and efficient teaching has resulted. The weakest phase of the work, from my point of view, lies in the general tendency to so far divorce method from subject matter that much time that ought to be devoted to underlying principles, to the consideration of a subject as a science, is frequently given to the study of mere devices. Pupils are thus brought into bondage to set forms instead of being rendered independent of them; they are made servile imitators instead of being made original thinkers; they are surfeited with plans and devices instead of being grounded in the principles that underlie rational method. As a result, they fail to distinguish form from substance, and the vehicle becomes of more importance than the object for which it was created.

A marked advance has been made in the character of the observation and practice work that is being done by the classes. More time has been devoted to it and more attention given to its systematic organization and supervision. There are, however, classes in which this part of the work is far from satisfactory—due chiefly to two causes: Incompetent teachers in the grades, and lack of time for adequate supervision on the part of instructors.

The condition of the pedagogical libraries is much better than it was a year ago. In some cases the addition has been large and valuable; in many others, it has been smaller but important. Most of the classes now have access to an excellent assortment of reference books on the prescribed subjects of study. There are still some few that have practically no such books of reference. I am of the opinion that this part of the work is of such vital importance that no school should receive an appointment to instruct a training class until it is satisfactorily equipped in this respect.

One of the most encouraging features that I have noticed has been the professional spirit manifested alike by members of the training classes, their instructors, principals, and superintendents.

Toward the latter part of the year, I inspected a few high schools and academies whose courses of study have been approved by you in accordance with chapter 1031 of the laws of 1895. I found most of these schools deficient in one or more of the requirements, but desirous of adjusting themselves to the new conditions. I am thoroughly persuaded that this statute will not only result in providing the state with more efficient teachers, but that it will also prove a blessing to the high schools and academies that come under its provisions.

CHATHAM, *August* 1, 1897.

REPORT OF WILLIS D. GRAVES

According to the provisions of chapter 1031, laws of 1895, no person shall be admitted to a city training school who has not graduated from a high school or academy having a course of study of not less than three years, approved by the State Superintendent of Public Instruction, or from some institution of equal or higher rank, approved by the same authority.

Upon the date of my appointment as inspector, May 1, 1897, forty-eight high schools, either public or private, had submitted courses of study which had been duly approved. These schools claimed to meet the requirements of the course of study prescribed for admission to city training schools, and I was at once assigned to the work of inspecting the facilities and instruction of such approved institutions. The schools visited, represented preparatory departments of colleges, city high schools, parochial schools, and other private institutions and academies; and the character of the work seen differed greatly in scope and thoroughness, as well as in respect to the facilities afforded. It was evident, however, that with few exceptions, these schools were earnestly striving to fully meet the requirements prescribed, and in some instances the superiority of the instruction imparted was most pronounced. Methods employed were by no means uniform. Certain representative schools exhibited much that is best in teaching. On the other hand, some of the schools inspected could be by no means as highly commended. Among defects noted, was lack of breadth in the instruction given. Often memory was the chief faculty employed by the student, and little was gained in way of mental discipline. In the teaching of science and mathematics, some schools were accomplishing little, compared with what these departments of study are designed to secure. The chief cause for this was undoubtedly the poor preparation of the teacher.

In way of equipment, nearly all the schools seen were supplied with excellent buildings and cheerful surroundings. Libraries and apparatus were in some cases very inadequate. This defect was partially remedied by making use of laboratory and library facilities outside of the school. In no instance were exceptions taken to the inspection called for by the superintendent of public instruction, and as a general thing no effort was made to withhold information desired. Suggestions were cheerfully received and often called for.

It is apparent that if the city training schools are to meet the demands upon them, they must supply teachers strong in subject matter as well as thoroughly trained in practice and methods. The work in subject matter is to be done in the approved schools. Upon it the work in the training school is to rest. It should be thoroughly supervised, and the work of inspecting approved schools is hereafter to constitute an important factor in determining the status of those teachers furnished by the training schools of our cities.

The city training schools visited were without exception accomplishing excellent results. The character and scope of the work in methods were worthy of high commendation. Systematic observation and practice in the actual grades of the city schools were afforded. This work was done under such supervision and limitations as to be of the highest value to the members of the training schools and with no detriment to the grades.

I did not see the work of the country training classes during the short time covered by this report.

DELHI, *August* 1, 1897.

REPORT OF W. E. STEARNS, A. M.

Inasmuch as my appointment was not received until May 1st, this report covers but a small part of the year.

I visited but a few training classes. These were well managed both teachers and pupils were earnest and enthusiastic, and the character of the work done was such as to convince me that the state is amply justified in contributing to their support.

I inspected nineteen schools having courses of study approved by you under the provisions of chapter 1031 of the laws of 1895. Not all of these schools were offering the full work of the course. This was largely due to the fact that there had not been sufficient time for them to adjust their existing courses to the new requirements.

All appreciate the advantage of a school having a recognized standing and are willing to provide whatever is necessary to equip it properly with library and apparatus. In too many of them the teaching force is inadequate. This is a serious defect and until it is remedied, such schools cannot hope to do the most efficient work.

Training schools must very soon feel the beneficial effects of the law, since pupils who enter them will have an academic education sufficient to enable them to appreciate the professional work based upon it.

ROME, *August* 1, 1897.

---

3. REGULATIONS FOR TEACHERS' TRAINING CLASSES

The following regulations governing teachers' training classes have been prescribed in accordance with chapter 556 of the laws of 1894, providing for the professional instruction of common school teachers in academies and union schools of the state.

Attention is called to the regulations adopted, to the course of study arranged, and to the provisions of the law relating to training classes.

I. Appointments

1. To receive due consideration, applications for appointments to instruct classes for the ensuing year, should be forwarded to the Department of Public Instruction by the first of May.

The consideration of appointments of teachers' training classes for the school year beginning August 1, 1897, will be based upon the following conditions:

No school will receive an appointment unless it can fulfill the following requirements, viz.:

(*a*) To furnish as instructor or instructors of the class for not less (each day) than three recitation hours of forty-five minutes each, a duly qualified teacher who is either (1) a college graduate with not less than three years' * experience in teaching in the public schools of the state; (2) a graduate of a normal school in this state from a higher course than the elementary course, so-called, of at least two years' * experience in teaching in the public schools of the state; or (3) one holding a state certificate granted in this state upon examination subsequent to 1875. Such instructor or instructors must be approved by the state Superintendent of Public Instruction, the same as teachers employed in the several normal schools of the state.

(*b*) To furnish a suitable room or apartment separate from all other departments of the school in which the training-class members shall be seated and no others, unless it may be the members of the graduating class of the current school year.

---

* Since graduation

(c) To furnish opportunity for the class or some members thereof each day to observe methods of teaching in the several grades of common school work, and, when practicable, to actually have an opportunity to teach in such grades under proper criticism and direction.

(d) To conduct the recitations in the several subjects belonging to the training-class work separately and distinct from all other recitations in such subjects.

(e) To maintain a legal class for at least thirty-six weeks in the year.

(f) To observe implicitly the conditions of admission to membership in the class.

2. In making assignments to institutions in the same county, reference will be had to the following considerations:

(a) The proper distribution of the classes among the school commissioner districts of the state;

(b) The location of the class to accommodate the greatest number of suitable candidates;

(c) Such equipment of the institution as will give assurance of doing substantial work, both in the theory and in the practice of teaching.

3. To meet the progressive demands of the teaching service, institutions fulfilling the requirements will receive an appointment to instruct a class for the school year.

4. The funds paid by the state for this instruction go into the treasury of the institution, and not to any individual. Trustees who pay a fixed salary to their principal cannot allow teachers to share in these funds as an extra compensation.

5. A blank form of application will be furnished to institutions requesting the same.

II. Qualifications for Admission

1. Candidates must be at least seventeen years of age at the time of entrance.

*2. They must subscribe, in good faith, to the following declaration: "We, the subscribers, hereby declare that our object in asking admission to the training class is to prepare ourselves for teaching; and that it is our purpose to engage in teaching in the public schools of the state of New York, at the completion of such preparation. We pledge ourselves to remain in the class

* Candidates should have their attention specially called to this obligation.

during the year, unless prevented by illness or else excused by the Superintendent of Public Instruction."

The principal and school commissioner must be satisfied that the candidates have the moral character, talents and aptness necessary to success in teaching.

3. Before admission they must hold as a minimum qualification, either an unexpired third-grade teachers' certificate and have attained a standing of sixty per cent. in Civil Government, under the uniform examinations, or must hold under the Regents a preliminary certificate and fourteen academic counts, four of which shall be in *English, two in American History, two in Civil Government, two in Physiology and the other four optional.

4. Candidates entering an examination, in order to qualify for entrance to any training class, shall present to the examiner a certificate from some reputable teacher, that in such teacher's judgment the candidate is capable of passing the examination and worthy to enter a training class. Such certificate shall be forwarded to the state Superintendent's office with the answer papers of the candidate.

III. Organization

1. The school year is divided into two terms of not less than eighteen nor more than twenty weeks each.

2. The class must consist of not less than ten nor more than twenty-five members.

3. The compensation allowed institutions for the instruction will be at the rate of one dollar for each week's instruction of each member.

4. To secure the most promising candidates, the following information should be fully announced prior to the organization of the class:

(*a*) The date on which the class is to be organized;
(*b*) The conditions of admission;
(*c*) The character and advantages of a professional course of study;
(*d*) The importance of this work in securing teachers' certificates.

5. Principals should consult the school commissioner with a view of securing from the schools under his visitation, as members of the class, those persons who intend to teach.

6. *Three periods of forty-five minutes each, every school day,* must be occupied with instruction on the topics laid down in the course of study. Outside of the time given for this separate instruction,

* The only subjects accepted under English are as follows: Advanced English, English Composition, Rhetoric, English Literature and American Literature.

only such members of the class as have time and ability may be allowed to pursue other subjects, for which, however, no tuition may be charged, but no person not an accepted member of the class shall recite with the class.

7. Free tuition includes all subjects embraced in the uniform and state examinations.

8. Two blank forms for notice of organization and two organization registers will be furnished to each institution. These blanks must be properly filled and one of each forwarded to the Department at the end of the third week after the organization of the class. The others must be retained by the principal for inspection by the proper school officers.

IV. Rulings and Requirements

1. No institution can be allowed more than $450 for any one term's instruction.

2. No allowance can be made for any pupil not shown by reports to have been eligible to enter the class.

3. No allowance can be made in the case of any pupil for first term for less than sixteen or more than twenty consecutive weeks.

4. In report for second term, all pupils who were members of class for first term for less than sixteen weeks, and who remain in second term sufficient time to make eighteen or more weeks consecutively will be allowed for such attendance, provided the total does not exceed thirty-six weeks.

5. In case pupils who attend first term not less than sixteen, and not more than twenty weeks, and who continue in second term a less period than eighteen weeks, allowance will be made for weeks attended in second term, provided the weeks of attendance in both terms have been consecutive.

6. No person shall be admitted as a member of the class after its organization except by permission first granted by the state Superintendent, and no such permission will be granted to enter the class later than the second Monday following the date of its organization.

7. Payment for instruction will be refused in all cases where members of classes fail to enter the examinations provided, unless such failures are satisfactorily explained in the principal's report.

No allowance will be made for any pupil who leaves the class before the expiration of the term, except by permission of the state superintendent, and no such permission will be granted during the year, simply in order that the candidate may teach.

8. When the class is organized, the qualification for admission of each candidate shall be entered in the place designated for

such entry in the "Teachers' Training Class Daily Register," and the credentials thereof filed for inspection.

9. A "Teachers' Training Class Daily Register" will be furnished for each class and the daily attendance of each member upon each recitation recorded therein. This "Register" must be forwarded to the Department at the close of each term with the report for that term.

10. The first term for the ensuing year shall begin not later than September 13, and the second term not later than January 31, 1898.

11. Training class certificates are granted only upon the completion of a year's work as prescribed in the course of study.

12. No person holding a training class certificate, or entitled to hold such certificate, is eligible to membership in a training class.

V. Course of Study

This course is designed to meet the requirements of the uniform system for teachers' certificates, and to satisfy the conditions of admission to advanced classes in the normal schools of the state.

FIRST TERM

First Recitation

Arithmetic

Subject matter and methods.

(One recitation daily through the term.)

Review of the following topics with special reference to teaching:

1. Definition of terms.
2. Notation and numeration.—Arabic and Roman notation.
3. The four fundamental processes.
4. Properties of numbers.—Classification; divisibility of numbers; factors; divisors; multiples.
5. Fractions.—Common and decimal.
6. Denominate or compound numbers, and their practical application in measurements.
7. Percentage.—Applications in which time is not an element;

NOTE—The methods should deal thoroughly with primary number. The order of the above topics is, of course, discretionary with the instructor. The study of the mere art of computation is not sufficient; the science of arithmetic must be considered, both the facts and the reason for those facts, how processes are performed and why they are so performed, are to be studied. Original problems illustrating the various topics are to be given by pupils. Instructors are cautioned against taking the time of the arithmetic class with obsolete and impractical processes. The spirit of the above suggestion is to be observed in the other studies of this course interest, simple, compound, and exact; partial payments by the United States rule; discount, true, bank, and commercial.

8. Ratio and proportion.

9. Involution and square root.—Their simple application in mensuration.

SECOND RECITATION

Geography

Subject matter and methods.

(One recitation daily for twelve weeks.)

Review of the following topics with special reference to teaching:

1. Definition of terms.

2. Mathematical.—Form, size, and motions of the earth; day and night; the seasons; latitude and longitude; local and standard time.

3. Physical.—The great mountain systems of the earth; the principal rivers, lakes, and other bodies of water; climate; soil; tides; ocean currents, and trade winds.

4. Description.—General description of the countries of the world.

5. The United States.—Boundaries and extent; states and territories; mountain and river systems; agricultural and mineral productions; industries or occupations; important cities; population; commerce and trans-continental lines of travel; general plan of government.

6. State of New York.—Boundaries and extent; mountains, rivers and lakes; counties; cities and important villages; agricultural and mineral productions; industries or occupations; commerce; railroads and navigable waters; climate; places noted for natural scenery; general plan of government; places of historic interest.

7. The principal countries of the world, especially those of Europe.

8. Races of men.—Location; characteristics; occupations.

Reading

(One recitation daily for subject matter and methods not less than four weeks of the term.)

FIRST TERM

THIRD RECITATION

History of Education

(Three recitations each week throughout the term.)

Drawing

(Two recitations each week throughout the term.)

SECOND TERM

FIRST RECITATION

Language and Grammar

Subject matter and methods.

(One recitation daily through the term.)

Review of the following topics with special reference to teaching:

1. Definition of terms.

2. Parts of speech.—Classes; modifications; inflections.

3. Syntax, and analysis of sentences.—Principal clauses; subordinate clauses; classification; sentences and clauses; analysis of clauses; modifiers—words, phrases, clauses.

4. Practical exercises.—Illustrations of the foregoing.

5. Composition.—Plan; subject, heads, thoughts. Compositions about familiar subjects. Letter writing, bills, orders, receipts, acknowledgments, introductions.

SECOND RECITATION

Physiology and Hygiene

Subject matter and methods.

(Six weeks.)

1. The skeleton.—The bones; their structure, composition, nourishment, adaptation, technical names of principal bones; kinds of joints, cartilages, ligaments.

2. Muscles.—Kinds; structure, use, mode of action; comparison of muscle, ligament and tendon.

3. Skin.—Structure; functions, glands; hair and nails; cleanliness; bathing; clothing.

4. Food and digestion.—Necessary element of foods; cooking of food; drinks. Organs of digestion; fluids; all processes involved in the conversion of food into tissue.

5. Circulation.—Object; organs; process; blood, amount, composition; rapidity of circulation.

6. Respiration.—Organs; process of breathing; muscles involved; effects on the blood; impure air; ventilation.

7. Excretory organs.—Skin, kidneys, lungs, intestines.

8. The nervous system.—The brain; spinal cord; cranial and spinal nerves sympathetic system; effects of stimulants and narcotics.

9. The organs of special sense.—The eye; ear; nose; tongue; skin.

It is required that under the several heads, the matter of hygiene and the effects of stimulants and narcotics shall be thoroughly taught, and that some of the lessons given during the time devoted to this subject shall illustrate the method of teaching physiology in the several grades.

School Management and School Law

(Twelve weeks. See Syllabus and books prescribed by the Department for uniform examination)

THIRD RECITATION

Art of Questioning

(Three weeks)

The remaining weeks to be devoted to a review of the work necessary for the final examinations of the year.

VI. Notes Under Course of Study

1. The Laws of Mental Development and Principles of Teaching are to be considered especially in the study of methods of teaching; but as these laws and principles are fundamental to the professional study of the teacher, they can be illustrated and developed in connection with any of the above subjects of study.

2. When the principal is not satisfied with the proficiency of any member in American History and Civil Government these subjects are to be studied in connection with the regular class work of the school. Under no consideration are these subjects to take any of the regular time given to the training class.

3. Instructors are permitted to spend more time in the study of topics of a purely professional character, provided the class is unusually proficient in the subject-matter branches. In such cases it is required that the Department be notified of the change in the course of study.

4. The subjects of Penmanship and Spelling should receive careful attention from the beginning to the end of the year.

5. Persons holding teachers' training-class certificates dated not prior to August 1, 1896, will receive full credit on the first year's work for all subjects in the training-class course, except Methods, History of Education, School Management, Drawing and Music.

VII. Observation and Practice Work

1. In addition to receiving methods of teaching on the authority of the instructor, it is very important that the members should be trained to critically observe and intelligently interpret the principles of teaching by being brought in contact with the pupils in the actual work of imparting instruction. To afford this training, it is expected that the critic teacher, at least twice a week,

will give an opportunity to witness practical work, either by taking the class to other departments of the school to observe the work of experienced teachers, or by bringing pupils from other departments to receive a model lesson from the critic teacher.

2. For practice work it is recommended that each member be given actual work in teaching, both by taking charge of a class in other departments of the school, or of the training class, as often as is consistent with the work of the school, and by having pupils brought before the training class to be instructed by a member designated for that purpose. At a subsequent recitation let this observation and practice work be reviewed by the critic teacher, the underlying principles clearly brought out and the proper methods forcibly presented. Observation work shall not take the place of the regular daily periods of class instruction.

VIII. Examinations

1. Special examinations in all subjects required for second-grade certificates, and in the additional professional subjects prescribed for training classes, will be held in January and June for members of training classes, and those members who attain a standing of at least seventy-five per cent. in these subjects shall receive certificates which shall be known as "professional certificates," which shall be valid for three years.

At the end of three years' successful teaching, such certificate shall be renewable the same as are first-grade certificates.

2. The examination of the training classes under the uniform system shall begin on the third Wednesday of January, and on the second Wednesday of June, and shall continue three days.

3. It is required that the name of every member shall appear in the report of the examination at the close of the term. The Department reserves the right of refusing payment for the instruction of members not entering the examination or not reaching a fair standing in the subjects embraced in the course of study.

4. Members will be exempt from reëxamination in those subjects in which they attain a standing of at least seventy-five per cent. at the next preceding examination held for teachers' training classes, but such exemptions shall not apply to subjects prescribed for that part of the year not yet completed at the time of the examination.

5. Inasmuch as the examination at the close of each term has been appointed with special reference to the convenience of these classes, it is required that the members shall enter no other uniform examination during the term of study.

6. The following extracts from the regulations governing uniform examinations state the requirements for training-class certificates and for certificates of the second and third grade:

Training-Class Certificates

Term.—These certificates will be issued for a term of three years.

Renewals.—Upon the expiration of three years' successful teaching, these certificates shall be renewable under the same conditions that first-grade certificates are renewable.

Qualifications of Candidates

Experience.—Candidates for a certificate of this kind must have been in attendance upon a training class for at least two consecutive terms, as provided in the training-class regulations.

Educational requirements.—Candidates must attain, in examinations held for training classes, at least seventy five per cent. in each of the subjects for a second-grade certificate, and in addition thereto a standing of seventy-five per cent. in all special subjects designated in the course of study for teachers' training classes.

Dates of examinations.—The examination of training classes shall begin on the third Wednesday of January and on the second Wednesday of June, and shall continue three days.

Note.—All other rules of the uniform system of examinations not conflicting with the rules under which these certificates are issued shall apply to and govern the issuing of these certificates.

Program; Training-class examination.—Wednesday, a. m., History of Education, School Management, School Law; p. m., Art of Questioning, American History, Orthography. Thursday, a. m., Civil Government, Drawing; p. m., Methods, Geography, Current Topics. Friday, a. m., Arithmetic, Physiology; p. m., Composition, Grammar, Methods (for those who failed in next preceding examination).

"Candidates for certificates of the third grade shall be required to pass a written examination in Reading, Arithmetic, Composition, Geography, Grammar, Orthography, Penmanship, Physiology and Hygiene, American History and School Law."

"Candidates for certificates of the second grade shall be required to pass a written examination in the following subjects: American History, Arithmetic, Civil Government, School Law, Composition, Current Topics, Drawing, Geography, Grammar, Methods and School Economy, Orthography, Penmanship, Reading and Physiology and Hygiene."

7. The regulations governing uniform examinations fix the time of holding such examinations as follows:

Examinations for certificates of the second grade, unless omitted in the discretion of any school commissioner, shall begin on the first Thursday of March and June; second Thursday of January and August; the fourth Friday of April and September, and shall continue two days.

Examinations for first grade shall begin on the first Thursday of March and the second Thursday of August, and shall continue two days. No examination shall be held upon any other date than those above enumerated, except by direction of the state Superintendent of Public Instruction.

8. A blank form for making a report of the organization and final examination of the class will be furnished by the Department. It is expected that this report will be forwarded within two weeks after the date of the final examination, as the apportionment of public money for the instruction will be assigned to the different institutions at that time.

IX. School Commissioner

1. The duties of the school commissioner to the training class are defined by title XI, chapter 556 of the laws of 1894.

2. School commissioners are instructed to accept one year's work in a training class as an equivalent for the ten weeks successful experience in teaching required in the regulations governing uniform examinations. Any member without experience as a teacher, failing to secure a training-class certificate at the final training-class examination, can become a candidate for a second-grade certificate at any subsequent regular uniform examination held within one year from the date of such final examination.

3. After visiting the class the school commissioner is directed to immediately forward to this Department a report concerning the number in the class satisfying the conditions of admission, the character and quality of the instruction imparted and the improvement of the opportunities afforded for observation and practice work. At the close of the term the results of the final examination must also be reported. Blank forms will be provided for these reports. School commissioners will be expected to inspect every class under their jurisdiction as often as once in each month during the term.

4. It is required that the members of the training class shall attend the teachers' institute held in the district in which the class is organized. Each member of the class shall keep a full record of the subjects discussed and methods presented by the instructors, and submit the same to the principal.

X. The Law Creating and Governing Teachers' Training Classes

CHAPTER 556 OF THE LAWS OF 1894, TITLE XI

TEACHERS' TRAINING CLASSES

Section 1. There shall be annually appropriated out of the income of the United States deposit fund, not otherwise appropriated, the sum of thirty thousand dollars, and out of the free school fund the sum of thirty thousand dollars for the instruction of competent persons in academies and union schools, in the science and practice of common school teaching, under a course to be prescribed by the Superintendent of Public Instruction.

§ 2. The Superintendent of Public Instruction shall designate the academies and union schools in which such instruction shall be given, distributing them among the school commissioner districts of the state, as nearly as may well be, having reference to the number of school districts in each, to location and to the character of the institution selected.

§ 3. Every academy and union school so designated shall instruct a class of not less than ten nor more than twenty-five scholars, and every scholar admitted to such class shall continue under instruction not less than sixteen weeks. Whenever it shall be shown to the satisfaction of the Superintendent of Public Instruction that any pupil attending such class or classes has been prevented from attending the same for the full term of sixteen weeks, or has attended the first full term, but not the full time in the second term, during any one year; or that for any reason satisfactory to such Superintendent, said class or classes have not been held for the full term of sixteen weeks, such Superintendent may excuse such default and allow to the trustees of the academy or union free school in which said class or classes shall have been instructed, pay for such scholar or scholars for the time actually spent in attendance, or during which said class or classes shall have been under instruction, at the rate of one dollar for each week's instruction, as provided in section five of this title. The Superintendent shall prescribe the conditions of admission to the classes, the course of instruction and the rules and regulations under which said instruction shall be given, and shall, in his discretion, determine the number of classes which may be formed in any one year, in an academy or union school and the length of time exceeding sixteen weeks during which such instruction may be given.

§ 4. Instruction shall be free to all scholars admitted to such classes, and who have continued in them the length of time required by the third section of this title.

§ 5. The trustees of all academies and union schools in which such instruction shall be given shall be paid from the appropriations named in the first section of this title at the rate of one dollar for each week's instruction to each scholar who has attended for the term of time as required by section three of this title, on the certificate of the Superintendent, to be furnished to the Comptroller.

§ 6. The appropriation provided by this act, for the instruction in academies and union schools in the science and practice of common school teaching, shall be deemed to include, and shall include, the due inspection and supervision of such instruction by the Superintendent of Public Instruction, and the expenses of such inspection and supervision shall be paid out of said appropriation on vouchers certified by the Superintendent.

§ 7. Each class organized in any academy or union school under appointment by the Superintendent for instruction in the science and practice of common school teaching, shall be subject to the visitation of the school commissioner of the district in which such academy or union school is situated; and it shall be the duty of said commissioner to advise and assist the principals of said academies or union schools in the organization and management of said classes, and at the close of the term of instruction of said classes, under the direction of the Superintendent, to examine the students in such classes, and to issue teachers' certificates to such as show moral character, fitness and scholastic and professional qualifications worthy thereof.

XI. The Law Transferring Teachers' Training Classes to Superintendent of Public Instruction

CHAPTER 137 OF THE LAWS OF 1889

AN ACT to transfer the management and supervision of teachers' classes in academies and union schools from the board of regents to the Superintendent of Public Instruction.

Passed April 15, 1889.

Section 1. The powers and duties conferred and imposed upon the regents of the university by chapter four hundred and twenty-five of the laws of one thousand eight hundred and seventy-seven, and chapter three hundred and eighteen of the laws of one thousand eight hundred and eighty-two, relative to the instruction of classes in academies and union schools in the science and practice of common school teaching, are hereby transferred to the Superintendent of Public Instruction.

§ 2. This act shall take effect immediately.

XII. To Encourage and Promote the Professional Training of Teachers

CHAPTER 1031 OF THE LAWS OF 1895

AN ACT to encourage and promote the professional training of teachers.

The People of the State of New York, represented in Senate and Assembly, do enact as follows:

Section 1. The board of education or the public school authorities of any city, except the city of New York, or of any village employing a superintendent of schools, may establish, maintain, direct and control one or more schools or classes for the professional instruction and training of teachers in the principles of education and in the method of instruction for not less than thirty-eight weeks in each school year.

§ 2. Towards the maintenance and support of these schools and classes established pursuant to this act, or heretofore established and maintained for similar purposes, and whose requirements for admission, and whose course of studies are made with the approval of the State Superintendent of Public Instruction, and under whose direction such classes shall be conducted, the said superintendent is hereby authorized and directed in each year to set apart, to apportion and to pay from the free school fund one dollar for each week of instruction of each pupil, provided, however, that said apportionment and payment shall not exceed in the aggregate one hundred thousand dollars in each year. Such apportionment and payment shall be made upon the report to the local superintendent of schools filed with the State Superintendent of Public Instruction, who shall draw his warrant upon the State Treasurer for the amount apportioned.

§ 3. If the total sum to be apportioned and to be paid, as provided by section two of this act, shall in any one year exceed the said sum of one hundred thousand dollars, the said State Superintendent of Public Instruction shall apportion to each school and class its pro rata of said sum upon the basis described in section two of this act.

§ 4. After January first, eighteen hundred and ninety-seven, no person shall be employed or licensed to teach in the primary and grammar schools of any city authorized by law to employ a superintendent of schools, who has not had successful experience in teaching for at least three years, or, in lieu thereof, has not completed a three years' course in, and graduated from a high school or academy having a course of study of not less than three years, approved by the State Superintendent of Public Instruction, or from some institution of learning of equal or higher rank, approved by the same authority, and who subsequently to such graduation has not graduated from a school or class for the professional training of teachers, having a course of study of not less than thirty-eight weeks, approved by the State Superintendent of Public Instruction. Nothing in this act shall be construed to restrict any board of education of any city from requiring such additional qualifications of teachers as said board may determine; nor shall the provisions of this act preclude the board of education of any city or village from accepting the diploma of any state normal and training school of the state of New York, or a state certificate obtained on examination, as an equivalent for the preparation in scholarship and professional training herein required.

§ 5. All acts and parts of acts inconsistent with this act are hereby repealed.

§ 6. This act shall take effect immediately.

XIII. Syllabus

The following outlines are presented to aid in the study of the methods of teaching. These outlines are given as suggestions to teachers for a plan of work:

Psychology

Brief outline to be used as a general guide.

The Mind:

Its nature unknown;
Only its phenomena can be studied.

How Studied { By introspection. / By observation.

Fundamental Divisions	Sensibility	*feels.*
	Intellect	*knows.*
	Will	*acts.*

Sensibility:

General physical sensibility;
Special senses;
Higher emotions and sentiments;
Consciousness.

General physical sensibility gives feeling of comfort, discomfort, rest, fatigue, hunger, thirst, heat, cold.

Special Senses: Smell, taste, touch, hearing, sight.

Kind of knowledge gained from each sense.

Smell, gives knowledge of the odors of material things.
Taste, gives knowledge of the savors of material things.
Touch, gives knowledge of form, smoothness, roughness, hardness, softness, pressure, temperature.

Hearing, gives knowledge of sound and distinguishes noises, musical tones, quantity of sound, quality of sound, pitch and timbre.

Sight, primarily gives knowledge of colors and forms of plane surfaces; secondarily, in connection with touch, gives knowledge of solidity and the distances and sizes of objects.

Law, ideas which belong to one sense cannot be obtained through another sense.

Consciousness, the internal sense accompanies all acts of the mind.

The Intellect:

Primary divisions
- Acquisitive faculties—Sense perception.
- Retentive faculties—Imagination.
- Reproductive faculties—Imagination.
- Elaborative faculties— Comparison. Judgment.
- Regulative faculties—The reason.

Attention: Its nature and importance; its necessity in the acquisition of knowledge; how secured and trained.

Law: The primary facts of knowledge, form, color, sound, weight, savor, odor, etc., can be obtained only by the direct action of material things upon the senses and cannot be taught from books.

Importance of training the senses in the acquisition of the primary facts of knowledge by object lessons.

Percepts and Concepts.

The Memory: Spontaneous and voluntary; how trained; most easily trained in early life.

Laws of association.

Imagination, kinds. Reproductive. Constructive.

Its value in education and in life.

The Elaborative Faculty: The power to judge, compare and reflect, and to work up the knowledge in the mind into new forms.

Inductive and deductive reasoning, analysis and synthesis.

Abstraction and generalization.

The reason: The power which regulates and guides all the other powers and faculties of the mind.

The Will: Necessity of training; motives; formation of habits.

Law: All the powers of the mind are strengthened by exercise.

History of Education

The following syllabus is intended to give the outline upon which the work in this subject will be based and not to present methods of teaching it.

It is expected, however, that this subject will be taught in a manner to inspire interest therein for its own sake, to arouse a professional spirit, to bring the class into intimate acquaintance and sympathy with the great educators of the past, to secure an intelligent appreciation of current pedagogical discussions, and to beget serious reflection upon the real nature of education and the true aim of the educator.

To secure these results, the class should

1. Become familiar with the mistakes, the struggles, and the triumphs of the great educators of the past;
2. Trace the growth and development of educational principles and systems;
3. Gain a clear conception of the diverse phases that education has assumed in different nations and ages;
4. Know how largely education and its results have depended upon the conditions of the times and the environments of the people.

Syllabus

I. Introductory: A general view of education among the old Asiatic nations. (Chinese, Hindoos, Israelites, Egyptians and Phœnicians.)

II. Education among the Greeks:
- (a) Comparison of Athenian and Spartan education.
- (b) Noted educators, including Socrates, Plato, Aristotle, Eucid, Xenophon, Strabo, Ptolemy and Pythagoras.

III. Education among the Romans:
- (a) Comparison of Greek and Roman education.
- (b) Noted educators, including Quintilian, Plutarch, Varro, Pliny, Seneca, Saint Jerome, Saint Augustine.
- (c) Effects of Christianity on education.

IV. Education during the Middle Ages:
- (a) Description and explanation of its general character.
- (b) The Benedictines.
- (c) Franciscan and Dominican friars.
- (d) The Liberal Arts.
  1. The Trivium.
  2. The Quadrivium.

(e) Noted educators, including Charlemagne, Alcium, Thomas Aquinas, Bishop Aldhelm, the 'Venerable' Bede, Abelard.

V. The period of the Renaissance:

(a) Characteristics and causes of the Great Renaissance.
(b) Noted reformers, including Erasmus, Melancthon, Luther, Sturm, Montaigne, Rabelais, Comenius, Ascham, Bacon.
(c) The teaching societies.
1. The Jesuits.
2. The Port-Royalists (Jansenists).
3. The Oratorians.

VI. Education since the Sixteenth Century:

(a) General characteristics.
(b) Special study of the following educators:
Fenelon, Locke, Rousseau, Basedow, Pestalozzi, Froebel, Jacotot, Arnold, Bain, Spencer, Mann, Barnard, Page.
(c) Leading facts in the development of common schools in America.
(d) History of the school system of the State of New York.
1. Higher education.
2. Elementary education.
3. Professional training of teachers.

Art of Questioning

Brief outline to be used as a general guide. Members of the class should be required to conduct recitations in different subjects, employing questions in accordance with instruction given.

1. The purpose of questions
   (a) To stimulate thought.
   (b) To develop thought.
   (c) To test knowledge.
2. The nature of questions
   (a) Clear.
   (b) Reasonable.
   (c) Definite.
   (d) Concise.
   (e) Pointed.
3. The origin of questions
   (a) With the teacher.
   (b) With the pupil.
4. The order of continuity of questions.
5. The manner of asking questions.

6. Different kinds of questions, *e. g.*, leading, alternative, direct, indirect.
7. Different forms of the same question.
8. Consideration of answers as to correctness or incorrectness

(*a*) Subject matter.
(*b*) Form.

School Management

I. Organization:

(1.) General appointments of school buildings.
(*a*) Lighting.
(*b*) Heating.
(*c*) Ventilating.
(*d*) Seating.
(*e*) Blackboards.
(2.) Care of school property.
(3.) Course of study.
(*a*) Length of sessions—recesses.
(*b*) Program of recitations.
(*c*) Program of study.

II. Classification.

Grading of Pupils.

III. Relation of teacher to:

(*a*) Trustees and boards of education.
(*b*) Patrons.
(*c*) Pupils.

IV. Discipline:

(1.) Object of:
(*a*) To promote order.
(*b*) To prevent disorder.
(*c*) To correct disorder.
(*d*) To promote study.
(*e*) To promote self-control.
(2.) Means of:
(*a*) By thorough preparation of the teacher.
(*b*) By keeping the pupils at work.
(*c*) By timely admonition and proper encouragement.
(*d*) By suitable punishments.

Methods in Arithmetic

The mental faculties developed by the study of Arithmetic.
The Idea of Number.

Concrete number.

Especial care given to the most approved methods of presenting the subject of number to beginners by means of numerical frame, pictures, counters, and the like.

Abstract number.

The gradual separation of the idea of number from any particular object. The cultivation of the memory by constant drill in the use of abstract number.

Methods of teaching number.

The Grube, the Pestalozzian, the two combined.

Notation and numeration.

The principles of the Arabic and Roman systems. The development of the idea of the order and relation of the figures in numbers, numbers of few orders being used.

The fundamental operations:

The elementary combinations in addition using all the digits. The steps leading from addition to subtraction; the development of multiplication and division. The use of signs.

Properties of numbers:

The classification and properties of numbers which naturally follow the study of the fundamental operations. The knowledge of the divisibility of numbers applied to factoring, and the application of factoring in determining divisors and multiples. The use of these principles exemplified in cancellation and the employment of cancellation in all possible operations.

Fractions:

The application of the principles already learned to the elementary idea of fraction primarily developed in the child's mind. The distinction between the fraction itself and the expression of the fraction. Decimals governed by the same principles applicable to whole numbers and fractions.

Denominate numbers:

A clear idea of the use of concrete objects wherever practicable, of the standard units of measure, common and metric, and a thorough memorizing of the several tables. The operations do not differ in principle from those already learned.

Practicable problems entering into the experience of the pupils are of special value.

Percentage:

The principles of percentage are identical with those of fractions, the denominator being the constant number 100.

The rules of business fractions are to be thoroughly known.

Ratio and proportion:

A development of the relation of numbers.

Review:

Unify the work, showing the relation of subjects.

Geography

1. Direction, right, left, points of compass.
2. Distance, units and their application.
3. Definitions of terms developed as far as possible from observation.
4. Map constructed from observation (not copied) of school room and school ground.
5. Maps of town and county, showing streams, villages, railroads, canals, etc.
6. Local industries, natural products, manufactured products.

Earth studied from an artificial globe:

1. Circles.
2. Zones—their climate and principal flora and fauna.
3. Grand divisions of land and water.
4. Transition from globe to map of the world.

Countries:

1. Location.
2. Drainage.
3. Climate and soil determining vegetable and animal products occupation and character of people.
4. Outline maps rapidly sketched by pupils.
5. Great cities, the natural causes that have determined their location and contributed to their growth.
6. Important facts concerning these cities.
7. Commerce—(*a*) Domestic and foreign. Principal exports and imports.
   (*b*) Great centers of commerce.
   (*c*) Great highways of commerce, railroads, canals, steamship lines.
8. Imaginary journeys.
9. Comparisons of geographical features of different countries.
10. Form of government.

Mathematical Geography:

1. Plane of ecliptic.
2. Relative position of earth and sun in the plane.
3. Movement of earth in plane producing day and night.
4. North star, how located.
5. Inclination and parallelism of axis.
6. Seasons, causes producing them.
7. Width of zones, cause determining.

State of New York:

1. Outline map sketched.
2. Relief map moulded; showing mountains, mountain passes, valleys, rivers, lakes.
3. Counties and important cities and villages in each.
4. Principal railroads and canals with important cities and villages along their lines.
5. Important facts associated with noted places.
6. Industries and natural products.

Language

Oral:

Object lessons.
Picture lessons.
Story-telling.
Sentence building.
Reproduction exercise.
Narrations.
Descriptions.
Quotations from classic authors.

Written:

A. Preparatory work.
Copying.
Dictation.
Completion of elliptical expressions.
Incorporation of given words and sentences.
Expansion—Substituting phrases for words, and clauses for phrases.
Contraction—Substituting phrases for clauses, words for phrases, and the use of elliptical expressions.
Choice of words—Involving definition, and the use of synonyms.
The parts of speech and their classification.
The classification and analysis of sentences.

Syntactical constructions.
English word analysis.
Mechanics—Involving capitalization, punctuation, headings, margins, and paragraphing.

B. Applications.

Letters.
Business and social forms.
Narratives.
Descriptions.
Paraphrase.

C. Criticism and correction.

Order of, in importance —
The thought expressed;
The language used;
The mechanics.
Corrections—T, tr., ∧, Caps, l. c., O, ¶.

Reading

1. Aim.
2. Blackboard exercises.—Charts.
3. Words selected from vocabulary already known by pupils.
4. Pupils taught to recognize by sight the words of a proposed sentence.
5. Sentence read silently, then orally.
6. New words taught, and new sentences read.
7. Necessary steps in reading:
   (*a*) Perfect word knowledge, (*b*) Silent reading, (*c*) Oral expression.
8. Oral reading of sentence not to be attempted until the thought is in the mind.
9. Elementary sounds with diacritical marks to be taught, (*a*) to give ability to call new words without help, (*b*) to improve articulation, (*c*) to correct defective speech.
10. General drills in pronouncing difficult combinations of elementary sounds.
11. Transition to reading books.
12. Supplementary reading, such as newspapers, histories, and standard literature.
13. Discussion of advantages and disadvantages of different methods of teaching reading.
14. How to conduct recitations in advanced reading.

Methods in Spelling

I. **Oral:**
   (*a*) Advantages.
   (*b*) Disadvantages.
   (*c*) Application.

II. **Written:**
   (*a*) Advantages.
   (*b*) Disadvantages.
   (*c*) Application.

III. **Syllabication and accent.**

IV. **Word analysis:**
   (*a*) Stems.
   (*b*) Prefixes.
   (*c*) Suffixes.

V. **Diacritical marking.**

VI. **Exercises in articulation.**

Drawing

I. **Value of a knowledge of the subject:**

II. **Color:**
   (*a*) Knowledge of six positive spectrum colors, viz.: red, orange, yellow, green, blue, violet.
   (*b*) Recognition of twelve standard hues, viz.: violet-red, orange-yellow, green-yellow, blue-green, violet-blue, red-violet, orange-red, red-orange, yellow-orange, yellow-green, green-blue, blue-violet.
   (*c*) Arrange hues and positive colors as here indicated, completing spectrum scale with eighteen colors.

Vlo R.	R.	O. R.	R. O.	O.	Y. O.	O. Y.	Y.	G. Y.	Y. G.	G.	B. G.	G. B.	B.	Vlo. B	B. Vio.	Vio.	R. Vio.

III. Form. Knowledge of geometric type solids:

Wholes—1. Sphere. 2. Cylinder. 3. Cube.
Bisections — 1. Half-sphere. 2. Half-cylinder. 3. Half-cube.
Quadrisections as New Wholes — 1. Square prism. 2. Triangular prism. 3. Square plinth. 4. Circular plinth.
Geometric Type Solids — Variations. (*a*) Spheroids. (*b*) Oblate spheroid. (*c*) Prolate spheroid. (*d*) Ovoid. (*e*) Cone. (*f*) Pyramid.

IV. Parts and their relation:

(1) Surface. (*a*) Kinds. (*b*) Parts—faces.
(2) Faces. (*a*) Kinds. (*b*) Number. (*c*) Shapes. (*d*) Location. (*e*) Directions. (*f*) Parts.
(3) Edges. (*a*) Kinds. (*b*) Number. (*c*) Location. (*d*) Directions.
(4) Angles—Right—Oblique { acute. obtuse.
(5) Curvilinear, mixtilinear and rectilinear geometric plane figures and their details as representing faces of the solids, *i. e.*, circle, square, half circle, oblong, triangle.
(6) Bisect spheroids and ovoid to obtain geometric figures, circle, ellipse and oval.
(7) Circle and circular figures. (*a*) Circumference. (*b*) Center. (*c*) Diameter. (*d*) Radius.
(8) Rectangles.
1. Square and similar forms.
2. Oblong. { (*a*) Diameters. (*b*) Diagonals.
(9) Triangles and similar forms. (*a*) Base. (*b*) Apex. (*c*) Altitude.
(10) Three kinds of angles used in industrial drawing.

V. Practical knowledge of use of tools and materials:

Mechanical:

(1) Scale, compasses, hard pencils and eraser are used.
(2) Lines—Should always be sharp and clean cut, but may be either dark or light.
(3) Measure—Proper method of marking off distances, ruling, use of compasses and of making erasures.

Freehand:

(1) Soft pencil, charcoal, crayon and blender.

(2) Lines—In drawing, the line must express as nearly as possible the character of the surface of the object, must be light or dark, fine or broad, abruptly broken or continuous, according to the contour of the object.

(3) Kinds as to { direction. relative position.

VI. Divisions of work:

Geometric drawing:

(1) Geometric plane figures and regular polygons.

(2) Working Drawings — Mechanical — Principles. (*a*) The representation of visible outlines and edges. (*b*) The representation of invisible outlines and edges. (*c*) Parallel cross sections, plans and elevations. (*d*) Oblique sections. (*e*) Drawing to scale.

(3) Freehand applications—Plans and elevations of objects based upon the type forms.

(4) Development—Pattern Making—First draw the developments freehand on practice paper, then accurately with ruler on paper or in the books. If the model is to be constructed from the pattern, draw on oak tag paper, cut, fold and glue. The developments may be used for constructing simple, useful objects in paper, leather, cloth or wood. The surface of the frustum of a square pyramid or cone may all be drawn radiating from a point. This should be illustrated by turning the model of a pyramid on its sides and tracing about each triangular face in succession.

VII. Decorative drawing.—(Instrumental and freehand):

Color. (1) Classification—Harmonies (*a*) Key colors; (*b*) tints, *i. e.*, modification of color by white or increased light; (*c*) shades, *i. e.*, modification of colors by black or diminished light.

(2) Dominant harmony is a symmetrical arrangement of any color with its tints and shades.

(3) Complementary colors—Composed of colors which together will produce white or grey.

(4) Complementary harmony—Composed of complementary colors.

(5) Analogous harmony—Composed of colors allied to the spectrum; borrowing tones from neighboring scales.

(6) Contrasted harmony—Any color found in the spectrum in juxtaposition with the grey of the atmosphere.

(7) Comparison of the colors. (*a*) Warm and cold colors. (*b*) Active and passive. (*c*) Negative colors.

Botanical Drawing.—Draw from the natural forms. Teach conventionalization. Draw leaf and flower forms conventionalized.

Historic Ornament.—(1) Study illustrations of historic ornament for (*a*) modified regular units; (*b*) bilateral historic units; (*c*) changes made from natural forms; (*d*) plan of construction; (*e*) bilateral main lines in the units both of borders and limited surface decorations; (*f*) the natural forms used, with adaptation and conventionalization of these forms; (*g*) the technical principles upon which the designs have been constructed, namely, fitness, order, growth, unity and repose. (*h*) Draw from a copy of standard decorative design, giving special attention to expression, character of line, accent and brilliancy, and beauty in execution.

Design.—1st. Principles — Contrast. Unity, strength, variety and rhythm. Units. based on the square and on other regular geometric figures. 2d. Principles—Growth, symmetry, balance and distribution.

(8) Study illustrations of (*a*) balanced curves, (*b*) bilateral main lines, (*c*) the law of balance; subtle radiation, tangential union of all parts, and the laws of plant growth. (*d*) Draw main lines in conventional but beautiful sprays, and clothe these with units, elements or forms of design.

VIII. Pictorial Drawing:

Knowledge of elementary pictorial art, based on the correct representation of geometric type solids according to principles of perspective, and the application of these same principles in the representation of other objects. The perceptive faculties should be quickened to a keen discrimination of proportion, and the accurate observing of form and representation of it should be stimulated. Practical and common sense methods should be employed to obtain good results; peculiarities and mannerisms should be avoided; simplicity and truthfulness should be the aim, and pupils should learn to draw by drawing.

(1) Representation of solidity—Expressed by shading.

(2) Principles—Fore-shortening and convergence.

(3) Problems—(*a*) Lines bounding unequal plane faces, equally fore-shortened. (*b*) Lines bounding equal plane faces, unequally fore-shortened. (*c*) Lines bounding unequal plane faces, unequally fore-shortened.

(4) Principle—Convergence at unequal angles, and use of diagonals to find centers.

(5) Relation of axes—When drawing, illustrate by rapid sketches many different type solids, as (*a*) ovoids and ovoidal objects in various positions, sketching main axes first; (*b*) cone and conical objects in various positions or on different axes; (*c*) pyramid and pyramidal objects on main axes; (*d*) cylinder and cylinderical objects. (*e*) Make finished drawings of each ovoid, cone, pyramid and cylinder and of some objects based upon them. (*f*) Draw groups of two or three objects based upon the type previously studied. Arrange groups artistically.

IX. Clear-cut definitions of principal terms and statements of important facts:

Under this division of the subject, practical applications—*i. e.*, ability to represent by drawings—of all curves, geometric plane figures, working drawings, sectional views, ground plans, elevations and fore-shortening are essential to a teaching knowledge of industrial drawing.

American History

I. America previous to Columbus.

The Northmen; the mound builders; the Indians, their character, habits, government, number, distribution, location of tribes, especially of the Iroquois and Algonquins.

NOTE.—Never miss an opportunity to study good pictorial art. Sketch in connection with history, geography and natural science lessons and learn to use drawings as a natural and easy means of expressing thought.

II. America, 1492–1607.

Exploration: (*a*) Spanish; (*b*) French; (*c*) English.

III. America, 1607–1754.

Settlement: (*a*) Spanish; (*b*) French; (*c*) English; (*d*) Dutch; (*e*) by the Swedes.

IV. America, 1754–1789.

The French war, the years preceding the Revolution; the Revolution; the time of the Confederation.

V. The United States, 1789, to the present time.

The different administrations and their leading events; the political parties; the growth of territory; the formation of new states.

VI. The history of the state of New York.

In addition to the topics usually treated in the text-books on United States history: The settlement of the Mohawk valley, and the contest with the French for central and northern New York; the Dongan charter; Leister's rebellion; the Zenger trial; the change from colonial to state government; the contest over the adoption of the constitution; the principal governors; the Erie canal; the public school system.

Civil Government

I. The different forms of government.

II. The Constitution of the United States.

Provisions; principles.

III. The revised Constitution of the state of New York.

Comparison with the National Constitution as to main features.

IV. The three departments of national and state government.

V. Officers, state and United States.

How chosen; eligibility; length of term, duties, extent and limitations of power.

VI. Government of the counties, cities and towns of the state of New York.

NOTE — In the study of the above topics the following details should be noted: the dates of the leading events, such as shown above; the approximate time and general order of time of other events; the causes and results of war, the number and condition of the people at the various times; the location of places historically important; inventions; men of letters and their writings; internal improvements, including canals and railroads.

VII. Citizenship.

How acquired; privileges; duties.

VIII. Electors.

Qualifications.

IX. Discussion of the fundamental principles of our national and State government.

X. Discussion of the fundamental differences of political parties.

XI. The functions of political machinery. (*a*) Caucuses; (*b*) conventions.

School Law

I. State Superintendent.

(*a*) Election of; (*b*) Powers of, pertaining to teachers; to trustees; to school commissioners.

II. School commissioners.

(*a*) Election of; (*b*) Powers of, pertaining to teachers; to trustees; to school districts.

III. Trustees.

(*a*) Election of; (*b*) Changing number of; (*c*) Powers of, pertaining to teachers; to districts; (*d*) Duties of, pertaining to teachers; to districts.

IV. Teachers.

(*a*) Qualifications; (*b*) Powers of, pertaining to school discipline; to methods of instruction; (*c*) Duties of, pertaining to school register; to school property.

V. District meetings.

(*a*) Annual—time of holding; powers of.
(*b*) Special—how called; powers of.

VI. Voters—Qualifications of.

VII. State and other school moneys, their apportionment and distribution.

REGULATIONS FOR TEACHERS' TRAINING SCHOOLS AND CLASSES IN CITIES

City Training Classes

The following regulations governing teachers' training schools and classes have been prescribed in accordance with chapter

1031 of the laws of 1895, entitled An Act to Encourage and to Promote the Professional Training of Teachers.

Attention is called to the regulation adopted, to the course of study arranged and to the provisions of law relating to city training classes.

I. Appointments

"The board of education or the public school authorities of any city, except the city of New York, or of any village employing a superintendent of schools, may establish, maintain, direct and control one or more schools or classes for the professional instruction and training of teachers in the principles of education and in the method of instruction for not less than thirty-eight weeks in each school year."

II. Qualifications for Admission

1. Candidates must be at least seventeen years of age at the time of entrance.

2. They must subscribe, in good faith, to the following declaration: "We, the subscribers, hereby declare that our object in asking admission to the training school or class is to prepare ourselves for teaching; and that it is our purpose to engage in teaching in the public schools of the state of New York at the completion of such preparation."

3. Before admission they must hold as a minimum qualification a diploma of graduation from a high school or an academy having a course of study approved by the state Superintendent of Public Instruction, or a diploma from an institution of equal or higher rank, approved by the same authority, as provided under the law. Additional qualifications may be prescribed by boards of education.

4. Graduates from institutions in the state of New York, applying for admission to these schools or classes, will be required to file with the local superintendent of schools a certificate from the principal teacher of the high school or other institution from which they were graduated, setting forth the fact of graduation on the completion of the required course, duly approved by the state Superintendent of Public Instruction. The Department will publish, from time to time, a list of the institutions whose course of study has been approved.

5. Candidates from other states, applying for admission, in order to qualify for entrance to any training class, shall present credentials of graduation from a high school or an institution of equal or higher rank, having a course of study at least equivalent to the high school course of study prescribed as a basis for en-

trance to training classes in this state. Such credentials shall be forwarded to the state Superintendent for approval.

III. Organization

1. The school year is divided into two terms, but no school year shall consist of more than forty weeks.

2. The compensation allowed institutions for the instruction will be at the rate of one dollar for each week's instruction of each member.

3. At least four hours every school day must be occupied in study or in instruction on the topics laid down in the course of study, or in the observation of model teaching or in practice work.

4. Two blank forms for notice of organization will be furnished to each institution. These blanks must be properly filled, and one be forwarded to the Department at the end of the third week after the organization of the class. The other must be filed by the superintendent of schools for inspection by the proper school officers.

IV. Rulings and Requirements

1. No person shall be admitted to the class after the report of organization has been forwarded to the Department.

2. No allowance can be made for any pupil not shown by reports to have been eligible to enter the class.

3. No allowance will be made for any pupil who leaves the class before the expiration of the year, except by permission of the state Superintendent, and no such permission will be granted during the year, simply in order that the candidate may teach.

4. When the class is organized, the qualification for admission of each candidate shall be entered in the place designated for such entry in the "Teachers' Training Class Daily Register," and the credentials thereof filed for inspection in the office of the superintendent of schools.

5. A "Teachers' Training Class Daily Register" will be furnished for each class, and the daily attendance of each member, upon each recitation, recorded therein.

V. Course of Study

This course is designed as a minimum to meet the requirements of chapter 1031 of the laws of 1895.

The subjects designated therein shall be completed in not less than 450 hours.

The number of hours to be devoted to each subject shall be determined by the local superintendent of schools. The number of hours placed opposite the several subjects is to be regarded as suggestive only, and as indicative of their relative value.

Minimum Course of Study in Teachers' Training Schools or Classes in Cities

I

1.	Psychology and Principles of Education	90	hours.
2.	History of Education	30	"
3.	School Management	20	"
4.	Methods in Mathematics	40	
5.	" " Nature Study { Plants, Animals, Minerals } and Phyisology and Hygiene	40	
6.	" " Reading, Spelling and Phonics	30	
7.	" " Language, Composition and Grammar	40	
8.	" " Geography	30	
9.	" " Form Study and Drawing	40	
10.	History, Civics and School Law	30	
11.	Physical Culture, with Methods	40	
12.	Methods in Music	20	

II

At least fifty hours shall be spent by each member of the training class in practice teaching.

VI. Examinations

1. The Department of Public Instruction will, on application of the local superintendent of schools furnish special examinations in the several subjects prescribed in the "Course of Study," in order that the members of the Training School or Class may become eligible to appointment to schools in this state other than those of their own city.

2. These examinations shall begin on the third Thursday of January and on the second Wednesday of June.

3. It is required that the name of every member electing to take the examination shall appear in the report of the examination at the close of the term. The Department reserves the right of refusing payment for the instruction of members not reaching a fair standing in the subjects embraced in the course of study.

4. Members will be exempt from reëxamination in those subjects in which they attained a standing of at least seventy-five per cent. at the next preceding examination; but members shall not be admitted to the examination in any subject which they have not regularly pursued in class.

5. Inasmuch as the examination at the close of each term has been appointed with special reference to the convenience of these classes, it is required that the members shall enter no other uniform examination during the term of study.

VII. Certificates

1. Members of training schools or classes who attain a standing of seventy-five per cent. in the several subjects in which they are examined will receive a training-class certificate if the city superintendent of schools shall state that he deems them worthy to receive such certificates.

2. Training-class certificates are valid for three years, and, at the end of such time of successful teaching, are renewable the same as are first-grade certificates, under the state uniform examinations.

5. STATISTICAL TABLES

(A) *List of institutions that organized teachers' training classes for first and second terms,* 1896–1897, *with amount of money apportioned to each institution each term, showing total for each county*

County	NAME OF INSTITUTION	First term	Second term	Total	Total by counties
Albany	Albany Training School	....	$1,140	$1,140	$1,140
Allegany	Alfred University	$282	244	526	2,911
	Cuba High School	322	340	662	
	Friendship High School	196	247	443	
	Genesee Valley Seminary	178	245	423	
	Wellsville Union School	196	239	435	
	Wilson Academy	203	219	422	
Broome	Binghamton Training School	....	844	844	2,037
	Union Union School	198	244	442	
	Whitney's Point Union School	213	220	433	
	Windsor Union School	119	199	318	
Cattaraugus	Chamberlain Institute	144	193	337	723
	Delevan Union School	179	207	386	
Chautauqua	Forestville Free Academy	227	245	472	1,017
	Jamestown Training School	....	545	545	
Chemung	Elmira Training School	469	434	903	903
Chenango	Norwich High School	221	174	395	395
Delaware	Margaretville High School	268	317	585	1,005
	Walton Union School	221	199	420	
Dutchess	Poughkeepsie Training School	....	666	666	666
Erie	Buffalo Training School	....	1,610	1,610	1,610
Essex	Port Henry Union School	179	219	398	717
	Westport Union School	175	144	319	
Franklin	Franklin Academy	200	175	375	375
Greene	Catskill High School	144	128	272	272
Herkimer	Ilion Union School	169	206	375	375
Jefferson	Watertown Training School	....	377	377	377
Kings	Brooklyn Training School	3,437	3,918	7,355	7,355
Lewis	Copenhagen Union School	144	172	316	1,047
	Lowville Academy	162	322	484	
	Port Leyden Union School	135	112	247	
Madison	De Ruyter Union School	322	299	621	1,282
	Oneida High School	345	316	661	
Monroe	Fairport Classical Union School	168	177	345	1,233
	Rochester Training School	....	888	888	
Montgomery	Canajoharie Union School	108	260	368	818
	St. Johnsville Union School	278	172	450	
Niagara	Lockport Training School	303	274	577	941
	Middleport Union School	177	187	364	

Oneida	Utica Training School	157	454	454	454
Onondaga	Baldwinsville Free Academy	188	243	431	
	Fabius Union School	223	219	442	
	Fayetteville Union School	390	450	840	3,611
	Onondaga High School		1,066	1,066	
	Syracuse Training School	224	240	464	
	Tully Union School	124	224	348	
Ontario	Canandaigua Union School	256	248	504	853
	Geneva High School				
Orange	Port Jervis Union School	228	244	472	472
Orleans	Albion Union School	231	289	520	520
Oswego	Fulton High School	286	299	585	
	Mexico Union School	170	226	396	1,978
	Pulaski Academy and Union School	316	231	547	
	Sandy Creek High School	232	215	447	
Otsego	Cooperstown High School	239	272	511	
	Morris High School	216	228	444	1,697
	Richfield Springs High School	174	211	385	
	Unadilla Union School and Academy	160	167	327	
Rensselaer	Hoosick Falls High School	164	161	325	
	Lansingburg Academy	216	220	436	1,955
	Troy Training School		1,194	1,194	
St. Lawrence	[illegible] High School	263	252	515	933
	[illegible]burg Training School	156	232	418	
Saratoga	Corinth Union School	230	367	597	597
Schuyler	[illegible] Academy	190	198	388	388
Steuben	Canisteo Academy	279	323	602	1,028
	North Cocheton Union School	224	202	426	
Sullivan	Monticello Union School	185	221	406	406
Tioga	Owego Free Academy	225	198	423	796
	Waverly High School	184	189	373	
Tompkins	Trumansburg Union School	236	250	486	486
Ulster	Ellenville High School	267	234	501	890
	Kingston Training School	186	203	389	
Warren	Glens Falls Union Free School	264	245	509	509
Washington	Sandy Hill High School	373	367	740	740
Wayne	Clyde High School	177	200	377	799
	Palmyra Classical Union School	214	208	422	
Wyoming	Arcade Union School	226	316	542	964
	Warsaw Union School	136	286	422	
Yates	Dundee Union School	195	166	361	727
	Penn Yan Academy	180	186	366	
	Totals	$18,726	$29,372	$47,998	$47,998

STATISTICAL TABLES — (Continued)

(B) *Statistics showing condition of teachers' training classes for the first term of school year, 1896–97*

County	NAME OF INSTITUTION	Number of Students Reported: Men	Women	Total	Visits by school commissioners	Number who had already taught	Apportionment to each institution
Albany	Albany Training School	.....	37	37	....	.....	....
Allegany	Alfred University	3	13	16	......	13	$282 00
	Cuba High School	3	15	18	2	6	322 00
	Friendship High School	2	10	12	1	...	196 00
	Genesee Valley Seminary	3	7	10	......	1	178 00
	Wellsville Union School	2	10	12	......	3	196 00
	Wilson Academy	2	9	11	......	4	208 00
Broome	Binghamton Training School	.....	24	24	......	.....	....
	Union [illegible]	3	8	11	1	6	198 00
	Whitney's Point Union School	.....	12	12	1	7	213 00
	Windsor Union School	6	4	10	.....	2	119 00
Cattaraugus	Chamberlain Institute	4	6	10	3	6	144 00
	Delevan Union School	3	7	10	2	.....	179 00
Chautauqua	Forestville Free Academy	9	3	12	......	6	227 00
	[illegible] Training School	.....	15	15	......	.....	....
Chemung	Elmira [illegible] School	.....	24	24	......	6	469 00
Chenango	Norwich High School	3	10	13	.....	8	221 00
Delaware	Margaretville High School	2	14	16	1	9	268 00
	Walton Union School	....	12	12	......	2	221 00
Dutchess	[illegible] Training School	.....	22	22	......	....	....
Erie	[illegible] Training School	1	42	43	......	.....	....
Essex	Port Henry Union School	.....	12	12	1	.....	179 00
	Westport Union School	1	9	10	2	7	175 00
Franklin	Franklin Academy	1	10	11	1	2	200 00
Greene	Catskill High School	.....	8	8	2	1	144 00
Herkimer	Ilion Union School	1	10	11	......	......	169 00
Jefferson	Watertown Training School	.....	12	12	......	......	....
Kings	Brooklyn Training School	.....	201	201	......	......	3,437 00
Lewis	Copenhagen Union School	6	5	11	1	5	144 00
	Lowville Academy	.....	12	12	2	7	162 00
	Port Leyden Union School	1	10	11	5	9	135 00
Madison	De Ruyter Union School	6	12	18	......	10	332 00
	Oneida High School	2	13	20	......	2	345 00

Monroe	Fairport Classical Union School	......	11	10	4	......	168 00
	Rochester Training School	......	21	21	......	......	....
Montgomery	Canajoharie Union School	8	2	10	......	......	108 00
	St. Johnsville Union School	5	11	16	......	8	278 00
Niagara	Lockport Training School	......	16	16	......	1	303 00
	Middleport Union School	1	10	11	......	2	177 00
Oneida	Utica Training School	......	15	16	......	......	....
Onondaga	Baldwinsville Free Academy	......	12	11	3	......	157 00
	Fabius Union School	5	5	10	2	1	198 00
	Fayetteville Union School	......	12	12	1	1	228 00
	Onondaga High School	7	13	20	4	7	390 00
	Syracuse Training School	......	37	37	......	......	....
	Tully Union School	3	9	12	3	......	234 00
Ontario	Canandaigua Union School	1	9	10	1	2	124 00
	Geneva High School	......	13	13	1	7	256 00
Orange	Port Jervis Union School	......	13	13	......	......	228 00
Orleans	Albion Union School	2	11	13	1	......	231 00
Oswego	Fulton High School	4	11	15	1	......	284 00
	Mexico Union School	2	8	10	1	6	170 00
	Pulaski Academy and Union School	2	15	18	1	11	316 00
	Sandy Creek High School	2	11	13	......	......	232 00
Otsego	Cooperstown High School	1	14	15	1	8	269 00
	Morris High School	3	10	13	3	1	216 00
	Richfield Springs High School	4	10	14	......	......	174 00
	Unadilla Union School and Academy	6	4	10	1	......	160 00
Rensselaer	Hoosick Falls High School	1	9	10	1	1	164 00
	Lansingburg Academy	......	14	14	1	2	216 00
	Troy Training School	......	33	33	......	......	....
St. Lawrence	Gouverneur High School	1	13	14	3	5	263 00
	Ogdensburg Training School	1	10	11	......	3	186 00
Saratoga	Corinth Union School	5	12	17	5	4	230 00
Schuyler	Cook Academy	1	10	11	2	7	190 00
Steuben	Canisteo Academy	2	14	16	1	11	279 00
	North Cohocton Union School	4	8	12	1	5	224 00
Sullivan	Monticello Union School	5	6	11	1	5	185 00
Tioga	Owego Free Academy	1	12	13	1	......	225 00
	Waverly High School	3	10	13	1	2	184 00
Tompkins	Trumansburg Union School	3	11	14	2	......	236 00
Ulster	Ellenville High School	1	17	18	1	11	267 00
	Kingston Training School	......	19	10	1	......	186 00
Warren	Glens Falls Union Free School	......	15	15	......	......	264 00
Washington	Sandy Hill High School	3	18	21	2	8	373 00
Wayne	Clyde High School	1	10	11	......	2	177 00
	Palmyra Classical Union School	1	13	14	2	......	214 00
Wyoming	Arcade Union School	2	10	12	2	2	226 00
	Warsaw Union School	2	8	10	6	6	136 00
Yates	Dundee Union School	3	8	11	2	3	195 00
	Penn Yan Academy	1	10	11	2	3	180 00
Total		161	1,211	1,373	90	237	$18,726 00

STATISTICAL TABLES — (*Continued*)

(C) *Statistics showing the condition of teachers' training classes for the second term of school year*, 1896–97

County	Name of Institution	Number of Students Reported: Men	Number of Students Reported: Women	Number of Students Reported: Total	Visits by school commissioners	Number who had already taught	Apportionment to each institution
Albany	Albany [illegible] School	.....	32	32	.....	.....	$1,140
Allegany	Alfred University	3	14	17	1	10	244
	Cuba High School	3	16	19	2	2	340
	[illegible]p High School	3	10	13	2	.....	247
	[illegible]e Valley Seminary	3	10	13	1	4	245
	Wellsville [illegible] School	2	10	12	2	.....	239
	Wilson Academy	2	9	11	1	3	219
Broome	Binghamton Training School	.....	22	22	.....	.....	844
	Union Union School	4	9	13	3	6	244
	Whitney's Point Union School	.....	12	12	3	6	220
	Windsor Union School	5	6	11	1	.....	129
Cattaraugus	[illegible]in Institute	3	8	11	4	7	193
	Delevan Union School	2	9	11	2	2	207
Chautauqua	Forestville Free Academy	10	3	13	1	3	245
	Jamestown [illegible] School	.....	15	15	.....	.....	545
[illegible]ng	Elmira [illegible] School	.....	22	22	.....	3	434
Chenango	Norwich High [illegible]	3	7	10	2	6	174
Delaware	Margaretville High School	2	15	17	3	7	317
	Walton Union [illegible]	.....	12	12	1	3	199
[illegible]chess	Poughkeepsie Training School	.....	19	19	.....	.....	666
Erie	[illegible]lo Training School	2	46	48	.....	.....	1,610
Essex	Port Henry Union School	.....	11	11	5	.....	219
	Westport Union School	.....	8	8	6	6	144
Franklin	Franklin Academy	1	9	10	3	1	135
Greene	[illegible]kill [illegible] School	.....	7	7	6	1	129
Herkim r	Ilion Union School	1	11	12	1	.....	206
[illegible]	Watertown [illegible] School	.....	12	12	.....	.....	377
Kings	Brooklyn Training [illegible]	.....	203	203	.....	.....	3,918
[illegible]is	Copenhagen Union School	5	4	9	2	8	172
	Lowville Academy	2	14	16	.....	8	322
	Port Leyden Union School	1	10	11	4	5	112
Madison	De Ruyter Union School	7	10	17	3	9	299
	Oneida [illegible] School	1	17	18	1	.....	316
Monroe	Fairport [illegible] Union School	.....	10	10	4	.....	177
	Rochester Training School	.....	25	25	.....	.....	888

Montgomery	Canajoharie Union School	3	8	11	1		390
	St. Johnsville Union School	3	7	10		6	178
Niagara	Lockport Union School		15	15			274
	Middleport Union School	1	10	11	4		187
Oneida	Utica Training School		11	11			454
Onondaga	Baldwinsville Free Academy		12	12	3		331
	Fabius Union School	7	5	13	2	2	228
	Fayetteville Union School		12	13	2		219
	Onondaga High School	7	18	25	4	8	450
	Syracuse Training School		33	33			1,046
	Tully Union School	3	14	17	4		240
Ontario	Canandaigua Union School	1	10	11	1	1	224
	Geneva High School		11	14	3	7	248
Orange	Port Jervis Union School		15	15	1		244
Orleans	Albion Union School	6	11	17	4		299
Oswego	Fulton High School	4	11	15	2	2	299
	Mexico Union School	2	9	11	2	4	226
	Pulaski Academy and Union School	2	12	14	1	8	231
	Sandy Creek High School	3	9	12	1		215
Otsego	Cooperstown High School	3	13	16		9	272
	Morris High School	2	10	12	1	1	229
	Richfield Springs High School	4	8	12	1	1	211
	Unadilla Union School and Academy	6	4	10	1		167
Rensselaer	Hoosick Falls High School	1	9	10		2	161
	Lansingburg Academy		11	11	2	2	220
	Troy Training School		33	33			1,194
St. Lawrence	Gouverneur High School	1	13	14		6	252
	Ogdensburg Training School	1	10	11		8	232
Saratoga	Corinth Union School	4	13	17	5	4	367
Schuyler	Cook Academy	1	9	10	3	7	198
Steuben	Canisteo Academy	3	14	17	2	11	323
	North Cohocton Union School	2	9	11	4	4	202
Sullivan	Monticello Union School	6	8	14		4	221
Tioga	Owego Free Academy	2	9	11	3		193
	Waverly High School	1	9	10	2	2	189
Tompkins	Trumansburg Union School	3	11	14	2		250
Ulster	Ellenville High School	1	15	16	2	11	334
	Kingston Training School		12	12	1	1	203
Warren	Glens Falls Union Free School	1	13	14	2	4	245
Washington	Sandy Hill High School	2	17	19	4	8	367
Wayne	Clyde High School	1	10	11		2	200
	Palmyra Classical Union School	1	10	11	3		208
Wyoming	Arcade Union School	3	16	18		2	316
	Warsaw Union School	5	10	15	6	9	246
Yates	Dundee Union School	2	9	11	3	1	166
	Penn Yan Academy	1	9	10	1		186
	Totals	169	1,201	1,370	146	226	$29 372

(D) Statistics showing by classes the maximum number of students reported either term, the number of candidates for certificates, and the number of certificates granted

County	Name of institution	Maximum number of students reported either term: Men	Women	Total	Number of candidates for certificates	Number of certificates granted
Albany	Albany Training School	......	37	37	30	16
Allegany	Alfred University	3	14	17	15	14
	Cuba High School	3	16	19	17	8
	Friendship High School	3	10	13	12	8
	Genesee Valley Seminary	3	10	13	10	8
	Wellsville Union School	2	10	12	12	11
	Wilson [illegible]my	2	9	11	11	8
Broome	Binghamton Training School	......	24	24	22	21
	Union Union School	4	9	13	11	8
	Whitney's Point Union School	......	12	12	12	6
	[illegible]or Union School	5	6	11	8	5
Cattaraugus	Chamberlain Institute	3	8	11	8	6
	Delevan Union School	2	9	11	9	8
Chautauqua	Forestville Free Academy	10	3	13	12	9
	Jamestown Training School	......	15	15	11	10
Chemung	Elmira Training School	......	24	24	23	21
Chenango	Norwich High School	8	10	18	13	10
Delaware	Margaretville High School	2	15	17	16	10
	Walton Union School	......	12	12	11	5
Dutchess	[illegible] Training School	......	22	22	19	10
Erie	[illegible]lo Training School	2	46	48	41	26
Essex	Port [illegible]nry Union School	......	12	12	9	5
	Westport Union School	1	9	10	11	5
Franklin	Franklin [illegible]y	1	10	11	10	8
Greene	[illegible]ill High [illegible]ol	......	8	8	7	5
Herkimer	Ilion Union School	1	11	12	8	6
Jefferson	Watertown [illegible] School	......	12	12	10	6
Kings	Brooklyn Training School	......	203	203	8	3
Lewis	Copenhagen Union School	6	5	11	8	7
	Lowville Academy	2	14	16	10	5
	Port Leyden Union School	1	10	11	8	3
Madison	De [illegible]r Union School	6	12	18	18	14
	Oneida High School	2	18	20	18	17
Monroe	Fairport Classical Union School	......	10	10	11	11

	Rochester Training School	......	34	36	34	21
Montgomery	Canajoharie Union School	8	8	11	11	4
	St. Johnsville Union School	5	11	16	16	18
Niagara	Lockport Training School	......	16	16	15	11
	Middleport Union School	1	10	11	10	6
Oneida	Utica Training School	......	16	16	12	9
Onondaga	Baldwinsville Free Academy	......	12	12	12	3
	Fabius Union School	7	5	12	18	7
	Fayetteville Union School	......	12	13	12	11
	Onondaga High School	7	18	25	18	11
	Syracuse Training School	......	37	37	20	15
	Tully Union School	3	14	17	11	7
Ontario	Canandaigua Union School	1	10	11	9	6
	Geneva High School	......	14	14	12	11
Orange	Port Jervis Union School	......	15	15	12	8
Orleans	Albion Union School	6	11	17	12	7
Oswego	Fulton High School	4	11	15	13	10
	Mexico Union School	2	9	11	9	7
	Pulaski Academy and Union School	2	16	18	17	14
	Sandy Creek High School	2	11	13	13	9
Otsego	Cooperstown High School	3	13	18	14	10
	Morris High School	3	10	13	13	12
	Richfield Springs High School	4	10	14	12	9
	Unadilla Union School and Academy	6	4	10	9	6
Rensselaer	H[illegible]k Falls High School	1	9	10	10	7
	Lansingburg Academy	......	14	14	13	5
	Troy Training School	......	33	33	27	20
St. Lawrence	Gouverneur [illegible] School	1	13	14	14	13
	Ogdensburg Training School	1	10	11	9	7
Saratoga	Corinth Union School	4	13	17	17	9
Schuyler	[illegible] Academy	1	10	11	11	11
Steuben	[illegible] Academy	8	14	17	17	12
	North Cohocton Union School	4	8	12	12	7
Sullivan	Monticello Union School	6	8	14	13	8
Tioga	Owego Free Academy	1	12	13	13	11
	Waverly High School	3	10	13	11	9
Tompkins	Trumansburg Union School	3	11	14	14	13
Ulster	Ellenville High School	1	17	18	18	16
	Kingston Training School	......	12	12	9	5
Warren	Glens Falls Union Free School	......	15	15	15	12
W[illegible]	Sandy Hill High School	3	18	21	20	15
Wayne	Clyde High School	1	10	11	11	10
	Palmyra [illegible] Union School	1	13	14	13	10
Wyoming	Arcade Union School	3	15	18	12	11
	Warsaw Union School	5	10	15	10	5
Yates	[illegible] Union School	2	9	11	9	3
	Penn Yan [illegible]	1	10	11	10	9
Totals		176	1,261	1,438	1,080	766

* Candidates for a certificate must have been in attendance upon a training class for at least one year

STATISTICAL TABLES — (*Continued*)

(E) *Teachers' training classes — General summary from* 1889 *to* 1897

TERM	Number of classes organized	Number of Pupils Registered: Men	Number of Pupils Registered: Women	Number of Pupils Registered: Total	Number of visits by school commissioner	Number who had already taught	Number of scholars allowed	Amount paid
1889-1890, First term	49	162	596	758	34	256	680	$7,932 00
1889-1890, Second term	59	225	814	1,069	36	327	928	10,863 00
1890-1891, First term	61	221	758	979	39	304	873	14,75[illegible] 00
1890-1891, Second term	56	236	726	962	26	291	808	13,087 00
1891-1892, First term	82	262	1,012	1,274	52	464	1,053	17,612 00
1891-1892, Second term	77	292	964	1,256	54	390	1,070	16,774 00
1892-1893, First term	95	304	1,120	1,424	78	456	1,153	19,580 00
1892-1893, Second term	100	339	1,179	1,518	81	516	1,370	21,740 00
1893-1894, First term	109	396	1,276	1,672	80	558	1,317	21,998 00
1893-1894, Second term	118	469	1,511	1,980	80	702	1,709	26,627 00
1894-1895, First term	127	531	1,621	2,152	189	681	1,655	27,189 00
1894-1895, Second term	140	642	1,840	2,482	283	799	2,212	36,063 00
1895-1896, First term	74	190	875	1,065	156	212	881	15,846 00
1895-1896, Second term	72	203	886	1,089	156	287	1,050	19,728 00
1896-1897, First term	88	161	1,211	1,372	90	257	1,242	18,726 00
1896-1897, Second term	88	169	1,201	1,370	146	216	1,268	29,372 00

EXHIBIT No. 17

CHILD STUDY

1. Report of Anna K. Eggleston
2. Account of formation of the New York Society for Child Study
3. Constitution of the New York Society for Child Study
4. List of officers
5. Proceedings of the First Winter Meeting held at Syracuse

CHILD STUDY

1. REPORT BY ANNA K. EGGLESTON

It has not seemed wise to issue during the past year a leaflet giving work along new lines for teachers already interested in studying children's hopes. Those teachers who were reading studiously the papers which their pupils wrote were getting in the best way suggestions for original investigation, and in many instances teachers were forming questions that were far better for their classes and more helpful to themselves than could have been formed by any one not possessing a definite knowledge of the children and their surroundings. In many localities of the state the plan for studying children's hopes had not until this year been presented, but in all cases, as in the preceding year, it was received with much interest by the teachers. As a result of their co-operation in the movement about 2,000 papers written by children have been received by this department.

The formation of desires and aspirations of childhood can be learned only from the children themselves. One who did not know something of that ability which children possess to touch with fancy the hardships of life, would marvel at reading the desire expressed by many to become farmers, for instance, when all their experiences have been gained on farms where the severest toil yields only a slight return. Accompanying a series of papers in which the children have expressed a hope of becoming farmers and farmers' wives is a letter from the teacher, saying the parents are all poor farmers and the land exceedingly rough and unproductive. In this connection it is interesting to note that the occupation of farming is an attractive one for children. It is impossible to read their thoughts upon country scenes and events without strengthening the conviction that it is rare good fortune to spend the first ten or twelve years of life where the planting and growing of agricultural products may be seen and a knowledge gained of this great industry.

The power which stories have to create ideals in young minds is illustrated in but few papers. One boy hopes to be a lumberman, because his father has told him stories of his own life as a lumberman. He wishes to begin work in the same place where his father did, so that he may have the same experiences that have fascinated him through the story that doubtless began, "When I was a boy." A boy wishes to be captain of a war-ship, the Texas, and describes her guns. Another longs to be a poet like Shakespeare, and there are many who wish to be hunters and travelers. A girl writes: "I want to be rich and travel all over the world and see many curious things. I can see all the different kinds of animals and I could see the tombstone of a man, it was 80 feet high, he had to pay $5,000 for it."

Frequently travels are described quite fully, as for instance, in the following: "I would like to be a sailor on a United States man-of-war, take a cruise around the globe and see the strange people of two hemispheres, visit many old sea-ports through Asia and Africa such as Tripoli and all through the Barbary States. Leave the ship at Hong Kong, travel through the Chinese Empire, see how the Mongolian race lives, go hunting lions in the jungles of India, also hunt the tiger. Go through Turkey, visit Armenia, but look out for the ferocious Turk, then come to Christian Europe visit all places of interest in Germany, France, Spain. Then go to the British Isles, visit London. Then go into the highlands of Scotland, view the 'bonny crags.' Then go across to Ireland, the Emerald Isle, inspect the land of the Irishman. Then go back to Liverpool, take a steamer for America. See all of interest in my own land."

Girls must have read or heard stories of queens, which called forth this desire: "I would like to be a queen, because they have everything and all the money they want, and have everyone come to see them and wear diamonds and pearls and all kinds of valuable stones." Another from the same class writes: "I would like to be a queen, because then I could have a great many nice things to wear, and I could have nice things to eat."

Those who know from experience in telling stories to children how in their imagination they often picture themselves as doing things heroes have done, will wonder why there is found in these papers so little evidence of this influence upon children's hopes for their own future greatness. Ought one to infer, therefore, that pupils in our common schools are not getting the best stories from literature?

Many papers lead to the belief that some children have been taught to express only school thoughts in school rooms. These papers are artificial and indicate a serious error in teaching. Others, however, show that the children are perfectly natural. In these instances frequent and enthusiastic references are made to sports and games. Pupils seem not to have lost sight of everything in life which does not pertain directly to the school room. It is the question, "What I want to do next year" that causes children to tell of their favorite games, and those who seem to have much love for sports write with great spirit of what they hope to be and do when they are men and women. There are suggestions that come from this seeming influence of games and sports which teachers would do well to consider. The energy, enthusiasm and desire to succeed, which are exhibited in play, are forces that are needed in school work, and a teacher's study of the games and sports of her pupils and the spirit in which they enter into them may be a means of bringing these forces to her aid.

Those who have expected some fundamental truths unknown to educators would be established from this study of children's hopes will be disappointed. If papers on any one theme are classified and examined, it is found that children have as varied opinions as have their elders, and the conclusions one might reach in examining the first 500 papers are often entirely overthrown by reading the next 50. Although no positive deductions have been made, the time and effort spent in studying children's hopes have not been fruitless. Through working out the plan submitted a year ago, some teachers have been stimulated to investigate along original lines this year. It is impossible in this report to record all that has been done, but a few illustrations are here given.

One teacher asked children who were doing the fifth and sixth year's work what they would do with $100 and, in her letter accompanying the pupils' papers, she says: "Knowing many things about each child's environment and training, I detect very few signs of affectation in this work."

Boy, aged 8 years

"If I had a hundred dollars I would have a very nice house, lots of horses and carriages, a coachman and a footman, a gold ring set with rubies and waiters and a lot of other attendants."

Boy, aged 11 years

"If I had a hundred dollars I would have a good time if I could do just as I wanted to with it. First I would put it into the savings bank and earn all the money I could. Then I would take my hundred dollars out of the bank and put what I had earned with it and start for New York city to see what there was there to see and then go to work again and earn enough money to build a cottage and rent it to city people in the summer."

Girl, aged 9 years

"If I had one hundred dollars I would get a silk dress and a gold watch and go to New York city and all around the world.

I would go to all the shows and have a flower garden with the dearest flowers in it. I would live in a brick house painted pink and tinged with light blue and go riding every day with a span of bay horses. I would spend the rest of my money on things I used on my table and get clothes for the folks."

Girl, aged 10 years

"I would have a lazy horse, one that wouldn't run away, and a nice carriage to ride in. I would live in a big house and keep boarders and lots of hired girls and have a negro cook and lots of cats and kittens. I would have a nice looking driver and be a school teacher and have him take me to school in the morning and come after me every night. I would make the scholars mind well. I would have a little boy to lead around and go riding with me and a dove and a rabbit. I don't dare to do anything more because I think my money is nearly gone. I want a bicycle though."

Boy, aged 11 years

"I would go somewhere and get some clothes for the winter and a gold watch and give the rest to my mother. Then she could do just what she pleased with it. I hope that she would help my two little brothers and little sister. Then we would enjoy my hundred dollars."

Girl, aged 11 years

"I would buy a fifty dollar organ and a dress that cost about five dollars and take about forty dollars for a bicycle and keep five dollars to spend for other things. I would get a dress for everyday and some aprons, I would have about two dollars left to go to S———— Lake with."

Boy, aged 11 years

"I think I would send it to the bank and when I was a man I would take it out and spend it on a house."

Girl, aged 11 years

"I would pay some of the store debt and make a payment on the place."

Girl, aged 12 years

"I would give mamma and papa some money and get me a bicycle. I would send some money away to the heathen and go away to school. When I came back I would teach school if I had enough education. A hundred dollars would not last long."

Boy, aged 13 years

"If I had $100 I would put it in the bank so that I could get interest and increase my money. In eight or ten years I would have quite a little money."

In one of the public kindergartens of the state the teacher recorded in an elaborate and interesting manner the answers which the children gave her to the following questions:

What I want to do next year and why.

What I want to do when I am grown up.

For what I am most thankful to God.

Which part of kindergarten work I like best.

The teacher writes: "As my children are too young to write anything in regard to their aspirations, I have tabulated the desired information as best I could. We have been studying for the past two or three weeks on the Thanksgiving theme, thankfulness to God for food, clothing, home, friends, help, etc., dwelling at length on the harvest time and learning of the development from seed to ripened fruit, grain and vegetables, consequently my children seem greatly in favor of farm life. It has been of help to me to know this, in that it proves that kindergarten training does influence the children."

Some of the things mentioned for which the children are most thankful to God are sweet potatoes, cabbage, Aunt Annie and potatoes, soup, meat, McKinley, Miss C——, papa and mamma.

One teacher sent the answers which her pupils, ranging from 11 to 14 years of age, wrote to the following questions:

What sound do you like best?

What book do you like best? Why?

If you could not be yourself, who would you rather be?

Who is your hero?

Name the five you love best.

Several teachers have written of their own childhood experiences, telling of hopes and aspirations they never dared to tell to anyone when children, as, one writes, "I am very sure that my childhood did not differ from that of other children, in that there was a great deal in my nature, disposition, hopes, fears, and aspirations that no one suspected." There surely must come a more intelligent sympathy with real child life to those who have looked deeply into their own experiences, thereby gaining a faith that children often have better things hidden in the depths of their nature than are brought to the surface.

In one district, where a great deal of interest in child study has been manifested for the past two or three years, a large number of teachers made a careful study of the children who are most troublesome. The evidences of stubbornness were set forth and some teachers made a very thorough analysis of cases. A few extracts from these papers follow.

(1.) "I have in my room several stubborn pupils, they are boys between 11 and 13 years of age. I am impressed that their troublesomeness is due in a measure to home surroundings and influences; also to the thought that the majority of the class is in advance and the 'don't care' spirit has got the better of them. In urging a boy, whom I will call A, to prepare his lessons more carefully, he remarked that, no matter how hard he studied, B always had the better lesson. I find that a few words of encouragement and leaving the impression that I expect a certain amount of work is the best way of obtaining results."

(2.) "My impression is that self-willed children are those whose motives are not understood, and who have been dealt with in such a way as to cause a feeling of rebellion. Most children will yield readily, I find, to reasonable requests, if treated justly and politely. One boy, coming into my school from a home where he had been roughly treated, was asked to comply with a simple request and refused, for no possible reason only a stubborn inclination to do as he pleased. When asked politely again to comply, because he would greatly oblige me, did it at once and never again refused to do whatever was required of him. This is but one of many instances."

(3.) "In my class-room I register 73 pupils and have a daily average of 63, some days more and some days less. * * * I haven't one stubborn child, but a little boy, J——, is very self-willed, mischievous, noisy, doing something naughty about all the time and it puzzles my brain to know how to punish him."

Parents' Meetings

There is a strong desire on the part of teachers to know more of children as they are when under the home influence. Parents have shown, in most instances, not only a willingness to give the desired information, but to co-operate in plans which teachers have presented. Parents' meetings, mothers' meetings and child study clubs have been organized and teachers and parents are working together in the interest of home and school training. The tact teachers have often displayed in getting parents into the schools show how earnestly and intelligently they are studying the interests of the children. In a district school the pupils filled a Christmas tree with gifts for their parents, who were invited to come to listen to Christmas exercises, the tree being kept as a surprise. The teacher knew how to use this happy event to further a plan for mothers' meetings. One district school has a class in United States history, because the teacher knew how to say the right thing to get mothers to buy the necessary books. It is not difficult to understand how that special class in history, for which mothers had worked, would lead them to an interest in other subjects taught in the school. Reports have been received from a few union schools where plans were formed to hold a meeting of teachers and parents once a month. In other schools it was arranged to have mothers' meetings in connection with first, second and third years of school work. In some districts the connection between home and school has been established through patrons' day.

In response to many inquiries received from parents and teachers, the following scheme for the organization of parents' meetings was prepared.

Organization of meetings for parents and teachers

1. Number of meetings

It is better to plan for one meeting each month as more frequent meetings may result in weak programs, and less frequent ones will scarcely sustain the interest.

2. Place of meeting

Hold the meetings in the school building and have the rooms and the decorations as attractive as possible. This is a means of cultivating a pride in the school and its furnishings.

3. First meeting

Teachers may issue to parents or mothers whatever form of invitation they wish. No children should be present at the meeting. Some general school topic may be selected, upon which one or two teachers may give a 15-minute talk. Some one outside of the school who would give an interesting address might be asked to do so. Prominent women may be asked to discuss some subject. If the meeting is for mothers, the afternoon, just at the close of school, is possibly the best time for holding it. If it is desired to hold the first meeting in the evening, interest some prominent gentlemen who are willing to talk. The mothers' Congress, which was held in Washington in February, 1897, is an excellent theme for the first meeting. An account of this Congress is to be found in the February and March numbers (1897) of the Kindergarten Magazine, published in Chicago. The work of mothers' clubs in connection with the kindergarten may be discussed with profit, and the fact brought out that teachers of all grades need the help which mothers can give. An effort should be made to make mothers feel that they can help teachers to understand children better, etc. Mothers should be encouraged to help in planning future meetings and to propose topics they wish discussed. At the close of the general meetings give an opportunity for private conference between teachers and mothers for the discussion of special cases. If some parent denounces any of the school work, teachers will gain much by quietly attending to all that is said and waiting before replying until the faultfinder has become more familiar with the workings of the school.

The following topics are merely suggestive. Those who have intimate knowledge of the towns, families, and schools for which the plans are being formed will know of other topics of especial local interest.

Topics for teachers and parents to discuss

I. The formation of habits of order

1. Children's care of their own property.
2. Their regard for the property of those they love, as mother's, father's, or a favorite brother's or sister's.
3. Do they deface the common home property, as chairs, tables, walls, etc.?
4. Their care of their own rooms at home.
5. Their care of their own desks at school.
6. Their regard for the property of school-mates.
7. Their care of common school property, as doors, windows, reference books, etc.
8. The ways in which teachers and parents may co-operate in training children to be orderly.

It is one of the great purposes of education to make an orderly individual. The training which homes and schools give along this line makes people careful or careless in both private and public affairs. The right training gives the ability to care for personal, town, county, or state property. One rightly trained serves state and country as faithfully as he serves the individual.

II. Promptness

1. Punctuality as shown in life at home. Punctuality as shown in school life.
2. Obedience to commands; trustworthy; conscientious; quick to hear a request; quick to respond.
3. Effects of tardiness on the character of pupils.
4. Ways in which teachers and parents may unite in training children to be punctual and obedient.

III. Children's activity in manual work, study, and play

1. Industry; regulated work at home. Are children required to do any work systematically and regularly at home? Parents' responsibility in providing manual labor for children. Teachers may give a talk on the importance of manual training and tell how it has grown to be a factor in education. Cooking, sewing, and all kinds of housework for girls. Sewing seeds, gardening, shoveling, using hammer, etc., for boys.
2. Study; hours spent in study at school and at home. Importance of having a special time devoted to study at home.
3. Play; sports. Hours devoted to play out of school and in school. Kinds of sports and their influence upon children.
4. A comparison of pupils' work, study, and play at school with their work, study, and play at home.

IV. Influence which makes children kind and loving

1. Influence of home, school, and town.
2. Study of children's toys, pets, etc.

V. Ways in which parents may co-operate with teachers in training the intellects of children

1. Reading with children along the lines of school work. Learning from the teacher what special books she wishes children to read
2. Conversation with children regarding their interests in school. Learn from the children as far as possible the effect upon them of various conditions of school life. As soon as parents think they have discovered an error in school management they should tell the teacher kindly, but frankly. The teacher whose only purpose is to do right, will always welcome council and enlightenment. Parents in turn should listen attentively to suggestions which teachers make regarding certain influences that are working against the children's interests.

The flood of enthusiasm for Child Study is at last finding its way into natural and proper channels. It seemed at one time as though the true relation of things might be lost sight of by a majority of the teaching force. Child Study seemed simple and interesting to many who could not master the subjects of the higher education, and they, too, often drew conclusions that had no foundation in fact. The philosopher and scholar looked on and laughed. If he would be an intelligent student of children, the teacher must first be a scholar, with a judgment that has been trained through the study of mathematics, history, literature and all that can give clear thinking, and then there must be a study of methods of teaching, based upon a knowledge of psychology and the principles of education. The short and very general study of psychology, which most teachers pursue before beginning the work of teaching, is not sufficient. It has simply furnished the groundwork for the definite study that ought to be carried on with the teaching. When investigating children's hopes for the future, their love for toys, their favorite games, etc., the best authorities on psychology should be consulted. There must be an intelligent insight, not only into the characteristics of children, but also into the laws which govern the growth of mental and moral qualities.

Every teacher who has a class of beginners in reading has an opportunity to study pupils as they learn the forms of words. Children are getting new sensations when they learn to think through word forms, and there is no place in the school life where teachers may observe the workings of children's minds in acquiring knowledge with better results than in connection with the reading lessons. Serious mistakes in teaching will be made until there is a clear understanding not only of the nature but of the cause of failures. To know that a child cannot remember the words which he sees, or is dull in numbers, is not sufficient. If he is to be rightly taught, his teacher must know whether he does not learn because of his unwillingness to apply himself, or whether his mind has not yet reached the stage of development when it is possible for him to learn what is being forced upon him. The needs of the individual must be considered, as well as those of the class.

It has been impossible for one person to care in a satisfactory manner for the correspondence that has come to the Department of Child Study, and the work of the institutes has made the examination of such large numbers of papers very difficult. It is a pleasure to announce to those who wish help or desire to unite with others .who are working along lines of common interest, that the New York State Society for Child Study has been organized for this purpose.

2. NEW YORK SOCIETY FOR CHILD STUDY

Account of Formation

At the meeting of the Council of School Superintendents, held in Utica, October 14-16, 1896, the following resolutions were adopted:

Resolved, That in the opinion of this council the time has come for the organization, upon a broad and reliable basis of a society or center for Child Study in New York.

Resolved, That the State Superintendent of Public Instruction be requested to appoint a committee representing such educational bodies of the state as, in his judgment, should be represented to proceed with the organization of a New York Society for Child Study.

In accordance with this resolution, Superintendent Skinner appointed, March 11, 1897, the following committee:

George Griffith, Utica, for the superintendents.
Miss Anna K. Eggleston, Buffalo, for the Department.
Prof. M. V. O'Shea, Buffalo, for private schools.
Miss Jenny B. Merrill, New York city, for kindergartens.
Principal W. H. Benedict, Elmira, for grammar schools.
Mrs. John G. Allen, Rochester, for women's clubs.
Prof. W. H. Squires, Hamilton College, for colleges.
Miss Mary E. Laing, Oswego, for state normal schools.
Dr. Albert Leonard, Binghamton, for high schools.

This committee met in Utica May 22, and decided to proceed with the organization of a New York Society for Child Study. Officers were selected to serve until July 1st, a sub-committee was appointed to draft a constitution, to be submitted July 1st, and it was decided to hold the first meeting in connection with the July meeting of the State Teachers' Association at New York city. Such a meeting was held as a section of the New York State Teachers' Association.

(The proceedings of this meeting will be found in the proceedings of the State Teachers' Association, elsewhere in this report.)

At this meeting a permanent organization was effected, a constitution adopted and officers elected for the ensuing year.

The constitution is as follows:

3. CONSTITUTION OF THE NEW YORK SOCIETY FOR CHILD STUDY

Adopted at New York, July 1, 1897

ARTICLE 1. NAME

The name of this society shall be The New York Society for Child Study.

ARTICLE 2. PURPOSE

It shall be the purpose of the New York Society for Child Study to promote in every way possible the rational training of children in home, church, school and college, and in the community life of town and city. To this end it shall aim to unite scientific studies in psychology, anthropology and other sciences with their practical application in the treatment of children of all ages. In particular it shall be the purpose:

1. To hold two general meetings a year, where all educational interests shall be represented upon the programs.

2. To establish and direct local Child-Study centers of parents and teachers.

3. To prepare outlines and other material for the instruction and guidance of parents and teachers.

4. To act as a bureau of distribution for the literature of Child Study.

5. To encourage and direct scientific studies relating to the rational treatment of childhood from birth to maturity.

ARTICLE 3. OFFICERS

The officers of this society shall be a president, a vice-president, a secretary-treasurer, and executive committee of not more than nine, in addition to the president and secretary-treasurer, who shall be members *ex officio*, and an advisory board.

ARTICLE 4. TERM OF OFFICE

The officers of this society shall be elected annually at the regular summer meeting of the society, except as hereinafter provided for.

ARTICLE 5. DUTIES OF OFFICERS

The duties of the president and vice-president shall be such as usually devolve upon these officers in similar societies.

§ 2. It shall be the duty of the secretary-treasurer to collect all moneys due the society and to pay out the same upon order of the president. He shall attend to the printing, publication and distribution of all matter recommended by the executive committee. He shall undertake all correspondence of the society, and, in general, shall have charge of all clerical work necessary in order to fulfill the purposes of the society. In order to discharge these duties he shall be supplied with such clerical aid as he may deem it necessary, and as shall be voted by the executive committee.

§ 3. The executive committee shall be composed of representatives of the various educational interests of the state in home, church, school and college. The executive committee shall include the president and secretary-treasurer of the society. It shall have charge of the general work of the society, and shall recommend to the secretary-treasurer plans for carrying on the work of the society. It shall further prepare the programs for the public meetings of the society, and shall endeavor to have Child Study given a place on the programs of the various educational meetings of the state. The executive committee shall appoint an advisory board at the time of the annual meeting of the society.

§ 4. The advisory board shall consist of distinguished representatives of the various educational interests and institutions for the dependent and defective of the state. It shall be the duties of the members of this board to aid the executive committee in planning and directing the work of the society. The executive committee shall, from time to time, submit plans to them as a body, or as individuals specially concerned, for their criticism and counsel. The individual members of the advisory board shall safeguard the society against confining its work to a too limited field, against undertaking responsibilities which it cannot wisely assume, and against promulgating doctrines as scientific which are as yet only speculative or uncertain. The advisory board, being composed in some measure of specialists in different phases of Child Development, shall be called upon from time to time, to advise the executive committee with regard to the preparations of plans and discussions relating to the treatment of children along their special lines.

ARTICLE 6. MEMBERSHIP

Any person interested in Child Study, whether in New York state or elsewhere, may become a member of this society by paying fifty cents into its general treasury. This fee shall entitle a member to all the publications and other benefits of the society during the year in which the fee is paid

ARTICLE 7. ROUND-TABLES

It shall be the purpose of this society to encourage the formation of local round-tables wherever there are at least five persons who wish to unite in the study of children. Such round-tables may receive direction in their work by the payment of seventy-five cents into the general treasury of the society. This fee shall entitle the round-table to receive plans for the prosecution of its work, and each member shall receive all the publications of the society during the year in which the fee is paid. It shall be the duty of such round-table to elect a secretary, who shall keep the secretary of the parent society informed respecting the work of the round-table, the number of members, and shall furnish such other information as the secretary may desire for the purposes of publication or for permanent record.

ARTICLE 8. MEETINGS

This society shall hold two public meetings a year, one in winter and one during the summer vacation, the place and the exact time to be decided by the executive committee. The latter meeting shall be regarded as the annual meeting of the society.

ARTICLE 9. AMENDMENTS

Amendments may be made to the constitution of this society in the same manner that is prescribed by the constitution of the New York State Teachers' Association.

4. LIST OF OFFICERS

President, Superintendent George Griffith, Utica.

Vice-President, Superintendent Edgar Dubs Shimer, New York city.

Secretary-Treasurer, Dr. Edward F. Buchner, New York University, Washington square, New York city.

Executive committee.—President and Secretary-Treasurer, *ex officio*, Miss Anna K. Eggleston, Buffalo; Dr. Jenny B. Merrill, New York city; Principal W. H. Benedict, Elmira; Mrs. John G. Allen, Rochester; Prof. W. H. Squires, Clinton; Miss Mary E. Laing, Oswego; Dr. Albert Leonard, Syracuse.

Advisory board.—Dr. Felix Adler, New York city; Prof. J. McKeen Cattell, New York city; Mrs. Lillian W. Betts, New York city; Superintendent A. B. Blodgett, Syracuse; Dr. Nicholas Murray Butler, New York city; Principal Gardner Fuller, Batavia; Mrs. John A. Goodale, Utica; Dr. A. W. Hurd, Buffalo; Dr. Walter L. Hervey, New York city; Ossian H. Lang, New York city; Superintendent W. H. Maxwell, Brooklyn; Prof. J. F. Reigart, New York city; Principal M. T. Scudder, New Haven Conn.; Prof. M. V. O'Shea, Madison, Wis.; Dr. E. R. Shaw, New York city; Dr. E. B. Titchener, Ithaca; Dr. C. G. Wagner, Binghamton; Dr. Z. V. Westervelt, Rochester; A. M. Wright, Albany.

NEW YORK SOCIETY FOR CHILD-STUDY

Proceedings of the first winter meeting held at Syracuse, N. Y., Thursday, December 30, 1897.

PROGRAM

FORENOON

Joint Session with Grammar School Principals' Conference.

9 o'clock.—"The Relation of the Home and School in Child-Study."

(a) From the point of view of the Home, Mrs. Harriet W. H. Green, Utica.

(b) From the point of view of the School, Mrs. M. H. MacElroy, State Normal School, Oswego.

Discussion: Superintendent R. H. Halsey, Binghamton.

11 o'clock.—"Child-Study for the Practical Teacher," Prof. L. H. Galbreath, Teachers' College, University of Buffalo.

Discussion.

AFTERNOON SESSION

2.30 o'clock.—"Child-Study in the High School," Principal John G. Allen, Rochester.

BUSINESS SESSION

Discussion: Superintendent Fox Holden, Olean.

3.30 o'clock.—"The Dullard." Dr. James P. Haney, New York city.

Discussion: Miss Annie K. Eggleston, Instructor in Primary Work, Teachers' Institute, Buffalo.

EVENING SESSION

8 o'clock.—"Child-Study by a Woman's Club," Mrs. Ella Hastings, New York city.

9 o'clock.—"Scientific Child-Study," Professor Edward Franklin Buchner, School of Pedagogy, New York University.

Discussion: Rev. J. H. Caughn, Geneva.

Adjournment.

The full minutes of this session are not available since the society was without a secretary, owing to the resignation of Mr. Myron T. Scudder, who removed from the state in September and a secretary *pro tem.* was not appointed. A report of the discussions during the forenoon session may be found in the proceedings of the New York State Council of Grammar School Principals for 1897. The following proceedings consist of abstracts of the several papers read before the society as indicated by the program. At the business session in the afternoon, the society elected Professor Edward Franklin Buchner, of the School of Pedagogy, New York University, to fill the vacancy in the office of secretary-treasurer.

EDWARD FRANKLIN BUCHNER,
Secretary-Treasurer.

THE RELATION OF THE HOME AND THE SCHOOL IN CHILD STUDY — FROM THE POINT OF VIEW OF THE SCHOOL

BY MRS. MARY HOLBROOK MACELROY, STATE NORMAL SCHOOL, OSWEGO.

From the teacher's standpoint which is the standpoint of the school, of what practical value has been the new science of Child Study? This question is beginning to be asked and must be answered, not by the theorists of the universities and normal schools, but by the teachers, actually and every day in contact with the children. Masses of observations have been gathered and stored as at Worcester; comparison and generalization have been attempted with more or less success at Leland Stanford and Clark Universities; and the same processes of study are being recommended and adopted in our own state. Principals and grade teachers are going to take up the work with energy and enthusiasm if it can be shown that it really adds strength and intelligence to class-room work, interest and sympathy to the wearing contact with immature yet ever growing minds. If it cannot be shown to have so much value then the most of us will lay it away on a shelf of useless experiments, forced upon us by amiable but unpractical people, of whose ambitious attempts to fit German theories to American school children this is likely to be the most unpleasant.

We must admit that all the sweeping reform in primary education in the last quarter of a century is due to the difference in comprehension of child nature by Pestalozzi and Froebel and the educators who preceded them. We may argue, too, that modern Child Study is a return to the methods by which those masters wrought their great effects, a swinging away from the narrow and unfruitful round of machine-made methods which grew out of ignoring the corner stone of their philosophy—child knowledge. Here indeed, is that which has been already gained in modern child study. Children are no longer to be dealt with altogether in classes and grades; fitted with this method in geography, that in arithmetic and the other in drawing, and so turned out by the score and hundred, patterned and moulded and managed alike, according to our grown-up notion of what children should be. An honest and intelligent Child Study will change all that; instead of studying the mould into which all child nature is to be run we have to look at the individual nature which will make or break the mould in the long run. Method is not discredited by the new science but is made yielding, adaptable, secondary in value.

What has been accomplished in the study of the physique of children is one of the most beneficent results of this individual study and if there were no other, this would be a sufficient reason for child study. In our own school a child was a long way up in the grades before it was discovered that her peculiar looking eyes did not indicate a sly and underhanded habit with which she had been carelessly credited, but a serious nerve weakness for which special care and treatment were needed; and a boy who seemed hopelessly dull under our methods of oral work, advanced with great ease when it was discovered that a slight deafness which he himself hardly realized had interfered to prevent his comprehension of the most important work.

Child Study, then, has proven its value at least in these two ways: It has drawn us from the making of method to the fitting of them through a study of the nature of the individual, and it has helped us to remedy some of the physical defects which impede intellectual progress. In this last effort the teacher may perhaps be altogether successful without help from the home; in the first, the character estimate on which instruction is to be based, the school is helpless without the home. Here indeed is the great danger of the new cult, and a danger against which the home has every right to protest. It is almost better to have no thought of child character at all than to have a narrow and prejudiced notion of it. What else can the teacher's idea be if uncorrected and unenlightened by the knowledge of the home? In the first place, the atmosphere of most school-rooms is unfavorable to any expression of the real nature of the child except in a very limited way. Very little opportunity is afforded for studying the children in their relations to each other for instance; and the relation between teacher and pupil is necessarily much less free and unforced than between children and the members of their home circle. If child study is to be genuine and thorough-going, certain changes must be made by which teachers will have opportunities of seeing children in other attitudes than those of study and recitation. Already this is understood in some schools and the recess time or the gathering time is the most interesting period of the day to the teacher who sees the significance of actions and expressions which are quite unguarded and natural, who is able to catch and interpret the school room chat and gossip, to watch the formation and decay of school room friendship, the subtle and wonderful influences which characters have on each other. In some schools, too, the social spirit is designedly cultivated; and the lessons are not less well done because an occasional picnic or class party or school reception come in to break and vary the routine. On all such occasions the interested teacher will get new lights and needed ones on her character study.

Even with these aids, however, the teacher will come continually upon puzzles which only the mother can help to solve. Here is a big, growing boy. He cannot or he will not attend to his class work, and his misdirected activity is the torment and despair of the teacher. Apparently every effort has been made to interest and profit the boy, but in spite of all he is developing such waywardness that one trembles for his future. The mother happens to be a clear-headed woman, one whose brain is of use to her as well as her heart. When you appeal to her, and she feels that you are studying the boy's best interests she tells you an odd thing. "The boy is like his grandfather," she says, "and he would never stay in school at all. He learned his lessons of thrift and energy and courage somehow though, and made an excellent business man and good citizen. I believe I can make him see that it is worth his while to learn." She did too, for the incident is a real one. I think one way she took for appealing to the practical and commercial side which she knew was in his nature, was to pay him so much for every excellent mark he gained. The teacher would perhaps have felt that this motive was a low one to strengthen—the mother knew differently and acted on her knowledge with great aid and comfort to the teacher. The mother knew that in the boy's heredity which the teacher could not possibly. I suppose all faithful and interested teachers have similar stories told them. Those do well who heed and use them in estimating the children in their care.

Environment as well as heredity must be taken into account also. Last winter in cold, bleak weather one of our teachers came to me with tears in her eyes. "I have been so wicked," she said, "I scolded and scolded little Dan in the primary because he did not attend to his work. I even threatened to punish him if he did not do better. And just now a neighboring woman came in and told me how his father came home late last night, dragged his mother out of bed and beat her half senseless, and for days the child hadn't had enough to eat." What can excuse a teacher who misjudges a child like that, except ignorance. And what business have we to be ignorant of a child's home life, if we pretend to estimate the child's character which is so largely moulded by the home influences?

Heredity and environment are not all, but they are much and they cannot be left out of account in any intelligent scheme of child study. When my last new class came in I had the curiosity to go to the directory and find out the occupations of the fathers. That told me a little about them. There is bound to be some difference between the children of a sailor, a politician, an unskilled laborer, and a business man, reputed to be perilously sharp. The occupation of the father is at least one factor in the problem of child study. Just to meet the parents of the children throws some light on their peculiarities. How this is to be accomplished by the busy teacher of yearly changing classes, it is a little hard to say. I have sometimes thought that the mother's meetings about which we are beginning to hear, might be an attempt on the part of some teachers to solve the problem. It is easier and perhaps better to draw the mothers to the school room, than to send the teacher to the homes. In our own school we have made a beginning in that direction which has proved as helpful as any other one thing in giving us real comprehension of the children we have to deal with. Whatever the difficulties in the way the teacher must have the light of the home on the problem of the child's nature, and the teacher who has not felt how altogether one sided, fragmentary, and unsatisfactory the mere school-room study has been, has no real understanding of its aim and scope.

We must try, as teachers, to make this study of the human intense and reverent, as well as scientific. No study can be intense which is not inspired by intelligence, sympathy; no sympathy can be intelligent which leaves out of view the moulding power of the home. No study can be reverent which forgets the one thing which forever differentiates the child from every other object of study—the divine—human ideal in itself according to which it is working out its destiny, helped or hindered by our narrow and partial vision. In working out any adequate conception of Child Study, the home and the school are inseparable agents. They are forever working, together, though apart, in building up the character of the children. They must work together consciously and intelligently if Child Study is ever to be made as broad, as practical, as fruitful as we hope.

CHILD-STUDY FOR THE IRACTICAL TEACHER

By PROF. LOUIS H. GALBREATH, Teachers' College, University Buffalo.

Can we, with show of reason, expect an average teacher to carry on child-study while teaching? Can teachers, working under customary conditions, wisely attempt a more systematic study of their pupils? A right kind of child-study will help the teachers in their work, and, consequently, they should cultivate it. This recently emphasized, if not newly discovered field of educational activity, can help to improve the practical judgment of teachers. Through its aid and in its spirit, teachers can become more skillful readers of the human nature with which they have to deal. Through it more points for observation and judgment can be had; a better habit of attention to, and a more critical discrimination cultivated with reference to certain classes of school affairs; a greater command of resources and more tact in their application, possessed; and a higher sympathy and deeper respect experienced for the child-life with which they work. These improvements will of necessity be followed by a heightened appreciation of the possibilities and responsibilities of the teacher.

But it needs to be said, and with some emphasis, too, that we should not expect scientific work of teachers. To many, this caution may not seem necessary, but the history of the movement justifies it. Leaders in child-study need it, because they are now and then advising work far beyond the province and preparation of teachers. Specialists themselves seem also to need it, for they have been striving to stimulate teachers for co-operation on a plane of work and to an extent quite beyond an ordinary teacher's capacity of response. Teachers, too, would benefit by this recognition, if thereby they could be led to see more clearly where to exert their efforts and could be shielded from the feelings of humility and discouragement, if not to say self-condemnation, for not being able to succeed in work for which they are, and of right, ought to be ill-adapted.

Though teachers cannot employ the intricate methods of the scientists and the delicate apparatus of the laboratory, still the benefits of child-study to the teacher are not likely to be overestimated and overstated. If through the spirit of this magnificent movement the teachers of our country could be induced merely to use the science, now at their immediate command, in determining the needs of pupils and how these ought to be met, greater blessings than have hitherto been imagined even, would come to the education of the children in America. Besides being led to better organization and use of their common sense, they can be helped to use their knowledge of physiology and school hygiene to a greatly increased efficiency in determining the pupil's physical constitution and its condition of life and growth, as a basis for a more wholesome guidance and a superior educational care and control. Further, they can be helped to apply their psychology, as only a few now do, in trying to ascertain the pupil's mental make-up at the time of being taught, its characteristics and possibilities. Further, still, they can be assisted to use their philosophy of moral conduct in seeking the weak and strong virtues in their pupils, so as to find the point of greatest need for ethical culture. The plea is for a study of children by teachers with the aid of, not for the sake of, science, a study which, though systematic, is not to be regarded in strictness as scientific. Science, as a means, is to be brought into requisition to aid in the construction of a system of questions and plans for use in education as an end.

Child-study for the practical teacher must be a study of children for teaching purposes. It must aid him to realize more perfectly his office. He must feel that some practical reward in some service to his work is at hand. Teachers are too deeply concerned in the care and culture of children to turn aside to collect and collate data for knowledge's sake. The immediate need of their pupils rather than the remote values of scientific knowledge very rightly lays claim to their time and energies. The development of science and the development of children give rise to two very different demands of training and equipment; the teacher and the school try to supply one, the scientist and the university, the other. It is true that teachers can and should now and then aid specialists, but from duty to their pupils as well as from necessity of preparation and opportunity, they must attend to the wants of the individual lives before them. They should not rob Peter to aid Paul. Their work may be compared to the practical gardener whose business it is to study the forces and conditions that affect the development of the growing plant, in order to control these agencies for its more perfect maturing. In this their work is quite unlike that of the botanist or scientific horticulturist. The study of children by a teacher in service is to be carried on, not to lead up to the solution of any abstract problem, but to understand a more abstruse puzzle, a living, acting, growing child, and particularly to arrive at a practical knowledge of the causes and conditions which affect this expanding life.

Child-study for the teacher, therefore, could better be called pupil-study, the direct study of children under conditions of school work for the purposes of teaching—management, training, and instruction. Whatever may be of interest to the physiologist, psychologist, or theorist in pedagogy, this study of a given body of children as they have been and are, under educational conditions, marks off unquestionably the principal interest of the teacher while at work.

Because of the complex nature and inherent difficulties of this task set for the teacher, no apology is needed for its proposed limitation. The concrete child is the teacher's problem. He presents himself to the teacher as a product of a very significant past. Heredity, environment, and education have been exerting their silent but strong influences in shaping his career. In teaching, the result of this influence must be reckoned with. What a child is as a product of these influences determines very largely what he can be made through instruction and training. Right teaching, therefore, must give no little attention to the influences that have been pouring into the young lives found in the school-room. These features and factors of growth, the teacher should search out, in some cases to act with them, and in others, against them. The teacher's office is to influence with purpose and power this changing life; he is to enrich its field of moral insight, elevate its plane of intellectual activity, and expand its world of doing and daring. How can this be done with adequate intelligence and effective means in the absence of a warm and intimate acquaintanceship with the pupils?

This separation of a field of child-study for the teacher should not be regarded as a forced distinction, though a much-needed one, arising out of the exigencies of the moment. It is probably true that the movement is at a critical point. Many things have been uselessly undertaken, and much unwise advice has probably been too freely distributed. It is not surprising that we see signs and hear rumors that interest is waning. But the distinction here pointed out of child-study by the teacher in contrast with child-study by the scientist is a serviceable analysis; it indicates two fields for continued cultivation; and the one for the teacher is in no wise of less significance and permanency. In the present age, as in no other time in the world's history, in America as perhaps in no other country, are we recognizing the debt of education to science, of methods in teaching to methods of investigation, and of the teacher to the scientist. In this age which seems in comparison with the past pre-eminently scientific, many of the practical arts are undergoing great transformation. An ever-deepening knowledge and broadening intellectual horizon is being applied to them. No wonder, therefore, that our thought of educational processes and activities is being modified. It is becoming more and more recognized that highly artistic teaching requires the attitude of a student not merely toward the subject-matter, but toward the pupils. The teaching processes necessitate a preliminary study of the pupils, and this in turn demands the application of a broad field of knowledge, the spirit of a student, and the means and methods suggested by the scientist.

For modified views and practices relating to child-life, education owes most perhaps to the science of physiological psychology. Influences emanating from it have led educators to think as if for the first time of the real educational relationship of mind and body. These have been too long treated as two orders of unrelated being, both in theory and in education. Physiological psychology presses home to us the fundamental truth of their interdependence. Philosophy of earlier times has emphasized the independence of mind; it has been regarded as a sustained and self-directing energy; and, in consequence, education of the past has regarded its province to be that of spirit too exclusively.

It is no longer to be called in question that the author of our being has seen fit to link mind and its operations with a nervous mechanism. Though separable in thought, they are indissolubly united in fact. The mind works on the world, and the world upon the mind through the body; and mastery of the world through thought, necessitates an educated nervous system. The teacher can come in contact with the soul-life of his pupils only through the medium of the senses and the brain. All impulses and resolutions awakened through education are practically valueless without a body and nervous system strong and skilful enough to give them expression and realization. The brain needs proper nourishment, stimulation, and exercise to get proper growth. If it fails in this, mental activity and development are affected. In teaching, therefore, one is not merely concerned with pure spirit, but with brain and nerves also, having a certain time-rate of activity, condition of health, and of blood-supply.

Old as these ideas may seem, they would, if properly applied, modify a great deal of our practice in education. They would often affect the kind and number of studies taken up by the pupils, the amount of work assigned by the teacher, the method employed, and not infrequently the temper and spirit of the whole work. There are pupils who are "born short" physically, or who have become "short" through disease or accident, or, mayhap, through school work. These the teacher will always have with him for discovery, diagnosis and treatment. Since thinking exhausts the brain, it is reasonable to hold that in grading and classifying teachers are to pay more attention to the workable energy of the various pupils. As it now goes, a weak, sickly child is given the same classifications and assignments as the strong, sound child. Unless the abnormality is very great, special allowance is not sufficiently planned for in our school systems. Teachers and parents do not, as a rule, give due weight to the far-reaching results of school work, of loss in sleep, or lack of proper food. After some days or weeks of absence because of illness which may have drained the whole body and brain of its reserved power and accustomed vitality, the student is given generally not less but more work "to catch up." Seldom do teachers inquire into the home rest, recreation, and relaxation of their pupils. The proper recognition of the rights of the physical child, and the disposition to find and sympathize with its natural limitations ought to modify very considerably much of school life. Justice and humanity are crying out loudly for this recognition.

The demand for this school room child-study is greatly enforced by that phase of modern psychology which passes under the name of apperception. The power to attend, to discriminate, to judge, in short, to learn, is dependent upon the stock of ideas on hand. That instruction will not proceed wisely and most effectively which does not regard this fact and aid the pupils to revive and to use this working capital. To do this at all well the teacher must be intimately acquainted with them.

How can a teacher proceed from the known to the unknown, from the concrete to the abstract in teaching, if he has taken no pains to find out what is known by the pupils, and what is not known, and what is concrete to them, and what not? He should labor to discover the strong and lively ideas in order to link on to them the weaker and less active ones of the new matter of instruction.

Do we not also grant at least theoretically that the general instincts and interest of a class, and the peculiar traits, tastes, and tendencies of individuals should play no little part in determining the work of instruction? How is the teacher to find this "point of contact?" Will general information, professional experience, or intuition supply the need?

The schoolroom child-study means a turning of the attention of the teacher from physiological charts to the actual hygienic or unhygienic conditions under which the pupils work, from the text-book to the child, from the ideas of an author to those of the pupils, and from the logic of his own mental movement to the movement in the learning mind. It is the child that is to be studied and should become the center of interest, because it is the child who is taught, not the branch of learning.

CHILD STUDY IN THE HIGH SCHOOL

BY JOHN G. ALLEN, PRINCIPAL FREE ACADEMY, ROCHESTER

The want of some practical plan whereby the teachers of the high school could definitely pursue the important subject of Child Study has long been felt. They have needed such information as parents and former teachers of their pupils could have given them. They have felt that for some time after their pupils have entered the high school they have been experimenting with them, and that the recitations and the examination results were inadequate. Some of the best educators in the country have given to this subject their deepest thought, and, as might have been expected, there has been at least one practical solution to the problem. I refer to the scheme which has been devised by Dr. Fred. W. Atkinson, principal of the high school at Springfield, Mass. It was my good fortune while attending the summer school at Clark University to hear him explain his scheme, a copy of which he afterward sent me. This plan appeared in the School Review last September, and, doubtless, many of you have seen it. By the aid of our enthusiastic teachers, this scheme was put into operation last fall in the Rochester high school, and I venture to describe it and give some of its details. It has not been long enough on trial to determine all its merits, but good has already come of it and more good is promised. The scheme consists of a memorandum to be made by the principal of the grammar school, one to be made by the parents of the pupil, one by the pupil himself and one by the teacher of the high school. The memorandum of the principal gives information as to school attendance, health, temperament, character, scholarship, his judgment as to the course the pupil should have chosen, as to extra work during the first year, greatest strength and interest, greatest weakness, outside interests, home conditions and the most helpful methods of instruction and discipline in case of difficulty of learning or fault in behavior. The parent tells about health, eyesight, hearing, as to sleep, appetite in the morning, the kind and amount of recreation and exercise, whether high school teachers require too much of the pupil, the kind and amount of reading done, steady likes and dislikes in school and out, and any other information the parent may be pleased to give to be of greatest help and encouragement to the child. The pupil gives information as to what books he has read since a given time, which of these he especially likes, the favorite character in these books, kinds of literature preferred, favorite author, kinds of newspapers habitually read, the magazines read and which preferred, and whether he draws books from the city library and how often. The memorandum to be kept by the teacher in the high school includes the following items: Name of pupil, date and place of birth, date of beginning the study of ———, height, weight, sight, hearing, health, temperament, character, general scholarship and character of mental development, greatest strength, greatest weakness, application, attention, ability to express orally and in writing, ability to think, ability to memorize, attendance, interests in school and out, controlling motives, general deportment and other additional data.

The parents of 162 boys and 115 girls made returns, and from these we glean the following information: Eighty eight per cent. of the boys and seventy-seven per cent. of the girls are reported as having good health. Twenty-nine and one-half per cent. of the boys and thirty-two per cent of the girls are said to have trouble with eyesight. While the difference is slight as to boys and girls, the proportion is so large that something ought to be done to ascertain the cause. Ten per cent. of the boys and seven per cent of the girls have trouble with hearing.

All the girls are reported as sleeping well and all but six of the boys. Average number of hours sleep of boys, eight and four-tenths; of girls, nine and four-tenths; just an hour's difference. Do girls need more time for sleep than boys? Ninety-five per cent. of the boys and eighty-four per cent. of the girls take time enough to eat a good breakfast.

Boys average three and one-half hours a day in recreation; girls, three. Boys take more physical recreation than girls. Forty-four per cent. of the girls spend not more than two hours in the open air; but twenty-three per cent. of the boys confine themselves to so little time out of doors. Bicycling is the leading kind of exercise with the boys and walking with the girls. Thirty-nine per cent. of the boys and fifteen per cent. of the girls ride wheels. Fifteen per cent. of the girls recreate in doing housework; *one boy* is so reported. Fifteen per cent. of the boys and sixty-one per cent. of the girls do not spend as much time in out-of-door exercise as their parents think necessary.

The teachers were pleased to learn that in the opinion of a large majority of the parents they do not require too much studying of their pupils. Thirty per cent. of the boys and fourteen per cent. of the girls could do more studying just as well as not. Boys study at home, on the average, three hours a day; girls, four hours. It seems from this that our girls are compelled to study an hour a day on the average more than the boys in order to do the same work. Can they do this four years with impunity? Is there an argument here against requiring as much work from girls as from boys in the high school?

Of the boys, twenty-four per cent. and of the girls, twenty-five per cent. draw books from the city library. The boys average two hours a day and the girls one and one-quarter hours a day reading books and other matter not connected with school work. An interesting showing was made relative to the kinds of home reading. The boys read chiefly fiction and history, and about the same amount of each; the girls read fiction largely. Many boys read travels; not a girl was so reported. Forty-five per cent. of the girls and twenty-one per cent. of the boys read fiction; eighteen per cent. of the boys and six per cent. of the girls read history. Of the boys, sixty-three per cent., and of the girls, fifty per cent., read magazines. Ninety per cent. of the boys and seventy-six per cent. of the girls read newspapers.

The question relative to steady likes and dislikes brought a variety of answers. Of the boys, the largest showings were for sports and athletics; of the girls, reading and music. Many parents said as to likes: "I do not know;" as to dislikes, "he (or she) has none." As to which of the high school studies is complained of as hardest, forty-six per cent. of the boys and fifty-five per cent. of the girls make no complaint. Thirty-two per cent. of the girls and twenty-one per cent. of the boys find physiology their hardest subject. Girls take more kindly to Latin than boys in the ratio of fourteen per cent. of complaint to thirty per cent. Four per cent. of the girls and twenty per cent. of the boys find algebra hardest. The use which the wise high school teacher can make of such data is apparent.

Parents were requested to state other things which principal and teachers ought to know to be of greatest help and encouragement to their children. This seemed to be a new departure in education. Some did not send replies, but a large majority sent many helpful and suggestive facts. From these we learn that many of our pupils suffer from nervousness in various ways; others need encouragement on the part of the teachers; some are sensitive and feel keenly the depressing effect of fault finding. It is gratifying, in view of the tendency to find fault, to observe how few have taken this occasion to complain of the school. On the other hand, many parents have come to the school to bring the memoranda, to commend the scheme and to personally thank the principal and teachers for the interest thus manifested in their children.

The memoranda of the pupils have been studied with great interest by the teachers, especially by those teaching English. It has been a revelation to them to learn what their pupils have been reading since last June. They have learned much about a large class of juvenile literature of which they were not informed. Some of us found ourselves asking, "Who is Henty?" The boys knew, for many of them had read from one to ten of his books during the vacation. Now, the problem which our teachers of English have to solve is, how to interest boys, whose favorite author is Henty, and girls who prefer Louise M. Alcott's writings to all others, in the works of Scott, Cooper, Irving, Bryant and Lowell, as prescribed by the regents. The summer reading of the boys has been a better preparation for their school work than that of the girls, for, next to Henty, Cooper is their favorite author; while only one girl prefers Cooper. The eighteen girls who have been reading the Elsie books during vacation will find the work in English rather heavy. One of the problems of Child Study is to determine the content of children's minds, so that teachers may base their work on that sound Pestalozzian principle of going from the known to the unknown. Do we not get a hint from the boys and girls, by the examination of these reports, as to the literary content of their minds on entering the high school? Should not their study of literature be based on what they already know of that subject? If such a line of inquiry should be extended throughout the state, should not the regents make its results a basis for the work in English, thus conforming to a true pedagogic principle? The entire time allowed for this paper and its discussion could profitably be spent in giving the results of a critical study of the reading of these 350 boys and girls as reported by themselves.

To the principals of the grammar schools the scheme was new. Some seemed to be afraid of it. They looked askance at it. Some thought it would involve too much time and labor. Some hesitated about giving information relative to the character of pupils, fearing that an unwise use would be made of it by the teachers of the high school. The great majority, however, responded promptly, regretting that their answers were so brief and so unsatisfactory to themselves, and saying that in the years to come they would be better prepared to give more helpful information.

The memoranda of the teachers of the high school are to be started by those of the first year, beginning with next term, and passed along to the teachers of subsequent years. We anticipate the growth of this information to that extent that it will prove even more valuable than examination results or the markings of daily standings. Comprehending the data of other memoranda, and faithfully and judiciously made, it will furnish valuable data for a school-life memorial which will be prized by many students more highly than their diplomas; or it will furnish data for certificates far more acceptable to the authorities of higher institutions than the evidence of the ability to pass certain examinations can possibly be.

As to the entire scheme, time and experience will reveal its merits, its defects and its value. It has great promise if wisely used. If it should bring the lower schools into closer touch with the high schools, if it should, by its suggestiveness, aid in establishing a system of parents' meetings, wherein they may confer with the teachers, thus bringing them into closer sympathy, in short, if it should be a means of making the schools more efficient, no one will regret having used it, and many will feel heartily thankful to him who devised so valuable a scheme of Child Study in the high school.

THE DULLARD

JAMES P. HANEY, M. D., SUPERVISOR MANUAL TRAINING, NEW YORK CITY.

"We hold these truths to be self-evident, that all men are created equal." Never was a pretended axiom more sadly false. Is there need to quote Lombroso or Ribot, to those who have to deal with the children of men, to prove that such children are far from being equal either in physical or mental stamina. That the Darwinian law recognizes " a fittest " in the cradle? It is to be feared, however, that there are many who fail to comprehend the law of cause and effect, many who are content to resort to an oriental philosophy which ascribes all things to an inscrutable providence. Kismet—it is fate!

Every school knows the dullard, the child whose height and years mark him as one who has been passed in the race, as one who vainly clutching at the skirts of his fleeter neighbors acts as a drag upon them and is at once a burden to his teacher and to himself. Of him it is often said, " He ought not to be in school," though of all that stand in need of schooling surely he is not the least. Denied the privilege of busying himself with work having for him pleasure, interest and profit, he is idle, and an idle child is ever a troublesome child. Those who have followed the annals of penology would rather asseverate, " He ought not to be let out of school." Too often does the dullard of ten become the delinquent of twelve.

To scientific child study, which has pointed to the many hygienic wrongs done to healthy children may we not look for aid in the case of the defective who so often bears the stamp of hereditary disease. But no superficial examinations will be of aid; the study must be conducted by those fitted by education to recognize and deal with conditions which required the life long labor of a Saegert and a Seguin.

To medicine, as well as to pedagogy, are we to look for aid in the solution of the problem of the dullard and what to do with him. Modern science does not, when at a loss for treatment, turn to the rod as a panacea, but essays to exercise the devil of drink or of dullness by more diligent study of the disease, as a disease, with a view to its amelioration if not its cure. It is, however, beyond our purposes to discuss the causes and pathology of this affliction or to differentiate between the cases of hereditary disease and those induced by other affections. The physical signs may rather claim our attention. Most characteristic is the defective physical condition; this is often marked. Associated with it, cranial abnormalities are frequently to be observed: the small head, narrow or lumpy forehead, low hair line, frontal protuburences, prognathus jaw, outstanding ears with lobes defective or absent, etc. All these point to the coincident cerebal abnormality, for when one part of the body presents defective development the brain is apt also to be defective. A tooth ground flat, a trembling hand, an overacting frontal muscle, all evidence defective enervation. Especially will this deficiency be shown in exercises requiring the performance of well cordinated movements of fingers or of lips. All expression of mind is by movement—an abnormal movement means an abnormal mind. The defects in hearing frequently [illegible] acquire good hearing. They are symptomatic of [illegible] defect. The special senses of sight and taste may be found as poorly developed as the special organs which contain them: the eye of the child may recognize color and form no more than that of an infant. The heart [illegible] may weaken and [illegible]. Each additional ailment aids to make the [illegible].

Some happily not all of this array of symptoms will as a rule be found to mark the dullard, yet at times all signs fail and occasionally we do find a boy or girl with good development of everything but that which we agree to call intellect. But the defective with feeble body and dull perceptions need cause no wonder at the feeble power of attention. Attention is absent from the absence of senses which make attention possible. With weak understanding he can but have weak will, uncertain memory and defective judgment. Moral perversion of the willing but witless is a symptom as much to be expected as pain from an open wound.

As to treatment one may premise with Beach that "unless physical conditions can be improved, no amelioration of the mental state can be expected." That care for the hygienic side of the child's life, which scientific child study has shown to be so necessary must in the case of the dullard be of prime importance. With systematic work he must have systematic play; each calculated to not unduly tax his powers, so soon fatigued. The treatment must be "Medico-pedagogical." Physiology has long since been pointed out as the means which must be sought to aid in the defective brain. Upon the senses depend the knowledge the mind has of the great outside. "Imperfect organs must be exercised to develop normal functions and functions must be trained to develop imperfect organs." But are physical and mental education not to be thought of as independent? Manual and mental training are one. There must be culture first of the external senses, co-ordination then of muscular movements and later a union of senses and movements in exercises requiring manual and mental activity. There must be no abstractions. In the language of Froebel, "the teaching must rest with the learning on actual fact and actual existence." It is, to be sure, impossible to supply facilities which are wanting, but as a rule few are wanting, they are only undeveloped: with the education of the intellectual, education of the moral faculties becomes possible.

The child must be with his peers. No physical touch of elbows with normal children can serve to cause mental attrition sufficient to point the wit of the dullard. The mental dwarf will not be aided by being made to stand with those who are to him as intellectual giants. For the dull child special teaching is necessary and it must be given by special teachers. Teachers who aim to educate and not to instruct. Teachers who can interpret signs given by children with little power to know and see, and little power to show what they know and see. Teachers who will accord the meed of praise to the effort of the dullard which is praiseworthy—too often it comes in for blame. Such teachers must be child students in every sense of the word. "It is necessary for them to think down to the plane of those with whom they have to deal." If they would aid these children they must learn to think *with* them, not *of* them.

It has been well said that the tone of a school system must not be judged by the height to which it rises, but by the depths to which it descends to raise its lowest members if but a single step higher.

No single course and class for instruction of both bright and dull boys can be satisfactory. In such a class the dull boy occupies more of the teacher's time than is his due, and yet, with the subject matter unadapted for him, he fails of the development which he might attain. His adequate instruction is difficult, is practically impossible, under such circumstances. No course but one distinctly manual has promise for the child who must do to appreciate the thing done. A separate class must be resorted to both for his own sake and the sake of his brighter fellows. A separate class, in which the individual pupil may in the course adapted to him, receive individual instruction, not an ungraded class which is to be taught by a teacher ignorant of that which has been pronounced most essential to success in this difficult task.

Would a parent submit to having a child consigned to a class in which are the confessedly dull? In London there are 17 such "Schools for special instruction" with an attendance of over 600 children. In Providence, where the plan has been tried, parents have moved nearer to the school to take advantage of its instruction. It has been said that teachers should know as much physiology as doctors, and doctors should know a good deal more. Teachers for such special classes would need special training in child psychology, medicine, and pedagogy. A few schools now offer, in part, this instruction, but more physiological knowledge should be given in normal schools and schools of pedagogy.

The dullard is apt to be a solitary brooder. In a course of study designed for him, the kindergarten games and others resembling them are of special value. The kindergarten spirit is helpful, communal. Ordinary class work fosters the isolation of the individual. The games and occupations should be such as develop the special senses. They should take advantage of the gift of imitation, which is often strongly marked in the defective. *Facta non verba* should be the mottoes in all the instruction.

The school-room should be furnished with benches and simple tools in addition to ordinary desks. The lessons should alternate between bench and desk, building and drawing, making in all its forms. From the things wrought are to be derived such lessons in number and language as the pupil can master. It is needless to add that all grades cannot be brought to the same standard of development or discipline. The years during which this training is of most advantage are from 8 to 12. It may frequently and with profit be continued until 15, but nearly all authorities recommend that it begin as early as possible.

Classes for the dull have long been known on the Continent and in England. Introduced in Brunswick in 1881, they were later instituted in Cologne, Dusseldorf, Crefeld, Gera and elsewhere. Those in London have already been referred to. In our own country they have already been introduced in several cities, and from each comes the report that the first signs of active interest, of quickened intelligence, of an unlooked-for skill were seen in the dullard upon his entrance into this special class. Says Fernald, "to my knowledge, no school for the deficient, has ever been given up."

CHILD STUDY BY A WOMAN'S CLUB

MRS. ELLA HASTINGS, PRESIDENT OF THE SOCIETY FOR THE STUDY OF CHILD NATURE, NEW YORK CITY

(Read by Mrs. E. H. Merrill, President of the Mother's Club, Syracuse.)

When our club was formed in 1889 there were no other societies of the sort in existence. We were actual pioneers, and were, as pioneers usually are, of different sorts and conditions. When a band of students engage in intellectual labor, they usually have had about the same prior training and possess about the same average mental outfit, but our terms of association merely demanded that its members take an interest in the study, and that they be aroused to a desire for the best methods of securing their uniform development. On this basis, we set to work to ascertain what was definitely known of the child's nature, and from such ascertained facts seek to draw that which would help us to aid the best unfolding of all children that might come under our influence. Indeed, all that we could hope for in our members was sincerity of motive and single purposedness of aim. When we commenced to work, we knew nothing even of the literature extant upon the subject.

We were fortunate in having on our earliest membership list Mrs. Felix Adler, through whose distinguished husband we were enabled to get at the best works on the subject of our study. There was no systematized course of instruction then, nor, as we have found, does such exist to-day. Hence, we were forced to do our own surveying — map out our own charts. And if, at times, we have strayed a little out of our course, owing to the absence of trustworthy guides, we may, nevertheless, say, that never, for long at a time, have we remained in strange waters. There has been published recently, in an educational journal, a list of books suitable for those about to pursue a course of Child Study, according to any of the methods now in vogue. These books have, without exception, entered into our work, either through careful perusal of the text or copious extracts, or as constant reference. It was not through a happy chance that we had at hand the best bibliography, but because the officers were determined to exercise the most careful discrimination, and were emphatic in their exclusion of all pseudo-scientific treatises.

Rousseau's radical "Emile," in an available form was our first authority. Erroneous as the method is, the underlying truths are so undeniable that we found it most suggestive, and its very fallacies refreshing. Next, we undertook Locke's "Thoughts on Education," and that furnishes, in a nutshell, a philosopher's idea of the educational method warranted to turn out an ideal English gentleman. It is extremely practical, and, incidentally, the truth can be learned that this method will, to some extent, aid in forming an American citizen.

Spencer's very didactic remarks on education are useful and productive of discussion, but they are extremely fallacious at times, and no longer considered altogether safe as guides, so we dismissed his treatise after brief study.

Up to this point our text-books referred to the boy child alone, as if he were the exclusive product of the human race. As we were somewhat interested in the girl child, we naturally desired to have some worthy guide who would recognize that the fundamental difference of sex necessitated at times difference of treatment. We found but little literature on this subject that was worthy of the name. Much of it is mere sentimental nonsense, and the rest full of glittering generalities, without any wise thought underlying any of them. We finally accepted a book that had no pretensions to exact knowledge, but was dedicated to the elucidation of the ideal relations that might exist between a mother and her daughters. This was by Richter. We found it exceedingly delightful and helpful to the judgment. Now we arrived at the necessity for having some fixed ideas on the proper training of children as to their ethical relations. Prof. Adler's book on "Moral Instruction," supplemented by our own contributions by the way of original papers, was quite adequate for our purpose and very convincing.

Then came a crisis. We had exhausted the list of books directly suited to our purpose; and we found that we must advance now on the psychological line. Many of our members were disinclined to take up the abstract study in genuinely student fashion—the only way, indeed, that satisfactory results could be obtained. We looked about for a book that would embody facts on this science that would be based on other philosophers' or scientists' investigations. Radestock's little treatise on "Habit" was the only work that at all answered our demands in this direction. So we assayed it, and, in spite of its being replete with references to the works of very advanced thinkers and experimenters, still we managed to extract a great deal of valuable information from it, although like younger learners, we skipped the hard parts, only using that which would show us how to go to work to form the right mental and physical habits. From the time of the completion of Raedstock's book, we have been forced to carry on our work in a less clearly defined manner. Then the sound of the syllabus was heard throughout the land, and a very stentorian voice it had. But as interesting as many of the syllabi undoubtedly are, and even though we spent months in making veritable gradgrinds of ourselves in our firm intention to gather "facts and nothing but facts," we did not find this syllabus work illuminating enough to continue it. For, although many of the syllabi are very enlightening, and give much material for discussion, they are, after all, better suited to the student who is interested in the completion of scientific thought on the subject of graded-school methods.

We have now reached our work of the present year. In the dearth of proper material for our work we considered it advisable to discuss such literature as was in circulation among our children, in order to arrive at some conclusion as to what books were entertaining and profitable for the young of various ages, at the same time endeavoring to analyze such as were apparently most in demand, in order to ascertain if such books were deservedly popular, or, in reality, meretricious or purely negative. Then we have ventured into the fields of fiction and biography, deducing such themes as would suggest the influence of various early conditions on the formation of the character of the subject under disquisition. This year we have had a number of extremely carefully prepared papers on the various topics. All the work of this winter has been evidently done *con amore*. The previous consideration that we had given to temperament, various traits and proper early influences has been of great value to us in this particular sort of study.

The running survey which I have given, incompletely as it has been done, cannot fail to impress my listeners with this fact that we have never lost sight of our main object, "How we can best assist in the proper development of children." And scoffed at, as our work has been by many a doubting Thomas, it is safe to say that no woman who has been a member of our club all these years regrets the time she has spent on this, maybe, incoherent study. There has undoubtedly been much time given to this work that if bestowed on some other intellectual labor would show a more complete return—more direct and tangible results; but the insight we have thus gained into human physical conditions and the mainsprings of human action, the definite knowledge we have gained of what to expect from our children under normal conditions will be of lasting value.

The very recent so-called Congress of Mothers, convened at Washington, although we may smile inwardly over the very little Child Study and the very much of everything else that entered into its deliberations, serves to convince us that a wide-spread interest is taken in the observation of child life, child conditions and child ideals, and that mothers wish to know the last word on the best ways of caring for their children spiritually, physically, mentally. Nevertheless, to-day we remain unique. No other club has done the work as we have done it, nor will there probably ever be one exactly like it, unless our own Child Nature Society continues on the same lines.

There are now offered manuals on Child Study that will serve better as guides, possibly, than those we have chosen, but that the study is still chaotic is in no way better evinced than in Sully's "Studies of Childhood." It is quoted as a valuable authority, and yet it is nothing but a collection of the phenomena of child life as observed by a psychologist of established repute. Such phenomena are, indeed, as familiar to every observant parent. Indeed the work that will make this study a veritable branch of human learning has yet to be written.

SCIENTIFIC CHILD-STUDY

BY PROFESSOR EDWARD FRANKLIN BUCHNER, SCHOOL OF PEDAGOGY, NEW YORK UNIVERSITY

Very much like the science of astronomy, child-study has won the attention of many investigators, not because of its commercial gains; for, as we all are so often found aptly saying, "there is no money in it." And, furthermore, unlike other sciences, any of its discoveries cannot be converted into gain through the practical channels of industry. The mathematics of a star in its movements, the strength of building material, or the alternating of electrical currents may swell the treasury of a steamship company, the bank account of a contractor, or provide a small manufacturing community with the needs of life. Scientific child-study does not lend itself to such gains. It appeals to us first and foremost as being a field of knowledge for the sake of knowledge.

Scientific child-study has been breathed about as though science were treasuring a few laws in its reticule, and going about seeking such facts as it might devour. It is asked, "Can any laws be formulated which might serve as general guides in our efforts to obtain deductions of mathematical accuracy?" Our answer must be yea and nay. I know many will clamor when I say that the pedogogics of science, molding it into text-books and into forms of instruction, is far more responsible for the rigidity in the laws of science than the conclusions of many of nature's workers themselves, who more than often specialize the laws of nature by the quotation marks of doubt and uncertainty.

The phenomena of childhood will become amenable to practical needs only as we succeed in the quantification of those phenomena. But, what is quantification? Can we measure this or that impulse, this or that growth, this or that function? As to scientific knowledge, however, quantification is the way of exact judgment. Unfortunately this ever remains relative to the standard of measurement erected. In general psychology this standard comprises the physical elements employed in science and adopted in ordinary affairs; usually this basis of science is not "nature," but lies in some governmental vault. In pedagogical science we are in part forced to add other standards which must come out of the activities of childhood itself. In this way the paradox arises that pedagogical psychology is of all the most natural in its standard of measurement, and not artificial as natural science actually is.

The quantification of childhood may proceed in two ways: simultaneously, or in sequence; in masses, or in individuals. Each child may offer its own standard of equality or inequality. Here appears the value of biographical records, and these can be secured only by comparing the sequence of days and weeks. Masses of children may be studied in one locality and the results compared with masses studied in another place, the former offering the standard.

In all fairness to the enduring endeavors of the past years, scientific child-study as yet contains "nothing but problems," and may be said to be very much like a cerebral psychology, which presents no solutions. Who is to blame for this state of affairs? No one in particular. Is there no demand for the results of scientific child-study? The results of no field are more eagerly awaited. On every street corner and in every school door—American at least—some one is anxiously waiting for the newest words from those whose pedagogic training entitles them to delve into the silent days and ways of childhood.

Each parent may know his child exhaustively, as Preyer, Baldwin, *et al.* This knowledge, while a force in calling attention to this field, is only personal and isolated; and, in the accumulation of data no store will be found more trustworthy. One of the needs of child-study is the means of reducing the facts thus obtainable to some quantitative expression. The results of a problem can be verified at a later time, or by another investigator only as those results are given exact statement. Qualities are only discriminable, and constantly require the presence of the student, while quantities become the one expression of natural objects and events which can pass current in any circle of scientists.

Is the quantification of childhood too high an aim for child-study? No true searcher can rest until his conclusions become verifiable a score of times, and pruned in the light of material gathered by gradually improved methods. Children are to be measured in every way that they are measureable. Whenever any change is detectable, there must our yard-sticks, balances and reaction keys be carried. No sensation, no movement, no representation is unworthy of being given a line in our record blanks. Who shall detain us by asking a pittance for the fetich altar of the "practical?"

The field of child-study has, unfortunately, been brought into disrepute among its sympathizers and co-workers by being divided by the lines setting the "unscientific" off from the "scientific." Alas! The impersonal logic of science is replaced by the animosities of the scientists themselves! Is child-study as undertaken by the specialist, trained in laboratory secrets, to be identified with the child-study open to and cultivated by parents and teachers? Let us not centralize a needful difference in methods into a fixed antithesis in material, shutting those windows which offer the largest views of that phase of nature we long to see. The observations upon infancy made primarily for the benefit of science, and the observations made primarily for the sake of the child in its welfare in the home and the school, may apparently lie far apart; but each mingles with the other in trying to reconcile the ultimate facts of the typical, physical and mental processes through which each one of us has been forced by the very functions of growth.

Scientific child-study, considered as being chiefly the psychology of childhood, cannot be brought to the exact methods which have been so forceful in promoting the recent developments in psychology. The data in this large chapter in genetic psychology receive considerable distortion before coming into hand for tabular treatment. The child can neither report nor reflect upon his own mental states. Laboratory records of the discriminative sensibility in children present great gaps in faithfulness, owing to the predominating disposition of children to react by word of mouth or reaction key in almost uniform disregard of the stimulation. This is true even in the case of adults, as was instanced in the laboratory of my colleague, Professor Bliss, only a few days ago, where an investigator found a normal subject who gave evidence of an illusory audition *uniformly* reappearing in a series of tests upon the lower limits of hearing, during the whole series of which there was actually no stimulus applied! Thus it is that a factual study of childhood presents the vast need and field of interpretation. The frontiers of the sciences are literally strewn with well or ill-formed hypotheses which have been offered in the hope of making facts more tangible.

One of the most abused terms at the present time is "science" and its derivatives. To make an appeal to it has become the supposed pass-word to truth! Let us not be led too far astray by a failure to distinguish properly those elements which enter into science. Science is safely summed up as consisting of that knowledge which is both *quantitative and genetic*. For a long time mathematical reductions of phenomena were supposed to be the true and only goal of the natural sciences. Now the field is changing. From the strong impulses of biological phenomena, the physical sciences are themselves becoming more and more genetic, and less and less quantitative. Witness the value of the nebular hypothesis and the theory of evolution. On the other hand, men are multiplying their attempts to reduce the phenomena of growth to quantities.

Genetic principles, however, are what contribute the knowledge that serves explanatory purposes. Fixing quantities, on the other hand, is rather the method of science, which shall be effective in sorting out the actual facts which are in need of explanation. Mere quantities are dead, inert, disparate. In the genetic aspects of any group of phenomena, the two great facts are *survival* and *variation*. These rubrics *can* aid us in exploring the field of childhood. Let us be just and generous to facts and theories arising from either point of view, but, let us not gnaw the bones of ignorance and scepticism if the child's nature and progress do not comport with our smoothly-flowing logical distinctions.

Our knowledge of the human individual has weaned us from a pangenetic view of that life. We no longer regard it as performed or moving forward as a totality. On the other hand, that the child is in a process of development, is the abiding fact. How is this fact to be tabulated and explained? It may be an evolution, an accretion, or a performed unfoldment, observing the utmost continuity. That childhood is a genetic fact, and must positively or negatively be regarded from that point of view, has given rise to the following general theories, which loosely group themselves as *phylogenetic*, which holds that the racial processes lead and are determinative, and *ontogenetic*, or that general view which maintains that the make-up of the individual is the important and better knowable fact. These theories, indicated by single terms, are those of original faculties and endownments, physical structure and function, heredity, environment, growth as energy, instinct, spontaneity, organic and selective reactions, imitation, sensation and conscious process, habit and accommodation, suggestion, inhibition, teleology, and individuality.

The next great step in child-study development will be a facing, in its own way, the relative values of these explanatory genetic principles. These ten distinct principles are not *forced* into child-study; but rather they have been appealed to again and again, yielding much confusion. The occasion for Rousseau's juggling with paradoxes lay in his unmitigated appeal to environment. Froebel stoutly maintained the principle of continuity of growth in which no sharp lines are to be drawn. The development of the human individual follows "originally an orderly and logical course." Heredity has been the watch word of a host of investigators. Taine, Guyau, Galton, Preyer, Haeckel, Baldwin, and others adopt for their starting-point the position that individual physical and mental development follows the lead presented in the racial development. Contemporary psychology is emphasizing the predominance of physical structure and function. Instinct and suggestion have no less been accredited by Morgan and Fouillée in accounting for the nature and sequence of physical and mental phenomena. While spontaneity, selective reactions, and inhibitions on the part of consciousness itself have scarce served in any quarter to systematize the phenomena in question.

The confusion arising is well instanced in Preyer and Baldwin who, while having much in common, show the influence of hypotheses in the parting of their ways. What, according to Preyer, is innate and inherited is, according to Baldwin, the latest products of evolutionary development. Much of our distress comes from our apparent inability to free our facts and conclusions from the antithetical influences of these various points of view.

While the revelations of new facts urge us to invoke increasingly the several foregoing principles, the probable outcome of it all is that no one principle can suffice. The morphology presented by childhood is delicate and intricate enough to find room for them all, and, perhaps even for more. The child's development is supreme in breaking away from the uniformity demanded by a thoroughgoing adoption of any one hypothesis, and organizing an *individuality*. The goal of human growth, as indicated by a careful psychological analysis, is found, not in the resultant likenesses of the members of the race, but in the differences each one presents in light of the reactions upon the intellectual and emotional content of his consciousness. The concrete truth is that each man shall be a species unto himself.

One of the present great needs in our inquiries is to turn them into a *quest for the standard child*. Can we fully assure ourselves as to that environment where the child is his standard self—in the home, or the asylum, in the street, in this or that school? True it is, that the child is actually forced into all sorts of environments. But, no teacher, for example, is entitled to label a child "bad" or "stupid" who chances to lack or exert the inhibitions in the school-room which the child *may* manifest elsewhere. Until we have the standard child, we lack the basis of comparison which is indispensable in all measurement of childhood. Our present studies of childhood do not offer us any conclusion in this matter. Only a few days ago, a judicial laboratory investigator of childhood unhesitatingly and naively assured me that "a child is always himself." But, is it true? I submit that it is not. Were the child a mere mass of unorganized or organized matter, we might have no hesitancy in admitting the child's uniformity with himself. It is his conscious elements—and the great Darwin and the lamented Dr. Cope both found it needful to regard consciousness as a real cause in the evolution and preservation of a species—under the forceful forms of imitation and simulation, which lead the child to be often other than himself. When this quest for the standard child shall have been successful, a common basis will be at hand to evaluate observations upon childhood from all points of view.

And what, finally, is the guarantee of scientific child-study? Will it teach us to *know* the actual child in actual life? Do not be over-hopeful. Curves and averages tell us a big deal. But *knowledge*—that fair vision of reality—may be, and actually is of larger import than a few figures. Columnar tabulations of one who has been exhaustive in fixing the numerical equivalencies given to his special problem by reactions and essays, may be the most helpful way of seeing the deeds of childhood; but they are the lenses only, not the actual field.

Does scientific child-study exhaust the field? Does it deny any right to the popular, unscientific efforts made in every school and hamlet? May not the truest scientist often be the most perplexed father, a struggling debtor, or a pious deacon?" "Scientific" and "unscientific" may be exclusive concepts, growing fat, feeding upon the principle of contradiction; but the actual life of every man brushes aside the structure of the astute logician!

The child, at best, or at worst, remains more than science in its totality can reproduce. While we patiently strive to nurture and prune what little may be known, verified, and rendered transferable to other members and aspects of childhood, let us not forget that life, in its very least, is a synthesis in an individuality which must be *felt* rather than discriminated by quantitative measurements. As our single and collective insights into the structure and potentialities of childhood grow from more to more, let us not pollute by unchaste "thought, word, and deed," the sacred chalice whence new life has come, and cause it to disappear. The Holy Grail of childhood can never again come by a successful Sir Galahad!

EXHIBIT No. 18

COMPULSORY EDUCATION

Reports of Inspectors under the Compulsory Attendance Law

COMPULSORY EDUCATION

REPORT OF A. M. WRIGHT, A. M.

In making my third annual report of the work accomplished in the enforcement of the compulsory education law, I wish first to acknowledge the hearty co-operation and sympathetic support of local school authorities and attendance officers and especially the earnest activity of my associates.

During the past year over 800 visits have been made to the various school districts of the state, many teachers' institutes have been addressed and some thirty-five meetings of trustees and attendance officers have been held.

The method of work has been practically the same as in the preceding year, although the visitations have been directed more to the distinctly rural schools. The visits of your inspectors in 1895-96 disclosed the fact that in a large majority of cases the cities and larger villages were enforcing the law, and did not need the stimulating influence of a visit from the state inspector, so only those places were revisited which seemed to fail in properly appreciating the work expected of them.

As the amendment made by the legislature of 1896, to section 7 of the law, would place in the field as assistants in its proper enforcement some fifteen hundred town attendance officers, it seemed necessary to call the attention of town boards to the requirements of the statute, that prompt and favorable action might be taken. The following circular was therefore sent to each supervisor and town clerk in the state.

STATE OF NEW YORK:

DEPARTMENT OF PUBLIC INSTRUCTION,
SUPERINTENDENT'S OFFICE.
ALBANY, *August* 20, 1896.

To Supervisors and Town Clerks:

Your attention is hereby called to section 7 of title 16 of the consolidated school law, known as the compulsory education law, which reads as follows:

"Attendance Officers.—The school authorities of each city, union free school district, or common school district whose limits include in whole or in part an incorporated village, shall appoint and may remove at pleasure one or more attendance officers of such city or district, and shall fix their compensation and may prescribe their duties not inconsistent with this act, and may make rules and regulations for the performance thereof; and the superintendent of schools of such city or school district shall supervise the enforcement of this act within such city or school district; and the town board of each town shall appoint one or more attendance officers whose jurisdiction shall extend over all school districts in said town, not by this section otherwise provided for, and shall fix their compensation which shall be a town charge; and such attendance officers appointed by said board shall be removable at the pleasure of the school commissioner in whose commissioner's district such town is situated."

This section is mandatory and places upon town boards the duty and responsibility of appointing one or more town attendance officers whose jurisdiction shall extend over all school districts in their respective towns, except union free school districts, and common school districts whose limits include in whole or in part an incorporated village. As the statute is silent concerning the term of office of such officers, appointments should be made annually. The services of these officers are required between October 1 and June 1 in each school year, therefore town boards should convene and make the necessary appointments before October first. These officers are town officers and should take the required oath before entering upon their duties. Trustees of schools are not eligible to appointment as town attendance officers.

The statute confers upon town boards authority to appoint town attendance officers and fix their compensation *only*, and they may not legally assume the responsibility of determining or limiting the duties of these officers.

School commissioners are charged with the responsibility of removing incompetent or inefficient officers, and are therefore the judges as to whether they are consistently performing the duties required of them and may direct and instruct them as to the same.

In determining the compensation of these officers it should be borne in mind that good service cannot be secured unless the compensation is fairly reasonable. The experience of the past year has shown that the most satisfactory method of compensation is by the day, *for actual services rendered*, with mileage. The prevailing price has been $2 per day and five cents for mileage, each way. Experience has shown that the best results are obtained when one good man is appointed with jurisdiction over all the districts of the town. I would, therefore, urge that only one man be appointed in each town, unless the schools be so numerous or so widely scattered as to render such action unwise.

I remind you of the importance of selecting competent and energetic officials, as their duties will often be of a very trying nature, requiring the exercise of sound wisdom and discretion. As soon as the appointments are made each town clerk should send to the school commissioner of his district the names and post-office addresses of the officers appointed.

CHARLES R. SKINNER,
State Superintendent.

As the officers thus appointed would be ignorant of the law and its application, also of their duties in its enforcement, the following circular was sent to each town attendance officer as soon as notice of his appointment was received.

STATE OF NEW YORK:

DEPARTMENT OF PUBLIC INSTRUCTION,
SUPERINTENDENT'S OFFICE.
ALBANY, *October* 1, 1896.

To Town Attendance Officer:

Dear Sir.—This book of blanks is sent you with the expectation that by its use a wise enforcement of the compulsory education law will result.

As soon as possible after receiving notice of your appointment you should visit each school under your jurisdiction, secure from the trustees the census of the school children between 8 and 16 years of age and compare the same with the actual attendance as recorded in the school registers. Should you discover cases of non-compliance with the law, you should immediately investigate them and secure the attendance of all children subject to its provisions. You should impress trustees, teachers and parents with your determination to enforce the law.

After your first round of visits, in most localities, the law can be consistently enforced if you promptly investigate the cases brought to your attention by the trustees and teachers, and dispose of them according to law.

Your school commissioner is charged with the responsibility of removing incompetent or inefficient officers, and is therefore the judge as to whether you are properly performing the duties required of you, and may direct and instruct you as to the same.

Respectfully yours,
CHARLES R. SKINNER,
State Superintendent.

In addition to the book of blanks referred to in the above circular, copies of the law and of a circular of information and instruction relative to the provisions thereof were sent to each such officer.

The following is a sample of the blanks contained in the book:

Date .... No. ....

Name of Child .... Age ....

School..

Name of Parent or Guardian } ....

Residence ....

Charge ....

Employer ....

Disposition of Case } ....

Remarks ....

....

....

Teacher's Signature } ....

Officer's Signature } ....

DUPLICATE

To be filled out and given to the teacher to be preserved for future reference

Date. .... No. ....

Name of Child .... Age ....

School..

Name of Parent or Guardian } ....

Residence. ....

Charge ....

Employer..

Disposition of Case } ....

Remarks..

....

....

....

....

Officer's Signature } ....

It further seemed advisable to spend considerable time during the year in instructing these officers as to their duties. To this end some thirty-five meetings were held in various commissioner districts, at which attendance officers were present and the interpretation placed upon the several sections of the law by the Department of Iublic Instruction was discussed. These meetings proved extremely beneficial, and I am confident that much of the time of your inspectors can be profitably given to similar work the present year.

The method of appointment of town attendance officers, however, is not entirely satisfactory, and the persons chosen are not always competent, or, if competent, efficient, owing to the attempt on the part of the appointing power to limit their compensation too narrowly. I am confident that much better results would be obtained if some other method of appointment was adopted, and would recommend the following:

It shall be the duty of each school commissioner, together with the supervisor of each town, subject to the approval of the state Superintendent of Iublic Instruction, on or before the fifteenth day of September in each year, to appoint one or more attendance officers for each town in his commissioner district whose terms of service shall be for one year from the first day of October, succeeding their appointments, and whose jurisdiction shall extend over all school districts in their respective towns, except those districts the school authorities of which are required by law to appoint attendance officers with local jurisdiction. The attendance officers so appointed shall receive two dollars for each day of actual service, to be audited and paid by the town boards of their respective towns, and such town attendance officers shall be removable at the pleasure of the school commissioner in whose commissioner district such town is situated. Any vacancy occurring among such officers shall be filled by appointment, as aforesaid, for the remainder of the term.

This method of appointment combines the elements of local judgment and general supervision, which, I believe, will give results much more satisfactory than can possibly be attained under the present plan.

I am led to make this recommendation not alone because the appointments made by the town boards have not always been wise, and their tendency to limit the compensation within too narrow bounds has often caused competent officials to refrain from the performance of known duties, but because it has been almost impossible to secure action at all by some of the town boards, and in many towns a large part of the school year passes without the services of such officers to aid in the proper enforcement of the law. When supervisors and town clerks were advised to take immediate action, it was urged that it would cost at least twelve dollars to convene the board for this special purpose, and more time is desired, until other matters should require the attention of the board, when action would be taken. Again, a like additional expense would be incurred in filling any vacancy which might occur. All this unnecessary expense would be avoided, and prompt action would result by amending section 7 of the compulsory law in accordince with the plan recommended.

Reference to the tables of statistics shows that the work of these officers has resulted most favorably in spite of the difficulties above enumerated. While the number of children of school age (5 to 18 years) in the state was increased by 17,091, the number attending school some portion of the year was increased by 27,125, and the average daily attendance by 48,200. The increase in average daily attendance I look upon as most significant and the most encouraging feature of the work. The average increase in average daily attendance for the past ten years has been 14,624, and the present year's increase exceeds the highest previous year, 1895, 11,569, or 32 per cent. These tables further disclose the fact that improvement has been most marked in the towns, for while the cities gained 32,105 in number of pupils registered and 33,878 in average daily attendance, the towns, though losing 4,980 in number registered, gained 14,322 in average daily attendance.

The following table summarizes the work done under the law in the cities of the state.

	Number children found truants or non-attendants and returned to school	Number found illegally employed and returned to school	Number children committed to truant and other institutions	Number of Parents or Guardians: Arrested	Fined	Imprisoned	Number persons, firms or corporations fined for illegal employment of children	Number attendance officers employed
Albany	85	29	58	0	0	0	0	2
Amsterdam	103	12	0	6	3	0	0	1
Auburn	32	2	5	0	0	0	0	1
Binghamton	214	48	47	43	0	0	0	5
Brooklyn	2,994	262	122	1	0	1	[illegible]	1
Buffalo	1,690	17	31	13	4	0	0	1
Cohoes	30	2	2	0	0	0	0	6
Corning	[1]	[1]	0	0	0	0	0	1
Dunkirk	102	0	0	6	0	0	0	1
Elmira	164	10	5	7	0	0	0	1
Geneva	[1]	[1]	7	8	8	0	0	9
Gloversville	86	15	0	1	0	0	0	1
Hornellsville	[1]	[1]	4	1	0	0	0	1
Hudson	50	8	1	4	0	0	0	1
Ithaca	154	6	0	0	0	0	0	1
Jamestown	133	5	2	0	0	0	0	1
Johnstown	46	0	0	3	2	1	0	1
Kingston	18	23	0	0	0	0	0	1
Little Falls	66	1	0	0	0	0	0	1
Lockport	215	0	17	0	0	0	0	1
Long Island City	77	0	11	0	0	0	0	1
Middletown	274	2	3	4	0	0	0	1
Mount Vernon	21	2	3	25	4	0	0	1
Newburgh	91	0	4	0	0	0	0	1
New York	18,528	*	172	13	8	1	0	20
Niagara Falls	416	7	2	22	1	0	0	1
North Tonawanda	[1]	[1]	1	0	0	0	0	1
Ogdensburg	50	0	0	0	0	0	0	1
Olean	20	3	1	7	1	0	0	1
Oswego	224	16	9	1	0	0	0	1
Poughkeepsie	[1]	[1]	10	0	0	0	0	1
Rensselaer	[1]	[1]	0	0	0	0	0	1
Rochester	744	55	108	0	0	0	0	7
Rome	40	0	3	0	0	0	0	1
Schenectady	334	2	2	2	0	0	0	1
Syracuse	712	57	76	0	0	0	0	1
Troy	364	0	51	0	0	0	0	2
Utica	98	18	3	7	2	0	0	2
Watertown	150	10	12	0	0	0	0	1
Watervliet	[1]	[1]	0	0	0	0	0	2
Yonkers	102	17	16	4	1	0	0	1
Total	28,552	568	798	180	34	3	0	87

[1] No report

* Referred to inspectors of mercantile and manufacturing establishments

In the towns 313 parents were arrested, 80 of whom were fined; and 484 children were arrested as truants, 98 of whom were committed to truant schools or similar institutions.

Many of the difficulties which confronted your inspectors in their visitations the first year no longer exist. The teachers are more careful and prompt in recording attendance and more earnest in securing the daily presence of their pupils; the attendance officers are better informed as to their duties and more efficient, and the school authorities are more systematic in carrying forward the work.

As many inquiries come to the Department concerning blank forms for committing children to truant schools or similar institutions, the following blanks prepared by the authorities of the Westchester Temporary Home are inserted for reference. Modified forms of these blanks can be used in committing to other like institutions.

[Blank No. 1.]

CONSENT OF PARENT

........................., N. Y., ... 189

I Hereby Certify, That I am the .... of the child ...., who lives at ...., and that such child is .... years of age. That he has sufficient health to render h attendance upon public instruction expedient; that he is a truant from school, and that I have been notified concerning h case, and an opportunity for a hearing has been given after due notice to said child.

And I Hereby Consent and request that such child be confined and maintained in The Westchester Temporary Home for Destitute Children at White Plains, Westchester County, New York, for such period and under such rules and regulations as the authorities may prescribe, not exceeding the remainder of the school year.

....

[Blank No. 2.]

ORDER OF COMMITMENT OF TRUANT TO THE WESTCHESTER TEMPORARY HOME FOR DESTITUTE CHILDREN, WHITE PLAINS, N. Y.

NEW YORK, ... 189

IN THE MATTER OF COMMITTING .... A TRUANT, TO THE WESTCHESTER TEMPORARY HOME FOR DESTITUTE CHILDREN	Order of Commitment

It having been made to appear that the child

....

who resides at No .... street, in the .... of ...., N. Y., is between eight and sixteen years of age, in proper physical and mental condition to attend upon lawful instruction as required by the Compulsory Education Acts, and is a truant therefrom;

And notice having been given to said truant and to the persons in parental relation to comply with such law, and having failed therein, and a reasonable notice having further been personally served upon such truant and the persons in parental relation to h...... that said matter would be considered by the Board of ....at a session thereof, held on the ....day of ...., 189

And said case having been duly considered, and an opportunity given for all persons to be heard in relation thereto;

And it further appearing from such proceedings that said child is now ....years of age, and is a truant from lawful instruction and in proper condition to attend thereupon and that he is not regularly and lawfully engaged in any useful employment or service, and upon the consent of the persons in parental relation to said child:

It is therefore hereby determined and ordered that said child be forthwith committed to said Westchester Temporary Home for Destitute Children, White Plains, N. Y., and be there confined, maintained and instructed for a period not exceeding the remainder of the current school year, or until paroled by the proper authorities, as prescribed by law.

It is further ordered that the attendance officers of this.................. .... convey said child to said Westchester Temporary Home for Destitute Children, and the Superintendent of said Home is hereby required to receive and confine said child according to the terms of this order, the provisions of law and the local regulations applicable thereto.

Given by direction and pursuant to action of the Board of..................................... of the............ ....of.......................... ......New York, this ....day of......... 189

....

....

Should parents refuse their consent to such commitment, children must be proceeded against as disorderly persons, and a modification of the following blank, issued by the Rochester Board of Education, could be used:

[Blank No. 3.]

WARRANT OF COMMITMENT

STATE OF NEW YORK,
.... COUNTY,
.... OF .... } *ss.* ....COURT, In the Name of the People of the State of New York.

IN THE MATTER OF COMMITTING
....
A TRUANT FROM INSTRUCTION, TO THE PUBLIC TRUANT SCHOOL AT ROCHESTER. N. Y. } *Commitment After Trial*

To any Attendance Officer of said Town, or Peace Officer of said County:

It having been made to appear to me on oath that the boy................ .. .., who resides at No............... .. ..street, in the ....of......................... N. Y., is between 8 and 16 years of age; in proper physical and mental condition to attend upon lawful instruction as required by the Compulsory Education Acts, and is a truant therefrom;

And notice having been given to said truant and to the persons in parental relation, to comply with such law, and having failed therein, and a reasonable notice having further been personally served upon such truant and the persons in parental relation to him, that said matter would be considered by the PUBLIC SCHOOL AUTHORITIES on the. ....day of ....189 ;

And said case having been duly considered at said time by said public school authorities, and an opportunity given for all persons to be heard in relation thereto;

And it further appearing that said child is now.................years of age, and is a truant from lawful instruction and in proper condition to attend thereupon, and that he is not regularly and lawfully engaged in any useful employment or service, and the persons in parental relation to said child refusing to consent to his commitment to a proper institution;

And thereupon it was ordered that such conduct of the child be deemed disorderly conduct, and that he be proceeded against as a disorderly person.

And whereas, the undersigned magistrate at once caused said truant to be brought before him, charged on oath with being a disorderly person within the meaning and intent of the statute; and such proceedings were thereupon had before me, pursuant to the provisions of chapter 606 of the laws of 1896, and the general statutes of the State relating to disorderly persons: That I, the undersigned, did adjudge and determine that said truant,............... ...., was guilty of being a disorderly person as aforesaid, and he was thereupon on the...............day of..... .... .189 , convicted of said offense by me, and it was adjudged and determined that he should be committed to the Public Truant School at the

City of Rochester, New York, and be confined and maintained therein for a term not exceeding the remainder of the current school year, said offender having previously been required to attend upon lawful instruction in a public school in this State.

And, whereas, a certificate of such conviction has been accordingly filed in the office of the clerk of this county,

These are, therefore to command you, the said attendance officer or peace officer, forthwith to deliver him, the said............................, into the custody of the City Public Truant School in the City of Rochester, N. Y., pursuant to the provisions of chapter 606 of the laws of 1896, to be there maintained and instructed until discharged or paroled by the Superintendent of Public Schools of said city, not exceeding the remainder of the current school year, or discharged by law.

Said Truant School, and the Executive Officer of said school, are hereby required to receive and detain him according to the terms of this warrant, the provisions of law, and the local regulations applicable thereto.

Given under my hand at the said..............of................, New York, this............ day of............, 189 .

....

Justice..........of.........................*

County of.................. N. Y.

* Name of office in full.

The present labor law, revised by the legislature of 1897, chapter 415, laws of 1897, requires that any child over 14, and under 16, years of age, desiring to work in a factory, shall have attended school the entire school year, during the year previous to his arriving at the age of 14 years. Section 3 of the compulsory education law should be so amended so as not to conflict therewith, and I heartily concur in the recommendation of the committee on legislation of the state Council of Superintendents that the said section 3 be so amended that children between 12 and 14 years of age shall be required to attend as many days, annually, as are now required of children between 8 and 12 years of age.

Those having charge of institutions to which truant children are committed complain that their efforts at reformation are often unavailing, owing to the fact that all the children so committed must, as the law now reads, be released at the end of the current school year. There can be no question that the law should be amended so as to remedy this evil. The suggestion made by the legislative committee of the state Council of Superintendents that all children under 14 years of age be committed up to that age, and that when those 14 or over are committed, their term of commitment extend to the age of 16, meets my hearty approval.

So many pupils are unable to avail themselves of the best offered in our schools, owing to a lack of requisite text-books, I am constrained to refer once more to the subject of free textbooks. The children in many of our cities and larger villages are enjoying these unusual advantages, owing to local liberality. Why should not all children enjoy like privileges?

The need of proper clothing also interferes with regular attendance. I commend to the attention of others the following plan adopted by the board of supervisiors of Saratoga county.

At the annual meeting of said board, the sum of $200 is voted and placed to the credit of each supervisor to be used exclusively for supplying indigent children with needed text-books and clothing. If, at the close of the year, any balances remain in these funds they are transferred to other funds. The work has progresesd so satisfactorily under this plan that I cannot refrain from urging its adoption by the other counties of the state.

The need of state parental homes grows more and more urgent each year.

The commitment during the past year, of nearly nine hundred children to local truant schools and to private institutions, the equipment of many of which is deplorably inadequate, would seem to justify and demand some action by the state. Educators frequently speak of the trinity of educational influences, the home, the church and the school. To these must be added the education of the street, an influence which the state, in its efforts to develop better citizenship, may not wisely ignore.

It was my privilege to attend, as a delegate from New York, the eighth annual convention of "The Boys and Girls National Home and Employment Association," held in Indianapolis December 13-15. The principal subject under discussion at this meeting was the American Curfew Ordinance, which is now in successful operation in some four hundred cities and towns in the western and west central states.

The consensus of opinion was that such an ordinance in force in every city and large village of every state in the union, would very materially decrease the expense of maintaining child criminals in reform schools. This ordinance requires children at the ringing of a bell or the blowing of a whistle, at eight o'clock in winter and nine o'clock in summer, to immediately repair to their homes and not again appear upon the streets unaccompanied by parents or guardians.

Mrs. May Wright Sewall, one of the delegates, in answering the arguments of certain opponents to this ordinance, said in part as follows: "The question seems to resolve itself into this; not whether we should interfere with individual liberty, but at just what point the individual shall be taught his relation to the community and his obligation to it. Taught it at some time he must be. Shall he be taught it by the policeman who arrests the child in the gutter; by the jailer who watches him during the days of his detention; by the executioner who meets him on the scaffold, or shall he be taught it by the sound of a bell which summons him to his parents side and makes both child and parent feel that they are not living by themselves alone, but that they are a part of the community life and that they may do nothing which will menace the safety and the happiness of the communal life; that they may not clog its intelligence by their ignorance, that they may not diminish its virtue by the mingling of their vice?"

It is the business of educators to think seriously of the public morals and the public health as well as of the public education of the children of this great commonwealth, and I am persuaded that all of these ends will be conserved by the passage of the curfew law. Feeling certain that truancy would be diminished and the administration of the compulsory education law greatly aided, I express the hope that the curfew law may soon receive state and municipal sanction in this the empire state. And why not enact an ordinance that will take the children from the streets after dark? We have enacted other humane laws, why not this?

The following from a recent issue of a leading New York daily is to the point in question.

CRUELTY TO CHILDREN?

The other afternoon a number of happy children, in charge of wealthy parents and relatives, gathered to take part in a Christmas pantomine given for a charitable purpose.

But the Society for the Prevention of Cruelty to Children intervened and, despite the indignant protests of the parents, prohibited the little ones from appearing in the roles for which they had been prepared with so much pains. The children and their friends were sorely disappointed, but the society said, "There is the letter of the law; we shall enforce it."

Along Broadway and other thoroughfares these bitter, freezing nights—at all hours, even after midnight—the pedestrian, chilled although wrapped to the chin, encounters half clothed and shivering little tots of eight or nine years. With frost pinched faces, toes out of their shoes and fingers stiffened with cold, they stand on the wind swept corners trying to sell newspapers or begging from passersby.

If it is cruelty to wealthy children to dance and sing in presence of their parents in a comfortable hall some fine afternoon—cruelty which the society is impelled to prevent—how about these friendless and half frozen waifs in the midnight streets?

REPORT OF A. EDSON HALL

My inspections during the year include 311 public, 41 parochial and 19 private schools. A large number of these inspections were made in the rural districts with gratifying results. Many of the town attendance officers and trustees did not comprehend the importance of their work in connection with the proper enforcement of the law. I, however, found them anxious for suggestions and in general ready to carry out my directions.

With a few exceptions, local school authorities have understood the object and necessity of the inspection and have promptly furnished the required information.

After my inspections I required certain school authorities to make a special report to you, and these reports, without exception, showed an increase in registration and a decided improvement in regularity of attendance. One district school required to make this report, doubled its registration and attendance. The authorities of one of the union free schools had nine parents arrested, eight convicted and fined, and as a result of this twenty-two pupils were added to the registration list. The attendance during the remainder of the year was all that could be desired.

Town boards, as a rule, are in hearty sympathy with the law, and have exercised great care in appointing attendance officers.

Many of the pupils that are required to attend school are poorly clad and without books. If the different boards of supervisors in the state would adopt the plan of the board of supervisors of Saratoga county, this difficulty would be removed. Each supervisor in Saratoga county has $200, to be used to clothe and provide for destitute cases, and it has materially aided in the enforcement of the law.

I have experienced some difficulty in some localities in adjusting the relations between the private schools and the public schools. The teachers of most of these private schools cheerfully and promptly furnish the required information to public school authorities and are willing and glad to report to attendance officers any irregularity in attendance or truancy. The records of attendance in many of these schools are imperfect and therefore of little value. The work would be greatly facilitated if the private schools were required to use the same kind of registers as the public schools.

Proper excuses for absences and tardiness have caused considerable trouble. A few parents have thought that the teachers were overreaching their authority by demanding reasons for absences and tardinesses. I have found many strange and sometimes insulting excuses. Example—"If you wish my boy to attend school send him a pair of shoes." "Please excuse George for all absences that may occur this school year." "I kept my boys out yesterday to put to practical use some of the knowledge that they have received this year."

We are realizing some of the benefits derived from truant schools. The majority of the boys that were sent away last year are this year in their home schools, studious and regular in attendance. Their training in the truant school has been a material benefit to them.

I would recommend that private school authorities be required to make stated reports in full to public school authorities.

Second. That the state establish and maintain one or more schools for truants.

Saratoga Springs, N. Y., *December* 1, 1897.

REPORT OF WILLIAM J. BARR

As indicated by daily reports inspections have been made as follows:

(a) Cities	14
(b) Union free school districts	117
(c) Common school districts	90
(d) Parochial school	36

In addition to such inspections, 125 schools have been visited thus far during the present school year.

Supplementary to formal inspections, teachers' institutes and association meetings have been attended and addressed relative to the provisions of the compulsory law. Several meetings of attendance officers have also been held. These meetings afford an excellent opportunity for local authorities to more thoroughly inform themselves as to their powers and duties in regard to the enforcement of such law. This feature of the work has been so helpful that it is my intention to make it more prominent during the present school year.

Too much cannot be said in praise of the amendment making provision for town attendance officers. In consequence of such provision, rural schools have received more attention and registration, punctuality, interest and general efficiency have correspondingly increased. Some have contended that the law could not be enforced in the rural districts, and, indeed, that it was never intended to apply to such schools. In reply to the former proposition I have simply to say that "nothing succeeds like success," and that the law is already operative throughout such towns as have received due attention. In many instances this includes not only towns, but entire commissioner districts. The latter proposition is an old stumbling-block in a new path, and, as usual, the rural school is the intended victim. The adherents of this proposition favor progress except for rural schools. They favor the law, but oppose its execution in rural schools. Happily the law does apply to these schools, and fortunately its application insures increased supervision. Observation indicates that there is no class of schools in which proper supervision will more readily obtain beneficial results and deterioration more rapidly follow neglect than in the average rural school. These schools must receive attention or die. Indeed, they have been neglected so long that death has already visited many of them, although the champions of the antique claim that it is simply a case of suspended animation. The compulsory law will certainly help to vivify these schools.

Rochester has continued during the greater part of the year to maintain a school for the detention and instruction of male truants. Although conditions at times have not been ideal, it would seem unfair to condemn one city for even imperfectly providing for both resident and non-resident truants, and fail to call attention to the fact that, with few exceptions, other cities have failed to make adequate provision for even resident truants.

I desire to mention St. John's Protectory, West Seneca, as a Catholic institution of much merit. The influence of this school is not only deterrent but reformatory. On account of limited accommodations, however, the influence of the school is largely local, so far as truancy is concerned. It is evident that the best attainable general results will not be secured through the action of local authorities, and that the establishment by the state of one or more schools for habitual truants has become a positive necessity.

I again recommend that private and parochial schools be furnished with registers and blank reports. This will secure uniformity and accuracy and will greatly facilitate the work of public school authorities.

Batavia, N. Y.

EXHIBIT No. 19

SECOND BIENNIAL SCHOOL CENSUS

---

1. The Law and Its Enforcement
2. Specimen Blanks Used
3. Summary and Affidavit of Enumerators
4. Tabulation of Attendance
5. Tabulation of Special Statistics

SECOND BIENNIAL SCHOOL CENSUS

The Legislature of 1895 enacted a law providing that school census should be taken in October, 1895, and every second year thereafter in all the towns and villages of the state having a population of 10,000 and upwards. In accordance with this law the first biennial school census was taken in October, 1895, and the tabulated results were published in the report of this Department for 1896, and repeated in the report of 1897. The second biennial school census was taken in accordance with the provisions of this law in October, 1897, and the results appear in the tables which form this exhibit. The law in full is as follows:

CHAPTER 550 — LAWS OF 1895

An Act in Relation to a Biennial School Census

Became a law May 7, 1895, with the approval of the Governor. Passed, three-fifths being present.

The People of the State of New York, represented in Senate and Assembly, do enact as follows:

Section 1. It shall be the duty of the State Superintendent of Public Instruction, to take or cause to be taken, in the next ensuing October after the enactment of this law, and thereafter in every second year in the month of October, a school census, in all towns and cities of the State having a population of ten thousand or upwards, which shall ascertain the following facts, and he shall embody a summary of the same in his annual report, for the year in which said census is taken, viz.: the names and ages of all persons between the ages of four and sixteen; the number of persons in each town or city coming within the application of this law, between the ages of twelve and twenty-one years, that are unable to read or write; the number of persons over four and under sixteen years of age who do not attend school because they are obliged to work within school hours; the number of persons between four and sixteen years who are attending other than public schools; and such other facts as in his judgment may be of importance in securing the information needed to carry out the requirements of article nine, section one, of the State constitution, or for the improvement of the common school system.

§ 2. In taking this school census, the Superintendent of Public Instruction is authorized to determine the work to be done by all of the common school authorities and employes under his superintendency, and it shall be the duty of all such authorities and public officers having any civil authority in connection with the common school administration of the State or of said city or town, to aid said Superintendent in all proper ways in the discharge of his duties under this act.

§ 3. Whoever, being any parent or person having under his or her control, or in his or her charge, a child between the ages of four and sixteen years, refuses or withholds information in his or her possession, sought by said Superintendent or his representative for the purpose of a school census, or falsifies in regard to the same, shall be liable to and punished by fine not exceeding twenty dollars, or by imprisonment not exceeding thirty days.

§ 4. The money required for the purpose of carrying this act into effect shall be paid by the towns and cities respectively included in the provisions of the act, and shall be paid for the service rendered in taking the school census, on the certificate of the State Superintendent that such census has been satisfactorily taken.

§ 5. This act shall take effect immediately.

A careful estimate based on the national census of 1890 and the state enumeration of 1892, placed all the cities of the state above the ten thousand population limit, and also six of the incorporated villages. The census was accordingly ordered for these places.

In explanation of the foregoing law the following circulars were prepared and sent out by the Department:

BIENNIAL SCHOOL CENSUS

STATE OF NEW YORK

DEPARTMENT OF PUBLIC INSTRUCTION
SUPERINTENDENT'S OFFICE
ALBANY, *September* 1, 1897

To City and Village Superintendents:

Under the authority conferred upon me by chapter 550, laws of 1895, entitled "An act in relation to a biennial school census," I have caused blanks to be prepared which you will use in taking the said census. These blanks are bound in book form, each book furnishing space for twelve hundred names. These books will be ready for distribution about the 15th of September, and will be furnished you in such numbers as you shall require at cost. Please forward to the Department at once your estimate of the number you will need, and make a remittance sufficient to cover cost of same at 30 cents per book. The books will then be shipped to you express paid and receipt given.

By a ruling of this Department, the census will be taken in all cities and also in incorporated villages of the state having a population of 10,000 or upwards. Villages claiming a population of 10,000 will have their claims taken under consideration. The census will be taken between the 1st and 31st days of October, and a sufficient number of enumerators should be employed to faithfully and accurately perform the required work within the time specified. Enumerators should study carefully instructions given on the " Specimen page," inserted in the front of each book, and you are earnestly requested to see that these instructions are understood and followed.

Each enumerator should be required after completing the census of his district, to fill out the " summary " in the back of the book or books, and make affidavit thereto, and a careful and accurate summary of the school census of the entire city or village should be compiled therefrom, the compilation for cities being extended by wards, as indicated by the " compilation blanks," which will be sent you with the census books. This will necessitate the taking of the census by wards, and care should be exercised in assigning districts, that ward lines are observed. General qualifications requisite for appointment of enumerators are good penmanship, accurate spelling, good general information, sound judgment and discretion. In certain localities special qualifications may be essential. Each enumerator will be entitled to not less than three dollars for each eight hours of service. The appointment of these enumerators is made from this Department.

The expense incurred in taking this census will be a charge against the villages and cities respectively, as per section 4 of the law, a copy of which is herewith enclosed. The books in which the census is taken will be the property of the city or village, and should be filed for future reference. The " compilation blanks," will be sent in duplicate, and one copy must be returned to this office as soon as completed.

Yours respectfully,

CHARLES R. SKINNER,

State Superintendent.

STATE OF NEW YORK
DEPARTMENT OF PUBLIC INSTRUCTION
SUPERINTENDENT'S OFFICE
ALBANY, *October* 5, 1897

To City and Village Superintendents:

In accordance with the powers conferred upon me by chapter 550, laws of 1895, I have appointed enumerators for the biennial school census in your city. These enumerators are directed in their certificates of appointment to report to you for instructions, allotment of territory and census books.

You are hereby empowered to direct and supervise the taking of this census so that it shall be done in the most efficient and expeditious manner possible and at a reasonable cost. I have assumed that the method of appointing these enumerators will guarantee efficient service, and should any enumerator prove to be incompetent he will be removed at once.

You should keep a close supervision over the work and insist that it be done in a manner satisfactory to yourself and in a manner calculated to secure the information required by the law. Each enumerator should make a daily report of the amount of territory covered and the number of names enrolled, and payment for a day's work should be based on a reasonable minimum of work accomplished.

All bills for enumerator's wages and incidental expenses must be approved by you before they will be certified by me to the city authorities.

I desire that this shall be the most accurate and reliable census yet taken and for this purpose delegate to you under section 2, chapter 550, laws of 1895, the supervising and auditing powers above set forth.

Yours respectfully,
CHARLES R. SKINNER,
State Superintendent.

The method of taking the census was practically that adopted for the first biennial school census. Enumerators were appointed by the state Superintendent of public instruction and the census was taken in accordance with the rules and regulations prescribed by this Department. The routine and technical details of the work were intrusted to the city and village superintendents where the census was taken, with the exception of New York city where by special request a superintendent of the census was appointed. The experiment tried in some of the smaller cities and villages in

1895 of permitting teachers to take the census during afternoons and half-holidays was abandoned, as the results did not seem to warrant a continuance or extension of this plan. In the city of Brooklyn the census was taken by the police in the same manner as in 1895 for the reason that the chaotic condition of the financial affairs of that city, owing to its approaching incorporation in the city of Greater New York, rendered it impossible for any other plan to be followed. We still object to this plan of taking the census inasmuch as the work is apt to be done in a perfunctory manner and the results less likely to be correct and reliable than those obtained where careful supervision of the work is exercised by men appointed especially for the purpose and where enumerators trained in the work of this nature are appointed. In the city of New York, as it then existed, (boroughs of Manhattan and the Bronx) special enumerators were appointed with supervisors over each corps of enumerators, the assembly district being taken as the unit. The plan worked well and gave satisfaction to the school authorities. It is my opinion, however, that in the future a larger unit of division should be used and a supervisor appointed for each senatorial or congressional district.

To take the biennial school census every two years as required by law seems to force upon municipalities an unnecessary expense and I have recommended in an earlier part of this report that the legislature amend the law so that the census be taken every four years. If once carefully taken the records can be revised by the attendance officers of the city or village yearly and kept in good working order for a period of at least four years. Some legislation is also necessary to determine the question as to whether the census should be taken in towns or townships as the strict letter of the law would imply or in incorporated villages as was evidently the intent of the legislature. Acting under the discretionary power vested in this Department, the census has been taken only in the incorporated villages having a population above the required limit.

The following tables show concisely the amount of work done, the methods of doing it and the results:

Number of enumerators appointed for each city:

Albany	21
Amsterdam	7
Auburn	6
Binghamton	13
Buffalo	54
Cohoes	6
Corning	6

Dunkirk		4
Elmira		9
Gloversville		5
Hornellsville		7
Hudson		10
Ithaca		4
Jamestown		6
Johnstown		4
Kingston		9
Little Falls		4
Lockport		7
Middletown		3
Mount Vernon		10
Newburgh		4
New York:	supervisors	38
	enumerators	318
	interpreters	12
Niagara Falls		4
North Tonawanda		2
Ogdensburg		4
Olean		4
Oswego		6
Poughkeepsie		7
Rensselaer		4
Rochester		50
Rome		7
Schenectady		2
Syracuse		46
Troy		30
Utica		18
Watertown		6
Watervliet		9
Yonkers		10

VILLAGES

Cortland	4
Glens Falls	4
Peekskill	6
Lansingburgh	4
Port Jervis	1
Saratoga Springs	15

This is exclusively a school census.—This book must contain only the names of persons over 4 and under 18 years of age.

SPECIMEN PAGE

1	2	3	4	5	6	7	8	9	10	11	12	13	14	15	16
RESIDENCE			AGE				BETWEEN 4 AND 8		BETWEEN 8 AND 16					BETWEEN 12 AND 18	
Name of street or avenue	No.	NAMES OF PERSONS OVER 4 AND UNDER 18 YEARS ONLY	Years old last birthday	Month of birth	Sex	Race	Attending public school	Attending private school	Attending public school	Attending private school	At work during school hours	Absent for other lawful cause	Truant from school	Can not read or write English	Remarks or name of parent or guardian
Prince	73	James Martin Underhill	6	Dec	M	C	X								Grammar School No. 11.
East 10th	214	Mary Ann Brown	11	Mar.	F	E							X		
Genesee	28	Charlie Ling	15	June	M	M					X			X	Refused admission.
Madison avenue	139	Agnes Cornelia Bristol	9	May	F	C									Invalid, blind, deaf and dumb, etc.
Spring	74	John Bruce	10	Nov	M	A			X						Genesee Street School
Front	198	Mary O'Hara	14	July	F	C				X					St Joseph's Academy

INSTRUCTIONS FOR ENUMERATORS

1. In column 1 write the name of street or avenue.
2. In column 2 write the street number.
3. In column 3 write the name of person in full.
4. In column 4 write figures indicating age last birthday.
5. In column 5 write abbreviation for month in which birthday occurs. (This column need not be used unless desired.)
6. In column 6 use the letter M to indicate male and the letter F to indicate female
7. In column 7 use the letter C to indicate Caucasian or white, the letter E to indicate Ethiopian or negro, the letter M to indicate Mongolian or yellow, the letter A to indicate American or red. In case of mixed race explain under 18, as father M, mother C.
8. In column 8 mark with X in case the person is attending public school.
9. Indicate facts for columns 9, 10, 11, 12, 13, 14 and 15 in like manner.
10. Give facts for persons between 4 and 8 years only under columns 8 and 9.
11. Give facts for persons between 8 and 16 years only under columns 10, 11, 12, 13 and 14.
12. Give facts for persons between 12 and 18 years only under column 15.
13. In column 16 write any explanation, e. g., name of public school, name of private school, reason for absence from school, or truancy, blind, deaf and dumb, cripple, etc. If the superintendent of schools prefers, he may use this column for name of parent or guardian, but the record of defective children must also be included

2. SUMMARY AND AFFIDAVIT OF ENUMERATOR

[illegible]

SUMMARY

1. Number of persons over 4 and under 16 years of age:

   Male

   Female

   Total ....

2. Number of each race:

   Caucasian { Male / Female

   Ethiopian { Male / Female

   Mongolian { Male / Female

   American { Male / Female ....

3. Number attending public school:

   Between 4 and 8 { Male .... / Female ....

   Between 8 and 12 { Male .... / Female ....

   Between 12 and 14 { Male .... / Female ....

   Between 14 and 16 { Male .... / Female ....

4. Number attending other than public school:

   Between 4 and 8 { Male .... / Female ....

   Between 8 and 12 { Male .... / Female ....

   Between 12 and 14 { Male .... / Female ....

   Between 14 and 16 { Male .... / Female ....

5. Number at work during school hours, or absent for other lawful causes:

   Between 4 and 8 { Male .... / Female ....

   Between 8 and 12 { Male .... / Female ....

   Between 12 and 14 { Male .... / Female ....

   Between 14 and 16 { Male .... / Female ....

6. Number truant from school:

Between 8 and 12 { Male ....
{ Female ....

Between 12 and 14 { Male ....
{ Female ....

Between 14 and 16 { Male ....
{ Female ....

7. Number between 12 and 18 who can not read or write English:

Male ....

Female ....

8. Number of deaf and dumb:

Male ....

Female ....

9. Number of blind:

Male ....

Female ....

STATE OF NEW YORK, }
COUNTY OF........................ } ss.:

...., being duly sworn, deposes and says that he is the person named in the foregoing enumeration or school census, taken in the town of.................... in said county, as the enumerator, and who signed the summary therein; and that the fore going census and summary are correct and true to the best of his knowledge, information and belief.

Subscribed and sworn to before me, }
this .... day of..........., 189 . }

....

....
Enumerator

SECOND BIENNIAL SCHOOL CENSUS

4. Compilation Blank No. 1. — Attendance

Population by cities and villages, of the school children between 4 and 16 years of age, classified by ages and sexes, also statistics as to school attendance, public and private

CITIES	MALES															
	Between 4 and 8			Between 8 and 12				Between 12 and 14				Between 14 and 16				
	In school		Out	In school		Out		In school		Out		In school		Out		
	Public	Other	Not subject to compulsory law	Public	Other	Employed and other lawful causes	Truant	Public	Other	Employed and other lawful causes	Truant	Public	Other	Employed and other lawful causes	Truant	
Albany	1,653	449	713	2,305	731	28	38	1,090	315	12	71	680	149	548	11	
Amsterdam	282	107	346	478	178	3	3	217	95	2	2	121	46	119	15	
Auburn	372	150	265	600	249	3	6	265	152	5	2	211	51	126	19	
Binghamton	877	36	104	1,158	45	8	1	489	26	8	2	281	21	73	2	
Brooklyn	15,679	6,321	20,637	31,178	8,136	558	186	13,586	2,652	988	115	6,865	1,618	8,698	34	
Buffalo	6,474	2,479	2,251	8,872	4,327	124	131	8,810	1,454	116	109	2,533	698	1,481	214	
Cohoes	418	163	244	425	444	4	4	198	184	21	5	106	91	408	2	
Corning	271	1	142	338	2	4	4	153	......	6	3	116	1	43	4	
Dunkirk	171	61	236	232	175	1	1	136	77	2	4	77	29	66	1	
Elmira	428	124	213	921	177	18	4	474	83	7	3	376	49	14	......	
Geneva	......	......	......	......	......	......	......	......	......	......	......	......	......	......	......	
Gloversville	338	11	189	460	10	4	......	243	8	3	1	146	7	57	6	
Hornellsville	251	35	109	289	71	4	3	139	38	4	5	128	27	47	10	
Hudson	145	52	......	221	61	......	......	105	27	4	......	63	14	44	1	
Ithaca	137	54	136	259	64	4	1	140	40	2	......	130	25	20	......	
Jamestown	498	13	144	680	45	9	......	357	21	4	1	178	13	126	5	
Johnstown	198	4	14	272	......	......	......	135	......	4	4	85	......	81	......	
Kingston	434	85	205	718	168	8	12	329	71	12	4	219	28	94	5	
Little Falls	121	42	56	235	88	4	......	106	47	2	......	104	32	63	1	

Lockport	298	70	198	468	102	3	4	214	60	8	7	191	29	61	16
Long Island City	847	180	750	1,712	154	40	2	689	47	34	2	306	38	221	1
Middletown	221	30	192	378	37	2	6	179	24	2	1	123	17	36	7
Mt. Vernon	386	127	151	590	114	5	1	262	38	12	1	177	36	54	2
Newburgh	434	117	243	670	175	3	13	321	90	3	8	251	77	184	1
New York	24,864	11,593	1,510	48,332	13,068	1,217	1,193	20,979	5,008	549	754	9,453	2,936	7,217	789
Niagara Falls	364	80	158	481	122	8	14	202	47	3	4	139	33	99	10
North Tonawanda	257	46	180	287	88	......	6	140	35	1	5	79	5	29	......
Ogdensburg	253	86	54	416	167	4	16	182	71	7	7	140	36	42	23
Olean	176	28	102	245	60	3	1	129	35	2	......	102	18	29	2
Oswego	470	139	168	620	203	4	2	319	92	9	5	211	33	178	2
Poughkeepsie	516	61	92	586	74	15	1	276	34	21	2	168	36	143	4
Rensselaer	166	88	77	179	120	6	......	90	43	6	......	69	33	57	......
Rochester	3,508	1,253	863	3,554	1,895	30	40	1,456	784	159	126	872	347	1,047	89
Rome	201	110	93	255	73	......	......	170	20	6	3	105	11	58	......
Schenectady	312	145	446	547	288	13	6	282	68	9	6	178	20	98	20
Syracuse	2,089	353	560	3,028	512	29	26	1,412	180	47	18	1,016	82	403	115
Troy	725	465	556	1,098	686	27	16	637	614	20	23	348	179	251	33
Utica	947	298	726	1,310	492	11	14	605	248	29	36	852	98	315	69
Watertown	369	60	184	601	29	6	2	274	12	7	1	172	1	55	3
Watervliet	207	108	164	294	164	8	16	130	83	5	10	65	63	73	9
Yonkers	868	384	295	1,021	374	9	1	411	141	30	2	202	68	244	3
Total	67,170	25,908	33,885	116,343	33,988	2,212	1,774	51,357	12,759	2,201	1,352	27,188	7,095	23,068	1,478
VILLAGES															
Cortland	133	40	82	175	82	4	1	90	40	3	......	83	53	8	......
Glens Falls	251	118	116	188	160	1	3	130	78	3	5	136	154	56	1
Lansingburg	315	62	12	348	78	3	1	209	35	......	2	98	26	20	1
Port Jervis	238	22	80	307	84	2	......	160	10	1	2	142	2	30	......
Saratoga	317	2	33	344	3	6	......	172	1	1	......	110	4	30	1
Peekskill { No 7	98	19	49	173	11	......	1	81	3	3	......	50	4	33	......
Peekskill { No. 8	69	7	56	141	9	2	......	60	3	......	......	39	3	10	1
Total	1,411	265	428	1,675	377	18	6	902	170	11	9	658	246	187	4
Grand total	68,581	26,173	34,313	118,018	34,365	2,230	1,780	52,259	12,929	2,212	1,361	27,846	7,341	23,255	1,482

COMPILATION BLANK No. 1 — ATTENDANCE — (Continued)

Population by cities and villages of the school children between 4 and 16 years of age, classified by ages and sexes, also statistics as to school attendance, public and private

CITIES	FEMALES															TOTAL POPULATION OF MALES AND FEMALES BETWEEN 4 AND 16 YEARS OF AGE
	BETWEEN 4 AND 8			BETWEEN 8 AND 12				BETWEEN 12 AND 14				BETWEEN 14 AND 16				
	In school		Out	In school		Out		In school		Out		In school		Out		
	Public	Other	Not subject to compulsory law	Public	Other	Employed and other lawful causes	Truant	Public	Other	Employed and other lawful causes	Truant	Public	Other	Employed and other lawful causes	Truant	
Albany	1,602	454	826	2,305	764	22	28	1,054	384	17	100	627	222	507	18	17,668
[illegible]	274	82	314	488	199	7	3	234	82	7	7	109	34	129	21	4,004
Auburn	371	139	294	619	246	5	2	280	167	14	5	221	74	129	22	5,064
Binghamton	911	83	111	1,148	68	20	......	530	25	15	......	429	26	104	......	6,641
Brooklyn	14,799	6,188	21,584	30,869	8,121	624	147	12,941	2,698	1,301	71	7,683	1,970	8,680	27	234,988
Buffalo	6,221	2,273	2,159	8,674	4,226	115	131	3,642	1,822	232	107	2,731	781	1,408	171	69,802
Cohoes	429	167	241	429	432	8	7	204	148	46	15	102	77	398	5	5,415
[illegible]	232	2	132	330	5	2	......	165	3	6	......	127	7	86	......	2,135
Dunkirk	165	70	220	231	171	4	5	125	96	2	12	102	86	74	......	2,582
Elmira	462	144	201	913	177	10	1	406	116	3	3	89[illegible]	64	75	3	5,987
Geneva	......	......	......	......	......	......	......	......	......	......	......	......	......	......	......	......
[illegible]ville	350	12	189	557	18	11	5	241	11	5	5	176	5	72	1	3,136
Hornellsville	210	46	100	273	81	......	5	149	41	1	3	132	32	25	8	2,286
Hudson	148	30	......	192	61	......	......	127	25	......	1	66	19	24	1	1,431
Ithaca	121	50	124	279	63	2	......	150	33	9	......	153	20	10	......	2,026
Jamestown	491	27	137	656	51	4	1	299	20	3	4	208	16	133	......	4,189
Johnstown	206	3	18	328	......	2	1	187	......	2	4	110	1	30	......	1,584
Kingston	451	117	349	690	191	9	6	326	83	19	14	218	36	131	6	5,159
Little Falls	113	62	71	173	99	2	......	101	51	4	1	79	30	76	1	1,764
Lockport	298	67	207	429	148	4	4	226	67	2	4	231	31	42	9	3,452
Long Island City	841	118	715	1,090	197	35	......	686	85	62	......	250	44	277	......	9,988

Middletown	226	36	194	378	48	2	3	163	25	8	9	149	26	18	15	2,550
Mt. Vernon	413	140	172	530	120	5	2	252	53	8	1	183	40	50	......	3,925
Newburgh	443	119	243	668	164	2	9	303	79	6	6	218	71	190	5	5,116
New York	34,240	11,419	1,528	47,449	13,988	1,208	1,114	20,478	5,202	631	1,002	9,446	2,810	8,146	1,088	299,176
Niagara Falls	375	75	181	498	117	5	6	212	43	7	7	196	28	69	10	3,608
North Tonawanda	225	35	186	282	81	4	8	131	38	1	9	91	12	47	......	2,308
Ogdensburg	228	83	65	349	151	5	14	157	79	14	9	145	35	54	20	2,912
Olean	180	42	97	261	80	1	......	132	23	2	......	118	23	15	......	1,905
Oswego	461	112	197	611	212	1	1	236	27	6	1	252	63	153	1	4,899
Poughkeepsie	508	68	83	641	82	19	1	306	32	40	1	198	41	165	2	4,216
Rensselaer	145	96	71	184	112	6	......	74	66	8	......	73	29	62	......	1,662
Rochester	3,189	1,271	906	3,569	1,878	47	55	1,364	722	182	182	944	388	988	117	31,840
Rome	206	85	132	258	86	......	......	162	27	2	....	136	21	51	......	2,268
Schenectady	325	118	322	494	272	10	11	243	99	17	8	152	50	119	19	4,767
Syracuse	2,119	430	455	3,015	642	28	10	1,454	247	70	19	1,041	148	364	81	19,942
Troy	634	574	562	963	887	12	16	501	414	32	16	334	220	299	20	10,862
Utica	852	297	668	1,360	483	26	15	649	155	41	37	351	72	264	58	10,828
Watertown	343	43	213	601	16	6	2	306	8	6	2	247	5	46	......	3,620
Watervliet	182	126	187	318	177	7	8	134	87	15	8	47	64	59	10	2,828
Yonkers	841	384	299	895	425	10	1	374	133	40	1	241	74	232	......	7,953
Total	64,826	25,634	34,818	114,587	35,289	2,280	1,622	49,654	13,075	2,886	1,674	28,692	7,745	23,766	1,738	816,059
VILLAGES																
Cortland	112	42	86	78	84	4	1	94	41	1	2	87	57	7	1	1,591
Glens Falls	241	98	98	23	154	6	6	168	80	12	11	146	56	55	6	2,790
Lansingburg	311	57	10	38	69	3	1	152	40	2	3	92	15	22	11	2,366
Port Jervis	228	21	75	21	20	2	......	150	8	1	2	118	5	23	......	1,999
Saratoga	354	2	40	31	11	3	......	184	14	5	......	160	30	24	......	2,202
Peekskill { No. 7	73	25	79	53	19	2	......	91	7	......	......	42	2	30	......	1,049
Peekskill { No. 8	68	5	52	122	6	2	1	68	2	......	......	38	6	17	......	787
Total	1,387	245	440	1,756	363	22	9	907	192	21	18	690	171	178	18	12,784
Grand total	66,213	25,879	35,258	116,343	35,652	2,302	1,631	50,561	13,267	2,907	1,692	29,382	7,916	23,944	1,756	828,843

SECOND BIENNIAL SCHOOL CENSUS

5. COMPILATION BLANK No. 2. — NATIONALITY, DEFECTIVES, ENGLISH LANGUAGE

Giving by cities and villages the number of persons between 4 and 18 years of age of each sex and race, the number of deaf and dumb, the number of blind, and the number of persons between 12 and 18 years of age who can not read or write English

CITIES	Number of Caucasian or White			Number of Ethiopian or Negro			Number of Mongolian or Yellow			Number of American or Red		
			(1)			(2)			(3)			(4)
	Male	Female	Total	Male	Female	Total	Male	Female	Total	Male	Female	Total
Albany	9,745	9,986	19,731	61	75	136	......	......	......	......	......	......
Amsterdam	2,311	2,260	4,571	13	14	27	......	......	......	......	......	......
Auburn	2,833	2,966	5,799	42	42	84	......	......	......	......	......	......
Binghamton	3,505	3,730	7,235	53	43	96	......	......	......	......	......	......
Brooklyn	123,694	124,254	247,948	1,229	1,375	2,604	6	4	10	1	2	3
Buffalo	37,064	36,386	73,450	96	102	198	2	......	2	......	3	3
Cohoes	2,947	2,973	5,920	......	......	......	......	......	......	......	......	......
Corning	1,196	1,168	2,364	9	13	22	......	......	......	......	......	......
Dunkirk	1,443	1,489	2,932	......	......	......	......	......	......	......	......	......
Elmira	3,415	3,448	6,863	67	80	147	......	......	......	......	......	......
Geneva	......	......	......	......	......	......	......	......	......	......	......	......
Gloversville	1,692	1,859	3,551	17	18	35	......	1	1	......	......	......
Hornellsville	1,337	1,294	2,631	10	4	14	......	......	......	......	......	......
Hudson	1,103	1,084	2,187	38	37	75	......	......	......	......	......	......
Ithaca	1,130	1,212	2,342	15	25	40	......	......	......	......	......	......
Jamestown	2,378	2,380	4,758	8	15	23	......	......	......	......	......	......
Johnstown	880	975	1,855	13	11	24	......	......	......	......	......	......
Kingston	2,764	2,914	5,678	44	63	107	......	......	......	......	......	......
Little Falls	1,028	990	2,018	5	6	11	......	......	......	......	......	......
Lockport	1,970	2,003	3,973	18	25	43	......	......	......	......	......	......
Long Island City	5,458	5,435	10,893	23	32	55	......	......	......	......	......	......
Middletown	1,391	1,389	2,780	38	50	88	......	......	......	......	......	......

Mount Vernon	2,169	2,190	4,359	16	22	38	......	......	......	......	......	......
Newburg	2,713	2,655	5,368	37	57	94	......	......	......	......	......	......
New York	195,125	195,935	391,060	2,168	2,339	4,507	50	22	61	1	......	1
Niagara Falls	1,846	1,956	3,802	7	9	16	......	......	......	......	......	......
North Tonawanda	1,334	1,304	2,638	......	......	......	......	......	......	......	......	......
Ogdensburg	1,718	1,622	3,340	3	3	6	......	......	......	......	......	......
Olean	1,048	1,063	2,111	8	18	26	......	......	......	......	......	......
Oswego	2,700	2,683	5,383	5	4	9	......	......	......	......	......	......
Poughkeepsie	2,096	2,201	4,297	50	58	108	......	......	......	......	......	......
Rensselaer	1,001	993	1,994	2	4	6	......	......	......	......	......	......
Rochester	17,193	17,550	34,743	44	54	98	1	1	2	......	......	......
Rome	1,346	1,408	2,754	10	14	24	......	......	......	......	......	......
Schenectady	2,695	2,588	5,283	8	9	17	......	......	......	......	......	......
Syracuse	11,313	11,627	22,940	89	98	187	......	......	......	......	......	......
Troy	6,016	6,073	12,089	25	41	66	......	......	......	......	......	......
Utica	6,108	5,862	11,970	24	25	49	......	......	......	......	......	......
Watertown	1,991	2,106	4,097	14	7	21	......	......	......	......	......	......
Watervliet	1,565	1,584	3,149	3	4	7	......	......	......	......	......	......
Yonkers	4,236	4,162	8,398	47	49	96	4	......	4	......	......	......
Total	473,497	475,707	949,204	4,359	4,845	9,204	52	28	80	2	5	7
VILLAGES												
Cortland	915	936	1,851	4	0	4	......	......	......	......	......	......
Glens Falls	1,409	1,424	2,833	4	7	11	......	......	......	......	......	......
Lansingburg	1,256	1,238	2,494	7	5	12	......	......	......	......	......	......
Port Jervis	1,154	1,141	2,295	14	14	28	......	......	......	......	......	......
Saratoga Springs	1,105	1,250	2,355	42	66	108	2	......	2	......	1	1
Peekskill { No. 7	558	527	1,085	10	14	24	......	......	......	......	......	......
Peekskill { No. 8	397	380	777	17	15	32	......	......	......	......	......	......
Total	6,794	6,896	13,690	98	121	219	2	......	2	......	1	1
Grand total	480,291	482,603	962,894	4,457	4,966	9,423	54	28	82	2	6	8

COMPILATION BLANK No. 2.— NATIONALITY, DEFECTIVES, ENGLISH LANGUAGE—(Continued)

Giving by cities and villages the number of persons between 4 and 18 years of age of each sex and race, the number of deaf and dumb, the number of blind, and the number of persons between 12 and 18 years of age who can not read or write English.

CITIES	Number of Deaf and Dumb: Male	Number of Deaf and Dumb: Female	Number of Deaf and Dumb: Total	Number of Blind: Male	Number of Blind: Female	Number of Blind: Total	Number Between 12 and 18 Years Who Cannot Read or Write English: Male	Number Between 12 and 18 Years Who Cannot Read or Write English: Female	Number Between 12 and 18 Years Who Cannot Read or Write English: Total	Total Population Between 4 and 18 Years of Age (Sum of Cols. 1, 2, 3 and 4): Male	Total Population Between 4 and 18 Years of Age (Sum of Cols. 1, 2, 3 and 4): Female	Total Population Between 4 and 18 Years of Age (Sum of Cols. 1, 2, 3 and 4): Total
Albany	7	3	10	3	.....	3	3	[illegible]	[illegible]	[illegible]	10,[illegible]	[illegible]
Amsterdam	......	......	......	......	......	......	[illegible]	[illegible]	[illegible]	[illegible]	[illegible]	[illegible]
Auburn	2	2	4	......	......	......	[illegible]	....	[illegible]	[illegible]	[illegible]	[illegible]
Binghamton	1	2	3	2	......	2	[illegible]	....	[illegible]	[illegible]	[illegible]	[illegible]
Brooklyn	48	95	143	[illegible]	[illegible]	[illegible]	104	[illegible]	[illegible]	[illegible]	[illegible]	[illegible]
Buffalo	[illegible]	66	155	5	2	7	170	[illegible]	[illegible]	[illegible]	[illegible]	[illegible]
Cohoes	1	......	1	2	.....	2	3	....	3	[illegible]	[illegible]	[illegible]
Corning	1	2	3	......	......	......	[illegible]	1	4	1,[illegible]	1,[illegible]	[illegible]
Dunkirk	1	2	3	......	......	......	11	7	18	1,44[illegible]	1,[illegible]	[illegible]
Elmira	1	......	1	1	......	1	....	....	....	[illegible]	[illegible]	[illegible]
Geneva	......	......	......	......	......	......	....	....	....	......	......	......
Gloversville	......	1	1				1	1	[illegible]	1,7[illegible]	1,[illegible]	[illegible]
Hornellsville	......	2	2				[illegible]	[illegible]	10	1,[illegible]47	1,[illegible]	[illegible]
Hudson	......	......	......				1	....	1	1,141	1,[illegible]	[illegible]
Ithaca	2	1	3				....	....	....	1,1[illegible]	1,[illegible]	[illegible]
Jamestown	2	1	3				[illegible]	7	10	[illegible]	[illegible]	[illegible]
Johnstown	......	......	......			1	....	....	....	[illegible]	[illegible]	1,[illegible]
Kingston	2	2	4			[illegible]	[illegible]	[illegible]	[illegible]	[illegible]	[illegible]	[illegible]
Little Falls	2	......	2				....	....	....	1,[illegible]	[illegible]	[illegible]
Lockport	1	2	3				....	....	....	1,[illegible]	[illegible]	4,018
Long Island City	......	1	1	[illegible]	1	3	4	[illegible]	[illegible]	[illegible]	[illegible],467	10,[illegible]
Middletown	2	1	3		1	1	[illegible]	[illegible]	[illegible]	1,4[illegible]	1,4[illegible]	[illegible]
Mount Vernon	4	2	6				[illegible]	....	[illegible]	[illegible]	[illegible]	4,[illegible]
Newburgh	1	2	3				[illegible]	[illegible]	[illegible]	[illegible],780	[illegible],718	[illegible]
New York	501	208	709	26	16	42	1,158	1,608	[illegible],760	197,[illegible]	[illegible]	[illegible]

Niagara Falls	......	2	2	1	......	1	4	2	6	1,853	1,965	3,818
North Tonawanda	2	......	2	1	1	2	....	....	....	1,334	1,304	2,638
Ogdensburg	......	1	1	1	......	1	2	6	8	1,721	1,625	3,346
Olean	......	3	3	......	......	......	1	....	1	1,056	1,081	2,137
Oswego	2	2	4	......	2	2	5	2	7	2,705	2,687	5,392
Poughkeepsie	......	1	1	......	1	1	5	2	7	2,146	2,259	4,405
Rensselaer	2	2	4	......	......	......	3	....	3	1,003	997	2,000
Rochester	72	79	151	2	1	3	7	3	10	17,238	17,605	34,843
Rome	......	......	......	......	......	......	1	....	1	1,356	1,422	2,778
Schenectady	1	1	2	......	......	......	7	6	13	2,703	2,597	5,300
Syracuse	6	6	12	......	......	......	8	11	19	11,402	11,725	23,127
Troy	1	1	2	2	1	3	3	2	5	6,041	6,114	12,155
Utica	5	3	8	1	1	2	17	7	24	6,132	5,887	12,019
Watertown	......	......	......	......	......	......	1	....	1	2,005	2,113	4,118
Watervliet	1	1	2	......	......	......	12	8	20	1,563	1,588	3,156
Yonkers	......	1	1	1	......	1	3	6	9	4,287	4,211	8,498
Total	760	498	1,258	75	58	133	1,678	2,110	3,788	477,910	480,585	958,495
VILLAGES												
Cortland	1	......	1	......	......	......	3	....	3	919	936	1,855
Glens Falls	......	......	......	......	......	......	....	1	1	1,413	1,431	2,844
Lansingburg	1	......	1	......	......	......	....	....	....	1,268	1,248	2,506
Port Jervis	2	......	2	......	......	......	1	....	1	1,168	1,155	2,323
Saratoga Springs	2	1	3	......	......	......	....	....	....	1,151	1,319	2,470
Peekskill No. 7	......	......	......	......	......	......	....	....	....	568	541	1,109
Peekskill No. 8	......	......	......	......	......	......	....	....	....	414	395	809
Total	6	1	7	......	......	......	4	1	5	6,896	7,020	13,916
Grand total	766	499	1,265	75	58	133	1,682	2,111	3,793	484,806	487,605	972,411

EXHIBIT No. 20

ARBOR DAY

1. Law Establishing Arbor Day
2. State Superintendent's Letter to School Officers and Teachers
3. State Superintendent's Letter to the Children
4. Arbor Day in Spain
5. How to Plant Trees
6. Suggestions for Programs
7. Specimen Programs
8. Selections Appropriate for Arbor Day Programs

It is no exagerated praise to call a tree the grandest and most beautiful of all the productions of the earth.-

GILPIN, *Forest Scenery*.

STATE OF NEW YORK

DEPARTMENT OF PUBLIC INSTRUCTION

ARBOR DAY ANNUAL

MAY 7, 1897

Let arbor day be devoted to the study of the best plans for beautifying school grounds, for the adornment of school buildings, the planting of trees and the proper care of those already planted; a study of birds and flowers and their influence upon life.

A tree in full leaf is a nobler object than a king in his coronation robes. -Bacon.

Chapter 196, Laws of 1888

AN ACT TO ENCOURAGE ARBORICULTURE

Approved April 30, 1888.

The People of the State of New York, represented in Senate and Assembly, do enact as follows:

Section 1. The Friday following the first day of May in each year shall hereafter be known throughout this state as Arbor day.

§ 2. It shall be the duty of the authorities of every public school in this state, to assemble the scholars in their charge on that day in the school building, or elsewhere, as they may deem proper, and to provide for and conduct, under the general supervision of the city superintendent or the school commissioner, or other chief officers having the general oversight of the public schools in each city or district, such exercises as shall tend to encourage the planting, protection and preservation of trees and shrubs, and an acquaintance with the best methods to be adopted to accomplish such results.

§ 3. The State Superintendent of Public Instruction shall have power to prescribe from time to time, in writing, a course of exercises and instruction in the subject hereinbefore mentioned, which shall be adopted and observed by the public school authorities on Arbor day, and upon receipt of copies of such course, sufficient in number to supply all the schools under their supervision, the school commissioner or city superintendent aforesaid, shall promptly provide each of the schools under his or their charge with a copy, and cause it to be adopted and observed.

§ 4. This act shall take effect immediately.

In those vernal seasons of the year, when the air is calm and pleasant, it were an injury and sullenness against Nature not to go out and see her riches, and partake in her rejoicing with heaven and earth.—Milton.

Note.—Remember Memorial Day, May 30; and Flag Day, June 14.

"There is no way in which we can more surely cultivate a love of home, native town, State, and country, than by a proper observance of arbor day."

SUGAR OR ROCK MAPLE—STATE TREE.

"The Maple is supple, and lithe, and strong,
And claimeth our love anew,
When days are listless, and quiet, and long,
And the world is fair to view.
And later—as beauties and graces unfold—
A monarch right royally drest,
With streamers aflame and pennons of gold,
It seemeth of all the best."

"The teacher in charge of a school who does not in any way observe arbor day should seek a new field of employment."

SUPERINTENDENT'S LETTER

To School Officers and Teachers:

The proper observance of arbor day does not consist merely in the occupation of a few hours once in the year with a certain round of exercises connected with the planting of trees or shrubs. These should be but the outcome of an interest in trees, shrubs and flowering plants fostered by appropriate readings on the part of the pupils in the schoolroom and familiar talks by the teacher, both in the schoolroom and by the wayside, reaching through the year. So the day should connect itself more or less with the whole course of school life and be, so to speak, but the blossoming out of the studies and observations of many months.

The day will be a fit time, therefore, for reviewing the past weeks and months and for laying plans for the future. It will conduce much to the interest of the day and of successive arbor days if the teacher or superintendent has a blank-book in which is recorded a detailed description of what is done both on the anniversary day itself and at intermediate times—the exercises in the schoolroom and the course of proceedings out of doors, the marchings, the music, the speeches, the trees or shrubs planted and by whom planted, the number of people in attendance, persons to whom trees were dedicated and everything of importance connected with the observance of the day or the subject of trees and tree planting, such as observations made in regard to the growth and condition of trees that have been planted. This record should be referred to and portions of it read from year to year as a part of the arbor day exercises, and after a few years it will become a history which will be cherished more and more with the lapse of time.

I would suggest also that as we have been improving many of our school grounds, and in part as the result of the premiums which have been offered for the purpose, we should give more attention than we have done to the interior appearance and furnishing of our school buildings. Estimated by the work done in it—the development of mind and character—the schoolhouse should be second in beauty and interior equipment to no building in town or village. Why should our boys and girls pass the best hours of the day and the most impressible years of life in rooms with bare walls and altogether unattractive if not uncomfortable furnishings? Why should there be so little in them to please the eye or cultivate the taste? Why should they contrast so strongly as they do with their own homes and other buildings? Habits of neatness, order and politeness should be taught in the school place [illegible] and the love of the beautiful and the good be fostered [illegible]. Pictures may be [illegible] copies of the finest specimens of architecture and the most beautiful works of sculpture are now so cheap that with [illegible] any village school room may be made most attractive and instructive and a place on which the pupils will look back in their mature years with pleasant memories. And if school boards are not ready to make the necessary appropriations for the purpose the pupils might be encouraged by the teachers to take the matter in hand. They might get up dramatic or other entertainments the proceeds of which could be devoted to the better furnishing of the schoolrooms. Friendly rivalry between the different schools of a town or village might be stimulated for the purpose, and if only a little should seem to be accomplished at any one time, in a few years a most desirable change for the better might be wrought in many of our places of instruction.

CHARLES R. SKINNER,
State Superintendent.

SUPERINTENDENT'S LETTER TO THE CHILDREN OF THE PUBLIC SCHOOLS

Dear Boys and Girls of the Empire State:

This springtime of 1897 marks the twenty-fifth anniversary of *arbor day*. The birds are welcoming with their sweet, cheery songs, for they love the trees and make their homes in them, and all lovers of trees ought to rejoice now because the trees are putting on their beautiful dress of green and decking themselves with many colored blossoms for our delight and preparing to give us in due season their various fruits.

Let us make this the best arbor day we have had. Let us grasp more fully than we have done before, all that the day means and how much of good there is in it for us and for many others. How the observance of the day has spread during the twenty-five years since it began. From far away Nebraska it has been adopted by state after state until now it is established throughout our great country and millions of school children engage in its pleasant celebration every year and many millions of trees are planted annually by their hands.

But not only has the custom of observing arbor day spread throughout this great land of ours, but it has been adopted also in other lands. It is such a beautiful observance that it has passed across the oceans and is now established in several European countries and in Japan. So it may be said to have gone around the globe in a few years. I can not think of another institution or observance which has spread so far in so short a time. And this has been done without any urgency or compulsion. It shows that it must be a good thing in itself, otherwise it would not have been adopted so speedily and so widely. It has been welcomed also by all classes of people. Last year it was adopted by Spain and with royal sanction and royal pageantry.

Let us think now how much good the day has already done. To how many schools in our land has it brought a pleasant holiday. How many companies of children have found it a delight and a lesson in well-doing and care for the welfare of others. To how many has it made the world around them a brighter and better world. How many beautiful trees has it caused to be planted in school yards and along the borders of streets and around dwellings. How many places it has caused to be sheltered from stormy winds. How much of comfort and pleasantness has it brought to many homes.

And now the lesson of all this is, and I would have you take it to heart to-day, the importance of little things, as we call them. I say, as we call them, for we often make a mistake in speaking of great things and little things. The little things are sometimes greater than those that we consider great things. Arbor day was a little thing seemingly when it was started far away in Nebraska, but now it is a great thing, spread over the whole country, and no one can measure its power for good. So the tree which you plant in the school yard, or on the roadside to-day may be small, hardly more than a twig, perhaps, but years hence it may be a great landmark and the admiration of all who see it. And so a good deed or a good thought may seem a little thing at the time but it may make one famous and be a benefit to thousands. Arbor day was only the kind thought of one man at the beginning, but has grown as the tree grows, and overspread the country and every year blossoms out in the beauty of these almost innumerable gatherings of teachers and scholars, and gladdens their hearts and encourages them to be good and to do good. Let us welcome the lesson and thank the Heavenly Father for giving it to us. As we plant the trees to-day, so we may plant trees of goodness, kindness and love in each other's hearts to grow there from year to year throughout our lives and thus have the blessing which comes from doing good.

CHARLES R. SKINNER,
State Superintendent.

ARBOR DAY IN SPAIN

It will interest the school children to know that arbor day has not only been established in Spain, but established by a king who is a boy not older than the boys of average age in our schools, and that a great company of the pupils of the schools were associated with him in its establishment.

On the 26th day of March of last year the Queen Regent of Spain—the king's mother—and her court, went with the young King Alphonso to some grounds about two miles from Madrid. There the king, with his own hands, planted with much ceremony a young pine tree. Flags were flying and cannon boomed at the time. After the king had planted his tree 2,000 children, who had been chosen from the public schools of the city as his associates, each planted a tree. All expenses of the occasion were paid by the city and each child received a medal inscribed thus:

FIRST FETE OF THE TREE

INSTITUTED IN THE REIGN

OF

ALPHONSO XIII.

Spain, 1896

Similar arbor days it is expected will be held yearly in all parts of Spain, and the plantations enlarged by the successive plantings. The children are to be taken periodically by their schoolmasters to inspect their plantations and see how their trees are growing, and they will be taught to encourage tree planting wherever and however it may be in their power to do so.

HOW TO PLANT TREES

Having prepared the ground, let the trees be taken up carefully on the day preceding arbor day, so that there may be no haste and no delay then. Be careful to break as few of the small roots as possible in taking up the trees, and if any are broken, cut the ends off smoothly with a knife and cut off a corresponding amount of branches, so that roots and branches may be equalized. Keep the roots from exposure to the sun or wind after being taken up, by wrapping them with mats or blankets while transporting them and by "heeling them in," as it is called, until the time of planting. Then on arbor day, removing the finely prepared earth where the trees are to stand, place the trees at proper depth in the holes and slowly and carefully fill in the earth around and among the roots, pressing the soil with the hands into all the interstices and finally bringing roots and soil into as close contact as possible by a firm pressure of the feet. If the soil is in a moist condition and is pressed closely about the roots no watering will be needed in the process of planting, but if dry a little water may be dashed among the roots when the holes are nearly filled with earth. When completely filled the ground should be smoothed over with a rake and covered with a coarse litter several inches deep and extending as far as the spread of the roots. This will prevent the evaporation of the moisture of the soil and the need of subsequent watering unless in very dry seasons.

Remember that what is worth doing is worth doing well, and that one tree well planted is worth many carelessly planted.

SUGGESTIONS

Programs

Full instructions regarding preparation of programs and planting of trees have been given in previous annuals. The following much-needed suggestions can not be too often repeated:

1. Make programs long enough to admit of pleasurable variety; but not too long lest interest in the exercises may flag.

2. Have as many children as possible from the different grades take part in the exercises.

3. Have a place in the program for an essay or talk on the beauty, utility and peculiar habits of the trees to be planted.

4. Interest the patrons of the schools in attending the arbor day exercises, and encourage the children to plant trees, vines or shrubs at their homes.

5. Have short talks by some of the school officers or other prominent residents of the district.

6. Give especial attention to the committing to memory by the children of selections on nature and patriotism.

7. Have children learn for that day some one of our national songs.

Tree Planting

8. Do not plant trees too near the school building.

9. Have holes for trees made large and partly filled with a good loam several days before arbor day.

10. When planting trees, use great care to see that none of the roots are doubled up.

11. When placing soil over the roots, see that it is properly packed.

12. Appoint a committee of pupils to take charge of trees planted and to see that they are watered and cared for during the year.

SUGGESTIVE PROGRAMS

These programs may be freely changed to meet differing conditions.

Program First

1. Music—Arbor day anthem—tune, "America."
2. Reading of arbor day law.
3. Superintendent's letter.
4. History of arbor day. Essay.
5. Music, patriotic.
6. Short recitations on trees, flowers and birds.
7. The trees our best friends. Essay.
8. Short talks by teacher, friends and parents.
9. Recitation—"Seed-time and Harvest."
10. Life of General Grant, and his recent entombment. Essay.
11. Music, patriotic—"My Country, 'tis of thee." Smith "America."
12. Planting of the trees —
    Recitation by three pupils—"What do we plant when we plant the tree?" Henry Abbey.
    Marching song.
    Dedication of trees and some account of the persons to whom they are dedicated.
    Planting with care, and brief recitation at planting of each tree.
13. Final song and dismissal.

Program Second

1. Reading of arbor day law.
2. Song—"My Country, 'tis of thee." Tune, "America."
3. Reading of Superintendent's letter to the children.
4. Recitation—"The American Flag." J. Rodman Drake.
5. The patriotism of arbor day. Essay.
6. How the trees chose their king—Judges, 9, 8-15. Recitation in parts by several pupils.
7. History and meaning of arbor day. Essay.
8. Bryant's "Forest Hymn" (part). Recitation.
9. Music —"Red, White and Blue."
10. Patriotic — "Flag of the Heroes who left us." Holmes Recitation.
11. Reading of letters and brief addresses.

12. Planting.
    Marching song.
    Short address as each tree is planted, about the tree or the person to whom it is dedicated, or a quotation from the writings of the person or some well-known author. The planting to be carefully done by several pupils designated for the purpose beforehand.
13. Final — "Star-Spangled Banner."

Program Third

1. Reading arbor day law.
2. Music — National song "America."
3. Recitation — "All Things Beautiful."
4. Letter of the Superintendent.
5. History of arbor day and what the day stands for.
6. Recitation — "Woodman, Spare that Tree."
7. Music — "Red, White and Blue."
8. What the trees do for the birds. Essay.
9. Recitation — "This is the Forest Primeval." Longfellow.
10. "Johnny Appleseed." Essay.
11. The tree I love best. Short addresses by six pupils.
12. Music.
13. Short talks by teacher and visitors.
14. Marching song and drill with flags.
15. Dismissal.

THE STATE FLOWER

SELECTIONS APPROPRIATE FOR ARBOR DAY PROGRAMS

Nature's Tree-Planters

Squirrels. The squirrels eat many nuts but carry a portion to some distance in every direction, where they plant one or two in a place. It may be the thought of the squirrel to return at

WHAT DO WE PLANT?

(To be read by three pupils)

First—

What do we plant when we plant the tree?
We plant the ship which will cross the sea.
We plant the mast to carry the sails;
We plant the planks to withstand the gales—
The keel, the keelson and beam and knee;
We plant the ship when we plant the tree.

Second—

What do we plant when we plant the tree?
We plant the houses for you and me.
We plant the rafters, the shingles, the floors,
We plant the studding, the lath, the doors,
The beams and siding, all parts that be;
We plant the house when we plant the tree.

Third—

What do we plant when we plant the tree?
A thousand things that we daily see:
We plant the spire that out-towers the crag,
We plant the staff for our country's flag,
We plant the shade, from the hot sun free;
We plant all these when we plant the tree.

—Henry Abbey.

INFLUENCE OF NATURE

Therefore am I still
A lover of the meadows and the woods
And mountains, and of all that we behold
From this green earth; of all the mighty world
Of eye and ear, both what they half create
And what perceive; well pleased to recognize
In nature and the language of the sense,
The anchor of my purest thoughts, the nurse,
The guide, the guardian of my heart and soul,
Of all my moral being.

—Wordsworth.

ALL THINGS BEAUTIFUL

All things bright and beautiful,
All creatures great and small,
All things wise and wonderful—
The Lord God made them all.

Each little flower that opens,
Each little bird that sings,
He made their glowing colors
He made their tiny wings.

The purple-headed mountain,
The river, running by,
The morning, and the sunset
That lighteth up the sky.

The tall trees in the greenwood,
The pleasant summer sun,
The ripe fruits in the garden—
He made them, every one.

He gave us eyes to see them,
And lips that we might tell
How great is God Almighty,
Who hath made all things well.

—C. F. Alexander.

LEAF-TONGUES OF THE FOREST

The leaf-tongues of the forest, the flower-lips of the sod,
The happy birds that hymn their rapture in the ear of God,
The summer wind that bringeth music over land and sea,
Have each a voice that singeth this sweet song of songs to me:
"This world is full of beauty, like other worlds above,
And if we did our duty, it might be full of love."

—Gerald Massey.

A little of thy steadfastness,
Rounded with leafy gracefulness,
Old oak, give me—
That the world's blast may round me blow,
And I yield gently to and fro.
While my stout-hearted trunk below,
And firm-set roots unshaken be.

—Lowell.

If thou art worn and hard beset
With sorrows, that thou wouldst forget,
If thou wouldst read a lesson, that will keep
Thy heart from fainting and thy soul from sleep,
Go to the woods and hills! No tears
Dim the sweet look that Nature wears.

—Longfellow.

Summer or winter, day or night,
The woods are an ever new delight,
They give us peace, and they make us strong,
Such wonderful balms to them belong;
So, living or dying, I'll take my ease
Under the trees, under the trees.

—Stoddard.

FOREST HYMN

The groves were God's first temples. Ere man learned
To hew the shaft, and lay the architrave,
And spread the roof above them—ere he framed
The lofty vault, to gather and roll back
The sound of anthems; in the darkling wood,
Amid the cool and silence, he knelt down,
And offered to the Mightiest solemn thanks
And supplication. For his simple heart
Might not resist the sacred influences
Which, from the stilly twilight of the place,
And from the gray old trunks that high in Heaven
Mingled their mossy boughs, and from the sound
Of the invisible breath that swayed at once
All their green tops, stole over him, and bowed
His spirit with the thought of boundless power
And inaccessible majesty. Ah, why
Should we, in the world's riper years, neglect
God's ancient sanctuaries, and adore
Only among the crowd, and under roofs
That our frail hands have raised? Let me, at least,
Here, in the shadow of this aged wood,
Offer one hymn—thrice happy, if it find
Acceptance in His ear.

—Bryant.

The World a Fairyland

The world we live in is a fairyland of exquisite beauty; o very existence is a miracle in itself, and yet few of us enj as we might, and none as yet appreciate fully the beauties a wonders which surround us. The greatest traveler cannot ho even in a long life to visit more than a very small part of our eart and even of that which is under our very eyes how little we se

What we do see depends mainly on what we look for. When turn our eyes to the sky, it is in most cases merely to see wheth it is likely to rain. In the same field the farmer will notice t crop, the geologists the fossils, botanists the flowers, artists t coloring, sportsmen the cover for game. Though we may look at the same things, it does not at all follow that we shou see them.

It is good, as Keble says, "to have our thoughts lift up to th world where all is beautiful and glorious,"—but it is well realize also how much of this world is beautiful.—Sir John Lu bock.

A Plea for the Birds

One of the most pleasing ideas connected with this arbor d work of planting trees is that we are thereby making homes f our precious singing birds. We are now close to the season building nests; may we not earnestly hope that parents eve where, and especially teachers in the public schools will give this matter of protecting the birds the most earnest and thoug ful attention. Let your voices and your positive authority be hea in this most humane work. I am also constrained to belie that hundreds of boys and girls reared in well-ordered hom who read these pages, will plead earnestly with those who dulge in the degrading, criminal practice of despoiling the ne of birds. The beautiful and graceful notes of the mother rob whose nest has been thus secured from desecration, will ling in memory for a whole lifetime.—Charles Aldrich.

The man who builds does a work which begins to decay soon as he has done, but the work of the man who plants tr grows better and better, year after year, for generations.

"Trees, plants and flowers talk to us grandly, lovingly, bea tifully. To learn their language we must give attentive ea eyes and minds; then their speech will minister continually our happiness."

A student who has learned to observe and describe so sim a matter as the form of a leaf has gained a power which w be of lifetime value, whatever may be his sphere of professio employment.—W. N. Rice.

Grass

"Next in importance to the divine profusion of water, light and air, those three physical facts which render existence possible, may be reckoned the universal beneficence of grass. Lying in the sunshine among the buttercups and dandelions of May, scarcely higher in intelligence than those minute tenants of that mimic wilderness, our earliest recollections are of grass, and when the fitful fever is ended, and the foolish wrangle of the market and the forum is closed, grass heals over the scar which our descent into the bosom of the earth has made, and the carpet of the infant becomes the blanket of the dead.

"Grass is the forgiveness of Nature — her constant benediction. Fields trampled with battle, saturated with blood, torn with the ruts of cannon, grow green again with grass, and carnage is forgotten. Streets abandoned by traffic become grass-grown, like rural lanes, and are obliterated. Forests decay, harvests perish, flowers vanish, but grass is immortal. Beleaguered by the sullen hosts of winter, it withdraws into the impregnable fortress of its subterranean vitality and emerges upon the solicitation of spring. It evades the solitude of deserts, climbs the inaccessible slopes and pinnacles of mountains, and modifies the history, character and destiny of nations. Unobtrusive and patient, it has immortal vigor and aggression. Banished from the thoroughfare and field it abides its time to return, and when vigilance is relaxed or the dynasty has perished, it silently resumes the throne from which it has been expelled, but which it never abdicates. It bears no blazonry of bloom to charm the senses with fragrance or splendor, but its homely hue is more enchanting than the lily or the rose. It yields no fruit in earth or air, yet should its harvest fail for a single year famine would depopulate the world."—John J. Ingalls.

The effect of nature alone is purifying; and its thousand evidences of wisdom are too eloquent of their Maker not to act as a continual lesson.—N. P. Willis.

The great demand is, that the school of the times shall blend nature in books with nature as it is in life.—A. E. Winship.

UNION AND LIBERTY

First voice.

Flag of the heroes who left us their glory,
  Borne through our battlefields' thunder and flame,
Blazoned in song and illumined in story,
  Wave o'er us all who inherit their fame!

Second voice.

Light of our firmament, guide of our nation,
  Pride of her children, and honored afar,
Let the wide beams of thy full constellation
  Scatter each cloud that would darken a star.

Third voice.

Empire unsceptred! what foe shall assail thee,
Bearing the standard of Liberty's van?
Think not the God of thy fathers shall fail thee,
Striving with men for the birthright of man!

Fourth voice.

Yet, if by madness and treachery blighted,
Dawns the dark hour when the sword thou must draw,
Then, with the arms of thy millions united,
Smite the bold traitors to Freedom and Law!

All.

Up with our banner bright,
Sprinkled with starry light,
Spread its fair emblems from mountain to shore;
While through the sounding sky,
Loud rings the Nation's cry,—
Union and Liberty!—one evermore!

—Oliver Wendell Holmes.

General Grant

Washington secured freedom of colonies and founded a new nation. Lincoln was the prophet who warned the people of the evils that were undermining our free government, and the statesman who was called to the leadership in the work of their extirpation. Grant was the soldier who by victory in the field gave vitality and force to the policies and philanthropic measures which Lincoln defined in his cabinet for the regeneration and security of the Republic. * * * As long, therefore, as the American Union shall abide with its blessings of law and liberty, Grant's name shall be remembered with honor. As long as the slavery of being is abhorred and the freedom of man assured, Grant shall be recalled with gratitude, and in the circles of the future, the story of Lincoln's life can never be told without associating Grant in the enduring splendor of his own great name. * * *

He rose more rapidly than any military leader in history, from commander of a regiment to supreme direction of millions of men divided into many great armies and operating an area as large as the empires of Germany and Austria combined. He exhibited extraordinary qualities in the field. His bravery among the American officers is the rule which has, happily, had few exceptions, but as an eminent general said, "Grant possessed quality above bravery. He had insensibility to danger, apparently unconsciousness of fear. Besides that, he possessed an evenness of judgment to be depended upon in sunshine and storm." * * *

General Grant in his services in the field never once exhibited indecision, and it was this quality that gave him his crowning characteristic of a military leader. He inspired his men with a sense of their invincibility and they were thenceforward invincible. The career of General Grant when he passed from military to civil administration was marked by his strong qualities. His presidency of eight years was filled with events, events of magnitude in which if his judgment was sometimes errant, his patriotism was always conceded.—James G. Blaine.

ANTHEM FOR ARBOR DAY

Tune—"America."

By Rev. S. F. Smith, D. D., Author of "America."

Joy for the sturdy trees!
Fanned by each fragrant breeze.
Lovely they stand!
The song birds o'er them thrill,
They shade each tinkling rill,
They crown each swelling hill,
Lowly or grand.

Plant them by stream or way,
Plant where the children play
And toilers rest;
In every verdant vale,
On every sunny swale,
Whether to grow or fail—
God knoweth best.

Select the strong, the fair,
Plant them with earnest care—
No toil is vain.
Plant in a fitter place,
Where, like a lovely face,
Set in some sweeter grace,
Change may prove gain.

God will his blessings send—
All things on Him depend.
His loving care
Clings to each leaf and flower
Like ivy to its tower,
His presence and His power
Are everywhere.

PRAYER FOR OUR STATE

Air—"America."

God bless our noble State,
And make her doubly great,
In progress grand.
Nor fear to right the wrong,
Protect among the throng,
The weak as well as strong,
By her command.

Long may her banner bright,
Wave in the morning light,
And all her laws,
Approved by justice stand,
Her sons a manly band,
Her daughters hand in hand,
The home her cause.

—D. R. Lucas.

O GLORIOUS FLAG!

O glorious flag! red, white, and blue,
Bright emblem of the pure and true;
O glorious group of clustering stars!
Ye lines of light, ye crimson bars,
Unfading scarf of liberty,
The Ensign of the brave and free.

—Edward J. Preston.

THE AMERICAN FLAG

When Freedom from her mountain height
  Unfurled her standard to the air,
She tore the azure robe of night
  And set the stars of glory there;
She mingled with its gorgeous dyes
The milky baldric of the skies,
And striped its pure celestial white
With streakings of the morning light;
Then from his mansion in the sun
She called her eagle bearer down,
And gave into his mighty hand
The symbol of her chosen land.

—J. R. Drake.

APPENDIX

EXHIBIT No. 1

VIEWS OF SCHOOL BUILDINGS

STATE NORMAL COLLEGE—ALBANY
Established 1844

ALBANY NORMAL COLLEGE—MAIN ENTRANCE HALL

ALBANY NORMAL COLLEGE—CHAPEL

STATE NORMAL SCHOOL—BROCKPORT
Established 1867

STATE NORMAL SCHOOL — BROCKPORT
Established 1867

STATE NORMAL SCHOOL—BUFFALO
Established 1867

BUFFALO NORMAL SCHOOL—CHEMICAL LABORATORY

BUFFALO NORMAL SCHOOL—Study Room

STATE NORMAL SCHOOL—CORTLAND
Established 1867

CORTLAND NORMAL SCHOOL—NORMAL HALL

CORTLAND NORMAL SCHOOL—LIBRARY

CORTLAND NORMAL SCHOOL—LIBRARY

STATE NORMAL SCHOOL—FREDONIA
Established 1867

FREDONIA NORMAL SCHOOL—NORMAL HALL

STATE NORMAL SCHOOL—GENESEO

Established 1867

GENESEO NORMAL SCHOOL—NORMAL HALL

GENESEO NORMAL SCHOOL—STUDY HALL

JAMAICA NORMAL SCHOOL—ASSEMBLY HALL

STATE NORMAL SCHOOL—New Paltz
Established 1885

NEW PALTZ NORMAL SCHOOL—ASSEMBLY HALL

NEW PALTZ NORMAL SCHOOL—SCIENCE LECTURE ROOM

STATE NORMAL SCHOOL—ONEONTA

Established 1887

ONEONTA NORMAL SCHOOL—Assembly Hall

ONEONTA NORMAL SCHOOL—LIBRARY

STATE NORMAL SCHOOL—OSWEGO
Established 1863

OSWEGO NORMAL SCHOOL—Reference Library

OSWEGO NORMAL SCHOOL—PHYSICAL LABORATORY

STATE NORMAL SCHOOL—PLATTSBURGH

PLATTSBURGH NORMAL SCHOOL—NORMAL HALL

PLATTSBURGH NORMAL SCHOOL—PHYSICAL LABORATORY

STATE NORMAL SCHOOL—POTSDAM
Established 1867

POTSDAM NORMAL SCHOOL—NORMAL HALL

APPENDIX

EXHIBIT No. 2

PROCEEDINGS

OF THE

Council of School Superintendents

October 20--22, 1897

COUNCIL OF SCHOOL SUPERINTENDENTS

OF THE

STATE OF NEW YORK

Proceedings of the Fifteenth Annual Meeting, Held at Canandaigua, N. Y., October 20, 21 and 22, 1897

OFFICERS OF THE COUNCIL

A. B. Blodgett, Syracuse............. President
Henry P. Emerson, Buffalo.......... Vice-President
Emmet Belknap, Lockport........... Secretary and Treasurer

The meeting convened in the court house, Canandaigua, at 3 o'clock p. m., Wednesday, October 20th, with President Blodgett in the chair. The attendance was large. During the three days session there were present Hon. Charles R. Skinner, state Superintendent of Public Instruction; attendance officers A. M. Wright, W. J. Barr and A. E. Hall; supervisor A. S. Downing and several other officials representing the state Department of Public Instruction; Hon. Melvil Dewey, secretary of Regents; inspectors C. N. Cobb and A. G. Clement of the office of the Regents; Mr. C. W. Bardeen, Syracuse; J. T. Thiery, Long Island City; Hon. John Raines, Canandaigua; principals Thos. B. Stowell, state normal school, Potsdam, S. D. Arnes, Palmyra, G. H. Ottoway, Canastota, J. G. Benedict, LeRoy; W. B. Chriswell, Bergen; Prof. Charles R. Wells, Rochester; Prof. A. S. Bickmore, Museum of Natural History, New York City; superintendent James W. Pierce, Westchester Temporary Home for Destitute Children; superintendent Wm. R. George, George Junior Republic, Freeville, N. Y.; superintendent F. H. Briggs, State Industrial School, Rochester; superintendents from thirty-seven cities and twenty-one villages in the state and numerous other friends of public education.

PROGRAM OF REPORTS AND DISCUSSIONS

WEDNESDAY, P. M.

Words of welcome, superintendent J. Carlton Norris, senator John Raines.

Should physical training be compulsory in public schools?

Requirements for and credentials of graduation from public schools.

Duties of a village superintendent.

WEDNESDAY, P. M.

The requirements in drawing under the uniform examinations.

The results in drawing in the grades.

Manual training in public schools.

THURSDAY, A. M.

Report of committee on legislation, Charles W. Cole, chairman.

Report of committee on licensing teachers, A. S. Downing, chairman.

What amendments are necessary to the compulsory attendance law?

The George Junior Republic.

The necessity of a state truant school.

What shall the smaller cities and towns do with habitual truants?

THURSDAY, P. M.

Teachers' training classes under chapter 1031.

Should Regents' diplomas be accepted for entrance to city training classes?

How may the work of class teachers be supervised and recorded so that teachers may receive proper credit for their work?

The place of business education in public schools.

Election of officers and selection of place for holding next annual meeting.

THURSDAY, P. M.

Science teaching in primary and grammar schools. What? How much?

How can pupils of all grades be encouraged to read good literature?

How can the school library be made easier of access?

School savings banks.

FRIDAY, A. M.

The necessity of laws requiring adequate lighting, ventilation, etc., in the erection of school buildings.

What is the highest function of the superintendent?

What is the ideal teachers' meeting?

Simplification of annual reports to different educational departments.

Adjournment.

Meeting called to order by president A. B. Blodgett.

It is with great pleasure with my natural timidity and considerable pride, a large amount of pride, that I call this fifteenth annual meeting of the superintendents of the state to order. As most of you will remember, especially those of you who are older in this work than others, our meeting has always been of a very informal order, nothing like formality has characterized our actions at any time that I know of.

This time we have departed a little from that, as we are going to give our brother, superintendent J. Carlton Norris, an opportunity to give us a few words of welcome. I am very glad to introduce to you J. Carlton Norris.

Superintendent J. Carlton Norris, Canandaigua.

My brother superintendents and gentlemen of the association of school boards.—With more pleasure than I can express I welcome you to my home. This year rounds out with me twenty-five years of work as a superintendent and principal. I need not say to you that these years have brought much pleasure as well as care and worry, and among the pleasantest things that have helped to sweeten a busy life, have been the warm friendships born and bred in such meetings as this. I believe that this state is second to none in generous care and liberality towards its public schools; and I believe further, that nowhere else have teachers' associations done so much to diffuse good, sound, educational thinking, inculcate that respect which every true teacher feels for a fellow teacher and encourage good fellowship. There are many faces here that are very familiar, many whose hand grasp I always receive with a thrill of pleasure, and many whose society I look forward to from one of these state meetings to another; yet most of these faces I never saw except in a meeting of this kind.

Now, gentlemen, one word in regard to our town—it is yours now—I suppose to you who live in the older sections of the state it may seem absurd to speak of Canandaigua as a historical town, for such it is. For many years, long before Rochester or Buffalo were thought of, Canandaigua was the center for all western New York, for law, finance, education; but I cannot speak at length of this. I call your attention to the old academy just up Main street, a little way above us; for, begun in 1795, now a century back, it has done a large share of the educational work of the state. And the old Ontario female seminary which stood on the other side of the street, for many years was one of the strongest institutions in the state. I hope you will be able to walk around our village and see our historical places; the Granger place school, just above the academy, an old mansion built by Gideon Granger, who was for some thirteen or fourteen years postmaster general under Jefferson and Madison, afterwards occupied by his son, postmaster general under Tyler. Across from the academy you could have seen a year ago the old Greig mansion which was our show place for years, and for years the finest mansion west of Albany. Just south of that stands the mansion where senator Lapham lived for years, built by John C. Spencer, who was a cabinet officer under Harrison, and whose life at that time was saddened by the execution of his son, Phil Spencer, for mutiny in the navy. I understand you have not come here to study Canandaigua history, but I do hope to show you some of our places. To-morrow afternoon, if the circumstances will permit, I hope to be able to extend some courtesies to you. But I understand you have come here to work, not to listen to me, and again most sincerely I welcome you. (Applause.)

President Blodgett.—That is an excellent send off to a meeting and we already feel at home, Superintendent Norris. We are now to listen to a few words from one whose name is familiar, to one whose fame is not confined within the borders of New York state, state senator John Raines. (Applause.)

Hon. John Raines, Canandaigua.

Mr. President, gentlemen of the boards of education and superintendents of the state of New York.—By holding your joint meeting here, a meeting of both your associations, you have made us twice glad. But that does not seem to me to afford any good reason why you should be compelled to listen to two speeches of welcome. I can only account for that in one way, and that is, that whoever arranged your program was so well acquainted with Dr. Norris that they deemed it best that whatever he should say should have corroboration by an unimpeachable witness. I therefore reiterate all the Doctor has said in the way of welcome, and may possibly add something to it.

We have here assembled superintendents and boards of education, we are also honored by the presence of the head of the educational interests of the state, Superintendent Skinner. These two associations largely represent one great department of the educational interests of this state, the department of supervision which perhaps is next in importance to that of the teaching force of the state. And these departments, boards of education and supervision have to do, as we are all aware, with great interests. How great those interests are will appear from the fact that there is an average attendance of something over a million of pupils in the public schools each year; that the teaching force numbers thirty thousand, and the expenditure is something over twenty million dollars of money. These great interests are committed largely to the hands of the gentlemen who have honored Canandaigua with their presence to-day. Now the state must have some reason for intrusting to these bodies so great interests. The state has assumed charge to a large extent of the education of the youth of the state. It does it on the theory that the education of the rising generation of children is necessary for the protection of the public, and to this end even reaches into our homes and compels the attendance of the children at the public schools. I may be pardoned if I call attention to the fact that in these later days it has been called in question by men who are at least theorists, as to whether by our educational systems we have accomplished the purpose which is was designed to accomplish. We have had two generations pass through the public schools and become citizens, a third is well under way, yet the other day a gentlemen, whose name is known through all of this great land of ours, who is now prominent in the eyes of the people of the whole state, in a public address raised the question as to whether, here in America it is not yet a debatable question as to whether a republic or a monarchy would be the better form of government. Another gentlemen who is also quite prominent to-day in the eyes of the people of the state, and who, by the way, is an educator of ability, as he occupies a position at the head of a college, calls your attention directly to this question as to whether the educational systems of the state had accomplished what it ought to do in making citizens who are capable of governing the state and governing themselves to the best advantage. Virtually saying by the position which he occupies in a contest now attracting attention in Greater New York, "that ninety per cent. of the people of the state who have arrived at adult age and who are voters and control the affairs of the state, are not competent to govern the affairs of the municipality of the Greater New York because they are partisans." Now if our educational system is such that it has resulted in the state of affairs that this gentlemen, these two gentlemen assume exists, it would be well, perhaps, that in your discussions you should consider whether it is not best to revise your system and see whether some improvement is necessary; whether something cannot be done that shall qualify the ninety per cent. of the citizens of New York, who believe in the government of the state through regular organized parties to properly administer the government of a municipality, rather than that we shall be compelled to believe that the ten per cent. that do not believe in government by party should be competent to govern a great city. For my part, gentlemen, I wish to state that I do not believe in the theorist or the theory. From the churches, from the homes and from the schools of this state, for one hundred years have gone out the men and women that have made this nation great. They have been able to preserve it through all trials and all storms and in the fiercest tempest, that have assailed it, and I believe that through the present educational system of the state, carried on as it has been carried on for fifty years, carried on as it will be carried on under the wise supervision which now governs the great educational forces of this state, we shall develop coming generations which will be as competent to preserve this great country and this state, and even this new municipality as any theorist that believe there is something in the far distance that we might possibly reach if we had the wings of an angel and could soar to the heavenly heights.

Gentlemen, I came to corroborate Dr. Norris and I will reiterate what the doctor has said and bid you welcome to our village of Canandaigua, and hope that this meeting of the superintendents and the boards of education will only result in good to the great commonwealth of which we are so proud and of which we are all members.

President Blodgett.—I wish to thank you, superintendent Norris, and also senator Raines, for these kindly words of welcome, for this reminder of the historic institutions connected with this place, as related by superintendent Norris; and also to senator Raines especially for his calling our attention to the questions which are to a certain portion of the state so vital at this time. And further, for myself especially for the earnestness that he has put in to his talk to us and the inspiration that he gives to me, and I hope to every one of us, and ought to give to us, as a body of school men, to build up men and women of character, of heart, and of life, that shall go out and live as men and women ought to live and keep this county of ours ever progressing upward and onward, as I believe it is within our power to do if we do our full duty. I thank you for your cordial words of welcome in behalf of the association.

We are glad to have with us the state council of school boards, while regretting that the number is not as large as expected, we are glad to have you with us this afternoon; and the state senator called my attention to it, as I had not thought of it in that light, that most of these questions here proposed, are questions pertaining as much to the one branch of the school administration as to the other. As much of interest to the school boards as to the superintendents, although prepared for the school superintendent's council, and I doubt not, that in studying these questions we shall find much of interest to us whether belonging to the school boards or superintendents of schools.

I think it now fitting that we hear from our State Superintendent a few words. I am sure we shall be glad to hear from him.

Hon. CHARLES R. SKINNER, *State Superintendent of Public Instruction.*—

Gentlemen of the council and association of school boards: I do not need to tell you again that it always gives me pleasure to look into the faces of those with whom we are all working to solve some of the problems of life through education. We have been twice welcomed to this beautiful village which has always seemed to me to represent among the villages of our state almost an ideal educational condition. I have watched the educational interests in this village for many years. Give to me a community which insists upon electing intelligent, wise, progressive citizens to its boards of education; give me a community which stands behind this board of education year after year; give me a board of education which believes in employing the best teachers in its schools; give me a board of education which believes in providing adequate facilities for its school children, and you have, what seems to me, an ideal condition for the best educational work that is possible. I believe you find these conditions met very largely here. Our good friend, the senator, while he occupies the proud position in state councils to-day, occupies what seems to me a higher position still, and that is, one of the educational leaders of this great village in this part of the state of New York. For ten years he has been president of the board of education; his inspiration goes through the whole school system. For more years than that he has been a directing influence, and no gentleman knows better than he what the common schools mean, and what they are for—the raising up of good men and good women for our communities; good men for other positions to which they may be called by the state and country. Our school system, if it is for anything, my friends, is to raise up men of influence, men of power and education, who believe in the highest type of American politics; not that I would put politics into education, my friends, but education into politics; so that we shall have the best politicians that any republic in the world can produce. These are what our schools are for. In this country, universal suffrage must carry with it the purpose of universal education, and if we are to have the highest type of self-government, so we must have the highest type of self-education.

Gentlemen, you have to deal, I believe, and you have been dealing for this many years, with the most vital questions in connection with education and the prosperity of our state and country. You have to do with school supervision as superintendents. The cities and villages of the state comprise more than half the teaching force. It is for you superintendents to lead and inspire these teachers and to so far influence them and to convince them that as you have faith in them, they may have more power to do the best that is in them. No man on this earth has the power to demonstrate to the world what sympathy can do, as a superintendent can demonstrate it through the teachers under his jurisdiction. What recompense has a teacher unless the patrons of the school, unless the superintendent, under whose direction they teach, has their sympathy and encouragement. I believe pre-eminently in the power of a good superintendent who has the faculty of infusing, his spirit, his love of education, his ideas of what is pre-eminently right and proper into his teachers' lives. Thus, as the senator says, I believe that the truest interests of education depend on the closer association between the homes and the schools. There is great power in a teacher in bringing about this condition of things, in bringing closer and stronger those relations which should lead to sympathetic, harmonious efforts between parents and teachers. In many localities in this country the experiment has been tried with good effect; the fathers and mothers uniting with teachers in considering questions of vital interest in the education of their children. Let the superintendents and your teachers learn all that is best in the boy or girl; that is the highest type of child study; then let education be given to that child as he is studied and understood. You, superintendents, have to deal with school discipline, school government. school methods. You, my friends of the board, have to deal with school administration. These phases of education comprise the mighty work for which our state puts out her money so liberally, and the reward she asks is, that you will give her back better citizens. As you go through the state to-day, the only places where you will find the stars and stripes from Albany to Canandaigua, are over the schoolhouses that we pass. The Constitution of the state gives to every child within our borders the assurance of an education. We have a compulsory law which says children must go to school, we have therefor the educational system by an act of law as no other state has therefor; and for what purpose? Simply that our schools may turn out our men and women citizens, true educated citizens to take the places of honor in county and state. Huxley says: "Education is the training of the intellect, guiding the laws of nature, and the education of the affections and the soul to obey these laws." After all, my friends, education is but nature being developed, whether it be in bird, or flower, or tree or man, all our work, all our lives are the development of natural laws, and education means the proper study of these laws and the training of the affection and will to obey them.

What our state is to-day in education is due to the efforts which day by day you are making in the rounds of your schools, in your associations with your teachers and in encouraging a deeper and a healthier public sentiment. I believe this condition, my friends, is largely due to your efforts, and I wish to say a word of encouragement to these earnest men who have been instrumental in organizing the association of school boards. I believe it will be an agency which will arouse this public sentiment, and we shall see progress which we have not yet seen and results which we hope for. Let me say to our friends, the ladies, that one of the healthy indications of educational sentiment in this state is the organization of women's clubs and organization of mother's congresses. I am not advocating that all things happy and healthful will come to women only when they belong to school boards. I believe that in every instance women will find their greatest power in making the homes what they should be, and in reaching out their hands to the thousands of teachers with a determination that they will know personally the men and women who teach their children. In a large city, not long ago, at one of those meetings of women interested in deepening the interests of the homes and schools, the question was asked of the thousands of women there, "How many of you know the teachers who teach your children?" and there wasn't a single response.

Let us not only put men and women as teachers into these rooms, men and women with heart and soul, who know children and have the power to love children, but let them be surrounded in their work with some of the conditions and some of the luxuries of life. There is a great part to do for every man and women who is thoroughly interested in educational work, there is problem after problem to be solved, there are revivals which should be made, and they will come in time, and, my friends, when they come, the people will understand that they have come through their friends and servants and representatives, the superintendents of our schools and the representatives of the school boards. (Applause.)

President Blodgett.—I think we have been exceedingly fortunate, having with us at the opening of the session our state Superintendent, to give us these words of advice and counsel. We will now turn to the program as it has been prepared.

Let me say to you, friends, that this program is rough — it was simply put together that we might have something definite to take up in case anything else didn't come up — only two or three are fixed. The subject of "Science teaching in primary and grammar schools" and the subject of "Training schools" are the only ones that are fixed for this special meeting. It is perfectly right for any party, at any time, to move the taking up of any question on the program. The supplemental subjects were not put there because they were less important than the others, and let me ask that all interested in educational work will feel at liberty to discuss any or all of these questions.

I was glad, while Superintendent Skinner was speaking, to see coming through the door the form of Dr. Clark, who has been known to many of us, and all of us, as a prominent factor in educational work in this section and through our state. His influence especially is felt throughout the state.

Dr. Clark, I am glad, as president of this association, to welcome you to our midst. We are glad to know you are still with us and hope to hear your counsel and advice on any topic that may come up here; and may I ask that any and all feel at liberty to speak.

The first three topics on the program put down for this afternoon, "Should physical training be compulsory in public schools?" "Requirements for and credentials of graduation from public schools" and "Duties of a village superintendent" were left over from last year's program. I have not arranged for anyone to discuss these topics, but put them at the beginning thinking they might be important to some, and thinking some might like them discussed.

Now, gentlemen, the meeting is yours. Will some one open the discussion on the first topic?

Superintendent C. E. Gorton, Yonkers.

Mr. President.—The president said he would be glad if I would say a word at the opening of this discussion. I suppose he thought that whatever hesitation there might be at the start, it better be provided against. He thought after the first start there would be no danger. In the attempt that we are making to produce competent, thoroughly educated men and women from the children in our schools, men that shall be independent, vigorous, God-fearing citizens, there is perhaps danger that we shall give too much attention to the intellectual and moral sides and too little to the physical. I was not aware until I saw this question on the program that it remained any longer a question, I thought that it was substantially settled that the schools of this state and the schools of the country ought to provide for the physical well-being of their children just as much as for their intellectual and moral welfare. There is not, in my judgment, the slighest question, especially as in many of the cities and villages of the state the daily sessions are much longer than formerly, with the intermission having been abolished there is now no question that some kind of exercises, some kind of physical training ought to be provided for every one. Only such physical conditions as will make necessary the excusing of particular children from exercises of any character, with that condition only I believe that physical training, methodical work, ought to be required of all the children in our schools. When we think that only a comparatively small number of the children receive any physical education whatever, anywhere except in the schools, the necessity for this becomes all the more apparent. The boys get more exercise, the girls get less, the girls especially in the high schools, girls fourteen, fifteen or sixteen years of age, get almost no exercise and no proper physical drill. Physieal culture, not athletics, such physical culture as will run very properly along with the hygiene we are teaching in all the schools of the state; such physical culture as will tend to develop and strengthen the lungs; such physical culture as will draw the blood from the brain and send it tingling all through the body; such training as will not only build up the physical condition of the child, but will also put him back in his seat ready to resume his school work in better condition than before, is what the schools of the state and the schools of the world need. Permit me to say just one word in explanation of this, and that is this, that this physical training to be good for anything ought to be methodical. That it ought to be worked out along such lines that it will be progressive from class to class; that it will be insisted on at stated times; that it shall not be dependent upon the whims of the teachers; that it shall not be dependent upon the likes or dislikes of the teacher, but that it shall take its place in the school on exactly the same footing as the study of hygiene is enforced by the state; as the study of reading and arithmetic there, which is enforced by the common sense of humanity. Such physical training as will preserve the old maxim of the Greeks and Romans, as will give a sound mind in a sound body, is what we ought to insist on in the public schools of the state.

Senator Raines.—I would like to ask a question. If the gentleman is now giving us a theory, it is all right. I would like to ask him what he practically does in the Yonkers schools.

Superintendent Gorton.—I will answer the question that the senator asks with a great deal of pleasure. After giving the subject considerable attention and visiting various places where the various methods of physical training in the public schools were tried and practiced, I brought before the school board the proposition to introduce the Swedish system of gymnastics as being the most practical and thorough system for the benefit of the children along all lines. It was introduced under the direction of a special teacher and has been continued in the schools under the directions of this special teacher ever since. We give every child in the grammar school systematic exercises twice in the morning and once in the afternoon. Every girl in the high school is given systematic training in the gymnasium attached to the school, at some hour during the day. It is not left to chance; the bells of the school room strike at one time so that the noise of these exercises will not disturb anyone else, and the exercises are all taken at the same time. We do not trust to chance at all, we know that every child in the school who is in a proper physical condition—I never have had a single objection raised by a parent or physician, except in the case of a child who has had a spinal disease or something of that kind. With this exception I never have encountered the least opposition to this course, while the people who have studied and watched it are all enthusiastic in its favor. And I have marked very closely its effect, especially upon the girls. Its effect in their change of posture, its effect in the development of their figure, and a certain air that I see, a very marked change. I have said several times very recently that I wished I had photographs of the lines of girls as they move through the class rooms taken twelve years ago, that I might compare them with photographs taken at this time. I know our children have improved greatly.

A voice.—What is the Swedish system?

Superintendent Gorton.—The Swedish system of calisthenics is a light system that can be used in the class room, except the special parts that are given in the gymnasium.

You may go into any school and hear the pupils read, or see them walk, or see them sit at the desk, and you will be impressed with the importance of this idea. Enough of gymnastic exercise to insure proper carriage, good lung development, vigorous, strong bodies that are able to stand the strain that shall be put upon them in the years to come, as they arrange themselves along the various activities of life. As you read the obituary of successful men who drop out by the wayside in the cities, how many times you read, he was born in, perhaps, Canandaigua, perhaps Oneida, or in this country town or that country town, was reared on the farm and used to hard work, and when he went to the city he was able to put in long hours of work by effective, systematic work along the activities in which his life had found its channel, because of the stock of vigor and good health and the full lung power that had been acquired as he raced over the hills in the country village or on the country farm, if you please. A business man, of all men, is the most practical. If you go into many of the best regulated banks and business houses in the city of New York what will you find? You will find that at a large expense they have fitted up gymnasiums close to their offices, and when the clerk begins to grow drowsy over his ledger or over his journal entries from footing up long columns of figures, his mind begins to be clouded and isn't clear, he does not think with definite, strong and steady purpose, he stops his work, goes into the gymnasium and takes some wholesome exercise, not to become an athlete, but to tone up and strengthen the body. They, I say, are practical men and business men, and I have had them tell me that in New York we find it pays; our clerks will do all the more work because of the little rest from their labors and the toning up of the body. And so I say, Mr. President, and to the gentlemen assembled, that I believe this subject ought to be made compulsory—the teaching of it under proper system, properly organized. I know in my own class in college three men who were known as the most brilliant scholars in the class, easily outstripped the rest of us, but who have hardly been able to do anything since their graduation, because they were not found on the ball field and in the games, but they put their entire time to their studies, and when they graduated they were physical wrecks and have not been able to do work that amounted to anything. The men and women who win in this practical day and age are the men and women who can turn their hand to something useful and put it through. The young man you want in your office, if you are business men, is the man with whom you can trust a piece of work and feel that he will put it through—that he will bring it to pass. The men who manipulate the railway that runs through your village here, are men who are able to bring things to pass, men who are able to cope with the problems that come to them, and have a physical endurance and power coupled with their mental endowments and requirements to bring things to pass along the various lines. And I believe as school superintendents, as school directors, that your first duty is to see to it that such an arrangement be made, such a system be organized and put in your schools as will insure, when your boys and girls graduate from your grammar schools and high schools, that they have such a physical constitution that, with the control they will have acquired over their faculties, they will be men and women to be felt, whose influence will be felt along the various lines of activity to which they will go in the great world. Realizing that only can the highest development be reached and the highest services rendered when the engine of our bodies is in perfect shape. Some of you came to this convention, or part of the way, perhaps, on the Empire state express. Did you realize there what it was, as you went hurrying along, to have a splendid engine with the very best of equipments, an engine that was capable of doing service that was put to it? When they mapped out the time table and said that train must make a mile a minute, the engine was the only possibility. If they put a weak engine on to the train it couldn't make it go and it couldn't do the service that was required of it, and so it is shown in our work. If our boys and girls come out of schools, no matter what their mental qualifications may have been, if their physical condition is weakened, they are slouchy in their carriage, they haven't the good address, they have not learned to walk upright, and to have that lung power, and have developed such a lung power as will enable them to supply the enginery with that which is necessary for the battles of life. Just as that engine, if it is out of order, will not make the mile a minute for the Empire state express; and so let us, in this Empire state, as we plan for the education of our boys and girls, let us put the corner-stone in the structure that we are to erect that shall be the pride of the great Empire state and of the nation. Let us put as a corner-stone, first and foremost of all, there should be a sound body in which to put a well-equipped man.

Superintendent Barney Whitney, Ogdensburg.—The modern theory of Psychology rests largely upon a physical basis, and no person attempts the study of Psychology unless he first arms himself in the knowledge of the physical constitution, and, if it is essential for this information, to study the body thoroughly in order to have a knowledge of the mind and soul, it certainly seems to be consistent that the subject of physical training receive special attention in the public schools. I need no more than call your attention to the fact that the medical profession assert, as a matter of fact, that in the average school boy and girl that leaves our school, the organs are from one and a half to four inches lower than the normal conditions, and no such persons can enjoy good health, they cannot possess a sound, vigorous mind, and, it seems to me, it is almost a crime to omit the subject from the curriculum of the school.

A year ago last summer we received at Thousand Island Park a thorough course of instruction in physical training, a course of training that was admirably adequate to work in the schoolroom; a system that could be practiced and the work could be done in every schoolroom from the kindergarten to the academic; and it is work that the ordinary teacher can easily master and easily teach, and since there is a system that comes within the reach of every teacher, I am prepared to say we have reached the point where this should be made compulsory. The first question that seems to arise is, is it possible for teachers to prepare themselves to do efficient work in the matter of physical training? Our experience has settled the point so far as we are concerned. About sixty per cent. of the teachers of our city took this training for three weeks; they were not quite satisfied, so they, at their own expense, employed the same teacher for three weeks, and paid her $150, and at the end of that time, one of the teachers, who had taken a special course, took charge of the work in the high school, and it has been eminently successful, the teachers doing the work most successfully. It has improved, not only the appearance of the pupils, but it has been the means of improving pupils wonderfully. I believe we have reached the point where this subject should be seriously considered and should be made compulsory.

President Blodgett.—I was very glad of the question senator Raines asked, "Is it theory or is it practical?" I think we should strike at the practical. I think experience is one of the best points to bring out. Who will add a word to this topic?

Superintendent J. Irving Gorton, Sing Sing.—I would like to make a suggestion in accordance with what we have heard about this physical training. According to all we have heard, it is important that physical training be made a part of our school system. If that be the case, if there are no opposing opinions, it must arise from two causes, that all here concur or that most people here are ignorant of the practical work, and regard it as a theory, rather than practical. In either case whichever of these assumptions is correct that everybody is in favor of it, or that everybody pretty nearly is ignorant of it, in either of these cases it seems to me, it calls for more examination, and I would suggest that that examination be provided for now, and that some steps be taken for a further and more satisfactory attention to this subject at our next annual meeting, if not before, either by the appointment of some committee which shall carefully examine and specifically report ways and means and processes, or in some other practical way. I will only say in relation to these processes, that a good many schools are attracted by those who carry on physical training in their schools. Some of these systems are better than others. I would suggest we now appoint a committee to take this matter into consideration, and to review as specifically and carefully as they are capable of doing in this matter; and I move you, if it be in order that such a committee be appointed.

time it seems to me that we have hit the very gist of the subject in the fact that there may be a difference of opinion in different localities of the state. I for one agree fully with the superintendent from Yonkers. As far as the city of Olean is concerned we have compulsory physical culture in every section of the school and in every grade. And I think, with a single exception, there has been no person in the city that has asked to be excused from taking these exercises. We feel that it is an excellent study and training. For several years we have had special supervisors in this branch; but when you say that it should be compulsory and that the law committee take it in charge, I apprehend that the meaning of the word compulsory is not that the local superintendent and boards of education should manage their affairs as they choose to manage them, but that it should be a law that should compel us to do everything in the same way. We have in the state of New York a grand school system; it is grand because we are a part of a great body politic. It is not a school here and there, or one city against another, but we are welded together by law, so that we are a part of one great school system. That is altogether to our advantage, but it would not be to our advantage to have legislation that would compel us further than we are now to do things in some particular way. If the lower Hudson is right and the upper Hudson is wrong, the best way to convert the upper Hudson is not by holding a gun over its head, but by showing what excellent results there are towards the mouth of the noble river. On the other hand we may not be sure but that the waters are purer above than they are below, and we would like to have a continuance of that stream of wisdom and experience coming down to us. In other words, what we want is not more uniformity, but more individuality, and consequently, while I will fully favor the word "compulsory" if it means that individual localities may exercise their own discretion, but I should be just as much opposed to that word "compulsory" if it meant uniformity throughout the state.

Superintendent Barney Whitney, Ogdensburg.—The word "compulsory" does not involve the word "uniformity." Uniformity would require the practice in a definite way. It seems to me superintendent Gorton has made that very clear. There are ten or twelve systems of physical culture that are practical. It seems to me, Mr. President, this has gone beyond the question of experiment. It seems to me it is not any longer experimental. The state of Pennsylvania has made this compulsory and I happen to know something of the results of their practice and experience and it is entirely satisfactory.

President Blodgett.—Perhaps I may be excused for saying a word. I believe it is one of the best things that can be put into any school system, and I think just as superintendent Gorton said, I would have liked several years ago to have had a camera and had a picture of a file of children passing in and out of the school building at that time compared with one taken in these later days. It would show a vast improvement in the physical condition of children. They stand better, they walk better, they go out of the building in much better condition. And then too it is one of the greatest teachers as to the matter of obedience. When the children are taught to put down the left foot at a given signal, when they can be taught that the left foot goes down on the emphasized note, when they can be taught to extend the arms, or raise the arms or lower the arms and do it at a given signal, there is a question of obedience comes in there that is very helpful in all school work.

Another thing I have found in my experience. Sometimes a teacher who is really not a good teacher, or is deficient in many things, will find there is something she can make a success of, and when a teacher has found one element in school work that she can make a success of, around that very thing she can wind the rest of her school work and thereby lift it up. I believe in physical training put in our schools and practiced daily, and when I can feel that from fourteen to eighteen thousand children are at this time taking physical culture, which is expanding their lungs, strengthening them up, making better men and women of them, I think it is a good thing. It is not a matter of athletics, it is to get these little crooks out of them and make them better men and women, and I think it is physical culture does it.

Superintendent Charles W. Cole, Albany.—I would second the motion made by Mr. Gorton that this subject be referred to a special committee. I feel that I ought to say that it expresses my opinion, that I do not believe that it is a subject of legislation at all. I think it is a very proper subject for us to discuss and examine and give some opinions upon the best way to get at it. And I believe that a committee should look into this matter and report the condition of this matter of physical culture at another session, but I do not believe that physical culture is a matter that should be made a subject of legislation at all; therefore I second the motion of Mr. Gorton.

President Blodgett.—I wish to say that my suggestion was not one looking to having a law passed, but thinking that that committee having studied the law of the state for a number of years, might be able to make a suggestion before the close of this gathering that would tell us what was best to do in the matter. The question is before you that a committee of three be appointed to consider this question of compulsory physical training in the school. Do you wish to discuss it, if not those in favor will please say " I." (The motion was duly carried; the chair later appointed as such committee, superintendents J. I. Gorton, George Griffith and James G. Riggs.)

President Blodgett.—I will ask that some one open the discussion on the second question, Requirements for and credentials of graduation from public schools.

Superintendent Gorton.—I should like very much to hear something from some of the officers of the board of Regents in relation to that; it is perhaps, more naturally in their line of work than anyone else.

President Blodgett.—Is there some one from the Regent's Department who will volunteer this matter?

Inspector Cobb of the Board of Regents.

Mr. Chairman.—When I observed that on the program, I supposed it had reference to the graduation from the district schools and from the grades. I thought that was the point from which it was to be discussed and I came here feeling intensly interested in the matter, and listened to the discussion, having no idea of saying anything about it.

So far as the work of the high schools is concerned, it seems to me that so far as we are concerned in the office, we have been striving for some years past to get the general opinion of the school men of the state with reference to what is substantially necessary for graduation from the school. Of course it is now recognized throughout the state generally that graduation from the secondary schools involves substantially four years study after having completed the grammar school work. I confess there is some doubt in my own mind as to whether it is feasible for a school as a rule to adopt the four year system and insist that pupils shall go through with that. I do believe that a four year course may be so arranged, however, that every pupil who comes in to it and stops at the end of the first or second year shall get the best possible training for the time that he is in school. It would seem to me, furthermore, that it is desirable that a pupil should not feel, if he stops at the end of the first year or second or third year that he has accomplished all that that school should give to them; therefore, I should say that, in my own judgment, I would not graduate a pupil from the high school or union school until he had completed four years academic work. I should desire also that that four years work be systematic work. I am inclined to think that it is not desirable that there should be uniformity throughout the state with respect to courses. I have been asked a good many times within the last few years to give my judgment upon the courses which have been outlined by school officers in different parts of the state; I have been asked to make a course, and I confess that I am unable to make a course that even I thought would be a good one, the most desirable one for the schools in all parts of the state. Now these persons who are on the ground and know the condition of affairs as prevailing in the towns and in the school districts it seems to me are in a better position to judge of how the high school studies should be arranged. I believe most thoroughly in the idea that eight years work should be done in the grades before going in to the high school, and I think it should be done most thoroughly, most carefully. I have no sort of sympathy with the idea of grading pupils ahead any faster than they are able to go. I have all manner of sympathy with making courses and regulations pertaining to courses so elastic that a pupil who is bright and strong and well and can get out two years work or a year and a half average work in one year, shall have the privilege of doing it. I believe we ought always to recognize that fact; and we ought not to require that a pupil shall spend so many years in school before he is permitted to graduate. If he has accomplished the work and done it faithfully and well, I believe he should be graduated. It seems to me furthermore, that the course which is adopted in some of the high schools of requiring more than eight years of grade work before permitting pupils to enter the high school, while it is probably wise in some places where the high schools are overloaded and they want to keep the pupils out of it and hold them back, it is not a wise course to pursue generally. There is a little tendency, I think, all along the line of education to strive to crowd in too much. I have a feeling that a boy or girl ought generally to get into life work before the most advanced age. It seems to me that those of us who are trying to do work to-day if we look back upon our own educational experiences will realize that if we spent eight years in grades, four years in high school and four years in college and three years in technical or professional school, we should be spending more time than most persons can afford to spend. Possibly this is a little heresy, but heresy you know sometimes become orthodoxy when the majority believe in it.

Superintendent Foster, Ithaca.—I rise to a point which is germane to this question, and I am not sure but it should be considered exactly with it. Ought not the requirements for the credentials to depend entirely upon the value placed upon the credentials? What is the value of the credentials anyway? Is the credential a diploma, a school certificate that this pupil is now ready for life of any kind? Is it a certificate that the young woman is ready to be married? Is it a certificate that this pupil is ready to go into business? What is the value of it? I have a particular question to ask. The question is why cannot the value of this certificate, as representative of the scholarship of the pupil, be accepted in other departments of life, outside of law and medicine and other professions? Why cannot they also be applied in the profession of teaching? It seems to me that this is quite an important question. Why is it not possible that these certificates should not be made of value in the profession of teaching, as representing this scholarship of the pupil? If they can be made of value in this way, as well as in other professions, the requirements leading up to these credentials would be determined, of course, by the value to be placed upon them.

Superintendent J. Irving Gorton.—There are three points in relation to this matter which I should like, for the interests of my own school, to have explained.

The fact is that in many of our schools the four years' course is impossible. In others it is impracticable. The pupil who cannot spend four years, perhaps, can spend three, but he is not going to have any graduation at the end of three years. Consequently, as he cannot go four years, and cannot get a diploma for three years, he goes two years, and he loses one year, which he would have had if the graduation had been given for thirty-six regents' scholarship counts, rather than forty-eight. It may be that some others who can stay three years would not stay four, and I think that there should be for some schools three years' graduation, and for those who can go four years a corresponding diploma.

Our state Department has provided for certificates for examinations in our rural schools that do not touch a rural-school child. I want to see examinations for rural schools — the district schools. With the smaller schools we cannot go very far on the certificates of attainments corresponding to their examinations.

State Superintendent Skinner.—The Department has prepared examination questions which commissioners are authorized to give to their pupils in district schools, and give them a certificate as their percentage. We can do nothing in relation to the graduation which is spoken of here further than is already done.

The commissioners' course of study is completed by the issuing of a little diploma to the scholar who has passed in the course of study and passed the examination which the commissioners provide. Oftentimes that little diploma is all the diploma those children ever have. I think the question asked by superintendent Foster, as to what this certificate of graduation means, is entitled to some consideration. What is it a preparation for? He asked why cannot that certificate of graduation be considered in the profession of teaching? I do not know of any reason why it should not be considered if there is any fixed understanding as to the thoroughness of the course of study and specifying the examination held. It seems to me that this is the trend of public sentiment throughout the state—is pretty well settled that no person should undertake to teach at least in the primary and grammar schools without professional training. Professional training to-day has its place in the cities and villages and the larger schools, and I do not believe it can be displaced.

Of course, the commissioners' course of study which was submitted by the school commissioners of the state, and which is carried into operation as thoroughly as possible in almost all the school commissioner districts, is doing a great deal for thorough education of those who can never get above the common schools. You will remember that ninety-six per cent. of the children in our schools never go beyond the common schools.

Superintendent Burgess.—Is the holder of a second-grade certificate entitled, under the present law, to teach in a city school?

State Superintendent Skinner.—I think not.

Superintendent Burgess.—Is the holder of a first-grade certificate entitled to teach in a city school?

State Superintendent Skinner.—He must have three years' successful experience. The holder of a certificate with three years' experience is entitled to teach in city schools.

Superintendent Burgess.—I do not understand why holding a first or second grade certificate was not included as one of the scholastic qualifications to teach in the cities. I have often wondered why these qualifications were omitted.

State Superintendent Skinner.—I think you could obtain that information by asking the council on legislation, for this council has prepared the law.

Superintendent Cole.—No uniform act can be recognized at present in the city of Albany, for the reason that the incorporating law of Albany gives to the board of public instruction the power to say who shall be the teachers, and there is no state law that compels them to take any of the uniform examinations as a criterion. The board is organized under a special act, and the power is given to the board to determine what persons shall teach in the city and what persons shall receive their certificates. We cannot recognize any of these other examinations, unless special acts are passed. For instance, there are many cities that do not recognize the normal schools. The incorporating act of the city of Albany does not. Many cities have accepted the normal-school diploma, and many cities have accepted the examinations called the uniform examinations.

Superintendent Young.—Is it or is it not true that a graduate of a training school in the city of New York is a legally qualified teacher under the law in the city of New York?

Superintendent Cole.—It is not true that any local board may not add other requirements, if they choose. The law says that they must have this course of study, and not less than three years in a high school, approved by the state Superintendent, and must also have a year of professional training. The law does not give any person who simply has professional training a right to teach in the city. The board of education may choose to require additional qualifications.

Superintendent Young.—According to the laws of the state of New York is not a graduate of a training class in the state of New York a legally qualified teacher to teach in the city of New York?

State Superintendent Skinner.—Subject to the pleasure of the board of education of that city. In many of the cities of the state normal school diplomas are worthless, although they carry upon their face the statement that the holders are licensed to teach in any of the public schools of the state. The state is satisfied with a life certificate, and yet many of the boards of education in cities throw them back as worthless. So in effect a normal school diploma says that this certificate is good to teach in the backwoods but not in the cities. There should be a uniform regulation and there is, I understand a movement in this association looking to a uniform standing as a recognition of the certificates in the cities, that is, that when any one holds a normal school diploma or life certificate, which is the best certificate to teach in the United States, we shall not have any board of education throw it back unless for other reasons they do not want to employ the holder.

Superintendent Whitney.—I desire information. I want to know if the provision that three years' experience is equivalent to three years' education in the high school, with a course of study approved by the Department of Public Instruction means training in a training class?

State Superintendent Skinner.—I said that that clause was the actual object of the law.

Superintendent Whitney.—I want to know if three year's experience in the rural schools in the Adirondacks or in any of our rural schools makes it possible for a teacher to be employed in the city of Ogdensburgh provided the board of education shall see fit to overrule the superintendent. Can it be done?

Chairman ruled this discussion out of order and to wait until Thursday.

Superintendent Emerson.—I believe the educational opinion is already in favor of lengthening the high school course and shortening the lower course.

When I became superintendent of schools in Buffalo, I found

rather a curious condition of things, namely: A high school course of three years and ten grades below it. The first thing I did was to reduce the lower school course, including the primary and grammar courses to nine years. Then I lengthened the high school course to four years. We have tried to make as good use of the nine years as possible and in the entire year we have been introducing higher subjects in the course, and have been reading United States history and taking the advanced English course. It may be that it is the best plan to omit the ninth grade in a city like Buffalo and do high school work in it so far as possible and then make it possible for bright pupils to complete this high school course in three years. Are there any other cities that have nine years in the grades?

Chairman Blodgett.—May I ask that the superintendents in whose schools there is a nine year's course preceding the high school, to please arise, including kindergarten.

Fifteen superintendents stood up.

How many have four years below the high school course?

Superintendent Norris.—Many of us have practically eight years in the lower school with four years in the high school. Our ninth grade is a transition period. Some pupils pass from eighth to tenth without even entering the ninth.

Chairman.—How many have the eight year course?

Twenty-one stood up.

Chairman.—May I ask how many practically finish United States history before the high school course?

Nineteen stood up.

Superintendent Babcock.—How many of the superintendents present believe that we should take length of attendance on the part of the scholar in a school as a criterion for graduation instead of the amount of work accomplished?

Superintendent Foster.—Two years ago I looked over the statistics of the public schools and I believe that in the average the years were less than nine, so that practically the majority of the pupils completed their course in eight years.

While I am standing I want to say that I believe in the professional training of teachers; and the only thing I was asking about was the subjects and work actually done in the school and to make these certificates of value on the professional certificate in teaching.

Superintendent Snow.—I would like to know whether they admit children at the age of 5 or 6 years. Some schools admit children at the age of 5 years and others keep them out until they are 6. I would like to know of those who have nine years' course in schools how many of them admit at the age of 5.

Chairman.—Nine.

I would like to know which of the towns here graduate pupils solely upon Regents' credentials, and I would like to know which of them graduate upon one, two, three and four years course; that is, graduate pupils from the high school course solely upon Regents' credentials? Twelve.

How many graduate from a one year's course from a high school? None.

From an English course of three years? Ten.

Superintendent Willets.—We have four different courses; three of them are four years each.

Chairman.—How many of the diplomas specify the number of years—in some way or other? Eighteen.

Chairman.—Another question has been asked. How many of the schools continue the subject of United States history in the high school? Twenty-two.

Regularly moved and seconded that this evening the subject of manual training be taken up. I fear that if it is put over until late in the session it will be passed over altogether. Motion carried.

October 20th, 8.30 p. m.—Meeting called to order at 8 p. m.; subject, Manual training in the public schools.

Superintendent George Griffith.—Mr. President and gentlemen of the Council: The president has "shut off" nearly all the speech I had prepared, by the limitation he has given in this discussion.

As to reasons for manual training I shall not take your time to discuss them to-night except, perhaps, to just mention them. My investigation of it leads me to believe that the one great reason for it is in its poorly educational state in the peculiar development, the peculiar training that it brings to those who have it, a training that in its main features cannot be secured by other work. It is an essential element of a complete, well-balanced mental training. We must realize that it gives an added dignity to manual labor in the estimation of boys and girls who are going out from our schools. It tends, to a great extent, to bridge over the chasm, the feeling, between the laboring classes, those who labor with the hand and those who labor with the mind, or who do not labor at all.

Another important provision, it seems to me, is that found in the fact that, rightly carried on, it gives that systematic or that general basic training that fits a boy to learn a trade or fits a boy to learn some of the professions. We cannot emphasize too strongly the fact that manual training in public schools shall never attempt to teach a trade or anything that borders upon it, but that it shall be taught for its educational value wholly and yet at the same time it gives the elements of a general training that fits the boy to learn the trade afterwards. Its training to accuracy of hand and eye is well known.

An experience of one year in our city has brought out a fact, and an important one. I presume that none of us who have had experience with a bad boy, or an incorrigible boy in our schools, have failed to recognize that very many such pupils are redeemed if we can find the one thing in school life or school work in which that boy is especially interested, and working with him on that one thing we bring him around until he does all the school work. I am finding that manual training is the one thing in many cases; it is the one thing in which the boy has an interest and we are able to bring him into line with the other work of the school. Another point; I believe it keeps the boy in school for a longer period. In the lower grades we have cabinet molding, folding and scrolling; in the higher grades modeling, iron work, etc.

We recognize two systems of manual training, by some called the Sloyd and the Russian systems. Of the Sloyd, the essential feature is a complete object. The essential feature of the Russian system is a series of graded exercises. I am firmly convinced that the trend of manual training work is toward the essential principles of the Sloyd system. I believe that this is the coming system and that the manual training specialists of the country are working toward it.

We all recognize that there are certain periods in the development of a child's life and character when certain things can best be attained, or a language can best be learned; and it seems to be shown that the training of the young can best be done at a certain period in the child's life. If that period is passed it is much more difficult, and in many cases impossible to give any training to the young. That period is pretty well passed when the high school period is entered upon. Therefore I believe it is a very important matter that they be started below the high school, as in the grades. I believe if we are to have manual training in our schools it must be made a part of our organic work, it must be a part of our course of study. It should be made an essential, organic part, as arithmetic, geography or languages.

As to the amount of work we have been able to do in Utica, only one hour every two weeks in the fifth and sixth grades, and one and one-half hours every two weeks in the seventh and eighth grades. We have not found that it has taken anything from the advancement in the other studies, rather it has added to it. It adds to the power of work in the other classes, and I believe there is no power lost in the other classes.

The only other point is that perhaps it may be of interest to the council to know just what we have done and what it has cost us.

We have, in fifteen ward schools, work in wood usually with knife, square, triangles, saw, desk covers upon the top of the desk for the boys and the girls for sewing—one hour every two weeks in fifteen schools in two grades—the seventh and eighth grades. We erected a building, the upper floor is fitted up with twenty-five carpenters' benches, with sets of tools, etc. The lower floor is fitted up as a cooking room, with gas burners, and lessons are given there of an hour and a half. We have the lesson for the four grades, including about twenty-one hundred pupils all told, employing four teachers, and if you care to hear I will give you the total cost. The knife work for fourteen schools, two grades—desk covers, tables and cases for holding the work—$575.

I will say that in one of our large schools the teacher made some experiments last year in paper Sloyd and in elementary work through the lower—the third and fourth grades—and they were found very satisfactory. We have also modified our drawing somewhat in the higher grades, so that it correlates with manual training work. The lesson in mechanical drawing will be work that will be supplementary work in the manual training school.

In answer to a question superintendent Griffith said that desk covers are boards that fit upon the top of the desks. The teacher of bench work designed them. The people seem to favor manual training pretty generally. The opposition has decidedly lessened. So far this fall I have not heard any opposition, and not more than half a dozen out of two thousand patrons offer any objections. The objection was principally in cooking, and the objection was that the girls could be taught at home. I think it would be poor work to set the girls at wood work.

Superintendent Cole.—Perhaps it would be appropriate at this time that something be said concerning the application of the general principles of manual training in a different way from that described by Superintendent Griffith.

We have had manual training proper in the high school at Albany for something over ten years, and we are well satisfied with the result. We do not have it in the elementary schools. We have work preparatory to courses of manual training, although we have in the primary and kindergarten grades, paper cutting, paper folding, stick work drawing and the like, leading to and preparing for a course in manual training. We hold certain connections in regard to placing wood-working with tools in the elementary school. We may be entirely wrong, but we came to the conclusion that the high school was the better place, and that the elementary schools do not offer the proper conditions for the use of tools. One reason why we do not use them in the elementary schools is that we do not believe that tools can be profitably used by children whose muscles are immature, or by those who are unable, through lack of sufficient strength to properly handle the tools, which, it seems to us, should be used in the wood work. We give manual training in the high school to both the boys and the girls. The plan of making the course compulsory upon every student, and the plan of having a special course, which all selecting this course must take throughout the entire four years in the result of the latter plan I will say that we have been disappointed—we find that the number who will take this special course, which was framed to give a good academic course and at the same time give due attention to manual training proper, is comparatively small. We have the result that in four years trial the number has decreased so very much, compared to the number taking manual training under the compulsory plan, that we shall undoubtedly return to the original plan. We do not have sewing. I must say I consider that sewing has no educational value at all. I can find no place for sewing in the public schools.

The Sloyd system is used for the girls in the high school. We have two years of Sloyd, followed by two years of wood carving. Our teacher is one who is especially skilled in this work. She received special preparation, first in the Teachers' College in New York and afterward completed a course at Naas in Sweden, and is very successful.

The girls take two years of Sloyd and this is followed by wood carving and work of that nature for the following two years. I believe that metal working should be introduced. I believe that we are not doing the right thing in confining the course to wood work. I believe that the chief value of this course is its educational value, and that so much should not be done in any one department as to lead to the idea that we are teaching a trade. Some of our boys become very skillful carpenters and then leave the high school.

The expense of maintenance of the manual training department is not, of course, nearly as low as in Utica. It costs us in salaries $900 for the boys and $800 for the girls. The expense of material is probably altogether about $400 more. The plant cost us a comparatively large sum. We have an electric motor and many other appliances which are very expensive. I should say that the plant itself must have cost altogether, probably, as much as $3,000, including all the tools. We are well satisfied with the general result although we regret our inability to vary the work by introducing iron work, etc. We are sure that we have held a great many boys and a great many girls in the high school who would never have completed the course of study in that school without the manual training.

As to the effect on the individuals, I agree heartily and thoroughly with superintendent Griffith, with one additional thought that I have heard expressed, that aside from the mental and physical development there is a very strong moral development in connection with wood work, because the boys learn from the exercises to hew to the line all the time in doing things well, truly and conscientiously.

Superintendent Montfort.—With us manual training is not compulsory. We have it in the five grades beginning with the eighth year. I have never known a boy to object to manual training for any reason. We desire to have it universal. I have an experience of eleven years and have found it entirely satisfactory. We have no difficulty in training the young at the advanced age of the high school and the work is remarkably well done. It has proved in many cases a study to enter Cornell and the wood work has been accepted at Cornell.

We have the ordinary wood working; in the first year the cabinet work, wood carving and drawing. We have an electric motor and our plant has cost us about $3,500. We pay our teacher $1,200 and think it is little enough. So far as the compulsory part is concerned, we have no trouble. We have sewing in four grades, beginning with the second year.

Superintendent Cole.—Do you have cooking? I do not think it has nearly the educational value that the tools, the construction, has for the girls. I want to say that one point that should be remembered, is that drawing is made a very strong adjunct to manual training.

Superintendent Halsey.—In cities of the class of Utica, is it advisable to have a separate manual training school or would you take the manual training simply a part of the high school work?

Superintendent Griffith.—I do not know. We have had no experience with that. My investigation of it would lead me to say that if we had a room in the high school building it would be preferable.

Superintendent Rogers.—I wish simply to say that I believe in manual training. We have done most of our work with the boys in the grammar grades from the sixth to the ninth inclusively. I believe that is a wise course with us and consideration of that matter, thus far, has been overlooked. It is not altogether a question whether it it is the best time to do the work but as to whether it will be done at all.

We have sewing in the grammar grades and cooking for the lowest eighth grade. I believe in sewing for the girls. I believe it is educational and has value in that direction. I am not afraid of having a child learn something in school he or she can use outside even if it may not be so highly educational. It helps to make school life valuable to his people, and in the lower grades we have carving and wood work. The question was asked me by visitors if this work is compulsory. Nobody knows. It goes right along and is very satisfactory to the parents. I want to see the work enlarged in the high schools.

Superintendent Gorton (Sing Sing).—I wish to know whether any of the pupils do careless work. In arithmetic they do careless work. Are the pupils universally taking the utmost pains with their work without being stirred up to it?

Superintendent Rogers.—I do not know that manual training is a cure-all for laziness and stupidity. There are pupils who do poor work in other subjects and who do good work in manual training.

Superintendent Marsh.—If you were to build a new high school building would you prefer to have the arrangements in that building in preference to a separate building?

Superintendent Rogers.—I would much prefer to have it in the same building to a room in a separate high school. There is a good deal of danger that people will misunderstand manual training. If you attempt to have a separate manual training school it would be almost impossible to give people the idea that there is an educational value.

Superintendent Halsey.—We have had somewhat peculiar circumstances in Binghamton in connection with manual training. A fund was left some years ago, about $50,000, and a manual training school was established. The board of education built a small building and equipped that in part. The difficulty is in the payment of salaries to teachers. We have begun at the wrong end because it is limited to pupils of high school grades and has not been introduced in the grades at all. I certainly would not advise a city of that size building separate manual training schools.

Superintendent Maxwell.—I do not know that I have very much to add to what has been so well said. There is one thing that struck me very forcibly throughout this discussion and that is, that no longer is there any question raised whatever in this assembly as to the value of manual training. It now seems to be admitted on all hands that manual training is in reality a part of the school course and the question carries itself to one of measures, to one of ways and means.

It seems to me that two questions have been raised for discussion to-night. The first of these questions is, whether manual training should be done in the elementary schools, at eight years as it is done in Utica, or whether it should be done in the high school course as it is in Albany, and in Binghamton. This seems to me to be an idle discussion because if manual training is a good thing, as I believe it to be, as evidently the gentlemen of this association believe it to be, it is patent that it ought to be in both departments—both in the elementary schools and in the high schools and I think it is particulary important that it should be in the elementary schools, for two reasons—and here I am speaking theoretically entirely because we have not that work in the elementary schools of Brooklyn. We have sewing for the girls and, of course, we have drawing, etc. We have not yet regular wood work for the boys in the elementary school, but theoretically speaking it seems to me that upon pedagogical ground the boys ought to have manual training. More and more every year is the work in our high schools becoming elective, and I think very properly so. In an address that I listened to a few days ago from professor ——— of Harvard, he took strong ground in favor of introducing electives as low as ten years of age. I would not go so far as that, but I do believe that one of the principles of electives in studies is to make a necessity for high school work. Now, if the boys and girls who enter our high schools are going to make a choice I think they will have to make a choice between a literary course and a manual training course, and I include under the word literary, all the subjects that are expressed in the regular high school course. If they are to make an intelligent choice between these two courses it seems to me that it is quite necessary that they should have some experience in manual training in the elementary schools before they enter the high school in order that they may make that choice intelligently. I do not think it is wise to compel the boys to take up a special line of work or duty unless they have an aptitude for it. I think, friends, that one of the great evils which society is laboring under to-day is that people are not put at the kind of work they can do the best. I believe that schools might, and must, do far more in the future than they ever did in the past in bringing up boys and girls to that particular kind of work for which the child evinces an aptitude. In order that a boy may select intelligently between a manual training course and a literary course, I believe it is essential that he have experience in manual training work.

As to the point raised by Mr. Halsey, such seems to me to be the second important point, that if you have a separate building for separate manual training work you are liable to have a rush of pupils to that school and away from the other schools because people find their children are going to become carpenters, blacksmiths and cooks and that that school will at once put them in the way of earning a livelihood. Still, I am not prepared to speak on this point from experience. We have four high schools in Brooklyn. One of them, I believe the largest high school in

America, three of these schools are literary high schools, teaching the languages, Latin, Greek, French, German, mathematics, etc., etc. In the fourth we have a course of lectures throughout the course, mathematic work, manual training, work in wood, electricity, model making and all those things that go to make a regular high school course, and my experience is that there is no rush of boys and girls from the literary school to the manual training course, but on the contrary, the great body of children go to the literary school.

One word of the experience of a friend of mine. The president of our board of education, who is fortunately able to speak all the Scandinavian languages, has been last summer in Sweden; and from being an opponent of manual training came back, after a minute inspection of the work in the schools in Stockholm, a complete convert to manual training and particularly to the idea of teaching cooking to the girls. He told me that in every school in Stockholm a warm wholesome lunch is served for all the children who desire to partake of it, those paying who were able to pay and those who were not able to pay getting their lunch for nothing and all the cooking is done by the girls of these schools. I do not know whether this business of warm lunch is one that has been brought to your attention, but I know that in my city, in the poorer districts, it would be almost of inestimable value.

Superintendent Cole.—Do you regard sewing as having considerable educational value?

Superintendent Maxwell.—I was not so trained myself and I do not profess to be a judge in the matter. So far as my observation of the work is concerned I think that in its elementary stages sewing makes a very slight call upon the intellectual powers and does not require any very great perceptive powers. When it arises to the dignity of dressmaking I confess that I am simply appalled by the intricacy of the whole business.

Inspector Charles N. Cobb.—I wish to say a word or two with respect to my observation on the method of manual training in the high schools and its effects on their work. In visiting the manual training high school in Brooklyn I have observed that the boys do almost infinitely better work in English, history, mathematics and other things than the girls do, and the only explanation that I am able to give of it is the fact that the manual training course for the boys is very much better than the course for the girls.

Superintendent Griffith.—I visited manual training schools in twenty or thirty places and in regard to girls' work and poor work done by the pupils, I think that the pupil can be taught to realize that he has done poor work, careless work, better in manual training work than in any other school work. Manual training leads to more careful, accurate work.

Superintendent Caswell.—I still believe in the value of sewing in manual training. He then related what he saw at Chautauqua in manual training class room there.

Superintendent Sawyer.—I do not know that as superintendents of schools our only business is to see about the educational value of work, and yet I confess that the matter of sewing and cooking for our girls has been to me a matter of real value. When I look at the homes from which these poor boys and girls come to us, what wretched places they are and why they are wretched, and understand and believe it is largely because mothers do not know how to take care of what is brought into the house, when we consider all these things it seems to me that some of the money that we put into other things would be a great deal better spent in furthering a knowledge of cooking and sewing and such things as boys and girls can carry home with them, and which will be of some real use to them after they get home and after they go out of the school.

Superintendent Burgess.—I have seen manual training in a reformatory school where we have sent a number of truants last year, and the testimony of the superintendent of that institution is that the work is exceedingly serviceable.

Superintendent Caswell.—It may be interesting to some of you to know how we succeeded in getting our manual training started in our city. It seemed to be impossible for me to get our board of education to realize the importance of the work or to do anything toward carrying it on. I said to one teacher that if she would look into the work and take lessons, I would see that she was given work. When she came back to Little Falls and began the school year I presented the matter to the board of education and they refused to pay her for a lesson a week on Saturday; but they did consent to giving her the use of a room in one of the school buildings provided she paid the janitor for his extra work. I was determined that the people of Little Falls should be educated up to the idea of the value of manual training in some way, and this young lady has gone about among the families and was able to secure fifteen or twenty little girls as private pupils for her Saturday morning class. She receives $2 for ten lessons from each of these children, and the parents are only too glad to pay her the $2 per week, and she could take as many more if she could take care of them. There is an interest growing that I hope will develop into something good. A philanthropic gentleman has already engaged this young lady to take a class of poor children to one of the churches on Saturday afternoons and he defrays the expenses of that.

Superintendent Gorton.—At an exhibition in the city of New York last year I saw what was to me a very remarkable exposition of manual training work.

Chairman Blodgett read the following telegram:

The board of school superintendents of New York city sends greetings to the council. We regret that we cannot be represented at the meeting of the council this year. We are unusually busy at this time.

JOHN JASPER.

Chairman Blodgett.—I think it is well settled that nothing should be put into the school that is not of educational value. On the subject of cooking, it seems to me that it is the duty of the schools to send out into the homes something of value, that is going to lift the home and to help it. It seems to me that the schools in this country owe a duty to the homes in that line. They should have the pupils in our schools take up the subject of cooking and have the children who come in from those homes, which really are not homes in many cases, get them to put on their white caps, wash their hands and get themselves in cleaner condition before taking up the cooking lesson. I believe that very much of that will go back into the homes of the children, and we do what we ought in that line, as well as by teaching religious truths, etc.

I am not in favor of putting in a separate building. I believe in having rooms set apart in the school buildings themselves for Sloyd work. I believe that if any of us should go into this work we should start it right, and I believe we do something for the homes of these children to bring this instruction to their homes and that is something of great help to them.

Superintendent Maxwell.—Is it your experience that in Sloyd work in the elementary schools the desk covers, such as we use in our truant school, are sufficient, or that a separate work shop should be fitted up?

Superintendent Blodgett.—We have separate rooms fitted up.

Superintendent Maxwell.—Would you think it advisable to try putting it into one ordinary class room as they do in Utica?

Superintendent Blodgett.—It seems to me the better way would be to have one separate room, and put them into Sloyd work in the sixth year and continue it up to seventh and eighth.

Superintendent Maxwell.—Do you consider it advisable to begin sewing at an earlier age with girls than in the sixth year in the school?

Superintendent Blodgett.—I cannot answer that question.

Superintendent Maxwell.—In both New York and Brooklyn we begin sewing at the commencement of the fourth year in school, and my experience is that children beginning at the fourth year of school take up the elementary work in sewing very much better than the older children.

Superintendent Foster.—We have manual training for boys in the sixth, seventh and eighth grades; and for girls we have the sewing in the same grades, and they take it as superintendent Blodgett advises—the boys in their manual training work and the girls in their sewing at the same hour. We are using the Russian system, and I do not think it is the best. It does not produce anything definite. We are in doubt as to whether we have our work in just the right place.

Superintendent Maxwell.—As to the question of when sewing should be commenced with girls, I am pretty well of the opinion that the beginning of the fourth year of school is the proper time. I have come to the conclusion that boys in the corresponding classes should be taught sewing as their beginning of manual training work. The boys in our schools are clamoring for sewing, and we are giving it to them as the beginning of their manual training work.

Discussion closed.

October 21, 1897.

Meeting called to order at 9.40 a. m. Owing to absence of chairmen of committees, the first subject taken up was: The necessity of a state truant school.

Superintendent Diamond.—I will give some personal experience in this matter. I had occasion, within the last ten days, in our town, to bring a couple of boys to our police court for assaulting their teacher. One boy was undergoing discipline and the other brother took a hand in and, between the two, the teacher got the worst of it. They were complained of before the magistrate and the boys were brought up. The magistrate was, perhaps, a little too hasty, and he sent them to the truant school at Rochester. Then we found that one of the boys was too young to go there. We then found we could do nothing as there was no place to which he could be sent. The age of the boy was 11.

Committee on legislation.—Superintendent Cole, of Albany, chairman, said: Mr. President and gentlemen of the council of school superintendents—The committee on legislation respectfully reports:

CANANDAIGUA, N. Y., *October* 21, 1897.

To the Council of School Superintendents:

Your committee on legislation respectfully reports that in accordance with instructions given at your last meeting, an act was prepared and presented to the legislature to provide for the furnishing of free text-books and school supplies to the pupils of the public schools of the state. The terms of the bill were mandatory, except as to common school districts. The act was introduced early in the session of the legislature and was duly referred to the senate committee on public education. Your committee was unable, however, to obtain a hearing from the committee until quite late in the session and even then it was not practicable to get the attention of the full committee. A patient hearing was given, however, and your committee presented the claims of this bill for favorable action at considerable length. The committee on public education declined to report the bill favorably. Apparently there was no opposition to the bill; that is, no one appeared before the committee in opposition. Perhaps the opposition was all the more effective because it did not appear on the surface. The experience of your committee is that a measure of this kind, which is rather sweeping in its provisions, is rarely adopted when first offered, and it will probably be necessary to urge its passage again and again before the desired legislation can be obtained.

Your committee was freely consulted by the Department of Public Instruction during its preparation of a state truant school bill which, all its friends were persuaded, would have a fair opportunity for enactment, because the governor had practically recommended the establishment of such a school in his message to the legislature. It seemed, however, that the time was not propitious for the establishment of new institutions, and the proposed law never emerged from the committee room.

The following resolution is recommended for adoption by the council:

Resolved, That the committee on legislation be and is hereby instructed to present again to the legislature of the state an act to provide for furnishing free text-books and school supplies to the pupils of the public schools, and to urge its enactment.

CHARLES W. COLE.
WM. H. MAXWELL.
CHAS. E. GORTON,
A. B. BLODGETT,
SHERMAN WILLIAMS.
E. W. GRIFFITH.

On motion, duly carried, the report was accepted and ordered printed in the minutes of the meeting.

Regularly moved and seconded that the resolution offered by the committee be adopted.

Superintendent Cole.—The committee found that there was no

argument presented against the theory of this bill, and I believe firmly that no one substantial argument can be brought forward. The objections to the passage of such a bill are entirely on the grounds of expediency. The old objections were urged, especially that it ought to be a matter of local option. The specious plea was brought forward that it interfered with home rule. It is well understood that any locality may, now legally adopt a system of free text-books if that is the wish of the citizens of that locality; but the real objection, the strongest objection in the minds of those who opposed the bill was that they were not ready for the enforcement of this kind of thing; that in one place they were building a new school house, enlarging their facilities and expending a great deal of money and that they could not feel that they should be compelled to raise additional funds for this special purpose. It was immediately pointed out to them that that argument, if accepted, would always hold good; that if this were proper legislation and desirable that this argument would hold against it at any time and therefore the present time would be as prosperous as any other time. I feel that in the future the only way in which this proposed legislation will be passed, will be entirely on this line and the opponents of this measure will not attempt to argue against the good policy of using a free text-book system and will rely entirely upon this argument of expediency.

I feel that public sentiment is in favor of this system and I am sure it is growing. Another position was taken by a member of the legislature, that he would not object to it at all provided we would exclude certain localities. Well, the question immediately rose where to draw the line. The first class cities have free text-books, one of the second and at least two of the others are well prepared to accept it, if not to urge it. In the smaller cities of the third class, the argument of expediency is very strongly urged, but no other. I feel that all that would be necessary would be to keep up the agitation of this subject, and although we may not succeed this winter or next winter, by continuing to ask for it we shall obtain it before long.

Superintendent Norris.—I for one will vote against this resolution. I do not agree with brother Cole that no argument can be made against free text-books. I think the time has come when in legislative matters it is well for us to go slow. Several things have happened within the last year or two that have made the people a little doubtful about some of the advancements that have been made. In legislation for school purposes the Regents' office and the Department are receiving a great deal of criticism from people who think that it is not necessary to furnish everything to children in our public schools. I do not agree with this sentiment entirely, but I do protest that the time is not come when the larger villages are ready for free text-books. I most sincerely oppose the resolution.

Superintendent Gorton.—I would ask to what extent in other states this system is prevalent.

Superintendent Cole.—I know that the states of Massachusetts, Connecticut, Maine and New Hampshire have the full free text-book law, and Pennsylvania also, most of them have had it in operation for eight years. I think it was eight years ago that Massachusetts adopted the law. Of course, this committee offers the resolution subject to the opinion of the council. If the council directs the committee that the proposed law should be changed in any way we shall obey your directions in every respect.

Sherman Williams.—As to a question of this kind, where we have large cities and villages, with great diversity of interests, what may be expedient in some parts of the state may not be in others. Speaking for the villages, which I represent, I am very clear that if they alone were to be considered, that a like movement would be desirable. I believe if they should vote upon that question at their next annual meeting, it would result in being carried in every village in the state. So far as the villages are concerned, if you say that they shall vote upon the matter you solve the question. I do not think it would be possible to have the cities vote upon it.

Superintendent Cole.—Such proposition as Mr. Williams has made would not be opposed by any member of the committee at all. I suggest that this come in the form of general instructions to the committee if the resolution is passed.

Superintendent Rogers.—I am heartily in favor of free text-books, but I believe there is a great deal of sound common sense in what superintendent Williams has said. I believe that the idea of free text-books is bound to prevail, and that it will be of much more service in these smaller towns if it comes by the will of the people than if it comes against it.

Superintendent Marsh.—It seems to me there is a good deal of sense in what superintendent Williams has said, but it also seems to me there is a flaw in his argument to this extent, that a large number of the smaller towns have already adopted free text-books, and we do not want to resubmit the question to these communities.

Inspector Barr.—It is absolutely valueless to crowd through a compulsory bill without watching for results in regard to bills that have already been passed.

Superintendent Cole.—The bill referred to I presume is the one giving our school districts the privilege of voting upon this question.

Superintendent Rogers.—I move that the law be optional and be submitted to a vote of the people.

Superintendent Caswell.—Do I understand that it is the idea of this resolution that it is compulsory on the part of all towns and villages to put this question before the people at this time or soon; that it must be submitted to the people? If so the cause is lost. If the question was submitted to the people next year it would be lost. In a few years it may become strong.

Superintendent Williams.—Why?

Superintendent Caswell.—Because they do not appreciate the advantages yet. It takes time to bring about the sentiment in favor of it.

Superintendent Willetts.—The cities of the second class should be recognized in this matter. On the matter of local option I represent a city of the second class, and there is a strong opposition to compelling that city or any other community to furnish free text-books for the pupils. Mr. Cole has referred to the defeat of the bill last year. I believe that is a local matter. I know it is with us, and I think it will be a great mistake if a law is passed compelling cities and villages or communities to do what they think is not for their interests.

Superintendent Blodgett.—For three years we have had a free text-book system in Syracuse. It was taken up by the laboring people and pressed through and passed by the legislature by a very large majority. It was only opposed by a few politicians who wanted to keep the tax budget down. You will have the working people with you in a matter of this kind.

Superintendent Kennedy.—I sympathize with the free text-book idea, but think there may be many here who are opposed to the compulsory text-book system or compulsion of any kind. We think it is an unwise thing to say the least. We have the power now to give free text-books. The principle of compulsion is an unwise one.

Superintendent Cole.—I do not represent the resolution. The committee stand ready to accept all amendments offered by superintendent Williams of having it include all localities, cities and villages except those that are using the free-text book system at present.

Superintendent Rogers offered the following as a substitute for the resolution of the committee:

Resolved, That the committee be requested to prepare a bill which shall contain a requirement that the question of the adoption of free text-books and supplies be submitted to a vote of the people in all cities and union free school districts that do not now make use of this system.

Superintendent Bullis.—I rather object to the restriction in regard to villages. The wording is not clear.

Superintendent Truesdale.—In many of the villages the school limits or boundaries do not correspond to those of the village.

Superintendent Gorton.—I believe that in the whole discussion not a word has been said about the district schools, and the law ignores them entirely. That is not right.

Superintendent Maxwell.—I think superintendent Gorton's remarks are wise. I hope Mr. Rogers will include in his amendment, where free text-books are not already in use.

Superintendent Foster.—Supplies are included with free text-books. Is it the idea to include supplies? In our city we furnish the text-books.

Inspector Barr.—Leave the motion by simply reading that the vote be required in all school districts of this state.

Superintendent Williams.—I think it is rather presumptious for us to take up that phase of the question. The school commissioners have a meeting next month, and they know more about it than we do. I think we ought to appoint a committee to confer with them.

Superintendent Maxwell.—I do not see why we cannot make this broad enough to cover all the schools in the state.

Superintendent Whitney.—I believe this is a matter of policy, a matter of courtesy, that the suggestion of superintendent Williams be carried into effect, and I believe this council should appoint a committee to confer with the meeting next month at Saratoga.

Question was called upon the resolution of Superintendent Rogers and it was adopted.

The council then passed to the consideration of the topic, What amendments are necessary to the compulsory attendance law?

Superintendent Maxwell.—My experience shows me that for the effective administration of a compulsory education law two amendments are absolutely necessary. There may be others, but the necessity for these two amendments first forces itself upon me very strongly. The first of these relates to the time during which a child must be in school. The existing law provides that the child must be in school from eight to fourteen years of age, except that during the two years between twelve and fourteen, he may work after he has been eighty days in school; that between fourteen and sixteen he may be at work all the time, but if not at work he must be in school. It was the intention of the committee on legislation, when this bill was adopted, that the whole time of child life between the ages of eight and fourteen ought to be spent in school; but owing to opposition at that time, to making so strong a measure, the committee were obliged to concede this plan. The children should be permitted to go to work after spending eighty days in any school during the two years elapsing between twelve and fourteen. Since the compulsory education law was adopted, however, the legislature of 1896 passed two acts, one known as the factory act; the other known as the mercantile establishment act. Both these laws forbid in the most positive terms any child being employed in cities and villages before fourteen years of age or until he is fourteen years of age. The enforcement of these laws is directly under the factory inspector and health commissioners of cities and villages. It is manifest, therefore, that there is now a conflict between the factory and mercantile establishment act and the compulsory education law. The compulsory education law says that a child may go to work between twelve and fourteen years of age if he has spent eighty days in school. It is doubtful in my mind whether the factory and mercantile establishment law have not repealed this section of the compulsory education law. If so, it is a very bad thing, because the compulsory education law is the only law that provides a penalty. The other laws are positive enough, but do not provide a penalty. Therefore, I believe the compulsory education law should be amended so that children would be required to attend school between the first of October and the following June, between the ages of eight and fourteen years. Personally I should be in favor of extending the limit upwards; but I know there would be so much opposition to that that I do not think it would be wise to recommend it at present, and if we can succeed in getting these it is all we would ask for.

The other is that provision which says that a boy could be committed to a truant school until the end of the current school year. The state Superintendent, as I understand, made a decision that the current school year ends on the thirty-first of July. Consequently all boys committed under the compulsory education law must be discharged on the thirty-first of July. The effect of that I find is exceedingly bad.

Of course I do not pretend to speak on this subject from any experience except my own. I think that in my own case, when boys are committed to our truant school in Brooklyn, say—in April or March or May—they know perfectly well that they have to be discharged on the thirty-first of July. They do not care whether they make any progress or not, and they do not try. We discharged, if I remember right, about seventy-five boys from our truant school and not one of these had any idea of reform. The *result is* that already this term—they have been sent back to us and many of the boys were in worse condition than when sent into the school first. When a boy is committed in November or October, and remains five or six months we turn him out a pretty good boy, who is willing and ready to go to school. But the boys who are committed in the spring know that they have to get out on the thirty-first of July; therefore it seems to me that this part of the law requires amending. What I believe in is the undetermined sentence, at least, to a certain extent, that is, that a boy may be committed until a certain age is reached. I am not clear in my own mind whether that certain age should be 14 or 16 years. Upon the whole, I am rather inclined to favor 14. My experience seems to point to this, that it is not desirable to have boys between the ages of 14 and 16 in our truant school. Their meeting with boys from 10 to 14 has rather a bad influence in many cases, a very bad influence. A boy of 14 years, who has the privilege of working or going to school and will not work or go to school should be treated as a vagrant, and sent to some reformatory.

I have drawn up this resolution, which I offer for adoption:

Resolved, That the committee on legislation be instructed to prepare and submit to the legislature two amendments to the compulsory education law, as follows:

First, That children between the ages of eight and fourteen shall be required to attend school the entire time the public schools are in session, from October 1, to June 1.

Second, That truants under fourteen years of age may be committed to truant schools until they are fourteen, but may be discharged at any time when they give evidence of reform; and that truants between fourteen and sixteen years of age may be committed until they are sixteen, but may be discharged at any time when they give evidence of reform.

Superintendent Rogers.—I am in favor of this amendment offered by superintendent Maxwell. There are one or two other points that have occurred to me. I offer it as a suggestion which I think will bear fruit some day, that we shall adopt not an exclusive time limit as a time that a boy or girl should be discharged from the school, but some minimum standard of attainment. It is not enough that a boy stay around and look at the clock until he is fourteen; but that he should be compelled to do something. The boy knows that when he is fourteen he has got to work, and the school interest disappears before that time, when if he knows he has some definite thing to do he will do it.

The age limit of time extends from October to June and should be extended to cities of the third class—and to schools in the rural districts, but I do not see how the compulsory education law could be continued through the entire school year.

Superintendent Maxwell.—With regard to that point, I do not see that we have any choice in the matter. These children by the laws I have referred to are prevented from working. As I understand Mr. Rogers he desires that in the city of Jamestown, children should be permitted to go to work between certain ages.

Superintendent Rogers.—No.

Superintendent Maxwell.—I have for many years been convinced myself of the wisdom of the suggestion that there should be a standard of attainment in school work before a child should be permitted to leave the school. Mr. President, you will remember the first compulsory law we submitted to the legislature, and it met with such tremendous opposition that it was absolutely impossible to pass it. We were obliged to withdraw that feature of the law. I do not think we can get this provision with regard to the attainment of a certain standard embodied this year, and now that I understand superintendent Rogers' amendment, that September and June be included I shall be perfectly willing to accept that. Possibly we may be able to word this amendment so that it may be optional in certain places, and if so, I am sure the committee will be glad to do it.

Superintendent Burgess.—The amendment of superintendent Maxwell is an excellent one, giving undetermined sentences. As the law now stands pupils committed to institutions have to be discharged on or before the first of July. It seems to me that it is not a good thing to discharge a boy during school vacation for the reason that having been in a truant institution where they have been under discipline and control and where they have partially acquired habits of regularity to throw them out of such school, back to their homes again where no school is in session, gives them an opportunity to recover their old habits and makes it doubly difficult for them when the schools open to return to them. We sent a number of children to White Plains. We sent them rather late in the year. There were eight or nine brought home on the 31st of July. Our schools did not reopen until the 14th of September and they would have had six weeks in which to get back into their old ways and the regularity and discipline which they had partially acquired in that time are almost totally lost. I think if a provision can be incorporated in the law it would be wise legislation.

State attendance officer A. M. Wright.—I am heartily in accord with the suggestion of the committee on the undetermined sentences. I want to emphasize what superintendent Maxwell has said in regard to the vast influence, which boys between 14 and 16 exercise upon other boys in the truant schools. I have been to the various schools and institutions where truants have been confined. I have visited them and watched with a great deal of interest the effect upon the young boys of 14 and 16 years of age. They are not only dangerous to the younger boys but they have habits which are extremely bad. Some of them they learn at home and carry them with them to the institution.

I am also in accord with the suggestion that the law should be made to conform with the other laws. There is one little trouble that arises in the enforcement of this law and comes before me very frequently in correspondence, and that is the part of teachers regarding the attendance law and in regard to keeping of these records by teachers of private schools. If the law is to be amended at all it would be well to amend it in these features which are found weak in the inforcement of the law.

Superintendent Cole.—As Mr. Maxwell is very chary of forming a judgment on an important matter solely upon his own experience, the only point concerning which I am in doubt in regard to the terms of the resolution, so far, is as to the age limit; whether it would be wiser to limit it to 14 years or to let it remain as it is now, to 16 years; that the person must be either attending school or be at work during the last two years. My personal experience is somewhat in the direction of the great benefit of retaining a hold upon the boys from 14 to 16 years.

We have been obliged to commit several of this class to truant schools and contrary to what has been said, in certain instances very excellent results have followed; even a complete reformation in several cases. I would say on the other hand that there were two cases where absolutely no change was made in the characteristics of the boy. There is one thing about keeping your hands on the boys until they come within these two ages. We know that period between 14 and 16 years is a critical one in the life of the boy. This is the time when some influences should be brought to bear that will bring a change for the better. Of course this is a reformatory matter, but the best result we can seek after all is the reform of individuals.

I feel at present that it would really be a loss of some fine opportunities if we let go entirely those boys who are between 14 and 16 years of age.

Superintendent Emerson.—The conflict between the compulsory education law and the other recent laws led me to ask from our legal advisor of the city of Buffalo, the corporation counsel, a decision as to the difference, and his decision was that the compulsory education law had substantially been amended by these recent laws and that such laws now requiring the attendance of pupils until the age of 14 years were not of any account; that the former provision which allowed pupils to work before 14 was amended.

This compulsory education law ought to be amended to conform to the factory law because it leads to misunderstandings. If both laws were alike not many questions would come up in that particular.

If you change the law so that children may be committed to a truant school until 14 years, I am afraid there will be trouble in getting them committed.

Mr. Maxwell.—Or until they are reformed.

Superintendent Emerson.—We have to deal with it in Buffalo. They do not want to have these boys a charge upon the city for two or three years.

Superintendent Maxwell.—As I said to the council, I am not clear whether the age limit should be 14 or 16 years. There is one point, I fear, on which there may be some misunderstanding. It is not proposed to relax in any way that provision which requires boys between 14 and 16 years, if they are not at work, to go to school. It is not proposed to relax that in any way whatever. If you have not the power to commit to a truant school between 14 and 16 decidedly you do relax that provision of the law which requires boys to be at school if they are not at work and I think that is a very strong point in making the age limit 16 years. Furthermore, while I grant a good deal of what Mr. Wright has said in regard to possible influences of boys between 14 and 16 on younger boys, that is but a question of administration in the truant school and handled there.

What I should like is that before this amendment is put the meeting of this council may vote as to whether the limit of age when the boy must leave the truant school shall be 14 or 16. If those favoring this shall exceed those opposed I shall insert it in my resolution.

Superintendent Beardsley.—Does the compulsory education law authorize the superintendent to commit truant children to the truant school?

Superintendent Maxwell.—Certainly.

Superintendent Blodgett.—As to inserting the number 14 and 16 years as the age limit, I find now that it is true by our experience in Syracuse, that we can in a large number of cases have the child committed, with the consent of the parents, to the truant school with an undetermined sentence. If that were absolutely fixed at 14 or 16 years you would have to go to the courts in nine cases out of ten. I should be in favor of fixing it at 14 and I realize that that means a great deal of court work.

Superintendent Williams.—The hold that we have upon the *pupil* 14 to 16 years is worth all that we have in the law. There are some boys that go to destruction between the ages of 14 and 16 simply because they have nothing to do.

Mr. Wright.—It strikes me that this matter is not necessarily fatal, that this law can be so amended to limit the age, as 14 years for those who are under 14 when committed and if it becomes necessary to commit a child over 14 that 16 can be put in; but it strikes me that you will make it necessary to have a pretty large number of truant schools before you get through with it.

I cannot see any reason why we cannot keep control of children between 14 and 16 years just as well. Still if you want to make the limit 16, if that seems wise, I certainly cannot forsee any serious objection to it except that these institutions have to be so conducted that there shall be sufficient force to look after boys carefully and closely.

Superintendent Benham.—Supposing a boy is 13 years old and bad, and I put him into an institution until he is 14. He is not reformed but his father comes after him and says I have work for him I have no course but to discharge him.

Superintendent Babcock.—An amendment something like this, that a boy committed to a truant school may be kept in such institution in the discretion of the managers for one year.

Superintendent Young.—I can conceive that possible in some other state than New York. There might be some temptation for the manager to keep the boy longer than he should be kept.

Superintendent Maxwell.—Boys who are committed to a truant school who are under 14 must be discharged when they reach 14, or if re-committed may be retained until they are 16. Because I thing the suggestion of my friend from Niagara is correct, when a boy is 14 the father comes along and says he has a job for him and you have to let him out anyway.

Those in favor of the resolution as amended by the suggestion of superintendent Wright please say aye. Motion carried.

Motion of superintendent Rogers lost and original motion of superintendent Maxwell carried.

Mr. Wright.—I find a great deal of difficulty arising from the interpretation of this section, which reads "Teachers' Record of Attendance, etc." I notice that schools, not the public schools, the private schools, have to keep these records and that these records must be open to the inspection of attendance officers or any other person duly authorized by the school authorities of the district and may inspect and copy the same. It seems to me that it would be well if we could introduce an amendment to the law, that such teachers shall, at stated periods, report to the superintendent of schools and the public school authorities of the district of their registers, not less than once a month. I know that in many localities, if abstracts of the registers, or attendance records, were furnished to the public school authorities a more accurate record of the attendance of children at private schools may be had. These abstracts, I believe, would bring the private schools into more direct relation with the public school authorities. Certainly the department cannot look to anybody but the public school authorities for their information.

Superintendent Rogers offered a resolution, to provide that in every village or union free school district all children shall attend school from September 1 to July 1.

Superintendent Maxwell.—I should be very much opposed to that resolution. I do not think it would be possible to get such a resolution passed by any legislature that has existed in the state of New York or in any American community. If there is anything the American people stand for it is individual liberty and what is the effect of this resolution? It practically says to the board of education of any city or village in this state that all the children within the city or village shall attend school all the time the public schools are in session and that means that it has the power to compel every private school that takes children within the age limits of the law to keep school the same time as the public schools are in session. It is perfectly idle for us to talk on such proposition as that. We would be simply laughed at if we went before the legislature with such a thing.

Superintendent Bullis.—I move that the resolution lie on the table. (Motion was seconded and carried.)

Necessity of a state truant school and what shall the smaller cities and towns do with habitual truants?

State attendance officer A. M. Wright.—There is no question in the minds of those who are observing the difficulties in the way of committing children to institutions under the truant law. I am receiving letters constantly asking where can we commit children and I am obliged thus far to confine my information, for the Protestant children to one institution, the Westchester Temporary Home, and to people residing in Erie county that is a good ways off and the expense of sending a boy across the state, with an officer, is certainly a very large expense. Of course, there are several institutions where children of Catholic parentage may be confined and I am very free to say that when children were sent to those institutions they have been well cared for and that they return from these institutions better boys.

I do not think it is necessary to ask this question. I think that, as teachers and superintendents and others interested in the schools of the state believe in it, the legislature should be asked this year to at least establish one such institution as an experiment, and I think the year will be more propitious for such result than last year. It seems to me that it is one of these things that if we do not get it one year we must keep at it.

A bill will be presented to the legislature of Massachusetts at its coming session which provides for four state institutions called "parental homes." They have adopted our idea of state supervision in the matter of attendance at school. Heretofore it has been left to the locality. They propose to have four "parental homes." If Massachusetts needs four of these institutions we will have need of many more before we get through.

Superintendent Benham.—I have come to the conclusion that it would be better far if we could establish in the county of Niagara a truant school of our own We might make it upon the county plan, or if that is too small, every county could maintain a truant school with these cities.

At present we can only send our truants to White Plains, and if by securing legislative enactment power was given to the county of Niagara to establish a county truant school we could do it without trouble or expense to the state of New York. The state truant school means too great an expenditure—too many people to run it.

State Superintendent Skinner.—I am satisfied that if we properly enforce the compulsory education law that the state must furnish some institution to which its boys and girls may be taken. I have thought that so long as the law provides that truants must be liberated at the end of the school year that to establish a truant school with the liability that a portion of the year there would be no pupils it would be idle to ask it.

Since the enactment of the two laws which have been referred to, which virtually amend the compulsory education law, I see the way clearer to the establishment of a truant school in which there shall be some semblance to class work; but if any class work is not possible, then we can safely come up with the proposition of individual instruction of each pupil.

As Mr. Wright has said, Massachusetts and other states have looked into this question. If Massachusetts can present to the legislature of that state an approval of four truant schools, surely there ought to be not the slightest objection to giving New York one, and I regret very much that we could not try the experiment and demonstrate its usefulness. The demand for it will increase from month to month. I had thought that the demand might be lessened, but the other day I took up the newspaper from my own home, Watertown, and I saw that a truant officer was starting for Rochester with four truants, and on the same train was an officer from Gouverneur with three. There

This teacher we pay considerably more than we do any teacher of the same grade of work in the city. We commit to that school, through the principal, any boy who is either a truant or who is disorderly under the terms of the compulsory education law. The principal of any school is given the power by the board to suspend in two ways. He may suspend temporarily for a day or two, or notify the parents to confer and settle the case. If, however, it is a case of persistent truancy or a case of persistent ill-behavior, the principal has the power to suspend the pupil indefinitely and send him to the ungraded school. The principal does not need to consult me. If he decides that the boy can no longer be well managed in his school, he may send him to the ungraded school, and he notifies the principal of that school of the transfer, giving a history of the child, giving his age, grade, work done and anything pertaining to him that will throw light upon the case. He also notifies, at the same time, the attendance officer of the section of the city in which the child lives. The attendance officer, on receipt of this notice, at his first opportunity, goes to the house of those in parental relation to the boy, and states that he has called to notify them that he has such a notice. He escorts the boy to his new school and the attendance officer knows that he is there. He installs him in the school. Now, you will notice that the suspension is for an indefinite period, an indeterminate suspension. We adopted a plan which I saw in operation in the Brooklyn truant school, to determine how long the suspension will last. We give a certain number of discredits to each boy on coming in. He is given 500 marks and is told that he may reduce the 500 by 15 marks per day, 5 for good work in his studies, 5 for punctuality and regular attendance and 5 for good conduct. In this way he may reduce the discredits given him, and when they are wiped out he is permitted to return to his own school, but, of course, how soon depends upon himself.

One marked feature of this plan is that we make it unpleasant for the boys by making them walk, in many cases, a great distance. They must go to that school. They must be regular attendants. The hours are different. The morning hour is half an hour later than the school hour. The reason for this is that they may not have any chance to mingle with the regular pupils of the building. They are kept over half an hour later. It is impressed upon them that they are not favorites, and that they are sent there for reasons not creditable to themselves, and that they can work their way out by good behavior.

I think we have saved at least $1,500 by maintaining this ungraded school beyond the cost of maintenance. Otherwise we should have been obliged to send most of these boys to reformatories. I think something of this kind is practicable in the smaller cities and smaller towns that cannot have a truant school and yet are reluctant to send boys so far away from home.

Superintendent Burgess.—We have some trouble with a few disorderly boys. I find it difficult to fill an ungraded school.

Superintendent Sagendorph.—I would like to ask whether we have the right to send children for disorder.

Superintendent Cole.—Yes, sir.

Superintendent Marsh.—We organized, three years ago, an ungraded room for these reasons, first, to take care of those boys that we did not care to send to an institution; second, to take care of the bad boy in school, and third, to take care of the boys who are too old to send back into the grades to which they belong properly. The result has been that we have taken the troublesome boys out of the schools. Furthermore, we have had great results, from an educational standpoint, which it has been impossible for us to secure before in the regular ways.

Superintendent Whitney.—Do they place, in those schools, the still boy with the disorderly?

Superintendent Marsh.—No.

Superintendent Foster.—Our experience has been almost exactly the same. We had a number of boys who had committed various misdeeds, which fitted them for the industrial school at Rochester, and it has happened in our case, where the boy was not fit for a room in our ungraded room that we have been able to send him to Rochester to the industrial school, which is a good place for him, especially at an age when it is impossible in the ordinary truant school to have him sit with the little children who may come there. We have less in the room now than we ever had, and perhaps we shall not have to get so many at any time. At present we have but three or four in the room and we have seats for eighteen.

Superintendent Marsh.—I would like to make another suggestion. Most small towns have a central school building, and our first two years' work was in that building. I believe that the rooms should be kept separate and the boys kept separate from the other pupils.

Superintendent Bullis.—We have had an ungraded room in Oswego for twenty-five years. We have done some good by means of it.

Superintendent Norris announced that the local committee had arranged to give the gentlemen present a trip on the lake, but as the weather was so inclement it has been thought advisable to postpone it.

THURSDAY, OCTOBER 21st, 2:30 p. m.

Meeting called to order at 2:38. Subject: Report of chairman of committee on licensing teachers.

Chairman Downing stated that the committee had no report to make, as it had not been called together; but wished the committee to be continued. On motion, duly carried, it was so ordered.

Superintendent Cole offered the following resolutions:

(1) *Resolved*, That this council hereby expresses its unqualified approval of the proposition that the state shall establish, support and control an institution or institutions for the purposes of confining, instructing and reforming such persons as may be committed thereto under the provisions of the compulsory education act.

(2) *Resolved*, That this council respectfully and earnestly urge upon the governor and the legislature of 1898 the enactment of a law which shall establish the institution or institutions described in the foregoing resolution.

(3) *Resolved*, That the president and secretary of this council be, and are hereby, instructed to prepare and transmit to the governor and to each of the members of the legislature of 1898 a memorial embodying the foregoing resolution, and to affix thereto, in addition to their official signatures, the names, official designations and addresses of the members of this council.

They were unanimously adopted.

Superintendent Snow was requested to make some remarks upon the death of Dr. Edward A. Sheldon. He said:

This matter comes up unexpectedly to me. I shall be very glad to pay a tribute to Dr. Sheldon commensurate with my estimation of the man. I have known Dr. Sheldon nearly fifty years. He was a college associate for three years, he being a year in advance of me, and I was intimately associated with him during his college course, belonging to the same societies in the college. I can say this of Dr. Sheldon, from what I know of him during his college course, that every duty that was assigned to him was faithfully and conscientiously performed by him. I think that this characteristic of him is one that has continued during his entire career. It was but a short time after his graduation from college that he was placed at the head of the Oswego normal school, in which position he has continued up to the time of his death, some two months ago.

It is not necessary for me to recount what Dr. Sheldon has accomplished in this position. He established an enviable reputation for himself and for the school, a reputation that was national, I may say, international. I think that the Oswego normal school has maintained a reputation for the excellence of its graduates that is surpassed by no other institution in this or any other nation.

The loss of the educational interests of the state in the death of Dr. Sheldon I will not undertake to set forth. You all knew him personally or by reputation, knew the work he accomplished, the esteem in which he was held and how deserving that esteem was. I think, then, that it would be proper that some expression of sentiment on the part of this body, gentlemen who knew him well, knew how much we are indebted to him in educational matters, that some expression be sent to the body that gathers there this evening for the purpose of preparing a testimonial and I most heartily concur in the movement to send such testimonial.

On motion, duly carried, telegram in accordance with the above was sent.

Dr. Stowell.—I want to second this motion, and suggest that it may seem fitting that a committee be appointed from this body to draft a suitable memorial that should be a matter of permanent record, more than simply a passing record, in view of the services of Dr. Sheldon, which have placed him among the foremost educators of this continent; and when time shall place him where he belongs there will be no man his equal. With such a loss it is only fitting that any educational body or meeting should take some special action relative to the loss of such a man. I move that the chair appoint a committee on such a memorial.

Motion carried.

Chair appointed Dr. Stowell, superintendents Snow and Bullis such committee.

Superintendent Snow presented the following resolution:

Resolved, That it is the sense of this council that the enumerators for taking the biennial census, under chapter 550, laws of 1895, should be appointed and employed by the board of education or other local school authorities of the city or village in which such census is to be taken, and that the committee on legislation be instructed to endeavor to procure an amendment to said law to that effect.

Superintendent Cole.—Whatever may be the present phase of this question, it seems to me that this is a matter that this council ought not to go into. I really feel that the effect of directing the committee on legislation to make an appeal to get such an amendment to the general laws is hardly in place. I really feel that it belittles the functions of the committee on legislation to ask them to do anything of this kind. You all know that there are many things connected with this business that are of a political nature. I feel that it would be ill-advised to ask legislation in a matter of this kind.

Superintendent Maxwell.—I very heartily agree with what superintendent Cole has just said. Had this resolution been presented when superintendent Skinner was present it might have been proper to discuss it. I think the resolution should be withdrawn.

Superintendent Snow.—I had no personal feelings whatever in introducing the resolution. I tried to get an opportunity to introduce the resolution during the time superintendent Skinner was present. There are representatives of the state Department here now. The school census is a matter that pertains simply to school matters. It is for the purpose of enforcing the compulsory education law, as I understand it, and it seems to me that the original act should have provided for the appointment of these enumerators. In our own city we can employ enumerators and have the census taken for at least half the money, and just as well as by any other authority. Will not the school authorities know better than any other authority can, the most competent men for this work? I appreciate the fact that the gentleman refers to what has taken place during the present year. If the committee on legislation are sensitive about introducing this matters to the legislature, and think it is too trifling for such committee, I would like an expression of opinion upon it.

Superintendent Maxwell moved to lay resolution on table.

Motion carried. Ayes, 33; nays, 16.

President Blodgett at this time introduced Mr. W. R. George, superintendent of the George Junior Republic, who said: I can assure you that it affords me the highest pleasure to be present to-day to speak with a body of gentlemen who are interested in educational matters. Each and every morning I receive about forty letters in my mail, a large percentage of them are inquiries as to what the Junior Republic is. I hope to be able to say, in fact I can say it at the present time, that the only difference between the Junior Republic and the great big glorious republic is in the age of its citizens. They are boys and girls from 12 upwards instead of men and women of 21 and over. Everything else is the same as nearly as possible, the same conditions, the social conditions, the civic conditions, the commercial conditions made to correspond to those as nearly as possible with the like conditions in our great republic. It is not a place where I am carrying out hobbies of my own. Like every other man I have my hobbies, but the Junior Republic is not the place to ride them. Its boys and girls are going out into the great big *world and* we want to teach them cause and effect. They are.

not playing at citizens of the republic. It is not play, if we get down to rock bottom, and I say the same conditions, and therefore, they are obliged to work or starve to death. A great many persons ask me that question, "Do you mean to say that you would allow a boy or girl to starve to death?" I mean to say that very thing, unless, of course, they are sick; but any boy or girl who is able-bodied and has all the faculties, should starve to death if he or she is not willing to work. I want you to eliminate from your mind, as I speak about this, any thought of an institution of any character, however good it may be, and there are lots of them. I do not want you to compare it with any institution for we are not anything that is like an institution and we are simply copying after our great republic. The same laws govern us; the boys are enforcing the laws of New York state. Only the other day the legislature passed a bill. It was a remarkable bill considering that it came from a boy.

The question of penalties largely rests with the judge. They would have to enact special laws for various cases, and we have such a variety of them. One day a boy arose in the legislature and proposed that for all criminal offenses that the penalty, the sentence by the judge, should be one one-hundredth part of the maximum sentence, and that one one-hundredth part of the minimum sentence prescribed by the penal code be added; and if a boy was tried and sentenced for larceny, the term was ten years, one one-hundredth part would be a few days. That was a good rule and it is working admirably. If they found the sentence was too light the legislature could enact a special law.

You will know, gentlemen, each and every one of you, that the majority of boys, the young fellows, are trying to get on in the world and a great many of them with as little personal effort as possible. They are depending upon a father or mother or a rich uncle or by a periodical appeal or something or other to carry them through life, and when their prop gives way they are all at sea. The first object of mine is to kick away all the props. When a boy or girl enters the place we allow him to stand, and teach him to stand on his feet, and thus he will acquire strength in his efforts to rise. They must work if they would eat. They are citizens. I could tell you stories of our every department of work, but I think you are ready to question me. If a question arises in your mind. "What do you do in your Junior Republic under certain circumstances?" I would answer by asking another. "What would you do in the greater republic under similar circumstances?" I think I will let you question me right off.

Superintendent Maxwell.—I think it would throw a great deal of light upon the subject if Mr. George told the council something about how he came to establish the George Junior Republic. I cannot think but it would be useful to every person present.

Mr. George.—In 1890 I became interested in the boys in New York city. I devoted a good deal of time, looking after boys and girls and forming the acquaintance of the little children in the city. One day I hit upon the plan of taking them to the country for a vacation. I went to my old home; went to see some friends, and asked them if they would supply provisions for certain days. They complied readily; and I brought the boys, the first being in 1890. I had no other idea than to give them all the fun they could get in two weeks. We had lots of fun, but in an evil hour somebody sent in a package of clothing to distribute among the boys. I distributed the clothes. When they returned to the city they brought a good stock along with them. After we returned to the city the parents became aware of the fact that I was trying to help the boys.

As to the question of punishment among the boys. I had about fifty, and they would steal green apples. The farmers complained, and they would come in and criticise long and loud, and I would have to settle bills. Then I was exasperated with the small boy. They answered me: "I did not do anything, Mr. George," or "I will never do it again." Then they would go out and at it again. To make a long story short, I flogged them; I mean I thrashed thirty-two boys for stealing apples. I had them in a large assembly building. Usually the small boy, when anything good is being given out, can say, here, sir; please, sir. There was nothing of that kind this morning. Corporal punishment in institutions should be administered. Something has to be done. In our republic we have the methods of law and order. A good, wholesome spanking does a small boy good. I made the laws and I had to enforce the laws. Well, one day I was in for experiments and I did not know whether I had better punish certain boys or not. Finally, I made up my mind that I would have a trial and let the entire company vote upon the fact. At the trial the boys decided that the young fellow should be punished, and I whipped him. Finally we selected a body of twelve boys and they would decide upon the offense, and if they concluded the boy should be whipped, then I would whip the boy.

How they did dread to work! Instead of whipping them I sent them to pick up stones. That was worse than whipping. We got the boys to work a certain number of hours picking up stones. I soon discovered the offenses beginning to lessen and, upon making inquiry of certain boys, I found they preferred to be whipped. On several occasions the boys came to me and suggested rules of conduct, and I finally concluded to accept some of their rules and, to my amazement, they were better rules than those I made.

The boys were finally put in companies, and they were sent out in charge of an adult who looked after them to see that they picked up the stones and to watch them all the time; but one day my adult keeper was sick and I was in distress, for having a large crowd of boys, and it was necessary that they should serve their sentence. I thought of a boy named "Banjo" and put him in charge, and to my great delight he got better work out of them than the adult. To my amazement, instead of being a law-breaker, he was my best assistant thereafter. He began to feel that the right thing ought to be done by them and get the same amount of work out of them.

When they returned that fall to New York city I made up my mind I had hold of something to begin and study. I lay awake nights thinking about it. I concluded that if they would work for their clothing why not for their food? They can get along without clothing, but not without victuals. I at once made up my mind that I would require them to earn their victuals. Then the thought naturally followed to work in certain lines, in digging, in carpentry and farming. The girls were taught millinery and cooking and dressmaking.

We are now getting along nicely. We have three or four good structures. The only thing particularly remarkable is that the boys and girls are governing themselves.

Superintendent Gorton.—Tell us what the plant consists of; how it is sustained; what the boys work at.

Mr. George.—The plant consists of forty acres of land valued at about $4,000. The boys, where do they come from? We have over 400 applications. They come from all over New York state. We hope to have some fine, equipped trade schools in time, but at present we have not. We have a little carpentry and farming and that is about all for the boys. For the girls, we have cooking, millinery and dressmaking. The boys are all sent by some charitable societies. The work is supported entirely by voluntary contributions. We have no stated time to keep the boys. They remain various periods of time. They come from the very worst class of homes; boys that have served terms of imprisonment, but that is one thing, they want the past forgotten. We have a school, of course, and that is one of the things that would interest you most, I suppose.

President Blodgett introduced superintendent F. H. Briggs, of the state industrial school at Rochester, who said:

Mr. Chairman and gentlemen of the council.—Since I came in, this evening, I have been trying to study out why the chairman invited me to be present, unless it may be as a horrible example. Some years ago I was principal of a union school and I had an ambition, looking to the time when, perhaps, I might be a superintendent of schools and have a seat in this council. Instead of that I find myself one of these institution fellows. I suppose that the most of you who are present know pretty generally of the work of the state industrial school. There are boys in the state industrial school from pretty nearly every city and village which is represented in this council. I suppose that one of the questions that you are asking is, what is done with the boys when they come there?

We have a common school system of manual training, the trade school system, and the military system. As superintendent Cole remarked this morning in regard to the teacher whom he put over his ungraded schools we select a couple of our very best teachers for our common schools that is possible for us to find. Our teachers are all secured from competitive civil service examinations, and they, perhaps, will embrace the quality of teachers which we secure when I say to you that not over 25 per cent. of those who enter the competitive examinations secure the standing therein which entitles them to an appointment. I say, without vanity and without boasting, that we have twenty-two teachers who are not to be excelled in any of the schools of the state.

When these boys, then, come to us from various parts of the state, after they have been bathed and supplied with clean clothing and have remained in the hospital until the physician has examined them, so that we may be certain that no contagious or infectious disease afflicts them, they are brought in and assigned to their proper grade in school. Their school work takes up four and one-quarter hours daily, for the older boys; and five and one-half hours daily for the smaller boys. In the schools, in addition to common branches, they are taught mechanical drawing in order that they may understand the use of the working drawing in their trade schools. They have free-hand drawing and vocal music. I believe we can sing boys into a better frame of mind than we can bring them in any other way. We have history in order that the truths of history may be impressed upon their minds as a guide to right conduct. We have also, in connection with our penmanship, the elements of bookkeeping and the elements of commercial law, these principles of commercial law which have to do with the making of contracts.

The time that the boy is not in trade school the first four months which he is there is taken up with various implements. At the end of four months he is put into one of the trade schools of the institution, our trade schools in iron working, blacksmithing, veneer work, machine shop, steam and gasfitting and electrical construction and operation. That is a mixture of the iron work and other work as well. In wood working we have carpentering and pattern making. We have also printing and bookbinding, painting, masonry, bricklaying and plastering, laundry, tailoring and shoemaking, upholstry, gardening and green-house work. In these trade schools the boys spend four and three-quarter hours daily. In military drill the larger boys have three-quarters of an hour daily, the smaller boys one hour.

The remark was made that it was impossible to manage an institution without corporal punishment; but if you, gentlemen will come to Rochester I will show you an institution that is managed without corporal punishment and in which no officer is allowed to strike a boy. The method of maintaining discipline is by deprivation of privileges, by work in the drill squad, or punishment squad as it is called, and by confinement in a room 10 x 14 feet, lighted by four large windows from the roof and in one of these rooms which is well ventilated and well lighted as you will see, the refractory boy who will not do as he is told is placed. There he remains until he signifies his willingness to come forth and do as he is told. For ordinary offenses they are placed in the drill squad. This drill squad marches up and down a garden about 200 feet in length for 15 minutes. For 15 minutes they will stand at ease and for 15 minutes military study and military exercises. Then the marching begins again, to be succeeded by a recess and by the calisthenic drill. For a slight offence the boy instead of going to the dining-room to partake of the abundance which is furnished the others, will eat bread and water for the meal.

Our granting of parols is based upon the progress which the boy makes in the common schools, in the shops and by his conduct. We require children to complete the work of the seventh grade in the common schools where they have the mental capacity to reach that stage of advancement. We find among our boys, however, that a great many of them reach a maximum development before they reach the seventh grade, or where it is impossible for a boy because of mental deficiency to reach that grade he is sent out at the end of three years anyway, and sooner if his conduct is such as to warrant it.

I do not know that I need take any more of your time. Briefly I have outlined the work, and any question I can will be gladly answered.

In answer to question by Mr. Wright, superintendent Briggs said: If any boy becomes incorrigible and we cannot reform him we have the power, by securing a court order, to send any boy over the age of 16 to the Elmira Reformatory. Where you find a boy of this kind, in justice to his fellows, he should be removed from their midst and put with others of the same ilk.

Secretary Dewey.—How many did you find it necessary to send to Elmira.

Superintendent Briggs.—There are 705 boys at the school now and 120 girls. During the past year we have sent between 16 and 20 to Elmira.

Superintendent Kneil.—Which do you find the most intractable, boys or girls?

Superintendent Briggs.—I would sooner deal with a very bad boy than with a very bad girl.

Superintendent Burgess.—If any of the boys committed there, if you consider them reformed and thereby discharged, are they permitted to remain there if they choose to do so?

No, sir.

Do you use your discretion as to how long they will remain there.

Superintendent Briggs.—I have this rule that when a boy has completed the seventh grade he shall go out, if his conduct is anywise hopeful.

Superintendent Diamond.—I had a little experience some years ago in a matter in which your institution was concerned. The father wished to turn his child over to the Erie county institution. During the father's absence from home, and on his return he was very much put out because he had been notified of the proceedings that had been taken against the boy and was very anxious to effect the boy's release and he used this language. He said that he had met a large number of people in the Erie county penitentiary and nearly all of them were graduates of the Rochester industrial school. If this is true I would like to know it.

Superintendent Briggs.—I shall have to answer that by making another assertion. Nine out of every ten boys who come to us have been in Sunday school.

Superintendent Maxwell.—I should like to ask if Mr. Briggs has any statistics to show what the result of his training in that institution was?

Superintendent Briggs.—No sir; the statement had been made before the national conference of charities and correction that the reform schools of the country were responsible for all the tramps that are now pestering a long suffering public. I had the agent make out for me a list of the number of children that had been paroled from that institution during the time that the agency system had been in effect. These reports show that 57 per cent. of all the children who had been paroled during these years were doing well; while but 20 per cent. of all the children that had been paroled during these years were doing badly. There are 23 per cent. which have been lost sight of by the agents. From the number of those who come back to the institution visiting and those who have been lost sight of and from those that I hear from indirectly, I am satisfied that one-half of those whom we have lost sight of are doing well. Taking one-half of 23 per cent. give me 11½, and which added to 57 gives 68½ per cent.

Superintendent Maxwell.—I would like to know if the inmates of the institution are given any voice or required to take any part in the administration or governing of the institution?

No, sir; to this extent: The unnecessary breakage, the unnecessary wear and tear of furniture and clothing is charged up to the division to which a cadet belongs, and when the value of that breakage, loss and wear and tear amounts to the value of their most cherished food, pork and beans, instead of having their pork and beans for that time, we have a slip on which is given all of this breakage, on the plate of each and name of the cadet who was responsible for the breakage or damage.

Superintendent Maxwell.—Am I to understand that the entire division is punished for the fault of the one member who committed the fault?

Superintendent Briggs.—Yes, sir.

Superintendent Wright.—Are these boys permitted to earn money in any way for their work either in the shops or in the school or in any work about the building or in any way?

Superintendent Briggs.—They are not.

Superintendent Norris.—What is the youngest age you can take a boy?

Superintendent Briggs.—We do not receive children under 12, except for felony.

Superintendent Norris.—Is there any way that, having an incorrigible boy indicted by the grand jury, a justice can send him to you?

Yes, sir; the justice in making out the commitment must state that he committed this felony and then state that in his discretion he tried him for such.

Superintendent Gorton.—How thorough a technical education is given in your institution?

Superintendent Briggs.—Let me illustrate by carpentry. The boys are placed on working drawings which involves the use of plans, up to the various work that a carpenter is called upon to perform. When that work is completed the boy is taken into a squad in charge of another foreman and called upon to do practical carpentry.

Superintendent Gorton.—Do you know of any place which the state of New York provides where boys can receive that education without having committed a felony?

No, sir; I do not.

Superintendent Maxwell.—As I understand the scheme of punishment, it is the means of bringing the power of public opinion upon the squad and if an individual who is disposed to be careless of the property of the institution or if one of the squad of 200 commits an offense the other 199 will have to suffer the same punishment that he does.

Superintendent Briggs.—Because the boy himself will be specially punished and at the same time he shares the punishment of the others.

Superintendent Maxwell.—I would like to ask if that has not resulted in inflicting private punishment on the unfortunate miscreant who did the damage?

Superintendent Briggs.—The practical result is that when the others see one fellow about to commit something that will result in loss to them, they will endeavor to restrain him.

Superintendent Sawyer.—When the boys lose their pork and beans are they deprived entirely?

No, sir; they have everything except that one dish.

At one time boys were paroled when they had earned four hundred dollars of fictitious money. For instance a boy earned so many dollars every week he was there. If he did anything that was deserving of punishment he lost part of his earnings and the idea got abroad that the boys were to get that amount in actual cash when they went out.

Superintendent J. A. Pierce, Westchester temporary home.—My motive in being present here to-day is simply to present some blank commitment forms, contracts, etc., and to listen to what may be said in relation to this truant work.

During the past year I have been receiving from different parts of the state some truants. I have listened to the very interesting remarks of Mr. George, also to the gentlemen from Rochester, and I feel that I am nowhere. Of course, our institution is very differently situated from those other institutions. In the first place Mr. George has only started, and on such different basis from ours that we can hardly compare it with that. On the other hand, Mr. Briggs is thoroughly equipped with working force; more than we are because he has more money at his hand.

The reason the Westchester temporary home was started was that the Catholic children in Westchester county were well cared for, but the Protestant children were comparatively neglected, and were the victims of the politicians. The one who had the most influence received charge of the children, and the money that should have been for the support and health of the children was used in other ways. Some of the better element of the people of Westchester county said, "This is all wrong," that the Protestant children should have as good a chance as the Catholic children. So we organized and opened a little building. The year previous Westchester supported about 60 children and costing about $110 per year; these ladies entered into a scheme of caring for the Protestant children and had in some way to get these children from the hands of the politicians and it was only by one way, by reducing the expense to us, they offered to take the children for $1.52 per week and this had to cover the entire expense.

The matter of expense was a very serious consideration. We could not do what we wanted to do because we did not have money enough. You know how it works where you are continually asking money it becomes continually harder to obtain it.

A good many of the politicians said: "These ladies will soon get tired of this and we will have the thing back into our hands" and there have been several times during the past eighteen years that it was tried to get it back just where they wanted it, and I am very glad to say that they have not got it. In 1885 our managers bought property in White Plains. We bought first what was a large frame structure with about 16 acres of land. Then one of the managers, who was and is the treasurer of the home to-day, authorized me to buy in addition to that, 23 acres of land making, say, about 40 acres of land which she holds in her own right and gives us the use of it.

At present we have a very pleasantly located building one to one and one-half miles from White Plains. Two years ago our frame structure was laid in ashes. The fortunate part was that no lives were lost. We have passed through another severe vicissitude at our home; we have passed through severe illness. I am glad to be able to say this to you to-day, that while we have carried 67 cases of scarlet fever we have never lost one, and out of a hundred cases of measles we have never lost one. The time we have been running we lost 16 children, and these died soon after they came to the institution and their disease was most thoroughly located and contracted before they came to us.

As to punishment for the boys. Up to the present we have never felt that a boy should be punished for what he does not deserve. We try to make the bad boy feel that he is not a hero among our boys if he does something wrong. In relation to our school and discipline we have the manual training class. We would like to have the means of going into carpentry more extensively. We are simply doing wood carving at present. No work in scroll work but simply with a knife, and I think I can say without boasting that two years ago we were invited to go to Madison Square Garden to show some of our work with the other institutions, and I think we compared very favorably in our institution with the handwork of other institutions.

The boys begin this work when about six or seven years old. The majority of those children who come to us come from careless parents. These boys and girls who come to us have to earn their living. They have to earn it by being taught with care and taught carefulness in everything they do and they cannot begin too early.

Question.—Do you have any trouble in keeping your boys there?

No, sir; we have had some run away, but in 18 years' experience had but one run away. We have 125 boys now and have room for 225.

Superintendent Gorton.—If children are committed to you by school authorities from a district school does not the school district pay the expenses?

If they have a superintendent of schools the school board has to pay the expenses.

Suppose a police justice sends them to you?

If there is a superintendent of schools the board must pay.

Superintendent Maxwell.—The compulsory education law specifically provides that truants committed under that law shall not be sent to any institution to which criminals are sent, so that I do not understand how it is possible to commit truants to this institution or school where criminals are received.

Superintendent Pierce.—I do not know that you can hardly call them criminals. They come for petty offences.

Question.—From schools where demand is made by the county, do you require the board of education from the small village schools to enter into contracts?

Superintendent Pierce.—Yes, sir; that is what I expect to do this winter. Our bill will be presented month by month.

Superintendent Belknap.—I would like to know as to the methods of discipline and whether you have military training.

Superintendent Pierce.—We have had various means of discipline in the institution. Some years ago, perhaps, some of the boys used to run away from us. Now we have no great fences, no locks, no bars and have not had a watch during last year. We go to bed like any other family and sleep through the night. When a boy runs away we put an anklet on when brought back, but the boy is allowed to go among the other children. There is no ball attached to it, but simply the chain, restraining him from running away. He has to perform his work with the other boys and that is kept on long enough to feel secure that he is safe from running away. We had, previous to that, as a last resort, used corporal punishment, only as a last resort. Every other humane means was used before the use of corporal punishment, but since a year ago last January we have not had to use corporal punishment, but we got into that position where we had to do something and we have consulted the authorities and they have allowed us to put in a lockup. This, perhaps, four by six feet, well ventilated and about six feet in height. We have twelve of these and for certain offences they are put in there for different lengths of time, and the first time they are in we give them their regular meals. If that punishment is not quite sufficient we give them bread and water for their dinner and regular meals morning and night.

We have had a system of military drill among our children. We have one boy who has been very successful in that. He is drilling the other children. The matter of drilling or marching for punishment is another thing we have instituted since the matter of corporal punishment has been discontinued. I consider marching better punishment than locking them up.

Mr. George continued his explanation of his junior republic. As to the boys' school work, they work hard eight hours. I believe in keeping them busy. All the arrests are on Sundays and idle hours and the police court is full on Monday. The boys wish to build up a city and come to live there.

Mr. Wright.—In this short period in which you have been running is there developing anything that tends toward politics?

Mr. George.—We have it there. Just as quickly as the conditions are the same issues will rise.

Superintendent Maxwell.—If any school districts, villages or cities thought of entering into an arrangement with you as representing the junior republic to have truants committed as truants are, would you care to receive them?

Answer.—We are willing to take your truants, we do not care how bad they are, we would be glad to take them, that is, if we had the accommodations. We are crowded to our utmost capacity at the present and we are building a cottage that will permit taking about twelve more.

Secretary Dewey.—How much would the average annual expense be as you estimate it?

Mr. George.—About a dollar and a half a week, cost.

The council then passed to election of officers.

Superintendent Caswell.—I nominate for president of this council a gentleman that all delight to honor and I name Thomas R. Kneil of Saratoga Springs.

Superintendent Snell.—I take great pleasure in seconding the nomination that has been made. I feel that nothing that I could say would add to the knowledge of this association concerning the man who has been nominated, so it gives me pleasure, without taking time, to second the nomination.

Superintendent Williams.—I move that the secretary be directed to cast one ballot for superintendent Thomas R. Kneil.

Carried unanimously.

Superintendent Prentice.—I nominate superintendent Rogers of Jamestown for vice-president.

Elected unanimously.

Mr. Bardeen.—I solicit the privilege of casting the ballot of the council for Emmet Belknap as secretary and treasurer.

Carried unanimously.

Superintendent Sherman Williams.—I would like to invite the council to Glens Falls and I will assure you that we will accommodate you there. In the 16 years of the existence of the council no convention has been held in northern New York. It was two years ago at Newburgh. On two occasions or more along the southern tier of counties. All other portions of the state seem to have the council in its territory and I would like very much to have you meet with us. If you decide to come we could take the council through Lake George and we would show it to you in a dress of beauty that very few of you have seen it. Lake George in June is not at all to be compared to Lake George in October.

Superintendent Burgess.—I also desire to extend a cordial invitation to the council to hold its meeting in Poughkeepsie. Such invitation was extended to the council last year. Before I came away from Poughkeepsie our board of education passed a resolution extending a cordial invitation to this council to meet there. The hotel accommodations are ample. There is an excellent restaurant near the hotel and there is an excellent place to meet in. There are excellent committee rooms off the main hall and I am sure that if this council sees fit to accept the invitation that you will be well treated. There is also near Poughkeepsie, Vassar College, I am sure many of the gentlemen here would like to make a visit there and I can extend to you a very cordial invitation to hold the next council meeting there.

Superintendent Cole.—I second the invitation of superintendent Burgess. I feel that the council will be in every way satisfied. I do not think anybody would treat you better than superintendent Williams would. I sincerely hope the council will accept the invitation from that beautiful city just half-way between the greater Albany and lesser New York.

Superintendent Diamond.—It occurs to me that this combined meeting of the school boards and of the superintendents is a permanent arrangement. Would it not be well to have a general committee to which this matter could be referred?

Moved and seconded that we proceed to ballot; 72 votes cast, 24 for Poughkeepsie, 48 for Glens Falls.

Superintendent Williams.—Gentlemen, I thank you and trust you will not regret it.

OCTOBER 21ST

Meeting called to order at 8:16 p. m.

Chairman announced we have a surfeit of good things on the program and I think we have one of the best of them for this evening. Something that we are all getting interested in and want to be interested in more than we are.

Science teaching in primary and grammar schools.

Prof. Bailey, Cornell University, was introduced and said: I feel somewhat diffident about coming before you, the actual teachers of nature study in the primary and secondary schools of the state. I am sure that we are all interested in the same thing and that is the instruction of the young, but I imagine that nearly all differ as to the methods which shall be employed in science teaching in the schools. I have some opinions which are personal ones with which you may not agree, but possibly we may raise some discussion. I should preface my remarks by giving a brief history of the movement in nature study.

Some four or five years ago the grape growers asked the experimental station at Cornell to investigate the cause of destruction to the grapes in their section. We replied that we had no funds to devote to that purpose. This was the last we heard of it until finally it appeared before the legislature in the form of a bill which was introduced by some gentleman and finally was passed and money was appropriated for the purpose of extending horticultural knowledge. This appropriation was for eight thousand dollars. The director of our experimental station was at that time in California and this new work of teaching horticulture fell to me and the work was enlarged to cover the whole State, with an appropriation of $25,000, composing the whole field of agriculture. This bill was drafted in a very liberal spirit allowing us to extend agricultural teaching in whatever way we choose, whether by issuing reports holding schools, or by the publication of results.

We began to handle what we call the horticultural schools in western New York in which we gave the whole day to that one particular topic, the grape and the peach. We always began these meetings with observation lessons. We passed around among the farmers a twig or an apple for about five minutes and then we ask what they had seen. From these observation lessons in horticulture schools there arose a desire on the part of the teachers who had seen this work for some instruction as to how they could carry on this work.

Simple suggestions, a little information, suggest a method of how a teacher can take up common things and interest children in them.

I should like to ask one or two questions in order to bring this matter before you forcibly. In the first place, Why do we want to teach science for the primary and secondary schools? The answer determines the whole course of our teaching. Do we want to teach science as a science for science's sake or for the pupils' sake? Our text-books are written with the idea that we should teach science for science's sake. I do not believe we ought to begin teaching that way. We teach for the pupil's sake alone. It is love and sympathy which we need to teach. I believe the teaching of science in a secondary school is a subsequent matter, but I believe the teaching of nature study is a primary matter, not for the purpose of teaching botany as a means to an end but for the purpose of awakening the sympathies, the observing powers of the pupil. I believe if we get the difference between these two ideas we get the difference between teaching science and nature study. Once in a while a pupil wants to be a botanist, he wants to take up botany as a science or he can take it up both as a science and mere study of natural principles of a plant. I believe there should be four general requisites for successful teaching of nature study. In the first place the subjects should be those that interest the pupil. In the second place, a pupil must be an investigator. The pupil must feel that he is doing the work, that he is seeing the things and must be told. I do not believe in some of the teaching in the colleges. They tell the pupil nothing. The pupils become listless through it. The teacher should guide the pupil.

In the third place, we should not give too much at once. Children are nearly all specialists and even pupils of ten to twenty years are more or less specialists when we come to analyze them. Sometimes a cobble stone would be enough for a whole day in work of this kind. If we simply give the child one day a thought which he can work out in some way and investigate for himself, I believe it is worth more than a whole basketful of information. So I believe we should not try to give too much. I do not believe with beginners in nature study that we should try to lecture them very much. Among the objects before them, to suggest deftly and casually that there are those differences, that there are those objects to be seen. Let it drop there and the child will take it up. The trouble is that when we try to teach nature study the child tries to take notes and that spoils the whole thing; yet if we put in one or two ideas there is so much gained. We must have this work guarded. We must have it laid out so that we know what is coming out of it. Every teacher can learn enough about one or two insects so that she can put them before the pupils and give instruction in nature study.

Superintendent Gorton.—How were the leaflets referred to obtained?

These leaflets are published by the state and they may be obtained by writing to the College of Agriculture, Cornell University.

Principal Wilson, Syracuse.—I may say that a committee of the state Science Teachers' Association is at work now and will make a report, or at least a partial report in December at Syracuse. I think Prof. Bailey is a member of that committee. There is to be a report on this subject at that time and perhaps you will be sufficiently interested to attend the meeting.

If we were requested to start a class in nature study in Canandaigua, we should choose a class of children, not a class of grown people. I would not choose you. It is very evident that little children are wide awake and those who have had experience in large cities have to confess that those from 15 to 18 are not so alert. They in some way become helpless. There must be something wrong with the teacher if that condition of things prevails. I am glad to find that I agree with Prof. Bailey in most of the positions he has taken in reference to this matter. The fundamental idea should not be information. It should be power. It should not in any sense be technical, but general, and around this line of work should be gathered those subjects which we have to carry along in the school.

It has been said by some the argument for this kind of work is to induce children to love it. This is unnecessary. Little children love it naturally; they are in sympathy with nature until we as teachers drive all this natural sympathy out of them by our methods of teaching. The care of the interests of the child should be the main idea in teaching, and practically we hold to the idea of teaching a subject with a book. Consequently a large amount of information that children receive, nearly all of it in the larger schools is second-hand. They have to take somebody else in that subject either written or oral; one of the main ideas then, I think, is to train children to get knowledge first hand and if we can train children to make original investigations, to get knowledge for themselves, we will surely strengthen them. I believe a child will develop as carefully and as perfectly as a flower if the child receives the proper training. As a flower takes in sunshine and air and water as it needs them, just so knowledge should not be forced into a child when he does not want it. Man is to be trained before he receives benefit from our high ideas and so the teachers main idea is to arouse the interest of the child and direct the attention of the child. There is great danger that we may mistake studying about nature for nature observation.

I would disagree with Prof. Bailey on just one thing that he has said. When he spoke of taking a plant to-day and a stone to-morrow or something else. I think a child may see a great deal in a sense but still see very little and so he should be directed. We should take up study in the ordinary way, not in any sense botany, not technically, but follow out some line so that when the child reaches a mature period of life he has something upon which he is to build. He has learned certain great truths about plants and it is in these larger truths that we should be schooled. The material used will depend to some extent upon the location of the school, the teacher, and the time of year.

In my own school we take 20 minutes a day to study plants. It is not possible to study plants in winter, so we then study the snow. The children study the idea that nature is going to sleep. I think it better to begin the study of plants in April and continue during the vacation and up to winter.

We started first with the whole plant. The children were asked to bring a plant to school. The teacher described briefly the different parts, investigated the parts, then each child was requested to select a specimen and press it in the first page of his book and the plant was pressed. Then we took the different parts of the plant, studied the roots and soil and studied stems. We are now studying leaves. The leaves are not selected at all, the children are asked to bring any leaves and from the leaves brought to the schoolroom we select certain formations. We do not talk very much, that is to say, pupils are not asked to state what they see for fear others will learn from hearing, and that is the thing we want to avoid; but after the subject has been studied and learned the children write what they have seen and after the writing then comes the talking. Along with this we have seed planting. We say, if any one wants to plant seeds, if you bring earth and a jar we will give the seeds. Everyone wants seeds or bulbs to plant at home. If this plan or something like it should be followed care should be taken to give out right seeds, seeds that are likely to germinate. Care should be taken not to discourage children. Children should study some things out of the book. We have not used a book so far, but by and by I should like to say, "Now that you want to know more about these things here is a book that will tell you."

The children should study things originally themselves and from actual observation and experience. I asked the teacher this morning before coming up here "What is the effect upon the class, of this work Does it interfere with their other studies?" "No"; she told me; "they do more." They are wide awake; they are alert. There is another strange feature about the home planting of seeds, that it is getting to be a bond between the homes and the school and it would surprise you to see the different views and thoughts that come up. For example when we were planting the first seeds the question of watering came up. I give you these seeds, I said, and it is your business to have them come up. If not, we will give them to somebody else. Then the question came up, must all seeds be planted? They thought they must. One little girl in bringing in a leaf said, this is soft on the under side. Another one in examining a leaf said, this is rough and has hairs on it. In studying stems we notice the coverings on the stem for protection.

I want to throw out another suggestion here, if I may. I think this nature study idea should prevail in our study of color. I cannot understand why we should paint or dye paper to normal colors and place it before children and call it color study. Why not study color as it is, not as we make it? Why not a color study of plants or of the rainbow or of the clouds? I think that knowledge is the thing that we should study and books are the ordinary helps. I may say I have some of the books here if any of you care to see them.

Prof. Bailey.—This is one of the best talks I ever heard on nature study. The difference between us is the difference of method, the difference in surrounding, etc. It seems to me one of the clearest cut studies of nature teaching I ever heard.

Superintendent Whitney.—I must disagree with the position taken by the two gentlemen who have spoken. To get at the question I raise another. What is the very first and most important question that arises in education? In other words, what is the first important question? Now, I grant that pedagogically it is the gaining of power. How is power gained? It is gained through knowledge and the first end and purpose of education is not the obtaining of power but the gaining of knowledge. The mind lives and grows by means of food and the food of the mind is knowledge. I would not endorse the idea that the acquiring of knowledge is not an important one and it should be, in my judgment, continually in the mind of the teacher, with all honesty, for the reasons that I have given, reasons that we all know well. If I take up a line of study I want to be convinced on general fundamental principles that it is right.

Another observation on the subject of nature study; if we grant two or three questions, first that education takes two lines, the line of original investigation, original knowledge, knowledge at first hand, that knowledge that is gained by the observation and experience of the individual child, and secondly that through books. Secondly, if it be granted that original knowledge at first hand, that is, every kind of knowledge, every kind of teaching, is absent, then nature study is absolutely essential in order to obtain knowledge from books and other oral instruction. Then again, if we grant another proposition, that elementary ideas and facts can be obtained only through the concrete, through observation, then it seems to me that it is clearly evident that there is no more important, I may say, no department of school instruction that is so vital and important as the subject of nature study. Just another point. I think that the subject of nature study should reach down also. It should reach the child that cannot read and I believe that the highest and best instruction that can be given is given to the little ones when they first come to school. I suppose it is possible that the elementary principles of science are perfectly comprehensible to the little child, so I say, teach the elements with the so-called science. It seems to me our teachers should be well grounded and it is a little dangerous for teachers to attempt to teach those, with a little smattering of the subject.

Superintendent Griffith.—This subject of nature study we have had in the Utica schools for three years and possibly a few words on the line of work may be of interest. In the first place, we have decided to begin it in the very lowest grade. We have nothing better as the basis of reading lessons, language lessons, than the lesson on a plant and flower or an animal instead of the conventional singsong which we have been teaching as reading, etc. The child expresses the knowledge gained from the observation of the plant as the basis of the language lesson. We do most of the study of plants in the spring.

After three years of experience of nature study in our schools we are very much in favor of it. It has produced very excellent results.

On motion meeting adjourned to unite in joint session with the Association of School Boards during the remainder of the evening.

FRIDAY MORNING SESSION

President Blodgett suggested the topic, simplification of annual reports to different educational departments, and called upon Hon. Melvil Dewey, secretary of the Board of Regents, to open the discussion.

Secretary Dewey.—From the nature of my work which consists in studying educational problems for the whole state rather than for the individual institution, or what might be called by the wholesale instead of retail methods, I am forced to make an unusually large and constant use of reports. I doubt if any one appreciates more keenly their practical value to those who interpret them intelligently and profit by the lessons they teach. Furthermore, I have often pointed out that many a report was worth all it cost because it compelled the local teachers and officers to sit down and systematically review the result of the years of work. Many minds are so constituted that except for coercion they would never take an educational inventory or make a balance sheet and would be working on impression rather than on reliable statistics. I think often if a report were burned when it was completed and never tabulated or printed, that it may have been worth all it cost for the influence on the reporting officers. Having said this in appreciation I shall not be understood as proposing a crusade against the time-honored custom when I say that I am convinced that we might materially reduce the labor connected with the various reports both in the schools and in state departments without materially diminishing efficiency. Every well managed business must have regular inventories and balance sheets, but the proprietor of a great department store who locked his doors and stopped his sales for three days out of every month to take an inventory so as to see exactly where he stood, would be voted in business circles impracticable. We can conceive of a business in perishable fruits where an inventory might be taken daily. In others it is required monthly or quarterly, but for ordinary business the annual inventory is found all sufficient. There are certain matters connected with our schools in which we should certainly take our bearings each year. There are others in which it is clear to me that a report once in two or three or in some cases in five years would be all sufficient for showing the trend and for deducing all lessons of value, and that to repeat this information every 12 months is as foolish as to pull up a plant every morning and examine the roots to see if it is growing satisfactorily.

Our public schools, like our educational departments, belong to the state and are supported by the taxpayers. It is only human nature that when the cost of doing a work is paid from any private pocket its frequency and necessity will be questioned much more sharply than when it is a charge on the general treasury. But I hold it to be our duty both as public servants and as public educators to study constantly to find any economy which shall not interfere with efficiency. I know of no educational field in which there is available as much money or as much time as can be used to advantage and it is little less than crime to use any part of it extravagantly. It is my judgment after some years study of this question that in all our educational reports it would be wise to reduce to a minimum the facts that are given every year, and for other tables and comparisons to fix on longer periods. With our state and national census working by decades and alternating we get our statistics once in five years. I think we should get the best results if we were to agree on say five groups of the information needed occasionally but not annually, and take one of these groups for study and discussion each year. Each annual report would then have the brief statistics repeated every year and would take up one of the five groups and discuss it exhaustively. Unless for special reasons that group would then be left till the other four had received attention. If the question were, for instance, school buildings, we should find full statistics and discussion at regular intervals of five years; and with vastly less labor than given to the present system we should have a more thorough treatment and secure results of greater practical value at much less expense.

Superintendent Tuthill.—I sometimes wonder whether the national report is the report, or whether the state report is the report, or whether the Regents' report is the report. Each one has finally hit upon the right form and best method. There seems to me to be some difference of opinion, and perhaps we may, therefore, differ in opinion as to some of the statistics. I am interested, perhaps, as some people are in our daily school work. I would like to know the value of these reports that I am making out with so much labor and care. Is it to be a report for this day or this year? We can look back and see how ten years ago we studied on these items and these matters. It seems to me that in making out these reports there should be some system or plan. Not a call for the statistics of the cause of education simply, and not merely a question of how many pupils there are in my schools or in certain schools. That is, doubtless, valuable, but the real foundation of our schools, it seems to me, is in the growth of the school, the progress we are making, what are the pupils doing, and how they are progressing? I would be very much pleased to know how other *schools are* progressing and advancing, and it seems to me there should be some philosophy of report-making—some system which would endure from year to year.

Superintendent Rogers.—It is not possible to find out certain things if we do not know what is wanted until towards the last of the school year. A very slight change will make it impossible to produce any valuable paper for a report. So far as my individual experience goes, if the various reports would call for the same thing so far as they cover the same ground, and there could be definite information sent us beforehand as to what would be required, I think the principal defects would be obviated. I think the gentleman who last spoke touched upon the limitation of the reports. I would like to know concerning other schools and the work of their teachers.

Superintendent Diamond.—My idea is not exactly in line with the views of the reports that have been presented, but certainly as closely related to it as any.

It has been suggested to me by comparison of figures we find in the state Superintendent's figures, given by the different superintendent's in their annual reports to such Department that there are certain items there which are so disproportionate in the reports of schools of about the same size, and they show figures that are so widely divergent that it seems to me there must be different bases of estimating the same in figures we find there. It must be that the superintendent has figured on a different basis. There is one other item. The average ratio of attendance, the average attendance and average registers. Albany reports ratio of 95 per cent.; Amsterdam, 97; Auburn, 97; Binghamton, 96; Brooklyn, 87; Buffalo, no report; Corning, 94. Down at the lower end of the state we find that Niagara Falls has only 81; North Tonawanda, 84, and my report shows 86. We are looking for instruction in the matter, and perhaps the gentlemen can tell us. Would it not be best to ask the Department what basis should be used — whether we shall mark the child withdrawn at the end of the week or at the end of three days or when?

Superintendent Maxwell.—This matter of keeping the register, I find, is one that is to be very carefully watched or it is going to affect the compulsory education law in its administration, at least that is my impression. If you have a rule that a child who is absent three or five days, or any other period of time, the name must be stricken off the roll and not included in the registry, it simply means that the teachers are going to make truants for you—they are going to weed out children that they do not like in school. We, in Brooklyn, used to have a rule that if a child was absent five days the name was taken off the register. Now the rule is that every child is kept on the roll until it is definitely known that the child has gone to another school, or is employed in accordance with the compulsory education law, or has moved to another city, or has died or for some other good reason is effectually out of school; but if you are going to enforce the compulsory education law, it seems to me absolutely necessary that names should be kept on the register until it is known definitely where they have gone. It seems to me that it is important to do this. Some ten years ago, when I became superintendent of Brooklyn, I found that there was a constant pressure in the schools to keep the children back from promotion. I managed to get that remedied so that children were promoted as they ought to be promoted. I remedied it by collecting the published statistics in regard to each school.

I do not believe in making voluminous reports if it can be avoided, but I believe that each year, once a year, there should be a report giving all the vital and necessary statistics about school work. As the gentleman from Tonawanda has pointed out, it would be very desirable to get some accurate basis for making such items in our reports. On the whole, I am inclined to think that all reports should be figured out on each of these three bases, the total number of children instructed during the year, the average register and the average attendance.

Superintendent Griffith.—Superintendent Maxwell has pointed out how these differences should be definitely stated. It seems to me that the dividend should be stated. The expense for new buildings is almost as great as all the running expenses, salaries, etc., of the school. It seems to me that the reports should include new buildings, etc. It is not fair to indicate that it has cost us double per pupil this year to what it did last year.

Superintendent Maxwell.—I think that is a very important matter that Mr. Griffith has suggested, and I would say that in my own case I have carefully watched that matter, and in giving the cost of instruction per pupil I am only instructed to supervise that alone, and the purchase of books, stationery and such supplies as are usually needed for school work.

H. C. Case, Department Public Instruction.—As a representative of the Department of Public Instruction, and the person through whose hands most of these reports pass I am, of course, particularly interested in this discussion and pleased to get any suggestions that may be offered by the superintendents.

The average cost of educating each pupil is easily ascertained by taking from the financial table, in which is found the amount expended for different purposes, and dividing this amount by the number of pupils. In this way you can ascertain whether any particular superintendent's report has included the amount expended for buildings, sites, etc., or whether it simply includes the amount of ordinary running expenses.

I can see that it is not fair to schools that have heavy bills for new buildings, etc., to include those in computing the average cost per pupil of maintaining their school. I think this matter can be arranged in the blanks for another year, but any person who wishes to estimate these items upon any particular basis can easily do so by taking the financial statements and taking from them the cost of teachers' wages, fuel, building and any other expenditures which he chooses and figure the matter for himself.

It has been the study of the Department to make these reports as simple as possible, and, as a representative of the Department, I shall be glad to receive any suggestions from any of the superintendents on this line, and would suggest that it might be profitable to have a committee of the superintendents appointed to confer with representatives from each of the educational Departments to see if these reports can be simplified and improved.

Superintendent Snow.—I supposed that the basis of finding the percentage in the state Superintendent's office was the same for all of it. We take the total number of days' attendance and then divide by the average attendance. Of course, it brings a pretty high percentage where you allow a day's attendance for only half a day.

Superintendent Sawyer.—There is another factor in this matter that is worthy of consideration. Of course, in large cities, I suppose, they have a clerk to figure up all these things, and the report is not so much of a burden as it is with those of us who have to do all this work ourselves. It becomes quite burdensome for us to make a report to Washington and one to the Regents and one to the state Superintendent and one to the board of education, and every one of them to be entirely different and based upon different statement of facts. If we could find some way that we could copy the financial statement, for instance, of the one we send to Washington and send a similar one to the state Superintendent, it would simplify matters exceedingly.

Superintendent Cole.—In making these reports it is necessary that the Regents' report be made for a different period of time from the state report and national report. It would be a very much simpler matter if we had to make these financial statements once in regard to special items. We have three different kinds of financial reports to make, and getting our balances all right takes a great deal of time.

Mr. Barr.—If children are absent four days during the week

that attendance is imperfect, and if they are absent five days the attendance is perfect.

Superintendent Prentice.—Here is a good suggestion from the representative of the state Department. They are willing to do just what the superintendents want done. Suggest a committee. It seems to me that if the chair would appoint a committee it would settle the whole business and be satisfactorily to all. I did wish that some items which concern both the state Department and Regents would cover the same ground.

Superintendent Blodgett.—I am glad you are all so interested. It seems to me we ought to find some way out of this.

Secretary Dewey introduced the following resolution:

Resolved, That the council of superintendents earnestly request the University and the Department of Public Instruction to formulate a uniform method for reporting such statistics and information as are required by both departments, and to give explicit instructions as to the proper interpretation of all items which are liable to be misunderstood or to be reported from different standpoints by different school officers. That a committee of three be appointed by the president to submit this request, and, if desired, to confer with the state departments as to the methods to be adopted.

Supervisor Downing.—I would propose that the chair appoint a committee of three to confer with the department of education of the state upon this matter of reports, in order to come to a fair understanding of the basis upon which statistics are reported.

Superintendent Maxwell seconded Secretary Dewey's resolution.

On motion, the resolution was carried unanimously.

On motion of the president, Mr. Blodgett was elected to act as chairman of the committee.

Mr. Case, Department.—I find no difficulty in getting the reports, but in looking over the answers to the questions asked in certain matters I find that they are not quite right, and this will make some difference. There is one difficulty in getting these reports on the same basis in different schools. If we can suggest a plan that will bring the superintendents to answer the questions as they are asked, rather than how they think they should be asked, it would help matters. The statistical work for cities is different from that for villages. Villages are the same as common schools. Cities have separate blanks.

Superintendent Snow.—I do not know why it should be expected that this committee should determine this question of the basis of statistics in different schools. I think it would be well to determine some basis upon which we can all agree.

School commissioner Stephens.—We have in the rural districts a great deal of trouble, and I would like to have some method whereby the reports could be simplified. We cannot get the ordinary trustee to make a report satisfactory, because they do not understand it.

Mr. Wiswell, Department of Public Instruction.—This matter of library reports is exaggerated. The difficulty is not in the report at all, but in that the officials are asked to make any report. As the commissioner represents the rural districts, a public explanation would not interest this body. I will explain privately to the commissioner all the points of difficulty in the library reports.

The council then took up the next subject for discussion: Teachers' training classes under chapter 1031.

Superintendent Maxwell.—This is a subject to which I have not given a great deal of attention, and I wish you had told me I was to open the discussion.

These classes have been organized, as I understand, in several cities of the state. A committee of the council met the state Superintendent and his assistants in his office and adopted a report setting forth what ought to be contained in the course of study in a training school or class. You will remember that chapter 1031 of the laws of 1895 authorized the state Superintendent to prescribe the rules and regulations under which these schools or classes shall be conducted, and hence these regulations, as issued by the Superintendent, which are in the form of a uniform course of study, have all the force and efficiency of law, and, I assume, are being carried out in all the training classes. So far as these rules and regulations go I, for one, have no criticism to make of them except this, that they are working well. I have no suggestion to make with regard to them, but I believe, however, as a superintendent, that this law, as Col. Parker stated, has been the greatest step forward taken by any state of this Union since Massachusetts first established the normal school in that state. As a superintendent I believe that no one should be allowed to enter a training class who is not a graduate from a high school or academy or institutions of high rank approved by the state Superintendent. Furthermore, each board of education in a city or village, employing a superintendent, is authorized to set up such additional and higher qualifications as they, in their judgment, may see fit. After giving considerable time and attention to this I am convinced of one thing, that simple graduation from the school approved by the state Superintendent is not sufficient guaranty of fitness to enter upon the course of training.

I am also quite sure that Regents' diplomas, which are, in many cases, the graduation certificate from schools and academies, ought not to be accepted as sufficient of themselves to entitle the holder to admission to a training-school class. A year ago, about the first week in February, and again in September, when the schools open in September, it was decided at once by the board of education of Brooklyn that the superintendent should be authorized and directed to conduct an examination of all applicants of graduates of schools approved by the state Superintendent, who may apply, and conduct an examination of all these applicants. There is one regulation prescribed by the state Superintendent that limits the number of pupils who may be placed in a training school, namely, that each one of them must have, during the year, at least fifty hours' of practical teaching of training class. That regulation limits the number whom we can take to 104 each term. We cannot admit more than that each term and give them the fifty hours' of practice teaching each term. We have about 200 applicants each term, and all of them come either with certificates of graduation from the Brooklyn high school or present Regents' diplomas from the academies or schools approved by the state Superintendent and under the Regents. In the last examination conducted by me, in September last, there were 24 graduates, each one of whom possessed a Regents' diploma. Of this 24, only 2 passed. The papers of the remaining 22 were of such a character as to show that they were absolutely unfit in point of scholarship. They did not have the basis of scholarship. They did not have the training that any sensible man would say is necessary to enter the course of professional training.

Our Superintendent should make it his duty to guard the entrance to the training schools, and I believe that can only be done by a thorough examination of the applicant. Of what should this examination consist? I do not believe it is proper in that case to use the uniform examinations of the state Department. Why? Simply because they do not cover the ground required in the course of study for high schools laid down by the state Superintendent, and if the Superintendent's minimum course for high schools is to be carried out, is to be insisted upon in the high schools to prepare for the training class, I claim that these entrance examinations should be conducted perfectly on the line, on the subject of study, laid down by the state Superintendent.

Supervisor Downing.—Superintendent Maxwell touched upon the points vital to the future successful working of chapter 1031, and I speak from close observation of results in the training-class work since this law has been in operation. The greatest danger to the cities in the operation of this law, the most fruitful source of trouble to the superintendent, lies in carelessness of admission to the training class. One or two cities have found that out within the year, and they have found it absolutely necessary to prescribe some additional qualification for entrance to the training school other than that in the law. Brooklyn, Syracuse, Albany, and Auburn which organized a training class this year for the first time, are guarding the door to the training school. It is not a question whether the training school can supply a sufficient number of teachers for the schools of Brooklyn, but it is a question of vital importance whether the persons supplied by this school shall be competent teachers when they get into the schools of the state. Auburn took care of this at the start.

There are eighteen cities organized under chapter 1031. A number of the cities have made no provision for additional qualifications for entrance, and what is the result? As the inspectors have said, in these cases, they find that there are a number of persons absolutely unqualified to take professional training because they have not the subject matter. We ought to have the course at least a year and a half, because the students coming into our training school do not know subject matter, and, therefore, are unable to take the professional training. In such cases I tell the inspectors, "The right way is to keep these people out. Cut the class down to 25, instead of 75 or 50."

For the training schools throughout the state you say we make very high standards. Yet, my friends, this chapter 1031 has done more for the cities, more for the villages, more for the country training classes than you can imagine. If you could sit in the state Department and read the correspondence that comes to the Department you would see how it has raised the tone of teaching throughout the state. So that now they are asking for a similar law for the teachers to be employed in secondary schools.

There is another question that will make some trouble unless you stop it before the trouble begins. We have been told that three years of experience anywhere, and of any kind, in the public schools of the state admits a person to teach in the public schools of the cities of the state. If the politicians of the state once find out that three years' successful experience will admit to your schools, you have no remedy, no redress, and in five or six years from now you will have just as serious a problem on hand as you had prior to the passage of the law. This is the weak point in the law.

Superintendent Snow.—I would ask whether he would make the requirements for admission to the training school greater than those for admission to the normal schools or to the colleges of the state.

Superintendent Maxwell.—As I understand the normal schools every young person may go into the normal schools after taking three years of high school work. The state training classes are exclusively for teachers; not for giving subject matter.

Superintendent Cole.—I want to speak especially with reference to the point raised by Mr. Downing in regard to the danger that may come from admission and allowing a teacher having three years' experience to have a certificate. Who is to be the judge of successful experience?

Superintendent Downing.—The first year that the advanced regulations went into effect we had 69 training classes with an attendance of about 1,028. Out of the 1.028 we got through 800 teachers duly licensed. With a membership of 2,500 the year previous in the training classes of the state they got less than four hundred duly licensed teachers. So that we have more than double the number of trained teachers to put into schools. This year with the advanced standard and conforming to the regulations more nearly than they ever attained, we have 90 schools with an increased number of attendance of 500, and with men and women for rural schools at least. who are qualified and have the minimum amount of training and the city schools have increased the number.

Superintendent Maxwell.—I would like to make this motion, that this matter of requiring the three years experience should be referred to the committee on legislation with instructions to confer with the state Department and if possible arrange for the appropriate legislation to secure the proposed remedy.

Motion carried.

Chairman Blodgett stated that he had hoped to be able to call upon Mr. Thiry, of Long Island City, to read a paper in regard to school savings banks. He suggested as there would not be opportunity Mr. Thiry's paper be spread upon the minutes of the council.

Mr. Bardeen.—I would also ask that the paper be included in the minutes of the meeting and go out as part of the minutes of this association.

Carried unanimously.

SCHOOL SAVINGS BANKS IN THE UNITED STATES

Gentlemen of the convention.—Of the many new formative influences brought to bear upon school children in various parts of the land during the past twelve years, not the least has been that of school savings banks, concerning which I am invited to offer some remarks. A savings bank is a benevolent institution for the deposit by the poor of small savings on interest. It is, in its nature, a direct incentive to such classes to make such savings. Its basic principle contemplates the promotion of self-help among the otherwise improvident. The economic value of savings banks is represented by the remarkable history of a century in Europe and of four-score years in America.

The incubus of poverty which hovered over England and the Continent, baffling all attempts at relief, both individual and state, was only lifted when the poor were taught that the remedy was in themselves. The inauguration of the "Friendly Society for the Benefit of Women and Children," in 1801, by Mrs. Priscilla Wakefield, Tottenham High Cross, Middlesex, was the dawn of that radiant economic day that followed, wherein savings banks were the recognized instrumentality of redeeming society from the threatening forms of improvidence and mendicancy. The great fact evermore and sternly abides that a poor man cannot be helped. He must help himself. Help him, and you weaken and destroy him. The poor laws and other parliamentary forms of state relief in England and the legislation of the state of New York, under Governor Clinton, so testify. The system of savings is creative of an opportunity of self-help, and by so much has enabled the indigent classes to work out their own salvation, by acquiring independence through frugality. France, with pardonable pride, justly claims for her people a fuller measure of contentment than characterizes the lot of almost any other nation, because of the prevalence of provident habits among the wage-earning classes.

Furthermore, a savings bank saves more than money. It saves more than the individual. It saves the state. A radical need of the day is lawful methods of accumulating wealth. Though, like the wind that blows, wealth seems to be the result of capricious circumstances and favoring conditions, beyond the reach and foresight of the average man, it yet has laws, precise, definite and fixed by the Creator for human guidance and welfare. Were it true of wealth in general that it was the product of obedience to the three fundamental laws of industry, skill and frugality, the economic condition of society would not be marked by those extremes of riches and poverty which are but the heights and depths of surging billows threatening all the fleets upon the

comed by the ideal teacher. Education is an art. Economy in the higher sense of the management of the duties and resources of life, is also an art. For both, the field of occupancy steadily widens, and educators and philanthropists are evermore scanning the horizon for recruits. I am firmly persuaded that school banking will advance to national adoption, because it is a development responding to a great need in social economy. Its coadjutors, I pray you all to be. If the century now closing shall, with the aid of philanthropists and educators, more firmly and widely establish this benevolent system in the schools of the nation, a useful heritage will be bestowed upon the succeeding centuries now fast approaching, and anticipated as ushering in the most brilliant era in the history of time. Teach political economy and practice its principles by the introduction of school savings banks in the schools of the nation, and the fear of a social revolution will vanish before the dawn of a social evolution.

Note.—For information relating to the introduction and practical working of the school banking system apply to J. H. Thiry of Long Island City, N. Y., and for the literature published apply to Anthony Stumpf, editor of the "American Banker," 29 Murray street, New York, who will send by mail for fifty cents one copy each of the School Savings Bank Manual and its supplements.

The secretary announced to the council that by the courtesy of state Superintendent Charles R. Skinner, the services of a capable stenographer had been provided for this meeting, and that a verbatim report would, therefore, be obtained of the discussions.

Upon his motion, a vote of thanks was extended to Superintendent Skinner for his courtesy and to Mr. Macdonald for his services.

The council also expressed its appreciation of the courtesy of the agent of the trunk line association for courtesies extended by him in the performance of his duties as such agent.

On motion, a vote of thanks was extended to Superintendent Norris and to local authorities for the welcome and hospitality extended to the council during its sessions.

Superintendent Maxwell.—I think we are all agreed that a very large part of the time and energy of the superintendent should be devoted to educating his board of education. After our experience of last night it seems to me that these latter meetings are an admirable opportunity for superintendents to educate boards of education. I would therefore move that it is the opinion of this council that its officers for next year should arrange, if possible, for one or more joint sessions of the two bodies.

Motion carried unanimously.

The chairman said.—I wish to extend my personal thanks. You are a pretty lively set of men, and I find only one place harder to fill, and that is presiding over a lot of school ma'ams. You have acquiesced honestly in the suggestions I have made, and I thank you for it most cordially, and I thank you all for your consideration, and esteem it the highest honor I have ever received in the way of educational matters to be allowed to preside over this body of men, which I consider only second to one other body—that is the National Education Association. It gives me pleasure to present to you the president for the coming year, Superintendent Kneil.

Superintendent Kneil.—Gentlemen of the Council: I thank you for the honor you have conferred upon me. With Superintendent Blodgett I appreciate that this is a great honor in educational work. I only hope that the mantle which he has so worthily worn during this session of the council will be worn by me as worthily during the next session. What is the further pleasure of the council?

On motion, council adjourned.

EMMET BELKNAP,
Secretary.

LATE DR. E. A. SHELDON

Memorial by the Committee Appointed by City and Village Superintendents

To the Council of City and Village Superintendents:

Gentlemen.—Your committee appointed to draft a memorial to the late Dr. E. A. Sheldon, beg leave to submit the following:

The lives of the great and good are our richest inheritance. Such a heritage is ours in the late Edward Austin Sheldon, A. M., Ph. D., principal of the state normal and training school at Oswego.

To-day we stand too near, to get the proper perspective for a fair estimate of the work of this man. The times do not permit of reforms like those instituted by Comenius; the laws of mental growth have been carefully studied and formulated; educational theories have been promulgated and tested; but in a day when the trend of American education was towards formalism, it was Dr. Sheldon who arrested pedagogical thought and insisted upon bringing childhood into touch with nature, thereby predicting scholarship upon experience.

For nearly half a century he devoted his talents and energies to the development and improvement of our public school system, during which period a host of disciples went forth from under his teachings, whose missionary work has moulded and improved the methods of teaching throughout the length and breadth of our land. A pioneer in the introduction of untried methods at a time when those in vogue were crude and unphilosophical, he devoted himself resolutely and assiduously to the work of reform. He declined honors and emoluments which broader fields of work offered; and steadfastly toiled where he believed his Master had called him. Happily, he lived to see in the fruition of his work a golden harvest of merited honor. His name stands enrolled among the most illustrious promoters of popular education of modern times.

Without claiming for Dr. Sheldon the credit of discovery or the invention of a new system of pedagogics, his work was so distinctive, his theory of training teachers so radically different from his contemporaries, that we do well to pause and to consider our indebtedness to his life, and to honor the memory of a man who has given form to the educational thought and the educational practice of a continent. When the future historian of pedagogics shall rewrite the changes in American education, the progress in primary education and in the training of teachers, Edward Austin Sheldon shall stand alone, the Pestalozzi of the new world.

Simple, unpretending, seeking to be taught that he in turn might teach, his sole aim was to discover and to establish a system of pedagogics, simple, logical, based upon the unfolding activities of childhood, which should fit man for humanity and for his eternal destiny. Dr. Sheldon's character was unique. He labored for a principle and subjected all minor considerations to its advancement. He was not an enthusiast, but a patient, persistent and hopeful worker. He was ever courteous, gentle and unassuming, under conditions which would have rendered a less noble character autocratic and pretentious. He was guileless and pure, a disciple of the Great Teacher in precept and in example. In fine, a christian gentleman.

His home, "Shady Shore," with its trees and vines, its bees and flowers, was an outward index of his sympathy with nature. Longfellow's tribute to Agassiz may well be applied to him.

> "Nature, the old nurse took
> The child upon her knee,
> Saying 'Here is a story book
> Thy Father has written for thee.'
>
> And he wandered away and away
> With Nature, the dear old nurse
> Who sang to him night and day
> The rhymes of the universe."

The grove, the garden, the vineyard, the lake were his teachers. In these, more than in books, he found the inspiration of his life. He read them, not as botanist, not as naturalist, but as a child to whom these were an open revelation of a divine intelligence; to him they were a boundless store of knowledge, in which he found much to contemplate, and the very contemplation was inspiration, joy, peace.

In reviewing the life of Dr. Sheldon for the purpose of finding the secret of his power, at least the following characteristic may be discovered, a genial, hopeful spirit, love for children, enthusiasm born of conviction of the righteousness of his cause, the elevation of humanity, catholicity of spirit, supreme faith in Divine guidance and aid, and that somehow through all his work the "purposes of God would surely work their own best way." His own words, in explanation of his declining flattering invitations to posts of honor, best reflect his real life. "I have endeavored to put myself in position to pursue the line of duty, without reference to personal inclination, seeking simply to know my Father's will and then to do it."

In his address of welcome to the alumni, on the occasion of the celebration of the first quarter century of the Oswego normal school, Dr. Sheldon said: "One of the surest elements of prosperity in any undertaking is loyalty to truth. To this more than any other thing, has our success been due. Thoroughly imbued with the belief that there are certain unchanging laws of mental growth which must form the basis of all true educational progress, we have made them the foundation stone of our structure." In speaking of the agencies which have contributed to the growth of the school, he continues: "All these I have emphasized as human instrumentalities; but rising far above them all, and in and through them all there has been infinite wisdom to guide, direct and control all efforts and all events, and give them success. The providence of God has been very marked in the whole history of this school. We can but regard it as an institution of His own planting and protecting, and to Him be all the praise of what we are and what we hope to be."

Dr. Sheldon will ever hold a conspicuous place among American educators on account of two lines of work, either of which would merit lasting fame. Himself an ardent lover of nature, he sought to put every child in touch with nature, that the young life might early feel the presence of the Creator, and early learn to love Him. To this end he gave prominence to the acquisition of knowledge through the senses in primary education, and in laboratory methods in advanced study. That primary knowledge is sensuous was not an original conception with Dr. Sheldon, but he brought the attention of educators to this fact by the emphasis which he placed upon observation lessons or "object lessons," as they were first termed. These views were stoutly controverted in educational gatherings, and a man of less profound conviction would have abandoned the field, but certain of his position he met argument with fact until his critics and opponents, convinced of the correctness of his position, became his warmest friends. His oft-repeated, "You may not see it now, but you will come to acknowledge my position," was his only personal rebuke offered those who differed with him in these debates. The present generation of teachers can hardly realize that what they accept as cardinal principles in education were advocated for years by Dr. Sheldon alone. His faith in the ultimate supremacy of truth made him a bold defender of a principle whose verity he had tested.

The second phase of school work in America for which Dr. Sheldon is responsible, and for which he alone is entitled to credit, is the so-called "Oswego theory of training teachers." A firm believer in the necessity of a clear comprehension of principles, Dr. Sheldon did not believe that such comprehension could be divorced from practice. Precept and rule derived their content from application, hence the basal principle in the training of teachers was the necessity of a school of practice, where principles could be tested and where habits of correct teaching could be formed. The place of the schools of practice in the normal school, as taught by Dr. Sheldon, was at first strenuously opposed in the state associations and in national councils, but the results obtained in the Oswego school soon vindicated the author, and to-day the numerous normal schools, based upon the original Oswego idea, are the strongest evidence of the far-seeing mind of this prince of educators. To Dr. Sheldon must be given the credit and the honor of demonstrating the necessity of the practice department in the normal school.

The members of this council who were present at the Buffalo meeting of the National association in '96 will recall the heated debate upon the "Organization of the Training School," and also the clearness with which Dr. Sheldon outlined his ideal normal school.

The serious if not the fatal defect in our educational system before the advent of the "Oswego movement" was the strange neglect of childhood, a system predicated upon the university and not upon the kindergarten. How to reverse this system was the problem which engaged the attention of this second Pestalozzi. But who was to instruct him, and where was material to be found? Some means must be devised to put the child into proper relation with life. His education must be helpful, uplifting and inspiring. Dr. Sheldon believed that "education should imbue man with respect for the circumstances and the events of his environment, and at the same time inspire him with faith in the inexhaustible resources of his nature, for only by producing better things can he elevate himself above his past."

Dr. Sheldon never hoped to see self-wrought reforms; he believed in tireless activity. "When I have dóne my best to persuade men to my ideas, I keep right on and trust to the vindication of results." His life was an incarnation of the masterful sentiment of Lord Bacon: "In this world, God only and angels may be spectators." His theories were not the result of accident, but were the logical outgrowth of mature reflection. He had faith in them. Willing to make minor concessions for the sake of gaining major ends, he never yielded what he considered a cardinal principle. No secondary considerations were allowed to infringe upon the unity of his ultimate purpose. To this everything was subordinated.

That childhood even might be so related to life that its early lessons would put it in sympathy with nature, with truth, with purity, with God, was the end sought. The words of Thomas Arnold fitly voice his sentiments, "What I want to see in the school is the abhorrence of evil." "To become one in heart with the good and generous and devout is, by God's grace, to become in measure good and generous and devout." In his searchings for means to relate the child to nature, Dr. Sheldon found in the imported collection of the educational appliances in the National Museum of Toronto the first help to his great system of "object lessons." His return from Toronto is thus described by his gifted daughter, Mrs. Mary Sheldon-Barnes: "Well do I remember the delight with which he returned from this visit, armed with some material appliances for accomplishing his desires. The dark shelves of the little closets opening off from the dingy office where my father lived and worked all day, as secretary of the board of education, became filled with wonders delightful to my childish eyes, and I think no less so to his own. Colored balls and cards, bright colored pictures of animals, samples of grain, specimens of pottery and glass." Here were the means provided by nature to put childhood into touch with herself and into sympathy with her. These, rather than books, should prove the inspiration which would make books and life itself intelligible. "The difference between a useful education, and one which does not affect the future life," says Dr. Arnold, "rests mainly on the greater or less activity which it has communicated to the

OFFICERS

President

CHARLES H. HOWELL, Riverhead.

Vice-Presidents

GEORGE G. ROYCE, Gouverneur.
ADELAIDE L. HARRIS, Ransomville.

Secretaries

CORA A. DAVIS, Whitesboro.
D. D. T. MARSHALL, Redwood.

Treasurer

FRANK W. McELROY, Bliss.

Transportation Agent

HENRY R. SANFORD, Ph. D., Penn Yan.

Committee on Legislation

JAMES S. COOLEY, Glen Cove.
WALTER S. ALLERTON, Mt. Vernon.
JAMES R. FLAGG, Frewsburg.

Local Committee

Inspector, A. EDSON HALL.
Superintendent, THOMAS R. KNEIL.

PROGRAM

Wednesday

Address of welcome, Senator E. T. Brackett, Superintendent Thomas R. Kneil.

Responses to adresses of welcome, Commissioner Charles W. Fordham, James M. Milne, Ph. D.

Discussion: Compulsory school law and its workings, Inspector A. M. Wright, A. M.; Commissioner Myra L. Ingalsbe, Commissioner Fred E. Duffy.

Report of Committee on Legislation.

Report of Committee on Visual Instruction.

Address: Hon. Charles R. Skinner, Superintendent of Public Instruction.

Thursday

Discussion: Should the powers of the commissioner be increased? Commissioner Walter S. Allerton, Commissioner S. L. Whitlock.

Paper: Elements of success in supervision, Superintendent Charles E. Gorton.

Election of Officers:

Paper: Aid teachers think they may obtain from commissioners, Miss Gratia L. Rice, State Instructor in Drawing.

Paper: Reading in the public schools, Commissioner Martha Van Rensselaer.

Paper: The commissioner in the schoolroom, Commissioner C. Edward Jones.

Address: A study in school economics, Superintendent F. J. Diamond.

Address: Hon. George W. Ross, Minister of Education, Toronto, Canada.

Friday

Discussion: Practical suggestions on how to make commissioners' supervision more effective, Commissioner Oscar Granger, Commissioner J. W. Scott.

Paper: How commissioners may be more helpful to the Department, Howard J. Rogers, Second Deputy Superintendent.

Report of Committees.

Adjournment.

NEW YORK STATE ASSOCIATION

OF

School Commissioners and Superintendents

PROCEEDINGS OF THE FORTY-THIRD ANNUAL MEETING OF THE NEW YORK STATE ASSOCIATION OF SCHOOL COMMISSIONERS AND SUPERINTENDENTS, HELD AT SARATOGA SPRINGS NOVEMBER 3, 4 AND 5, 1897

The forty-third annual session of the New York State Association of School Commissioners and Superintendents assembled in the theatre Saratoga, Saratoga Springs, N. Y., Wednesday, November 3, 1897, and was called to order by President Charles H. Howell. After a song rendered by pupils of the public school led by Professor D. M. Kelsey, senator Edgar T. Brackett, of Saratoga Springs was introduced and delivered the following address of welcome:

Mr. Chairman, ladies and gentlemen of the convention.—We have discovered, as no doubt all of you have, that the pleasure of having the door open, and of seeing the nicety of the house does not depend upon the length of march which the person who open the doors give, but rather in the heartiness of the inasking. It is not expected of me, in thus welcoming you to our village, that I shall occupy your time with any set speech or any formal welcome. We welcome you as workers in and for and through our magnificent school system of our state. We welcome you as coming from different parts of the state.

Twenty years ago George William Curtis in a burst of that brilliant oratory which made him the leader of his time, said: "Thank God that in this day and generation it is not necessary to justify the benefits of popular education." Now, on behalf of the village of Saratoga Springs, a place where you have chosen to meet at this your session, you who are, as I said before, engaged in the upbuilding of this system, that has done so much for good citizens, decency and high living; and in all that goes to make up the elements of mentality and morality, I welcome you and give you the right hand.

Superintendent Thomas R. Kneil was introduced and extended further welcome on behalf of the board of education and school officers of Saratoga Springs, as follows:

Mr. President, ladies and gentlemen of the association and you who are interested in education.—I don't know why two addresses of welcome should be necessary this afternoon. The good one has come and gone. All that I can do is to add somewhat to the words of welcome which the senator has spoken. In behalf of the people of Saratoga Springs, I invite the convention to a social spread to be given at the Worden, after the exercises of Thursday evening shall be concluded. We consider that this, in a very mild manner, typifies the greeting that we have for you.

I realize that I am addressing a company of people that have in their hands the public school system of the state of New York—a school system which stands second to none among the states of the Union—a school system which is worthy of the very best efforts of the very best men and women of these United States of America.

Our school commissioners come very closely in contact with that, which a great many consider as the bone and sinew of our school system, the district school, the common school. If it be true that out of the common school come the statesmen, the business men, the successful men in every line of work in these United States, it seems to me that in you is laid a tremendous responsibility to see that these schools are made the very best possible. We are banded together, one and all, for a magnificient work. No petty jealousies, no lack of enthusiasm, no questioning as to what is expedient, should stand in the way of our giving to the people of this commonwealth the best common school system possible. I believe that the great need of the school system of the state of New York to-day is closer supervision. (Applause.) I believe that the day is coming, and coming very soon, when there will be in the state of New York, a system of school supervision which prevails in the state of Massachusetts. The great need of our school system to-day is not to tell how to teach, but to breath into the teaching force of the state the breath of life; so that the teachers shall be spurred on by inspiration and enthusiasm to do for the state what every one, who takes upon himself the sacred name of teacher, ought to do.

Commissioners of the state of New York, fellow superintendents of village schools, again on behalf of the people of Saratoga Springs; on behalf of the teachers of Saratoga Springs; yes, in behalf of us all, I bid you welcome to our village.

Response by school commissioner Charles W. Fordham, of Suffolk county:

I am so glad that in the Empire state we can say ladies and gentlemen. I think it is a sign of advancing civilization. I hope to live to see every door to honor and profit in the state and the United States, open to both sexes.

The president lately told me that I was alone in answering the speeches of welcome. But when he afterwards told me that that ripe scholar, and that genial gentleman of college attainments would stand by my side, the burden rolled off. I am only introductory to the morning star and sun that cometh. The superintendent told us what an important body we are. I agree with him; don't you? If you will tell me what the superintendents, commissioners and teachers are to-day, I will tell you what the governing policy of the government will be to-morrow. Our teachers are kings and queens to further the laws and policies of the government in the future. A very distinguished person in a prominent city said, "The only hope of getting out of the grasp of the corruptionist, is the common school of Brooklyn." The only hope of our state and United States is the common schools. We are here for a purpose, a great purpose. We are here to confer and to consult with one another; to see if we can not gain ideas that will be of benefit, and, we are here, to get inspiration from one another.

Response by James M. Milne, Ph. D., of the Oneonta state normal school:

We, too, can extend the hand and grasp yours cordially, one with the other. We give thanks for the welcome from the good people of Saratoga, from the teachers and the children. We thank you for all the instruction that you have pointed out to us in that close supervision. We should remember that with all supervision, with all studies, unless these are vivified and fed and directed, they will fail. Man must stand for an idea—he must stand for an inspiring idea. There are two extremes: the extreme where we trust too much in books, and the one where we trust too much in methods for practice. Between these two extremes, and, shall I say, putting our arms around these two extremes must stand the power of personality. My predecessor said, "If you tell me what the teachers are to-day, and the supervisors, I will tell you the citizens of to-morrow." He can only tell the leaders of the citizens of to-morrow. He can only tell of what kind, because they are simply the effervescence of the plant that produced them. So will our exercises prove to you the greatest possible thanksgiving, prove that community of interest that will breathe the thanks.

We offer another hope, that those who are now here, and will come, will in our day prove our thanks to you for your welcome.

COMPULSORY SCHOOL LAW AND ITS WORKINGS

A. M. WRIGHT, STATE INSPECTOR

The school commissioner is mentioned in the law but once, *i. e.*, in the closing of section 7, where he is clothed with authority to remove, at his pleasure, town attendance officers. This is a duty which is not always a pleasure to perform. I am confident that in the appointment of these attendance officers men are often selected because of some favoritism, or because they are willing to act, or not, as directed. In many cases the town boards have accepted and acted upon the suggestions of the state Department, that the compensation of these officers shall be fixed at, as we suggest, the sum of two dollars per day and mileage for actual services rendered. That act on the part of town boards in thus fixing the compensation will result in more energetic work on the part of these officers. I want to ask the commissioners to look at this part of their work from my standpoint, if possible. My standard in regard to the enforcement of this law is about as follows: The teacher is an important factor in the enforcement of the law. If the teacher is not willing to do her part, to know how many children should be in attendance, to carefully see that all pupils in the district are registered, to ascertain from day to day whether these children are absent, and use her influence to enforce attendance, the law will not be very effective. But side by side with the teacher must stand the school commissioner, ready to lend assistance whenever needed. The trustee is the responsible party; he is the executive of the district. If the law is not complied with the district loses its public money. There is no doubt but that the district could sustain an equitable claim against the trustee for thus losing its public money. In the enforcement of the law, we have had the town attendance officers for one year. It has been extremely gratifying to me, in reviewing the abstracts of the commissioners, to find that in the enforcement of this law very effective work has been done the past year by these officers. There has been an increase in the attendance of nearly five per cent. in one year. We stand in need of one very important feature of the law, that is, some place to put the boys and girls who are found willfully truant from school.

A state truant school is the logical sequence of the law. The state Department assures a hearty coöperation with you, and we are ready to give any assistance to aid you in the enforcement of the law.

Commissioner Myra L. Ingalsbe.—In prosecuting the enforcement of the compulsory law in the second district, Washington county, very little of what might be called actual discouragement has been met. Some obstacles have been encountered and some opposition, but with the law back of us, and with the press of the country with us, the law has been enforced with a comparative degree of smoothness. The secret of the proper enforcement of the law lies in the appointment of the attendance officer. A man of good judgment, of firmness, of pleasing address and of some social standing in his town meets with but little serious opposition in executing his duty. I have failed to experience an instance in which the town board has not been desirous of appointing capable men for this office.

Early in November, Mr. Wright, by arrangement with the commissioner, met the attendance officers at Whitehall. The town officers were notified to be present at said meeting and charge expenses to their respective towns. The commissioner holds she was justified in such action, and, furthermore, she acted only after consultation with those in authority.

As a result of this meeting, officers were not only instructed as regards the interpretation of the law and methods of enforcing the same, but they were convinced that the law was to be enforced, and through reports of the meeting, both verbal and printed, the education of the people, as regards the law, was carried on. Keep the law before the people, through visits from the attendance officers, notices in the press, reminders from the commissioner, and in all intelligent ways.

Visits from the commissioners and talks in the presence of the pupils are a great support to the teacher, who virtually meets the brunt of the law. Our school authorities have been obliged to call upon the state attendance officers several times, and have always found them ready and willing to render assistance, even to visit with some town officer a little district school. We have met with the greatest difficulty in enforcing the law in the thinly settled outlying districts, where man is virtually a law unto himself, and regulates his actions according to his own inclinations, without any consideration whatever as regards his social or civil obligations. During the past year I have devoted a great share of my energy to the enforcement of this compulsory law. I have given time to its work when I would have loved to spend it with the children in the various schools. Realizing fully the need of education in these times, I have turned from the work that I love to that which presents itself to me as duty, knowing well that each child whose feet are kept upon the first rounds of the ladder of learning may yet " climb to the stars."

Commissioner Allerton.—It would seem that there are one or two weak points in the law at present. I agree with Miss Ingalsbe that the school census is one of the most important things in the enforcement of this law. I am of the opinion, very decidedly that the school census is at present taken when it is least calculated to give good results. It should be taken earlier in the spring or later in the fall. I find that in some districts we are depending too much upon the teachers to enforce the law. The teacher should know the children in the district and know whether they attend school.

This is not possible in all districts. It is impossible to teach the school properly and at the same time keep track of the children to see whether they register or not. It is the duty of the teacher, of course, to understand why the children who are registered do not attend. To properly answer the questions relating to attendance at private schools, our officers ought to be put where they will know all about the children attending these private schools. I believe, before we can enforce this law, the state Department must declare that we must have a law that will compel the private school to keep a register, and give the attendance officer a right to examine the register to ascertain about the children attending there.

Mr. Wright.—I think that if the commissioner will read the law he will see that whenever a child attends upon instruction elsewhere than a public school, the teacher of such a child shall keep a register of such attendance; and that the school officers of that district are empowered to examine said register. It is a misdemeanor on the part of anyone having in charge such children to refuse to give information when they should.

Commissioner Allerton.—Who is to enforce the law against the people who infringe? These schools will not admit any person to examine the registers. Who is to enforce the law against them?

Mr. Wright.—The only persons are the public school authorities, and it becomes their duty to obtain the information in order to give it in their reports.

Commissioner Cooley.—The state of Pennsylvania has just adopted the compulsory law, which has a provision for requiring all private schools and private teachers to furnish to pupils or their parents, once a month, a record of their attendance. It is a good plan to have meetings with trustees and boards of education to talk over this compulsory law. We have found them very helpful. Much good results from these meetings.

Commissioner Rice.—Inspiration is aroused by meeting with the trustees and attendance officers. Often illiterate people are chosen as officers, because of necessity. It is hard work for such men to enforce the law. If you can get that man to a trustees' meeting, he will go home and do the best he can. The attendance officers are limited to their own town. They should have jurisdiction over the entire district.

Superintendent Kneil.—When we get down to hard pan and work harmoniously, there will be no trouble about the enforcement of the law.

Commissioner Stephens.—Upon whom will come the burden of proof as to whether children, who receive instruction at home, are properly educated?

Commissioner Cooley.—If the trustees are satisfied that proper instructions are not given, would they be justified in arresting the man and taking him before a justice of the peace?

Mr. Wright.—There is no question about it.

REPORT OF COMITTEE ON LEGISLATION

In obedience to the requirements of section 2, article 8, of the constitution and by-laws of this association, the committee on legislation, appointed at the close of the last convention, begs leave to report as follows:

Your committee came into existence just previous to the adjournment of the Niagara Falls convention, last January, and there was no opportunity for the members of the committee to confer together, before returning to our several districts. Furthermore, your honorable body gave to the committee no instructions whatever, and made no recommendations for their consideration, as to what legislative action should be undertaken or encouraged. Consequently, like a ship captain without sailing orders or port of destination, your committee was left free to navigate the troublous waters of legislation as, in the best judgment of its members, seemed proper, and as the shifting winds and tides of legislative possibilities made necessary. A statement was accordingly prepared and the same was submitted to the state Superintendent.

1. Substituting, for two assembly bills, already introduced, an amendment, providing for the purchase of text-books for the use of all pupils in all schools.

2. Providing an educational qualification for candidates for the office of school commissioner.

3. Providing additional compensation for school commissioners.

4. Placing all special act school districts under the jurisdiction of school commissioners, and giving to school commissioners exclusive authority to examine and license teachers therein, not possessing the qualifications mentioned in subdivision 5, section 13, title V of the consolidated school law.

5. Striking out the word "altered," in section 6, title VI, so that territory may be added to school districts upon which there is a bonded indebtedness.

6. Providing that any school district may, by vote, include in its annual expenses, the cost of conveying to the school building those pupils who live remote from the building.

7. Striking out the eight hundred dollar limit, in estimating the cost of a suitable new school house, where the old schoolhouse has been condemned by the school commissioner.

8. Reducing from five per centum to one per centum, the fees paid to collectors by county treasurers, on taxes returned by them as uncollected.

9. Providing that the employment of teachers in common school districts by the trustees shall be subject to the approval of the school commissioner.

10. Providing that the closing of schools during institute week, in districts employing a superintendent, shall be at the discretion of the school commissioner, instead of at the option of the board of education.

After some further discussion and consideration, it was decided to incorporate into a single bill five of the ten amendments to the consolidated school law, proposed in the committee's statement, and to secure the introduction of the same into both houses of the legislature as soon as they could be prepared.

These amendments were as follows:

1. Placing special act school districts under the jurisdiction of school commissioners.

2. Striking out the word "altered," from section 6, title VI.

3. Striking out the eight hundred dollar limit for the estimated cost of a new schoolhouse where the old schoolhouse has been condemned by the school commissioner.

4. Reducing the collectors' fees on taxes returned to the county treasurer as uncollected.

5. Providing for the closing of school during institute week, in school districts employing a superintendent, at the discretion of the school commissioner.

Your committee secured interviews with senator Wray and Col. Sanger, the chairmen, respectively, of the committees on public education of the senate and of the assembly, to whom these proposed amendments were fully explained. The members of your committee desire to express their sincere gratitude for the kind and courteous attention which was accorded them by both of these gentlemen, and for the interest manifested by them in the welfare and progress of the public schools of the Empire state.

The committee's bill, prepared in duplicate, was introduced into both houses of the legislature, early in March, and soon after, a circular letter was prepared, stating briefly, the action of the committee and giving the provisions of the committee's bill. Four of the five amendments proposed by your committee thus became a part of the school law. In securing these gratifying results, your committee received very material assistance from Deputy Superintendent Ainsworth, and the sincere thanks of the committee and of this association are due him, as without his aid it is doubtful if so much could have been accomplished.

That your committee on legislation may be more permanent in character, we recommend the following amendment to the constitution and by-laws of this association.

Amend sections 2 and 3, of article VIII, to read as follows:

Section 2. There shall be a standing committee on legislation consisting of three members, which shall be appointed immediately after the adoption of this amendment. The members of the committee first appointed under this section, shall hold office for one, two and three years respectively, as they may determine by lot. At each annual convention thereafter, the president shall appoint one member of this committee for three years, and also fill any existing vacancies, at the opening session of the convention.

§ 3. At the opening session of each convention, the president shall appoint the following committees, viz.: On resolutions, on treasurer's report, on transportation, on the time and place of the next meeting, and on school supervision. The last named committee shall present a written report at the next meeting after their appointment.

Your committee would also recommend, for your consideration, the following amendments to the consolidated school law, and would suggest that some definite hour be assigned for their discussion, that our successors upon this committee may have some definite understanding of the wishes of this association.

1. Amend section 7, title V, so that it will read as follows:

§ 7. Every school commissioner shall receive an annual salary of eighteen hundred dollars, twelve hundred dollars of which shall be payable, quarterly, out of the free school fund, appropriated for that purpose, and six hundred dollars of which shall be payable quarterly, by the several county treasurers, out of money raised by tax upon the several towns for that purpose.

2. Strike out section 8 of the same title.

3. Amend section 9 of the same title, so as to read as follows:

§ 9. Each school commissioner shall be furnished, at the expense of the county in which his commissioner district is situated, with such necessary stationery, printed matter and advertising as may be allowed by the board of supervisors.

4. Insert, after the word "superintendent," in line five of section 13, title I, the following words:

"Or does not possess the qualifications for the office which are required by law."

5. Insert, after the word "situated" in line six of section 3, title V, the following clause: "And who possesses one or more of the following educational qualifications, viz., a diploma from a college or university, obtained after not less than four years' attendance, a New York state certificate, granted upon an examination, a New York normal school diploma of not less than three years' standing a first grade commissioners' certificate of not less than three years' standing, or not less than three years' experience as commissioner.

6. Add to subdivision 7 of section 14, title VII, the words "or by ballot;" insert after the word "ascertained" in line two of section 18, same title, the words "by ballot or;" insert the same words after the word "ascertained," in line seven of section 19, same title; also, insert the same words in line 16, section 10, title VIII.

These last amendments are for the purpose of making the manner of voting uniform, in authorizing the levy of a tax, in directing that a tax shall be collected in installments, in designating a site for a school building and in changing the site, in any school district.

7 Strike out the words "altered or," in last line but one of section 30, title VIII, to make the section agree with the amendment adopted last winter.

8. Amend section 7, title VIII, as amended by chapter 466, laws of 1897, by striking out of lines four and five the words, "other than those whose limits correspond with those of an incorporated city or village." The purpose of this amendment is to allow boards of education in villages the same privileges, as to appointing a clerk, as are possessed by other boards.

9. Amend section 4, title X, as amended by chapter 512, laws of 1897, by striking out from lines 12 and 13 the following words, "at the option of the boards of education in such districts," and

inserting in their place the following: "as may be deemed for the best interests of the schools of such districts, in the discretion of the school commissioner in whose jurisdiction such districts are situated."

10. Amending sections 59 and 60, title VII, by changing the date of taking the school census from June 30th to September 30th, so that it may give a more correct list of the children of the several districts who are subject to the compulsory law.

Your committee would also commend to the favorable consideration of this association the following modifications of the compulsory education law, some of which are found in the Pennsylvania law, recently enacted.

1. Providing that the period of compulsory attendance shall commence with the opening of the school term and continue until the school closes, at the end of the school year, during the time that the school is in session.

2. Providing that the school authorities of each district shall furnish to the principal or teacher of the school, at the opening of the school term, a complete list of all children in the district who are subject to the provisions of the compulsory law.

3. Requiring principals or teachers to notify those in parental relation to their pupils, at the end of each week, of all pupils who have been absent, during the week, two days without a lawful excuse.

4. Requiring principals or teachers to report to the attendance officer, on Monday of each week during the school term, a list of all pupils who were absent three days during the previous week, without lawful excuse.

5. Requiring principals of private schools and other educational institutions, and teachers giving private instruction, to report absences, the same as teachers in public schools, and also to furnish, monthly, to each child under his instruction, or to the person in parental relation to such child, a certificate, duly signed, that such child has been, or is being instructed as provided in the compulsory law.

6. Providing that school commissioners, superintendents and trustees shall have authority to visit and inspect all private schools, and other educational institutions and teachers giving private instruction in their several jurisdictions, and requiring the principals and teachers of all such schools, and all teachers giving private instruction to keep an accurate record of attendance in registers furnished by the Department of Public Instruction, the same as is required in the public schools.

7. Providing that a residence of two miles or more from the schoolhouse, by the nearest traveled road, shall be a proper ex-

cuse for non-attendance, in the discretion of the school authorities of the district.

In closing this report, it is perhaps proper to add, as explanatory of the statement at the outset, that your committee received no instructions or recommendations from this association to guide its action, that until the distribution of the bound volumes of the report of the state Superintendent, in June, we were not aware that resolutions had been adopted at the last convention, recommending amendments to the consolidated school law, allowing any school district to contract with any adjacent district for the instruction and transportation of its pupils, establishing one or more state truant schools, and providing for the purchase of text-books for indigent pupils. Another excellent reason for amending the constitution and by-laws of this association, as recommended by your committee.

All of which is respectfully submitted,

JAMES S. COOLEY,
WALTER S. ALLERTON,
JAMES R. FLAGG,
Committee on Legislation.

SARATOGA, N. Y., *November* 3, 1897.

Mr. Maxson.—It seems to me that in this report which has been given by the committee, we have received some very valuable suggestions. Work of this kind should be taken up very carefully and considered.

On motion, the report was adopted and ordered placed on file.

A vote of thanks was extended to the legislative committee for their excellent report.

Superintendent Kneil moved that immediately after Superintendent Skinner's address, the recommendations of this committee be discussed in order. Carried.

Under the head of miscellaneous business President Howell called for an expression of the association relative to closing the session Thursday evening. After some discussion it was decided by vote of the association to continue the session as per program.

The treasurer, Commissioner McElroy, was reported absent.

On motion of Superintendent Kneil, Commissioner C. Edward Jones of Oswego county, was made treasurer pro tem.

WEDNESDAY EVENING, NOVEMBER 3, 1897

Meeting called to order at 8 p. m.

Report of committee on visual instruction.

Commissioner Baldwin.—At the closing hours of our last meeting, a resolution was introduced appointing a committee to confer with Dr. Bickmore, of the American Museum of Natural History, in regard to extending visual instruction in commissioner districts. As chairman of that committee, I have endeavored in various ways to get facts regarding the work. I think, perhaps, it would be well to review the growth of this work as it began in New York city; how it has extended to the normal schools and to the union schools. With the lantern and tanks, the institute conductors do excellent work. If the work is valuable for pupils and teachers in the cities, it is most certainly valuable for the rural schools. The committee have had to meet several objections. One was this: "Why, this is a wild scheme! It is impossible for the state to supply 114 lamps and the views." Thirty-eight lanterns would be enough. A good point in regard to this work in the rural districts is, that it gives us opportunity especially at the noon meetings, of talking with the people of the district, interesting them in the educational work.

The committee would recommend that some time during the session, or at the next meeting, this question of extending the work be thoroughly discussed. Second, that a committee be appointed to continue the investigation of this work, and report at our next meeting.

ADDRESS BY SUPERINTENDENT SKINNER

After a brief introduction, Superintendent Skinner, in substance, said: Our school superintendents are doing an important work, and doing it well. The essential point in the quality of a superintendent is to be able to know a good teacher and how to judge of his work. So far as my knowledge goes, there is no state more fortunate in the efficiency of the work of supervision. You all recognize that the main requirement is a knowledge of the value of the instruction given and a supervision of that instruction. Good morals are as important as good methods in the schoolroom. I believe there is not a system of education in any country on the globe equal to that which we are making possible in the state of New York, and the progress made is largely due to your faithful and loyal service. The army of school teachers in our state represents an element in our population possessing the highest characteristics of the human mind, and, under our system, they are continually working for the benefit of our schools and the proper education of our children.

I speak for the teaching of good morals and good manners. A well-rounded education means an education which is to prepare our children to fight their way through life. I fear there is not enough of life in the school days of some of our boys and girls which should impress them with the necessity of thoroughness in securing what they should have in preparation for college. Those who have ambition to enter the university should have a thorough preparation for its higher courses of study.

In our educational system the office of school commissioner can be made of great power. Magnify and dignify your office. You should have additional power, trustees under you should have additional power, school district meetings should have additional power, and among these additional powers school commissioners should have power to settle many of the questions which are now brought before the Department of public instruction.

As to school legislation, our laws are many years old, and every year something needs strengthening, and the tendency is to give more direct power to school commissioners. But we should not encourage radical changes in school laws.

The past year has been the most progressive school year in our history. The compulsory education law has demonstrated its usefulness.

The teachers' institutes, the training classes, the examination department, have all worked thoroughly and satisfactorily. Our great system of normal schools, in spite of increased requirements for admission, are full and overflowing. There is a constant demand for better teachers and these schools are striving to provide them.

Discussion of the report of the committee on legislation was taken up at 9.30 p, m., and Dr. Cooley read from the report the different points to be discussed by the meeting.

Commissioner Lester.—I cannot see why a college man should be eligible to the office of school commissioner, when he cannot teach school without a third-grade certificate. I think he is no better qualified than a normal-school graduate. If you accept three years from a normal-school graduate, why not from a college man?

As to monthly payment of commissioners, Commissioner Rice said.—I do not see any reason why a manufacturing concern should pay once a week about $7,000, and the commissioners are paid only once a quarter.

Superintendent Skinner.—Sometimes it is pretty hard work to induce the commissioners to accept their pay once a quarter. (Laughter.) There are about fifteen school commissioners in the state who do not transmit to the Department their receipts for salary without being written to three or four times. So far as the clerical work is concerned, it is altogether a matter of bookkeeping in the treasurer's office. The Department has never objected to monthly payments.

Commissioner Allerton.—I think if we ask for $1,800 we may get $1,500, and if we ask for $1,500 we may not get more than $1,200. I think the committee may say that they have looked the matter over very impartially.

Conductor Stout.—There has been, in the last twenty-two years that I have been connected with the Commissioners' Association of the state of New York, not less than five attempts to establish an educational qualification for school commissioners. It has failed in every instance, and it will fail in every instance so long as you endeavor to have any qualifications put in it. There is only one way that you will ever get it and that is to make it more simple. A year ago last winter it was arranged that we should have it. Letters were had from all over the state, and two-thirds of the commissioners opposed it.

President Howell.—I believe that the commissioners of the state can have their salary raised when they stand united. I believe we should advocate one standard salary, and $1,800 is what it ought to be.

Commissioner Woodward.—One man killed the bill when it was brought before the committee. If we can overcome one man the organization is of some value.

A motion was made that the recommendations offered by the committee on legislation be accepted, and that the committee on legislation, appointed at this session, introduce a bill embodying educational qualifications and also one raising the salary.

Commissioner Fordham.—I move to substitute that this whole subject be left to the wisdom of the committee. Let them do the best they can for us.

The original motion was passed.

President Howell appointed the following committees:

Resolutions.—Commissioners Granger, Kaufman and Jones.

Auditing.—Commissioners Van Rensselaer, Rice and Wymbs.

Time and Place.—Commissioners Baldwin, Kniskern and Whitlock.

Transportation.—Dr. Henry R. Sanford, Commissioners Van Wie and Mickle.

THURSDAY, NOVEMBER 4, 1897

Meeting called to order by President Howell at 9.40.

Song by pupils of the village school.

SHOULD THE POWERS OF THE COMMISSIONER BE INCREASED?

Commisioner Allerton.—My own convictions upon the question are that in many respects the powers of the school commissioners should be increased. It seems to me that, as I look at the educational system of this state, that there is something wanting in it; that there is a gap that ought to be filled. The commissioners should have more control over the engagement of teachers — the appointment of teachers in the district. I believe that this is a question that has at least an interest to our rural schools, our common school districts, our little country schools. One of the greatest evils we have to contend against, especially in our rural schools, is the employment of incompetent and inefficient teachers. We are well aware of the fact that in many districts we have incompetent trustees. In many districts a trustee is pushed for the office, and is elected because he can run the school cheaper than any other person in the district. The result of this is that we have a man who is utterly unable to select a competent teacher—a teacher who is adapted to the work that has to be done in the school. There is no authority in the legislative system of this state to prevent it. How can we remedy it? I believe we should have a law saying that no trustee can make a contract with a teacher until he has submitted the proposed contract to the school commissioner and obtained his consent in writing. It is an unfortunate fact that all qualified teachers are not competent. The fact that a teacher can pass an examination is not conclusive evidence that he will be a success as a teacher.

The office of school commissioner is one of great responsibility. We know that the statute creating the office says that we shall use our utmost efforts to improve the teachers and the schools under our charge. This is a great responsibility thrown upon us, but, unfortunately, the law has not given us any power in this respect to carry out its provisions. We are told that we are the supervising officers of the state. I hear, time after time, at our meetings, about the importance of thorough, intelligent supervision. The supervising officer, when he sees mistakes, ought to have power to remedy them. The commissioner has no such power.

I think we ought to have some authority over the course of study. We have a commissioners' course of study approved by the Department, but we are powerless to compel any school to adopt it. When complaints are brought to us, we ought to have power to look into these matters, and, if we find them wrong, we ought to have power to say to the teacher or trustee that this thing is wrong and ought to be checked.

Commissioner Whitlock.—I most heartily concur in what commissioner Allerton has said in regard to the powers of the commissioners.

Commissioner Wymbs.—We are introducing the course of study in our schools. I told the trustees that I would provide a course of study, and asked their coöperation in introducing it into their schools.

Commissioner Royce.—In St. Lawrence county we simply took the course of study and put it into the schools, and told the teachers they must adopt it. Public sentiment favors the course of study.

In regard to the increased power of school commissioners, I think that the power ought to be increased. In our county we would meet with some difficulty if the trustee could not contract with a teacher without the consent of the commissioner. The main difficulty is that we are short of teachers. It would be well to give the commissioner more power in settling disputes, yet I am not sure but that more trouble would arise.

Commissioner Baldwin.—I have objected to providing teachers for trustees, because when a trustee comes to me for a teacher he looks upon me as a teachers' agency. He thinks I am obliged to find a teacher for him. I would like to have the commissioners' powers increased in this, viz.: The power of appointing a town board of trustees—five or more in number—subject to the approval of the town board.

Commissioner Jones.—I find that the great majority of our trustees are men who are interested in good schools, and I believe that they are doing what they believe to be for the best interest of the schools in their districts.

Commissioner Cooley.—Mr. Allerton did not wish the commissioners to be authorized to appoint the teacher, but that he should have the right to approve the action of the trustees.

The commissioner is authorized to approve the choice of a new site in a common school district and the district cannot change the site of the school without the approval of the commissioner. It is quite as essential that the teacher in the schoolhouse shall be satisfactory to the commissioner as the site on which the schoolhouse is situated is satisfactory to the commissioner.

Commissioner Sheffield.—I believe it is the intention of the Department to do what is right. When the commissioners exercise the power they now possess, we can do much more towards bringing our schools to a higher standing. It is because the commissioners are afraid many times to exercise the power that lies within them, that they fail.

Commissioner Fordham.—My friend does not touch the point. We have no law in operation in reference to hiring teachers with the approval of commissioners. We ought to have a law to govern that. Commissioners may talk about executing the law we have, but we have no law here whatever.

Commissioner Cooley.—The difficulty that we have had in my district was from teachers who received many years ago state certificates and who are incompetent.

State Superintendent Skinner.—If, in the estimation of the commissioner, a teacher is utterly incompetent, it is sufficient reason for the annullment of the teacher's certificate.

ELEMENTS OF SUCCESS IN SUPERVISION

ADDRESS BY CHARLES E. GORTON

The conditions under which supervision is exercised vary greatly. In country districts with small widely separated schools the only inspection is by the commissioner on his infrequent visits, or perhaps still more rarely by a trustee whose standard of requirements and instruction is fixed by what they did in school when he was a boy. The principal, much of whose time is devoted to other duties, is the supervisory officer of the graded school. In large villages and cities superintendents and their immediate assistants exercise direct supervision, but with widely varying degrees of differentiation. In some cases their duties are almost purely educational, in many others, they perform a great variety of services, and as agents or representatives of the school board, are largely men of affairs.

In his notes on American schools and training colleges, Dr. J. G. Fitch says of the superintendent, "Within his state, county or city, the superintendent combines in himself, the character of a minister of public instruction, an inspector of schools, a licenser of teachers, and a professor of pedagogy. Under the sanction of his board or committee he draws up regulations for the work of the various classes of the schools, and often appends notes and comments prescribing the method in which each subject shall be taught. He conducts examinations for determining promotions of scholars from grade to grade. He sets the questions, he examines candidates for the office of teachers in his district and awards to them diplomas or certificates. He holds institutes and instructs those teachers who have not been previously trained in the work of their special classes. He also conducts conferences of the older teachers, and gives lectures to them on the philosophy and history of education." In many places, as indicated before there is added a great variety of miscellaneous duties to Dr. Fitch's enumeration.

The existing conditions are noted here to show the difficulty that arises in an attempt to treat this subject as if the same kind of service were uniformly required from supervisory officers. The essential qualities, attainments and methods will, however, not vary as widely as the range of duties and localities, but will be found to be pretty nearly constant quantities. No voice will dissent from the proposition that the schools are established and maintained solely for the children. "It is to and for the pupils that the superintendent's greatest force, thought and study must be directed. All effort has lent one aim, all instruments and means one object. All interests center at the children. The schools are for them. The advancement of the pupils is the desideration of all school management." Only those who are profoundly impressed with this view have fitly a place in the supervision of schools. He is a traitor to his position and profession who will ever for a moment regard the school as a place of refuge for incompetency or unfitness, or a place where personal or political favors are to be paid. Devotion to study, loyalty to the children, I place as the fundamental element of successful supervision.

The successful supervisor should be broadly humanitarian. Everything that makes for human progress and elevation should be of interest to him and within his province. The supervisor of schools should possess not only the spirit of the philanthropist, seeking the uplifting of humanity through the children, but he should possess faith in the individual, and should see in every boy or girl all the possibilities of good citizenship. He must never lose faith in the child and must often impart his own hopefulness to others. He will seek to know more of the operation of the child's mind, its development and its efforts. Dr. Thomas Arnold said the sternest reproof and most profound lesson of his life was received from a stupid boy whom he chided for his dullness. The boy with rising tears looked the doctor full in the face and said, "I am doing the very best I can, sir."

The successful supervisor must either have prepared the course of study or must be familiar with its details and spirit. He must comprehend the results sought to be reached by the course as a whole and by every part of it, in order that he may properly direct its execution in the class-room. It does not follow, that he must know the details of all subjects taught.

The successful supervisor must be a constant and profound student of method. To know the course of study minutely, to comprehend its objects fully, to understand the subject matter

The election resulted as follows:

President.—Commissioner George G. Royce.
First Vice-President.—Commissioner Lincoln A. Parkhurst.
Second Vice-President.—Commissioner Myra L. Ingalsbe.
Recording Secretary.—Commissioner Cora A. Davis.
Corresponding Secretary.—Commissioner D. D. T. Marshall.
Treasurer.—Commissioner C. Edward Jones.
Transportation Agent.—Dr. Henry R. Sanford, Penn Yan.

Report of committee on time and place was received, and, upon motion, the recommendation of the committee, naming Binghamton as the place for holding the next annual meeting of the association, was unanimously adopted.

The time of next meeting will probably be October, 1898.

Adjourned until 2 p. m.

THURSDAY AFTERNOON

After the opening exercises, President Howell read the following telegram from Miss Gratia L. Rice, who was unable to be present:

"Will not be present, therefore send the drift of my paper, which is based upon words from class teachers. The teachers think the commissioners might give direct help by creating more enthusiasm among patrons; by instituting encouragement for teachers from parents and by prompting appreciation from principals; also by their usual attitude of general interest, to be made manifest by an occasional request for class work, for exhibit and by encouraging the children in taking an active part in producing work for local fairs, etc.; above all to make plain to the *patres familias* the practical value of the subject of drawing."

Commissioner Cooley.—There is one point which Miss Rice makes in her telegram which may be of interest to us all—the relation between the home and the school. In one of our cities meetings are held, to which parents are invited to meet the teachers. If parents have any grievances, they can state them. In this way misunderstandings between parents and teachers are adjusted.

I think we, as commissioners, should aim to bring more harmonious relationship and better understanding between the home and the school. We should all work together. All forces should be brought in harmony along the same line, and not one working antagonistic to the other.

READING IN THE PUBLIC SCHOOLS

COMMISSIONER MARTHA VAN RENSSELAER

Reading receives the most indifferent teaching of any branch in the public schools. It is the most important branch, because it is the basis of all school work, and upon intelligent interpretation depends excellence in all other lines of work and ease in acquiring the full meaning of the text. It is the open door to literature and reveals, to a correct interpreter, the best thoughts of the best writers. Enjoyment of good literature is enhanced by faithful and correct methods in reading, thereby securing a means of improvement which is of life-long benefit.

Reading is a most difficult subject to teach, and it is impossible for a visitor in a school to comprehend the difficulties in this line. We expect, nevertheless, when we consider that twice a day the children in the lower grades are called upon to recite, unusual results. The mere mechanical work done in school, which you and I have listened to, perhaps, is doing a vast amount of harm. Things sometimes appeal to the senses without being present in the mind, and the same mechanical calling of words, as is often heard in reading-classes, is exceedingly detrimental. Have you had any experience in trying to find out whether a child has any idea of the thought in a lesson? If you had you were astounded at the lack of thought.

When a child cannot intelligently read, it is very difficult to secure good results in the other branches. We often hear teachers say that they have drilled and drilled on that principle, but cannot make that child understand. I do not believe that the trouble is with the principle. I believe that the child cannot read the example and, therefore, cannot do the work. Much harm is being done by our teachers allowing classes to use a history for a reading-book. Do you not know that people can sing "America," "Star Spangled Banner" and other poems without having an idea of the thought of these poems? I am always delighted when anything is said to us about becoming familiar with these poems, and yet it seems to me that great familiarity with them makes it almost impossible for us to observe them.

One reason why the teachers do not pass better examinations is because they do not know how to read. This is a broad statement, but I believe it to be true.

Correct reading, as a means of expression, is of value in making good conversationalists and good speakers. A class in reading affords an opportunity for physical culture and many graces which other branches do not suggest.

Charles Lamb said, "How we do all like to be liked!"—and then when being liked means a position and a livelihood, it is not surprising that we sometimes find the energies that should be directed to education in the school soon spent in courting favor. Over 15,000 teachers, most of them in rural schools with no true standard of judgment for their work—think of it! and we are forced to realize the need of able guidance and supervision. Therefore the antagonizing conditions to be harmonized by the commissioner in the school room are these—the great need, and the little time.

The state Superintendent's report shows that a large majority of the commissioners are experienced teachers, many of them college or normal graduates. And those who are neither have carefully equipped themselves by professional study, till so far as educational qualifications are concerned, they are a body competent for the work they have to perform; but in the matter of supervision there are other considerations that should not be neglected. Some days we have felt that we could grasp the conditions of a school and master them, others that the schools were so many dramas, try as we would, we had no part. This is what I have had to learn, and I presume you have had the same experience, that supervision requires more vitality than teaching, that while a fatigued teacher may do something, a fatigued commissioner is of no help to the school, and we must go to our work in the best physical condition if we mean to cope with the problems of the schools and give inspiration or direction. From the moment a commissioner enters a school-room, he must be recognized as master. Not an autocrat ruling by virtue of some paltry power, but one who from his wider study and experience is fitted to govern, and who is himself mastered only by his desire to give his best thought and work for this school. Lack of time requires that the commissioner shall be alert to see the greatest demands for his help. He cannot elaborate or work out details, but he must grasp the situation, see what needs encouragement, what needs correction, what introduced and what rejected. Every commissioner in the school-room should aim to be what Charles Dana Gibson is in the field of art, working in bold, vigorous strokes, and often accomplishing results with lines omitted, and only the blank sheet to suggest his purpose. True, there are a few details that must receive attention. Personal appearance of the teacher is a matter that influences directly the broader education of the child; and neatness and propriety should receive the keenest observation. The register must be carefully kept and a program should be on the wall, time of classes marked, and rigidly followed. I want to emphasize this point because it is my experience that teachers, while they may have a program, fail to follow it accurately.

How many times have we felt that our visit to a school was useless because the teacher was embarrassed, the students were therefore unnatural and we finally went away wondering what sort of a school it really was under normal conditions. Then the first thing for a commissioner to do upon entering the room is to put the teacher at ease, and this is another duty that requires tact. His visits are infrequent and short, and the question is how to accomplish this in the briefest possible space of time. Sometimes a single remark will do this; it may be about some improvement she has wrought in the room, some exhibit work on the walls, or something of only personal interest to her; what the remark is, matters little, but what it does, matters much. Whether it be the subject matter, method, discipline, or scheme that is at fault, the fault must be detected and corrected. Model lessons are frequently of greatest value in illustrating a point. These may easily be given even in discipline, and so given that neither teacher nor students realize that it is done in a spirit of criticism.

Many fail, too, from a lack of preparation, but here it is not the commissioner's forte to instruct. Time will not permit, but he should be able to tell the teacher what will assist her, and where she can find it. She fails often to appreciate the resources of her environment. I have had a teacher bewail the fact that she did not have a set of sand-trays, but around the school-house were hills and valleys, a typical watershed, and within a few rods a stream with capes, islands, peninsulas, and other land and water forms, but she had not seen them. If we can lead our teachers to appreciate what a very small part of the child's education comes from the school-room and that it is not for examinations so much as for life that they are making preparation, and persuade them to take advantage of the opportunities close at hand, we have done our schools a lasting benefit.

At the beginning of each school year the commissioner should have a definite plan of work. He knows what his schools most need, and through institutes, letters and personal visits he can emphasize these needs. Be it reading, penmanship, or whatever it may be, we get the best results when we give a teacher to understand that for that particular year we expect special excellence in some branch of work. She will in consequence do professional reading, and instead of other subjects being slighted, a deeper interest will be aroused in all she does, and this brings me to what I consider the most important work for the commissioner. I have frequently asked, "Why are you giving that particular lesson" in drawing, arithmetic, or some other subject, and received the answer, "It is what we were taught at the institute," or "That is what comes next in the book."

Our teachers will never succeed, never do the best they can till they appreciate the absolute necessity for a definite plan of work, not for a day, nor for a week, but for a whole year. They frit away time on this or that, and fail to grasp a scheme of work —they are flitting from flower to flower, but laying up no stores for the winter. If we have one supreme duty in the school-room, it is to lead the teacher to see the end from the beginning. In graded schools she has some helps, but in the ungraded school with as many classes as students this is not so easy a matter, and here the teacher should have assistance, she should be made to realize that each lesson is not a thing by itself, not a stone added to a pile of stones, but a part of the year's work, a carefully fitted block for the structure she proposes to erect—and no more in lessons than in discipline. What will I endure this month, what will I check next? What lesson in character shall I emphasize, how far along the road to self-government may I have the school in eight months? This is one of the first essentials of success, and the teacher should be made to realize it, and urged for her welfare not to let the first two weeks of her school go by without having made plans for the whole year's work.

Criticism should be given where it is needed. I have no sympathy with that supervision that looks only to the commendable. By all means give a teacher credit for the good work she is doing, but do not hesitate to point out her errors, even to the point of telling her, if it be true, that she is a complete failure. If she has the character necessary for the school-room, she will improve; if she is of the kind that becomes discouraged from knowing the truth, she has no place in a school-room, and the sooner she knows it, the better both for her welfare and for that of the scholars.

Again, let us sympathize with the teacher; let us win her confidence that we may help her the more. There is not in all this land a more earnest, conscientious, faithful body of workers than the teachers in our schools. Then give to them the help of your broader education and withhold not the help of the heart that will often lift the burden of discouragement and give them a happy consciousness of their power that will make them feel that they are factors in the uplifting of mankind.

Commissioner Fordham.—Much need be said concerning the ventilation of the school room. I have been in school rooms and found the children inattentive and listless simply because of bad r.

In the absence of Superintendent Diamond, Superintendent Kneil, of Saratoga, read the following paper. Before reading Superintendent Kneil said: "I wish to present to you a study in social economics, and renew to the convention of commissioners and school superintendents the invitation we extended yesterday on behalf of the business men of the village of Saratoga Springs, to a banquet to be served at the Worden, at the conclusion of the address by Minister Ross, of Toronto. We want to see every school commissioner and village superintendent and every member of the association present at the banquet. It is unnecessary to say, we assure you a hearty welcome."

A STUDY IN SCHOOL ECONOMICS

SUPERINTENDENT F. J. DIAMOND

The two uses of the word *economy* are familiar to everyone, the later and more common use which has reference to those practices which are associated with frugality and saving; and the earlier, but now more technical meaning, which refers to the system of internal adjustment and operation of organisms—plant or animal—and also to the analogous organisms which we find among human institutions, government, the church, the home, etc., in all of which we look for a more or less perfect adjustment of parts, one to another in ways resembling in their action the systematic arrangement which we find in nature. Of the various creations of man's constructive genius the most wonderful and perfect in all its parts is, of course, the system of school economy as we find it in America, and especially in the Empire state.

By that happy intuitive perception of the true inwardness of things, of which the student of language finds so many instances in the usage of those who have given language its form, it was long since perceived that only when the parts of the organism or the institution were in right adjustment and properly functioning, would there be found the highest efficiency and the minimum of loss; and economy thus came to mean either a gain in efficiency or the prevention of loss, or both.

From these preliminary remarks we easily deduce the proposition that, the most perfect scheme of school economy is the one which yields the largest results in school economies; and while this is not a theme that can lead up to any startling discoveries, or that is likely to call forth strikingly new or original ideas, there lies within it the possibility of bringing a group of related facts into such a juxtaposition as may give a new significance to the whole subject.

That existing conditions are not altogether satisfactory is evidenced by the restless activity which prevails in educational circles, and nowhere more manifest than among the leaders of educational thought. To the demand for economy must be attributed all the agitation in favor of correlation and concentration, and the genesis of the three famous committees, the Committee of Ten, the Committee of Fifteen, and the Committee of Twelve; and as their recommendations gain currency, we may hope to see improvement in the economic conditions prevailing in the schools, in two directions: A negative gain through the saving in time to the pupil, in money, to the taxpayer, in nervous force to the teacher, in friction to departments of administration; and a positive and permanent gain in the quantity and quality of the results achieved.

It is a maxim in mechanics that the earlier forms of any machine are more cumbersome and complicated than those appearing later; and by analogy we might be led to expect a like transformation in the body politic. The contrary is usually the case. And at the close of the century we find the educational system of the state suggesting in its operation nothing so much as a North river ferry boat, an administrative double-header, with a pilot at each end.. That the pilots are not in full accord would appear from the fact that each educational department is conducting a separate system of secondary institutions, having nearly parallel courses, neither one giving more than partial credit for work done in the other. Add to this condition the further fact that the higher institutions, the colleges and universities, are practically independent of all state control, and it need cause no surprise that our state educational craft is somewhat erratic in its movements.

We learn from the latest handbook compiled by the Department of public instruction that the normal schools of the state were maintained during the decade ending with 1895, at an expense aggregating three and one-half millions of dollars, and that during this period they graduated about seven thousand students, each of whom was certified as duly qualified and licensed to teach in the common schools of the state—a form of certificate which is highly gratifying to the holder thereof until he, or she, has occasion to seek a position in one of the larger cities of the state, New York, Brooklyn, Albany, or Buffalo, when it is learned that the common school system of the state has not yet extended to those mediaeval towns—towns whose authorities evidently look upon the state Superintendent as an enlarged copy of the rural school commissioner, and upon his office as being mainly concerned with the rural schools.

Of the seven thousand graduates referred to above as having been turned out during the preceding ten years, and the several thousand who had been graduated previously, there were not quite four thousand employed in the schools of the state during the year 1895-96; certainly a small proportion of the entire number. Assuming that matrimony and more lucrative employment in other states are in the main responsible for this deficiency, there would seem to be no remedy for the difficulty short of the imposition of an export tax on all normal graduates going out of the state, and the requirement of a certain degree of plainness in all young lady applicants for admission to the normal schools. There is, however, one additional factor instrumental in bringing about the early disappearance of a large number of normal graduates from the teaching force of the state, and that is the questionable practice of granting unconditional life certificates to every graduate of these schools—a practice which lessens the value of a normal diploma and gives a show of reason to the cities refusing to recognize them, and warrants the supposition that there are many holders of such diplomas who quickly find out their own unfitness for teaching and soon drop out of sight. A first-grade license, under the uniform examinations, should easily take precedence over an untested normal diploma.

While on the subject of licenses, I am prompted to say that several instances have come under my personal observation in which there has been real hardship and worry and nervous strain growing out of the requirement that the holder of a second-grade certificate shall come up for reëxamination in the whole list of subjects at every renewal, and this regardless of the grade of work in which she is engaged or the character of her experience. Though she be a tower of strength in our primary department, she must continue at stated intervals to post up in civil government and history and drawing, if she would continue to teach baby songs to the little ones.

Of the various duties entrusted to the educational officers of the state, there is probably none more important than that of supervision. This fact is recognized by the state to the extent of about $200,000 annually, which sum is contributed towards the salaries of commissioners and superintendents, and which is largely increased by the several communities receiving the services of these officers. About one-third of the teachers of the state are in the district schools, and the only supervision which they enjoy is that which the hundred odd school commissioners of the state are able to bestow. What this supervision amounts to is quite within the comprehension of a layman after he has learned that there is an average of about one hundred teachers to each commissioner, and that they are spread over an average extent of territory of four hundred square miles.

In view of the generous remuneration received for this service, it may be aptly described as the combination of a long-distance supervision and a narrow-gauge salary.

That the educational system of our state is open to improvement is sufficiently indicated by the yearly attempts made in that direction through the legislature. Such faults as exist have not been created or fostered by any one individual or set of men; they are a growth by accretion rather than by evolution. Ultra-conservatism and the unwise zeal of the reformer have both contributed to bring about existing conditions. Apparent discords among the educational forces of the state are due to statutory provisions, rather than to the perversity of individuals; and with all its faults the school system of the Empire state is easily first among the states, and we may safely rely upon the professional spirit of its teachers and the public spirit of its citizens to maintain its present rank in the years to come.

TONAWANDA, N. Y., *November* 1, 1897.

President Howell introduced James W. Pierce, superintendent of Westchester temporary home, who spoke of the work the pupils are doing in the school of which he is superintendent, and cordially invited the members of the association to ask any question they wished concerning the truant school, and to be free to inspect the work which was on exhibit.

THURSDAY EVENING

Meeting called to order by the president at 8.15.

On motion of Commissioner Baldwin, a committee was appointed to draft suitable resolutions in regard to the work of Dr. Sheldon.

The following committee was appointed: Sherman Williams, Charles E. Gorton and James S. Cooley.

Commissioner Cooley.—I think the association should take some special action relative to our late president, Mr. Elwood. I move that a special committee be appointed to prepare resolutions to the memory of our late president, Mr. Elwood, and that the following be appointed: Commissioner Cosad, of Wayne county; Commissioner Cora Davis, of Oneida, and Mr. Wiswell. of the Department.

Carried.

President Howell, introduced Hon. George W. Ross, Minister of Education, Toronto, Canada, who spoke as follows:

"Mr. President, Ladies and Gentlemen:— I am here to-night feeling that I am in no way qualified to address such a meeting of experienced educators. We do in Toronto a great deal of progressive work, encouraged by the pioneers of education on this side of the line. In fact, we owe to this side the one school system of my province. We owe to you the free text-book system, and, perhaps, we are quite as familiar with the works of the great educators as you may be in some parts of the United States. We know Horace Mann, Dr. Sheldon, Dr. Harris, Judge Draper and more than a score of others that I need not mention. These names are quite as familiar in our cities as they are in your cities; and we thank you for all the benefits they conferred upon humanity.

"About the school system of Ontario we find some things in common. I do not know that we are quite as democratic as you are. I do know that we are more arbitrary than you are. I do not know that we are more prompt in receiving reforms than you are. I shall not make comparisons; that would be invidious."

The speaker then gave a detailed explanation of the school system in Ontario, from the kindergarten to the university. He spoke of the powers and duties of the Minister of Education, as to his appointment, manner of introducing educational bills in Parliament, and his power as to the equipment of the public and high schools. He explained concerning the powers and duties of inspectors of schools in his province.

"If we do not train our boys and girls to pursue knowledge and give them a love for knowledge in the public schools," the speaker said, "then the real object of the state in promoting free education is, to a great extent, lost."

"If the teacher who teaches reading does not inspire a pupil with a love for good and a taste for high-class literature, then the work of education is in vain. We have so inoculated our young people in our high and public schools with a taste for the literature of the great masters, the great poets and historians—the literature of your country and our own—that fiction in the ordinary sense of the term is not sought as it was ten or fifteen years ago. If we are to have great men, stalwart, rugged, vigorous men and women to bear the burdens of this state and to keep a clear head, you must indoctrinate them with the knowledge of the best literature of this and past generations."

"Under a democratic system, such as yours or ours, the great danger is that demagogism will have sway, or that some great leader will stampede the ballot-box.

"What is to be the steadying force in the state? I answer, educating our young people for citizenship. The value of education is felt in the solidity of the state, in the continuity of legislation, in the steadfastness of civil government."

"The Duke of Devonshire, in a recent address said that the public schools are the first line in the defences of the nation. They lie at the foundation of all other systems of education."

"Character building is the great work of the teacher. If pupils are not trained to be honest, persevering, energetic and progressive, to be well balanced in their character, all their knowledge is in vain. This country is looking for strong men, for leaders, for steadfast men, for men of character in every position in life. We look to our public schools to lay the foundation of that character, the high schools to continue the structure and the universities to fit for other professions in life."

"The anchor of our hope for the future of our country is the young people, and we forge the anchors of our hope in the most interesting workshops that any people can have — the public schools under skilled leaders."

Commissioner Sheffield.—I believe I voice the sentiment of this association that we have all been instructed and helped in our work by listening to the admirable address of the Minister of Education from Ontario. We want to express in some degree our gratitude for the grand and noble thoughts expressed to us, and I would move you that the association tender him a vote of thanks.

The motion was carried by a rising vote.

After the address, upon invitation of Superintendent Kneil, on behalf of the board of education and citizens of Saratoga, the members of the association convened at the Worden, where a sumptuous repast was in waiting.

The reception was a pleasant one, and fully demonstrated the hospitality and generous liberality of the citizens of Saratoga.

FRIDAY MORNING, NOVEMBER 5, 1897

PRACTICAL SUGGESTIONS ON HOW TO MAKE COMMISSIONERS' SUPERVISION MORE EFFECTIVE

COMMISSIONER OSCAR GRANGER

The supervision in which the commissioner is concerned relates mainly to conditions found in rural districts and the smaller village schools. That supervision is accomplishing the most possible, under the influence of which every teacher is obtaining the best results that individual ability and tact will effect, and which promotes the interests of the pupils in as high a degree as the instructor's capacity will permit, although the end gained may not, in all cases, reach the maximum standard of excellence. The influence of a supervisory officer is needed more in some schools than in others. So far as possible, weak teachers are to be strengthened, and all should be encouraged. No supervision will make any teacher as good as any other teacher, nor can the commissioner supply a teacher's deficiencies by conferring the advantages of a complete normal school course, or that of the training class. His work should assume that the teacher has the necessary preparation and should be advisory and directory. It should direct the ability of the teacher into the channels of the greatest usefulness, and by constant watchfulness keep it there. The greatest possibilities of the teacher are to be developed, and willing co-operation is needed to effect the most satisfactory results, besides a better relation on the part of the teacher with the commissioner is thereby secured. Perfunctory supervision may cause perfunctory teaching, either or both of which is destructive of educational vitality.

The graded course of study and examinations constitute a powerful influence and facilitate greatly the work involved in the commissioner's supervision. Occasional visits are useful so far as they go, but are unsatisfactory, for the reason that the information they afford is insufficient, and possesses little knowledge of detail required for intelligent supervision. The schools should be within the range of the personal influence of the supervisory officer frequently, and this influence should be so directed as to be felt by the greatest number. In the smaller areas the advantages to be obtained by personal observation are greater than in those districts covering wide extent of territory. In the latter, business matters are correspondingly increased, consume much time, and by necessity take precedence of other matters. In such districts especially, the question of obtaining by correspondence, information more frequently, relative to affairs of the school-room suggests itself. The best way of obtaining such information is by means of a blank something like the following:

Number	*Town of*.......... *School Dist. No*... *Teacher*.......... *Date*......... 189.. NAMES OF PUPILS REGISTERED (*Add names of all others of school age residing in the district*)	Age	ATTENDANCE FOR WEEK ENDING ...., 189 (Copy of register)					ARITHMETIC				GEOGRAPHY					GRAMMAR										SPELLING					READING										PENMANSHIP				PHYSIOLOGY				DRAWING						
			M	T	W	T	F	Grade	No. recitations daily	Length of recitation	Topic	Grade	No. recitations daily	Length of recitation	Oral lessons	Map or topic	Grade	No. recitations daily	Length of recitation	Language lessons	Definitions	Parts of speech	Parsing	Oral analysis	Diagram	Composition	Grade	No. recitations daily	No. of words daily	Oral	Written	Grade	No. recitations daily	Length of recitation	Phonics	First	Second	Third	Fourth	Fifth	American history	No. of copy book	Daily practice	Vertical	Slanting	No. recitations daily	Length of recitation	Oral	Topic	Daily practice	Definitions	Color	Pictorial	Geometric	Decorative	Botanical
										m				m					m															m									m				m			m						
1																																																								
2																																																								
3																																																								
4																																																								
5																																																								
6																																																								
7																																																								
8																																																								
9																																																								
10																																																								
11																																																								
12																																																								
13																																																								
14																																																								
15																																																								
16																																																								
17																																																								
18																																																								
19																																																								
20																																																								

Advantages of Blank

1. It will supplement the personal visits of the commissioner and afford information concerning the schools when such visits are impracticable.

2. It gives information of the order in which the divisions of each subject are pursued by comparing the different reports from the same school.

3. It affords data to be furnished to the attendance officer when of a character requiring his services, and stimulates activity.

4. It will bear information as to the manner in which the register is kept.

5. Any work will be better executed when the same is to be submitted to the inspection of a supervisory officer. This being the case, teachers become expectant, more careful, more thoughtful, and exert better effort, which will consequently result in increased benefit to their schools.

6. The information obtained will show where there is most urgent need of the personal visit of the commissioner.

7. A record of individual work of each pupil is obtained instead of that information gained in a general way by other means.

8. It will reveal defects in school organization and often suggests the remedy.

9. It will furnish opportunity for the teacher to present difficulties and seek the advice of the commissioner on matters that might never in any other manner come to his notice.

10. The material submitted by the teacher may, in some instances, be compared with the work of the school-room when making a personal visit.

11. A closer relation is established between the schools and the commissioner, which intervening distance prevents by personal observation.

12. It brings to the teacher's attention the requirements and suggestions of the manual.

13. Teachers will keep their schools more directly in line with the graded course of study.

14. It suggests the assistance and direction needed by the teacher.

15. Omission of the instruction in any subject will be apparent.

16. It will show, by the comparison of different reports, the progress pupils are making.

Mr. Wright of the Department.—I am satisfied that this blank would be a very effective means of keeping the attendance up. It seems to me that if the inspector or commissioner could receive reports, as indicated, on these blanks, it would place in his hands the statistics that would make it possible for them to indicate what action to take by the local authorities.

Conductor Sanford.—The organization Mr. Granger has effected in his county, of trustees and attendance officers, is having a great influence in carrying on the work of the schools.

Commissioner Baldwin.—I would like to ask the commissioner if his board of supervisors furnish him with these blanks and pay the postage, or do the teachers?

Commissioner Granger.—We have not asked the board of supervisors to meet the expense. They allow me $400 for expenses, and by being reasonably economical, it is met with that amount.

Superintendent Kneil.—If I understood him, through this system he is $175 in the hole.

State Superintendent Skinner.—We have an object lesson here. If Commissioner Granger can do that with two hundred districts, it seems to me that in the commissioner districts with half that number of schools, the work ought to be pretty well systematized if the commissioners have the courage with the power.

Commissioner Granger.—The blanks will not do what personal inspection will do. It is not the primary work of a supervisory officer to teach methods.

Commissioner Whitney.—What do you consider the primary work of school commissioners?

Commissioner Granger.—I believe the first work that should take our attention is business matters. In large districts much time is necessary for this work. We should visit the schools as often as practicable.

HOW THE COMMISSIONERS MAY BE MORE HELPFUL TO THE DEPARTMENT

HOWARD J. ROGERS, A. B., *Second Deputy Superintendent*

Commissioners of the state of New York; Ladies and Gentlemen.—When the request of your respected President to speak on the topic, "How commissioners may be helpful to the state Department" was first received, it was accepted with a number of misgivings. The title seemed attractive and many lines of development were apparent, but I thought I could see also the possibility of this period proving to be, instead of a peaceful symposium, something of the nature of an old-fashioned experience meeting where there was considerable speaking out in meeting. In fact there was uncertainty as to whether I had had put into my hands for use a golf stick or a boomerang; or whether I was expected to do some preliminary sparring in order that some muscular commissioner might be given an opportunity to effectually cross-counter.

But a fair interpretation of the request would seem to be that your president's inner consciousness confesses the fact that there are many short-comings on the part of commissioners towards the Department; that his experience emphasizes the counter-fact that there are many things that can be remedied in the treatment of the commissioners by the Department; and that his judgment prompted him to arrange this period of this meeting so that the facts might be set forth freely face to face and a better understanding obtained.

Acting on this view it would seem to be only courtesy to him that the Department's case be set forth in the plainest English that I can command; and let me say that we thank you for this invitation for we should have hesitated otherwise to have obtruded into the meetings of the commissioner's association anything which might seem to savor of criticism.

I am reminded by our position of a story that G. Stanley Hall tells. The scene is laid in the stirring old days of rural New England when the courtships were attended with a rugged romance that we do not find in these latter days; when John after finishing the chores on a Sunday evening drove five or ten miles across country to see the object of his affections, and after being cordially greeted by the whole family and talking crops and prices and neighborhood gossip, would finally, as one after another slipped from the room on various pretexts, be left alone with Susan. And in this particular instance it happened that though there were plenty of chairs in the room only one was occupied; and though there were two persons in the room no one was standing. And after this statu quo had been preserved an indefinite length of time a wave of compassion swept over Susan's heart and she said, "John, I'm real heavy; aint you tired holding me so long?" But John toed the mark like a major and says he, "No, Susan, I ain't tired a mite. My knees was kind of tired about an hour ago but I'm real numb now and I don't mind it." So there have been times when the Department has been a little tired, but we have grown somewhat numb now and are glad of a chance to change knees anyhow.

It was Charles Lamb who divided all mankind into two classes: those who borrow money and those who lend it. On the same general lines I would divide commissioners into two classes: those who know their business and those who have yet to learn it. Of course I am aware that there are none before me this morning but those who belong in the first class; for that reason

I can speak with less embarrassment and with no chance of giving offence.

You can first be helpful to the state Department by being loyal to the Department. By this is meant not alone personal loyalty to the state Superintendent as your chief executive. We expect that; nor necessarily political loyalty, though we would appreciate that; but first, essentially first, loyalty to the educational policy of the Department. You are state officers, paid by the state and responsible to the state Superintendent of public instruction for the performance of your duties. You are parts of one great system which controls and shapes the education of the children of our state. If you are in harmony with that system and work in accord with it, your interests and your success, and our interests and our success are proportionately advanced and heightened. If, on the contrary, you are a discordant element, and execute the policy of the Department in a half-hearted or captious manner, you not only bring discredit on yourself, but weaken the power of the Department and lower it in the estimation of the people. Now, do not misunderstand me on this point. We would not for a moment interfere with the right of any commissioner to think for himself on any educational topic; we would not presume to question the correctness of his judgment on any matter connected with his schools; but we do insist that when a policy or plan of action has been decided on either by legislative statute or Department regulation that it is the duty of every commissioner to sink his individual preferences and act in accordance with his instructions from the central authority. In no other way can the school interests of our state be properly administered and developed. If a law or regulation is enforced in Suffolk county, and evaded in Sullivan county, the effect is to weaken its administration in every other part of the state. No good soldier receives orders with any other intent than to obey them. One of the most efficient commissioners to-day in enforcing the compulsory education law is one who questions most seriously the extent to which the state can trench upon private rights. We honor him! The Department does not seek to restrain individuality; it does insist upon a concerted and loyal enforcement of laws and regulations.

Commissioners may be helpful to the Department by being self-reliant. By this I mean that they should get such a grip upon the provisions of the consolidated school law and upon the principles of school management that they feel absolutely competent to entertain and decide any question of school policy which may come before them. Don't attempt to mortgage the opinion of the Department on questions which have been decided over and over again from the term of Rice to the term of

Skinner, and over which you have original jurisdiction. What would you think of that lawyer who should attempt to extract from a judge before whom he was to try a case some intimation as to the judge's opinion of the merits of the case. Hardly a week passes that we do not receive one or two communications running something like this:

"Dear Sir.—There is in such a place in my commissioner district a very bad condition of affairs. I feel it to be necessary and expedient in view thereof to undertake such and such a plan. If I do this will the Department stand by me?"

The Department will stand by any commissioner who performs an act dictated by common sense, common law or common justice. We ask only that he exercise a wise discretion and observe the forms of law. If you honestly think a schoolhouse should be condemned, condemn it. If you think the school interests of a community would be promoted by dissolving a district, dissolve it. Don't ask us about it. It is not any of our business till you get get through with it and some one brings an appeal. Then if your action is based upon the motives I have just mentioned, you need have no fear of lack of support from the Department. And then, too, I beg of you don't get into a state of trepidation because your action may possibly be reversed by the state Superintendent. It won't hurt you if it is. "It's better to have loved and lost than never to have loved at all." We don't think any the less of you because we may be obliged to differ from you in a legal ruling. It's a mighty poor lawyer that never lost a case. The chances are that he never had but a few.

Commissioners may be helpful by studying understandingly the rules and regulations issued by the Department. This statement may seem to be in the nature of an indirect accusation, but I assure you that it is based upon the most obtrusive facts. It's the little trivial details of life which disturb the equilibrium of things. A six-penny nail in the cog-wheel of a great engine may jolt the machinery of a mill and destroy many dollars' worth of woven cloth. Burnt chops and leaden biscuits rank very high as promoters of divorce suits. A cold and muddy cup of coffee may promote an indigestion causative of more mischief than the diplomacy of a nation's cabinet can undo. So inattention to instructions issued, or carelessness in interpreting them may cause annoyance and vexation between commissioners and the Department, and is oftentimes the cause of an injustice to teachers or trustees. Now, do not think that I am exaggerating in this statement or conjuring up an imaginative train of evils. I can give you reams of documentary evidence in support of it from the letter files of the Department. It was only a few days ago that we received from a most excellent commissioner, to whom we had sent a circular announcement that hereafter only five uniform examinations would be held yearly, a letter asking if we really meant it. I have no doubt that this commissioner knows how regulations emanate from the Department; that they are first drafted by the head of the sub-departments; then submitted to the Superintendent for approval; perhaps considered in a full council meeting; then sent to the printer, put in cold type, and lastly mailed broadcast over the state. And yet, he wonders if we mean it. We do!

We also receive many letters asking for interpretations of regulations which have been more fully and carefully discussed in circulars that we could possibly do by letter; and if we answered the letters we would simply be obliged to reiterate the statements in the circulars. Many letters indicate that the commissioner has lost the circular mailed him, instead of preserving carefully a file of every printed statement sent him.

Here are one or two other cases in point. Frequent requests are received for questions for vocal music examinations. No such examinations have ever been provided, and the regulations for the past two years have stated that such certificates are issued only on application and proof of efficiency. Still another late case in evidence. The examination department in August, 1897, issued regulations altering the dates of examinations for the current school year. A number of commissioners issued institute programs this autumn giving the examination dates as they were last year. This come pretty near being personal, but truth is mighty and will prevail. This very circumstance means about four hundred letters for us to answer as to which date is the correct one. A useless letter is an unnecessary expense to the state. It means the following routine: Opening on receipt, and I presume I feel as deeply on this point as anyone, as this work is a part of my duties, enough of a perusal to catch the import of the letter and a reference to the proper department; a careful reading by the head of that department; dictation of a reply to a stenographer, the stenographer's time in preparing the letter; reading for correction; submission to the superintendent or his deputies for approval and signature, copying in the letter press, mailing, posting and finally indexing and filing. Now multiply this letter by thirty or forty and you have nearly the time of one clerk spent in useless labor besides the cost of postage and stationery. Closely allied to this is another way in which commissioners may be of help, viz., prompt attention to personal correspondence. Spare us from the class of communications beginning, "I have written my commissioner on this point and have been unable to obtain a reply." And above all don't advise people to write the Department for information when in the same epistle or the same conversation you could give it to them exactly as well.

Again the Department asks your help in the prompt filling out and returning of blanks for information. You have not possibly a clear conception of the annoyance and delay caused us by three or four commissioners holding back these blanks and thus delaying the tabulation of the returns often beyond the desired time of using them. We have often been forcibly reminded that the Department was gradually making clerks of its commissioners, but the implication is unjust. I assure you that we take no delight in concocting this species of torment for you and none of us lay awake nights devising complicated statistics. But in the development of any line of policy it is absolutely necessary that we have all the data and information bearing on that subject which can be collected in the state and we have no one on whom to depend for it but our commissioners and superintendents. This source has been ample and sufficient at all times and you must pardon us if we seem to draw upon it too often and too freely. I confess I have often sympathized with you in this respect, especially in the number of blanks required in the routine of certain departments, but we are cutting them down as rapidly as possible. You must recall that certain of our departments are in a state of rapid evolution and the changing conditions which are continually confronting us call for a corresponding change of methods. As soon as we can approximate a perfect system the blanks will be fewer and more stable.

Commissioners may help the department by arranging to devote to the duties of their office their undivided attention. I am aware that this is a delicate subject and I shall not enlarge on it. It is not necessary to do so. The mention of the subject carries with it the arguments pro and con. It is a matter for you to square with your oath of office. We realize and have said many times that you are an underpaid body of men; your services, your standing and the nature of your work call for a salary so high that you can afford with justice to your families to devote your whole time to school duties. The position of the Department on this matter is well known to you. It stands where it stood in 1896 and will co-operate with you on that basis whenever you are ready to meet it. At present you seem to be under the same dead weight of public apathy that holds our teachers' wages to the lowest average consistent with decency. It is to the eternal discredit of our race and to our boasted intelligence that that profession which forms and develops the human intellect should be the last for which a special training has been demanded, and an adequate compensation paid. The only reason possible for it is, that that which touches the pocket of the animal, man, is more quickly felt than that which touches his mind.

The greatest help which commissioners may afford the department is by close adherence to the duties prescribed in the consolidated school law. Section 13 of title 5 of that law is the cloud by day and the pillar of fire by night which should guide the course of every commissioner in the state. Look at its chief provisions: " Every commissioner shall have power and it shall be his duty to inquire into and fix the boundaries of districts, to visit and examine all schools, to inquire into modes of school management, courses of study, methods of instruction, text-books, discipline, etc." What a boundless field of usefulness is here opened up for the work of an earnest commissioner—a fallow field ready for the seed of suggestion and encouragement. I sometimes think that the country school-room with its ungraded intellect its bright boy far in advance of the others, its dullard, and its mischief-maker presents the most fascinating picture of school life possible. Those bare legs dangling from the whittled benches are the sturdy under-pinnings of our future merchants, lawyers, statesmen, and financiers waiting only maybe for a chance word, or an approving smile to rouse their pluck and ambition. Canvass the business street of any city for the antecedents of its successful men and you will find the course of the majority led through the one room, cross-roads, country schoolhouse. There is not a metropolis in the world that would not rot out in two generations from internal decay, were it not for the fresh life-blood poured into it from the country. Here then is a work worthy of your efforts, to preserve the individuality and virility of our common school system. The bane of our educational world for the last fifteen years has been the cloud of theories which have settled down and obscured our vision like a miasmatic mist. Less theory, fewer studies and more common sense will improve nine-tenths of our curriculums to-day. There are gratifying signs of a return to a simpler order of things in our elementary schools. Correlation, thank Heaven, is dead and buried; buried with its twin brother co-ordination in a common grave, where the sods of public objurgation will continue to correlate and co-ordinate over them till a mound as high as an obelisk marks their resting place for the avoidance of future generations.

The ideal of our common school education is to teach every child to read. To read: not to spell his way through a paragraph, but to read it. Why? Because this opens to him every branch of learning, no matter what his occupation; no matter what his opportunity of future study. If he can read, you have put into his hand a key which will unlock the temple of every science and art, where he can wander at his leisure. Commissioners, you have it in your hands not only to help the Department, but to help the development of the race, by insisting that a few studies, taught thoroughly, outrank in educational value a crowded curriculum with its smattering of methods.

"To examine the condition of schoolhouses and sites; to inspect libraries; to advise and counsel with district officers; to recommend studies and courses of instruction. To direct repairs to buildings; to abate nuisances, to condemn schoolhouses; to examine and license teachers under the regulations of the Department." I must stop a moment here, because this is a power fraught with the gravest consequences. You are the only authority that can determine the teaching ability of the 16,000 teachers employed in the commissioner districts of this state; and the only judge to decide upon their right to remain in the school-room. Teachers may pass 95 per cent. in every subject under the uniform examination system; may talk glibly of methods and management but unless they have the power to attract and draw out children, to gain their confidence and inspire their work, they have no place in a public school-room. Incompetent, careless and inefficient teachers, you will of course weed out at the earliest opportunity. Their power for damage exceeds any pestilence that ever swept the face of the earth. Prune them unmercifully as you would any noxious weed that chokes and obscures the growth of flowers. In the language of Thomas Arnold "There is no sight more pitiable than the yoking of a bright and gifted boy to the neck of an incompetent teacher." There is no duty of the commissioner which calls for more independence and at the same time is of so public a benefit. We are aware that the pressure brought upon you to favor weak teachers is sometimes very strong, but the test of your fitness to hold office is the strength with which you resist such pressure. You are not dealing with inanimate things—you are temporizing with a power which may make or mar a human mind—a human soul.

"And generally to use his utmost influence and most strenuous exertions to promote sound education, elevate the character and qualifications of teachers, improve the means of instruction and advance the interests of the schools under his supervision."

This is your magna charta, under the warrant of which you may undertake any measures likely to further the interests of your schools and train intelligently the children of your district. Under it the question to perplex the earnest commissioner is, not what I may do to help the state or to help the Department, but how much will my strength and my time permit me to do.

Gentlemen:— There are many other topics which we might discuss, such as the formation of teachers' associations, promotion of legislation, and the development of institutes, but the time will hardly admit of it. I have spoken somewhat plainly, perhaps, of some of the common things which you and I in the drudgery of this daily life have to contend with. I trust that you will receive it exactly as it is intended, and "nothing extenuate nor aught set down in malice." No one commissioner does all these things; few commissioners do many of these things; but most commissioners do some of these things. We thank you again for allowing us to call your attention to them. (Applause.)

Commissioner Royce.—We have a great many third grade teachers. They are inexperienced but they must have their experience sometime. They may fail in one school and be a success in the next one. I would gladly rule out incompetent teachers but until the conditions change it is absolutely impossible for me to do so. We have not enough teachers to fill our schools. I wish there never was such a thing as a temporary license.

Commissioner Wymbs.—A teacher with a temporary license would be preferable to an incompetent teacher.

Commissioner Royce.—My best teachers who fail on examination do not want a temporary license. It is the incompetent who wish them.

Commissioner Kniskern.—I was compelled to ask for fourteen temporary licenses in order to open my schools, and I found in almost every instance, the young and experienced teachers were the most eager to receive them.

Commissioner Webster.—It seems to me that if we can get a young man or woman who is trying to get along we would have better work. I would rather have one of that kind than a first grade, indolent, lazy teacher.

Superintendent Kneil.—I would like to ask how many school commissioners have refused to renew a first grade license, even to an incompetent teacher when the license came for renewal? It is not a lack of power on the part of commissioners, but a lack of backbone.

Commissioner Wymbs.—If we refuse to renew a certificate, we ought to have some data to substantiate our action.

Commissioner Jones.—It would be a good plan if the visiting books sent, could be made with blank spaces on which we could write our notes in regard to teachers. The circular letters sent to trustees are very helpful. Much labor is saved and business is more legally conducted. If that be true, would it not be well, whenever a change is brought about, if the Department would issue a circular letter explaining the subject in full? We could thus save them many questions.

The report of the auditing committee was adopted as read.

The committee on resolutions presented the following report:

Resolved, That the forty-third annual meeting of the New York State Association of School Commissioners and Superintendents recognizing the valued service of President Charles H. Howell and its other retiring officers, and appreciating fully the efforts made by them in bringing the work of the program to a satisfactory close; and of the local board, Messrs. A. Edson Hall and Thomas R. Kneil, in their untiring efforts to meet every want of the association, returns to them its cordial thanks.

Resolved, That the considerate action of the Saratoga Board of Education in closing its schools during the meeting, also of D. M. Kelsey in furnishing so excellent music merit our sincere gratitude.

Resolved, That as we grasp the liberal hand of hospitality extended by the business men of Saratoga in the banquet of Thursday evening, we have with that hand the assurance of reciprocal good-will, kind regards and thankful hearts.

Resolved, That we tender our thanks to Hon. George W. Ross, Minister of Education of Ontario for his presence and very able and instructive address; and that we thank Deputy Superintendent Howard J. Rogers for his helpful suggestions.

Resolved, That we appreciate the loyal support given us in the administration of our respective offices by Superintendent Charles R. Skinner, that he has inspired us to further efforts and given us high ideals of our responsibilities and duties, and that we pledge him our hearty co-operation in the broad and liberal education he is so earnestly promoting in the Empire state.

OSCAR GRANGER,
WM. P. KAUFFMAN,
C. EDWARD JONES,
Committee.

Superintendent Kneil spoke of the inspiration the association had been to the community, and thanked the members of the convention for meeting in Saratoga.

The report of the committee on transportation was accepted.

Superintendent Kneil.—It is an open question whether we have not too many educational meetings in the state of New York, and whether by concentration we may not get better results and at smaller expense than we do now.

I would move that a committee of three be appointed by the president of this association, to consult with a committee, which may be named by the Council of Superintendents and School Board Convention, looking to a joint meeting of these several associations as soon as it may be arranged for.

Conductor Sanford.—I wish to second this motion. I do believe that one body under a new name, whatever you may think best, made up of school officers of these three bodies, can be made very effective.

State Superintendent Skinner.—In our annual report two years ago, I urged the formation of an educational association, an educational union, if you please, which would be broad enough to include all superintendents, all teachers and all boards of education, of all men and women who are interested in the cause of education in New York state. Why is it not perfectly practicable to hold a state educational meeting at some point either permanent or temporary? Let the forenoon session be made so attractive as to bring together all educational forces from all directions. Let the afternoon session be devoted to exclusive consideration of interests in different departments. I believe the effect upon the education of the state, the effect upon the communities of the state would be a great inspiration and a grand educational movement which would be felt throughout all the veins of our system.

Dr. Sanford.—I do not believe in having too many associations. I therefore move an amendment that the committee be directed to correspond with all the educational bodies in this state to bring about a union such as our state Superintendent recommended.

Amendment accepted and motion carried.

RESOLUTIONS IN MEMORY OF ELLIS D. ELWOOD

Whereas, Since the last annual session of the New York State Association of School Commissioners and Superintendents, Ellis D. Elwood, who presided over this body but a few months ago, has been removed from our midst by death; therefore, be it

Resolved, That we deplore our loss and express our sense of his worth. Endowed with a remarkably strong and well balanced intellect, which was improved by a liberal education, he began his career with the prospect of unusual success. His choice led him into the educational field, in which his early experience gave promise of great influence. His stalwart form, which seemed to typify the character of his mind, could not, however, prevail against the might of sudden disease; and we are left with the memory of a noble and generous brother, while the state has suffered the loss of one who bid fair to serve it faithfully and efficiently for many years.

Resolved, That to the bereaved family we offer our warm sympathy, and point them hopefully to one who has promised to comfort the widow and the fatherless.

Resolved, That to the bright and attractive child, his father's joy and pride, too young to realize fully the loss of his natural protector and friend, we pledge an especial and perpetual interest.

Resolved, That these resolutions be spread upon the minutes of this association, and that the secretary be directed to send a copy thereof to the family of the deceased.

SAMUEL COSAD,
CORA A. DAVIS,
LEON O. WISWELL,
Committee.

Superintendent Skinner.—I think I voice the sentiment of all who knew Mr. Elwood, when I say that those who knew him best loved him best. He had a noble character and he had the characteristics which go to make up a noble manhood, faithfulness to duty and loyalty to those with whom he was associated. The best of all, he was a true husband, a loving father and a noble man. He sought his duty; he sought and found his work and then he did it. He had before him a career of great usefulness because underlying his noble character, there was an honesty of purpose and a determination to do good things which must always win in life's battle. It is very appropriate that his associates, who loved him, should sprinkle these flowers over his grave.

Secretary was instructed to send with the resolutions a copy of the remarks of state Superintendent Skinner to the bereaved family.

The death of Dr. E. A. Sheldon, principal of the Oswego normal school, was officially announced, and the following memorial and resolution was unanimously adopted as expressing the sentiments of the association:

The death of Dr. Sheldon removes from our number one of the foremost teachers of the state and nation. He has been actively identified with educational progress for almost fifty years. All that period he has been a teacher in his profession, and has guided thousands of teachers to higher intellectual attainments and more rational methods. Probably no other man of his time has exerted so much influence as he in favor of improved methods of teaching. Dr. Sheldon was a great teacher. He was equally an advanced humanitarian. The motive of his life lay in his love of children and his faith in humanity. He laid down his work only with life's close. It is permitted to but few to accomplish so much, and, dying, to leave behind so pure and noble a record. Of him it may not only be said that the world was better for his living, but also that the world will continue to gain priceless riches from his teachings.

Resolved, That the foregoing memorial be published with the proceedings of the association, and that a copy thereof be signed by the secretary and transmitted to the family of Dr. Sheldon.

SHERMAN WILLIAMS,
CHARLES E. GORTON,
JAMES S. COOLEY,
Committee.

Commissioner Howell thanked the members of the association for their courteous treatment and generous support while acting as president of the association.

President George G. Royce was then presented to the association.

Commissioners James S. Cooley, James R. Flagg and Walter S. Allerton were reappointed committee on legislation.

Committee on school supervision, appointed by the president.—Superintendent C. E. Gorton, Commissioner Oscar Granger, Commissioner Martha Van Rensselaer, Inspector W. J. Barr.

In compliance with a resolution passed by the association, the president appointed the following committee to effect, if possi, ble, a union of all the educational organizations of the state: Superintendent Thomas R. Kneil, Dr. Henry R. Sanford, Dr. William J. Milne, Commissioner Millard W. Baldwin, C. W. Bardeen.

Adjourned.

LIST OF

Persons attending the annual meeting of school commissioners and superintendents, held at Saratoga Springs, November 3, 4, 5, 1897.

DEPARTMENT OF PUBLIC INSTRUCTION

Chas. R. Skinner.......................................Albany.
Howard J. Rogers.......................................Albany.
A. S. Downing.......................................Albany.
T. E. Finegan.......................................Albany.
A. R. Macdonald.......................................Albany.
L. O. Wiswell.......................................Albany.
C. W. Halliday.......................................Albany.
A. Edson Hall.......................................Saratoga.
A. M. Wright.......................................Waterville.
W. J. Barr.......................................Batavia.
S. W. Maxson.......................................Adams Centre.
Wayland E. Stearns.......................................Rome.
Frank H. Wood.......................................Chatham.
H. O. Case.......................................Allen's Hill.
Henry R. Sanford.......................................Penn Yan.
I. H. Stout.......................................Geneva.
Welland Hendrick.......................................Cortland.
Percy I. Bugbee.......................................Oneonta.
Chas. A. Shaver.......................................Clayton.
Florence B. Himes.......................................Albany.
Anna K. Eggleston.......................................Buffalo.

REGENTS' OFFICE

Chas. F. Wheelock.......................................Albany.
Chas. N. Cobb.......................................Albany.

NORMAL PRINCIPALS

William J. Milne.......................................Albany.
Francis J. Cheney.......................................Cortland.
Frank S. Capen.......................................New Paltz.
James M. Milne.......................................Oneonta.
Edward N. Jones.......................................Plattsburgh.
Thomas B. Stowell.......................................Potsdam.

SCHOOL COMMISSIONERS

William H. Woodward.......................................Watervliet.
Oscar M. Burdick.......................................Little Genesee.

Mrs. Mary L. Kniskern.............................Deposit.
Erwin B. Whitney.........................Chenango Forks.
Martha Van Rensselaer.............................Randolph.
Edwin S. Manchester..............................Scipioville.
James R. Flagg.................................Frewsburg.
Jess S. Kellogg.................................Horseheads.
E. Everett Poole.........................Lincklaen Centre.
Seth S. Allen......................................Peru.
John D. Mickle..................................Chatham.
I. W. Van Buskirk..................................Preble.
Frank L. Ostrander..............................Masonville.
Luke D. Wymbs...................................Glenham.
Luther L. Stillman.............................Red Hook.
Fred V. Lester..................................Westport.
Willis E. Leek.................................Johnstown.
Joel A. Loveridge..................................Batavia.
D. D. T. Marshall...............................Redwood.
Samuel Whitlock..............................Springwater.
Carlos J. Coleman................................Madison.
Lincoln A. Parkhurst...........................Canastota.
Albert D. Sheffield..............................Nelliston.
Adelaide L. Harris...........................Ransomville.
Cora A. Davis.................................Whitesboro.
Selden L. Harding................................Camden.
James McCullough...............................Remsen.
John H. Stephens........................Clifton Springs.
Wm. P. Kaufman..................................Otisville.
Thomas O. Young.............................New Haven.
C. Edward Jones..................................Pulaski.
Myron N. Webster............................Elk Creek.
Millard F. Agor..........................Mahopac Falls.
William M. Peck.............................Whitestone.
James S. Cooley...............................Glen Cove.
Byron F. Clark..............................Hoosick Falls.
Edwin S. Comstock..............................Brainard.
George G. Royce..............................Gouverneur.
Walter E. Andrews.............................Pierrepont.
Edwin F. McDonald..............................Norwood.
Frank L. Smith..................................Birchton.
John T. Rice......................................Corinth.
Minor G. Foster..................................Wheeler.
Charles Marlatt.............................Troupsburgh.
Charles H. Howell..............................Riverhead.
Charles W. Fordham...........................Bay Shore.
Oscar Granger...............................Tioga Centre.
Charles Clum..................................Saugerties.

Millard W. Baldwin.............................Port Ewen.
Roxie G. Tuttle.............................Glens Falls.
F. W. Allen.............................Bolton Landing.
William H. Dennis.............................Greenwich.
Myra L. Ingalsbe.............................Hartford.
Samuel Cosad.............................Wolcott.
Rufus N. Backus.............................Palmyra.
Walter S. Allerton.............................Mount Vernon.

CITY AND VILLAGE SUPERINTENDENTS

R. H. Halsey.............................Binghamton.
Henry Delamain.............................College Point.
Thos. R. Kneil.............................Saratoga Spa.
Sherman Williams.............................Glens Falls.
L. O. Markham.............................Haverstraw.
H. H. Snell.............................Hoosick Falls.

SCHOOL BOOK AND SCHOOL FURNISHINGS REPRESENTATIVES

Frank D. Beattys.............................New York.
Edwin S. Parker.............................Albany.
J. S. Adams.............................Albany.
Randolph McNutt.............................Buffalo.
L. F. Stillman.............................Cortland.
K. N. Washburn.............................Springfield, Mass.
E. L. Cummings.............................Springfield, Mass.
R. A. Kneeland.............................Rochester.
H. W. Childs.............................Syracuse.
A. D. Perkins.............................Syracuse.
C. W. Bardeen.............................Syracuse.
Geo. Fenton.............................Broadalbin.
Geo. H. Bryant.............................Batavia.
E. A. Winchell.............................De Ruyter.
W. R. Glen.............................New York.
H. P. French.............................Albany.
W. A. Choate.............................Albany.

PRINCIPALS OF SCHOOLS

Walter S. Knowlson.............................Saratoga Springs.
Oliver B. Kipp.............................Saratoga Springs.
A. A. Lavery.............................Crown Point.
L. W. Bishop.............................Schroon Lake.
W. A. Good.............................Bath-on-Hudson.
Jas. W. Pierce, superintendent of Westchester Temporary Home.............................White Plains.

APPENDIX

EXHIBIT No. 4

New York State Teachers' Association

1. Proceedings of the Fifty-first Annual Meeting at Rochester, July 6 and 7, 1896
2. Proceedings of the Fifty second Annual Meeting at the Normal College, New York City, June 30 and July 1, 2, 3, 1897

NEW YORK STATE TEACHERS' ASSOCIATION

1. FIFTY-FIRST ANNUAL MEETING AT ROCHESTER, JULY 6 AND 7, 1896

OFFICERS, 1895-96

President

CHARLES E. WHITE, Franklin School, Syracuse.

Appointed by executive committee to fill vacancy caused by the resignation of Dr. Wm. J. Milne, President elect.

Vice-Presidents

FRED V. LESTER, Westport.
MARTHA VAN RENSSELAER, Randolph.
ANNA K. EGGLESTON, Buffalo.

Secretary

WELLAND HENDRICK, Cortland.

Assistant Secretary

SCHUYLER F. HERRON, Elizabethtown.

Treasurer

PERCY I. BUGBEE, Oneonta.

Assistant Treasurer

GUSTAVE STRAUBENMULLER, New York.

Transportation Agent

ARTHUR COOPER, New York.

Superintendent of Exhibits

WALTER S. GOODNOUGH, Brooklyn.

Executive Committee

CHAS. E. White, Chairman ex officio.
GEORGE E. HARDY, New York.
J. E. YOUNG, New Rochelle.

TERMS EXPIRE, 1896.

CHAS. F. WHEELOCK, Canajoharie.
WM. J. O'SHEA, New York.

TERMS EXPIRE, 1897.

JOHN H. HAAREN, Brooklyn.
GEO. H. WALDEN, Rochester.

and whether by concentration we may not get better results and at smaller expense than we do now.

I would move that a committee of three be appointed by the president of this association, to consult with a committee, which may be named by the Council of Superintendents and School Board Convention, looking to a joint meeting of these several associations as soon as it may be arranged for.

Conductor Sanford.—I wish to second this motion. I do believe that one body under a new name, whatever you may think best, made up of school officers of these three bodies, can be made very effective.

State Superintendent Skinner.—In our annual report two years ago, I urged the formation of an educational association, an educational union, if you please, which would be broad enough to include all superintendents, all teachers and all boards of education, of all men and women who are interested in the cause of education in New York state. Why is it not perfectly practicable to hold a state educational meeting at some point either permanent or temporary? Let the forenoon session be made so attractive as to bring together all educational forces from all directions. Let the afternoon session be devoted to exclusive consideration of interests in different departments. I believe the effect upon the education of the state, the effect upon the communities of the state would be a great inspiration and a grand educational movement which would be felt throughout all the veins of our system.

Dr. Sanford.—I do not believe in having too many associations. I therefore move an amendment that the committee be directed to correspond with all the educational bodies in this state to bring about a union such as our state Superintendent recommended.

Amendment accepted and motion carried.

RESOLUTIONS IN MEMORY OF ELLIS D. ELWOOD

Whereas, Since the last annual session of the New York State Association of School Commissioners and Superintendents, Ellis D. Elwood, who presided over this body but a few months ago, has been removed from our midst by death; therefore, be it

Resolved, That we deplore our loss and express our sense of his worth. Endowed with a remarkably strong and well balanced intellect, which was improved by a liberal education, he began his career with the prospect of unusual success. His choice led him into the educational field, in which his early experience gave promise of great influence. His stalwart form, which seemed to typify the character of his mind, could not, however, prevail against the might of sudden disease; and we are left with the memory of a noble and generous brother, while the state has suffered the loss of one who bid fair to serve it faithfully and efficiently for many years.

Resolved, That to the bereaved family we offer our warm sympathy, and point them hopefully to one who has promised to comfort the widow and the fatherless.

Resolved, That to the bright and attractive child, his father's joy and pride, too young to realize fully the loss of his natural protector and friend, we pledge an especial and perpetual interest.

Resolved, That these resolutions be spread upon the minutes of this association, and that the secretary be directed to send a copy thereof to the family of the deceased.

SAMUEL COSAD,
CORA A. DAVIS,
LEON O. WISWELL,
Committee.

Superintendent Skinner.—I think I voice the sentiment of all who knew Mr. Elwood, when I say that those who knew him best loved him best. He had a noble character and he had the characteristics which go to make up a noble manhood, faithfulness to duty and loyalty to those with whom he was associated. The best of all, he was a true husband, a loving father and a noble man. He sought his duty; he sought and found his work and then he did it. He had before him a career of great usefulness because underlying his noble character, there was an honesty of purpose and a determination to do good things which must always win in life's battle. It is very appropriate that his associates, who loved him, should sprinkle these flowers over his grave.

Secretary was instructed to send with the resolutions a copy of the remarks of state Superintendent Skinner to the bereaved family.

The death of Dr. E. A. Sheldon, principal of the Oswego normal school, was officially announced, and the following memorial and resolution was unanimously adopted as expressing the sentiments of the association:

The death of Dr. Sheldon removes from our number one of the foremost teachers of the state and nation. He has been actively identified with educational progress for almost fifty years. All that period he has been a teacher in his profession, and has guided thousands of teachers to higher intellectual attainments and more rational methods. Probably no other man of his time has exerted so much influence as he in favor of improved methods of teaching. Dr. Sheldon was a great teacher. He was

Remarks.—Professor E. C. Colby and Principal Walden.

Above motion carried unanimously.

Moved that the convention be held in Rochester in 1898. Declared out of order.

Dr. James M. Milne, chairman of the committee on resolutions, reported the following resolutions:

Whereas, The State Teachers Association of New York recognizes the continued progress of educational spirit and methods in this state, which, remarkable as it has been for the past ten years, has never been more constant and far-reaching than during the past year, and as representing the teachers of the state desires to express its approval of and sympathy with some of the most important new measures. Therefore be it.

Resolved. That the uniform examinations, which have done so much to lift the calling of a teacher to the rank and pay of a profession should be so extended that a certificate granted under the authority of the state shall be required of every teacher in the state for whom any school in the state receives a teacher's quota.

Resolved, That we approve of the added dignity given to the calling of the teachers by raising the lowest limit of age to eighteen years, and by the increased requirements for admission to training classes and normal schools.

Resolved, That we express our gratification at the results of the compulsory law, which seems now for the first time to become practical and far-reaching throughout the state.

Resolved, That we take pride in the ever increasing spirit of patriotism fostered in our schools, the patriotic ardor of our people, the love of flag and love of country, and we welcome all legislation that shall deepen and awaken the appreciation of the glory of American citizenship and the grandeur of American institutions, and we give unquestioned loyalty to the plans of peaceful arbitration, which is commanding the attention of the best minds in our country.

Resolved, That we recognize in the two bills passed by the last legislature for the consolidation of weak districts, and especially for the transportation of children, two important steps toward the adoption of the township system, the next great measure of educational and civil reform which is needed to place New York in this respect on an equality with her sister states.

Resolved, That we extend to the superintendent and teachers of Rochester thanks unmeasured for their cordial welcome and for their efforts to make our stay pleasant.

We recognize the self denial with which they have yielded to what would seem to be an equitable claim for a complete meeting here next year, and we pledge our efforts and ourselves, not only to bring the meeting of this association to Rochester in 1898, but to make it memorably successful in the annals of the association.

JAMES M. MILNE,
EDWARD W. STITT,
W. F. O'CALLAGHAN,
J. C. NORRIS,
C. D. McLEAN.

Moved to adopt as read. Carried.

Report of Percy I. Bugbee read, $1,145.45 in hands of treasurer.

Moved to adopt. Carried.

ELECTION OF OFFICERS

President

CHARLES E. WHITE, Franklin School, Syracuse.

Vice-Presidents

MILTON NOYES, Rochester.
FRED LESTER, Westport.
MARTHA VAN RENSSALAER, Randolph.
ANNA K. EGGLESTON, Buffalo.

Secretary

SCHUYLER F. HERRON, Elizabethtown.

Assistant Secretary

WM. F. O'CALLAGHAN, New York.

Treasurer

S. McKEE SMITH, Chatham.

Assistant Treasurer

GUSTAVE STRAUBENMULLER.

Transportation Agent

ARTHUR COOPER, New York.

Superintendent of Exhibits

JAMES LEE, New York.

Executive Committee

Terms to expire in 1898.

WALTER B. GUNNISON, New York.
VICE-GEO. E. HARDY.
JOHN T. NICHOLSON, New York.
VICE-I. E. YOUNG, New Rochelle.

Adjourned.

NEW YORK STATE TEACHERS' ASSOCIATION

2. Fifty second Annual Meeting at the Normal College, New York City, June 30 and July 1, 2, 3, 1897

OFFICERS, 1896-1897

President

CHARLES E. WHITE, Franklin School, Syracuse.

Vice-Presidents

MILTON NOYES, Free Academy, Rochester.
FRED V. LESTER, Westport.
MARTHA VAN RENSSELAER, Randolph.
ANNA K. EGGLESTON, 45 Wadsworth street, Buffalo.

Secretary

SCHUYLER F. HERRON, Canajoharie.

Assistant Secretary.

WILLIAM F. O'CALLAGHAN, 24 East 47th street, New York.

Treasurer

S. McKEE SMITH, Chatham.

Assistant Treasurer

ABRAM FISCHLOWITZ, Grammar School No. 40, New York.

Transportation Agent

ARTHUR COOPER, 100 Washington Square, New York.

Superintendent of Exhibits

DR. JAMES LEE, 235 East 124th street, New York.

Executive Committee

CHARLES E. WHITE, Chairman ex officio.

TERMS EXPIRE, 1897

CHARLES F. WHEELOCK, Canajoharie.
WILLIAM J. O'SHEA, 87 Pike street, New York.

TERMS EXPIRE, 1898

JOHN H. HAAREN, Brooklyn.
GEORGE H. WALDEN, Grammar School No. 10, Rochester.

TERMS EXPIRE 1899

WALTER B. GUNNISON, Erasmus Hall Academy, Brooklyn.
JOHN T. NICHOLSON, St. Nicholas avenue and 117th street, New York.

Local Organization, New York City

OFFICERS

Executive Committee

President.—Edward A. Page, Grammar School No. 77, 400 East 86th street.

Vice-Presidents

Henry P. O'Neil, Mary E. Tate, Julia Richman, Hester Roberts, Andrew J. Whiteside, John H. Grotecloss, Jr., Henry C. Litchfield, Sarah J. J. McCaffery, Teresa L. Atkinson, Hattie L. Davidson, Evander Childs, Abner B. Holley, George W. Harrison.

Secretary.—John T. Nicholson, 75 West 132d street.

Treasurer.—Gustave Straubenmuller, 146 Grand street.

Superintendent of exhibits.—Dr. James Lee.

Chairman committee on halls and spaces.—Hugh P. O'Neil.

Chairman committee on entertainment.—Walter B. Gunnison.

Vice-chairman committee on entertainment, Joseph H. Wade.

Chairman committee on reception.—John W. Davis.

Chairman committee on press.—William J. O'Shea.

Chairman committee on music.—Alfred T. Schauffler.

Chairman committee on printing.—John T. Nicholson.

Chairman committee on transportation.—Arthur Cooper.

Chairman finance committee.—Gustave Straubenmuller.

PROGRAM

WEDNESDAY EVENING, JUNE 30, 1897, 8 O'CLOCK

Music.—Waltz, "Symposia" .... Bendix.

Orchestra of male department, Grammar School No. 77, Louis Roeder, Conductor.

Music.—Selection, "Carmen" .... Kochkeller.
Orchestra.

ADDRESS OF WELCOME

SUPERINTENDENT JOHN JASPER

Mr. President and fellow teachers.—To me has been assigned the pleasant duty of extending, on behalf of the teachers of the city of New York, a welcome to the visiting teachers and their friends to the fifty-second annual session of the New York State Teachers' Association, the first session of that association to be held in our city.

Strange though it may seem, this metropolis has had within its limits that great variety of free schools that puts its school system in touch with the entire educational work of the state—beginning with the grand institution in which we are meeting to-night and its kindred institution, the boys' college, extending through a grammar and primary school with its daily attendance of more than 3,000 children, and ending with a school of one teacher with many grades—from the stately building located in the midst of the densest population to the one-story frame school-house in the suburbs, into which the children are gathered from the remote parts by means of conveyances furnished at the public expense. Hence it is that those interested in our school work here are, naturally, in sympathy with what is helpful to our fellow teachers throughout the state and feel that a victory gained here in the cause of the school or teacher is, by the example, a victory partly gained for those struggling elsewhere to accomplish the same end.

In this direction we are glad to find that the life tenure of office of the New York city teacher, as distinguished from the system of annual appointment so generally prevailing, forms the basis of an argument for permanency of position for teachers in other communities—a permanency that removes from the intelligent and faithful worker the doubt and uncertainty that so frequently arise from changes in appointing boards.

In like manner, the enactment of the law creating our "teachers' retirement fund" has been followed by similar legislation for other teachers, and it is not at all improbable that many within this hall to-night will see the teachers of the common schools of the state of New York living and laboring under the provision of a general law guaranteeing comfort and rest to those who have given up the best years of their lives to the service of these schools.

The meetings of this association are annual, so that there would be but little value to be found in the proceedings if the work or the influence of the work came to an end with the end of the session. The same spirit that will prevail here should animate each one when he returns to his community, in which on each school day he will have full opportunity to give to his pupils the benefit of the best that he may have heard or seen.

The teachers of our own city schools live, I might almost say, in a series of teachers' conventions, beginning with September and ending only with the summer vacation. Conferences with superintendents, conferences with principals, grade conferences, conferences in societies of a pedagogic nature, and, lastly, attendance on pedagogic courses in a university—all these are indications of the interest already taken by the great body of our instructors in the perfecting of their methods and in the elevation of their profession; yet I feel safe in saying that your presence here will add to that interest no matter how great it may already have become, and that their appreciation of the inspiration of your counsel and the encouragement of your example will be shown by a year of such progress as shall make this session a landmark in the history of our school work.

It is my sincere hope that in your attendance upon the meetings which form the program for this session, and in your inspection of the exhibit you will find much to repay you for the time spent, and that you will take to your homes the remembrance of friendly intercourse and of pleasant associations to be renewed at successive annual meetings and, when possible, at more frequent visits.

My duty on this occasion would not be properly done, if I failed to pay a tribute to my associate teachers to whom is due the credit for the reception of this great convention. The underlying principle of success, whether it be in a nation, in a community, or in an association, is loyalty—loyalty to the cause; and, from an experience of a quarter of a century in the Department of superintendence, I can say and do say most truly that the teachers of *the* system have never failed to do their duty freely and fully.

The substantial unanimity of the response to the call for their support in the effort to make your visit an unqualified success is most remarkable, and for this they are entitled to my personal gratitude and, in due season, will receive a proper expression of my official thanks. Co-operating with our own teachers in this reception we find hundreds of earnest representatives of our sister school system of Brooklyn—men and women with whom it is at once a pleasure and an honor to be associated. And now, on behalf of the five thousand teachers whose sentiment I voice, I bid you, Mr. President, and through you the visiting teachers and friends of the New York State Teachers' Association a most cordial welcome. May the benefit derived from the proceedings of this session be manifold, may the pleasures planned for the occasion be more than realized, and may you and your associates carry hence at the end of the session nothing but the pleasantest memories of the teachers of the Empire city.

ADDRESS OF CHARLES BULKLEY HUBBELL, PRESIDENT OF THE BOARD OF EDUCATION

Mr. President, Ladies and Gentlemen of the New York State Teachers' Association.—The man who tries to fill the place of Mayor Strong in any capacity in which that gentleman assumes to act, has a most difficult contract to perform, and I regret that some accident or circumstance beyond his control has prevented his appearing before you and extending on behalf of this city, the hearty welcome and cordial hospitality which he would have delighted to have done. On behalf of the board of education, I would most cordially welcome you to our beloved New York and assure you that your presence here is at once an inspiration and a joy to us all.

We welcome you to a city where we believe from the school masters' point of view there is much to interest, may I hope something to instruct you. A city that has nearly six thousand men and women as its army of teachers; where there are nearly two hundred school houses and nearly three hundred thousand children in scholastic relations to our department of public instruction cannot fail to invite study and investigation. It is not the vastness of the system that I would commend to your consideration so much as some of the features of which we in New York are very proud, and which you will find in some measure indicated in the exhibits that are displayed in this building to-night. Notwithstanding a change in the law relating to the administration of our school affairs that were radical and opposed by many of our teachers, I think I may claim to-night that a spirit of co-operation and kindliness exists between the administrative and the executive departments of this great system. We believe that our schools are good, but we think it no evidence of disloyalty to strive in every way to make them better. In this aspiration, teachers of all grades and officers of every class seem to share.

If an instance of the policy of the state with reference to local expenditure is desirable of mention, I would remind you that at the last session of the legislature, New York city by special act was permitted to expend the enormous sum of ten millions for the purchase of new sites and the erection of new schools, and two millions and a half for the construction and equipment of school houses to be devoted to the purposes of secondary education, and when those measures came before the mayor of this city for his approval and an opportunity was afforded to the citizens of New York to appear and oppose them if they saw fit, be it said to the credit of my fellow citizens, there was not one who ventured to raise his voice in opposition to the proposed expenditure. Therefore it is that we are proud of our city and our state in this connection.

The recollections of the very hospitable treatment received at your hands on the occasion of the annual meeting in Saratoga, three or four years ago, makes my appearance before you to-night most agreeable to me. Some of you may recall that on that occasion in return for your hospitality I ventured to offer you a cigarette—for discussion only—and some of you will remember how delighted I was to find that you fully realized the danger that lurked within that innocent-looking roll of paper and decided with me that so far as school boys were concerned, " the cigarette must go." You will recall too, the genial and kindly young man who presided over your deliberations on that occasion who within a few months has passed away and gone to the reward that awaits the schoolmaster who is weighed in the balance and not found wanting. George Hardy was one of the most earnest and successful men, I believe, engaged in the work of public instruction in this city. You all know his career; how, after a brief apprenticeship of less than five years as a teacher, he found himself in a principal's chair where in addition to the efficient service rendered in that office, he continued his study of English literature making most valuable contributions in the form of publications relating to the study of his chosen subject, and you will recall the brief but brilliant service rendered by him when subsequently summoned to the chair of English literature in the college of the city of New York. His career was all too short as measured by those who watched the usefulness of his life which gave promise of the ripening of rare fruits, which, alas, never came to maturity. You will all join with me, I am sure, in laying upon his grave to-night the wreath that I tenderly place there. I rejoice that this opportunity has been accorded me to testify to the worth and usefulness of one of the noble school masters, your former president, who has passed to his reward.

I believe that public school education in this state is keeping pace with this advance in science and in art, and that the noble men and women who are gathered here to-night are fully abreast of the demands of the times as related to themselves.

George S. Morrison, a celebrated engineer of this city has called attention to the wonderful demands made upon education by what he terms the manufacture of power, that is to say, the transference of force by mechanical or other means, from inanimate matter, as for instance, steam from coal and electricity from its original conditions. A vast field has been opened which makes necessary a better education in its relation to a larger number of our people than was ever made necessary before. Must not the man who stands upon the platform of a cable car charged with the mechanical management of that vehicle of transportation and death, be called upon for the exercise of a broader intelligence and greater alertness than that which was formerly required of the amiable and not over intelligent driver of the horse car of former years? Competition has become keener in every department of life, and the man who wins in the struggle of to-day was once the boy who availed of the best methods of education in their relation to his physical, intellectual and moral development.

I have no fear whatsoever of over-educating the masses. The masses of yesterday are the classes of to-morrow (if we admit that there is to be any distinction observed in this country). It is wrong in my opinion to withhold from any youth, competent to profit by it, any grade of instruction in connection with which he has the capacity to acquire and to improve.

The demand is made to-day of every teacher that he or she should know the latest truths contributed by anatomists and physiologists as related to psychology, so that each particular child can be led forth and developed up to the full possibility of his capacity for development, and not by reason of a lack of understanding of the conditions that prevail in the child, fall into the error of condemning the child as stupid or unresponsive. Such a model teacher should be equipped with a cultivated voice, sympathetic in its tone and encouraging in its influence that commands the attention and unconsciously calls forth the affection of the child. Such are some of the reflections that occurred to the mind of one that has been concerned in the administration of school affairs in this city for a number of years. The outlook for us is most hopeful. The spirit of self-improvement I see everywhere indicated among our teachers. We find in New York the best of them, that is to say the greater number of them, responsive to every effort that is being made for the improvement of our schools or methods of instruction, and in all things we observe that co-operation that is necessary for successful school administration where the school officer and the school master are concerned.

We rejoice in your presence here, and assure you of our determination, teachers, superintendents, inspectors and school commissioners, to make the school system of the city of New York so excellent in all its features, that hereafter when a convention of school masters is held, you will have to come to us here, because you will find here that which is best in connection with school administration and school teaching.

RESPONSE BY PRESIDENT CHARLES E. WHITE

Ladies and Gentlemen, teachers of the state of New York.—It is a great privilege to respond to these most generous words, conveying as they do so much of genuine hospitality, as well as of courage and of good cheer to the teachers of the State of New York. I know that I speak the unanimous voice of this association in saying to his honor, Mayor Strong, and to you Superintendent Jasper you have extended to us the "glad hand" and we are already at home.

Fellow teachers we are honored by these cordial welcomes, coming as they do from the highest municipal and educational representatives of the greatest and grandest city of the American continent. For fifty-two years the New York State Teachers' Association has been migrating from city to city, throughout this state, and why this is the first visit to your city, I know not. Your teaching force is an army in itself. Your field is broad, and your experience is large. And permit me to say to the teachers of Greater New York, we welcome this opportunity of knowing you better, this opportunity for a free interchange of experiences, so long denied. Our cause demands that the educational strength of this imperial state be one vast unit, "Each for all and all for each." Let this meeting, the largest in the history of the association be but the beginning of a closer fellowship, of a truer teaching spirit, of a broader, higher conception of the duties and principles of our profession.

The greatness of Greater New York was never more deeply impressed upon our minds. We realize more than ever that this is the metropolis of America, with all its greatness, great men, great learning, great institutions, great industries, great commerce, and great population. It is difficult for your country cousin to believe, but it is true, that if one of your large cannon were fired from the front of normal college one-half of the inhabitants of New York state could hear the report.

We wonder at the vastness of these things and while we wonder our minds turn backward and feed on the historic past of this island, and note the happenings and the conditions that have led up to this glorious present.

We see Hudson, cautiously feeling his way through the narrows, up the bay, and into the river, which now most fittingly bears his name, searching for that still undiscovered Northwest passage. This intrepid mariner, with prophetic vision, was the first to see the physiographical advantages of this island as a great future commercial center, with its boundary rivers and adjacent shores for harbors, its broad bay for anchorage, and "the Narrows" for defense. His glowing accounts soon resulted in the settlement of New Amsterdam by the Dutch.

We note particularly that this island was purchased for $24 in goods upon which there was an enormous profit. We see the rotund Dutchman, felling the forests, fortifying the town, building their houses, and tilling the broad acres now completely covered by pavement and piles of masonry.

We recall how New Amsterdam was declared a city by Stuyvesant; how he named the first officers, all highly respectable men; how he set apart a pew for them in the church, and how early Sunday mornings these worthies would leave their homes and families and proceed to the city hall, from which, preceeded by the bell-ringer, and carrying their cushions of state, they marched in solemn procession to church. No cartoons were printed in those days. These men served without emolument. We learn that now the city fathers do not serve without emolument; and that each public servant from the mayor down to the humblest schoolmaster, attends church, unostentatiously in peace and with his family.

The schoolmaster was also abroad in those early times. We have not been able to learn what were his emoluments; but it is well known that he received his salary in beaver skins, and in addition to his duty as instructor he also served as bell-ringer, choir leader and grave digger. We learn that these last three functions were long since considered unprofessional by the schoolmasters of New York, and abandoned.

It was my intention to tell you more of the early history of your city, but as I have no cyclopedia with me, and as you undoubtedly know it better than I, I desist, and simply say that from its earliest history this city, in the matter of possession, has passed through more reverses than any other city in the land. It was first occupied by the Dutch—captured by the English—retaken by the Dutch—recaptured by the English—occupied by Washington—captured by the English—and finally, occupied by the patriot army on evacuation day, when the English left our shores forever. Perhaps I should say that, politically, you have had like reverses. But through all its adversity it seems to have kept right on growing, and now occupies second place, among the cities of the world. And the time is not far distant, when the city of New York will outrank its only rival, London, even if it has to annex Syracuse, Rochester and Buffalo.

Lastly, without bloodshed, this great city has to-night been surrendered, unconditionally, to the New York State Teachers' Association for a three days' occupancy.

Song.—" Eva dell' Aqua "........................... Vilanelle.
Miss Adeline J. Holley.

REMARKS BY DR. JAMES LEE

Fellow Teachers.—I have been requested by the president, Mr. White, to make a few announcements concerning the exhibit of school work and the locations of the places for section work. I thank you for your very kindly greeting. It gives me a great deal of pleasure for I feared that you might blame me for being the chief instrument in placing extra labor upon you in preparing for the exhibit. This greeting, I take it, is hardly an evidence of any ill-will on your part. I congratulate the principals and teachers of the city of New York for again showing their readiness to place before the profession and the public generally the work done in our schools. You with the principals and teachers of other parts of the state who have sent the work of their pupils here have prepared and placed before this association the greatest exhibit of school work, I believe, ever seen in this state.

And now let me state the plan which has been followed in placing the exhibits. So far as individual schools are concerned the work in the tables is arranged to present the efforts of pupils from the kindergarten or lowest primary grade to the highest grade in the grammar or high school. Every pupil is represented in the packages of class work found on the tables. The age and grade of pupils and other information useful to educators will be found in each piece of work presented. Special work is marked as such. In the hallway leading from this chapel you will find samples of work from all the manual training schools of this city, both grammar and primary. To those interested in this feature of education I commend this part of the exhibit. At the same time I would say that very many schools not known as manual training schools, show many evidences indicative of attention to training in this line. In Room 11 off this same hall the manual training exhibit from the teachers' college will be found. The sections on nature study, Herbart, normal training, and grammar work will meet in rooms off this hallway. These rooms are designated by printed cards placed prominently in view. In the new calistheneum on the top floor and in the hallway just below will be found all the grammar and primary departments—omitting the manual training schools mentioned before—from No. 2 to No. 102 inclusive. Grammar school No. 100 is missing because of the prevalence of contagious disease among children who attend it. In the main hallway, entering from Park avenue, the primary schools not already noted will be found. Following these and continuing on the ground floor you will see the work sent from the evening high schools of this city and out of town schools. You will find exhibits from the Waterford public schools, the superintendent of which was the first to respond to my invitation as superintendent of exhibits. Then comes the city industrial school of Rochester. From the principal who is on hand, I learn that all the instruction in this school is given by female teachers. Considering the character of the manual work shown this will certainly interest every female teacher who examines this particular exhibit. Barlow school of industrial arts of Binghamton sends an exhibit of manual training. Yonkers makes a full and interesting exhibit, as does Lockport and Utica. I commend to your notice the plans of the last named.

Glen Cove sends many things characteristic of its location—in wood, iron, and rope. The ladies will be interested to see the variety of knots and bows made by the girls in these schools—out of rope! Freeport, Far Rockaway and Henrietta union free schools and Rosebank public school are represented by excellent work in all lines. Two schools in Auburn send a fine collection of mounted pictures which are circulated among the schools of that city. In the old calistheneum will be found an extensive and interesting exhibit of school books, periodicals, and other educational appliances. The character and location of each school as well as the name of the principal will be seen on cards at the top of each table. Teachers' names will be found on the packages sent from their classes.

The sections on high school, elocution and child study will meet in the rooms designated for the purpose off the main hallway. The proper cards will be found over the doors of these rooms. The conferences on primary work, kindergarten and manual training will be held in grammar school No. 76 across the way from this institution. In room 4, off main hallway, will be found a complete exhibit of kindergarten supplies.

In conclusion I desire to thank the board of education, especially its executive committee of the normal college and the committee on supplies for the assistance given to me in preparing and placing this exhibit. To President Hunter I am also indebted for many courtesies. At the proper time I shall ask you by resolution to show these gentlemen proper appreciation of their kindness.

To the superintendents, principals and teachers who have united to make the exhibit a success, I extend my most cordial thanks. I have but one word to add further. Remember, I am not down on the program for a speech. You have heard all that President Hubbell wisely said with reference to what you have done and can still do through co-operation—what Superintendent Jasper has so truthfully said of your loyalty to the system in which you work and what that means to the system and to you. Let me present to all who are desirous of learning it, the grandest evidence of your remarkable ability exemplified in the great exhibit which to-night fills every available spot in this immense building.

REPORT OF THE SUPERINTENDENT OF EXHIBITS

NEW YORK, *July* 10, 1897.

To the Officers and Members of the New York State Teachers' Association:

The following circular was sent to the officials connected with the state Department of Public Instruction, to every school commissioner, city and village superintendents, the principal of every school in the state that could be reached by mail, the supervisors of special subjects, in fact to every teacher and school official in the state who might be interested in the work of public education.

NEW YORK STATE TEACHERS' ASSOCIATION

ORGANIZED 1845

NEW YORK *March* 20, 1897.

The fifty-second annual convention of the New York State Teachers' Association will be held in New York city on June 30, July 1, 2 and 3, 1897. Through the courtesy of the board of education, the local committee has secured the normal college for the place of meeting. This is a large and commodious structure, occupying the block bounded by Park avenue, Sixty-eighth street, Lexington avenue and Sixty-ninth street. The chapel will accommodate 3,000 persons. Ample room will be found for round-tables, discussions, conferences and other meetings.

It is proposed to have an exhibit of school work from all parts of the state as one of the features of this convention. Every department and school in the city of New York will take part in the exhibit. As this convention will have representatives from every part of the state, the local committee requests superintendents, principals and others engaged in education to encourage and further every means to have the schools in which they are interested take part in the exhibition.

Table surface will be provided for the exhibition of work which may be placed in a horizontal position. These tables will be 30 inches wide and 8 feet in length. At the back of each table there will be an upright frame *44 inches in extreme height,* having three bars each 3 inches wide—one placed at the top, one at the middle ond one resting on the table. Work to be exhibited vertically should be placed on 22-inch cardboard or strawboard, which cards can be readily arranged one above the other to fill the vertical space. It is proposed that the vertical space shall be given to the school or schools using the horizontal space on any given table, so that the exhibit of said school or schools shall be seen as a whole. You are requested to notify the undersigned at your earliest convenience as to the amount of space you desire to occupy.

Work sent in packages should be fastened to keep it intact, and it is suggested that the accompanying information be placed on the outside of the top sheet of each package:

Name of school.
Location. (County, city, village.)
Grade of class. (Year or term in school.)
Number of pupils represented.
Average age.
Superintendent or commissioner.
Name of principal or head of school.
Name of teacher of the class.

All work sent for purposes of exhibit should be prepaid and directed to the undersigned at the normal college at least two weeks before the opening of the convention. The local committee will attend to placing the work sent without any further expense or trouble. Those desiring the work returned must make arrangements for such return, otherwise it will be disposed of at the discretion of the local committee.

It is hoped that the schools of the state will take part so as not to make this exhibit a strictly local affair.

It is expected that through the courtesy of the board of education one of the days will be devoted to visits to the schools and inspection of actual class-room work.

[illegible]

[illegible] New York [illegible]

[illegible] naturally [illegible] and [illegible]

[illegible] is period- [illegible]

[illegible] great [illegible] was [illegible] greatest [illegible] brought to- [illegible] magni- [illegible] was [illegible] striking feature [illegible] gave it a [illegible] the courses of study, as shown by the individual work of each child from the kindergarten to the high school, was its most attractive educational feature. Besides the great number of teachers in this and neighboring states who saw the work, parents and the public generally visited and examined the work during three days following the convention.

In conclusion, I desire to thank all who coöperated with me to make this feature of our fifty-second annual convention the success which I feel it attained. Their active and sympathetic interest deserves the highest commendation.

JAMES LEE,
Superintendent of Exhibits.

Music — Selected. Orchestra — Cornet solo by Frank Reissmann.

PUBLIC AND PRIVATE SCHOOLS

HON. GILBERT H. CRAWFORD

Mr. President, Ladies and Gentlemen.—Not long ago a Scotsman interested in public education visited this city. He was chairman of the school board in one of the smaller cities of Scotland, and was himself an interesting character, thoughtful and and energetic, who had risen step by step from an obscure position until he had become the master of one of the large ship-yards on the Clyde. After seeing something of our public schools he expressed profound astonishment at the rapidity with which our foreign population is assimilated. In one down town school, where he spent several hours, it was difficult for him to distinguish between the children of European parents and the few who were there of strict American descent. To tell the truth, his own broad, Caledonian pronunciation of the Queen's English seemed to amuse some of the boys, who in their homes heard nothing probably but some dialect of southern Italy. Our friend was moved to remark that no one could fear for the stability of republican institutions after such an object lesson in our capacity to absorb alien elements. It was marvellous, he said, that types of humanity which retain a stubborn individuality in Europe century after century should lose themselves here in the short space of an early childhood. The transformation which bewildered the Scottish shipmaster has become a commonplace to American teachers who are ever mindful of the hackneyed but immortal lines of Terence: "I am a man. Nothing is foreign to me if it is human."

The public schools are in the first line of battle. They are the leaders in great and permanent improvements in the art of education. This might be expected, for the people demand that their schools shall be the best and they spare no expense to make them so. No private enterprise can hold its own in such a competition. Inspired by the energy and sustained by the resources of the people, the public school is destined to hold a position of undisputed educational preëminence. What we can see now is but the beginning of what shall be. We have seen the public school taking great strides in the last three decades, but look ahead and you will see them becoming the greatest of all the influences that fashion social and political life, more powerful than the legislature, the courts of justice, the pulpit or the press. Even now it must be admitted upon any impartial consideration of the case that the people's schools are in possession of the field of elementary education, and the time will surely come when the people's colleges will equally dominate the field of higher education. The people's hand is on the plough and they will run the furrow to the farthest limit of the globe.

There are good reasons for this. Men of wealth, and let us not forget to honor them for their generosity, contribute munificent endowments to found colleges, but almost invariably they fetter them by restrictions which are like a ball and chain on a man's leg. There are exceptions. I will refer to one—a citizen of this state—who, if he had lived till last Friday, might have seen the red and white colors of the people's college he founded sweep victoriously past the crimson and the blue of the oldest and proudest universities of America. Ezra Cornell put no shackles on Cornell University. Peter Cooper put none on Cooper Institute. Hopkins put none on his great university. But these men stand out in shining contrast to the throng of benevolent, but less liberal, college founders who could not resist the temptation to make their benefactions a propaganda. When the people build a college they write over the door, "Sacred to free thought. We know no differences of race or religion here."

Still another reason for the rapid development of our public schools all over the state is the periodical frequency with which they are made the object of public criticism. Everybody is free to find fault with them, quite irrespective of any knowledge he may have of the subject.

If, leaving these general considerations, I were asked for some tangible evidence of the leadership of the public schools in the world of education, I should point to this convention, the successor and prototype of numberless similar gatherings, which for many years have been a prominent feature of American school life. Sometimes it seems as of a few inspired teachers had caught a glimpse of a scheme of public school life so elastic and so wisely planned as to enable every child to make the most of his natural faculties.

"Education by battalion," the phrase is not mine, is unfavorable to variety of type, and many teachers think the tendency of popular education is more and more to crush out originality in the child. But there are others who are equally confident that this tendency can be corrected, and that the cultivation of the individual is quite compatible with that instruction *en masse* which seems inevitable under existing conditions. These hopeful teachers are not looking much in the direction pointed out by the philosopher of Geneva, who qualified himself to write a book about the education of children by sending his own offspring to a foundling asylum. Their verdict is that Emile, the book, is full of fancies as beautiful and as elusive as the summer clouds that float over a country schoolhouse; and that Emile, the child, is an inconceivable unreality. No. the philosophic schoolmaster of the future will keep both feet on the solid earth, and his ideal will be a human child whose mind and body have been symmetrically developed to the highest point without waste of time or strength.

This ideal may or may not be a mere dream. What we call waste seems to be one of the economies of nature. Every great success is preceded by seeming loss of time and energy. Every successful man spends years of preliminary preparation which are marked by an apparently useless destruction of force, and even the supposed exceptions to this rule turn out not to be such upon closer inquiry.

Dumont said he should never have known how much could be done in twenty-four hours, had he not known Mirabeau. From the conception of a plan to the execution of it, he said, not a moment was lost. But Mirabeau was forty years old when the states general met in 1789, and before he became the first man in France he had thrown recklessly to the winds vast resources of strength and vitality which might have been of priceless value to his country. Dying of sheer physical exhaustion after less than two years of arduous public service, his genius still resplendent as ever, but his robust body worn out by willful excesses, Mirabeau is the most splendid example in history of magnificent waste going before magnificent performance.

Jefferson had some such idea as this, and so did his rival, Hamilton, and when one founded the university of Virginia and the other the university of this state, the two great statesmen took long strides towards each other. If the children of the people were taught politics as they are taught the history of their country, Hamilton would not fear universal suffrage and Jefferson would not fear a strong executive. The two opposing theories of government suggested by these illustrious names would be reconciled in the supreme enlightenment of the people.

I might cite the great name of Herbert Spencer in support of what has been said, but time forbids. It is for you, ladies and gentlemen, to determine what the next step shall be. It is for you to say whether you will strengthen the fabric of republican institutions at the very foundation.

Music — "Cocoanut Dance," Herman orchestra.

President White appointed the following committees:

NOMINATING COMMITTEE

Chairman, George Griffith, Utica; W. B. Gunnison, Brooklyn; A. B. Blodgett, Syracuse; Edward A. Page, New York; S. P. Moulthrop, Rochester; Dr. Wm. A. Ettinger, New York; Myron Scudder, Albany.

FINANCE COMMITTEE

Chairman, George H. Waldon, Rochester; John H. Harren, Brooklyn; John T. Nicholson, New York.

RESOLUTIONS COMMITTEE

Chairman W. K. Wickes, Syracuse; J. G. Riggs, Plattsburgh; Schuyler F. Herron, Elizabethtown; Dr. John Allen, Rochester; Dr. James Lee, New York.

INSPECTORS OF ELECTION

Chairman, Col. Samuel C. Pierce, Rochester; Principal E. N. Jones, Binghamton; W. H. Dumond, Brooklyn; C. E. Lawton, Auburn; Jos. A. Tripp, New York.

THURSDAY MORNING, JULY 1, 1897

Music — Polka, "L'Allegria," Mandolin orchestra of Grammar School No. 23, Bernard F. Cecire, leader.

Mr. Griffith presiding as chairman of nominating committee.

Nomination for president.--Superintendent J. C. Norris of Canandaigua and Dr. James Lee. Mr. Norris withdrew in favor of Dr. Lee.

For vice-presidents.—Wm. J. O'Shea, New York city, first vice-president; Arthur E. Goodrich, Utica, N. Y., second vice-president; Mary E. Tate, New York city, third vice-president; Mary E. Laing, Oswego, N. Y., fourth vice-president.

Memebers of executive committee.—Chas. N. Cobb, Albany, and George Griffith, Utica.

For secretary.—Schuyler F. Herron.

For assistant secretary.—Wm. F. O'Callaghan.

For treasurer.—S. McKee Smith.

For assistant treasurer.—John Dwyer and Abram Fischlowitz.

Transportation agent.—Arthur Cooper.

Superintendent of exhibits.—E. C. Colby, Rochester.

Mr. Page, Chairman of local committee, then spoke in favor of Rochester, as next place for holding convention. Motion seconded by Mr. Walden and carried.

Inspectors of election then named.—W. H. Beaumont and Joseph A. Tripp of New York.

Music.—Waltz, "Sobre las Olas"......................Rosas.
Orchestra.

THE RELATION OF THE HOME AND THE SCHOOL

DR. WALTER B. GUNNISON

The one thing in this class that the limit of this paper permits me to dwell upon is the changes that have taken place in the relations of the home and school.

There have been governments in which the accepted policy was to place the education of the young entirely in the hands of the state. The interest of the home ceased just as soon as the child had arrived at the age at which it had been determined that the state should assume the charge. The state was the end and aim of all public energy, and, with this as the central idea, the plan was right. The enlightened civilization of to-day, however, has rejected the whole proposition as a preposterous one and has made the state a servant of the individual, and the family and the home the unit of organization and endeavor.

In many respects the country schools of twenty-five or thirty years ago realized more perfectly the ideals of education than any plan that has since resulted. The schools were small, an absolute essential for the most effective work. They were mixed, thus furnishing the natural conditions of all social life. They were removed from all distractions. The teacher worked with the individual pupils. Such things as grades, by which it was attempted to perform the impossible, in trying to have forty or fifty pupils of differing attainments and differing capacity move along at a uniform rate, were unknown. There was no course of study. Each pupil was made to perform just what he was able naturally to perform. The teacher lived in the homes of the pupils, and many a brilliant leader in our cosmopolitan life of to-day will trace his first incentive to enlarged efforts to the advice and assistance that came to him years ago, during those long winter evenings, from some ambitious collegian who was "keeping school" to raise the wherewithal to pay for his next term in college. Above all, the teacher knew his pupils and the parents of his pupils, and thus was able to shape his instruction and to modify his discipline so as to accomplish the most desirable results for his pupils.

The above conditions of the earlier schools are fundamentally necessary in order to attain the highest results in education, and just as we have departed from them, whether deliberately or from necessity, just so far have we removed ourselves from the ability to attain the ideal. Of necessity large schools have taken the places of smaller ones. The distractions of the metropolis have taken the place of the quietude of the country. Individual work has been displaced by grade work. Courses of study have become a necessity. The bright pupil must be more or less kept back and the dull pupil must be more or less urged to more than his normal capacity by reason of the creation of what is termed "the average child." The teacher rarely meets his pupils outside of the walls of the class-room and never sees a parent, except to answer to some supposed infraction of the rules or to defend himself from some supposed injustice. With all these changes, all for the worse, have doubtless come many compensating advantages, finer buildings, better equipment, more skillful teachers, expert supervision, more adequate salaries, and an undisturbed tenure. How far these have gone toward making up the evident loss caused by the changes must remain wholly a matter of opinion, and we will not enter upon a discussion of the question involved. My aim is to ask you to consider whether something may not be done to restore in part, at least, the advantages we have lost. Are our very large schools and our abnormally sized classes a necessity? The answer will readily come, I suppose, from all, that this whole matter rests with the taxpayers. This is true, but cannot something be done to show to the dispensers of the public funds that very great injustice is being done to the young people of our cities by too greatly reducing the tax rate, and that by so doing we are failing to accomplish properly what so many millions are being expended yearly to bring about. Right here is the most urgent need of reform. It is useless to say that the lack of efficiency in our schools is due to incompetent teachers—to our poor courses of study—to the character of our supervision—all these things are merely incidental. It is the crowding of our children into classes of abnormal size that is responsible for most of the inefficiency. Let the classes be restricted to twenty-five or at most thirty pupils and the other troubles will quickly disappear. We as professional educators have a duty far greater than merely to teach the rudiments to the children. Our work should go out to the masses of the people, and from the vantage ground of our experience with the actual working of our schools, we should aid them by clearly showing where the real difficulties lie. The first steps necessary to accomplish this education of the people is through the establishment of a closer relationship of the schools with the people than at present obtains. The people, those who have children in the schools and who are, therefore, most vitally interested, know little of them. They have gradually turned the matter of the education of the young over to the school authorities. They no longer visit the schools. Thus it is that the children lose the benefits which come from a more intimate acquaintance of the parent and the teacher. No education can be properly directed unless the teacher knows fully the motives, the home life and the general environment of the pupil. No parent on the other hand can properly support and assist the teacher unless he knows fully the aims, the objects and the character of the teacher. To bring about this desirable result, however, will involve much education and a vast amount of missionary work all along the line. In the first place, we teachers need to become fully imbued with the necessity of this reform. We have so long conducted our schools without the co-operation of the parents that we fail to recognize its importance.

We all believe that every teacher intends to do her work faithfully and efficiently—that she wishes to do the very best possible for the children committed to her care—yet how often do we hear her motives questioned and her methods and actions criticized. And yet these criticisms arise largely from the fact that her acts and words are reported by the children, and the parents, knowing nothing of the individual, except on the hearsay evidence, regard the facts as established. Could they be brought together in mutual conference, all this would largely cease.

Our schools are so large that it is not feasible to urge the parents to visit them very much during the regular sessions. There is no place for them. While they should be made welcome at all times to visit and inspect the work as it is going on, it must be recognized that the continued interruption would prove injurious to the best interests of the school. The most practical solution seems to be to invite the parents to meetings at stated intervals. Have these after the regular sessions of the day. Have the teachers remain in their rooms so that the parents will feel free to go to them and to confer with them in regard to their children. It would seem to me that one or two days a month

[illegible]

[illegible] a wrong conception of what their position and attitude should be. A doctor does not consider that it is anything derogatory to his dignity [illegible] to make the fullest inquiries in regard to all the [illegible] of his little patient. The lawyer [illegible] to be under[illegible] from the different people who are conversant with the facts everything that has any bearing upon it, no matter how remote this may be. When these are all learned then the man of science and of law applies his rules, and independently uses his experience and judgment in the proper handling of his case. It is the solemn duty of the teacher, who more than any other has a sacred office to fulfill, to know everything that has the remotest bearing on the question, of how best to properly develop the young mind intrusted to his direction and care.

If there has been one thing that has worked against the dignity of the teacher, it has been that he has been willing to assume the position of one "who knows it all," and has attempted to perform the delicate work of education in accordance with fixed and arbitary rules and "must" formulas. The lawyer and the doctor who should attempt to pursue these methods would soon find reason for going out of business. The only thing that keeps such a teacher in office is our fixed tenure and the utter ignorance on the part of the parents of the working of our schools. In this matter we must take the dignified position of the men in the other professions. We are or should be experts, and entitled to respect as such. We should invite the parents freely to confer with us for the simple reason that we cannot properly teach their children unless they do so. We must know from them the things about which they know vastly more than we can ever hope to know—the pupil's habits of study and their personal habits, their natural inclinations, their attitude toward their work, the opportunities for study, their interest in certain lines, the length of time they are to remain in school, what their probable life work will be, etc., etc. When these things and a hundred other things equally important are fully known, then we, as teachers, will be ready to assume charge and intelligently direct the studies and not until then.

In things pedagogical we should need no assistance from the parents, and the parent who assumes to dictate in such matters can usually be classed among the freaks. Questions of school management and organization often arise, which make friction, and are frequently questions in regard to matters about which the judgment of a level headed business man is of the greatest importance.

If such a case arises it is the part of the teacher or principal to recognize that his will and judgment are no better than that of any other man of equal general experience, and a conference upon such a matter should be one in which he should look simply at the good of the school and the pupil and not allow himself to feel that his dignity will be impaired by not persisting in his opinion.

From every view I have been able to take of this matter I can find none that does not strengthen me in the position that there is nothing more promising that we can do as teachers and principals than to take positive grounds on the need and the helpfulness of furthering every move that will seem to draw closer the bonds which should hold the home and the school in the closest relationship.

That the methods I have briefly outlined are the best to accomplish the result aimed at I do not pretend. They are those that we have tried to follow out in the borough across the river. That they have done good there no one who knows the work will deny. If this or any other plan which may be devised will further the good work we should all rejoice. Once let the parents of our schools become thoroughly acquainted with them and

I feel confident that the time will be short in which it will be possible for the authorities in any school to allow 50 or 60 or 70 children to be herded together under one teacher, and unless I greatly err the great and beneficient work of public education will receive an intelligent and a helpful impulse.

March.—" El Capitan "............................... Sousa.
Orchestra.

Mr. Blodgett moved that the secretary be instructed to cast ballot for the nominations, except for assistant treasurer. Motion seconded and carried. Ticket declared elected. The inspectors of election reported Abram Fischlowitz elected treasurer.

THURSDAY EVENING, JULY 1, 8 O'CLOCK

Assembly.—Bugle and drum corps, grammar school No. 66. George Gorman, drum major.

Ball drill.—Pupils of female department, grammar school No. 96. Under the direction of Dr. M. Augusta Requa, supervisor of physical training.

First sergeant's call.—Drum corps.

Educational gymnastics.—Boys from grammar school Nos. 6, 18, and 96.

(a) Free exercises.
(b) Swimming drill.
(c) Hurdling.
(d) Short contest.
(e) Postures.

Adjutant's call.—Drum corps.

Aesthetic drill.—Girls from female department, grammar school No. 76.

Dismissal.—" G. D." Drum corps.

THE SCHOOLS AND THE STATE

CHARLES R. SKINNER, *State Superintendent of Public Instruction*

Mr. President, Teachers and Friends.—It is our pleasant privilege to meet in the metropolis of the western continent, in what will soon be the second largest city of the world.

Little more than a century ago the last soldier trod these streets, till then under the British flag which he served. The phenomenal growth in arts, commerce, manufactures, population, power and wealth of that colonial town is one of the greatest marvels of the age. From the day in 1633 that Adam Roelandson, the first schoolmaster, landed with Wouter Van Twiller, the director-general, thus antedating two years the first school in Massachusetts; from the signing by Governor Clinton of the first act of the legislature for the establishment of common schools, New York has marched in the front in educational progress, and to-day occupies a commanding position. To be first is not the ambition of New York, but to be the best. To give every child an education that shall swing wide the doors of future usefulness and success, and admit to the highest honors and the purest life — this New York is resolved to do.

It is appropriate that the educators of our state should assemble in this fair city, where new conditions are presenting to this people the greatest educational problem of our day. The solution of this problem, the adaptation of these new conditions to the great municipality that is to be, calls for discriminating wisdom of the highest character. Our hope is as strong as our faith that the problem will be speedily solved, and that a school system will be established here efficient in its working, satisfactory in its results, as it will be mighty in extent and in its triumphs— a magnificent example to great cities and nations, and the pride of the educational world.

It is a lesson worth learning to note the provisions made here for education and to contrast them with those of our rural schools. Provision for the expenditure of twelve millions of dollars for school buildings! Nearly as much as there was paid last year throughout the state for teachers' salaries. It gives a higher idea of how money can be used, to note the great buildings in which the poorest child may be trained for a useful life, if one will keep in mind the forlorn country schoolhouse, so bare, so uninviting, sometimes so repulsive, without and within.

It is interesting to compare the schools of this great city with their 354,566 pupils and 7,693 teachers, with some of the schools in our rural communities. In this city, our friends will show us a single school, which has a village population in itself, with 3,420 pupils and 71 teachers, more pupils and more teachers than any village in the state can count, and more than comprise the school systems in twenty of our interior cities. Contrast this great grammar school with the rural schools with one, two or three pupils and one teacher—with the teacher often waiting for the one pupil to appear. Contrast the millions expended upon the schools of this city with the country district, which maintains its school, pays its teacher and buys its supplies with the teachers' quota of $100 apportioned by the state. Sometimes a serious problem is presented to the district in determining what disposition shall be made of the surplus on hand at the close of the year.

It is an education in itself for our interior teachers to visit the metropolis and look upon the magnitude of its educational equipment. Will they not return to their work convinced that some means should be devised to improve, by consolidation or otherwise, the condition of our country schools. Is there not a "rural school problem" demanding solution? Professor Bickmore recently exhibited to the primary pupils in one of the schools of this city a view of a country schoolhouse, showing teacher and group of children, but not one of the pupils could tell what the picture represented.

More than twice the population and many times the wealth of the thirteen colonies when the British evacuated New York now find home within the limits of this city and state. What may not such a commonwealth, great in its past history, its resources, its opportunities, its people, its future outlook, do for the eduucation of its children and youth? What it can achieve is the measure of its duty. To do less is to betray its trust. To fail in lifting its schools, its colleges, its universities, to their highest efficiency, in providing the best instructors in every institution, in securing the most exact and thorough supervision, in sending pupils out into life prepared for its responsibilities, prepared to set the standard of municipal, state and national life on loftier heights, as well as to elevate and ennoble the mental and moral and spiritual life of the people—to fail in doing this is to dishonor the history and to stain the fair fame of the Empire state.

While congratulating, as we do most heartily, this city, the board of education, the superintendent and assistants, the schools, the teachers, the pupils of Greater New York on the work here accomplished and contemplated; while we clasp hands cordially with educational enthusiasts and co-workers, presidents, professors, superintendents, officers, commissioners and teachers, from Lake Erie to the ocean, it seems fitting, in the discussion of "The Schools and the State," to seek an answer to each of two questions: First. What have the schools the right to expect from the state? Second. What has the state the right to expect from the schools?

In answering these questions, one fact is as clear as the sunlight: That schools and education exist for the state; not that the state exists for the schools. In every thing pertaining to its life and power, the state is paramount. No division or class of divisions of the state, however important, can possibly equal the state. Whether the state be monarchial, republican or democratic in its government matters nothing as to its supremacy. Authority belongs to the state, inheres in it always, must be its prerogative; for its exercise the state always must be responsible. Every part of the state must acknowledge its authority, must submit to it, must defend and uphold it. Confusion, anarchy, disintegration, destruction await the state unless its authority is supreme. Its inherent right is to perpetuate itself. The welfare of its people, the support of its institutions, its honor among the nations are solemn obligations binding the state to enact such laws, enforce such control, provide such defenses as shall unalterably secure its unending duration. To secure this the state must, in every way possible, promote the intelligence and culture of its subjects. Its control over the education of its people is absolute. Its obligation to provide education is imperative. It can never safely surrender its control nor honorably evade its obligation. It has been well said that "The end at which the state aims is a noble life."

A republic like our own must insist upon the education of its citizens, for upon their intelligence and virtue its own existence depends. Other republics have flourished, but to-day are not, and their fall resulted from the defective education of their people. It behooves every lover of freedom, every loyal citizen, every patriotic American, to strive resolutely, with high and low, rich and poor, old and young, to secure for our country the blessings of a good education for every child in the land. Our work is not for New York only, but for our whole country. Our history, our position, our example in educational affairs largely influence other states. If true to past privileges, if faithful to present obligations, if alive to future possibilities, as educators, as parents, as citizens, we will make our schools a vital part of the noblest work of the state; we will make the state the living support of the highest education the schools are able to give.

But while schools exist for the state, let it never be forgotten that they are a vital part of the state. In proportion as their life is healthful and strong, so the state gains in resources, in character, in position, in power. As they are neglected and ignored, the state loses its capacity for progress and achievement, and falls to the rear. The first duty the state owes to itself is self-preservation. The surest way to accomplish this is to advance and elevate the schools; to increase the physical, mental, moral and spiritual powers of its citizens by careful, systematic, thorough education.

In view of the relation they sustain to each other, consider briefly what the schools have a right to expect from the state. This may be condensed into a single sentence: The fulfillment of the obligations of the state to the schools. In one sense the schools are the wards of the state. They possess untold riches. The state is to protect them. They have large, undeveloped resources. The state must unfold them. They inherit enormous capacities. The state must expand and strengthen them. They hold unlimited powers for good or for evil. The state must secure their exercise for the good. In doing this, the state not only fulfills in part its obligation to the schools, but most surely insures its own preservation.

Some particular features of the obligation of the state to care for the schools come into view. To provide for the elementary instruction of all the children is to repeat a truism, but its repetition will not be heard too often. Not till every child of school age is actually in attendance every day of the school year, unless prevented by good cause, will the state have fulfilled the initial part of its obligation to the schools. Non-attendance, or irregularity of attendance, is an injury to pupils, classes and schools, to the community and to the state. The state must compel the attendance of children in school through the entire period demanded by law.

But the state must also provide for pupils whatever is needed for their comfort and success in school. Not only in this center of wealth and power should buildings in every way suitable for their purpose be provided, but in villages, towns and rural districts, throughout our entire domain, care should be taken to secure grounds and buildings, commodious, well appointed, perfectly adapted to the needs of the children who spend so many hours each day within them. The proper arrangement of rooms, their ventilation, lighting, seating, warming, furnishing with maps, apparatus, books, pictures, engravings, ought to be insisted upon by the state for pupils in Hamilton and Warren counties as truly as for pupils in Greater New York.

In the buildings which it is hoped the state of New York will some day provide for all the children in our schools will be found teachers whose qualifications must be adequate for their work. In studies they must be accurate; in professional spirit, genuine and true; in zeal, untiring; with largeness of vision to see the magnitude and responsibilities of their high and honorable office. There will never be too much care in the selection of teachers, nor too much work given to prepare them for their duties. As the family, unfortunately, is thrusting constantly upon the school the discharge of its inherent duties in the moral as well as mental training of children, teachers are of necessity obliged to watch over pupils unceasingly to protect them from evil influences, and to surround them with whatever is pure and virtuous and noble in manly or womanly character.

The state must supplement the work of teachers by the ablest supervision possible. Only masters of the art should be called to this work. It is a true saying that "The people are the most intelligent and civilized, not merely where the most money is spent for education, but where the governmental supervision of the schools is the most complete." No subject to-day demands more intelligent treatment that that of the supervision of schools. In no other department are the needs so apparent. Prudent directors elect as president of a bank or of a railroad a man with special knowledge of the work to be done, as well as one of executive ability. Even an engineer on the Empire state express or on the steamer "City of Paris" is appointed because of his knowledge and experience in his calling. But supervisory officers for our schools are often chosen for other reasons than efficiency. Sometimes personal considerations or other causes enter too largely into the selection. Fitness often gives way to favoritism.

Men of unquestioned moral character, of unimpeachable integrity, of stainless purity, of sterling honesty, should be chosen supervisory officers of schools. They should also be well-educated men. It is a strange reversal of position for an official to have power to decide upon a license, a certificate or diploma, who cannot pass the examination the teacher is obliged to take who receives it at his hands. It should also be considered part of the equipment of a supervisory officer that he be a gentleman, courteous in manner and obliging in disposition. Give us always men of pure morals, of sound education, of courteous manners for supervisory officers, and the state of New York will take a long step forward in educational interests.

The work of supervision is not progressive only, it is also uplifting. Every visitation of a school by supervisors of the right character, let their official title be what it may—superintendent, supervisor, inspector, commissioner—gives teachers new insight into the powers and possibilities of their work. It cheers and inspires, even when methods of teaching are criticised and faults exposed. True supervision is the teacher's strongest support, as it is also the pupil's greatest encouragement. Many a teacher has been saved to the profession and many a pupil has been brought back to honorable position in school and society by the timely help of proper supervision.

To fulfill its obligations to its schools, the state must not only provide elementary instruction for all the children, but must also provide secondary education for those who seek it. Pupils in the elementary course often acquire a thirst for knowledge which cannot be satisfied with that course alone. High school or academic instruction is as needful to them as elementary. Buildings and grounds as thoroughly adapted, and teachers as well qualified, and supervision as exact and uncompromising, must characterize secondary schools as surely as elementary. If the educational foundations are strongly laid, the superstructure ought to be as wisely and securely constructed. Many pupils, many teachers, too, are content with superficial attainments. Examinations are passed, commencements held, pupils graduated, and teachers—take their vacations. But lessons carelessly learned, studies imperfectly understood, examinations passed by crowding or by collusion, leave ugly proofs of the pupil's folly and the teacher's crime. When the life work is begun, after school days are over, the mistakes and faults of an imperfect education show plainly as the unseemly fissures and sagging walls in buildings of poor material and defective workmanship. There never can be good common schools without good teachers; there never can be good teachers without the highest grade of secondary education, supplemented by the best technical training received in first-class normal schools and training classes.

Respecting higher education and the state, it is certain that secondary schools can never attain the highest efficiency unless their teachers receive an education superior to that given in these schools alone. Principals and teachers in high schools and academies should be graduates of college or university, should have more thorough preparation for their duties in instructing pupils, who will themselves be teachers in elementary schools, than these pupils can possibly receive there. It is only as the highest grade of scholarship and perfect efficiency in management are combined that principals of academies and high schools, of normal schools and training classes can be secured whose influence will perpetuate itself for good in the institutions of which they always must be the inspiration and controlling force.

Education, whether elementary, secondary or higher, is one in spirit, aim and purpose; the improvement and elevation of men. The welfare and prosperity of the state depend upon all the schools it fosters and protects. As the conservator of whatever is energizing, uplifting and ennobling for its people, the state will realize that education is an integral part of its life; and that it must not be content with less intelligence and culture in its citizens when greater can be secured.

Inasmuch as the interests of the schools and of the state are one in fact as truly as in theory, inasmuch as education is not for one class of citizens nor for one section of the state, therefore the state, in order to complete and perfect its system of schools and education, is pledged to the liberal expenditure of money for their support. The authority of the state ought to be exercised in rural districts, in villages, and in cities compelling the construction and furnishing of school buildings and proper care of school grounds. The many unsightly and unhealthful buildings and grounds now in use should be condemned and abandoned. If children are to be educated properly, let schoolhouses always be places of health and beauty and life.

The state ought to be generous also in salaries to teachers. Make entrance to the profession difficult, set the standard of qualifications high, bar out relentlessly unworthy applicants, demand the best and exact the fullest service, then pay salaries proportionate to the work they do for the children and the state. When hod carriers and street cleaners receive larger wages than the state allows teachers for salaries, something is wrong. Teachers are building the character of our children for time and for eternity. Surely their work is worth as much as the work of men employed in building our houses and places of business. A school commissioner recently stated that a trustee said to him: "I am paying my teacher $4.50 per week. Can you tell me where I can find one for $4.00?"

Teachers have a right to expect fair treatment, to be considered as men and women belonging to an honorable profession. A few years ago a party of teachers from one of our cities spent their vacation on the shores of Lake Ontario. They refused to make known their profession because they feared they would not be allowed the same privileges as other guests. Admitting that all teachers do not come up to the required standard of professional courtesy and learning—do all lawyers or physicians? Should more be demanded of teachers in these respects than is demanded of those in other professions? Whatever can be done by the state to ennoble the work of the teacher; to lift higher the standard of admission to the profession; to enlarge the privileges of those worthy to enter it; to secure their tenure in office; to provide adequate salaries; to protect from the infirmities of age those grown old in service; these returns, men and women who devote their lives to the grandest work of the age, have a right to expect from the state of New York.

Executive officers of the right sort should also have good salaries—large enough to atract men of the greatest brain and the noblest heart to the service of the state. With the examples set by banking, railroad and insurance companies in the salaries paid their officers, it is time the state determined to give adequate salaries to the officers who manage its educational interests. Horace Mann toiled for years as the secretary of education in Massachusetts on a less salary than a merchant gives his office clerk. Massachusetts to-day is far richer in the schools he advocated and established than it possibly could have been had he never served the state. Henry Barnard's name and fame will endure as long as education holds place in the hearts of men, and yet Connecticut kept his salary small, turned him out of office and refused the reward his age, his services, his great abilities justly entitled him to receive.

At Riverside, beneath a monument reared by loving admirers, sleeps the great soldier whose brilliant generalship and commanding will contributed so largely to give us peace with honor. We cannot revere his memory too highly. We never will exalt the mighty trio of American heroes, Washington, Lincoln, Grant, on pedestals too lofty for our love and praise. Give them grandly and nobly their due. Then turn and contrast the undistinguished place where lie the ashes of the first schoolmaster of New York and read once for all the lesson of the ingratitude of the state of New York to teachers and educational workers during the centuries since he died.

The school children of Massachusetts have told the story of their love in the monument in Boston commemorating the services of Horace Mann. Let the state of New York express its gratitude in suitable school buildings and grounds for the children, in generous salaries to teachers and supervisory officers, and it will build a monument worthy of its name and fame.

The state has a right to demand from the schools that children be trained first of all to thorough mastery of the studies in the elementary course. Less than this, schools ought not to expect to give. Less than this the state must not accept from the schools. Every pupil in every school in the state of New York ought to be required to master that course before school life is over. Whatever else may be had by the pupil, that course must be mastered, without exception of a pupil or omission of a study. With elementary studies as the foundation, pupils may go onward and upward in their education, but the foundation in every instance must be laid strongly, honestly, thoroughly.

But with these studies should be taught courtesy of manner, politeness of speech, refinement of thought and genuine culture of life. The state has a right to expect also that pupils, from the beginning of their course, be imbued with the spirit of honesty, with the love of truth and purity, with integrity of thought and action. Education to be successful can never be one-sided. Children cannot be trained physically and mentally with no moral and spiritual culture without loss to themselves, to parents and to the state. While it is never the province of the state to teach religious truth after the distinctive tenets of any form or belief, it emphatically is the duty of the state to see that children are taught the highest and purest morality. Inasmuch as this is a Christian commonwealth, the state must demand that the schools inculcate Christian morality.

Has not the state also a right to demand that colleges and universities shall so use their privileges and opportunities that students shall become not only educated men and women of high character, of noble purpose, of lofty purity, of unquestioned loyalty, of incorruptible patriotism, trained to know what is right, and to do it, to love what is good and to seek to reach it? Has the state a right to demand these results from the schools, colleges and universities it supports and protects? Have they the right to refuse the demand?

The state has a right to expect from the schools receiving its benefactions absolute loyalty. Loyalty not only in outward subjection to law, but loyalty of the spirit; the recognition of the right of the state to order its system of instruction after its own conception of the needs of the state, and of the highest interests of the schools; a loyalty that finds its best expression in the efforts of pupils, teachers, people to build up lofty ideals of manhood and womanhood, and of the broadest and noblest citizen ship.

The state has a right to expect in return for its enormous outlay an enthusiastic public spirit fostering and sustaining all efforts to develop and elevate the schools. Public opinion behind the machinery of instruction should be alert to see that moneys expended by the state are rightly and honestly expended. In no branch of public service would fraud of any sort be so peremineutly wrong as in the management of moneys expended to educate the children of the state. There ought to be such keen interest and unceasing watchfulness on the part of the public that corruption in this line would be impossible.

The state has the right also to expect that public interest in schools will show itself in the selection of competent, honest officers, even though those officers serve without salary. No work done for the state by its officials is more far-reaching in its results. The success of teachers, the advancement of pupils, the elevation of schools, depend upon the efficiency of those working without other reward than to do their duty, to benefit the children and the state, and to win the approval of their own conscience and the approbation of their fellows. All honor to faithful trustees and self-denying members of boards of education willing to do this work. No greater service is rendered to the state.

While there must always be difference of opinion respecting methods of management and modes of administration, the state has the right to expect honest and intelligent criticism of its work for the public schools. No system is perfect, no method so good that a better may not be devised. Schemes long proved successful may be superseded by those more efficient. It is not only the privilege, but the duty, of those interested in the public schools to see that they are freed from every defect of management, that their supervision is exact, that every provision is made for their advance. Fault-finding, censorious judgment, sweeping verdicts of condemnation effect little good. Effective criticism is constructive. If the old building is torn down, it must be to lay deeper and broader foundations for the new, to erect a larger and better structure than before. The state has the right to expect that the people will not only second every such movement, but will take the initiative themselves and point out the paths needed to reach desired results.

The state has a right to expect progressive methods in education. It has a right to expect that no foothold shall be given that old conservative policy which is advocated by those who believe that what was good enough for their grandfathers is good enough for their children. When we hear such men plead, we feel that they would turn the wheels of progress a cog or two backward. Such men would prefer the stage coach to the express train, the caravel to the ocean steamship, and the tallow candle of their fathers to the incandescent light of the present day.

Two hundred and eighty-eight years have passed since Hendrick Hudson, in the "Half Moon," sailed up this bay to the river which bears his name and fame to succeeding centuries. It is difficult to name a state in history which, in less than three hundred years, has done more to deserve an honorable place in the annals of men, than New York. In wealth, in population, in magnitude of resources, agricultural, mineral, manufacturing; in extent of commerce and trade, in social advancement, in political liberty and power, in religious freedom, in the character of its citizens, their intelligence and their culture; in the true, the beautiful and the good; in whatever exalts and glorifies a state, New York stands proudly in the presence of her sister states, nor does she fear comparison with the nations of Europe, with which she is so intimately related through the bond of commercial and friendly intercourse. Under the government of the state, this city, the metropolis of America, holds proud place, justly deserved through commanding pre-eminence in all the arts of peace. Rather than indulge glowing fancies of what shall be the future grandeur of the state and city, let us go forward with unflagging zeal, with lofty enthusiasm born of certain prominence of triumph, with undying courage, with unconquerable faith in the magnificent achievements yet to gladden the hearts and lives of the generations to follow. Let us consecrate ourselves anew to the work in our hands to do now for the city and the state we are proud to call our own. Their past history is safely written in honor. Their present position is superb and strong. Their future will be determined largely by what we of to-day do for their upbuilding and beautifying. The schools of the city and the state of New York are the realization of past labors and successes; they are the prophecies of grander success in the future.

If we teach our children to love the flag that floats over us to-day; to do their duty as American citizens; to be men and women worthy to inherit the privileges and blessings won by the courage and sacrifices of our ancestors, then those far-off centuries will witness here, and throughout this grand commonwealth, a happy, prosperous, Christian people, living under a school system made strong and helpful by a loyal public sentiment, proud and glad as are we, to have a city like Greater New York, and a state worthily and conspicuously recognized as the Empire state.

Friday morning, July 2, 9 to 10 o'clock

Preliminary business

Music.—(a) Ave Maria....................................Abt.
(b) The Forest Home.....................Bendedict.
Chorus of girls from female department, Grammar School No. 68, Miss Charlotte Richardson, conductor.

Music.—(a) Prayer....................................Weber.
(b) Old Folks at Home........................Foster.
(c) Departure.............................Jul. Stern.
Chorus of boys from male department, grammar school Nos. 20 and 70, Dr. Philip H. Grunenthal, conductor

PHYSICAL CULTURE

M. AUGUSTA REQUA, M. D., PD. M.

To-day the laws that govern health are better understood than formerly. What we should do, what we should leave undone, we now declare with more certainty. We are more scientific, more systematic. Note the great strides that have been made in prophylaxis and therapeutics. Among physicians the great study of the day is how to prevent disease. All kinds of investigation; chemical and physical tests, microscopical study and exhaustive examination of cases from every conceivable standpoint are being made to discover how to render the individual immune from disease and to give and keep him in physical strength and vigor. Antisepsis has given place to asepsis. The physician is not alone in studying preventive measures, the sociologist and pedagogue, in their work for the bettering of the race, also find that prevention must enter into their calculations and methods. Oliver Wendell Holmes wrote: "Some people think if the doctor had been called in early enough the child's life might have been saved." "Yes" he says, "that is true, but soon enough was 200 years ago and physicians are not usually called in at that time." We of to-day are the "200 years ago" of the future generations. Let us profit by his advice and at once take measures to prevent future troubles.

Each child, even the youngest, is to be started in the right direction; we must at once institute our preventive measures, and at the same time carefully nurture and develop all that is best. The old saying "Train up a child in the way he should go and when he is old he will not depart from it," is entirely in keeping with our modern theories.

I trust that the time is coming when every student of medicine shall be thoroughly instructed in pedagogical, corrective, and medical gymnastics. Galen, the most eminent physician of the second century, remarkable for his learning, and accomplishments, and for more than 1,000 years an authority in medical matters, said "He is the best physician who is the best teacher in gymnastics."

After the physician comes the nurse, who should also, in connection with the regular training be well instructed in all such branches of physical culture as pertains to the child in his earliest years. The mother should be as carefully trained how to develop the highest physical possibilities of her child as in sewing, cooking, or any other department of home life.

After a child has finished his elementary education, which should consist of as definitely drawn lines in his physical as in his mental acquirements, he should then receive instruction from special teachers or experts. These experts should be college or high school graduates.

We now come to the consideration of the exercises themselves. It will aid us very much in choosing what kind of work to adopt if we can decide upon what we desire to accomplish. Here we find a remarkable unanimity of opinion among teachers of physical culture. All agree that we desire first of all health, then strength and lastly grace. The difficulty arises when we come to discuss the question, what physical exercises shall we use to bring about these desirable results. Perhaps we will be able to arrive more quickly at a unanimous decision if we can more definitely state some of the underlying essentials of health, strength and grace.

We all agree that these essentials are as follows:

1. A correct carriage of the body in sitting, standing and walking.

2. Respiration should be full, free and there should be a development in lung power.

4. The exercises should aid functional activity.
5. The exercises should aid mental development.
3. An harmonious muscular development.

It then remains for us to discover what system brings about most thoroughly these desired results. I unhesitatingly answer, the educational gymnastics of Ling. This decision is made first, upon the statement of Dr. Edward M. Hartwell, director of physical training in the public schools of Boston. He says: "I have no hesitation in saying that the Royal Central Gymnastic Institution in Stockholm, is the best school for training teachers of gymnastics in the world;" second, Dr. Alice T. Hall, of the Woman's College, Baltimore, says, "Then I went to Sweden, and the first thing that impressed me was the magnificent carriage of the men, women and children. They walked without music; they held themselves erect; their heads were well poised; their step was firm; they had, in a word, perfect control of themselves to an extent that I had never seen in any other country. I went to the schools. I saw the children exercising at their desks, with little apparatus. Their attention was something remarkable. Every eye was in the right place; they were not looking at their neighbors; their motions were perfect, and they were as interested as they possibly could be. Then and there I decided that the Swedish system was the one that could be used to the greatest advantage in America, until we had taken what was best in all, and made a system of our own. That is what I believe we are coming to." Third, my own observation. I have never seen equalled, in any gymnasium or class room, where other systems were used, the results obtained from the Swedish pedagogical gymnastics. We have then results that cannot be gainsaid. The Swedes have proved their claim; we do but lose time and argue ourselves ignorant of the facts, if we do not know what this system has done and is doing along the five essentials in physical culture. Therefore as these educational gymnastics have proved what they can do on these fundamental lines, they should be taken to form, at least, the basis of any plan of work in physical training. I have taken it as the basis of the work in the public schools of Manhattan borough.

With regard to military training; it is a specialization, a training as its name indicates, for a special work, and it is carried along special lines; it is not a system of physical training. It may be deemed advisable by some to give this special training; but at its best it is still special and cannot be substituted for all around physical development.

There should be a systematic arrangement of the physical exercises in lessons. Each one of these lessons may be called a "gymnastic day's order." We are acquainted with the Swedish day's order; but if you have followed my arguments and agree with them then it becomes necessary to adjust the distinctive exercises of other lines of work to the already existing groups in this day's order and in such a way that its value is not injured.

To-day I simply suggest a plan for your future consideration. Further thought, investigation and experience may modify the plan here proposed.

The proposed gymnastic day's order.

1. Introductory exercises:
   - Deportment.
   - Order movements.
   - Introductory movements.
   - Relaxing movements.

General:
2. Arch-flections.
3. Heaving movements.
4. Balance-movements.

Special:
5. Shoulderblade-movements.
6. Abdominal exercises.
7. Lateral trunk-movements.

General:
8. Slow leg-movements.
9. Leaping.
10. Aesthetic movements including deportment.
11. Voice building.
12. Respiratory exercises.

The progression of the new groups of exercises introduced should be as carefully planned as those already in the Swedish day's order.

I would advise erecting a gymnasium building, adjoining each large school. This building to be three stories high, and each story a gymnasium connected by a covered bridge with the corresponding story of the school. By such an arrangement, the extra going up and down stairs is avoided and children without loss of time pass to and from the gymnasium.

With regard to apparatus, what kinds shall we use? Just for a moment recall the actions of a class when it has been allowed a few minutes freedom in a gymnasium. What do we observe? That the children, as a rule, do not go for the light apparatus. No. They begin to jump, to vault, to climb. The so-called "heavy work" is the most attractive to them. This natural impulse is a good, a right one. Long before a child uses a dumbbell, wand or club, he should jump, run and climb. These exercises aid in his physical development, while dumbbell, wand or club may intensify his defects, increasing deformity, interfering with respiration, circulation and digestion. If a child cannot stand and sit correctly, because his muscles are not strong enough or educated enough to keep him in the correct postures, why put a weight into his hand which can only add to the difficulty.

But physical culture deals with more than systematic exercises. Games, out-door sports and athletics, also form a considerable part of the work. These latter, however, should all be conducted according to gymnastic principles, and the children not excused from taking part in them, with the exception of athletics, unless for good and valid reasons.

With regard to athletics in preparatory or secondary schools, I heartily approve of them if wisely conducted. One of the governing principles should be that no child puts forth his maximum effort; but always is stopped at the safe point, his optimum, which is always less than his maximum.

The gymnastic dress also claims attention. Each child, girl or boy, should have an appropriate gymnastic costume. The present style of dress enables one, with a little management, to easily change from the dress of the class room to that of the gymnasium. The amount of time that should be given to physical culture, is, in my estimation, at least one-half hour daily. This amount of time should be divided into two periods, one of about ten minutes in the forenoon, to games and sports; and one of about twenty minutes in the afternoon, to systematic work.

Goethe has well summed up the aim of culture in the following words:

" Self-culture aims at perfection and is the highest fulfillment of the law of God. It means perfect symmetrical development of all our powers of body, mind and spirit."

DISCUSSION

Dr. Henry Ling Taylor, of New York, said, that the aim of physical training in the public schools was to aid in fitting the pupil to give and to receive the greatest benefit from the conditions and activities of life. In this it did not differ from the other branches of the curriculum, of which it should therefore form an integral and co-ordinate part. The effects of proper physical training were health, beauty, strength and stamina on the physical side; grace and dexterity through the correlated activity of the mental and physical; and certain definite results in the mental and moral sphere, among others cheerfulness, order and self-reliance, consideration for others and self-command. These results were to be obtained by trained and inspired teachers working according to hygienic, physiologic, pedagogic and common sense principles, but bound to no unyielding system.

Teachers of physical training should be able to guide the children mentally and morally as well as physically. We have so much of one side of the shield, the aim to build up health and strength, that we sometimes forget that physical training has another mission.

I thoroughly agree with Dr. Requa in favoring an eclectic system of gymnastics, using the best from each method. I believe the Swedish system should be used as a basis. Instead of executing a series of movements, learned by rote, requiring only the mental faculty of memory, Swedish gymnastics are executed to word of command, one movement following another in unexpected succession, or unexpected combination, demanding strict attention from the pupil. I think all teachers realize that anything is valuable that will increase the power of *attention*.

The will stands guard over muscle and nerve. The motor nerves telegraph the muscles needed; they instantly respond, and the result is a quick, vigorous movement. The muscles cannot act except through the medium of the motor nerves, and in the same way that the muscles, by exercise, keep their tone and strength, so does the function of the motor nerves remain intact through physical exercise.

Discipline, like another Minerva, leaps full armed from the head of physical training, and true discipline is also a mental training. I think it was United States Commissioner of Education, William T. Harris, who said—"From cradle to grave, humanity must always obey some power,— parent; school; city and nation. When the child realizes this, he learns to render obedience because it is right, not because it is demanded by brute force: He realizes his life's lesson that discipline means liberty to each individual."

Anything that makes a human being symmetrical and graceful builds up pride and manliness. Anything that destroys self-consciousness tends toward sincerity and self-control. Systematic, thorough physical training will beautify the human form, and it will do away with self-consciousness.

A delight in schoolroom gymnastics lays the foundation for an interest in games, athletic sports and outdoor occupations.

Ada F. Thayer.—The hardest work should come in the morning when pupils are fresh. The studies should be arranged in order of decreasing difficulty, the lighest work coming in the afternoon. It is wise to place the two subjects requiring greatest mental effort from 9 to 10 a. m., physical training following from 10 to 10.15, succeeded by singing or reading.

After intense mental effort the blood moves slowly through the brain, circulation is decreased by sitting position, and a heavy, tired feeling is the result. Gymnastic drill increases the respiration and circulation; clears the brain, jogs the motor nerves; revives the will power, and puts the child in a better condition to resume mental effort.

Last of all, art is under a debt of gratitude to the Greek gymnastic life for the purest specimens of, beauty in the human form, known to man. A beautiful human form, created by generations of physical training was an inspiration to the artist, who re-endowed the marble representation with an emotion. This combination became an inspiration to the gymnast of succeeding ages for the development of soul life within the body life. "The Greek artist represented the noblest human type,—giving his ideal conception of a human attribute. Jupiter, lord of Heaven, became the embodiment of the strength of will."

Physical training through its various phases so frees and limbers the body from stiffness that it becomes flexible and willing to translate the soul life. This is physical training in its highest sense. This is the aim of the Delsarte gymnastics, and as it appeals to the maturer faculties of the mind, it should come as the last step in our educational gymnastic ladder.

Music.—(a) The Chimes........................Mendelssohn.
(b) Lift Thine Eyes....................Mendelssohn.

Chorus of girls from female department, grammar school No. 50. Miss Teresa J. Pearson, conductor.

FRIDAY EVENING, JULY 2, 8 O'CLOCK

Joint session of the New York State Teachers' Association and the New York State Art Teachers' Association, Mr. W. S. Goodnough, President of Art Teachers' Association, presiding.

Song.—The Holy City...............................Adams.
Mrs. Nina Norman Adams.

Address.—Art in its Relation to Practical Life.—
William Ordway Partridge, Esq.

Song.—The Three Wishes..........................Pinsuti.
Miss Teresa J. Pearson.

THE TRIUMPHS OF THE TEACHER

JOHN P. CONROY, M. D.,

Instructor G. S. No. 83, New York City.

In a government like the United States, where the enactment of laws and the direction of public affairs are in the hands of the people, where no class nor caste controls the reins of legislation or administration, where from the lowest stratum of our society may come those to whom shall be entrusted the destines of our country, the necessity of a high morality and a broad intelligence among the people is manifest—if our republicanism is to be preserved, and the heritage handed down to us by our ancestors is to be enjoyed by our posterity.

Now, among the institutions to which we must look for the development of the moral tone and the intelligence of the people, so essential to the stability of society in general, but particularly so under our form of government, and for the settlement of questions now or to come before the people for decision, the solution of which may involve our very existence, there is none more important than the teacher and the school.

Though the population of New York city, according to the census of 1890, was nearly one-half foreign born, the children of our schools, many, if not most, of whom have homes in which must be felt the impressions of foreign rule, quit the schools with as great a love for and as intelligent a knowledge of our institutions, as great a loyalty to our flag, and all that it embodies, as the lineal descendant of the fathers. And what has been accomplished so well here, has been equally as well done elsewhere, wherever the teacher and the school have been properly provided. The immigrant is alien, but his child is American, and to the teacher is due the change. Well has it been said that the teacher has made the children of the Saxon and the Norman, the Celt and the Teuton—Americans, types of the moral, intelligent, and independently-acting man. Surely this is a triumph of which our teachers may indeed be proud.

The present conditions, under which this noble work of training is carried on, are not the growth of a day, but the outcome of an evolution, extending over the past fifty years, beginning with the growth of cities, as Dr. Harris has pointed out, and continuing as they grow. In the first half century the teacher and the school were of a poor quality. The schools of that period possessed few of the marks that distinguish those of the present. Scattered throughout the country, ungraded, with scant facilities for instruction, supported by a policy of niggardly appropriations—some remains of which still persist, like the appendix vermiformis of man in *his* evolution, and with like disastrous possibilities—with little or no intelligent supervision, the sessions very short, discipline maintained by fear of the rod, the teachers poorly paid, the school occupied no such place in our scheme of government as it does to-day. And the teacher was in keeping with the school. He took up teaching as a makeshift, spending the intervals of school-keeping in some other business upon which he depended chiefly for his support. Without general culture, or special training for his work, he lacked a knowledge of the principles and the methods of teaching. His place in the community was determined, not by his teaching, but by his work in other lines. And if, perchance, he had no other calling, he held an anomalous position in society, without the respect given to the professional man or the man of trade.

But a change came with time. Like a prophet who looks into the future, and anticipates the conditions that would obtain in the progress of his country, and noting the necessity of a change in the school and the teacher of his time, if the future of the republic was to be assured under the new conditions, and animated with the belief, as a part of the divine plan, that every child had a right by virtue of birth alone, to the proper development of his faculties, and that opportunity for such development should be provided by the state, a teacher, an educational statesman, as he has been called, arose in the person of Horace Mann. With tongue and with pen he exposed the weakness of the existing system, and roused the educational forces of America to the need of improvement. With unfailing enthusiasm and untiring energy, he brought the subject of education home to every citizen, and compelled attention to the lamentable condition of affairs. To him every believer in republican government owes a lasting debt of gratitude.

Nor was he iconoclast merely, for he pointed out the lines along which advance should be made, and out of the clash with conservatism which his attacks evoked, aided by the progressive spirit of our people, just then beginning to show itself, and which has resulted in such immense material improvement, began that evolution of the school and the teacher which has continued to the present, the forces of which are now so active, and the best results of which are seen in the great centres of population.

The teacher has risen from the place of a mere craftsman to the rank of a professional man. By study, observation, and discussion in societies or associations for the promotion of educational interests, of which the one now sitting in convention is an example (New York State Teachers' Association), and in a press of his own—an outgrowth of his evolution, the teacher of to-day prepares himself to meet every problem presented in the complex phenomena of the growing child.

By such means has the teacher triumphed, and carved out for himself a place in the community by the side of the physician and the lawyer. Such has been the progress of both teacher and school that to-day no single institution in our country has such reverence and hearty support as the public school; none of which Americans are so justly and so deservedly proud.

The teacher's work is hard. Life is spent in contact with crude minds, at times with natures perverse by inheritance or by lack of proper home control, the direction of which makes calls upon physical and mental energy unknown in other professions. The workers in other lines are under a less constant strain, have brighter prospects, are better appreciated, have less false standards to be judged by, are less subject to personal indignity, and if the state would maintain the high standard set up, and have the schools partake of the general intellectual advance, it must assure the teacher of reward equal to that offered to similar attainments in other directions. Otherwise, teaching on its present high plane will be followed, not as a vocation, but as a makeshift, and it is the duty of those having direction of affairs to see to it that such reward is offered.

America.—Sung by audience.

SATURDAY MORNING, JULY 3, 10 O'CLOCK

Committee on Resolutions

By the members of the New York State Teachers' Association assembled in Greater New York for their fifty-second annual conference, it is hereby

Resolved, First, That the most appreciative thanks of the association are due to President White and his executive associates for the months of steady and silent work which have made this present gathering possible and actual;

Second, That we deem it fortunate that in this mighty company the idea of section work has prevailed; that we deem it wise that morning and evening sessions only have been held and summer afternoons been free for rest or recreation;

Third, That in the kindergarten section, under the able leadership of Inspector Hughes, of Toronto, the crowns of scholarship and loving regard were laid at the feet of childhood for the enriching and glorifying of their young lives;

Fourth, That the primary section, in the skillful hands of Miss Anna K. Eggleston, has shown very clearly the limitless possibilities of the rising generation in respect to things educationally interesting and profitable;

Fifth, That the grammar school section, James M. Edsell, chairman, has demonstrated the truth of the dawning of new and plastic powers in this formative period of youth;

Sixth, That we commend the high school congress of the association, Principal Wickes, chairman, for an earnest endeavor to strengthen the bond between the association and the secondary schools of the state, for the presentation of a program aiming at the elucidation of certain cardinal doctrines of all true education; and we regret that a mid-day excursion summarily barred the congress from a delightful sail among the channels of thought under convoy of President Raymond and Professor McAndrews;

Seventh, That the normal school section, at whose head was Dr. Cheney, of Cortland, must remain as now it is, a great and steadfast reliance of the state in its efforts to furnish the boys and girls an education pedagogically sound and intellectually strong;

Eighth, That the child-study section, whose presiding officer was Superintendent Griffith, of Utica, merits our warm regard for its keen and constant study into the deep things of the child nature—and receives our congratulations upon the forming of an association for the further exploration of that vast realm of life;

Ninth, That we recognize in the scheme of the manual training section, Dr. Haney, chairman, the continued shaping into ever greater symmetry of a course of study and work designed to give to boys and girls a lasting grip upon many practical things of life;

Tenth, That the nature-study department, Gustave Straubenmuller, chairman, is to be commended upon its attempt to call back our thoughts to nature—mother of us all—and to enlist the service of the young in studying out her delightful secrets;

Eleventh, That we bow to music, Dr. Schauffler, chairman, in recognition of its claims upon our gratitude and regard—for it is the lightener of the cares of the teacher and the doubler of the joys of the child;

Twelfth, That the department of elocution, Richard E. Mayne, chairman, believes in the getting away from the "strutting and bellowing" which Shakespeare condemned, to the using "all gently," to the suiting of "word to action" and "action to word," which the great master of expression so commended;

Thirteenth, That the Herbartian section, Dr. McMurry, chairman, handling such philosophical themes as "the imagination" and "creative power," furnishes that nice counter-balance for the practical, so much needed in our self-absorbed age and land;

Fourteenth, That, as members of the general association, we cordially welcome the State Art Teachers' Association, Walter S. Goodenough, president, to a share in our deliberations, and thank them for the impulse given toward the cultivation of the aesthetic and the beautiful in the nature of youth;

Fifteenth, That the thanks of this association are due to the local committee of arrangements, Edward A. Page, chairman, for the ample provisions made for this meeting, for exhibition drills, gymnastics, and music, vocal and orchestral, performed by pupils of the public schools. The great work entailed by the exhibits, under the direction of Dr. James Lee, deserves our gratitude, as do also the committee on entertainment, who generously provided an excursion for visiting teachers free of charge; and Principal Davis, a whole committee in himself; the committee on printing and the press, especially each and every newspaper of New York city, Brooklyn and of other cities, which have given valuable space for our proceedings, share in our gratitude;

Sixteenth, That while regretting the absence of Mayor William L. Strong, from the initial exercises, we extend special thanks to Superintendent Jasper, to President Charles B. Hubbell, and Hon. Gilbert H. Crawford, for the cordial welcome to the metropolis accorded the association. We commend the fitting response made by the president in the name of the association.

Seventeenth, That we tender our sincere and heartfelt thanks to the board of education of the city of New York for its generosity in assigning the normal college for the purpose of holding our fifty-second annual convention, for its courtesy in authorizing the exhibit of the work of the schools under its jurisdiction, and for closing the schools during sessions of this convention; that the executive committee of the normal college and the committee on supplies of the same board are particularly deserving of the thanks of this association for offering every facility to make this convention a success; that we tender our thanks to President Hunter of the normal college for his courtesy in extending every facility to the officers of this convention; that the thanks of this convention be extended to Chief Bonner of the fire department, to Captain Grant of the police department, and to the officers under them for their efforts looking to our comfort and security during this convention; that the persons named in these resolutions be furnished with copies signed by the general secretary and countersigned by the president of the association;

Eighteenth, That we congratulate the state association on its full entrance into the second half-century of its existence, and upon the inspiring presence and work of the State Superintendent of Public Instruction, Hon. Charles R. Skinner—to whom we, as teachers of the Empire state, are much beholden for many deeds helpful in the strengthening of the true life of education;

Nineteenth, That we heartily thank Mr. Ordway Partridge for dropping his chisel, and Charles Dudley Warner for laying aside his pen to speak to us on high themes of art and life; they speak with authority—we listen with profitable pleasure; we commend their spirit of helpfulness to others—for all life is education, and we would fain have all education to be life.

Respectfully submitted by the committee on resolutions,

PRIN. W. K. WICKES, Chairman,
SUPT. J. G. RIGGS,
PRIN. JOHN G. ALLEN,
DR. JAMES LEE,
PRIN. SCHUYLER F. HERRON.

INTRODUCTION OF OFFICERS, 1896-1897

President, Dr. James Lee, assistant superintendent, New York; vice-presidents, Wm. J. O'Shea, New York; Arthur E. Goodrich, Utica; Mary E. Tate, New York; Mary E. Laing, Oswego; secretary, Schuyler F. Herron, Elizabethtown; assistant secretary, William F. O'Callaghan, 54 East Ninety-eighth street, New York; treasurer, S. McKee Smith, Chatham; assistant treasurer, Abram Fischlowitz, grammar school No. 40, New York; transportation agent, Arthur Cooper, 100 Washington Square, New York; superintendent of exhibits, E. C. Colby, Rochester; executive committee, Charles E. White, chairman ex officio. Terms expire 1897, Charles N. Cobb, Albany; George Griffith, Utica; terms expire 1898, John H. Haaren, Brooklyn; George H. Walden, grammar school No. 10, Rochester; terms expire, 1899, Walter B. Gunnison, Erasmus Hall Academy, Brooklyn; John T. Nicholson, St. Nicholas avenue and One Hundred and Seventeenth street, New York.

Address of Dr. James Lee, assistant superintendent of schools, New York city, newly elected president of the New York state teachers' association.

Fellow teachers of the New York state teachers' association.—I am deeply grateful for the honor you have conferred upon me in electing me your president for the ensuing year. I am not unmindful of the responsibilities attached to the position, especially when I consider the possibilities of a body of teachers such as we have seen in this our fifty-second annual convention. I can assure you, however, that I shall make every effort to advance the interests of this great and important organization. Whatever may have been its membership and its influence in the past, I am certain it never possessed a more enthusiastic and united membership than the enrollment shows to-day. Let me congratulate you on the magnificent showing of 7,000 active members present at this convention. This means much, I hope, for the profession in our glorious Empire state. We at this end of the state extend to you from less populous sections the right hand of fellowship. We trust that you feel that everything has been done to make this a successful meeting and that the promises made at Rochester a year ago have been made good.

The number of teachers of every grade and standing in our state and the individual interests represented naturally give rise to a number of organizations. I make a plea to-day for a union of all these educational forces. We are all engaged in training the youth of the state, and each part of the machinery employed in this work is essential to success. A union of the forces employed in every grade of school, from the kindergarten to the university, "the roots, the trunk and the bloom and fruit," as president White, our new ambassador to Germany, puts it, must insure to the general benefit of all concerned. There is no reason why we should not take the initiative in forming one grand state organization. There are many teachers here to-day who are aware of my sentiments concerning the solidifying of all such organizations into one great body. A glance at the grand program of this meeting with a thought of the success of the various meetings held by the art teachers' association, the sections devoted to normal, grammar, and primary work, nature study, child study, Herbart, kindergarten, manual training, music and elocution will convince any one interested that a union of all the educational organizations of the state is entirely feasible, and a grand annual gathering the most impressive manner of emphasizing the existence of such an organization. I take no credit for originality in expressing this view. I place it before you because of the great numbers present at this meeting, because I know many are anvious to see the consummation of such a project, and because I believe the present time ripe for concerted action among the teachers of the state. Besides the many benefits to be derived from a pedagogic standpoint there is much that we could obtain by unity of action through legislation looking to the benefit of the schools and of the teachers. The passage of laws looking towards a uniform pension law, providing tenure of position during good behavior, the proper licensing and retirement of teachers, and the enlargement of the use of libraries for pupils are among the many matters which vitally interest us as teachers.

The teachers of this populous section of the state and those from up the state have, I hope, through this grand convention learned to think better of each other. Gatherings of this nature and the exhibit of our every day work in our classes tend in a marked degree to help the social side of our nature. We are enabled to compare notes, talk over our difficulties, show each other how many features of our work may be made less irksome, gain enthusiasm and encouragement such as can only come by coming in contact with great numbers interested in the same line of work, and generally by such contact with others broaden our views of life and our work. Thus we get away from the monotonous routine, the disagreeable ruts, and the narrow methods into which we as teachers are liable to fall.

Hence I trust that all who have attended this convention will be with us at Rochester next year. To the teachers in the Metropolitan district I earnestly appeal to return the compliment of the effort of the teachers up the state who have come here to help make this convention a success. Let us make our next meeting as great a gathering as this. It will advance the teachers' cause.

In conclusion I ask the co-operation of the seven thousand teachers now members of this association to further its interests in every possible way. Its interests are yours. Induce every teacher who is not now a member to join. Make it the representative body of teachers as a state organization. With the pleasant prospect of meeting you all at Rochester next year, I again thank you for the honor you have conferred upon me, and now await your further pleasure.

MUSIC SECTION

A. T. SCHAUFFLER, *Chairman.* ELIZABETH E. BLAIR, *Secretary.*

THE CHILD VOICE IN SINGING AND SPEAKING

EMILE C. CURTIS

JULY 1, 1897

Let us omit all scientific description of vocal physiology, and follow the example of the tradesman, who places over his door the sign "Practical hatter," a most delightfully suggestive sign, for one's imagination is immediately aroused to wonder what a theoretical hatter may be. A man cares little on what scientific principles his hat has been formed; but he does care to buy a hat which will produce a good effect when he wears it. Let us consider the voice from the same standpoint—not from its scientific beginning, but from the end, the end that reaches our ears—that is, the result. This is why I ask you first of all to listen and be critical. All the science in the world will not enable you to improve the voices of your pupils, unless your ear can distinguish between a tone quality which is pleasant to hear and one which is the reverse—between a smooth, clear tone and a rough, rasping one. (This was illustrated.) What is the cause of the difference between these two qualities?

The tones of the voice are produced by the vibrations of the vocal cords—two little, delicate bands or edges of membrane which are held in position by the framework of the throat. Cut a slit in the center of a piece of paper; hold this paper in a horizontal position and run your finger up through the slit; imagine the finger to be the column of air passing from the windpipe up into the throat between the vocal cords; as it passes them, their elasticity causes them to vibrate and to communicate their vibration to the column of air above them. We have three factors to consider: (1) The breath, or the column of air which, when caused to vibrate, becomes the tone which is heard; (2) the vocal bands, which cause the vibration, and (3) the surroundings of all this—the walls of the throat—the case which holds it all. Do all these factors require equal consideration, or, if not, which one should be chiefly considered? Without doubt, the last is the only one which gives us much trouble. I do not say that it makes no difference how we breathe; I do not say that the condition of the vocal cords themselves is of no consequence; but I do say that if we give our first and chief attention to the walls of the throat the rest will almost take care of itself. Stretch your hand open so that the palm forms a smooth, concave surface. Let this represent the upper part of the throat, and consider how this surface may act like the sounding board over a pulpit, to reinforce the tone already generated and throw it forward through the mouth into the air. Now draw the fingers together and contract and break into ridges the surface of the palm. When the walls of the throat are contracted in this way the roughness of the surface breaks up the tone—it is not thrown out as a round, full, smooth tone, but some of its overtones are rendered too prominent and it reaches the ear of the listener as a rough, unpleasant, shrill sound. This is all the science that we need to know. We hear a smooth, round tone. How is it made, or, rather, shaped? By a smooth, round throat, that holds itself back from the tone, and gives it plenty of room. We hear a rough, rasping tone, which seems covered all over with ridges and prickles. How is this shaped? By the speaker contracting the throat and squeezing the tone all out of shape. I sometimes hear tones in which I can distinctly detect a shrill, screeching overtone three octaves above the foundation tone, and they are far from agreeable.

Do you know how many persons speak and sing with rough voices, and how easy it is to change this quality? Simply open the mouth wide, and then sing as low down in the throat as possible, with the throat stretched open as in yawning. The effort to sing low in the throat is important, for if this effort be not made, the larynx, which holds the vocal cords, is apt to rise on the high tones, and thus lessen the space in the throat. I generally point to the upper part of the throat and say: "Do not sing up there or up in the nose, but sing way down low in the throat, in a hollow voice. Keep the throat away from the voice. Sing with the voice itself, not with the throat." If the throat has become rigid and will not readily expand, the best thing to do is to use more breath than is necessary. Just as blowing into a toy balloon expands it, so puffing the air rapidly through the throat makes this expand and grow more elastic. That is to say, more breath should be used than can be converted into tone; some of it should pass the vocal cords unused, and the result should be a breath-y, whisper-like tone. This is my first principle: Sing low in the throat, with a great deal of extra breath.

My second principle is this: Train all voices from the top down. At the lower end of the voice is the chest, or thick register, and if singers, especially children, sing chiefly from the lower end up, they are very apt to carry the chest quality too high. Moreover, it is much harder to keep the throat in an open, smooth condition in singing up than in singing down. If, therefore, you will simply reverse the old order of things and always sing scales downward, you will find that there is no necessity for knowing or thinking about registers at all. Even the boy who has forced his chest register up to "D" and been unable to reach high tones at all, will soon have a smooth, even quality throughout the voice, with no break at all.

Another thing that you will discover, if you train voices downward is the indisputable fact, too long ignored, that children have high voices and can sing high much more easily and safely than they can sing low. The average child's voice has one or two more high tones than the woman's and one or two fewer low tones; while all the low tones are naturally weak and the high ones are the strongest.

Where the throat has been greatly contracted and the voice forced, the low tones often appear the strongest, and sometimes there seem to be no high tones at all. But this is not as nature intended, and the wisest thing that we can do is to work with nature and not against her. Children ought to sing plenty of songs and exercises that run as high as "G" above the staff, and no sight singing-books should begin as low as middle "C." In part songs for children, the second part should be a second soprano rather than an alto.

SECOND MEETING.—FRIDAY, JULY 2

The meeting was called to order at [illegible] by the chairman who introduced as the principal speaker, Mr. F. E. Howard, director of music in the schools of Bridgeport, Conn., and chairman of the music section of the National Education Association.

SCHOOL MUSIC AS VIEWED BY THE TEACHER AND AS VIEWED BY THE MUSICIAN

F. E. HOWARD

To one who observes the course of events in educational matters there is something very significant in the rapid introduction of vocal music as a regular study into the schools of our country. It has been added to the course of study in at least one thousand cities and towns during the last decade.

It seems to me that music has been introduced into our schools through the efforts of the teaching profession itself, who were the first to perceive its value as an educational factor. A little deeper analysis will disclose that in the public mind there is an undercurrent of thought that the public school should not only give to the pupil that knowledge and training which will enable him to cope with others in the business and social world, but should also inculcate moral principles and love of country. More than that, the child should be taught to see and to love the beautiful. That man or woman is no less intellectual who is alive to the forms and coloring of nature, and whose eyes are open to the beauties of art in any form which the genius or industry of man has given it, and, with all the materialistic tendencies and cool practicality of the American people, there is still an appreciation of the artistic side of life among us which exhibits itself a little hesitantly yet, but is more in evidence every year.

The average citizen and parent does not expect the musical knowledge his child obtains at school is going to aid his earning capacity. He is rather inclined to say that it is a good thing and let it go at that. At any rate, vocal music is in the schools, and there is a deep-seated conviction among all classes concerned that it ought to be there. There is an instinctive feeling that music is an influence for good, that it makes school life more cheerful and awakens sensibilities that, as they grow stronger, tend to good associations and happy upright lives. However, it is not my purpose to dwell upon the ideal in school music. The dream of the enthusiast, in which he hears only the sweetest of songs from childish throats, and where, in all school singing, the children are under the influence of emotion as powerful as his own, be it love of country, of home, or rejoicing with the birds, the trees and the flowers, that dream is as yet only a dim prophecy. I am not sure, even, that some of the rhapsodies which fervid souls outpour, wherein little children are supposed to be emotionally fevered whenever they sing of home, love, or country, are not a barren waste of words. The emotional gamut of the child is scarcely greater than that of the adult, and morbid sensibility is in the case of neither a necessary condition of musical performance.

Can teachers be expected to apply the same tests to the singing in the school room as would the average musician? How can you expect such a thing—I imagine some teacher saying—when I know nothing of music? But knowledge is not what you require in this case. It is taste rather, or say the exercise of common sense in music. Every one can distinguish between harsh tone and smooth tone, between loudness and softness in voice, and can tell whether a song is sung with a good rhythmical swing or not.

But why spend so many words to prove what you all know? Because I wish to emphasize very strongly the thought that responsibility for the musical or unmusical character of school singing rests upon principals and teachers as much as upon the special instructor or supervisor, and because, while everybody knows that bad singing is wholly undesirable, yet such is the force of long practice, and the conservatism of bad habits, that it is difficult to excite interest in this question among those concerned.

It is just as easy to teach children to use their voices properly in singing as it is to teach them to do otherwise. It is far easier, even, for then all the parts concerned are discharging their functions in a normal manner. In short it is emphatically true that the singing of children in the school room can be, though the music be simple to a degree, so beautiful and satisfying that fastidious musicians will listen with pleasure.

It was Mark Twain, I believe, who classified singers as those who sing by note, those who sing by rote, and those who sing by main strength. Well, there are instructors who, in the schoolroom combine these divisions, who teach children to sing by note, by rote, and always by main strength. I have encountered the same sentiment among church people, with reference to the singing of choir-boys, and am personally cognizant of a case in which a choir-trainer was forced to resign because he would permit his soprano boys to use the head tone only. This incident, however, occurred several years ago, and before surpliced choirs were general, or the principles of voice-training as applied to boys' voices were so well understood as they are at present. This sentiment in favor of loud, hearty singing is singularly strong; and, in spite of the fact that I have combated it for some time, it interests me very much. Does it spring from the idea that when a child is making noise he is happy, and the more noise, the greater joy? It is quite easy, of course, to understand the position of those who speak of singing as a useful exercise from the hygienic standpoint; as they say, it strengthens the lungs, promotes digestion, quickens the circulation, etc. These philosophers who rank school singing as a physical exercise are strictly logical in demanding loudness and vigor. It is very odd, though, that people who know good singing when they hear it, and who, keenly sensitive to niceties of tonal shading of voice or instrument at concerts, at church, or at home, who would never dream of measuring the intensity of the singer's emotion by the mere loudness of his tone, are so illogical in their views, or absence of views, about the singing of children.

But whether people like to hear children shout their songs because they themselves love to hear it, or because they suppose the children love to do it, or because they know no better, the fact stands out with startling clearness that until the teaching force in our schools unite with, and support supervisors in their efforts to supplant school shouting with a good singing tone, the character of school music, except in a town here and there, will remain unchanged. Again let me assert that good singing is as easily secured as that which is not good. It is possible for every teacher in the land who is not tone deaf to determine the character of the tone her classes shall use, and to learn how children should use their voices in singing. If principals and teachers will use the same care and taste, and apply the same critical faculty to music work that they do to other school work, the singing will become satisfactory from the musical as well as from the educational standpoint.

Mr. Schauffler nominated Mr. Frederick A. Lyman, of Syracuse, for chairman of the music section at the next year's convention. The nomination was seconded and Mr. Lyman was unanimously elected.

DEPARTMENT OF KINDERGARTEN

Inspector JAMES L. HUGHES, Toronto, Chairman
Miss JENNY B. MERRILL, New York, Secretary

MOTHERS' MEETINGS

BY MRS. C. E. MELENEY

One great beauty of normal kindergarten training is that it fits young women for their womanly duties as mothers, teachers, helpers. Mrs. Theo. Burney, president of the mothers congress held at Washington, said in her opening address—that all higher education should be secondary to that which shall fit young women to know the needs of childhood and thus be ready with head and heart and hand to serve the cause of helpless infancy in any emergency. The least experienced of us know how too often the young mother stands helpless before her growing child and longs for the power to lead her little one aright. Froebel understood so well this longing of motherhood and gave to the mother the keyenote of hapiness with her child, the conscious unfolding of its nature.

This yearning of motherhood to know and to be able to deal intelligently with her children has helped to create the wide spread interest in child-culture. There has been a tendency everywhere for mothers to meet together. Clubs have been formed for the study of different phases of child-life. To the investigations of the scientists in the schools, mothers are contributing their observations of the children in the home, they are seeking to bring the home life of the child into harmony with school-life—and are asking that the school life may be the enlargement of the ideal home where the spirit of the teacher is the true mother spirit and the child develops according to the laws of natural growth.

It was a pleasant experience to me a short time ago to meet a company of women and talk with them about their home life and lead them to a better spirit in governing their children. They looked worn and weary beyond their years yet many a kindly face among them told of motherly affection. From these an occasional nod of approval encouraged my effort. A kind-hearted physician preceded me with practical talks on the value of cleanliness, good ventilation, care in the preparation of food, lessons in infant feeding, etc. With this as a basis my task was more easily accomplished. Thoughts suggested in these meetings I bring to you in the hope that they may help any who are engaged in similar work. A little tact on the part of one dealing with hardworking women will help to gain their confidence. Once let them feel that you respect the hands that do honest labor, and know the burdens that they bear, and they will be ready to listen eagerly to the message that you bring. Early in the meeting, therefore, gain their confidence by familiar talks about home life, making prominent the child's great desire for love and sympathy. The kindergartener may make use of her gift as a story teller to aid her in this work. The lesson will be more forcibly taught if she selects two stories by which the thought is brought out in contrast.

Those of us who have been at the sea-shore in the autumn enjoyed watching the clouds that hung heavy and dull, blending their soft colors with the ocean beneath them. There is beauty everywhere for eyes that see. In selecting a story for the mothers, I took the short chapter entitled "choice of colors" from Helen Hunt's "bits of talks about home matters." She pictures a poor young girl standing at a shop window choosing the bright colors so dear to the child heart, and in her happiness she murmurs, "I choose that color, and I choose that color, and I choose that color," as though they were her own. She says in closing, "To be without is not always to lack, to reach is not to attain, sunlight is for all eyes that look up, and color for those who choose." Tell the mother how she may watch for and encourage this love of beauty in her children; by making the bright ball for the baby; allowing the little ones to seek and find the bright spots in the room; showing them how they may add brightness here and there to make the home more attractive. Let them think what the earth would be without color. We should not want to stay, our eyes would tire of the dullness, and yet we could not bear it if the earth were more brilliant than it is. After the brightness and beauty of the summer we are rested by the dull and sombre colors of the fall and winter. In the summer we have the warmer colors, red and yellow; in the winter blue and grey and purple are in the landscape. But the children will say "where do the colors come from?" and the mothers must be ready to answer their question, and tell them how the sun gives light, and color and beauty. How the children rejoice in the sunlight; how the baby hands reach out and try to grasp the shine and shadow. Show the mother how she may take a mirror and cause the sunlight to reflect upon the wall, moving the glass gently the shadow will flit back and forth delighting the baby heart. Little hands will reach out and try to catch the dancing light as it flits about the room. Show the mother how she may take a prism and letting a sunbeam fall upon it, have the light broken up into all the beautiful colors. The older children will call it a rainbow, and will be as pleased as the little brothers and sisters. During a talk of this kind the kindergartener may give to the mother hints on home decoration. Show how with a little thought a room may be made attractive at small expense. Try to have the mother catch the thought of harmony. As we look about us we see how beautifully God has made all things to harmonize. The delicate blue of the sky in summer harmonizes with the brighter colors that cover the earth. When the earth loses some of its brightness the sky becomes a deeper blue. In November we see the delicate hazy mist that covers the earth and we are happy that as good mother nature sinks to rest she is so beautiful. Then comes the winter with its pure white snow, full of lessons for the little ones. Show the mother how she too, may be filled with the spirit of the merry little dancing flakes. "Snow flake game." May the lesson of its purity come into our hearts and lives as we try to teach our children.

Practical lessons may be of great advantage on the value of putting children to bed early and leaving their rest undisturbed. The hours of rest are all too short for many a weary mother. The merry voices of the children are heard in the early morning hours. The activities of the day have begun, unless the mother is on the alert the day will not start aright. She must give the keynote to the family life.

What does the day bring for the children? "Life and activity," and if the activities are properly directed, power. Let the early morning hour be happy. A cheerful "good morning," a song of praise, a prayer for guidance, a word of greeting to each member of the family as they gather at the morning meal tend to make each one feel that he occupies an important place in the household. But these duties over, the children are ready for work. Urge the mothers to let the children help about the household duties; they learn by doing, and if the mother gladly receives the help of her children, even though the tasks are imperfectly done, she may be sure of future helpers when they have increased in power and strength.

The last topic that I shall outline this morning we will call "home joys." The winter is just the time to discuss home topics with the mothers. It is the time when family life is emphasized. The warmth of the fireside draws the members of the family nearer together. As the spring months come on topics from nature again suggest themselves to our minds. The wind, the rain, the birds, the flowers, all have messages to bring—but in the month of February while mother nature is still sleeping and the fireside is still warm, home joys shall be our subject with the mothers. I know of no better picture to bring as an ideal of contentment and happiness than the chapter from Pestalozzi's Leonard and Gertrude which shows the family ready for the day of rest. This I would bring to the mothers. It is a humble picture, yet how it brightens as we see Gertrude, her duties all performed, her house all in order, the children prepared in body and mind for the coming day. It is earnest, intelligent work that has accomplished this result, and the mother has called the children to her aid that each may feel that he has some part in making the home happy. From babyhood when the little child first shows his anxiety to help, Gertrude has given him work that he could call his own and he has been able to assume harder tasks as he has grown in years. How restful to the weary father is this home. He opens wide the door and as he hears the song, the words, "God bless you" are on his lips and tears are in his eyes. The mother fosters love for the father in her children; the father enobles the work and influence of the mother; the children's love for both complete the unity of the family.

Show how the hand represents this unity, the fingers its members. We may also show to mothers who come under our influence how the child may be led through this experience of unity in the home to realize that he is a part of the great family of earth and to understand in time the fatherhood and motherhood of God.

KINDERGARTEN METHODS IN THE PRIMARY SCHOOL

MARY H. WATERMAN

In the kindergarten, nearly the whole range of possible experiences and relationship has been given the child in a vague and general way. Centers of interest have been formed, the whole gamut of feeling has been aroused, budding points for future study have been given and the germs of impulse to all future education aroused. The first like the faint impressions on wax; the primary and following advanced grades repeat and deepen those impressions. What was seemingly forgotten responds to the magnetism of allied subjects and the pupil craves a broader view of relationships in a higher plane. These vital centers constantly return in seasons, national festivals and anniversaries in which childhood joins humanity in community of interest and participates in the world-spirit.

As in the kindergarten, so the child in the primary may have objects which he can observe and compare to find resemblances or detect differences. I saw a little boy on the street cars returning from the park or woods with a handful of flowers; he selected two and showed his father the differences in their stems, arrangement of leaves, and flowers; I knew at once that he had been to the kindergarten; it was done in a perfectly spontaneous, unconscious way; he had formed a habit of so doing and carried it into practice everywhere.

In kindergarten, while the knowledge of the particular object may be forgotten, the power developed remains and is there if the primary teacher will recognize it and build upon it. The kindergarten has trained the child to classification, illustration, generalization, forming of judgment, and the exercise of his reasoning powers.

In kindergarten and home the child has opportunity for making the internal, external, for taking in impressions of external objects, his mind is filled with such concepts and he longs to see them put in a form where he can recognize them without the object being present. He now comes to the school; he has reached the time for instruction. Froebel characterizes this period as one in which the child makes the external internal. He realizes that he must work industriously to acquire what he longs for—so we get the beginning of conscious work. The kindergarten lays stress upon the development of the child giving him training; the school places emphasis upon the subject and its relations. The intermediate school must form the transition. Gradually objects are withdrawn and mental images and concepts replace them. The pupil goes from the thing to its representation; so signs, which stand for these concepts and ideas are longed for and mastered by him—figures, letters and words—and in the period of school he is ready to recognize them as representing these correspondencies in his experience and to benefit by the store of knowledge others have gathered for him.

As in kindergartens the room and environment are considered as having a powerful effect on development. So in the primary the temporary illustrative material may gradually be withdrawn and replaced by permanent, artistic pictures. People who love the beautiful and look for the development of the true from the beautiful, are uniting to procure and place works of art where they may do their elevating and ennobling work. Patriotic sons and daughters of the revolution are combining with them to furnish flags and pictures that shall augment the patriotic spirit roused in the kindergarten. We educate by ideals, and should place them not at too remote a distance to discourage and defeat aspiration, but must steadily advance with each step gained toward the "mighty ideal which is never overtaken." And it is of many kinds: Ideals of politeness, helpfulness, punctuality, obedience, industry and altruism, in practical living. The ideal must help to perform the daily duty or it is worthless.

To develop self-activity is the aim of Froebel. The child is led through contact with the world of objects to abstract qualities belonging to all material things. He would not make it the aim to store the mind with the knowledge of such qualities and attributes, but would have such analyses followed by a new synthesis of abstracted qualities—an invention, a reproduction, bearing the stamp of his individuality, his God-like power to create, and revealing himself to himself as one akin to artist, poet, sculptor, musician, a creator of things, of his own character.

Will not this training, furnished by the wise teacher following the exercise of receptive and reflective powers, develop a character of executive ability who can carry plans into action and see his ideals realized in external form, his knowing and his doing one? Nor must these three powers be separated and rele-

[illegible] in different ages and stages of development they must be [illegible] at every age and assist the individual to realize his highest [illegible] at each stage.

A visit was made to a primary room where there was earnest [illegible] for the new education. Each child had on his desk a jar of newly germinated [illegible] and told in turn what he saw of their growth and [illegible]. The teacher told the class that they might write about what they had seen. Without an exception each [illegible] "Mother Nature gives us food, clothing and shelter." There was not a deviation in form, even to the tiny [illegible] drawn at [illegible]. The old method was so unconsciously strong that the "stamping-moulding process" was holding its own against the developing method. The unity was that of uniformity, not a varied individual expression of the experience. How different was another room where each was allowed to tell "the story of eight." There were boxes of pebbles, shells, seeds, blocks, pictures, counters, all kinds of objects from which to choose. Each child made his choice with pleasure and alacrity, and the different combinations corresponded to the number of pupils. There was self-activity.

One vital principle of the kindergarten is to give the child opportunity to discover the thing we would have him know, not to rob him of the pleasure and development. Watching children at free creative work, the teacher may see the very forms invented which she would have imposed upon him from without, while now she knows they were within the mind, only waiting to be made conscious thro' external expression. Supply the material and conditions for the child to discover the law which he has evolved, he will formulate it for himself. This method may be followed in any subject or lesson.

We must see to it constantly that the proportion is maintained between the knowledge and power acquired and the means of self-expression, only so can true growth be secured. Our method must be "experience, observe, assimilate, reproduce, create!"

In the primary grade we expect as an outcome original sentences, problems, stories and designs.

Physical exercise developing the body in play demands continued use in school; that the developed unity be not broken and that each power may keep pace with the whole. But as the pupil passes out of the symbolic stage, games adapted to his new stage of development are to be supplied. Such as call for skill, running, leaping, and ball games in great variety. Surely the education of body and mind together, begun in the kindergarten, are necessary in school. "Experiment and study must determine which physical exercises best promote the normal growth of the brain."

Reverence for life developed through nurture of life should receive careful attention in all primary schools. Children should sow seeds in boxes or garden beds and tend to the plants themselves. Not like a kindergartener who grasped a hoe, rushed out after the children were gone, and hoed the garden beds to remove weeds, and pulled radishes, because she felt they should be sent to the gentleman whose kindness had furnished the garden. Why should she deprive the children of these delights of nurture and from gathering the reward of the harvest they had sowed? What was the object of the garden? Show, or to fasten the nurturing instinct in the child? Not the thing but the spirit in which it is done is valuable.

We should help the child to discover laws in nature identical with those in his own life and pointing to the unity of source. Let him see the whole process of life in one plant that he may see evolution and development. To deepen the love for nature let them learn poems touching and developing the imagination, and listen to myths of them and of animal and insect. Animals to nurture, as well as plants, should find a place in every school room. Nature is the correlating study.

The transition room should use the more advanced gifts, especially the box of fourteen crystal forms (to be found in minerals and to be reproduced in modeling). The completion of Froebel's course of study demands their use, and the resulting development of the child fully justifies it. There should also be geometric paper folding, cutting, drawing, painting, card-board modeling, and music, built upon the foundation laid in the kindergarten.

Love, happiness, and helpfulness, are possible in the school. It is the spirit of the play and occupations which makes it vital. All materials used are merely paper, sticks and stones if not used in the right spirit. "It is the spirit of the school which makes the transition from the kindergarten possible. Both phases of the work demand a knowledge of the same underlying principles and a training that shall include both. When these principles are consciously held by all educators we shall have unity of purpose and variety of detail.

The leaflets of child-study, psychology, and science, sent out by universities, show an effort to make every interest appeal to children in the right way, and these lay the foundation for future scientific work.

When kindergartners and primary teachers hold the same principles and use the developing method, there will be unity of purpose and continuity in all work.

The whole gamut of feeling has been aroused in the kindergarten, furnishing budding points for future studies. These vital centers constantly return in seasons, national festivals and anniversaries, in which childhood joins humanity in community of interest.

The kindergarten has enabled the child to see his powers revealed in what he produced. He has formed the habit of looking behind effect to cause, and of seeing everything in its history. His powers to observe, compare, assimilate and reproduce have been cultivated. The primary teacher who knows his training can utilize it and furnish new opportunities for its further exercise in number work, reading, natural science, geography, form, tone, color, etc.

The kindergarten lays stress on training the child through play. The school lays emphasis upon the subject, instruction and calls for work. The concepts formed in his experience, he longs to see represented by signs, figures, letters, words, that he may benefit by stores of knowledge gathered for him. He goes from the object to its representation. Will-power must now exercise itself in a higher stage of executive ability. Primary teachers must so grade difficulties that the child's conquest shall be blest with victory.

In the new word-getting there is still necessity for analysis and synthesis, but let the process which called the word into being (its essential activity) be produced, that action, word and object may mutually interpret each other. Bridge the new by the familiar, that associated ideas may recall it at many points of contact. Balance all necessary mechanism of school work by creative work in material adapted to self-expression. The concentric plan of work is possible in the school. Nature study is the correlating subject, the excursion may form the basis of other work, with stories to embody the experience and universal truth.

As the environment assists or retards development, and the true and good may grow from the beautiful, let artistic picture or cast in the room do their ennobling work. Educate by ideals of politeness, punctuality, obedience, industry, truthfulness and altruism. To give exercise to self-activity and to develop creative power, must ever be the aim of the teacher, that the pupil may not only create things, but his own character.

Spontaneous gifts of handwork brought from home point to such results, and remind the teacher of the principle to "follow the child" in development of mind and subject. Some form of manual training seems to be demanded by these gifts.

Give opportunity to discover what we would have him know; evolve that from the mind, not impose it from without. Definition is the end of the process; he may formulate the law he evolves.

Suitable games and physical exercises must mutually develop body and mind, but calisthenics will not replace recess; relaxation comes through caprice, that the will may be ready for new effort. Play is the safety-valve for unused energy and furnishes a hint to the child of "his ideal self realized in institutions."

Pupils should sow seeds in garden beds or window boxes, and cultivate them, to foster their nurturing instinct and develop reverence for life. Let them see the whole process of development in one plant. Remember that Froebel believed from every "object in nature there was a way to God."

Poems of nature deepen the love for it and touch the imagination.

Secure plants and animals for the school-room and help the child to discover laws in nature identical with those in his own life, pointing to unity of source.

The demand has already called forth beautiful nature readers and classic literature in a form for supplementary reading, and charts for beginners, looking on the primary year as a whole and giving connected, artistic and scientific work.

Parents will attend meetings and coöperate with the school in vital concerns of child-life.

The transition class should continue the use of the higher gifts, especially the box of fourteen crystal forms (to be found in minerals, and reproduced in modelling). The completion of Froebel's course of study demands their uses and the resulting development of the child fully justifies it. There should also be paper-folding, cutting, drawing, painting and cardboard work and music, built upon the foundation laid in the kindergarten.

"It is the spirit of the school that makes the transition from the kindergarten to the grades beyond possible." The same principles underlie both phases of work. When kindergartens and primary teachers have a knowledge of these and use the developing method, there will be a unity of purpose and continuity in all work.

THE MUSIC OF THE KINDERGARTEN

Miss Sara L. Dunning, of New York city, said in part:

First of all I want to repeat what some of you have so many times heard me say that perhaps I ought to beg pardon for repeating it—that for music the kindergarten is the most important place of all, the lowest primary next, and so on up till the colleges and universities will take care of themselves. Of course, very little should be done in the kindergarten, but that little is of the greatest, the gravest importance, for there the lasting impressions are made. Because music is so intimately associated with almost all they do, they must first be led to love it, to love only good music, and to enjoy only a good quality of tone.

Let the little songs never be pitched too low, and also let them not be pitched too high. Very many of our present kindergarten song-books contain this first error, and it is not easy for every pianist to transpose the accompaniments. I hope it is not necessary to say let the pianist never pound her instrument, and let the teacher never sing or speak in a loud or rasping voice. In my opinion, the work in a real kindergarten should be almost entirely by rote, but in a kindergarten where the youngest children are five years of age, very much more than this may be done. Even with the youngest I should teach the scale, beginning it at the top and singing the complete scale down in the key of F, E, E-flat or D. They could also sing the same from a ladder representation, and these scales written out on a blackboard, with their proper signatures of flats or sharps. Let the representation be a true one, but the little mind need not be burdened with it. They will enjoy singing part way down and jumping back to the upper "do," and also holding up their little chubby fingers in imitation of the five lines of the staff and singing from them.

If violent motions, like chopping wood, are desired, let some of the children chop and the rest sing, but do not let both be done at the same time by any child.

In my opinion, motion songs should be used sparingly, the attention being centered more upon the proper enunciation and pronunciation of words, proper movements of lips, tongue and teeth, and the gaining of correct musical conceptions.

NORMAL SECTION

FRANCIS J. CHENEY, *Chairman*, Cortland

FRED V. LESTER, *Secretary*, Westport

Meeting was called to order at 11.40 a. m., by the chaiman, Dr. Cheney, of Cortland.

The chairman then introduced principal Francis B. Palmer of Fredonia, who read the following paper:

INFLUENCE OF NORMAL SCHOOLS ON THE PUBLIC SCHOOLS OF NEW YORK STATE

First consider the influence of the normal schools in favor of a higher standard of scholarship. It is not forgotten that the noble institutions that did everything that was done, and everything that could be done for secondary education from the '30s to the close of the war of secession did not gain in financial support equal to their merits, nor adequate to the growing demands, and that over-worked and under-paid teachers together with such devices as were contrived for keeping these academies running from September to June, had too heavy a burden laid upon them to give any attention to advancing the scholarship of the times. When we compare the college entrance examinations of thirty years ago with those of the present the differences which will strike us most will not be the added number of new subjects required, but the change of requirements in English, mathematics and history. To enter college now means some proficiency in these subjects which even good penmanship and correct spelling on the part of the candidate will not completely cover. When the law of '66 was passed it was a part of the purpose of its framers to establish a few schools on such a basis and with such support that they might venture to aim at a higher standard of scholarship without fear of breaking down their teachers or failing financially. Many other things could be named as contributing to better scholarship, but the normal schools were the first of all our secondary schools to demand it and adequately to provide for it. The first of the new schools established under the law, the normal school at Brockport, at once took high rank for the scholarship required, and it was not till several years of this advance that any of our colleges made higher requirements for entrance. It should always remain to the credit of the normal schools that they not only advocate good scholarship, but that at a time of decided depression they set an example that has been followed largely and that has led to the building up of a higher ideal in the class of secondary schools known as union and high schools which has made it possible for our colleges to advance their standard of requirements for admission. This work did not seem germane to the normal schools, and it has brought down much criticism upon them, but they have done the public schools of the state no better service than thus to set the standard of scholarship high.

The second class of influences of the normal schools is that which relates to methods of teaching. To the influence of the normal schools on the public schools of the state in improving the methods of teaching the practice schools are the key. The normal schools have laid great stress on the importance of developing the activities of children by skillful questioning, but if I were to claim any merit for originality in the art of questioning I should be very properly asked if we had never heard of Socrates. We have dwelt much on the importance of the inductive method; but some one will wonder if we had never heard of Bacon. Most of all, perhaps, we have insisted on the value of observation and the study of nature; but some one will immediately read us a lesson from Pestalozzi. The normal schools have not been original in these things, nor do they forget the debt they owe to the distinguished educators whom to name in this connection would be unpardonable pedantry and offensive patronizing. But the normal schools of this state have done more by their practice schools to make these principals practical than any if not all other influences that can be named.

It was a theory of Wordsworth that a writer could not open a new field of literature to the world by writing a book. He must not only write his story, but he must develop a sentiment, he must educate an intelligence, he must create a constituency to appreciate his story. If a new thing has to be done a new instrument has to be invented, and men have to be trained to use the new instrument. Many an inventor has failed because he has not trained his workmen or has not worked up a constituency. The story of better methods of instruction was attractively told in Leonard and Gertrude, and has been told thousands of times, but teachers have not been trained to use the better methods successfully, nor has a constituency been educated to appreciate them. The pre-eminent work of the normal schools of this state has been along these lines, and the thought of the school has found expression in its practice department.

Let us consider a few moments what the normal schools have done in this direction. In the first place they started out to emphasize objective methods of teaching. Object methods were the bane and the blessing of Oswego for years, now she is only blessed for them. Many of us can remember how the schools all over this state were invaded by the Oswego teachers only to rouse the parents of pupils taught by the objective system and teachers of the old rote system into fiercest opposition. Undoubtedly many a bungling attempt to handle the new tools was responsible for a part of the opposition, but the best examples of the class were not fairly appreciated, and the best examples were few. But Oswego had its influence on the other normal schools, and they came to her aid, and from all the schools, trained teachers were sent out in sufficient numbers to command respectful attention. After sufficient time and opportunity to adjust the new methods to the circumstances of the schools, and to bring the best features to the knowledge of the patrons of the schools, the objective method of presenting truths was received with all the credit due to its importance.

The objective method was developed from its beginning in object methods and was applied to the study of nature by observation instead of by text-book and picture, and under this form it is called nature study. It included the study of the *natural* sciences experimentally, and under this head is known as the laboratory method of studying sciences. The same method is applied to the study of mental and moral science and is denominated child-study. I do not believe it is too much to say that the schools of practice connected with the normal schools of this state have been essential to the development of these methods into realities. Time and talk would never do what has been done in the work-shop of the normal school system and made a reality before the eyes of the world. When all due credit has been awarded to theorists and high scholarship, the proof of the theory for the jury that must be convinced, must be credited as the work of the normal schools.

What has been said with reference to objective teaching is true also of the inductive method. The inductive method is, in fact, but a corollary of the objective. Children should be taught facts by experience and observation. This is objective; that a large number of facts is necessary to justify a scientific conclusion is the essence of induction. There are three steps in the process of induction; first, facts from direct knowledge; second, concepts from facts thus experienced; third, the conclusive. No person goes through a course in any one of our normal schools without having impressed by precept and practice the importance of facts from observation, and the importance of experience in gaining clear, accurate, and correct concepts. The first steps of induction are thus matters of habit, and the tendency to avoid loose thinking is greatly strengthened. But it is easier to generalize from one or two facts than to seek for many and it requires the perseverance that comes only with right training to withstand the temptation to take the shortest way. This development of a habit of inductive process comes with the work of teaching in the school of practice as it comes nowhere else.

PAPER BY INSPECTOR FRANK H. WOOD

The normal school and the training class are especially related in their work. Though sometimes apparently rivals, they are virtually supplementary institutions. The normal school cannot and I think was not designed to supply the demand for teachers in the common district school. In some favored localities (mostly confined to a few counties) the normal schools are equal to the demand and it is gratifying to know that the common schools in such localities are to quite an extent, availing themselves of the opportunity. But the normal teacher is beyond the average district school. In order to secure the expert opinion of local educational authorities upon the value of training class work, a circular letter addressed to superintendents, principals and commissioners was issued under date of May 17th, by the

State Superintendent. Two hundred fifty letters were sent out and one hundred seventy-eight replies have been received. The opinions rendered are remarkably uniform, in their general tone, and are practically unanimous in its favor. The few adverse criticisms that are made relate almost entirely to some special phase of the work, e. g., the examination in certain subjects, or they refer to some condition peculiar to an individual class.

The normal school receives many of its best students from the country districts and sends them to the village and the city. Were there nothing to counteract this tendency, the normal school would in its immediate effects prove a detriment to the out-lying districts, rather than a benefit. The training class, however, receives many of its members from city and village and sends them to the district school—thus tending to restore the equilibrium.

But the term "local needs" is not only applicable to the ungraded rural school, but to quite an extent also to the graded village school. Many grade positions are annually filled by training class teachers who have had a successful experience in the rural school—some without that experience—positions that otherwise must have been filled by untrained teachers.

There is another class of grade positions that forms a kind of "neutral zone"—not exclusively within the province of the normal school or the training class—but occupied by each. Here there would appear to be some opportunity for rivalry. One principal reports, as follows: "Members of the present class have been engaged to succeed normal graduates—nine of them will locate in union schools." Another says: "The present requirements open the doors of union schools to graduates of training classes. Formerly only normal graduates and first grade teachers were engaged in such work." One city superintendent says: "Trustees and school commissioners have informed me that the graduates (and even some members that failed to graduate) of training classes were doing as good work as graduates of normal schools working in the same county."

Objection has been made that the training class will tend to lessen the number of candidates for normal school, but I am of the opinion that the point is not well taken. In the first place, comparatively few of those who join the training class would enter the normal school. Again frequently students through their work in the training class are stimulated to pursue higher professional training, moreover these two institutions are mutually helpful in creating public sentiment, in awakening a desire for special preparation, and in creating a demand for trained teachers. Here as elsewhere, action and reaction are equal. The field is wide and it all needs cultivation.

The demand for our graduates is rapidly increasing. Little

difficulty is experienced in securing suitable positions. This is due to several reasons--first, the recent act referred to above, both by its direct requirements in the city and its reflex influence elsewhere is increasing the demand. In addition to this there is a growing tendency on the part of school authorities to hire trained teachers. Again, many schools now rely entirely upon the training-class for their teachers. Another important factor is the present standard of the uniform examinations which is creating a healthful scarcity of untrained third grade teachers.

It is an encouraging indication that the greater the number of classes in a locality, the more difficult it appears to be to supply the demand for teachers.

The amount of wages received by our graduates, varies greatly in different sections of the state. It seems to vary directly as the number of graduates employed. The average wage is apparently less than that received by the first grade teacher and more than that received by the second grade teacher. The average relative wage, however, is steadily increasing. This estimate does not, of course, apply to the teachers employed in city schools.

In further evidence of the efficiency of the work that our graduates are doing, I quote some statements from the replies referred to above. First from school commissioners: "Wherever I find a training class teacher, I find that he knows something of the art of imparting instruction to his pupils. I find trustees pleased with these teachers and are anxious to retain them for the ensuing year. I can invariably pick out a training class graduate after one-half hour in the schoolroom. I have done so repeatedly."

"It has been a very material aid to the district school in this loctlity. It has given a better tone to many of our schools."

"We get more competent teachers from training classes than from any other source."

"The schools are very largely what the training class teachers make them—either directly or by setting the pace."

"I think the value of training class graduates is not fully appreciated, but have seen better results the past year and the class in this district has done much to arouse public interest in professional training."

"When the difference between the work done by training class teachers and the teachers with no training is once known by trustees only the former will be employed. The demand is greater than the supply at present in my district."

During the current school year, in my official capacity as inspector of training classes, I have visited all classes in the state but ten, spending a day in each school. In these classes, I have found a body of young men and young women whose average age was nineteen years—as earnest and intelligent a class of students as can be found anywhere. They united with the training class to prepare for teaching, not to seek immunity from the payment of tuition in academic work, as had been done to a large extent in former years. Instead of averaging three academic subjects per member, as in many classes prior to last year, they have taken practically no academic subjects—the average per member throughout the state being a small fraction.

Whatever the results of the final examinations recently held, I am prepared to say that these students teachers have done thorough, conscientious, well-directed work, and that they will enter the schoolroom prepared to do credit to themselves, to the school and to the state.

The instructors of the classes are well equipped for the work. they have improved greatly in efficiency, and there will be still further improvement as soon as our brethren of the normal school fraternity are in position to provide us with more thoroughly trained teachers.

Eighty-one classes have been under instruction throughout the current school year. Upwards of a hundred will be under instruction during the coming year, and I predict that within five years the classes will double in number, and treble in aggregate membership.

One of the greatest needs at present is more time for the work prescribed, and some time for work that is not prescribed. But this and other important problems belong to the future, and they will be met in the fullness of time.

DISCUSSION OF PAPER BY DR. F. B. PALMER

The main point which I arise to emphasize is the influence of the normal schools in bringing before the teaching force of the state the final cause or the purpose of the school. I do not undervalue scholarship, I do not believe that the teacher will teach more than he has himself experienced, but I am persuaded that much depends upon the teacher's procedure. I therefore emphasize the teaching ability of the teacher. I may be able to set before you in stronger relief my thought in this connection by stating that to my mind the final cause of education is the realization in the pupil of the maximum effective energy from the minimum outlay of time and energy, or "the realization of all the possibilities of humanity as a whole in each individual," or the perfecting of the self.

The energy of the soul is innate; it is not conserved or correlated "Radiant Energy." An impassable gulf lies between the various forms of radiant energy and the manifestations of soul. I speak advisedly when I say impassable and not merely "not yet passed:" The fact that all forms of radiant energy are sensuous; that they are cognized as distinct from the self and extraneous to the self; that they may be cognized simultaneously by any number of observers; while not one of these conditions is true of soul manifestation, establishes the impossibility of referring soul to correlated radiant energy. I say then that soul energy is innate; that each child comes into the world with his aggregate energy fixed; and the problem for solution is what proportion of this inherent energy shall be developed. The aggregate potency plus kinetic (active) energy is constant, but the ratio of the kinetic to the potential is variable; or to concrete the proposition the query is, shall the condition of the child at six years be ninety units of potency and ten units of available energy, or shall it be seventy-five potent and twenty-five available; shall the youth leave school with ninety units potent and ten available, or with his undeveloped energy at ten and his available power at ninety. Of course these figures have no significance beyond showing the constancy of the "aggregate." The idea of a mysterious influx of some extraneous power is a relic of the earlier failure to recognize the unmeasured, the infinite possibilities of a human being.

It must be borne in mind that this potency can be reached only through the physical; the neurine responds to the peripheral stimuli, the sensorium (cortical brain cells) is automically modified by extraneous stimuli, and these sensorial modifications effect corresponding changes in soul. The recognition of this law is basal, and has done much to improve the character of the instruction in the public schools. The erroneous conception that the subject-matter must be adjusted or adapted to the pupil, instead of the converse is prolific of much of the poor teaching of to-day. I find in our schools of practice, teachers in training who have had from one to twelve years experience, teaching geography and not children. They fail to recognize that the child must respond automatically to stimuli presented; he must be raised step by step to the level of the plane on which rests the truth which he is to master, and when he is brought face to face with truth after such adjustment, he never fails to apprehend it, to apperceive it. This then is the distinctive work of the teacher. Teaching is the adjustment of mind to the subject-matter, and determining the accuracy of such adjustment.

Professor John F. Reigart, of the New York College for the Training of Teachers, was then introduced to discuss "How best to utilize Child Study in the training of teachers."

Our great fault in the schools, or rather danger, is that we plan to do so much work and then devote ourselves to working off that plan.

The professor presented an outline of work and the following references:

THE TEACHERS' STUDY OF THE CHILD

References:

Royce. Is there a Science of Education? Educational Review, Vol. I.

Sully. The Service of Psychology to Education. Educational Review, Vol. IV.

Bradford. Heredity and Education. Educational Review, Vol. I.

Preyer. Infant Mind, chap. II.

Psychologies—

Ladd, Primer, chap 13.

Psychology, chap. 27.

Sully. H. M., Vol. II, chap. 19.

Lotze. Outline, p. 137.

Hoffding, pp. 348-350.

Pedagogical Seminary, March, 1893; June, 1891.

Warner. The Children; How to Study Them.

Hertel. Over-pressure in the Schools of Denmark.

Clarke. Sex in Education.

Burnham. School Hygiene. Ped. Sem., June, 1892.

Burnham. The Study of Adolescence. Ped. Sem., June, 1891.

Hall. Training of Children and Adolescents. Ped. Sem., June, 1891.

Howell. A Boy's Town.

Royce. Mental Defects and Disorder. Ed. Rev., 1893.

Russell. Exceptional Children in School. Ed. Rev., December, 1893.

1. Tests for the Senses.

(1) Sight.

Cohn. Hygiene of the Eye; Scripture in Ed. Rev., January, 1893.

Jeffries. Color Blindness.

Cattell. Ed. Rev., March, 1893.

Risley. Defective Vision. Ed. Rev., 1892.

(2) Hearing.

Chrisman. Ped. Sem. December, 1893.

Cattell and Scripture. Ed. Rev., 1893.

Wiltse. Sound Blindness, in the Place of the Story in Early Education.

2. Intellectual Processes, etc.

(1) Memory.

Jacob's "Mind," Vol. XII, p. 75.

Bolton. American Journal Psychology, Vol. IV.; Scripture, Ed. Rev., January, 1893.

(2) Imagination.

Types, eye-mindedness, ear-mindedness, constructive imagination.

Galton. Inquiries into Human Faculty.

Jastrow. Popular Science Monthly, Vol. XXXIII, p. 597.

Burnham. Ped. Sem., March, 1893.

Mrs. Bryant. Testing the Character of Children, Ped. Sem., June, 1891.

(3) Thoughts and Reasoning.

Brown. Ped. Sem., December, 1893.

Hall. Contents of Children's Minds. Ped. Sem., June, 1891.

Barnes. Theological Ideas of Children. Ped. Sem., December, 1893.

Hall. Children's Lies. Ped. Sem., June, 1891.

3. Motor Activities: Language, play, work, voluntary power; reflex, instinctive and voluntary movements.

Preyer. Infant Mind.

Baldwin. Mental Development.

Sully. Studies in Childhood.

Shinn. Notes of a Child.

Preyer. Mind of a Child.

Tracy. Psychology of Childhood.

Wiltse. Children's Collections. Ped Sem., June, 1891.

Barnes. Children's Drawings. Ped. Sem., June, 1891.

Royce. Imitation. Century, May, 1894.

Haskell. Imitation. Ped. Sem., October, 1894.

TEACHERS' INSTITUTES AS A MEANS FOR PROFESSIONAL TRAINING

ISAAC H. STOUT

The interesting fact to be especially noted, is that the inception of the work was with the teachers themselves, and was the direct outgrowth of two widely differing ideas—one, the consciousness born of experience that better equipment was needed for successful teaching; the other, the desire on the part of the educators of all grades to have teaching recognized as one of the professions. The same causes are operating still, and account for the intense earnestness and constant endeavor concentrated upon professional training to-day.

The province of this paper is to point out to some extent the place and value of the teachers' institute in our scheme of professional training, but this is a difficult task, because from the very nature of the case, the work and functions of the institute must ever continue more complex than those of the training class or the normal school.

The early institutes, antedating as they did the establishment of the first state normal school, aroused an interest in professional training that was an important factor in securing the necessary legislation and appropriation for the establishment of the school at Albany.

All teachers, whether they have or have not had the advantages of the normal school and training class, may be classified according to certain stages of evolution or development. Superintendent Kratz of Sioux City, Iowa, in a discussion before the National Educational Association, Department of Superintendence, happily described these three stages substantially as follows: First, the imitative stage, chiefly characterized by careful imitation of the manners, methods, and devices of some former favorite teacher, but by little thought. Attractive methods are industriously sought out, and eagerly swallowed without any thought of analysis or assimilation. Some teachers never evolve out of this stage and may be classified as cases of arrested development.

Second, the irrational stage, in which much is said about pedagogical principles and doctrines, and but little done along the line of their wise application. In this stage we hear about "from the concrete to the abstract," but see the order frequently reversed in the school room. We hear glib talk about appreciation, interest, concentration, and correlation, but fail to see their intelligent application in school-room work.

Third, the thoughtful stage, when everything that enters into school-room work, whether principle or material or method or device is subjected first to thoughtful scrutiny to determine whether it commends itself to the judgment, and if so, is then subjected to the still more critical test of results in school work. This is the stage that is characterized by enthusiasm, growth, progress, and ever-increasing efficiency and power.

Both the history of past institutes and the analysis of the class of teachers included in the membership of those of the present, suggest that at least six lines of work must lie within the province of the institutes of the present, but it is also to be remembered that as the teaching force improves, there must, as in the past, be a continual readjustment of these several lines as to the time and force to be devoted to each.

1. Subject-matter—but only to reconcile widely differing business applications, to unify the varying terminology so common in language subjects, or to give a clue to the rapid and accurate study of some subject which the times demand, but which was not included in the courses of study when the great mass of the teachers were themselves pupils in our schools.

Also school-room devices—but only for the purpose of interesting teachers of the imitative stage in better methods and in the study of pedagogical principles of which the devices are an application.

2. To broaden and liberalize the views of teachers in regard to methods employed and results secured by their co-workers in the educational field, a side to professional training that must not be overlooked. No agency is more potent than the institute to correct and check the narrow spirit born of the isolation forced upon teachers by the very nature of their work—a state which has so frequently produced the pedagogue who seems to believe that the universe revolves around his school as a center, that to dispute either the correctness or the exclusiveness of his methods is, at least, akin to sacrilege, and that neither family necessities, social amenities, religious functions, nor school authorities, have any right to exist, if in any way they conflict with his peculiar notions as to the conducting of a school.

3. To continue the work of the normal school and the training class by stimulating their graduates to continued effort and investigation, and to draw from every available source the material necessary for success—not only the old that time and experience have proved to be good, but also the more modern applications and adaptations of old truths.

4. To bring from the great educational associations, both state and national, the latest discussion of educational needs, methods, and equipment, for consideration and study. By this means our teaching force may be kept abreast of the times in familiarity with educational theories, and ready to utilize those that prove their worth by surviving the experimental stage.

5. To cultivate and stimulate an active professional spirit in full and intelligent sympathy with the educational system of the state, a spirit that by the French is so aptly styled *esprit de corps*—the spirit that prompts the individual to labor unitedly and in harmony with others for the advancement of the common cause, to smother personal jealousies, to subordinate self to the good of the profession, to make sacrifices of money, time, or effort when they will tend to conserve and uplift the educational interest of the state.

purpose and the value of our work. We do not need to cite those prominent in the history of education and their advocacy of this idea that we may have a hearing, nor do we have to call upon leading scientists or educators of the day to attest the worth of our claims. Not indeed because it were not possible so to do, to quote Comenius, Basedow and Fichte, Rousseau, Pestalozzi and Froebel, Bacon, Locke and Spencer, Huxley, Playfair, Magnus and a host of others in support of these claims, but because, as has been truly said, "This part of the manual training battle has been fought," and the justice of the cause made evident the world over, in twice a thousand schools.

It is not my intention, however, to dwell upon the general progress of manual training in the educational world. this I leave to a speaker on the program of the morrow, who is well qualified to rehearse the triumphs of the needle, the pencil, the spatula and knife. A few words on the development of the manual training idea may, however, not be out of place.

First, perhaps, in point of time may we consider the suggestions of far-sighted educators, men who realized, as one of them put it, that the educational coach would have to be turned around and started in new direction. Comenius, Pestalozzi, Froebel, each in turn, reiterated what I may term the educational plea for hand work, work which meant not the mere learning of a trade, but the learning to do many things—by doing them, the setting free of the self-activity of the child.

But with many inventions, and altered economic conditions, came other and grave problems to the guardians of national education in the European states. The multiplication of industries, the division of labor, the introduction of machinery hastened the death of the apprentice system. Increased ease of transportation quickened the struggles for supremacy in the markets of the world, and the result upon the school system was inevitable. Thus, alongside the manual training idea in education crept in the industrial idea, and they were of mutual aid — without question. Indeed, they became, in measure, so well thought together that we are now bending our efforts to thinking them apart again; to distinguishing carefully between the industrial school and the manual training school; but it was the industrio-manual theory which first called manual training into prominent notice, the industrial idea to a large degree making the manual—or better, the educational—idea possible. In America these notions of the manual and the industrial were but partially differentiated at first, but became more and more distinct as a broader philosophy viewed the needs of the child and of the state. Though distinct as ideas, however, do not understand me to say that one is right and the other wrong, or that the pursuance of the one means the abandonment of the other.

Some of you may remember when in 1885, the national educational association, resolved "that we trust that the time is near at hand when the true principles of the kindergarten will guide all elementary training and when public sentiment and legislative enactment will incorporate the kindergarten into our public school system." But what is the true principle of the kindergarten? Dominant to details, to song, to game, to gift, is the fact that in the kindergarten the child lives a real life, a communal life, working for his fellows, enjoying the delights of one who is of some use in the world.

It is in the kindergarten that we find the child's interests centered about this absorbing business of life, about food and clothing and shelter, these coves of concentration as some might call them. "We are training no American craftsmen, and unless we devise better methods than the old and obsolete apprentice system, much of the perfection of our almost automatic mechanism will have been achieved at the cost not only of the manual but also of the mental development of our men."

But any hint of public industrial instruction is apt to bring to mind thoughts of the obstacles in the way of its introduction into this country, despite the fact that many trade schools are upon the continent supported by the government. But the difference in the industrial system of the continental states, the fact that their governmental forms permit schemes of education impossible in this country, fear of the enmity of the trades unions, the impossibility of teaching all trades, and the narrowness of trade teaching in general, all unite to deter any but the most ardent advocate of such instruction from urging the establishment of public trade schools.

To the few however, the economic arguments appeal with superior claims for recognition. To them the fact that private benevolence has for some time maintained in this and other cities, schools giving individual instruction, with the knowledge, and in some instances with the assistance of the trades unions, is an answer as to the possibility of establishing and maintaining these institutions amid our industrial conditions, while the serious and comprehensive schemes for the public education of the artisan which are now being carried out both in England and upon the continent are evidence of the desirability, if not necessity, of offering like assistance to our American workman who competes with his state-trained brother in the markets of the world, in which, even now, we send abroad much raw material to be manufactured and resold to us at many times our selling price.

in this direction has been achieved and with results markedly excellent. The incorporating of motor activities into schoolroom work in order that the formal acquisition of knowledge may become easier to the child, and that a firmer and stronger mental structure may be built up, is the next step to be taken in pedagogical progress and economy, and an end towards which the inventive powers and skill of onward-looking teachers should be directed.

SEWING, AS CONDUCTED IN THE PUBLIC SCHOOLS

MISS ANITA M. EARL

Normal College, New York City

Sewing is first taken up in the third year of the child's school life, and is continued one hour a week for four years, passing from the primary after one year and a half to the grammar grades, where it is taught for the remaining two and a half years. Cookery then takes the place of sewing in the three highest grades.

In the older schools into which manual training has been but recently introduced, no room can be spared for a kitchen in which to teach cookery, owing to an overcrowded condition. This enables us to carry the sewing to a higher state of perfection in the upper grades, and to introduce a system of practical dressmaking.

All of the new schools, however, possess a large, well-lighted, well-ventilated room set apart solely for the purpose of sewing. It is fitted up with long tables containing drawers for the various materials and pieces of work, chairs adapted to the height of the children—a most important matter—a closet for the accommodation of supplies, and a large blackboard, upon which the diagrams may be left from time to time for different classes. The change of room is of added interest to the children, and seems to inspire them when they reach its atmosphere.

It is the intention to further adorn the walls with cabinets containing specimens of the raw materials, various textile fabrics, and other objects of interest in connection with the sewing, which prove of special value on a dark and cloudy day, when practical work is necessarily discontinued. The time devoted to these talks is most profitably spent, as in this way the children gain a comprehensive knowledge of the origin and nature of the tools and materials which they are using. These lessons include instruction in the manufacture of needles, thimbles and thread; the growth of cotton and weaving of cloth, wool, silk, flax and the different textile fabrics made from each; dyeing and printing; the quality of material, color, tints and shades. It would be well

to relate briefly some of the advantages of such a course to the child—advantages not limited to sewing only, but which have their application to other subjects as well.

The prescribed course of instruction commences with the correct position of the body while sewing, the proper manner of holding the work (both of which are of far more importance than the mere taking of stitches), and the use of the various implements. These initial steps are conducted mainly as drill lessons, until the tiny fingers have become used to their new but welcome friends. Then follow even basting stitches, outlining geometrical designs with the running stitch—different colored threads being used to indicate degrees of proficiency; instruction in the combination and harmony of colors; running and backstitched seams; overcasting; French fells; bias fells; gathering applied to small aprons; putting on of bands; gussets; button-holes; sewing on of buttons; patching; hand weaving; developing the idea of selvedge, warp and woof threads; dress-darning; stocking darns; night-dress opening; sleeve opening; skirt opening or placket; piecing bias facings; tucking; Kensington stitch; catch-stitch; feather-stitch, and hem-stitch; drafting child's underwaist; gored skirt, model size, and a small model shirt waist.

In large classes it will necessarily follow that some children will complete their work more rapidly than others. To them is given what is known as extra or busy work. This is very desirable, not only as a reward for good results obtained, and as an incentive to renewed effort on the part of the more indifferent workers, but also as a means of applying the designing powers to the sewing in a fuller way than is always possible in the regular course. Children who are skilful enough to have extra work given them should require less of the teacher's attention, thus permitting her to devote more time to the remainder of the class.

The good results of the work depend largely upon systematic teaching. Keep the children interested and busy, and the hour will prove a profitable, and what is equally important, a happy one for all. This is not so difficult as at first may appear, owing to such large classes. The children are well disciplined; the order maintained as in other studies, and the noted reluctance with which the work is put away gives evidence to the fact of their love for the work.

It is necessary to study the child in order to obtain the best results. To consider the temperament, environment, inherited qualities, so that the best powers may be developed. Needless to say, different stimuli are required to meet the wants of varying natures. Love engenders love; and a cheerful teacher will produce a cheerfully working class. Children are particularly susceptible to the atmosphere about them. Praise, carefully bestowed, acts as a powerful incentive in producing good work, and a striving to do better invariably follows. Often, I have seen a child's face brighten perceptibly when told that she might take her completed piece home. Inspection, whether by parents at home, or through the means of an exhibition similar to the present one, stimulates endeavor and arouses a feeling of pride and satisfaction. Careless work should never be accepted. One untidy seam allowed to pass without correction induces future carelessness. Every time a child corrects a piece of work cheerfully, a tendency is formed to create a love of industry. It is so hard for the immature mind to realize that "practice makes perfect," and that "what is worth doing at all, is worth doing well." It is invariably necessary for the teacher to bring into play that most wonderful and rare of all possessions—tact—to smile away with words of encouragement any feeling of impatience which may arise. A most necessary element of manual training is exactness, and in order to secure this, considerable individual attention is necessary.

I think many do not know how largely the foreign element prevails in some of our schools. In the primary department in Mulberry street, twenty-nine nationalties are represented. Fortunately, the sewing teacher possesses a knowledge of four different languages. In grammar school No. 13, in East Houston street, there was but one child of American parentage out of one hundred and fifty. Possessing all the inherited traits of different nationalities as these children do, we confidently hope to make better women of them by means of the training they are receiving.

The child who has finished the sewing course should be well equipped with the problem of making and repairing her clothing, and have gained an independence which will increase her resources and add to her individuality. The pupils learn to appreciate good workmanship, and to regard with greater intelligence and respect the vast industrial world.

Looking at the subject further, from the standpoint of utility, the knowledge which they acquire of domestic science will certainly fit these girls to assume the manifold duties which present themselves in that most important phase of life—the making of the home. The lack of this very knowledge has often wrecked the home, which should stand as the foundation of our national prosperity.

Morality and religion are built upon industry, and a spirit of of discontent and anarchy is seldom found in a community which can bring a knowledge of trained labor to bear upon the successful issues of its work. The moral influence is a very essential part of our manual training. Neatness of attire engenders self-respect. A thorough knowledge of the industrial arts increases one's love of industry, and permeates the entire system with energy and healthfulness. Briefly stated, the purpose of this society must be to furnish help to the teachers of the state, that they may more enthusiastically and intelligently serve the children of the state.

Right here I want to emphasize one point, already mentioned by Professor O'Shea. Child study is not the study of little children alone. It must include the child until he is a man. All honor the importance of the work of the primary teacher. I should be the last one to detract from the greatness of her task. But people are pretty well aroused to the importance of the little child already. While interest and effort here should not be abated, but rather increased, this society will fall far short of its mission, if it fails to do much to further the study of older boys and girls, those in the adolescent period particularly. We have here as grave a problem as is to be found in the whole range of school life. It is during this period that the tobacco habit becomes fastened. At this time many drop out of school never to return. And after all due allowance is made for those who must help earn the family living, there is still a great number left, who are no longer in school. These should be retained; they may be retained, if the teacher and superintendent know how to hold them. This society can do no grander service to the state and to the profession, than by earnestly taking hold of the great problem of the study of the intermediate and grammar school pupil. There is no time to-day to speak further of the details of this problem. Let this society take hold of it in earnest.

There still seems to be need of the caution that machines must have a minor place in child study. Weight and height and strength tests, et cetera, are well, but they are after all only externals—means to a greater end. I am sure much harm has resulted in certain quarters by subjecting little children to conscious tests. Too much emphasis can hardly be given to the statement that tests of eye, ear, et cetera, especially with little children, must be in the nature of "games." They are too ready to take suggestions. Tell a child to hear or see a thing in a certain way, and he will probably do it, whether his eye or ear tells him to or not. Many teachers and supervising officers in our state need emphatic enlightment on this point.

ALTERNATIVE COURSES FOR SHOPWORK

MR. CHARLES A. BENNETT, *Professor of Manual Training, Teachers' College, New York*

I will call your attention to three lines of work that may be successfully taught to pupils of grammar school grades in the ordinary school-room; namely,

I. Bent iron work.
II. Knifework in wood.
III. Work in cardboard and paper.

I. The bent iron work shown in the exhibit illustrates a kind of works that may profitably be done by children in their fourth or fifth year in school. The operations are simple, not requiring too high a degree of accuracy, and the forms studied may be such as to help their work in drawing. The pupils are not asked to go through a long tedious series of operations before they get a result that looks like something.

The tools for this work are a rule, pencil, flat-nosed pliers and round-nosed pliers for each pupil, and snips or some other instrument for cutting off the iron. At first the teacher cuts off the pieces of iron; later the pupils may do it themselves. Most of the work should be done from drawings furnished the pupils by the teacher, because in the grades I have mentioned the pupils are not able to make drawings that are accurate enough to work from. So far as possible the course should consist of useful (including ornamental) articles that involve the desired principles of working and that are interesting to the children.

I see no good reason for extending the course much beyond what may be done in an hour and a half a week during one year, unless it is taken up from the standpoint of designing; and if taken up from that standpoint it seems to me to belong to the high school, or to the very highest of the grammar grades. Such a course as I have here mentioned might be given in the fourth or the fifth year, and another in connection with designing in the eighth or the ninth year.

II. None of the lines of work have received so much serious attention in this country as the knifework in wood; none can be found in so many schools to-day.

The tools used in this work are a rule, pencil, compasses, knife, and try-square, and a 5-inch x 7-inch pad of paper for the drawing which accompanies the woodworking. A few extra tools for general use such as a bit and brace, hammer, awl, etc., should be in the hands of the teacher.

The method generally followed in this work is to make (1) a class study of the model; (2) a freehand working sketch of it; (3) a mechanical drawing from the sketch; and (4) the object in wood from the mechanical drawing. Sometimes the mechanical drawing is omitted, the object being made from the working sketch; sometimes, both the freehand sketch and the mechanical drawing are omitted and the pupil required to work from a drawing or sketch furnished by the teacher.

The models, or objects, made should be useful to the child who makes them, in some sphere of his activity—at home, at school, or at play. At least, this should be the aim of the teacher in planning his course. The course should involve considerable geometry and form study, but should be designed especially with reference to the series of tool-exercises involved in making the models. Models involving simple knife-carving may profitably be introduced into the course. The course may also be enriched on the art side by introducing models involving free curves, especially if it is to be taught to pupils of the seventh as well as of the fifth and the sixth grades.

III. The kind of cardboard work to which I wish to refer is well illustrated by the course at the Leipsig manual training school. (That course has been translated into English, and published by O. Newmann & Co., of London.) It involves many of the processes of paper-box making and of book-binding. On the practical side, it opens the way to a group of industries connected with working in paper, cloth and leather. On the educational side, it is rich in problems in descriptive geometry and in accurate cutting, fitting and fastening. It affords an opportunity for the study of color. I have often thought, too, that growing out of this cardboard work might be some simple but artistic work in leather.

The tools used are a T-square, triangles, scissors, knife, brush for paste, bone folder, pencil, rule, paste box, and brush rest. A convenient outfit of tools has been designed by professor Mason, of the teachers' college.

The principal objection to this work in upper grammar grades, so far as I have observed it, comes from the use of paste and glue. So much of this is needed that great care must be taken or it will get on the hands, the clothing, and desk, and the floor. I believe that it is possible, in part at least, to overcome this objection.

THE PROGRESS OF MANUAL TRAINING

DR. HENRY M. LEIPZIGER, *Supervisor Free Lectures, New York City*

No "idea"—if that term may be so used—in education has met with so much popular aproval as the "manual training" idea.

The history of the growth of this idea may be found in the dissatisfaction with that education sometimes called humanistic—better called narrow—which trained the memory and neglected the senses. Froebel says: "Only that which he makes or is able to make is intelligible to the growing man." On the other hand, emphasize as we may, as advocates of manual training, its great value, a mistake is made if it is exalted into a substitute for all other training or as a panacea for all existing social evils.

Whenever, in manual training schools, deftness in manipulation is the desideratum, then such school ceases to be a purely educational institution.

The progress of manual training has been on the lines of most educational ideas, *i. e.*, from the higher schools downward. Technical schools have proven in the European countries great stimuli to the development of commerce, art and industry. These technical schools gather about them a class of students that exercise brain power of as high an order as that exercised by classical students. Gradually a standing for the technological school is attained, and the true university of to-day recognizes the laboratory as of equal value to the seminary, and the degree of bachelor of science as an equivalent to the degree of bachelor of arts. The advance in the natural sciences calls attention to the need of man for power to modify and control natural objects and phenomena, and this power is found to be developed through manual skill and large brain power. The mass of the people in all lands are workers, and for them it is now seen that a broader training is absolutely essential. Hence the demand for its introduction into the public school system.

England has, during the last ten years made, perhaps, the most notable advance of any country on the globe. Through the influence of the national society for technical education, the United Kingdom has been studded with technical schools and evening science schools. In the London board schools, manual training is introduced. In Germany, while there are some of the best technological schools and special mining and weaving schools, manual training in the elementary school is not interwoven with the curriculum. In Sweden, the Sloyd system is becoming a part of the general curriculum, and Switzerland has an excellent system of manual instruction. The manual training school of to-day is, however, a truly American product.

The type has been set by the admirable manual training school of St. Louis, under the direction of Prof. Woodward. Since its establishment nearly every great city except New York has organized a manual training high school: Boston, Denver, Cincinnati, Atlanta, Brooklyn, Philadelphia; and Chicago has two. These schools are intended for pupils who leave the grammar schools at an average age, say, of fourteen years. There are in both New York, Philadelphia and Brooklyn excellent trade schools. But what is of greater importance in the consideration of the progress of manual training is its incorporation in the curriculum of the elementary school.

I am happy to state that in New York city, too, that day is not far distant when there will be a well equipped mechanics' art school. One of the new high schools soon to be established is to be such a school. A new course of study has just been adopted whereby manual training is to form part of the curriculum in every school of the city, and the great advance in the adoption of the "idea" in New York city is shown by the following clause in the new charter for Greater New York, which reads as follows: "A school board shall have power to establish kindergartens, manual training schools, trade schools and truant schools."

As a compeller of its introduction, the kindergarten may be considered as a most efficient cause. In the kindergarten the pupils' activity is employed and directed, and a continuation of that manual activity is demanded. In New York city shop-work, paper cutting, designing, clay modelling, sewing, cooking and mechanical drawing are part of the regular curriculum in twelve schools. The wood-work is only for boys.

In Boston, wood-work is given in the grammar schools to girls as well as boys, and the superintendent reports that girls are in no respect inferior to the boys in their work at the carpenter's bench. Several of the teachers are women.

In the schools of Chicago, Washington, Springfield (Mass.), St. Paul and several smaller cities, the manual training is incorporated.

That a three days' session of manual instructors is soon to be held, that great institutions like the Young Men's Christian Associations are going to incorporate work, trade and technical classes indicate what hold the subject has on the minds of the present generation. In conclusion, two thoughts present themselves: (1) That manual training in elementary schools, *i. e.*, grammar schools, should be closely welded with other forms of instruction, and that the methods used should be calculated rather to develop thought than imitaion; (2) that the teachers should themselves, besides manual skill, possess the broad foundation of a liberal training.

The new education, including manual training as a feature of instruction, is based on physiological psychology, and from this study we receive the strongest argument in favor of manual training education. Eminent specialists have established the fact that the "brain is not as it was at one time supposed, a single organ acting as a whole, but a congeries of organs capable of more or less independent action." The brain has a sensory and a motor area—the latter presiding over groups of muscles. Each set of muscles has a special motor center which moves as the will dictates. Our mental states are dependent, therefore, as much upon the motor centers as upon the sensory centers. Dr. Browne says: "As the hand centers hold a permanent place amongst the motor centers, and are in relation with an organ which, in prehension, in touch and in a thousand different combinations of movement adds enormously to our intellectual resources, besides enabling us to give almost unlimited expression to our thoughts and sentiments, it is plain that the highest possible functional activity of these hand centers is a paramount consequence, not less to mental grasp than to industrial success." The writer of the above sentences shows that the brain, to be serviceable, must be used, and the motor centers in particular demand exercise. Hence he concludes that it is a requisite that exercises of the hand should commence at a very early age—as soon after the fourth year as possible.

Here comes the value of the kindergarten, the spread of which must delight all who believe, with Pestalozzi, that every human being is entitled to the development of the faculties he was born with. In the kindergarten, all the child's activities are brought into play, and here, at a time when the joints are supple, the child's fingers are trained. As the impression of the first seven years of childhood are among the most enduring, how important it is that the great years between three and six should not go to waste.

Nor should economic reasons be entirely disregarded. The great industrial opportunities afforded by our land should be developed by our own skilled workmen, not by those of other lands. We should not have our schools turned into workshops, but do we not practically bias children when we do teach them book-keeping and keep them ignorant of the use of the hammer and the saw? Do we not prejudice them against honest labor by keeping them ignorant of it?

The race of modern life is very keen, and the fittest alone survive. Our system of education, beginning with the kindergarten, should include not only the ordinary schools where manual training methods are adopted, but technical and trade schools. The university of to-day, with its school of mines and electrical engineering, illustrates the march of progress. So that manual training is necessary to preserve our national skill.

As an aid in physical upbuilding, statistics would prove the immense value of some form of manual training, and men engaged in sedentary occupations would call that teacher blessed who had given them an interesting "hobby" as a rest and recreation.

The nineteenth century has witnessed much progress in what may be termed the realms of science. It has seen, too, progress in the popular estimation in which the teacher is held. The good time is coming, we trust, when the chief citizen in the community will not be the banker, the merchant, the politician, but the moulder of character, the former of citizens, the teacher, and in that day the budget of our large cities will show but a very small proportion of its taxes paid for police purposes and the largest share for education. This consummation will be in a large measure brought about by the introduction of manual training, if properly understood.

THE ARTIST ARTISAN

JAMES HALL

William Morris and his work are growing more familiar to us here in America, since the recent death of that poet, socialist, and artist craftsman. In the last number of Scribner's is the best article upon him that I have seen, by his brother artist, Walter Crane.

His factory at Merton Abbey was an ideal workshop, with artist workmen, whose "work was pleasant to do, and worth the doing." Morris often worked with them, both there and at Kelmscott Manor, where was the famous press that has given such exquisite books to the world, and has started the revival of artistic printing which we are beginning to feel even in some of the cheaper work in this country.

Morris in his workshop quite exemplified the teachings of Ruskin, and machinery and modern contrivances of manufacture are ruled out of Ruskins' creed. But in this respect, the arts and crafts society has broader doctrines, and they are of their own times. They believe that although hand work has the highest charm, that machine made products can be artistic, if only they be frankly made, and the limitations of material, as well as its possibilities be recognized. They believe in "catching the mood of to-day" and embodying it in works of true beauty and originality; but that only is possible, when the workmen have an intelligent appreciation of the traditions of the past. Above all, the society hopes to do something toward making the public desire beauty rather than ugliness in common surroundings, to prefer the better to the poorer, to appreciate honesty of workmanship.

It is then an event of some significance, that in America we have had an exhibition this past season of the arts and crafts. Boston has already formed its society on the same lines as the one in England. The exhibition showed much reason for encouragement and hope for the future, and to me it was the most interesting event in the American art world during the season.

England saw the necessity of art education among her workmen, when she established through Prince Albert, the South Kensington museum, and schools of art throughout England. With all their faults, these art schools have done much for England, and the fine collection in the museum has probably done much more than the schools to aid English designers. England's recognition of the fact that her workmen could not compete with those of other countries where the art element entered more largely into the manufactures, led some intelligent people of Boston to make the movement which led to the establishment of drawing as a required study in the schools of Massachusetts, in 1870. The normal art school was opened for the study of industrial art teachers, and the wave of art instruction, so called, began its movement over the schools of the country.

The conception of what constituted industrial art, has been in many cases a crude one, if not altogether hazy, and much of the instruction given in the schools in this country to-day under the name of art, is of a kind to do more harm than good. Much of it has been so mechanical that of late, as a result of the protests of the artists and dissatisfaction of a partially intelligent public some drawing supervisors seem to have forgotten the industrial aim of the work, and are committing all kinds of extravagances in their efforts to get "artistic freedom." Art seems recently to have been parading in cap and bells, and any freakish production has passed as "clever" and "artistic," so it is not strange that this influence should have invaded the ranks of the drawing supervisors and led them away from the true path.

Perhaps I am wrong, but it seems to me that the true aims of art instruction and of manual training instruction are nearly identical. Certainly art training that does not consider the sturdier constructive side, is flimsy indeed. Manual training that does not consider honesty of workmanship, appropriateness of design to the material employed, justness of proportion of the parts, and harmony of the whole in every pattern made, will do doubtful good, and all these are elements of beauty, and beauty thus considered is art. It is a mistake to think that an object must be decorated to be beautiful. Mere knowledge of processes obtained in making inartistic models tends to degradation of our industries; for ugly things worked thus into the brain blunt the sensibilities instead of educating them to desire things beautiful. Machine power and the resultant subdivision of labor has so far destroyed handicraft that all sense of propriety in the use of material and suitability of design has well nigh disappeared. Let us strive to regain this sense by vitalizing the study of design, by bringing together the art courses and the manual training.

In the first place the surroundings in our schools should be beautiful. I do not now refer to casts and pictures, but to the architecture and construction of buildings, school rooms and furniture. Until this is considered a necessity, and not a luxury, art and fine craftmanship, and the love of beauty, cannot grow naturally. Art will remain an exotic, instead of being the simple, beautiful wayside flower, sweetening our walks of everyday life, blossoming joyously at every turn in the road, hardly noticed by the passerby, and yet giving forth its wholesome fragrance all the while for his delight. Our school houses should be built in the spirit of the Boston public library. That would be too costly you say, but there are many ugly buildings in Boston that cost far more than that chaste and beautiful one. Good taste is not so much a matter of cost as men are apt to suppose. It is possible to produce buildings, simple, beautiful and harmonious, at cheap cost. We shall begin to learn how to do this, let us hope, at no distant day. Professor Norton hardly ever speaks to his classes at Harvard without dwelling upon the importance of surroundings that are refined and beautiful, and he laments continually the lack of beauty in Harvard's own buildings, saying that they have a daily tendency to vulgarize the taste of the students. The rooms should have in them a few choice things rather than many inferior ones. All non-essential articles should be removed and a sense of fitness should prevail. The school rooms should be a constant example of refined simplicity, and teach the lesson that nowhere should there be ornament for ornament's sake.

Every school should have its museum of examples of fine craft. This is possible to a limited degree everywhere, for pictures, photographs and various reproductions can be obtained at small cost if fine original work cannot be afforded.

Here in New York visits to the Metropolitan museums by pupils would be practical in connection with the work in manual training, and such visits could be made most stimulating under proper direction; for pupils can appreciate the beauty of work in a material in which they have tried to express themselves, and they see the glorification of the crafts in the works of the masters.

And just here it seems to me comes a most important thought in our teaching. We should so present the work in each of the various materials that a high ideal of its possibilities is instilled into the minds of the pupils, and the famous men in the different lines of work should be familiar to them. Thus we can bring about a feeling of respect for what may have been a despised calling. We can teach "the nobility of labor, the long pedigree of toil." The drudge is the man without ideals. He is hopeless because he sees nothing before him, but if every workman could be made to see the whole ideal of which he may be working out only a small part, and to feel it within his power to strive for eminence in his calling, how much would be done to give joy to the workman. Then he might live to work, rather than toil to exist.

As many mediums and materials should be employed as seem practicable, for the key to good craft is the understanding of the possibilities and limitations of material. No material is inartistic if properly employed, but designs should be in harmony with the material, should grow out of its character, never should one material be made to imitate another.

The test of our work is found in the thought and interest that the pupils display in observing outside objects. Recently in Newton some boys were heard discussing the iron pickets on a fence, from the standpoint of constructive design. That showed good art training.

Finally our aim is not so much to give great skill to our pupils, as to make them appreciate what skillful work is, that they may have high ideals if they become craftsmen, and that they may at all events know the better from the poorer, and prefer the simple and the true and the beautiful to the tawdry and sham. Our aims should be similar to those of the arts and crafts societies. Thus shall we help to bring about in the next generation a more beautiful home life and a more beautiful public life.

MANUAL TRAINING AND MENTAL HABITS

DR. FREDERICK MONTESER, *Ethical Culture School, New York*

Surely a subject that contains such possibilities ought to stand in the very center of education, and the question of time which was formerly so often raised against it, ought to be simply pushed aside as a triviality.

Nevertheless, if any defence in this particular were needed, I should say that the experience of that school has amply demonstrated the fact that the time given to manual training is by no means lost to the traditional subjects of the curriculum, and the reason for that is twofold. In the first place, as every teacher knows, there is a time limit beyond which it is impossible to teach the purely theoretical subjects and get the full results of the teaching. Spelling, for instance, taught 45 minutes per day does not produce three times as good results as when you teach it only 15 minutes a day. Manual training, with its appeal to an entirely different set of brain centers, with the pleasurable emotion attending every kind of moderate physical exercise, affords the needed rest and relaxation. The beneficial effects of manual training are not only visible in subjects where we are prepared to find them, as in mathematics, geography and natural science, but they can be made to pervade the whole curriculum, even those subjects where the connection might seem less obvious, as history, language and literature.

But I do not intend to dwell longer on the intellectual value of manual training, although much might be said and has been said as to its effects on the development of the preceptive faculties, on the power of forming concepts, on the growth of imagination, and the training of the judgment. The aspect of manual training which attracts me most, and which is most in accord with the fundamental principles of the ethical culture schools, is its value as a means of the formation of character. A boy is not much disturbed by mistakes in spelling or language, but an ill-fitting joint, a carelessly drawn line stare him in the face, he cannot rest satisfied until he has produced something which harmonizes with his own mental standard of perfection. If he has studied a history lesson in a hasty and superficial manner, he may perhaps by a glib use of the tongue deceive others and himself. But there is no such possibility of hiding the result of error or negligence in manual work; the work itself proclaims it, so that everybody can judge, including its maker. Thus the student learns to despise sham and to respect honest work. But just as the bad piece of work stands out to speak for itself, so does the good too, there is no need of the teacher to tell the boy that he has done well. The very pleasure which he feels in the work shows him that it is right. The feeling of self-reliance, the independence of other people's opinions, this leaning on one's own judgments lies at the very foundation of a strong character. Furthermore, the consciousness of having performed a useful piece of work about as well as it can be done is invaluable, especially for the growing boy. It gives not only confidence in his own powers, it is not only an incentive to further efforts, but it imparts to him a certain dignity, a just and reasonable pride which is the best safeguard against all sorts of meanness and falsehood. In this way, manual training becomes a great school of industry and persistence. A boy who can take up his piece of carving or architectural drawing week after week working at it cheerfully until it is finished has learned a lesson of patient endeavor such as has produced all the great and enduring work in the world.

No wonder then that such an experienced observer as Mr. Larkins says " he has never met so potent a factor in ethical cultrue as manual training." More than in any other department it is true in ethics, that we learn to do by doing.

THE TRAINING OF THE SEWING TEACHER

The thoughtful teacher, in visiting schools where sewing is taught, to judge of its advantage as a part of the school curriculum, finds the greatest diversity in methods of teaching it and in the results gained. She also notices three classes of teachers at work in the field.

First. Sewing throughout most of the country is still regarded from its industrial and utilitarian standpoint. This idea, in many instances, has influenced the selection of teachers for their technical skill alone, and the work, though often faithfully given, has lacked continuity and correlation. If the aim of the educator is determined by the range of thought he brings to the subject, how can we expect educational results when we employ teachers who have never studied these problems and, in fact, have often but a grammar school education?

The second class of teachers is those who already are teaching in the grades or in other class work and have been appointed to teach sewing in addition to their other work. These are also unsatisfactory from the lack of interest they take in a subject of which they know almost nothing, and for which they have no time to prepare.

The third class—the teacher of sewing trained along pedagogic and professional lines—is slowly coming to the front. Her work shows the ability to meet the statement of educators that sewing should be a powerful factor in a girl's education.

The aim of the trained teacher of sewing is to touch the child physically, mentally, morally. To know how to train the brain through the hand she must never cease to study the child and its development, so the possibilities of all ages of children may be understood and utilized by her. By the materials in use in the work she trains the sense of touch to discriminate between qualities; the mind to judge of their appropriate use; and by the study of their manufacture she seeks to open the eyes to interests in the world without and create sympathy with work and the worker. The principles underlying the healthful and beautiful covering of the body, and the making of those articles, are but part of the study of ideal living and home keeping, which she should treat in such a way that ideas of home perfection may lead to a conception of honesty and beauty in the state. To accomplish this a regular training of several years is needed. Courses covering this ground are already formulated and are offered in parts of the country.

A SUCCESSFUL EXPERIMENT

Mr. Wm. W. Locke

New York City Truant School

The New York truant school is too recent an experiment to be quoted as a success, for the true success of such a school is to be tested by the general influence it has upon children who do not attend even more than upon those who are its inmates. The educational and other advantages of that school may induce children to play truant, in order to attend there. The opportunity for learning manual training may be so attractive, that pupils will be disorderly in their classes for the sake of securing the desired instruction. In much the same spirit, men have broken the plate-glass windows of a famous restaurant in order to obtain free board for a term of 30 days, or committed some crime in order to learn a trade in a penitentiary, which they had no chance to learn as an ordinary apprentice. The greatest success a truant school can accomplish is therefore not to be judged by the effect of its system of manual training upon its inmates, but by its deterrent and educational effect upon the children of public and other schools. A discussion of the larger sociological and economic importance of drawing, sewing, clay modeling and wood work as a part of public education might be of interest in connection with the subject of manual training. Courses of study have been determined too much by men of professional interests and not enough by men who had an intimate knowledge of manufactures, commerce and trade. No experiment in manual training can be thoroughly successful unless it reaches out towards the solution of the great industrial questions of our time. But the successful experiment I would call your attention to, is that of developing and strengthening character by means of manual training. This experiment of manual training which proves so interesting and educational to all children, is even more attractive and necessary to children of limited powers, who find no pleasure in books and study. Even the incorrigible truant and the child who is mentally deficient are glad to find that they have some powers for usefulness and are not altogether bad. For many years the truant was arrested during school hours, taken to the police court and sentenced to some reformatory for one or two years. This was clearly an injustice to the boy.

It is not recognized sufficiently that much of the truancy is not due to poverty, neglect or viciousness, but to the inadequate methods of the schools and the impossibility of adapting the teaching to individual needs. In the city of New York, where there are so many children of the foreign class and so many of the overcrowded tenement districts, there is special need of more flexibility and readiness to adapt the course of study to the needs of special classes. Much is done in a philanthropic way through the technical school of Baron De Hirsch, the educational alliance, the Italian schools of the children's aid society, etc. Hundreds of backward and overgrown girls and boys are given instruction in these schools, which they would otherwise obtain only in classes with children of four or five years younger than themselves. Hundreds of them realize that they cannot expect an advanced education and must necessarily belong to the laboring class. It is chiefly from this ignorant and undisciplined foreign class that the majority of the truants come. They are not proper subjects for reformatory institutions.

During the past winter 30 of these boys, who have been suspended from various public and parochial schools, were gathered together in an ungraded class. Some of them had been arrested by the police for disorderly conduct, larceny, etc. Some seemed to have no faculty for reading and spelling, although they were good at arithmetic and drawing. Some were partially deaf and mentally deficient, but only one boy was found to be so ungovernable that it was necessary to commit him to a reformatory institution. They became very much interested in mechanical drawing and wood work. They made good progress in clay modeling; their excellent sewing was a surprise to the dressmaking class of girls in the same school and their cooking class was the envy of all their companions. Although spending a large part of their time in manual training, they learned more than they ever did before in the ordinary English branches. It was difficult work for the teacher, and success was largely due to her kind, patient and determined efforts. But it was work that paid. The parents had less to complain of in regard to disobedience. Several of the boys who were almost of the vagrant class, secured employment at the end of the term and earned $3 a week. During the short term in which the truant school has been in operation, the same results of manual training have been observed. The boys have gained in attention, neatness, order and perseverance. They seem to have more life and ambition and self-respect. The protection of other schools was secured by having these boys attended to, the deterrent effect of their temporary confinement and discipline had its good influence upon their former companions in the neighborhood, but finally, not only has the city saved many hundreds of dollars, which would eventually have been spent upon these children in penal institutions, but has gained a number of young citizens, saved from any stigma of criminality, trained to useful service at some industrial occupation and made worthy of the birthright of their citizenship.

NATURE STUDY SECTION

Asst. Supt. Straubenmueller, Chairman

Henry G. Schneider, Secretary, grammar school No. 90

As chairman of the section, assistant superintendent Straubenmueller cordially welcomed the throng of teachers and then outlined the work of the section.

The papers presented, said the chairman, were prepared by teachers of New York city and would embody the results of their class-room work and experience in presenting nature study to city pupils. A special effort would be made to explain to teachers how, even in crowded city districts, true work in nature study could be done. As the first speaker, he introduced Mr. J. D. Hyatt, principal of grammar school No. 85, who presented a paper, "The use of the miscroscope in public schools."

Miss H. A. Johnson then presented a paper, "What can be done in nature study in crowded city districts." Then chairman Straubenmueller introduced Miss Eliza A. Jacobs, P. D., No. 77, who discussed the topic, "How children may be interested in the study of leaves." After brief discussion, the session was adjourned for the day.

The session of July 2 was opened by Mr. L. H. Hoysradt, grammar school 63, who dealt with the topic, "How to mount leaves and flowers."

Mrs. J. I. Northrop then spoke briefly of the attempts of the normal college alumnae to provide the downtown schools with nature study.

The next speaker, Henry G. Schneider, grammar school No. 90 discussed, "A trip to the Museum of Natural History—its educational uses to scholar and teacher in our city schools."

Mr. Wm. J. Timmons, grammar school No. 85, read a brief paper, "How should literature aid the objective study of nature?" Mr. W. H. J. Sieberg, principal grammar school No. 43, contributed a brief talk on "The study of minerals in the public schools."

The last paper was a plea for the earliest introduction of physics in the course of study because of its aid in the comprehension of such topics as climate in geography. Mr. John Doty of grammar school No. 103, entitled his paper "Introductory physics."

The chairman then declared that nominations for permanent officers to be the next business of the section.

Mrs. J. I. Northrup, 500 Warburton avenue, Yonkers, was then nominated and elected chairman of the section for 1898.

Miss Marie L. Sanial, primary department grammar school No. 90, was then nominated and elected secretary for 1898.

Mr. E. W. Stitt then moved a vote of thanks for the labors of chairman and speakers at the session and to the committee of arrangements whose efforts had resulted in making the sessions of the nature study section so successful and so enthusiastic.

NATURE STUDY WITH THE MICROSCOPE IN PUBLIC SCHOOLS

J. D. HYATT, *grammar school No.* 85, *New York City*

While to the profesional student of nature the microscope is an absolutely essential accessory to his appliances for investigation, that instrument has hardly yet been considered of such importance in the instruction of pupils in our public schools as to be placed upon the "list of supplies."

A small insect, or some portion of its anatomy, such, for example, as the compound eye of a beetle, the swarming animalculæ in a drop of stagnant water, or, most wonderful and instructive of all, even to people of more mature age, a view of the circulation of blood in the foot of a frog, will awaken a thoughtful interest and leave upon the mind a practical lesson in physiology that will remain long after all book lesson and lectures on the subject are forgotten. That the view of such an object may not be left as a mere matter of curiosity or amusement, pupils, after receiving such instruction regarding it as may be necessary, are cautioned to examine what they see very carefully, as they will be expected to make a rough drawing of it, and then write a brief composition containing a description, and the principal facts they have learned from its inspection.

In a manual training school, however, where cooking is taught to a certain extent on scientific principles, it would be quite impossible for teachers to carry out intelligently the requirements of the manual of instruction provided by the board of education for her guidance without the use of a fairly good microscope. Among the requirements of this manual the pupils must be instructed in such matters as the "nature and nutritive value of various articles used for food," the "germ theory and the causes of decay and decomposition of organic bodies." To make any intelligible explanation to children of these rather abstruse subjects without a good microscope would, it seems to me, be quite impossible, while with such an instrument any explanation is often quite unnecessary. As an illustration, place under the microscope some beef tea, the flavor of which shows that the process of decay has begun, or some mouldy bread or fermenting preserves, and the swarming bacteria in the first, and the thread-like mycelium and numerous reproductive spores of the others make the cause of decay so evident that the pupils would draw a correct conclusion as to the cause of decay without a word from the teacher. With regard to instruction respecting the "relative nutritive value of different kinds of food," an incident that came under my observation will serve to illustrate the great value of the microscope in determining some important points of that kind.

A TRIP TO THE MUSEUM OF NATURAL HISTORY—ITS EDUCATIONAL USES TO TEACHER AND SCHOLAR

H. G. SCHNEIDER, *grammar school* 90

We hear much of our disadvantages, as residents of a great city, in our lack of facilities for the study of nature. Yesterday's papers, and these exhibits of classwork from No. 90, justify our chairman's prediction that our sessions would demonstrate to our teachers that excellent work can be done even in schools situated where the only growing things are the children themselves. To-day I shall try to prove that our city children have advantages superior to those of their country cousins for real nature study. Our suburban parks are available for materials, and the suburbs of the Greater New York can supply all the material needed by the 4,000 teachers and the 200,000 pupils in our schools. Make up your mind that you will get the material, and you will find ways to get it.

The munificence of our city government, first in the world in the amount of money invested in buildings and equipment of our public schools, also provides an unrivalled institution for the recreation and instruction of our millions of fellow citizens of the Greater New York. Our Museum of Art and our Museum of Natural History can become very important features of our educational system if we teachers do our duty. Our Museum of Natural History is an institution of incalculable value in illustrating our daily class lessons.

To show what a great advantage the museum gives our city children, let us compare their facilities for true nature study. The country boy or girl is surrounded by the materials for nature study. While he has every opportunity for observing and collecting specimens, yet this very familiarity and accessibility often dulls his curiosity. To the city child, who sees a butterfly, a bird's nest or frog's eggs for the first time, the novelty and rarity of the experience makes him observe them with a keener curiosity than do his country cousins. In the country, the multiplicity of specimens is somewhat of a disadvantage for careful study. The city child's attention is concentrated to the one specimen in his class-room and not distracted by a variety. It is for the same reason that you must not try to give a formal lesson while out on a collecting trip with scholars; there are too many causes to distract their attention. But how is the country boy to bridge over the gap between the specimen and what man knows of it? How is he to name and classify the myriad observations he has opportunities to make? If he needs help, how is he to obtain it? The city child, on the contrary, has access to a noble institution, where he can see not only a specimen like his own, but also a label which tells him its place in the scheme of science, and its relations to all other manifestations of nature.

Every teacher knows that we must persuade and encourage the scholar to go to the dictionary, and train him in correct habits in using and referring to it for information, so in teaching him to avail himself of the museum's advantages, it is not enough to tell him to go there. We must take the children there and teach them to make a proper use of the trip only asking them to note one particular specimen that attracted their attention, and to observe that carefully for at least ten minutes. It is better to assign topics through the week, to separate groups of scholars, one for instance, to the relics of the mound builders mentioned in the school history; another to the race types illustrated by life-size figures in the hall of ethnology; another to the minerals and ores mentioned in the geography lesson; another to the trees and vegetable productions of the same continent we were studying; while other groups report on the animals in the museum pictured in our geography lesson.

The scholar who is trained to go to the museum for study of this kind digs out for himself what he wants to know. Very often he can outstrip his teacher's knowledge of the works of nature. In life, our scholars must see, think and compare for themselves, from the real things and conditions. In our observation lessons we should not, as we too often do, try to "cram" information which we have obtained from our reading. No! Get the real specimen before the pupil, let him find out what he can for himself by using his own senses. Never tell him what he can find out for himself; at most lead him by a skillful question to note the peculiarity you wished him to observe, and you will find that he will tell you more about the specimen than the books do. Teach him to use his own powers, and you will send into the world scholars able to think and learn for themselves.

HOW CHILDREN CAN BE INTERESTED IN THE STUDY OF THE LEAVES OF TREES

BY ELIZABETH A. JACOBS, *primary school No. 77*

The study of leaves in my class was introduced from the nasturtium seeds that my pupils had planted, and in whose development and growth they were deeply interested, evinced by the fact that on their entrance to the class-room the children immediately went to the window to see if their plants had grown over night. After we had discussed in previous lessons the root, stem and seed leaves, we began this talk about the true leaves, at that time very prominent on these little nasturtium plants, by my telling the children to observe the way the leaf was fastened to the stem, its color, its shape, and from this we passed on to the leaves of other plants.

"I shall speak of trees as we see them, love them, adore them in the fields where they are alive, holding their green sunshades over our heads, talking to us with their hundred thousand whispering tongues, looking down on us with that sweetness which belongs to huge but limited organisms."—O. W. Holmes.

Having aroused their interest by the selection and from their own plants, I gave each child a leaf obtained from various trees found in our central park. The children were delighted with them and many of them described the leaves in thir own language. The thought gathered from the children's observations and handling of the leaves was many sided and related to their shape, color, venation, sap, arrangement on stem, movement on tree; and the deduction followed that no two leaves were exactly alike.

The point that I wished to call particular attention to, and for which I was going to work, was the use of the leaves to the tree and to us; so I asked, where did these leaves you have come from? Of what use were they to the tree? What makes the tree grow? Here I would show two plants, one fresh, the other wilted, asking the children to notice in what way they differed. The response being, one of them needs water, and then would follow the use of water in feeding plants and the explanation of how the roots, acting as mouths, force the water through the stems to the leaves, where it passes off through their openings.

If possible, let the children look at their leaves under a magnifying glass, seeing the little cells, which are filled with the food called sap. Next the pupils noticed the number of veins in each leaf, and I told them the veins they saw when they looked, and of which there are so many in a leaf, carry the food, called sap or juice, to the cell in the same manner as our veins carry our blood.

What is it that makes leaves grow, besides food and air, was the next point I brought forward, and the pupils instantly said the sun's light, and they were right; for without the sun's beams a leaf or plant cannot properly perform its life-work any more than we can. At this juncture I explained to the class that it is the sun's light that colors the leaves green, and that to know this fact, they could place a plant in the dark for a time, and then they would be able to see its leaves lose their coloring matter.

For the lesson next time, I told my children to look at a tree. If no tree had been available, I would have said another plant, and then I would draw from their observation God's goodness in spreading out leaves on every part of the tree exposed to the light and air.

I now explained briefly how, by means of these cells in the leaves, which act as lungs to the plant, it breathes. Following it by: What is it we breathe? Air, was the response. Children, is the air always fit for us to breathe? No, the answers come, it is filled with bad gases. That is so, I said, and leaves of plants make the air pure again for us to breathe, by absorbing into their leaf cells the impure gases of the air which are good to make the whole plant grow. Then I drew attention to the way leaves clothe or dress the tree, and, considering how many leaves there are, they never get in each other's way. In my next lesson I'd talk about how dreary it would be were there no trees with their leaves, and how grateful we ought to be for the shade they offer us on a hot day. In all lessons I would endeavor to fix information, obtained by examination and observation, to enable children to draw and write about the matter learned. In subsequent lessons I would again dwell on the beauty of trees and their use; and have children memorize a few selections relating to the leaves, and try to plant within their minds the idea, the great thought, that the leaves are always working and helping to do their part in God's great plan.

GRAMMAR SCHOOL SECTION

JAMES M. EDSELL, *grammar school No. 101, Brooklyn, Chairman*

DR. L. H. WHITE, *grammar school No. 94, Brooklyn, Secretary*

THURSDAY

Channing Stebbins, grammar school 77, Brooklyn, was not present to discuss the question of departmental teaching.

James M. Edsell, grammar school 101, Brooklyn, chairman, opened the discussion. He claimed that while there were advantages in the departmental system, there was a great danger in such specialist emphasizing the importance of his own subject to the extent of overloading pupils with work.

Superintendent Norris, Canandaigua, speaking from experience in his own schools, claimed a great advantage in scholarship for departmental teaching.

Prin. Preston, of Mount Vernon, thought the conditions of discipline were more favorable in the departmental system, and feared that the improvement in scholarship was given in exchange for character development.

Dr. W. T. Vlymin, grammar school No. 5, Brooklyn, argued that the desirability of the departmental teaching was a question of conditions or environment.

Prin. John H. Haaren, grammar school No. 10, Brooklyn, claimed a great advantage in departmental teaching in the opportunity afforded to assign work according to special adaptations of teacher.

Friday

At the opening of the session, the permanent organization of this department for the coming year was completed. E. E. Lawton, of Auburn, was elected president; George E. Atwood, Long Island City, secretary.

GRADATION AND PROMOTION

Frederick H. Lane

That there shall be grades in large schools and that some effective method shall be provided to determine when the steps between the grades shall be taken, is pretty well established; how these grades shall be arranged and what shall constitute fitness for taking the step, has provoked much investigation and, possibly, more discussion. It has been extremely fashionable to criticise the formalism of schools, to deprecate the "Procrustean bed" of grades and to long for the freedom of the district school, but yet the escape from this indictment has not effectively or at least, generally presented itself. There is, unfortunately for system, no uniformity in mental development and therefore, there can be no gainsaying the assertion that pupils cannot be graded for mental progress as a company of grenadiers may be for alignment and length of step in marching. Granted that the start be even, it will be impossible to retain the equality for any length of time, some must be held back, an injustice with little defense, or others must be pushed, without understanding, over the ground for the sake of the progress fitting the brighter pupils.

The explication of this phase is far-reaching and the best attention has been given to it.

Pupils started with accomplishments as near equivalence as they can be ascertained, will not long remain in company. Abilities are unlike and require different methods of fostering; it will not be long before the particular sort of instruction received will have different effects upon the varying qualities of intellect affected and, entirely without intent, a classification will be set up. In the mental make-up of any grade there are roughly three classes—the bright, the dull, and the average; for which of these the class will be conducted is important but uncertain. The temptation to work along lines of least resistance, is clear and not too often withstood. On the other hand, the teacher may be hyper-conscientious or the grade standard low enough that the conduct may be for the duller. Or, as is general, the class may be carried on for the average members of it. In any case the injustice is certain. The brighter pupils will have been held back from their full capability and will acquire habits leading to mental rust and satisfaction with moderate instead of high achievement; the slow will have spent a year in the stultifying position of continual failure and growing depth of disbelief in self; while, save that the ideal is kept too near realization, the average pupil may have been well cared for. Although on the principle of "the greatest good to the greatest number," the quantity benefited does not seem to bear out the strict text of the precept, and other methods may claim to produce a larger good and in a proportion greater.

It must be admitted, however, that to criticise yearly gradation and promotion is to question the system in use in some of the foremost schools of the country (Cleveland, Worcester, Yonkers, Buffalo, Springfield, Brookline and Chelsea), and it savors of temerity to attempt it.

If a pupil deserves to be put forward, it must be for one year. The work yet remaining in his grade and all which has been done in the following grade must be skipped. If the course of study is well laid out, the omitted work is necessary for progress in the new grade and the pupil must be strong enough to do this without aid and beside, to maintain his place in a class one year in advance and one which has had careful instruction in the work of which he, in most cases, knows nothing. It lays down an injunction against the promotion of a pupil who cannot do, not only, two years' work in one but one of these unaided. Either this, or work is laid down in the course which may be omitted with impunity, in which case it has no place in the course at all. Naturally, ability of this marvelous strength is rare and effective promotions proportional. Too often the pupil irregularly promoted will fail from the over-burden thrust with the best of intent upon him and he will be found with the average members of the class from which he was promoted, dulled and discouraged with the feeling of a failure in which he had no voluntary part and his abilities stunted for future work. Such a method of grading is defective from the absolute damper which the long interval places upon individuality of any progressive sort, and from the time lost in passage through the grades. A shorter grade term seems the natural solution, and plans for meeting it are various.

A few schools have broken loose from all attempt at formalism as to time limits or grade integrity and classes are permitted to subdivide into what seem natural divisions for carrying on the work, especially in the more important subjects, and attention is given to each division according to its need. Promotions are made from division to division, according to merit and the incentive of constant progress is at hand. Its exponents claim that there is none of the loss incident to the usual grading and that the course for able students is shortened, abilities kept at their keen edge and general progress promoted. That these ends can be attained and that such a method of grading is free from most of the features which have given the usual gradation its bad name, is doubtless true, though it is not so certain that it is free from certain objections of its own.

To divide a class into sections will multiply the work of the teacher, seemingly by the number of sections, while the benefit to the pupil will be divided in something like proportion. It places the burden of two, three or more classes upon the teacher for whom one will be found ample for effective work. The use of such a system implies an infinitude of detail in supervision and the possession of a very high order of wisdom and strength by the teacher in charge. As individual teaching becomes possible, classes must diminish in size and it is difficult to see how this method can be successfully employed where the common illiberality in this respect prevails. It would be interesting to know if it could be effectively used in any of the larger systems, hampered with inadequate supervision, crowded classes and too frequent inexpertness in the teaching force.

The wisdom of subdivision will be properly questioned, since the breach will generally widen rather than close. Teachers with one class are sufficiently burdened and it would seem the wiser way to use every effort to maintain the integrity of the class, by giving to one division greater attention to enable it to get on an equal footing with the other, rather than to widen the gap and increase the labor of the teacher while diminishing the aggregate attention which the members of the class would receive if handled as a unit. There is unquestionably a middle ground to be maintained in the matter and it may not unfairly consist in a course which by shortness of interval will permit promotion and demotion without great loss to the pupil affected and which will, yet, maintain grade lines pretty intact within those limits.

The usual arrangement of grades, in most systems, is unfitted for the natural influx of pupils. In September new pupils enter the lowest primary grade and in April another detachment presents itself. The first will have fitted into the grade and gone on regularly while those entering in April will find the work two-thirds through under the yearly system or that of the spring class part completed, where the half-yearly system prevails. It would seem manifestly better if the grades terminated here as they would in the quarterly system or if the class entering in the spring could be retained by the same teacher until one year from that time. Some such arrangement is the more important since the initial year in school is that of greatest loss, as more pupils are kept from promotion in that year than in any period succeeding. The extra year obtaining in the nine year courses is generally due to the necessity for adjustment in this first year class.

On the question of promotion, I am unable to find a single school system of prominence in the United States which will admit that examinations are made the only basis for promotion; in one only, and that in New York State, that method is used in two of the upper grammar grades. In two systems the class record and examination are made the basis, in eleven the teacher's or principal's recommendation is the sole test and in all others, from fifty of the most prominent systems of which inquiry was made, a combination of examination, class record and teacher's recommendation holds. It is possible that a wider inquiry would develop a less favorable showing and it is probable that a much less encouraging exhibit would have been made by the cities in question, if the inquiry had been made a few years earlier. The exposition seems to indicate that there is little to rave over in the methods of promotion in use in the grammar schools of the country. It would seem therefore that examinations, as a test for promotion, have had their day, and that polemics in that field will soon fall futile. As a test for memory and self-possession, the examination will retain its value and it will remain the only method in which a person can exhibit his knowledge at short notice, to one unacquainted with his equipment; to the teacher as a final test for work done entirely under her eye and subject to the daily and hourly examination of the class room, it is not necessary. It sometime occurs as a query whether as much would have been made of examination, at least for so long, if they had not afforded a convenient refuge for the teacher to explain failure to promote pupils when approached by over-estimating parents. In several cities in which promotion is entirely upon the teacher's estimate, upon request pupils who fail to be recommended for promotion, are permitted to try an examination and are promoted if they succeed in passing, an event of no great certainty. It often seems that besides the question of how to find when pupils are fitted for promotion, decisiveness, bravery and backbone in the promoting power are quite as important and too infrequent.

To all methods of grading objections may and will be raised. With the yearly system the length of interval is cited; to a shorter grade term the duration of a good teacher's influence seems wanting and to procedure by sections, the integrity and unity of work. The ideal method would undoubtedly group pupils according to their ability and advance them in proportion to their power. To attain it there must be provided a course of study sufficiently elastic to admit of promotion at the time set, with the understanding that the following grade continue from the point left or promotions must be made only when the pupils complete the work assigned, regardless of time. Therein are involved the manifold questions of subdivision, number in a class, expertness in teacher and supervisor and the confidence of the public in the good sense and intent of those conducting the school. Towards this we are slowly working but to it we are not, nor are the leagues yet few.

CHILD STUDY SECTION

President—GEORGE GRIFFITH, Utica.

Vice-President—EDGAR DUBS SHIMER, Ph. D., New York City.

Secretary and treasurer—M. V. O'SHEA, Buffalo.

Called to order by the president, Superintendent George Griffith, of Utica.

He referred to the growth of the movement and commented on the wide-spread interest in child study. He sketched the movement that led to the formation of the New York state society for child study and then continued in substance as follows:

To study children is not new. All thoughtful parents, all true teachers, for all time, have been students of children. Their study has been loving and sympathetic, but desultory and empirical. In these days the effort is to interest all teachers in this study, and to make it systematic and scientific. It will be a mistake if it is allowed to become any the less loving and sympathetic. It is hoped that this and similar societies will widen the interest and will guide the study into the most helpful channels.

Years before last some of my teachers and myself were anxious to do some systematic child study. We knew almost nothing about it but got some help and began. Mistakes were made that had been made by others beginning as we did without proper guidance. Doubtless there are teachers and groups of teachers throughout our state that have learned just enough about the movement to see some of its possibilities and desire to begin systematic work. It is hoped that this society will be able to help such to start the work on right lines and to guide them in it. It has seemed to me that much material is being secured by child study throughout the country that if collected and examined by some central competent committee would reveal helpful lessons. Such a society as this can provide for this.

While I believe there should be great caution and becoming modesty in formulating and promulgating conclusions in the form of educational principles and pedagogical directions, I am equally certain that child study, rightly directed and its revelations intelligently interpreted, will result in many such principles and helpful directions for teachers. The New York society ought to have upon its committees men and women competent to do this wisely and well.

One word more. I read in the constitution of a similar society that the society was primarily for the good of the teachers, and secondarily, for the good of the children. If I understand this statement correctly, I wish to voice an emphatic protest. The good of the child should be the ultimate end of any and every similar movement. A newspaper criticised the child study movement and argued that the children were sent to school to be taught and not studied! Unless we study the child, that we may teach him better, unless better teaching of the child for his ultimate good shall be the great purpose of our child study movement, I believe we shall miss what should be our sole aim.

THE PURPOSE, SCOPE AND METHOD OF CHILD STUDY

PROF. M. V. O'SHEA

I

In the evolution of any people, there comes a time when they realize that progress is dependent upon the systematic education of childhood, and institutions are established to accomplish this purpose. Education in this sense has been considered in the past to consist in imparting to the youth of any generation that useful knowledge which preceding ages have discovered at a cost of much trial and suffering. Such a conception of educa tion does not take account of any essential differences between the child and the adult, and the instruction of the latter would proceed in substantially the same way as that of the former. The next step in the progress of a people is to realize that the development of an individual comprises something more than mere growth in size; and the adult is more than and different from a grown child. If our education, then, would be most effective in leading the young to realize more and more fully the ideals of the race, we must know what the laws of the development of childhood are, and must base our training upon these. This idea seems to be gradually disseminating itself in the minds of men to-day, and its embodiment in practical, active form has received the term of child study. There is a consciousness, not clearly defined, however, that the mental and physical development of an individual from birth to maturity is in obedience to definite principles of growth, and we may gain acquaintanceship with these only by concrete, inductive study in the same way that we have obtained a knowledge of the operations of inorganic nature.

Child study represents, then, first and foremost, an effort to apply the inductive method of investigation to the study of child development. One hears now and again some criticism of this movement, maintaining that it is not new, and that it has nothing in particular to acomplish, since the race has always studied its children and has based its training upon their needs and capacities at various stages in their development. It must, of course, be true that children have always been studied in a way, and that there has been some effort made to treat them in a manner conforming to their powers and interests. Chamberlain has shown us that even in the most savage homes among every tribe and people the child is recognized as differing in some important measure, be it ever so little, from the grown members of the family or community. In the literature of Greece and Rome, as Scudder says, there is frequent reference to the training of children based somewhat upon a comprehension of their needs and capacities. And as we come nearer our own day, we may point to Froebel, Pestalozzi and their disciples in evidence of the fact that children have, in reality, been studied before the present decade in the development of the race. But all this study has been principally of an incidental or intuitive kind, just as before the time of Bacon nature was studied intuitively. Bacon and his followers did not have to discover *de novo* the whole universe of physical laws. The experiences of the race had already established a considerable body of scientific knowledge; but the apostles of the inductive method, accepting what had already been accomplished, went forward to add a vast deal more and to show that much that had been implicitly believed and acted upon was false, since before the advent of this method the pseudo sciences of the middle ages, as chiromancy and astrology held, far greater sway over the people than did the exact sciences.

It purposes to marshal all the sciences that relate to human life to aid in this great undertaking. It has in view not only to discover how the child develops naturally if left to himself, but what effect various educational agencies have upon that development, either in hastening it toward a desired end or retarding or diverting it into wrong channels.

There are those who feel that any attempt to thus study childhood scientifically must result in doing violence to the spiritual nature of the one studied, and in stifling the sympathies and affections of the investigator. We all have the feeling, which is surely a wholesome one, that the soul of man transcends the possibility of being revealed in its essence by scientific studies, and we dread to have the word scientific applied to anything relating to matters spiritual, as though there were some irreparable conflict between the truth which science gives and that which resides in the human soul. But if any are thus afraid, they may dispel their fears, for in so far as child development, physical or spiritual, is not dependent upon laws, it cannot be determined by scientific study; but to the degree that it is thus dependent, it is most important that we know what these laws are. If we did but realize it, we are all scientists in a way with our children. We know that certain modes of treatment will invariably produce characteristic results. For instance, we have observed enough of the uniformity of law in child development to see that evil companions corrupt good manners, and that a deceitful parent begets a deceitful child. In our daily contact with children most of us try to ground our behavior, unconsciously many times perhaps, upon a knowledge of the fact that one kind of conduct will universally be beneficial, while another will as certainly be detrimental. Now it is to make these laws explicit, to greatly extend them, and to correct erroneous ones that is the proper field for scientific child study. No greater injury can be done to the spiritual nature of the child by such scientific study than is done every day by the parent or teacher who carefully calculates in his methods of dealing with his children what the effects will be. There need be no fear, then, that an earnest, sympathetic attempt to discover how the child develops and how various agencies influence him will have any other effect than to make our dealing with him more rational, and so more beneficial.

As the knowledge of nature only increases the mystery of her ways and constitution in a certain sense, so a profounder knowledge of child-life only magnifies our wonder and our reverence and our sense of gratitude and of responsibility.

II.

Child-study has another aspect which is not less important but rather more so than the first. As an outcome of modern psychology we are beginning to appreciate as we have never before that every individual is the product of many factors which give him a distinct personality—which determine his needs and which limit his capacities. It was at one time believed, and is still held by some persons, that every child could be made like every other child in intellect and temperament by proper instruction and discipline. One may even now hear teachers speak of a pupil who does not make satisfactory advances in the studies of the school as dull or stupid or lazy, and it is often believed that these conditions may be remedied by sufficient punishment; and if a pupil does not conform graciously to the regulations of the school his will is thought to be perverted and it can be changed only by a generous use of the rod. But an era of more rational things in education is being ushered in, and it is being appreciated that when a child is dull or vicious or exceptional in any way, there are definite causes which must be removed or modified in order that his nature may be changed. We have, then, a need for the study of individual children in order to ascertain their peculiar needs and capacities as an essential condition for their proper instruction and training; and this is perhaps the most important aspect of child-study. Every science has its phase of application where its laws are applied to particular conditions; and the science of child-study, if we may say that there is yet a science, has as its ultimate end the intelligent training of individual children in home, church, and school.

In our day every individual is deemed worthy of the most careful attention. All the influences at our command must contribute to his highest development. Unlike the farmer who cares little for any particular stalk in his corn field, the parent or teacher cares everything for every plant whether weak or strong in her child garden.

III.

The term child-study has not been a happy one in all respects to designate this movement, since it has been interpreted to relate principally or wholly to the period of early childhood. As a result the interests and attention of teachers in secondary and higher education have not been enlisted in any effective degree. There has been a noticeable tendency on the part of high school and college teachers to refrain from manifesting any enthusiasm in child-study, as though their pupils did not need to be studied after they passed the elementary school, or as if the teachers of these older children had some subtle power of determining the true nature of childhood which rendered it unnecessary for them to ally themselves with a movement of this kind. This is the more remarkable since it is being generally recognized that the high school and early college period constitute the most vital years in a child's life. While perhaps not much of value to teachers has yet been established by science respecting the period of adolescence, still it is at least certain that it is a time of rapid development, fluctuation, and uncertainty. This is probably the period where there is the least adaptation of instruction to the real needs and capacities of those being taught. Secondary and higher education seem to have responded very slowly if at all to the efforts to determine and conduct studies and discipline according to the nature of pupils. Rather the chief energy of the teachers of these older pupils has been given to developing scientifically subjects of instruction; and scholasticism has been and still is exhalted above everything else. We know how during the middle ages, and until a late period after the Renaissance, scholasticism was deified even with the youngest children. The wise men of those days maintained that if the child did not natively have a love for abstract knowledge, and that logically presented to him, why he ought for his own future well-being to be constrained thereto from the outset. There seems always to be the danger that teachers will give more heed to developing the subjects they are teaching formally than to adapt them to the children being taught; and while in elementary education this has been somewhat mitigated it appears to continue unmodified for the most part as you ascend the scale of grades in our educational system.

IV.

In the elaboration of any science one of the most serious problems is to devise practical and reliable methods of investigation. Scientific method always demands two things: First, an abundance of data; and second, this data must have been accurately obtained. In the sphere of child-study these conditions are particularly hard to be realized on account of the nature of the materials dealt with. While physical objects and phenomena may be experimented upon concretely and indiscriminately, such liberties may not be taken to any great extent with human beings. The problem is such an intricate one for science that people have despaired of ever solving it in the psychological laboratory. The child-study movement has been derided more for the methods of study pursued by some investigators than for any other reason. There recently appeared in the London Journal of Education an account of the way a father influenced by the ambition to contribute to the science of human development set out to study his little child. He first secured a long list of disagreeably tasting stuffs and proceeded to try each one upon his child so as to observe the character of his reactions. The first test produced such vigorous results both on the part of the child and its mother that the father could not describe them with scientific accuracy and he decided he had better try the other senses. Having a similar experience all round, he finally gave up child-study in disgust, and generously berated the whole movement as did all his friends and neighbors who had heard of his adventures.

It may be well to mention briefly some of the methods which have given us reliable data already in the hands of competent persons. There is first the biographical method employed by Preyer, Porez, Miss Shinn, Bowditch, and others, wherein the development of a child is observed for a considerable period of time, and the principal facts of his growth noted. The studies made thus far by this method relate in the main to very young children, but we would be greatly benefited by having them carried on with older children. Malling-Hausen, Lands, Bowditch, and others have studied a number of children for quite a long period of years with the one purpose in view to ascertain periods of physical growth, but we need studies to show if there are regular periods in mental growth, in the appearance of predominent interests, and so on. Then there is the method employed recently by Dr. Stanley Hall in his syllabi covering various phenomena of childhood, as anger, fear, etc., the data upon which are to be gained from parents and teachers. In the third place there is the syllabus method devised, I believe, by Barnes which give a number of questions calling for tests upon children, the questions to be answered by teachers. More lately professor Barnes has had children write essays upon some topic involving their ideas of time, of justice, and so on; or he has asked them to illustrate some story by drawing, and then the essay or drawing is examined. Fourth, there are the studies upon growth by weighings and measurements of the whole and different parts of the body. Finally, there is the truly scientific method of study with delicate apparatus in the laboratory to discover, speaking generally, the character of children's reaction upon stimulus under different conditions as in a state of fatigue following upon either physical or mental effort, and so on. These methods are not designed at all for teachers and parents; and much of the criticism of child study has resulted from a misunderstanding as to how scientific data were to be obtained and who was to secure them. The business of a teacher or parent is not to rear a science of child study, or to furnish to any great extent the data for such a science, for two reasons; first, they have not the time or opportunity; and secondly, they have not ordinarily the scientific training which would make their observations of great value.

The brain condition determines of course the intellectual and temperamental characteristics of the individual. For instance, one child may be found to give forth a great deal of energy upon the slightest stimulus. His reaction will be very much greater than the stimulus demands; while another pupil in the same class and of the same age will react slightly upon the same stimulus, perhaps not as much as the stimulus would warrant. Here are two types contrasted with each other whose characteristics are determined by fundamental physical conditions. Of what infinite value should this knowledge be to the teacher in dealing with these two children· So in the same way when a simple task requiring control and inhibition of movement is set two children in the same class one controls himself admirably in the effort to accomplish the task, while the other shows little power of inhibition, but goes off by explosion, as it were. Here again are fundamental differences which must show themselves in all the work of the school and which must explain many problems which constantly perplex and discourage the teacher.

V.

It should be the purpose of the New York society for child study to make use of all good methods in the study of children which while practicable are at the same time thoroughly scientific. And it should distinguish at all times between scientific investigation for scientific purposes and practical investigation for practical purposes. It should recognize that scientific methods require special opportunities and specially trained persons; but when results are reached they should be of definite practical value, and should then be given to teachers and parents and their concrete bearings indicated in as great detail as possible. With the purpose kept constantly in view to thus unify science and practice in every phase of child growth, and permeate all with the truest sympathetic spirit, this society cannot fail of distinguished success in promoting the rational treatment of children everywhere.

Professor J. McKeen Cattell, Columbia University, said that a science must precede its application. The phenomena of physics must be investigated and understood before we can have the steam engine or the electric motor. So we must understand the child's growth and development before we can intelligently direct it. It is wrong to regard knowledge as valueless because we cannot at once see its practical applications. We must, of course, do the best we can with our present knowledge, and an association such as this can accomplish much by mutual counsel and encouragement and by developing sympathy with the child and its point of view. But one of its objects should be to use the knowledge we have and to increase this knowledge.

The speaker then briefly described the physical and mental measurements made on students at Columbia University in the laboratory of psychology, and recommended that such measurements be also made in the schools.

SECTION OF READING AND ELOCUTION

THURSDAY

MARY HURLBUT BALDWIN, *Secretary*

RICHARD E. MAYNE, *Chairman*

Session called to order at 11 o'clock by Richard E. Mayne, chairman, with the following address:

Systematic elocutionary exercises in the public schools of New York city have met with many obstacles. The belief has long prevailed, for instance, that a mercantile section demands a mercantile education, and that of this, elocution is not a part. A more liberal view shows that its exclusion, even in an admittedly commercial center entails sacrifices too great to be longer borne. So many now share this view, including educators of every rank, that the attempt is being made to show how far and in what manner elocution can be utilized in the way that nature intended, that is at the service of the multitude of children upon whom rests the future of American speech.

I begin by substituting the name oral expression in place of elocution. This name stands for the larger and more essential part of the art of elocution, it conforms to the original meaning of the word, and it presents in a familiar and intelligible form what, under other terms, the school teacher has too long regarded as alien. It has been quite common for people to understand by elocution something having more to do with gesture than with speech. Nothing has done so much to keep the distance wide apart between the art and the great numbers who could make use of it as this damaging misconception. In public schools generally the actual exercises, under the name of elocution, have consisted of some extracts in prose or verse memorized and declaimed by a few pupils, and of selected recitations prepared to entertain friends at commencement; and this, without any definite means, like ex-

[illegible] Now, [illegible] vast [illegible] which it [illegible] is such a [illegible] primary [illegible] can [illegible] by an [illegible] monopoly [illegible] three-fourths [illegible] speak, that is [illegible] English. [illegible] then, a [illegible] consonants. Only [illegible] trained, the ear [illegible] and the weeds [illegible] from taking [illegible] lessons in [illegible] province of [illegible] in oral ex- [illegible] How much the in- [illegible] orderly de- [illegible] of sympathetic [illegible] Only in such [illegible] those faculties [illegible] soulless [illegible] would exhaust [illegible] disparaging words in the language. Composition-writing offers an interesting analogy to speech culture. Instead of this we need the flexibility of tone that responds to every quiver of thought or pulse of emotion, and projects with exquisite sufficiency the inner to the outer world of being. All good speakers and readers possess it and in it they have the rarest jewel in the treasury of the art. Each volume of sound coming from the larynx is like a sunbeam impinged upon the spectrum, whose variety of tints is limited only by the power of the organ that perceives them.

As already intimated, the right starting place in dealing with children is the primary department. The invariable regulation pertaining to the language lesson in that department prepares the way for improvement, requiring, as it does, instruction in the vowels and consonants. The new addition will, therefore, seem not as an innovation but as progression along the line already started. To facilitate the work a set of charts could be devised with exercises for frequent repetition. Among the advantages of the chart is one that is often overlooked. Its constant presence makes reference to it very easy, and it engenders a habit of attending to its behests unconsciously; in the same way the presence of a clock enables one to tell the time without the trouble of looking, except for verification. Another medium for practice is the quotation. If short, as it ought to be for the lower grades, twenty or thirty examples can be heard in part of the time now allotted to reading and language. I have on several occasions heard fifty, and found time for a word of correction or approval for each speaker, all in thirty minutes. The utility of speaking aloud is manifold. It is especially good as a test of pronunciation. The delivery being pitched on a large scale, beauties and blemishes are magnified and become more noticeable to the children who are listening. This is true alike of all grades and is, of course, more emphatic in proportion to the size of the room in which the speaking is done. Again, the young speaker learns how to address others directly—to convince or persuade—which is the ultimate end of all training in expression, instead of repeating the words merely to elicit correction from the teacher. No positive time can be stated when the elements of speech and the quotation ought to be laid aside; they could be continued above the primary. After the higher grades are reached and conscious attention is drawn for the first time to the principles of interpretation as such, pupils may refer back occasionally to the early lessons for review. In any of these exercises, but especially those of the first two or three years, strict attention should be given to the correlation of tongue and ear—that most necessary and at the same time most neglected of wise precautions. I need scarcely add that at all times spontaneity of utterance is the best of all things, and if it be added to the knowledge of principles so far spoken about, the reading lesson is soon changed from the thoughtless to the thoughtful.

However good these exercises may be for children, they will fail unless supplemented by the teacher's hearty co-operation. Teachers' training schools should provide a course in accordance with the most scientific methods. One or two hours weekly would suffice for the purpose. To pass the examination in a normal course a candidate should manifest a general knowledge of the art, and in particular be familiar with these details: know how to train memory, remove defects of speech, cultivate the ear sense, understand the bearing of expression on character building. She or he should understand why it is the foundation of literary criticism, be able to explain in what way the emotions are to be exercised so as to secure a flexible and responsive voice. The candidate should realize and keep in mind above all other things the importance of bringing out the best qualities of each pupil, with a view of facilitating the broadest and completest development of the individual.

Such is an outline of the place of elocution in public instruction. Such details as grading the exercises, fixing the amount of time for each class, promotions, and the selecting of literature for practice can be arranged to suit various tastes or requirements. Since the future American speech is based on it, its adoption in the public schools of the country is the next step to be taken in the progress of education.

DISCUSSION

Professor S. H. Clark.—I think, as conscientious teachers, we are ready to admit that the great failure of the public school curriculum is in the realm of reading. The fault does not lie with the teacher that he cannot teach it; but in the fact that the teacher receives no training whatsoever in the pedagogy of reading aloud.

Why is reading aloud the great untaught subject of the public school curriculum? There are two great difficulties to be overcome, which are inherent in the subject itself: First, the intangibility of vocal expression; second, the complexity of that composite result which we call "reading aloud."

Let me explain what we mean by intangibility. Perhaps that is best done by showing what is a tangible subject. When a student hands in a paper containing twenty words of spelling, the teacher may take up the paper and say, there are fourteen correctly spelled, and six incorrectly. But when we get into that realm of mental action that is manifested in reading, the expression is gone in the uttering. In a sentence of 100 words, the pupil does a hundred things. He may read quickly or slowly; his key may be high or low; his inflection may be incorrect; his melody may wobble around like a rudderless ship; his voice may not carry far enough. There are so many things occurring at every moment that when the pupil finishes the reading of a given paragraph the teacher stands incapable in the presence of the mistakes.

In the second place it is the complexity of the vocal expression that makes difficult the teaching of reading. Take a half a dozen words, and let us see what elements there may be in the reading of them. The phrase may be read slowly; it may be read in a high pitch or low pitch; it may be read with a great deal of force, or with an absence of it; and so, at one moment, upon a few words, we may have all the elements of vocal expression—the time, the pitch, the stress and what not—all of which elements manifest certain states of consciousness. Here, then, in a few words, are the two elements, the difficulty of which lies at the bottom of our inability as teachers of reading aloud—the intangibility and complexity.

We, as teachers, must understand the relation between the vocal signs and the activities of the mind that create those signs. Then the difficulties of reading must be presented to the pupil step by step until all the ground, so far as we are able to perceive it, has been covered.

The trouble with our students in their history lessons, in their geography lessons, and in their arithmetic lessons is, that the words do not present and convey ideas; and until the printed page becomes the speaking voice, all study in whatsoever department is utterly valueless, or haphazard in its results at best. I stand to-day to plead, not for reading aloud as an art, (that comes later), but for accurate, careful silent reading. After that, reading aloud becomes a comparatively simple process. No student who enters the public school, with very few exceptions, but has the possibility of becoming a good, if not a great, reader. The first thing that must be impressed upon him is, that these are not mere words, but are ideas, are representations of pictures, of thoughts, which he first must grasp in their entirety. After that comes the second stage. He must not only get the thought, which many can do, but he must be trained to keep the thought. We may have had the thought of the passage, but when we stand upon our feet it leaves us; the details elude us, as is so often manifested in public speakers, preachers and the like. And the third step is, you must give that thought. There is a great trinity. I am no lover of combinations or patent symbols, but there is the great trinity of reading—get the thought, hold the thought, and give the thought.

Miss Caroline B. LeRow.—It is almost impossible to talk upon this subject without talking too long, and talking over too much ground, for, as stated by the president of the board of education, of New York, in a most admirable address yesterday, given before the national elocutionists' convention, "this work is at the basis of all school work." I should say it is at the basis physically as well as in all other ways, and I do not hesitate to make that claim for it. The training in physical culture, which is so closely allied with the training in vocal culture, is one of the greatest blessings which can be given children in our schools, and will prevent them from growing into the round-shouldered, hollow-cheeked, weak, crooked speciments with which we have to deal in our different classes. I claim too, that all this work, barring the intellectual work of which Mr. Clark has spoken so eloquently, can be done and should be done before children are ten years old. The phonetic work, which is the very best form of physical training, should be done, and can be done, with intelligent children of six years of age. It seems to me, and I think many of you from your own experience will be willing to admit the truth of the proposition, that it is asking too much of grammar and high-school teachers, that they should be expected to teach reading to pupils who have never been taught to stand or to sit properly, who know nothing whatever of filling their lungs, or of the first principles of articulation.

After Miss LeRow's address a nominating committee was appointed, of which Mr. J. E. Souers was made chairman, with instructions to report on Friday, July 2d.

The chairman, Mr. Mayne, then brought the session to a close.

FRIDAY

When the session opened, Chairman Mayne began as follows: Our section enjoys a visit from some distinguished visitors this morning. It is my pleasure to announce that in response to the invitation sent by us to the National Association of Elocutionists, that body appointed a delegation of representatives. But this is not all. Besides gracing our meeting by their presence, those ladies and gentlemen will join in the discussion.

Prof. Thos. C. Trueblood.—We, as teachers, need, especially in our work in the earlier grades, to take care of the child physically, first, by looking after his positions as he stands in the class-room, his attitudes and movements; to care for his articulation, enunciation and the clearness with which what he says impresses itself on the ear. No child can give good expression in reading who stands in a languid way on the floor, with body let down, with shoulders forward, the head down and chest compressed. I would urge upon teachers as one of the first things, then, to get the body up. God intended that we should be developed mentally, physically and morally; that the three sides of man should be developed and developed evenly, and that the perfect man should stand erect.

Then, as to the vocal organs, of which the lungs are a very important part, I should certainly use some simple exercises in breathing. I would have the little fellows inflate the lungs as you lift the hand, and exhale as you lower the hand. The windows ought to be open and the air, as nearly pure as possible, so that these lung gymnastics may be taken to best advantage. These exercises develop lung power, so that when you desire vocal power you can get it a great deal more readily than if your lungs are not strong.

Now, in regard to the vocalization, I think there are certain light exercises in vocal culture that should be given to young pupils, although I do not believe in severe exercises. These will add amazingly to the strength, the purity and the general flexibility of the voice. There are three or four things that ought to be considered when you are talking about voice building. One of them is force, another is compass, another is flexibility and another is carrying power. These are not dependent upon each other. You can have wide compass with a very weak voice; you can have a flexible voice and not a wide compass. You may be able to use three or four tones of the voice very skillfully up and down the scale, and that is flexibility without wide compass. There are certain exercises in inflection and vocal culture that may be given in notes up and down the scale that will not hurt the child's voice nor strain it in the least, and yet will give it that pitch and flexibility of tone which are so charming in the child and later in the grown person. Remember that I would insist on making these exercises light, just as you make your exercises in physical culture light. You do not put children into Swedish gymnastic exercises, but you give them light, free movements of the arms and hands and feet; so with vocal exercises, which is a physical exercise. The voice depends upon muscular power; it is largely physical and should be developed gradually and rationally. Then, in connection with these exercises in voice culture and articulation, many of which I would be very glad to give you if there was time, the moment the child begins to read I should begin to apply the laws of emphasis. There are two chief laws of emphasis, and I believe there are only two. They are these: First, a word that is an important part of a new idea must be made strong; and, secondly, when a word has been made strong, unless it is repeated for emphasis, it should be made light. For instance, if I should say, as I have often heard it read, "Let me have a *country*, or at least the hope of a *country*, and that a free *country*." You see, all of you, that that reading violates the second law of emphasis. The proper reading is this: "Let me have a *country*, or at least the *hope* of a country, and that a *free* country."

It seems to me the best way to teach the child emphasis is simply to say to him: How many words of that sentence can you leave out? The words that you cannot omit are emphatic words; the other should be plainly articulated, but not emphasized. I think the child can soon eliminate unimportant words from a sentence; but perhaps the better way is to ask them to underscore the words that mean the most to them! What is the thought here? And then when they have read from the book, ask them to tell what new idea they have found in the sentence, and then their speaking becomes easy, natural.

The very fact that a good thought is well expressed by one pupil will inspire another to impress his thought equally well. Then everybody will be on the alert to listen to the reading lesson, because this recitation, properly conducted, means the bringing out of good thought. Then one can get voice culture by getting at the thought and having pupils impress it by those subtle questions which bring out the thought, and help him to read it in a natural, easy way that gives him flexibility and directness. Now, this is one of the things that we, as teachers of oratory, urge most upon our students—directness—as I said yesterday, in the convention. And that means, that when you say anything it shall come right at those to whom it is addressed, and will not be given out in a monotonous, listless way so that nobody can appreciate it.

Mr. F. T. Southwick.—With regard to reading, I don't believe in teaching emotional reading in the schools. I teach only the simplest gestural action, but I do believe in that because it is normal. I don't beleive in teaching these subjects in school as art, simply as means of expression. There is a distinction between teaching these things as art, as you do for dramatic work, and for personal culture, as we should in schools.

One word in regard to the province of reading. If your pupils study literature for the purpose of expression, they learn to find out what literature means, because it is only good literature that has got anything in it worth expressing. What I do with my pupils is to endeavor to teach them, first of all, the comprehension of thought, and, second, to have a distinct purpose to express that thought, and there is where the action of the eye is important.

Miss Martha Fleming.—It is the thought of the department of oral reading to have a piece of good literature, something dramatic, full of images and closely related to their other work constantly on hand, and to have some little time each day given to studying and reading it. For example, when the subject in nature study was "Air," the children in third and fourth grades made a study of "The Wind and the Moon," by George Macdonald.

They read it carefully or it was read to them and they were first asked to express on paper or on the blackboard the images they received. Then they were asked to tell about their own picture orally. Different parts of the poem appealed to different children. Then we took it up stanza by stanza, each one trying to give what he saw in the lines, the teacher helping by questions, drawings or in any other way that she could. The children soon learned the poem and were as delighted to repeat it as they were to sing their favorite song.

Oral reading is a most complete educative act. The mental is brought into action in getting the thought from the printed page. The motive — giving thought to others — cultivates the moral side of the nature; and in expression, the whole body is brought into action. The expression of thought and emotion through the body is not only the highest object of physical training, but it is the highest form of physical culture. No other mode of expression is so prolific of good as all round oral reading.

A teacher who would make a successful use of oral reading in the schools must know the children. She must study them in their homes, know something of their inheritance and environment; study them in their games and plays. One can learn more about children in their games and plays than in any other way. It is their own natural mode of expression, and I think the time is surely coming when we shall recognize the educational value of dramatic plays and games, not only in the kindergarten, but among the older children.

A study of the children here would clear up many of our difficulties.

Q. To Miss Fleming—You state in regard to text-books that you think the words beyond them, but afterwards you spend so much time in regard to the literature that I think no one can mistake that you have the best literature before the child from the very first. It seems to me in the teaching of reading, the same as in the teaching of music, the child may be given the simple classics to begin with. Do you not think so?

Miss Fleming—By classics, I suppose you mean the best literature. As I said the child should never read anything but good literature. There is not much that is literature in the ordinary readers prepared for the little children in the first grades. The myths, stories and folklore of the old literature may be adapted to the children, as the myths of Thor and Balder and the stories of Hercules.

Do not talk about words to a child at all, unless you wish him to image words alone, in which case there will be no room in his mind for anything else. How to get the thought, is the great question, and each teacher must answer it for himself. I know of no unfailing method. A method or way of doing a thing is always individual. One may succeed, and another fail with the same method. A teacher with dramatic power can, by skillful questions, help the children to get the images, or they may study the text until they get them, and then give them to the whole school in either their own words or the words of the book.

Mr. Southwick—Do you, in your work, ask your pupils to be critics of the work of other pupils, in other words, do you say: "Now tell me what is wrong in that line?"

Miss Fleming—No; I do not; I think one difficulty with children is the consciousness of self, and when I ask a child to criticise another it seems to me I put a damper on that child who is trying to express himself. His fear of criticism stands in the way of expression. I never correct or ask a child to criticise the way in which a thing is done. By every means in my power I keep the attention away from the form. I judge by the child's expression whether he has grasped the meaning of the text or not, and if I am not satisfied I lead him by questions, or in some other way, to a closer observation of the text, or I may have several children give what they get from the lines; I am not very sure about what is done in the department of numbers, although I am sure of the principle underlying the work. The child is led by the conditions put before him to add, subtract or multiply as the case may be. If the answer is wrong he has not grasped the conditions, and there is necessity for more and closer observation.

Mr. Mayne brought the session to a close with the following remarks:

I regret very much to be obliged to close this exceedingly interesting session. I will now call for the report of the chairman of the nominating committee.

The report was submitted nominating:

Richard E. Mayne, chairman; Sydney Marsdon Fuerst, vice-chairman; Caroline B. LeRow, secretary.

Motion made, seconded and carried, that the persons above named be elected to the offices set opposite their names respectively.

Adjourned without date.

RECOMMENDATIONS

The section makes the following recommendations:

1. That a paper on the influence of the home and the school on our common speech be delivered before the full body at the convention in 1898.

2. Interest in speech culture and desire for knowledge on the subject are daily becoming more manifest throughout the country. State pride makes it incumbent on every teacher in the Empire state to aid this important educational movement.

3. That all efforts to facilitate the work of oral expression for children must begin in the primary department.

4. That the exercises in this branch should be under the supervision of persons who, besides possessing expert ability in the branch itself, have had practical experience as teachers of children according to the most approved methods.

5. That the course of study in training schools for teachers should include exercises in the theory and practice of oral expression.

6. In addition is is suggested that the name of the section be changed to, section on reading and oral expression.

HIGH SCHOOL SECTION

GREETING

By PRINCIPAL WICKES, *Chairman*

The speaker hoped it would not be considered invidious to extend a greeting to this particular department of the association. For he had a strong reason, he said, for so doing. He had long felt that the bond which united the secondary schools of the Empire state to the state association was a very feeble one. The great body of principals were wont, at each holiday season, to meet in Syracuse for an educational conference; and upon the closing of schools each June, the same body has gone on a pilgrimage to Albany, our educational Mecca, to hear learned men and to pay homage at the shrine of the literature fund, whence so many of our pecuniary blessings flow. The speaker thought the effect would surely be to bring about neglect of our annual state association meetings, and, perhaps, the sundering of the bond. Against this the speaker protested.

He then spoke with favor of the plan of this year's meeting, by which it became possible for the "men of like degree"—the secondary school teachers of the state—to come together in a congress of their own and to listen to themes on principles rather than policies, on tendencies rather than technicalities, on matters fundamental rather than superstructural.

The speaker then gave greeting to his young student-friends as the first to address the congress.

Then, with brief allusion to the prospect of a delightful trilogy upon practice and principles, conservatism and radicalism, "letter" or "spirit," all as related to education, the speaker declared the High School Congress of the State Teachers' Association to be duly in session and ready for the special order of the day.

A PLEA FOR ATHLETICS

BY S. CARL WEBB, *Student*

The time has gone by when a weak body indicates a strong and healthy intellect. We need no longer go into the country to search among the farms for lads to represent strength.

No, we can find them in our own cities. What has produced them? Athletic training.

In these times the population of our state is centered in crowded cities containing places where the sun seldom, if ever, sheds its beams, and where the air is poisoned with every germ and form of disease. It is here that the boys who are to rule our nation grow to manhood. Oh, with what care we should watch and foster the development of our scholars. "A sound mind in a sound body" is the best foundation for a liberal education.

I claim that the morals of a boy who, in athletic training, abstains from those petty vices which destroy the muscles and health, are raised above those of the common masses and placed upon the higher plane of physical perfection. From inaction of the muscles and lack of exercise comes fatty degeneration, impeding the operations of the heart and intellect, resulting in death. And yet this is but one of the evils, ending in death, resulting from a lack of muscular exercise. It is absolutely necessary that man be strong to stand the competition of modern life, which, with every succeeding year, tends to grow stronger, crowding out the weaker ones, leaving only the hardy, intellectual men to wage the fight. Nations in the past have yielded to physical strength, from which comes a nation's strength, and nations in the future must admit its importance. Gentlemen, you are to-day educating a nation of the future. How carefully you seek to develop the mind in every branch of education, yet the body, in which the mind must dwell, is passed by without a thought.

The educational system of our state is so good that every year witnesses a large increase in attendance. The result is that our school buildings are, many of them, overcrowded. The inevitable result of an over-crowded building is poor ventilation, consequently students spend the greater part of their working hours in close and over-heated rooms. This tends to stunt their minds and deaden their ambitions, when, by the simple encouragement of athletic sports these same students will spend a certain amount of time exercising in the open air, breathing in pure oxygen, which is so vital to all of God's creatures. Athletics make men manly, strong and ready—in a word, vital with the best of vitality. From such exercises result precision, decision, presence of mind and endurance, qualities which make a nation strong.

Gentlemen, I have endeavored to demonstrate to you the necessity of athletics, the necessity of encouraging health and strength that the welfare of our nation may be promoted. I pray you, gentlemen, seek to develop the body with the mind, remembering that " He who is alive moves that which he touches."

A PLEA FOR AESTHETICS

BY G. FRED HURD

My predecessor has set forth the necessity of physical cultivation of the student, but surely education must not be limited to merely a matter of bone and muscle. Inclosed within the human frame lies the mind, where are stored the fancy, the imagination and the reasoning powers. Without these faculties man would be incomplete, nay useless, absolutely unfit for this battle of life. No man ever performed any noteworthy deed, unless he was spurred into action by his ever-working imagination. Every human nature has an imaginative side; every student possesses more or less of this faculty. It is for the cultivation of these aesthetic elements in the student's nature that I speak.

If the instructor would have the student who has shown artistic genius or the student who has displayed literary ability reach that degree of excellence of which they are really capable, he must not be satisfied with merely cultivating the muscles of the hand which so skillfully wields the pen, the brush or the pencil; he must train the inner elements which guide and direct these deft fingers and give them the power to express thoughts and sentiments which lie far beneath the physical being of the student, however healthy.

With the training of the imagination the reasoning powers must be cultivated. Common sense must counter-balance the flights and fancies of the imagination. Let the instructor neither neglect nor ignore the important aesthetic elements, the fancy, the imagination and the reasoning powers that the character of his pupils may be rounded and complete.

A PLEA FOR CIVICS

By A. A. Webb, *Student*

We are to consider the element in modern education which is of primary importance for the happiness of the individual, for the welfare of his nation and for the advancement of the human race and civilization—the study in our academies and high schools of civics and of that which will aid in the proper discharge of the duties of citizenship.

It is a common thing for some of our best citizens to scoff at and to ridicule our congress, our legislatures and our common councils, and to speak lightly of corruption in politics; thus the boys, the future citizens and lawmakers grow up under the impression that all government is vicious. Can anyone conceive of a more sacred office for education than the counteracting of this tendency?

Gentlemen, you to whom is entrusted the future, are not doing the full measure of your duty when you simply hang out a flag from your school building and cause those in your charge to sing "America," "The Star Spangled Banner" and "Hail Columbia." The needs of our country demand the teaching of the fundemental and primary duties of citizenship. This training should begin when the child is young, in the lower grades of the grammar schools, for impressions made at that period are rarely obliterated in later life. The reading books should contain sketches of great men's lives, of great deeds done, and of great sacrifies made in the formation of our government. This course of reading would make a firm foundation for the more advanced high school studies, consisting of civics, political economy and a critical study of United States history.

As a practical aid to civil instruction an organization similar to that which exists in the Syracuse high school, known as the S. H. S. congress, stands without a rival. This society is modeled, as nearly as possible, after the United States congress; bills introduced by its senators and representatives are debated, and the young legislators acquire by experience, a real knowledge of the spirit of our government, of its history and institutions, and attain an understanding of current events and political affairs which could be gained in no other way.

You, the instructors of the youth of this land, have in your powers the future of this great nation. Every true man may show his patriotism in the future, at the ballot-box, if you will now store his youthful mind with the proper knowledge.

FRIDAY MORNING

Meeting called to order by the chair.

Professor John G. Allen was nominated and elected president of the high school congress and professor Lewis H. Miller, as secretary for next year.

THE ART OF EXPRESSION

JAMES G. RIGGS, *Plattsburgh*

WHAT KIND OF BOOKS TO READ

Our aim is the noble expression of English, the means at hand for cultivating it, books, and our problem, what kind of books help to noble expression. In other words, what kind of books unseal the lips, and make a facile pen; what books make pupils want to say something, and call for utterance of thoughts which great souls out of the past have spoken to them; what books put pupils in the way of getting great thoughts, and lodge ideals in the soul which become motives in the developing mind?

De Quincey's classification of literature in two divisions, literature of knowledge and literature of power, will not help us, for they overlap too much for our purpose. We need to select those books which make pupils see, feel and appreciate the great thoughts which have been seen, felt and appreciated. They must be led by the paths along which noble expression has come. They cannot in reality traverse the identical lines, but they may through the imagination feel the same impulses which have come to expression in our rich English speech. There is not at our command to place about pupils the atmosphere which nourished Greek art, nor the breadth and fertility of the Elizabethan age to invite their effort, but the creative faculty is still the same— "not dead, but sleeping." Those books which arouse the dormant faculty and liberate the imaginative, are the material to which we may look for help.

Now the imagination is a faculty which has not had its due consideration in the making of school courses. We have been more concerned in preparing pupils to win in the warfare for beefsteak and potatoes, as an ultimate aim—with settling the furniture of our surroundings, and adjusting our elementary existence. The synonym for the imaginative has been the visionary, the unpractical. As a result our development in some degree is one sided. Your money-getter will cry out against the imagination and its cultivation, that it is vague, dreamy and unbusinesslike. Yet it is this very faculty which selects his goods from his buyer's standpoint, and arranges his bargains beforehand. Your most successful lawyer, is he who knowingly or intuitively puts himself into his clients' or witnesses' place, or in the jury box to look at the matter from their point of view, that he may be able to grasp the case in all its relations. The successful doctor or pastor is he who can imagine the ills of the body-sick and soul-sick, and thus enter into their needs with the wine and oil of healing. The imagination has a most practical and essential relation to every man's life and achievement.

> "Because a man has shop to mind
> In time and place, since flesh must live,
> Needs spirit lack all life behind,
> All stray thoughts, fancies fugitive,
> All loves except what trade can bring?"

Without the imagination there would have been no Venus di Milo, no sculptured yet speaking Moses, no heavenward pointing spires at Milan, no reverberation through the soul's chambers of the thoughts entrusted to music by the gods, no bridge to span the East river, no White City built by the lake to remain in memory a joy forever. This faculty directs the telescope of the astronomer, the hammer of the geologist, and the re-agents of the chemist. It enables a man to appropriate the beauty of nature and of art, and lifts him above sordid things. It leads him below the mind of a thing to the heart of it. The imagination projects and constructs. It builds up, and reaches out. Says Lowell, "What a witch is this imagination, who sings as she weaves, till we seem to see the music in the growing web!" It invents and plans, it elevates and inspires. It breaks up the self-center of a man and enables him to live with all humanity. It makes him,—

> "Alive to gentle influence
> Of landscape and of sky,
> And tender to the spirit touch
> Of man's or maiden's eye."

Above all the imagination helps to disclose to him his ideals, to feel his possibilities to come into completer self-possession. By it childhood climbs the bean stalk to the giant's house, or builds a hut with Good Man Friday; through it studenthood shares the trials of the wandering Aeneas, or strikes a blow for Caesar in the senate house; by it manhood lights the lamp which discloses the way of his footsteps toward truth. Separately the imagination is of little importance, but acting with the other powers of the mind it becomes their mainspring.

Now the reading of books is not to put something into the mind from without, which was not there before. It is rather for "opening out a way whence the imprisoned splendor may escape." It is rather for the purpose of furnishing the reader some world experiences and universal motives beside which in parallel lines, he may place his own meager experiences and lesser impulses, until by the contact they become charged with greater meaning and an informing spirit which calls for utterance. This mutual attraction of spirit to spirit—call it sympathy if you will—brings about a confirmation of one's half-formed purposes, and an adjustment of his relations.

If we would train a lad to be an artist, we will put him into the atmosphere of the highest art; if to be a musician, he must become acquainted with the work of the masters. If noble expression in words is sought, here is our own rich English literature ripening through twelve hundred years of growth and development. It invites the mind to a wide range through the past, and a broad acquaintance with men and things, and summons the imagination to a participation in great events and noble deeds which are nothing on the printed page, but only as they are lived again in thought and deed. The Athenian youth became a hero because he had heard of heroes from his mother's knee. The knights of chivalry were brave and bold because of the harper's song in the hall.

What is beautiful in thought, elevating in character, refined in spirit, literature holds—all in shapely form and order; and if the mind feed upon and assimilate the food, it will take color from its supply, become possessed of its nature and enriched by its wealth. It is thus the mind comes to nobler expansion, the first step toward the expression of "thoughts that breathe, and words that burn." It is thus the informing imagination brings the pupil to see, feel and appreciate the nobleness of other minds, which, reacting, summons up his own.

It remains to suggest what kinds of literature should appeal most strongly to high school pupils in shaping their expression. They are at a point where their opinions are unformed or at least not strongly held, and where motives have not taken definite shape. They are ready to think deeply, but have not yet had time, and they take things quite as seriously as at any other period of life. Says Chateaubriand, "There is no period of life more poetic than the fresh affections of a heart of sixteen years. The morning of life is like the morning of the day, full of purity, full of imagination and harmony." It is well to select readable books which deal with the great motives of life, and the universal truths so set in words that they leave the imprint in the mind of their presence there. Two classes of books may be named, first, those which contain tales of life and varied experiences of society; second, the great poems of the language which belong to no class, no locality, no time, but are universal and exemplify the continuity of life. The great novels not only command the pupil's interest, but demand the best in his intellect, heart and conscience in settling the great questions of life and conduct as there set forth. In other words they make him think. So engaging is the scene, so direct the appeal, that consciously or unconsciously, he allies himself with his hero, and this is the state from which may be expected the best expression from the pupil.

Such books are Scott's novels, Cooper's tales, Thackeray's and George Eliot's great works. The selection made by the association of colleges for entrance requirements is most excellent. The essayist must not be passed over but judiciously administered.

Prose literature is the result of long culture and reflective thought and requires more of the pupil. There was a time when prose and poetry were not severed. The literature of all lands begins with poetry, and to this day it partakes more of fresh, spontaneous life than more formal prose. As poetry is the product of the higher self and the deeper realities of feeling, so does it speak at once to the highest within us and call forth expression consonant with our impulse.

There is one essential to the pupil's appreciation of poetic literature, it is that he be introduced to it by some one who has appreciated it, has felt the divine afflatus, and is able "To make the Englis swete upon his tongue."

The silent reading of poetry is not likely to accomplish much, but the speaking voice interprets as nothing else can. Tennyson, so his son said, used to read his poems to a favored few, in a chanting, deep voice of swelling richness. So much is the expression an integral part of the sense.

Poets who speak the universal language should be selected, Homer, Dante, Milton, Shakespeare, Burns, Wordsworth, Shelley and Tennyson and Browning, who instructs:

> "Which, be they what they may,
> Are yet the fountain light of all our day,
> Are yet a master-light of all our seeing—
> Uphold us, cherish, and have power to make
> Our noisy years seem moments in the being.
> Of the eternal silence; truths that wake
> To perish never."

In the selection of books to read which may lead to noble expression, we must turn to those which make for the training of the imagination, the awakening of the sympathetic feelings, and the stirring of "the inward spiritual activity having for its characters, increased sweetness, increased light, increased sympathy."

The nobility of the thought will determine its nobility of expression, and only as it is noble will it enter into noble minds. Increase of knowledge does not make the soul larger. It is the power to feel which expands us. The man who feels goes deeper than he who thinks only.

"To have the heart open, and the eyes clear, and the emotion and thoughts warm and quick, and not the knowing of this or the other fact, is the state needed for all mighty doing in this world," says Ruskin.

So led in paths of literature, not by those who dismember it for sake of what they call study, but by those discriminating teachers who come sympathetically to its heart, pupils may be expected to feel what they express and express what they feel. To them, there is no mystery in the lines written above Tintern Abbey:

"I have felt
A presence that disturbs me with the joy
Of elevated thoughts; a sense sublime
Of something far more deeply interfused
Whose dwelling is the light of setting suns,
And the round ocean, and the living air,
And the blue sky, and in the mind of man:
A motion and a spirit that impels
All thinking things, all objects of all thoughts,
And rolls through all things."

THE TEACHING OF PUBLIC SPEAKING IN SECONDARY SCHOOLS

PROF. DUNCAN C. LEE

Public speaking occupies an unenviable position among subjects taught to-day. It is laughed at for its surface efforts, derided for its unscientific methods, scorned because the public appearances of those who have been taught are parodies on public speech. The causes of this feeling are such as make the result natural. The teaching has not touched the inside. The elocutionary charlatan has been allowed to introduce his tricks and to impose on our school methods artificialities, extravagances and mechanical movements, falsely called gestures, until the students of public speech seem content with imitation, and quite ashamed of original and individual expression.

In some schools public speaking as a subject to teach and to study is never heard of; in others, it is persistently neglected. The subject has, however, many claims to recognition. It multiplies power; it trains the mind; it would teach a mastery over self and over others; it may be made a leading culture study of our schools.

To teach spoken English demands special talent and adaptability. This subject should not be intrusted to "odds and ends" teachers, but to those specially trained for the work; to teachers of liberal thought and culture, who understand the principles of pedagogy, who have a true feeling for words, language and literature, who believe in the sacredness of individuality as well as of speech, and whose ideals of life are high and worthy of emulation.

That the training of our youth in the theory and practice of public address is not to be left to the college and the university alone, is attested by the awakening interest in the subject among the leading high schools and academies. The secondary schools send the great body of their students and graduates at once into active life; they are becoming sensible of the burden of their responsibility to the nation. A like responsibility should be felt in the college preparatory course. We are now practically agreed that the real training in English writing should be given in the secondary school. This paper would affirm that there is the same ground for insisting that the real training in English speaking be given in the secondary school. The secondary schools will not fulfill their duty to this subject if, in any grade of grammar school, high school or academy, written English and spoken English are not made to go hand in hand. One of the means which may be used to bring about this closer interrelation of oral and written English, to make them educationally helpful to each other, is oral reproduction. English composition or literature can hardly be taught effectively without oral reproduction. If the reading exercises of the school are in charge of a teacher full of enthusiasm and who loves the subject, reading will be a good preparatory training for public speaking. But definite and systematic work in public speaking should also be carried on. It should comprise the delivery of selections from orations, or of original composition committed, and extemporaneous speaking.

In the secondary schools declamation is best taught in classes like any other subject, special stress being laid on individual interpretation and expression. Declamations should be fresh; instructive; something the student believes and feels; preferably not oratorical or dramatic.

In preparation the following scheme may prove beneficial:

1. Read the declamation silently three or four times; find the meaning of every unusual word, obscure phrase or historical reference; grasp the sequence of thought by paragraphs; by sentences; note any echo.

2. See every picture, every movement; hear every sound; feel every emotion as personal. Get a perspective of whole; but do not vocalize a word until this process has been carried faithfully thus far.

3. Assimilate the thought of speaking aloud quietly so as to satisfy the ear of the meaning of every sentence. Bring out the key ideas. Now test the memory and complete the committing by a review of these steps.

4. Speak or drill in preparation as though an audience were before you; try to convince and persuade. Let the mental action determine the expression, vocal and actional.

Closely related to oral reproduction is extempore speaking, in which it is expected that the thought but not the form of the sentences has been previously decided upon. Debating and literary societies should be connected with every secondary school. The form of the organizations may differ; but the aim of all should be training in public speaking, literary appreciation and good citizenship.

In closing let me suggest a few of the incentives to the pursuance of elocutionary study in the secondary school.

1. The secondary schools are filled with students at such an age that their voices are flexible and yield naturally to suggestion.

2. In a Republic like ours many of our citizens are drafted into official positions where some ability in public address is a necessity. Unless the secondary schools give the rudimentary training, the majority of these public servants will be thrust into public life without proper qualifications.

3. So far as woman is concerned, the modern multiplication of social and civic clubs, benevolent and religious organizations, prophesies an increasing demand for women who are qualified not only to think but also properly to express their thought for the influencing of others.

4. A training which unpacks and sharpens the tools which the mind uses in the every day affairs of life, must be approved by every man.

A subject which makes the mind the regal factor in life, and claims for it the services of the entire body, must be interesting to every teacher.

ESSAY WRITING IN HIGH SCHOOLS

PROF. BRAINARD KELLOGG

There are two things to be achieved by this exercise—the pupil's growth in ability to think and in ability to express his thought. Of the two, thinking is chief. To think true thoughts, to think connectedly, to think logically, to think exhaustively, is the thing of primary importance in the writing of essays or of anything else. I emphasize the thought picture of it as I do because, in this day of infinite talk about the art of composition, I am confident that we have been so engrossed with the expression, that we have given little attention to the getting of thought to express. We have forgotten that the soul of a sentence or a paragraph outranks its body—that the matter of discourse is more than its manner.

And this brings me to expression, the other end to be secured by essay writing. We express thought in order to communicate it to another. We strive to lodge in his mind just what is rankling in our own. He must not, through our careless choice of words, or slovenly arrangement of them, fail to grasp our thought. We should not compel him even to search for it. I go further. I disallow the dictum some critics nowadays are pronouncing—the dictum that the pupils in our high schools are not to be instructed and exercised in what are termed the graces of expression. I heartily concede that imagery, humor, variety, beauty of expression are not to take the place of what is more fundamental—clearness, simplicity, directness, energy, individuality. The graces of style must not supplant these basic elements of it, but they may supplement them.

The getting of the best thought and the best expression for essays depends largely upon a wise choice of subjects for them. Of these subjects I have but this to say: They should take the pupil into fields where he is at home. The facts he is to brood over should, in large measure, be facts he has himself observed. The knowledge he is to use should be knowledge self-obtained and self-verified—first-hand knowledge, not knowledge gleaned from books. His trouble in writing will not then be paucity of matter, but surfeit. The writing of essays will then be to him not a duty he dreads, but a pleasure he anticipates; the essay will have a flavor of freshness and originality alluring to him and delightful to his listeners. And as the subject is drawn from his life, so will his words and their collocation in the sentence be. The pupil must avoid, on the one hand, bookish terms and idioms, and, on the other, slang. Of the two offences in his style, I know not which most sternly to condemn. But the subjects I am commending will draw the pupil toward neither—rather away from both. The handling of matter familiar to him will stimulate his fancy, spur his imagination and lead him to the occasional use of figurative language; and with what delight you will welcome an appropriate image of the pupil's courage I need not here remind you.

And now a word upon your criticism of these essays and I close. You cannot accomplish very much by marginal notes except in correcting orthographical and grammatical blunders or mistakes of punctuation. You cannot summon every pupil into your presence and go over with him in detail every essay of his. I suggest that you come before them with an essay picked out of the previous batch. This essay you have, in the interval, taken home and have thoughtfully and minutely studied—have acquainted yourself thoroughly with all its faults and defects, and with all its merits as well. Read aloud to the class the faulty, the defective, paragraph or sentence—read it just as it was written. Point out closely what, in your judgment, is open to criticism in it. Then read the sentence or the passage as you would have it, and as you have taken the trouble to make it. And be certain that in your mending it you have improved it; and that the whole class is convinced that you have improved it. Go through the essay sentence by sentence, page by page, in this way. If your work is done aright and in the proper spirit, you will have begun the slow reform. And commend unstintingly whatever in thought and expression you have found to be commendable.

RADICAL ATTACKS ON SECONDARY EDUCATION

PRINCIPAL W. A. MCANDREW, *Pratt Institute*

"*Whereas,* The time is one of agitation, experimentation and change,

Resolved, That the spirit of radicalism in the things of education threatens the overthrow of a temperate conservatism therein."

So it does! It's a good thing! The secondary school system seems to be undergoing almost constant attacks in one quarter or another. This is making the schoolmaster a student of his art. It is only by such threatening that his conservatism is preserved in its most favorable form. It is by such threatening that conservatism makes for progress, by retaining the known good of the past; instead of becoming a clog upon advancement, by retaining all the past, good and bad. How does the spirit of radicalism threaten us at this moment?

In the magazines printed in the years just passed we find most radical suggestions in the Cosmopolitan, whose editor finds the present system inadequate, wasteful and misdirected; in the articles of Dr. J. M. Rice in the Forum; in the educational articles of the Atlantic Monthly, aimed at the status of the schoolmaster as regards his salary; in the article in the Review of Reviews, upon the need of pensions for teachers and in the Journal of Education, agitating paying women the same salary as men.

These movements have been concerned largely with the general problem of education. The spirit of radicalism has attacked particular features in the conduct of the schools. It has assumed that there was a great deal of unwise procedure in teaching. Now the question suggests itself may not this be true? Why should we assume that while science, politics and religion are undergoing a constant change in response to radical attacks, we of the educational system whose place it is to keep up with the world for which we are fitting our boys and girls, should be left stationary?

Dr. De Garmo and the Herbartian radicals shake us up to a fresher realization of interest and correlation. The art-in-the-school room radicals, the child study radicals, those who want college entrance requirements changed, the anti-Greek fighters, the advocates of military drill, those who attack the honor system and assert the stupidity of commencement exercises and those who attack that very conservative element of school management, the examination, all these do us good by their very attacks and among them I see no radical movement that I should be glad to annihilate. I can not see any imminent danger of a loss of force in the school master through this radical uneasiness.

In all the instances where radicalism has threatened, I have been disposed to see the beneficial side of the attack. We cannot shut our eyes to the immense value that radicalism has been to the progress of every movement in this world. "Radical" means pertaining to the root of things. Who is there that needs to go to the root of things more than the teacher? There are growths in my system of teaching to-day that have no root. There are things passed down from one generation of teachers to another and preserved only because we do not think about them. Radicalism makes us think. It forces to go to the root and ask the everlasting why. If we cannot answer, then, perhaps, radicalism is right. Radicalism is necessary for a temperate conservatism. Radicalism always gives a reason. It wants a change because it claims to have something better. Conservatism often stands on precedent, and wants to keep things merely because it has them. It is only when forced by radicalism that conservatism ventures any reason whatsoever.

Then let us agree that the resolution is true and let us rejoice in it. Let us be glad that there are forces at work to hinder us falling into a rut. Let us rejoice that there is something to keep us awake and to keep us alive to the aims for which we busy ourselves all our life long.

APPENDIX

EXHIBIT No. 5

To Promote Patriotic Study in the Public Schools

REPORT OF SPECIAL COMMITTEE APPOINTED BY COL. ALBERT D. SHAW, DEPARTMENT COMMANDER OF THE DEPARTMENT OF NEW YORK, GRAND ARMY OF THE REPUBLIC

"Whatever we wish to see introduced into the life of a nation must first be introduced into its schools."—Baron Von Humboldt

To Promote Patriotic Study

IN THE

PUBLIC SCHOOLS

Report of Special Committee Appointed by Col. Albert D. Shaw, Department Commander of the Department of New York, Grand Army of the Republic, in

GENERAL ORDERS, NO. 6

Issued August 9, 1897

PUBLISHED BY THE
DEPARTMENT OF PUBLIC INSTRUCTION
STATE OF NEW YORK

[redacted]

Extract from General Orders, No. 6

HEADQUARTERS, DEPARTMENT OF NEW YORK,
GRAND ARMY OF THE REPUBLIC,
CAPITOL,
ALBANY, N. Y., *August* 9, 1897.

VI. The great importance of the development of a uniform system of teaching patriotism and civics in our public schools, is now generally acknowledged by our best authorities. It is in line with the highest sentiment of Christian citizenship. The only safety for our union in the future lies in the wise and unselfish patriotism and virtue of our whole people. The steps of future generations will not stumble if their National pathway is graded with right principles and safe-guarded with noble inspirations of justice, law, liberty and religion. To the end that the question of how best to practically evolve and introduce these right and patriotic teachings in our schools, it has been deemed wise to place the consideration of the same in the hands of an able committee of leading comrades in this department whose experience in public life, and in studying the objects aimed at in this line of action, eminently fit them for this delicate and commanding investigation and report.

VII. This action is based upon the view that comrades of distinction in civil life who periled their all for their country, in their early manhood, are best fitted by experience to consider this whole subject. It is admitted that the quickened sentiment of patriotism and loyalty to the flag, born of the late war, has caused the stars and stripes to float over the school houses in many states. Surely no more sacred work can fall to comrades, in the evening of their days, than to empty the spirit of freedom and lofty ideals of patriotism into the hearts of the children of generations to come. If this is wisely done in periods of peace it will foster freedom's grandest forces in uplifting our civilization to the highest plane of a free people's government.

VIII. The following comrades are hereby appointed a special committee of the Grand Army of the Republic of the Department of New York to examine and report to the department as soon as convenient upon the best practical methods of teaching patriotism and civics in our public schools.

MEMBERS-AT-LARGE

Charles T. Saxton, Post 173, Clyde.
Albert Vander Veer, Post 121, Albany.
Charles S. Baker, Post 4, Rochester.
Jos. A. Goulden, Post 165, New York, Chairman.
Henry H. Adams, Post 140, New York.
Wm. C. Morey, Post 4, Rochester.
A. C. Pickard, Post 285, Jamestown.
Geo. H. Stowits, Post 9, Buffalo.
Noah Tebbetts, Post 327, Brooklyn.
W. H. Scott, Post 151, Syracuse.
Chas. H. Searle, Post 53, Utica.
C. A. Rubright, Post 276, Corning.

The members of this committee will meet in conference at department headquarters, Ellicott Square, Buffalo, on Thursday, August 26th, at 10 a. m. It is important that every member should be present as the objects in view will be fully discussed.

By order,

ALBERT D. SHAW,
Department Commander.

Official:
G. H. LESTER,
Assistant Adjutant-General.

Meeting in Buffalo

The committee met at department headquarters in the city of Buffalo on August 26, 1897, at 10 a. m., the Hon. Joseph A. Goulden presiding. The following members of the committee were present:

Joseph A. Goulden, Chas. T. Saxton, Chas. S. Baker, Henry H. Adams, A. C. Pickard, Noah Tebbetts, W. H. Scott, Chas. H. Searle, George H. Stowits and William C. Morey.

There were also present by invitation Hon. Charles R. Skinner, State Superintendent of Public Instruction, William T. Salter, of New York city, George Fenton, of Broadalbin, Isaac H. Stout, of Geneva, and William J. Barr, of Batavia.

Commander Shaw also participated in the deliberations of the committee.

Noah Tebbetts was elected secretary pro tem.

Chairman Goulden briefly stated the objects sought in the formation of the committee, and brief addresses were made by those present favoring the purpose expressed in the order appointing the committee.

It was voted that the temporary officers of the committee be made the permanent officers.

The committee, after a general discussion, voted that the matter before the committee be divided into three parts, viz.:

Civics and history.

Patriotic exercises, and

Public celebrations,

and that committees of three be appointed for each part.

The following committees were appointed:

Civics and history.—Professor William C. Morey, chairman, Hon. Charles S. Baker, and Prof. W. H. Scott.

Patriotic exercises.—Col. Henry H. Adams, chairman, Hon. Charles T. Saxton, and Noah Tebbetts.

Public celebrations.—Prof. George H. Stowits, chairman, A. C. Pickard, and Charles H. Searle.

The Hon. Charles R. Skinner was appointed a member of all the sub-committees, and the thanks of the committee were extended to him for the interest displayed by him in the work of the committee.

It was voted that the committee have power to add to its membership. The meeting was then adjourned, subject to the call of the chair.

Meeting in New York

Pursuant to a call issued by Colonel Goulden, chairman, the committee met at Hotel Manhattan, in New York city, November 19 and 20, 1897. The following named persons were present at some time during the sessions of the committee:

Col. Joseph A. Goulden, Chairman,
Hon. Charles S. Baker,
Col. Henry H. Adams,
Prof. William H. Scott,
Charles H. Searle,
Prof. George H. Stowits,
Prof. William C. Morey,
Col. C. A. Rubright,
Col. Noah Tebbetts,
Hon. Charles R. Skinner,
Gen. John P. S. Gobin, Commander-in-chief of the G. A. R.,
Adjutant-General Thomas Stewart, of Penna.,
Col. Albert D. Shaw, commander of the department of New York,
Col. Josiah C. Long, commander Lafayette Post No. 140,
Prof. William L. Felter,
Major Heman P. Smith,
Prof. Edward H. Boyer,
Rev. W. R. Maul,
Mrs. Ada G. Mohr, President of the W. R. C. of the department of New York,
Hon. John L. N. Hunt,
Prof. A. H. Dundon,
Capt. E. L. Zalinski,
Col. W. T. Salter,
Miss Jennie M. Davis, and
Assistant Superintendent A. W. Edson.

On Friday, November 19th, the committee visited the normal college of the city of New York, where they were most cordially received by President Thomas Hunter and members of the faculty, and introduced to the twenty-four hundred young ladies of the college. After the opening exercises, which consisted of songs and quotations of a patriotic character, were concluded, Col. Goulden pleasantly introduced Commander-in-Chief Gobin, Department Commander Shaw and Superintendent Skinner, who made stirring addresses touching the objects of the committee and the methods of teaching history and patriotism to the young.

The speakers received frequent applause from the young ladies of the college.

After this inspiring visit to the normal college, the committee "moved immediately upon" public school No. 77, where they were warmly received by Principal Edward A. Page and Assistant Superintendent Edson. More than five hundred boys participated in the patriotic exercises which followed. The flag was saluted by all the boys. The scene was impressive. Patriotic recitations were given and brief addresses were made by General Gobin, Col. Shaw and Superintendent Skinner. The visitors were impressed by the attention, appreciation and appearance of the pupils.

The committee next visited public school No. 87 on Seventy-seventh street and Amsterdam avenue, where they were cordially welcomed by the principal, Prof. Edward H. Boyer, and introduced to the school. The flag was brought in, escorted by the color guard of the school and saluted by all. The boys were drilled in the "setting-up" drill, and in marching they showed that they had been well and carefully instructed. Recitations of a patriotic and humorous nature were delivered and national songs were sung with great heartiness. Short addresses were made by Adjutant-General Stewart, the Commander-in-chief, the Department Commander, the State Superintendent of Public Instruction, and Principal Boyer. The school was dismissed by the principal, and the need and value of thorough discipline in large schools was proved by the fact that the building was cleared of students in three and one-half minutes.

The committee adjourned to meet at Hotel Manhattan, Saturday morning, at 9 o'clock.

The committee met again on Saturday morning, and Chairman Goulden called for reports of sub-committees.

HISTORY AND CIVICS

Professor William C. Morey, of Rochester, submitted the following report of the committee on civics and history:

The undersigned, your sub-committee, appointed to consider and report upon the subject of history and civics, and their proper teaching in the public schools of our state, having given the matters so referred to us our most careful consideration, have the honor to submit the following observations and recommendations:

To emphasize the sentiments of patriotism and loyalty is one of the chief objects of the Grand Army of the Republic. We believe that the strength and prosperity of any nation are dependent upon the zealous support of its citizens. A firm devotion to the great principles upon which our republic rests, is, we believe, indispensable to a healthy and vigorous national life. To maintain as well as to exalt these principles, is the duty of every patriot. It is not unreasonable, therefore, that those who were called upon to defend the country in the hour of its greatest peril, should in the time of its prosperity, seek to preserve that patriotic spirit and that loyal attachment to our institutions, which form the strongest pillars of the state.

No efforts to cultivate the spirit of loyalty and patriotism can, we believe, be more beneficial in their influence or lasting in their results than those which are directed towards the rising generation which is preparing for the duties of citizenship. Whatever can be done to create in the minds of the young an enthusiastic devotion to their country, will contribute much to the well-being of the republic. We believe that the cultivation of this spirit should form a necessary part of every system of education. But it seems especially fitting that efforts of this kind should be made in connection with that part of our educational system which is supported by the public. Our public schools are an essential part of the American system. In them are being trained the reserve forces of our country; and they afford the best field, not only for diffusing an intelligent knowledge of our institutions, but also for cultivating that deep, patriotic impulse, without which no nation can long exist.

What are the best methods of promoting the spirit of patriotism in schools is a practical problem which is, perhaps, not easy of solution. But we would urge upon all those who are responsible for the education of the young, the great desirableness of the end to be attained, suggesting only in broad outlines the methods which might be adopted. That patriotism cannot be taught by any direct process of instruction, like mathematics or language, is quite evident, since patriotism itself is a sentiment or emotion which can be cultivated not so much by instruction as by inspiration. But every emotion is capable of being called into action and developed by presenting in an attractive and imposing light the legitimate object of its exercise. The love of country may be cultivated by the study and sympathetic contemplation of all those elements and characteristics which make our country what it is—its wonderful geographical features, its remarkable historical growth, and its superior political institutions. A true patriotism, which is something more than a blind and boastful pretense, must be based upon knowledge and not upon ignorance. Its strongest support is an intelligent conviction. It must also rest upon broad sympathies, and not upon narrow prejudices. To promote such an intelligent, broad and permanent national spirit is the purpose which we have in view in emphasizing the importance of certain studies as an element in American education.

One of the first subjects which may be mentioned as suitable to promote the feeling of patriotism is the special study of American geography. No American boy can contemplate the wide extent of our country, the variety of its climate, its magnificent river systems, the superb and imposing grandeur of its mountain ranges, the vastness of its mineral resources, the fertility of its soil and the bountifulness of its agricultural products, the extent and variety of its manufactures, the industrial enterprise, the inventive genius and superior plane of living of the American people, without feeling proud that he was born on American soil. Without depreciating the importance of the study of general geography, we believe that not only could more definite scientific results be attained, but a more valuable benefit could be conferred upon the future citizen, if a greater attention could be paid to that important part of the earth's surface which constitutes his fatherland, and upon which he, himself, is to live and labor.

Of greater importance than the study of the physical and economical features of our country, is the study of its history, and especially the growth of its institutions. It may seem to some a difficult question as to how American history should be taught so as to arouse the feeling of patriotism. But for those who have had experience in teaching this subject, it is difficult to see how it can be faithfully taught at all without exciting in some degree the sense of patriotic pride. The American boy who breathes the native air of freedom, whose soul is stirred by the stories of heroic deeds, cannot fail to be moved as he dwells upon the noble record of the struggles and triumphs which give lustre to the pages of his country's history. The point which we would especially enforce is not so much the matter of methods and details as the imperative need of making the study of American history an important part of the education of every American citizen.

The one who would appreciate the greatness and true significance of American civilization must understand the sources of its development, the conditions of its growth, and the process of its evolution. He must imbibe the spirit of liberty, which in great measure prompted the colonization of this land. He must study the foundations of our local governments as they were laid by the early colonists, and follow these pioneers of the new world through the vicissitudes of their industrial, religious and political life. He must understand the nature of those constitutional rights to which they tenaciously clung and from which arose the majestic fabric of our free institutions. He must be translated to the days of 1776 and comprehend the great questions involved in the war of independence. He must enter into the struggles which attended the formation of the Constitution. He must understand the terrific issues which culminated in the civil war, and the political principles which by that war became established. He must, in fine, see in the successive stages of our history the progressive growth of a great republic, stretching from ocean to ocean, which is at once democratic, representative and federative, "an indissoluble Union of indestructible states." To eliminate emotion from the study of our country's history would be as difficult as to repress the feeling of awe when contemplating the grandeur of its natural scenery. There are elements of greatness and sublimity in the expanding life of our nation which cannot fail to touch the soul of any sympathetic student.

In the teaching of American history we believe that the analytic and accurate study of facts should be co-ordinated with a broad, synthetic study of principles. We do not sympathize with any disposition to distort the facts of history, with the mistaken hope of thereby giving greater emphasis to some historical truth. The principles of history are embodied in the facts of history; and the disposition to pervert the one furnishes the presumption that there is a desire to misrepresent the other. The broad outlines of our nation's history are not so vague as to be easily mistaken. In the two greatest crises of our history, when passion and prejudice were the bitterest—in the war of independence and the war for the Union—the salient features and issues of both stand out in clear relief; and whatever honest differences of opinion may exist regarding men and motives, the material facts and essential principles of each remain indisputable. We do not, therefore, see any adequate reason why an honest history of the republic, which is suited to one section of our country, is not equally suited to any other. We are a single nation and have a single history. Although the historic stream was once lashed by a tempest and threatened to part in twain, its separated waters have reassumed their united channel; and as they have descended from a common source, they are now flowing on to a common destiny. Every fair and conscientious historian must recognize the fact that American history is essentially one and that, although its tranquillity was disturbed, its continuity was not broken by the civil war. We may be standing too near that portentous event for any American to record all its details without some taint of prejudice or partiality. There may be differences of opinion regarding the character of certain men or the expediency of certain measures. There may not be an entire uniformity of judgment in matters of military skill or strategy. But it still remains true that there need be no diversity of views in respect to the great issues which were involved in that war, or the nature of the principles which by it received a final vindication.

We believe that the study of American history should be taught in all the schools of all the states of our land, not for the purpose of stimulating or aggrandizing any section, or of furnishing capital to any political party; but for the purpose of giving to our youth a clear knowledge of the facts and conditions which have made our country what it is, of giving to them broad views of American civilization, and also of exciting in them a worthy and just pride in their own people and in those political institutions which are their glorious heritage.

Another subject which may be conducive to patriotism and which must be regarded as necessary to prepare the young American for the duties of citizenship, is the study of civil government, or what is sometimes called "civics." No one can have an intelligent appreciation of his own political system without some knowledge of the nature and ends of the state; the distinguishing marks and comparative merits of different forms of government, the nature of sovereignty and the distribution of coordinate and subordinate political powers and other kindred subjects which properly belong to the study of theoretical politics.

But we believe that in the elementary stages of education, the study of political theories should be made subordinate to the study of political facts. It may be questioned, even from a scientific point of view, whether any other country can afford such a significant array of political facts as that afforded by our own. Here we find the best illustration of popular institutions; the highest development of the representative system, the most complete form of constitutional government based upon written law, the greatest example of a well-balanced federative Union that the world has ever seen.

When we go further and consider that the main justification of our public school system is based upon the needs of an intelligent American citizenship, the special and thorough study of American institutions seems an imperative necessity.

The boy who is to become an active and worthy citizen should be given a practical knowledge of the whole political system under which he lives. He should become familiar with the local governments which are nearest to him, his own town and county, his ward and his city; the public officers in each and their duties; the several courts and their jurisdiction over civil and criminal cases; the mode in which taxes are assessed and collected, and the purposes for which they are raised. He should be made acquainted with the government of his own state; its constitution and the division of its various powers and the relation of the state government to that of his own locality. He should have made clear to him the nature of the federal union, the character and provisions of the constitution as the supreme law of the land; the structure and function of the federal government and its relation to that of the states. He should, moreover, have explained to him his constitutional rights as an American citizen, and his duties to his fellow countrymen; and should be taught that the security of his individual liberty depends upon the supremacy and enforcement of law. He should, finally, be imbued with a public spirit and be made to feel that the welfare of the whole country is paramount to the advancement of his own personal interests. By these means he will acquire some idea of the political organism of which he is a part, and his native impulse to care only for himself will be broadened into the recognition of the patriotic duties which he owes to the community, to the state and the nation.

In addition to the indirect effects which may be produced by instruction given in the branches of study mentioned, it is believed that the patriotic impulse can be directly appealed to by bringing before the pupil the best specimens of patriotic literature. The burning words which have kindled the love of country in times that are past, will continue to warm the heart in the years that are to come. American literature is rich with the poems of patriotism, and with these every boy and girl should be familiar. There are innumerable passages of oratory from the time of James Otis to that of Abraham Lincoln which should not be consigned to forgetfulness, but which should be stored up in the minds of our youth and be used to keep alive the love of country in each succeeding generation.

But the highest expression of the patriotic spirit is to be found in the lives of patriotic men. If the children in our public schools could have kept before their mind the example of our nation's heroes, of the men who have remained firm at the helm of state in the times of stress and danger, who have risked their fortunes and their lives in the hour of peril, who have maintained their country's honor in the face of temptation and obloquy, they would receive an inspiration which could be derived from no other source. By studying the lives of Patrick Henry and Samuel Adams, Washington and Franklin and Hamilton and Jefferson and Jackson and Lincoln and Grant, they would perceive the materials of which patriotism is composed. They would see that the love of country is not a vain and boastful spirit, but one of the marks of a broad mind and a noble manhood, and they would be inspired to emulate these high types of patriotic example.

In suggesting these methods by which the spirit of loyalty and patriotism may be cultivated, we realize that the end to be attained is more important than any particular set of means which may be prescribed. To make our country great and strong by having a living support in the heart of the nation, is the main purpose which we have in view.

The kind of patriotism which we, as survivors of the civil war, would seek to promote and foster in the young is not a spirit born of discord and strife, but a sentiment inspired by the love of our common country, and a desire that all its citizens may be bound together by the possession of common rights and the recognition of common duties. It was for the preservation of the Union and the integrity of American institutions that we once fought, and it is for the same objects that we would still continue to labor. We are proud of the records of the war for the Union, but we are more proud of the Union which that war made perpetual. Not in the humiliation of the men who were defeated, but in the vindication of the principles which were triumphant, do we most sincerely rejoice. "With malice towards none, but with charity for all," we would maintain the unity and the honour of our great republic, the supremacy of its laws, and the spirit of absolute loyalty which must everywhere form an element of the truest citizenship. With all due respect for the bonds of local interest and the obligation of party ties, we believe in a patriotism which is not confined to any section or to any party, but which is as broad as the boundaries of our great nation, and which comprehends in its scope the highest welfare of the whole American people.

Professor William H. Scott submitted a supplementary report, in part as follows:

"It has been left for me to assign some reasons for the position taken in the complete report which has been submitted. A large number of histories have been carefully examined with a view of determining whether the charges of unfairness and want of patriotic spirit shown in the writing, or, rather in the compiling of these books, are well founded; whether the facts are distorted or falsified, as to data; whether an unfair discrimination has been made by any author in the presentation of subject matter.

"Your committee would feel that it had assumed an unwarranted authority were it to condemn histories which are accepted as standard text-books in our schools, when we consider the fact that each compiler refers to the same authorities. It is needless here to give these authorities at length.

"We are not ready to say that the writers or compilers of the various school histories of the United States have garbled these authors, much less intentionally misquoted them. Inasmuch as the great question at issue with us is the accuracy of that part of history which relates to the war for the preservation of the Union, let me quote from a few books what is said, first, as to the cause of the war; and second, concerning the greatest battle of that war.

"Omitting names of authors and substituting numbers therefor, we quote as follows concerning the cause of the war:

(1.) "Why did the Southern States secede? To be fair to them we must seek the answer in the speeches of their leaders. 'Your voters,' said Jefferson Davis, 'refused to recognize our domestic institution (slavery) which pre-existed the formation of the Union—our property (slaves) which was guaranteed by the Constitution.'"

(2.) "What took these seven States, soon to be followed by four more, out of the Union? The answer is, it was first their conviction that slavery would thrive better by being separated from the influence of the North; and, secondly, it was their belief in 'States' Rights.'"

(3.) "The advocates of slavery thought that the Republican party would leave no stone unturned to deprive them of their established institution, and therefore decided that the time had come to take very radical measures for the preservation of slavery."

(4.) "The Southern leaders, believing that in the growing strength of the Republican party there was a peril to slavery and, as a consequence, to the power of the South, thought and talked of secession."

(5.) "The government did little to hinder this slave trade (the illegal landing of slaves captured in Africa in Southern ports) and it went on growing in dimensions until it was stopped by the Civil War."

(6.) "The States' Rights doctrine had found a good many adherents in the South, and in the present excitement the extreme Southern States claimed that, by exercising the rights of individual States, they might lawfully secede from the Union." The author leads up to this conclusion through a discussion of the question of slavery.

The following quotations relate to the battle of Gettysburg:

(1.) This author gives a page and a half about the battle and concludes by saying, "Gettysburg was really the dawn of a new day."

(2.) "Gettysburg is rightly regarded as the greatest battle of the war, and every regiment engaged has taken a just pride in marking the positions it held during the three awful days of slaughter."

(3.) "The Confederates then made a tremendous assault and broke through the center of the Federal Army, but they were soon driven back, defeated."

(4) "At Gettysburg, July 1-3, there ensued a terrific battle * * * * * Lee was defeated, but not very decisively, and retired slowly to the Rapidan, where he remained until the next spring."

(5.) "The Federal army gained the greatest pitched battle of the Civil War—the greatest war fought on the American Continent."

(6.) "It was the end of the most stubbornly fought battle of the war; nearly 50,000 brave men had fallen in the contest; Lee had failed."

"We have also examined the estimates given of the battles of Bull Run, Nashville and Chickamauga. From the quotations made above, and others in a similar vein not here presented, it appears at once that in almost every particular the authors agree, and the conclusion is irresistible that they made use of the same authorities as references. Much of the adverse criticism we have heard is therefore baseless. I do not refer to that class of books, a few copies of which I have seen, which for the purpose of inculcating sectionalism purposely distort facts. Such books are not histories and should be ruled out of the schools of every state.

"Again we are met by the charge that so much is omitted, the books are not accurate. The average school history contains about 400 pages. Such a book can give only a limited number of facts. We must have the history of the early settlement of each colony and its development; the rise, growth and ripening of the causes which led to the colonial and revolutionary wars; the chaotic existence of the federation and progress toward and the making and adopting of the Constitution; the establishing of the elective franchise and its kindred subjects; the progress of events during the administrations of the presidents from Washington to McKinley; the history of political parties and the great questions at issue between them; the progress of literature, art and mechanics; the history of the rise and progress of slavery from 1619 to its final culmination in the rebellion and its consequent abolition; the war of 1812 and the causes which led to it; the Mexican war, its causes, results and injustice; the civil war with its 2,265 engagements; together with the momentous questions arising; the financial history of the country from the time of Hamilton to the present; and lastly the great industrial development of the country. Proper consideration to all these great questions cannot be given in an ordinary text-book on history. Many attempts have been made to accomplish the result, and in many instances the work has been very well done.

"It is not for me to say how this subject is taught in our schools, but I may be allowed to offer the suggestion that where the teacher is thoroughly imbued with a spirit of patriotism there should be little trouble to find material that will arouse enthusiasm and lead to the best patriotic teaching.

"Regarding the subject of civics, the difficulty has been to find books that were elementary and suited for children ranging from eight to fourteen years of age. We are glad to note, however, that such books are now being prepared and many of them are excellent and worthy of our careful consideration."

PATRIOTIC EXERCISES

Col. Henry H. Adams presented the following report:

A considerable number of your committee have been actively engaged in the study of patriotic exercises in the public schools of the United States for the past several years. They have followed the practical lines throughout all its progressive stages and have been close observers of all of the advantages accruing therefrom.

Moral development.—The committee fully concur in the fact that patriotic exercises improve the student morally, stimulate his integrity of character, impress him with the responsibility of coming citizenship and elevate his ideas of manhood.

Intellectual development.—The records of such schools as have given most attention to the matter of patriotic exercises show that the students of these organizations stand the highest in scholarship, and that under thorough discipline, marked development in method, exactness, tenacity of purpose, and kindred qualities are conspicuous results.

Physical Development.—The "setting up" drill is a blessing to any boy, be he a scholar in the public school or otherwise. It is a noticeable fact that on entering a schoolroom of boys who are under military training, you find them sitting erect and most attentive and respectful. The pupil who is unaccustomed to this discipline, when asked to recite, half rises or stands in a stooping posture, supported by his desk and in an inaudible tone responds to the call; whereas, with the boy under training, he rises quickly, stands erect, and in a prompt manner, with clear enunciation gives his recitation. These facts are derived from the records of several of the prominent schools in New York city and from schools in the country, from Pennsylvania, Connecticut and other states.

Method.—Your committee would therefore recommend that in the fifth year, or in other words, in the year next to the graduating year of the grammar grade, military instruction should be introduced and maintained, embracing the "setting up" drill, and company formations properly officered, and that instruction should be given by officers of the state militia at such times and places as can be made convenient.

Uniforms.—Your committee would recommend that no uniforms be worn by the students of the public schools so organized.

Use of armory.—Your committee further recommends that proper efforts should be made to obtain the use of local armories for the purpose of drilling, at stated periods during the week, *after school hours*, of the pupils of the public schools of the state, *when accompanied by militia officers*. And further, that the endorsement of the legislature of the state, be obtained for measures embracing military instruction of some kind in the public schools. Your committee further suggest that military instruction in the public schools *shall not be made compulsory*.

Grades.—That there shall be one or at the most two grades, as above indicated, which shall receive military instruction.

Arms.—Your committee suggests that the drill with arms be entirely *voluntary* and *under such restrictions* as may be exercised by the *principals* of the schools.

Graduating class.—Your committee finds that the graduating year of the grammar school boy is one in which the student is required to use his entire time in perfecting himself in his studies. Having passed through the *experience and discipline incident to military instruction* he should be freed from all duties interfering with his last year's graduating work.

Drill masters.—Your committee further recommends that the state be asked to furnish such commissioned or non-commissioned military officers as may be available to give instructions in the "setting up" and other forms of military evolutions at such times during the week as will meet the requirements of the schoolboys and make available the service of the military officer.

PUBLIC CELEBRATIONS

Prof. George H. Stowits submitted the following report:

Since the birth of this nation, a little more than a century ago, it had been demonstrated, again and again, at great cost of blood and treasure, that this people are able, in the spirit of patriotism, wisdom and strength, to hold its integral parts together.

The star spangled banner symbolizes liberty, justice, free thought and free speech; and what this people are now to do, is to make good citizens of the millions born and to be born; not scholars all, but broad-minded, intelligent, enterprising, and patriotic citizens, devoted to country, its institutions and the flag; willing to give their lives, if need be, when country calls, that the glorious stars and stripes may float in honor and in peace over all the land.

This is our creed, and we believe that every true lover of his country is willing to give his life to preserve it, which was proven in the late struggle for national unity. To stimulate and keep in life that same sentiment should be the work of all good citizens who are interested in whatever tends to the general good. It is evident that the burden of patriotic culture must fall upon the teacher. That the teachers of this great state are imbued with the spirit and desire to advance the sacred work of patriotism in any and all ways, that school authorities may order, need not be questioned.

From the many duties required in the modern curriculum of studies, teachers see but little time for special instruction in patriotism, except incidentally as an exercise for the pupils' relief from the monotony of school work.

To enter upon this important work, as a part of the child's education, our teachers must feel that they have the moral and legal support of the executive officers in charge of school affairs. Our short existence as a nation, from colonies to states, is fruitful of what can be woven into a clear and entertaining ritual for the every day interest and profit of the children in our schools. Teach the history of the flag, its changes and final adoption by Congress, June 14, 1777, and named the Cambridge flag, with its beauty of unexcelled and striking splendor. This warmth of expression, is the growth of sentiment, deduced from the contrast of the flags of other nations with our own. The child's school life and home life should be filled with a patriotic atmosphere, charged with a sentiment that our flag is supreme as an object of veneration, a typical emblem of our country's glory. Our literature, modern as it is, teems with patriotic sentiments and soul-stirring expressions ennobling in their character, as testimony of a pervading reverence for our flag and country.

These printed sentiments should be memorized, burned into the minds and hearts of the millions of children, companionship for their active and meditative hours. Then, their love of fatherland would be exemplified, as that shown by the patriot Tell, on his return to his native land, when out of the fullness of his heart, he exclaimed: "Ye crags and peaks I'm with you once again," etc., etc. We are surprised when we read the preserved sentiments of Washington, so intensely patriotic with a fervent solicitude, that the people should lay aside their selfish prejudices and cultivate that national pride which would contribute to a more perfect Union.

The generations as they come forward to take our places must be taught not to undervalue the cost in blood and treasure, to preserve and sustain our free institutions, the Union and our homes from the dawn of the Revolution until now.

Patrick Henry indicated the probable sacrifices to secure independence when he exclaimed: "Give me liberty, or give me death"; Samuel Adams, that inflexible and true-hearted patriot, calmly announced: "I should advise persisting in our struggle for liberty though it were revealed from heaven that 999 were to perish and but one of a thousand were to survive and retain his liberty; as one such freeman must possess more virtue than a thousand slaves."

These were the patriotic sentiments that animated the minds and hearts of our revolutionary fathers, as they intelligently realized the sacrifices to be made by the wager of battle with the mother country; here independence and constitutional liberty could be secured, and attain a place of honor and recognition among the nations of the earth. The public services of these patriots and their compeers and those of a later period, conspicuous, as statesmen, poets, historians, judges and divines, in their several spheres, should be studied and treasured in the memories of our children and assimilated as elements of character, together with that brilliant galaxy of names, that clustered around the immortal Lincoln, as aids in the management of the ship of state, during that gloomy period of the great civil war; supported, strengthened and encouraged by the chieftains of the Union army, whose heroic deeds of valor are recorded on the pages of our histories, to be read and re-read by the multiplied generations as they rise and fall in the land, that they may know the facts of that unparalleled struggle for national life, as written in blood from 1861 to 1865.

To know this, that the real value of country may be estimated, these growing minds should be taught daily, with method and plan, that they may have a just conception of the cost of our cherished institutions, and in view of known results, that the price of a Union saved was not too high to secure the bountiful blessings that flow, as the fruits of liberty, with a well-regulated system of wise and judicious laws.

DISCUSSIONS

After an exhaustive discussion of the various reports they were unanimously adopted.

Hon. John L. N. Hunt, secretary of the board of assistant superintendents of New York city, was present and in a few brief remarks explained the absence of Superintendent Jasper, and conveyed to the committee an assurance of the Superintendent's interest in its work. Secretary Hunt suggested a plan of teaching history by placing a character like Lincoln as a center and grouping all the facts connected with his history around him.

Professor Stowits said, "The object lesson furnished to the children of Buffalo at the national encampment, held in that city in August, was of incalculable value in teaching them lessons of love of country and its history."

Colonel Adams said that eighty-eight per cent. of the population of New York city is foreign or of foreign born parentage. In Chicago the per cent. is 91. In Milwaukee, 96. Foreigners come here because they want to better their condition or to escape military service, very different from those who came here in the Mayflower for their principles alone. There are twenty-eight millions of foreign born in this country and that means four millions of voters. Therefore, we must be at work while we may. They must be taught loyalty to the flag. There is no other way to save this nation.

Professor A. H. Dundon said, "You have to deal with a foreign born population. The men do not speak English. Ask yourselves what interest they have in America, in the Constitution, and what respect they have for the flag of our nation. You must take the children into the public schools and there mould and fashion them."

Professor Felter said, that in Brooklyn the boys and girls all join in the salute to the flag.

Professor Boyer said, the boys in his school were under military drill and were trained to stand erect, look people in the eye and obey orders the moment they heard them. At a recent accident to the steam pipes in the school he called "attention" in a loud voice and every boy jumped to his feet at once, and at the next command marched out of the school room down the stairs in regular military order in spite of the noise from the escaping steam, and when the pipes were repaired soon afterward every boy marched back to his business. With military drill the boy is not afraid of you, because he is a soldier. The highest type of manhood is he who subjects his will to law and the right because it is right.

Colonel Goulden said, in a Christie street school 98 per cent. of the pupils were of foreign born parents. Recently one of the children was injured and when it became known crowds of people gathered around the school; but the boys had had military drill and organized into four companies of the American guard. They were ordered out at once and drawn up in two lines inside and out to prevent the frightened little children from leaving the classroom and keeping out 500 women anxious to reach and look after their little ones. It was all over in twenty minutes, and the police could not have done better. In every school where there is military training, the schools are much better in discipline.

Superintendent Skinner said that the greatest enemy to the public schools is public indifference. He believed that history and civics should form a part of the course of study in every public school.

Professor Morey spoke of the custom of observing Washington's birthday in Rochester with appropriate services at the public schools and the selection by the teachers of thirty-four boys to be the custodians of the flags presented to the thirty-four schools of that city by the George H. Thomas post.

Brief and spirited remarks were made by Mr. Searle, Professor Scott, Department Commander Shaw, Professor Stowits, Mr. Baker, Col. Rubright, Major Smith, Commander Long, Rev. Mr. Maul, and others.

A PLEASANT INCIDENT

A message was received under a "flag of truce" from Hon. John W. Vrooman, asking for a "cessation of hostilities," and inviting the members of the committee to a lunch at the Union League Club at one o'clock on Saturday afternoon. The committee "surrendered unconditionally" to the request of Comrade Vrooman and shared with him the generous hospitality extended. The following gentlemen were seated at the lunch table:

Hon. John W. Vrooman,	W. R. Maul,
J. A. Goulden,	Charles H. Searle,
William L. Felter,	E. L. Zalinski,
A. H. Dundon,	H. H. Adams,

Charles R. Skinner,
Warner Miller,
C. A. Rubright,
William T. Salter,
Eugene H. Conklin,
Charles S. Baker,
Albert D. Shaw,
Josiah C. Long,
Heman P. Smith,
Noah Tebbetts,
George H. Stowits,
W. H. Scott,
William C. Morey,
Charles K. Darling, Boston, Commander-in-Chief, Sons of Veterans, U. S.,
Alonzo Williams, Providence, Professor of Literature, Brown University,
E. M. L. Ehlers, Grand Secretary Masonic Grand Lodge.

At the conclusion of the lunch the host made a brief and happy speech, closing with the sentiment that the comrades of the Grand Army of the Republic never grow old, and believed that "the best part of life is yet to come."

RESOLUTIONS

The committee unanimously adopted resolutions as follows:

1. Thanking Hon. William L. Strong, mayor of the city of New York, for the deep interest taken by him in the welfare of the comrades of the Grand Army of the Republic, and expressing its appreciation of his sympathy with all efforts to encourage patriotic teaching in the public schools.

2. Congratulating Department Commander Shaw upon his wisdom and foresight in appointing a special committee to consider how patriotism can best be promoted in the schools of our state.

3. Thanking Commander-in-Chief Gobin and Adjutant-General Stewart for their presence and encouragement.

4. Making Hon. John L. N. Hunt an honorary member of the committee and thanking him and his associates in educational work in New York city for their manifest approval of the purposes of the committee.

5. Approving the excellent system of public instruction in force in New York city and the efficient methods pursued in the patriotic education of the pupils in the schools.

6. Thanking the State Superintendent of Public Instruction for his interest and encouragement.

7. Acknowledging the courtesy and hospitality extended by Comrade John W. Vrooman.

8. Thanking the management of the Hotel Manhattan for attentions received and accommodations furnished.

9. Complimenting Chairman Goulden upon his ability and fairness as a presiding officer during the session of the committee.

Letters

FROM COMMANDER-IN-CHIEF GOBIN

LEBANON, PA., *December* 1, 1897.

MY DEAR COMMANDER.—The position you have taken in your Department relative to the public schools on patriotic teachings and civics therein, is deserving of more than ordinary comment. The gentlemen selected by you as a committee have evidently appreciated the great possibilities of a conscientious work in the direction you have indicated; and the work already accomplished in the schools of the city of New York is potent evidence of their success. I take this occasion to congratulate you and them upon this great advance already made in patriotic teaching and observances—all of which must bear such fruits as will unite the hearts of citizens in a deeper and more abiding love for country, and all its institutions.

Very truly yours,
J. P. S. GOBIN,
Commander-in-Chief, G. A. R.

COL. ALBERT D. SHAW,
Commander Department of New York.

FROM DR. VANDER VEER

ALBANY, N. Y., *November* 30, 1897.

Col. ALBERT D. SHAW, *Dept. Commander of New York G. A. R.:*

My Dear Colonel.— I have just completed a careful study of the report of the committee appointed by yourself on teaching patriotism and civics in our public schools, and desire in a most positive manner to give it my most earnest, frank endorsement. I have seldom read a report so conservative, yet so full of patriotic incentives. It is directly to the point, and must result in great good to our present and oncoming generation of school children. It is also the best reading for the American adult, teacher, parent, soldier or civilian of the present day.

It was with great regret that I was unable to attend either of the meetings of the committee at Buffalo or New York, owing to urgent professional work I could not leave.

I congratulate you upon the work so well done.

Believe me, sincerely yours,

A. VANDER VEER.

General Orders, No. 10

The following extract from General Orders, No. 10, is inserted by direction of Department Commander Shaw:

HEADQUARTERS, GRAND ARMY OF THE REPUBLIC,
DEPARTMENT OF NEW YORK,
CAPITOL, ALBANY, *December* 23, 1897.

General Orders,
No. 10.

EXTRACT

V. The department commander gratefully acknowledges the great interest manifested by the Hon. Charles R. Skinner, Superintendent of Public Instruction of this state, in the subject under consideration by the committee appointed in General Orders No. 6, on patriotic teaching and civics in our schools. Superintendent Skinner has aided the committee by his fruitful counsel and suggestions, and to him we are indebted for the publication of this important report made by the able committee in question. The comrades feel deeply indebted to the superintendent for his most helpful and valuable co-operation in this important patriotic work, which lies so close to all their hearts.

By order,

ALBERT D. SHAW,
Department Commander.

GEORGE H. LESTER,
Adjutant-General.

APPENDIX

EXHIBIT No. 6

REPRINT OF THE

REPORT OF THE COMMITTEE OF TWELVE ON RURAL SCHOOLS

NATIONAL EDUCATIONAL ASSOCIATION

REPORT OF THE COMMITTEE OF TWELVE ON RURAL SCHOOLS

APPOINTED AT THE MEETING OF THE NATIONAL EDUCATIONAL ASSOCIATION, JULY 9, 1895

WITH APPENDICES

PUBLISHED BY ORDER OF THE BOARD OF DIRECTORS OF THE ASSOCIATION

NATIONAL EDUCATIONAL ASSOCIATION

REPORT OF THE COMMITTEE OF TWELVE ON RURAL SCHOOLS

APPOINTED AT THE MEETING OF THE NATIONAL EDUCATIONAL ASSOCIATION, JULY 9, 1895

WITH APPENDICES

PUBLISHED BY ORDER OF THE BOARD OF DIRECTORS OF THE ASSOCIATION

CONTENTS.

REPORT OF THE COMMITTEE,	5
INTRODUCTION TO THE REPORT,	7
REPORT OF SUBCOMMITTEE ON SCHOOL MAINTENANCE,	20
REPORT OF SUBCOMMITTEE ON SUPERVISION,	55
REPORT OF SUBCOMMITTEE ON SUPPLY OF TEACHERS,	77
REPORT OF SUBCOMMITTEE ON INSTRUCTION AND DISCIPLINE,	94
APPENDICES,	121
INDEX,	209

REPORT OF THE

COMMITTEE OF TWELVE ON RURAL SCHOOLS.

To the National Council of Education:

The undersigned Committee of Twelve on Rural Schools, appointed at the meeting of the National Council of Education, Denver, Colo., July 9, 1895, has the honor to submit the following report discussing the rural school problem in its four several aspects, each of which has been the special care of a subcommittee of three persons, who have submitted their results from time to time to the criticism of the entire committee. These subcommittee reports are preceded by a general introduction, written by the Chairman of the Committee of Twelve, in which a history of the formation of the committee is given, together with a brief summary of the recommendations of the several subcommittees. In the appendix will be found a number of valuable contributions illustrative of different points made in the severai reports.

HENRY SABIN,
D. L. KIEHLE,
A. B. POLAND.
C. C. ROUNDS.
J. H. PHILLIPS,
B. A. HINSDALE,
S. T. BLACK,
W. S. SUTTON,
L. E. WOLFE,
W. T. HARRIS,
L. B. EVANS,
C. R. SKINNER.

REPORT OF THE
COMMITTEE ON RURAL SCHOOLS.

INTRODUCTION.

To the National Council of Education:

The undersigned, Chairman of the Committee on Rural Schools appointed at the meeting of the National Council of Education, Denver, Colo., July 9, 1895, would respectfully submit the following report:

At the meeting of the Council on July 5 the Committee on State School Systems made a report on the Rural School Problem, through its chairman, Henry Sabin. C. C. Rounds, President of the Council, urged immediate action, in view of the importance of the subject, and of the growing interest in the question of improving the condition of the rural schools. Other members joined in the discussion, and, on motion of B. A. Hinsdale, the chair was directed to appoint a committee of five, who should submit a plan for the further investigation of this subject.

July 9 the committee reported as follows:

Resolved, That there be undertaken, under the auspices of the Council, an investigation of the subject of Rural Schools, embracing such topics as revenues and expenditures, the constitution, organization, and duties of boards of management and control, and the provision of suitable teachers. More definitely, said investigation shall be conducted in general on the lines laid down in the report of the Committee on State School Systems submitted to the Council at its present session.

Resolved, That a committee of nine be appointed to conduct this investigation, said committee to consist of the following persons: Henry Sabin, of Iowa; D. L. Kiehle, of Minnesota; A. B. Poland, of New Jersey; C. C. Rounds, of New Hampshire; J. H. Phillips, of Alabama; B. A. Hinsdale, of Michigan; S. T. Black, of California; W. S. Sutton, of Texas; and L. E. Wolfe, of Missouri.

Resolved, That the Board of Directors of the National Educational Association be urgently requested to appropriate, at some session to be held during the course of the present annual meeting, the sum of two thousand five hundred dollars, or such part thereof as may be necessary, to defray the expenses of this investigation, including the publication of the report of the committee.

Resolved, That the committee should report within the period of two years, in such form as it may determine, and that it be authorized to publish its report.

Respectfully submitted,

B. A. HINSDALE,
G. P. BROWN,
D. L. KIEHLE,
J. R. PRESTON,
EARL BARNES,
Committee.

[illegible]

The committee held its first meeting July 10, 1895, at which time, on motion of Dr. Hinsdale, the committee was increased from nine to twelve by adding the following persons: W. T. Harris, Washington, D. C.; L. B. Evans, Augusta, Ga.; C. R. Skinner, Albany, N. Y.

Messrs. Sabin, Kiehle, and Hinsdale were constituted a special committee to formulate a plan of work and furnish members with copies of the same; also, to divide the committee into sections and to assign appropriate work to each.

The committee as finally constituted consisted of the following gentlemen:

Henry Sabin, Des Moines, Ia., Chairman; B. A. Hinsdale, Ann Arbor, Mich.; D. L. Kiehle, Minneapolis, Minn.; W. T. Harris, Washington, D. C.; A. B. Poland, Trenton, N. J.; C. C. Rounds, Plymouth, N. H.; J. H. Phillips, Birmingham, Ala.; S. T. Black, Sacramento, Cal.; W. S. Sutton, Houston, Tex.; C. R. Skinner, Albany, N. Y.; L. B. Evans, Augusta, Ga.; J. F. Wolfe, Kansas City, Mo.

The special Committee of Three met in Chicago October 25 and 26, 1895, and, after consultation, divided the entire committee into four subcommittees, and assigned certain topics to each for investigation and report. These subcommittees were constituted and the work assigned to each in accordance with the following schedules:

I. School Maintenance.—Subcommittee: B. A. Hinsdale, Chairman; W. S. Sutton, S. T. Black.

This branch of the subject was divided for convenience into three subheads:

1. Revenues.—Permanent school funds; taxation, general and local; [illegible] state, county, township, and district taxes; miscellaneous sources of school revenue, such as fines, licenses, etc.

[illegible]

which the funds reach the schools, and the rules and methods governing their distribution and application.

3. Organization of Business Administrative Machinery. The county, district, and township-unit systems; the consolidation of schools; the transportation of pupils; county, township, and district high schools; the relation of rural schools to city schools. Inquiry should be made into the main social, industrial, and economical factors that condition rural education, as density of population, wealth, means of communication, etc.

II. Supervision. Subcommittee: L. B. Evans, Chairman; C. R. Skinner, Henry Sabin.

1. The manner of electing the superintendent, state, county, district, or township.

2. Minimum qualifications required of each, and term of office.

3. The relation of the superintendent, state, county, district, or township, to the teachers and pupils as officer and adviser.

4. The relation of the superintendent, state, county, district, or township, to school officers, and their duties.

5. The relation of the state superintendent to the county and township superintendent.

6. The relation of the superintendent to the public at large, as creating and shaping public opinion in rural districts.

7. The relation of the superintendent to school buildings, architecture, sanitation, and hygienic conditions.

III. Supply of Teachers. Subcommittee: C. C. Rounds, Chairman; J. H. Phillips, D. L. Kiehle.

1. An inquiry into the assistance rendered rural schools by the following facilities for preparation:

(*a*) Normal schools.

(*b*) Training schools in high schools and academies.

(*c*) Summer training schools.

(*d*) Institutes.

2. An inquiry into the means provided for the improvement of teachers already in the service.

(*a*) Teachers' meetings and associations.

(*b*) Reading circles.

(*c*) Libraries and current literature.

3. An inquiry into the manner of electing, employing, and paying teachers.

(*a*) By what authority examined and certificated.

(*b*) By what authority employed.

(*c*) Terms of engagement, certificates, and salaries paid.

IV. Instruction and Discipline. Subcommittee: W. T. Harris, Chairman; A. B. Poland, L. E. Wolfe.

1. Methods of teaching and government peculiarly affecting rural schools.

2. Courses of study, text-books, and other appliances.

3. Working programmes.

4. Gradation and classification of pupils.

5. The relations of rural schools to their environments: as to farm life, mining life, etc.

It was also provided that the investigation of the several subdivisions of the general subject should follow two main lines:

1. The condition of rural schools now existing.

2. Changes to be recommended; what is, and what should be.

It was not thought necessary that the committee should go into history or development farther than to make the conditions that now exist, and the reforms that are recommended, intelligible. It was also recommended that changes to be made, or reforms to be proposed, should have respect to existing facts; that they should be practical in the rational sense of that word.

It was further left to the several subcommittees to determine the methods to be employed in carrying on their work, and to exercise the greatest freedom in enlisting aid from every possible source.

Each subcommittee was thus left free to formulate such questions as seemed best designed to elicit the desired information in the most definite form.

The committee met at Jacksonville, Fla., February 18 and 19, 1896, for consultation and comparison of results. An informal meeting was held during the sessions of the National Educational Association at Buffalo in July, 1896, at which time it was determined to hold a meeting of the full committee at Chicago November 18 to 21, 1896. The chairman of each subcommittee was also directed to have such preliminary matter ready at that time as would embrace all the essential points necessary to a fair understanding of the scope of the final report to be made to the Council in July. It was also voted to ask certain experts in rural school matters to meet with the committee, in order that it might have the benefit of their experience.

The committee met at the Auditorium in Chicago, as determined. The entire committee was present at each session, with the exception of D. L. Kiehle, who for satisfactory reasons was not present until Thursday morning. The following gentlemen were present upon invitation of the chairman:

John MacDonald, editor of the *Western School Journal*, Topeka, Kan.; W. W. Stetson, State Superintendent of Maine; J. L. Pickard, of Iowa

City, Ia.; O. T. Bright, County Superintendent of Cook county, Ill.; Albert G. Lane, City Superintendent of Chicago; D. E. McClure, County Superintendent of Oceana county, Mich.; W. H. Chandler, of Madison, Wis.; President F. W. Parker, of the Chicago Normal School; G. R. Shawhan, County Superintendent of Champaign county, Ill.; John Trainer, of Decatur, Ill.; T. C. Chamberlin, of The University of Chicago; J. J. Schobinger, of Morgan Park, Ill.; W. S. Jackman, of the Chicago Normal School; A. W. Edson, State Agent, Boston, Mass.

Wednesday and Thursday were devoted to general discussion, one half day being allotted to each of the four subcommittees in the following order: School Maintenance, Supervision, Supply of Teachers, and Instruction and Discipline. Friday and Saturday were devoted to the consideration of the preliminary reports submitted by the chairmen of the respective subcommittees. The sessions were held from 9 A.M. to 12 M. and from 3 to 6 P.M. In order to facilitate discussion printed or typewritten copies of the main propositions in each report were placed in the hands of those present. During Friday and Saturday the reports were read section by section, and, after alterations and amendments as suggested by various members of the committee, they were adopted.

It was further ordered that the reports of the different subcommittees should appear in the printed volume in the following order:

1. School Maintenance.
2. Supervision.
3. Supply of Teachers.
4. Instruction and Discipline.

On motion the entire matter of printing the report, when completed, was intrusted to the charge of the chairman of the committee, with the suggestion that he confer with the United States Commissioner of Education in regard to securing the co-operation of the national bureau for publication purposes.

T. C. Chamberlin, of The University of Chicago; W. S. Jackman, of the Chicago Normal School, and F. H. King, of Madison, Wis., were requested to prepare a discussion of the possibilities of a course of study especially adapted to agricultural environments. This discussion constitutes *Appendix G* of this report.

Appendix A, consisting of a paper read by B. A. Hinsdale before the Department of Superintendence at Jacksonville, is published by order of the committee. The course of study for rural schools and the paper by Dr. White, designated as ***Appendix I***, and the paper by F. W. Parker, *Appendix H*, are inserted by the same authority. The other matter in the appendix has been placed there in accordance with a vote of the committee, leaving the selection to the choice of the chairman of each subcommittee and of the general committee.

The date for publication of the report was fixed at from four to six weeks before the meeting of the National Educational Council at Milwaukee. After determining that the chairman of each subcommittee should send a typewritten or printed copy of his report to each member of the committee before publication for suggestions or amendments, the committee adjourned.

In the foregoing historical statement no attempt has been made to follow the exact order of proceedings, but only to gather from the Secretary's records such main points as will give the Council exact information of the methods adopted by the committee.

As soon as possible after the adjournment of the committee the chairman of each subcommittee prepared his report, and printed or typewritten copies were sent to other members, and also in all cases to persons who were supposed to be able to point out omissions or to suggest alterations. As a result these reports represent the combined experience of many competent persons besides members of the committee. This method led to much correspondence on the part of the chairmen, but it has undoubtedly aided them very materially in making a broader and much more comprehensive report. The committee found itself confronted from the beginning with the fact that the environments of schools differ so much in various sections of the country that it is impossible to make other than very general suggestions. Conditions vary so much between Maine and California, or Minnesota and Texas, that what would be an excellent system in one would possibly fail in the other.

SCHOOL MAINTENANCE.

Those who read the following reports will find that several recommendations are made by more than one subcommittee. Thus in the matter of organization the necessity of adopting a larger unit than the district, as the township or the county, is very strenuously insisted upon by two or more subcommittees. It is a fact of such great importance that other essential points hinge upon this. The arguments are very fully stated in the report of the Subcommittee on School Maintenance, but the general committee is fully agreed upon the desirability of effecting this change wherever the district system at present prevails. It would conduce to effectiveness and simplicity of organization: to economy in the use and distribution of funds; to the equalization of the burdens of taxation, and to a system of supervision which would produce better results from the instruction given in the rural schools.

Again, all the subcommittees are strongly in favor of the consolidation of schools which are too small to employ profitably the time of one teacher into larger schools, when practicable, in order that better instruction may be provided than is possible under the present system. This involves also paying for the transportation of pupils to some central school at the public expense. The different subcommittees have reached this conclusion, each from its own standpoint. The inferences drawn from facts and figures are too obvious to need any argument. The conclusions arrived at in the discussion of the two points, organization and consolidation, are very broad, and would seem to be applicable to some section of nearly every state in the Union.

The manner of raising and distributing the revenues has been carefully investigated, and the subcommittee having that subject in charge seems to have reached very wise and just conclusions. The township, or special district, in which the parents of the pupils reside should contribute to the school funds, as should the county and the state. Every interest concerned in the education of children should bear a proportionate share of the burden of taxation. In the distribution of school funds, because of the community of interests involved in popular education, the strong and wealthy must contribute to the support of schools in weak and impoverished districts. It may not be possible to provide equal school facilities in every part of the state, but every district in which a school is established should be assured beyond all doubt of a sufficient sum of money to employ a competent teacher for the minimum number of months or days fixed by the law. The duty of providing for the pupils of the rural schools the means whereby they can have the benefit of high schools in their neighborhood has not been overlooked. It is not necessary to discuss fully these points. Attention is invited to them as set forth in the report of the Subcommittee on School Maintenance.

SUPERVISION.

The subject of school supervision is discussed under the general divisions of state, county, township, and district. The task assigned this subcommittee is difficult because, as far as rural schools are concerned, there are no well defined lines of work upon which there is a general agreement. There is great need of supervision which is intelligent and which carries with it some degree of authority. As a general thing, the officer known as state superintendent has only advisory authority. He can make suggestions, but they carry with them no more force than there is in the character and influence of the officer who makes them. He is too far removed from the rural schools, and is too much engaged in other matters connected with his office, to come into close touch with them and their present interests.

No one questions that supervision should be compulsory. In fact, such is the case in most states today. The great question connected with it is how to make it effective. A supervisor who has charge of a hundred schools or more, scattered over an entire county, finds it impossible to control and direct them in accordance with well-devised plans. Accordingly the subcommittee urges township or district supervision where it is practicable, or that each supervisor should have such deputies or assistants as will enable him to reach every part of his field. Again, if supervision is to be effective it must be the product of skill and intelligence. As well put an ordinary seaman, selected from the crew by lot, in charge of an ocean steamer, with its precious cargo of lives and wealth, as to place a raw, uncultivated man or woman, selected by the chances of a political convention, in charge of the schools in which our youth are being trained for citizenship. The subcommittee is of the opinion that certain qualifications, moral and mental, with some experience in teaching, should be exacted from everyone who aspires to the duties of a supervisory office. The duties which are incumbent upon a supervisor of schools have been so minutely discussed that it is not necessary to restate them here. It is sufficient to say that knowledge and skill, enthusiasm and patience, sympathy and forbearance, firmness and justice, are requisite in one who would discharge his duties conscientiously and with due regard to the highest good of all concerned.

The importance of bringing the school into touch with the farm and the home has been dwelt upon at some length (*Appendix O*). To this end the supervisor should make himself thoroughly acquainted with peculiar conditions of life in his supervisory district. It is not enough that he visit the school and consult with the teacher. He must meet school officers and parents, awaken their sympathy and arouse their interest, if he would do his whole duty. He must have a controlling influence in the selection of teachers, in the erection of school buildings, especially as concerns sanitation and hygiene, in teachers' meetings, and in general school work throughout his entire territory.

A wise supervisor cannot fail to observe carefully the environments of the school, which exert a powerful, though unconscious, influence upon the character of the pupils. The bearings of the æsthetical upon the ethical side of the child's nature, the relations of music and art as determining the development of the child along right lines, should be observed and guarded as well in the rural as in the city schools.

SUPPLY OF TEACHERS.

The question of the support afforded teachers is one great hindrance in the way of improving the rural school. The following table showing the average monthly salaries paid teachers in rural schools has been compiled from answers to circulars sent out to state superintendents. It is unfortunate that in most states the statistics make no distinction between city and rural school-teachers. Consequently many of the returns are estimated. They are valuable, however, for purposes of comparison and general information.

	Males	Females		Males	Females
Alabama	$25	$20	Missouri	$40	$34
Arkansas	33	30	Montana	60	45
California [1]	67	56	Nebraska	35	30
Colorado [2]	50	45	Nevada	85	60
Connecticut	30	30	New Hampshire	30	30
Delaware	35	33	New York [4]	37	37
Illinois	30	25	Ohio	35	29
Indiana	40	35	Pennsylvania [5]	42	33
Iowa	35	30	Rhode Island	40	36
Kansas	40	32	South Carolina	30	27
Kentucky	36	34	South Dakota	36	31
Louisiana	40	33	Utah	53	37
Maine	35	22	Vermont	39	27
Maryland	29	29	Virginia	28	25
Massachusetts [3]	32	26	West Virginia	36	36
Michigan	29	25	Wisconsin	46	30
Minnesota	40	31	Wyoming	45	40

In connection with above table we must take into account that in only a few states is the average length of the school over eight months. This includes cities and towns, as well as rural districts, so that it is fair to conclude that in general the country teacher finds employment not to exceed seven months in a year, and often not more than five or six.

The subcommittee regrets that so few are able to apprehend the qualities essential to a good teacher. Professional fitness is ignored in nearly every case. The smaller the unit of organization the greater is the disposition to engage teachers for short periods of time. All engagements should be for one year at least, and frequent changes of teachers should be discouraged.

Perhaps the most important subject intrusted to this subcommittee has reference to the training and preparation of teachers. There is no doubt that the normal school in most states does not reach down and take hold of the common district school. There is room, as indicated in the report, for a series of normal training classes with a course of one year, or at most two years, not modeled after a state normal school, but suited in all respects to the needs of a class of young people from whom we draw nearly all our rural school-teachers. Instruction for one year in such a school could be made to so inspire students with a desire for knowledge,

[1] Includes schools of not more than two teachers.

[2] Includes the schools in the agricultural sections only.

[3] Based on fifty-two male teachers and 143 female teachers in towns under $500,000 valuation.

[4] $9.26 a week, counting thirty-three and one-third weeks in a year.

[5] Not including the city of Philadelphia.

to so fill them with the teaching spirit, as to work a most beneficent change in the schools coming under their charge. The proposition to establish continuous sessions in normal schools, as set forth in the sub-committee's report, is full of promise for the improvement of rural school-teachers without withdrawing them from active service. The terms and courses could, under the plan, be so adjusted as to enable them to attend a normal school for work in regular courses of study during that large part of the year not occupied in teaching. A course for one year is indicated below. If extended to two years, the extension should consist not so much in the introduction of new branches as in doing something more than elementary work in the branches already in the curriculum.

COURSE OF STUDY FOR ONE YEAR OF FORTY WEEKS.

General Divisions	First Term	Second Term
Language.	Reading and Literature.	Grammar. Elements of Rhetoric.
Mathematics.	Arithmetic. Algebra.	Geometry.
Natural and Physical Science.	Geography. Elements of Chemistry.	Botany. Elementary Physics.
History.	U. S. History. Civil Government.	General History. Biography.
Professional Studies.	School Economy. Elementary Psychology Practice Teaching.	Physiology with special reference to hygienic conditions. Practice Teaching.

The number of lessons in each branch per week must be determined by the conditions and necessities of the class. Singing and drawing should have such a place as their importance demands. At least two lessons per week for each of them should be insisted upon.

The course of study to be completed in one year is arranged according to relation of subjects and not according to order of study. It embraces, so far as elements are concerned, those subjects which are necessary in order to enable a teacher to deal with organic and inorganic nature, with history and civil government, with literature and language, and with so much of music and art as the conditions of the school will admit. While provision is made for professional training, the success of such a course as this as a means for preparing teachers for their work will depend almost entirely upon the good judgment and skill of those who are intrusted with the management of the school. The tendency to overload such a course, to crowd two years' work into one, will have to be very carefully guarded against. The entire course is intended to be only elementary, and is for the benefit of a large class of teachers who have but little preparation, and are not able from various reasons to devote more than one year's time to attendance upon a normal school. The advantages of a school of this nature would be greatly enlarged by the possession of a carefully selected library, and of sufficient apparatus for purposes of illustration and experiment. If the students could be taught to make this apparatus, with maps, charts, etc., for use in rural schools, it would add to their usefulness as teachers. Very great advantage would accrue to the pupils from coming in contact with disciplined minds in the persons of their instructors. But few rural teachers know how to study or how to get the most out of the books which fall into their hands.

Summer schools, reading circles, and institutes have received their share of attention. The whole ground has been well covered and will repay a careful perusal.

The scheme for the examination and certification of teachers has been thoroughly digested. There will be some who may not agree with the subcommittee in all particulars, but no one will dispute the fact that too many teachers in the rural schools are contented with the lowest grade of certificate which will answer the purpose of the law. There is a great necessity for some scheme such as is here recommended, whereby teachers can rise step by step in their calling, if they earnestly desire to improve. On the other hand, this scheme furnishes a reasonable excuse for not affording further professional recognition of any kind to those who show no disposition or no ability to do anything better in the line of preparation for their work.

INSTRUCTION AND DISCIPLINE.

The report under this head will be found to embrace several important recommendations. Some of these will provoke discussion, but most of them are of such a nature as to commend themselves to every thoughtful person. The report opens a broad field of inquiry, which must of necessity receive more attention as the wants and necessities of rural schools are better considered.

The evils of attempting to grade the rural school as the city school is graded are very clearly set forth, accompanied by the suggestion that those normal schools which as part of their work train teachers for rural schools should carefully impress upon such teachers the necessity of considering the size of the school in determining the uses and abuses of grading and classifying pupils. This suggestion is all the more pertinent in view of the movement in many states to require some previous professional training as a prerequisite for entering any public school as a teacher.

Considering that the course of study for the rural school need not differ in any material point from that provided for the city school, it is urged that the aim of such a course is to enable the pupil to recognize the conditions of inorganic and organic nature, and to pursue the studies of literature, language, and history, as they are necessary for his entrance upon civilization. The difference in courses of study for rural or city schools is found to be in those collateral branches which relate to the environment of the pupil or to the neighborhood in which he dwells. The report upon this point is very full and will repay a careful study of its details. The subcommittee calls especial attention to the relation of the course of study to the system of grading and classification. The suggestions made are of great practical value in any discussion which endeavors to determine the method of adapting a course of study to the wants and conditions of rural schools. It cannot but be very helpful to be told that the course of study is the measuring rod used only to determine at what point in his work the pupil has arrived, and not a Procrustean bed used to give the work the lifeless beauty of a dead uniformity.

The consolidation of those schools which have become so reduced in numbers as to render it unprofitable to maintain them separately, the transportation of pupils at public expense to other schools than their own, and the concentration of higher-grade pupils at a central point, are urged as means of lessening many of the evils from which rural schools are suffering. This provision, having been grafted into the law of several states, bids fair to prove of great benefit. Wherever it has been tried it has commended itself as economical, and as a means of affording better teachers and consequently better schools. The matter of improved roads enters incidentally into this discussion, as having great bearing upon the question of transporting children to central points for school purposes.

In connection with school exercises at the town or county center, once or twice a year, competitive examinations are not recommended unless they are very carefully guarded. The feature of social intercourse, the stimulus which comes from meeting with his mates, have advantages which ought not to be overlooked or neglected.

Home reading, with what is termed school extension, is dwelt upon at such length as its prominence demands (*Appendix O*). To carry good reading material, whether of science, literature, or fiction, prose or poetry, into the schools and homes of the rural districts must be a part of any educational scheme which has for its object making country life more endurable or more attractive. The various recommendations of this part of the report are worthy of careful consideration at the hands of those even who may not wholly agree with them.

CONCLUSION.

Your committee has called in the aid of a number of persons whose time and thought have been largely given to matters connected with the management and instruction best suited to the wants of rural schools. It was found impossible to embrace the entire matter placed at our disposal in the body of the report. We have, therefore, printed much of it in the form of an appendix, believing that it will add largely to the value of this report. It is not to be supposed that every point has been covered, or that the entire subject has been exhausted. The committee has endeavored diligently and to the best of its ability to throw some light upon what may possibly be regarded as a collection of subjects embracing a very large field. While there are many points worthy of especial attention, I have gathered up the following as a brief summary of those which may be considered of most pressing importance:

SUMMARY.

1. For purposes of organization, maintenance, or supervision, nothing should be recognized as the unit smaller than the township or the county; the school district is the most undesirable unit possible.

2. Every community should be required to raise a certain sum for the support of its schools as a prerequisite for receiving its share of public money. A certain definite sum should be appropriated to each school out of the state funds, and the remainder should be divided in accordance with some fixed and established rule, a discrimination being made in favor of townships most willing to tax themselves for school purposes.

3. One of the great hindrances to the improvement of the rural school lies in its isolation, and its inability to furnish to the pupil that stimulative influence which comes from contact with others of his own age and advancement. The committee, therefore, recommends collecting pupils from small schools into larger and paying from the public funds for their transportation, believing that in this way better teachers can be provided, more rational methods of instruction adopted, and at the same time the expense of the schools can be materially lessened.

4. There is a tendency to fill the rural schools with untrained, immature teachers. The establishment of normal training schools, under competent instructors, with short courses, each year of which shall be complete in itself, would do much to remedy this evil. The extension and adjustment of the courses and terms of the state normal schools so as to constitute a continuous session would enable them to contribute more directly than now to the improvement of the teachers of rural schools (*Appendix S*). The state would then be justified in demanding some degree of professional training from every teacher in the rural as well as in the city schools.

5. The establishment of libraries, the prosecution of the work of school extension by lectures and other means, the introduction of such studies as will have a tendency to connect the school and the home, especially those having a direct bearing upon the everyday life of the community, and the necessity of applying the laws of sanitation to the construction of rural schoolhouses, demand immediate attention.

6. The rural schools are suffering from the want of official and intelligent supervision. In every state some standard of qualifications, moral and intellectual, with some amount of actual experience, should be demanded by law from those who aspire to fill the office of superintendent or supervisor of schools.

7. Good morals and good manners constitute an assential part of an educational equipment. The inculcation of patriotism, of respect for law and order, of whatever tends to make a good citizen, is of as much importance in a small as in a larger school. Regularity, punctuality, obedience, industry, self-control, are as necessary in the country as in the city school. Country school-teachers should call to their aid the beautiful things in nature, that with reverential spirit they may lead the children to reverence Him who hath made all things good in their season.

HENRY SABIN,
Chairman.

REPORT OF THE SUBCOMMITTEE ON SCHOOL MAINTENANCE.

The maintenance of an efficient state system of public instruction involves numerous sociological factors of an important character. This is particularly true in a democratic state, where public opinion gives the final sanction to all public activities. Moreover, there is good reason to think that it is even more important to consider such factors carefully when providing rural schools than when providing urban schools. The bearing of the wealth of the state, both in the aggregate and in relation to population; the density of population and the ratio of rural to urban population; the ratio of the adult or wealth-producing population to the population of legal school age; the facilities for travel and the character of the people in respect to race elements – the value of such factors as these in the problem is almost too plain for argument (*Appendix A*).

The organization and administration of the powers of government must also be considered. The government of the United States stands to all the members of the Union in the same relation; that is, within the states it has no proper educational function whatever. The state government, however, is a constant factor: it exercises the central state authority. But when we take the next step we are at once confronted by contradiction and confusion. First, we find in New England the town system of local government. Here nearly all the local governmental functions are performed by the town; the county exists, but it is more a judicial than a political unit, and in Rhode Island it is wholly judicial. The town is much, the county little. Secondly, the county system, which exists throughout the South and in several of the western states, more than reverses these conditions. The county is the organ of local government, and the township does not commonly exist. The county is divided into districts for the purpose of defining the jurisdiction of justices of the peace, into election precincts, and sometimes into school townships. Here the county is everything, the town nothing. Thirdly, the old middle states and most of the western states have what is called the mixed or compromise system. In these states the township is less than in New England and the county more, the county less than in the South and the township more; in other words, both township and county are employed in something like equal measure. Again, two types of the mixed system are found in different states. In New York and the states that have imitated her the county legislative and executive board is composed of supervisors elected by the several townships, while in Pennsylvania and the states that have followed her example this board is composed of commissioners elected by the county at large. The county is, therefore, a governmental organ in all the states, while the township is found only in two groups of states. Moreover, in those states where the town or township is found it varies considerably in powers in comparison with the county. These elementary governmental facts it is necessary to remember, because they directly affect the matter in hand. Manifestly, the people will not be apt to create local organs of government for any one single purpose unless they deem it absolutely necessary; on the other hand, they will manifestly use for any such purpose, as far as consistent, the same organs that they use for other local purposes. This is just as true of schools and education as of other public interests. Except that Vermont has a county examiner of teachers, no mention is made of the county in any New England school law;[1] no mention is made of the town or township in any southern state; while the states that have the compromise system use both the county and the township as organs for carrying on their schools. It will be seen that no account is here taken of the city or municipality, because this is common to all the states and does not relate to rural schools.

[1] Vermont, Maine, and New Hampshire once enacted laws creating the county superintendency, but these laws did not remain long on the statute books. No state is likely to use the county for an administrative school purpose unless it uses it for other administrative purposes.

An ambiguity in the use of the term *town* is also to be mentioned. The *township* of the middle and western states corresponds in general to the New England *town;* while in these states the *town* is a village, hamlet, or even city. All the recommendations made in this report will recognize distinctly the facts now stated.

Still another preliminary explanation is called for. The term *district*, as used in school legislation and in educational discussions, is very misleading. The two leading senses of the word must be sharply discriminated. This can be done by describing the two principal forms of local school organization.

1. *The Town- or Township-unit System.*—This is something wholly different or separate from the town system of local government described above. The two systems may exist together, but not of necessity so; the town- or township-unit system, called also the *town-district* system, is found in connection with both the town and the compromise systems of local government; it could not exist with the county system, as a matter of course. The town system of local government relates to local affairs generally; the town- or township-district system to schools only. The name *township-unit system* means only that the town or township is the ultimate unit of school organization and administration. This unit, with such assistance as it receives from the state or county, provides and carries on its own schools independent of any other unit. It raises funds by taxation and expends them, subject only to the law of the state. It is the organized town or township, a body corporate and politic, under its educational aspect. The local authority is sometimes a school committee, as in Massachusetts; sometimes a board of education, as in Ohio, and again a township trustee, as in Indiana. Again, the township-unit system does not necessarily involve the consolidation of rural schools. The school children within the unit may all be brought together in one central school at some advantageous point, or they may attend a plurality of schools scattered through the township. In the second case, the limits or boundaries of the several schools must be marked off for the regulation of school attendance, unless indeed pupils are permitted to attend such schools as they please, and these areas are commonly called *districts* or *school districts*. In Ohio they are known as *subdistricts*, and they serve also as units of representation in the township board.[1] Here then are

[1] The explanation of the Ohio law on this point is historical. Previous to 1892 the township was the school district proper, but this was divided into subdistricts. The township board of education raised all the local funds by a tax levied on the taxable property of the township, and apportioned them among the subdistricts; the subdistrict boards of directors employed the teachers and carried on the schools. The voters of the subdistrict, in annual school meeting, elected the three directors, one every year, for three years, and these again elected one of their number clerk, who represented his subdistrict in the township board. Under the Workman Law of 1892 all the old powers of the directors

two clear uses of the term *district:* one is the town or township, and the other a part of the town or township defined primarily for the regulation of school attendance, but also sometimes serving as a unit of representation.

2. *The District System.*—Here *district* is used in quite another sense. Geographically, the school district is now commonly a subdivision of a town, as in Connecticut, or of a township, as in Michigan, or of a county, as in the county-system states. Ordinarily it is a body politic and corporate, and is the ultimate unit of school organization and administration. It has its own school committee or board elected by the voters of the district, in school meeting, and, with such help as it receives from the state or county, it builds its own schoolhouse and provides and carries on its own school or schools. It is, therefore, a taxing as well as an administrative unit. Under this system the district is the controlling factor of school organization. Not only is it the most democratic form of school organization, but it has been called "probably the most communistic as well as democratic feature of our political institutions, and is certainly the smallest minor civil division of our system."[1]

Still other districts are mentioned in the laws and reports, as special districts, city districts, borough districts, joint districts, and the like; but these names do not present any new features of an essential character.

These explanations premised, the subcommittee will divide this report into three grand divisions, *viz.*, Revenue, Distribution, and Organization. The last topic, however, will be considered only so far as relates to school maintenance. By school maintenance is meant the provision and support of public schools.

REVENUE.

The subcommittee submits that the first essential to the material improvement of the rural schools of the country is the provision of revenue sufficient for their adequate support. Accordingly, this is the first subject to be considered.

The educational items in the budgets of all progressive countries have assumed great proportions, and are all the time growing. The Commissioner of Education reports the expenditure for common schools in the states of our Union for the year 1894–95, not including payments on bonds, at $178,215,556. Seven states expended more than $5,000 000 and less than $10,000,000 each, and five more than $10,000,000 and less

were transferred to the township board, but the subdistrict was left for the regulation of school attendance and to serve as a unit of representation in the township board.

[1] Mr. Wellford Addis, Specialist in the Bureau of Education. See chap. xxxiv. of the Report for 1894–95, "The Social Unit in the Public School System of the United States."

than $20,000,000 each. New York alone stood above $20,000,000. In 1888–89 the total for the country was $132,129,000, and in 1883–84 only $103,909,528. But, unfortunately, we have no statistics showing the division of these vast sums between the rural districts and the towns and cities. A *city*, in the dictionary of the National Census Office, is a concentration of population containing 8,000 people or more of all ages, and in 1894–95 there were 574 cities in the country. The Commissioner of Education reports for the year 1894–95 that 3,302,841 children were enrolled in the schools of these cities, to 10,894,911 enrolled in other schools. He reports further that the maintenance of these city schools cost $74,721,332, of the others $102,876,359. But this is no proper division of rural and urban schools, since the educational conditions existing in many centers of population containing less than 8,000 people are the same as those existing in the 574 cities. At present it costs much more to school 1,000, 10,000, or 100,000 children in the cities than in the country, but this is mainly due to the fact that the education furnished is so much greater in quantity and so much better in quality. It is not improbable that, if rural schools were brought as near as possible to the level of urban schools, they would be quite as costly. At least, it is evident that the first condition of good rural schools is a sufficiency of funds with which to provide and maintain them. How shall these funds be provided?

I. A century ago the American people began to take an interest in the creation of permanent school funds or endowments. This interest was originally stimulated, if not created, by the policy that Congress foreshadowed in 1785, and subsequently firmly established, to endow the common schools in the public-land states with liberal grants of public lands. In every state in which Congress has exploited the wild lands either one-thirty-sixth or one-eighteenth part of such lands has been dedicated to the public schools. Beginning with Connecticut in 1795, nearly all the non-public-land states have also created such endowments out of their own resources. Several of them devoted the United States deposit fund of 1837 to this purpose. At the beginning of the century no one dreamed to what proportions public education would grow in one hundred years; and men thought, not unnaturally, that permanent endowments would greatly ease the burden of taxation for school purposes, and would keep the educational machinery of the state constantly running and well regulated. It will not be denied that, relatively, these funds have come far short of meeting the expectations of those who laid their foundations. There can be little doubt that, in many of the states, and particularly when such states were new and poor, they have hastened educational development; but it is quite certain that they have often done great harm, causing the people to rely upon the feeble income derived from them, and to turn their faces away from the only adequate source of school maintenance, that is, public taxation. Texas has been gazetted as having the most magnificent possibilities of any state in the way of a permanent school fund, but some citizens of that state are now questioning whether these possibilities may not prove other than an unmixed blessing (*Appendix B*). The fact is, public schools in the United States have far outgrown all present or prospective endowments. In 1888–89 the income from such funds was $9,825,000 in a total of $132,-125,111; in 1894–95 the corresponding figures were $8,336,612 and $177,-597,691; that is, the per cent. fell from 7.4 to 4.7 in six years. New York and Ohio derive less than $300,000 each of their great school revenues from permanent funds, and Pennsylvania derives nothing from such a source. In fact, it would require a permanent fund of $400,000,000 to carry on, at the present scale of expenditure, the common schools of either New York or Pennsylvania. The subcommittee submits, therefore, that all permanent school funds, either state or local, should be carefully husbanded and wisely administered; that they should be preserved intact, and the income be scrupulously applied to the support of schools; that, under special conditions, it may be wise to augment old funds or create new ones, as when certain miscellaneous revenues can be devoted to that purpose; but that such funds must necessarily play a constantly diminishing part in popular education. Massachusetts is committed to the policy of adding to her fund $100,000 a year, raised by taxation, until a total of $5,000,000 shall be reached, and New Jersey to the policy of similarly dedicating the proceeds of certain riparian rights that belong to the state; and to this there is no objection; but for these states, or any others, to lean heavily upon such funds for school maintenance would be a most fatuous policy. Public education is, or at least should be, a recognized function or service of the state, the public schools of the country are civil schools, created and carried on by the civic authority, and they must rest ultimately upon the same general means of support as the other functions or services of government. As well, therefore, endow any other branch or function of the state government, such as the asylums and hospitals, the judiciary, the civil service, or the militia, as the state schools!

II. Gifts to popular education should be sedulously encouraged. Education has long been a favorite object with public benefactors, as the annals of every progressive country show, and none more convincingly than our own. No doubt when the public mind is aroused to the advantages of popular education, and school taxes are abundant, such persons who choose an educational object for their beneficence will rather be inclined to seek some other form or kind of education. Still, the constitution or laws of nearly every state, if not indeed every one, provide for the acceptance and use of private gifts for school purposes, and there are generous persons who are peculiarly interested in the common schools. Scattered over the country are many local public school endowments that had a private origin, and such gifts have not come to an end. The subcommittee is not aware that there are any statistics showing how far private benevolence contributes to public education, but it is apprised that the contribution is by no means contemptible, and it believes that it might be made considerably larger than it is. The favorite forms of such contributions, under existing conditions, are most likely to be land for building sites, and apparatus and libraries for schools; and the subcommittee is of the firm opinion that much more could be done than at present in all these directions, and particularly in the way of procuring apparatus and books for the schools in communities where the public funds that are available for these purposes are meager or insufficient.

III. The great resource of the public school *is*, and ***must continue to be***, some form or forms of public taxation. The ratio of the total school revenues derived from taxes to those derived from permanent funds is all the time growing, and it will continue to grow. At two periods separated by six years the sources of the common-school revenues expressed in per cents. were as follows:

Year	Taxes	Permanent funds	Other sources
1888-89	85.9	7.4	6.7
1894-95	85.7	4.7	9.6

Manifestly such areas or units of taxation should be created, or continued if already in existence, as will fully develop the sound American principle, that ***the whole wealth of the state shall be made available for educating all the youth of the state.*** This is both right and necessary, for it must be remembered that, in the United States, education is a civil, or state, function, to be supported like other similar functions. What shall these units of taxation be? The subcommittee names those following as coming under the principle just stated:

1. *The State.*—A liberal provision of funds from the state treasury, to be distributed according to some rational method, is indispensable, as a rule, to the maintenance of a good system of state schools. Formerly the burden was mainly or wholly thrown upon the local units. The old Massachusetts plan was to throw upon the towns the whole burden of maintaining their own schools. But the greatly increased cost of schools, growing out of enhanced salaries, longer terms, and improved material equipment, long ago demonstrated that this plan must be materially

modified. Many local taxing units are too poor to carry such a load, and they must either abandon all hope of good schools or they must receive assistance from the state or social whole. This fact began to gain recognition as early as the middle of the century. When the constitution of Ohio, adopted in 1851, provided that the legislature should make such provisions, by taxation or otherwise, as, with the interest arising from the permanent school fund, would secure a thorough and efficient system of common schools throughout the state, the law-making power hastened to levy upon all the property of the state, as rated by the assessors, a state school tax of two mills on the dollar, to be distributed on the basis of the school enumeration. Taking the country together, the cost of public education is divided between two or more taxing units. Still the fact remains that the part which falls to the local unit is often disproportionate. In 1888–89 the per cent. of the total amount of school revenues raised by local taxation was 66.8 to 19.1 per cent. raised by state taxation. In 1894–95 the corresponding per cents. were 67 and 18.7. The ratio of the two elements is variable in different divisions of the Union and in different states of the same division. The per cents. raised by state tax, as reported, range all the way from zero to a maximum of 83.2, found in North Carolina. We should naturally expect the southern states, since local government is there less fully developed than at the North, to rely relatively much less on local taxation and much more on state taxation, and such is the fact. But political habit is not the only factor that enters into the problem; economical conditions also assert themselves. In a state where wealth abounds, and is somewhat evenly distributed throughout its limits, as where manufacturing and commercial towns are frequent, there is not the same necessity for the state, as a unit, to assume a large proportion of the whole burden that there is in a state where wealth is meager, and where such wealth as exists is largely found in a few concentrations of population, leaving large areas thinly populated and poor. These remarks will throw light on the per cents. of school moneys raised by state taxation and local taxation in the five divisions of states that the Census Office recognizes. The date is 1894–95. (See also *Appendix B.*) No account is here taken of income from other sources than taxation.

Divisions	State taxes	Local taxes
North Atlantic States	19.4	68.2
South Atlantic States	38.1	51.3
South Central States	48.4	31.7
North Central States	9.9	75.4
Western Division	23.0	61.3

In some of the states, as will be shown hereafter, local taxation must be more fully developed than in the past or present; in others, and these principal states too, the same may be said of state taxation.

2. In all states where, for other local purposes, the county is the sole unit of taxation, a liberal county tax should be levied for the schools. This proposition applies especially to those states where the county system of local government prevails. In states where, for such purposes, the county is a large unit of taxation, it may be wise to levy a county school tax; that circumstances must determine. This remark applies to the states having the mixed system of local government. Under the town system county taxation for schools would be out of harmony with the social and political traditions of the people, and could be accomplished only through a change of habit; perhaps this end is attainable. For the year 1894–95 the Commissioner of Education shows that 67 per cent. of the total school revenues of the country came from local taxes. The scale ran from 1.7 per cent. in North Carolina to 98.2 in Massachusetts. Unfortunately we have no statistics showing from what sources the local taxes come; how much from districts, towns, and counties respectively. The point must, however, be strongly pressed that local supply for public education should be forthcoming as well as state supply. It is a great mistake to teach the people to look altogether, or mainly, to the state treasury for school maintenance. They should rather be taught to depend in due measure upon themselves. It is the confident opinion of the subcommittee that some states are now committing this mistake. Many states having the county system of local government have in the counties a resource for school maintenance upon which they have never adequately drawn.

3. In those states where the town or township is a large taxing unit for other local purposes, it should also be made to contribute liberally to public education. This recommendation it would be idle to urge in most of the southern and in some of the western states, because the civil town or township does not exist, and it would be vain to urge its creation for school purposes exclusively. But in those states where the town and mixed systems of local government exist, a township school tax would be congruous with the general social and political habits of the people. The desirability of local taxation for school purposes was urged under the last head. Such taxation develops self-reliance and local character, and tends to awaken and keep alive the interest of the people in the schools. The town was the sole school-taxing unit in old New England, and it is still a prominent, sometimes almost an exclusive, one throughout the northern states. The local school taxes of New England are town and district taxes, and, taken together, they range from the minimum of 69.2 per cent. of the whole in Maine to 98.2 in Massachusetts. It can hardly be

doubted that the New England states, as well as some others, now throw the burden too heavily upon the towns and districts, and that they will find it advantageous considerably to raise the ratio which state taxation bears to local taxation. The other New England states will probably follow, sooner or later, the example of Maine, which raises nearly one-third of her school money by state taxation. In some states, no doubt, the townships should carry a heavier weight than at present, at least as compared with districts; at all events, the township should bear a reasonable part of the cost of its own education.

4. Special districts, as incorporated villages, towns, and cities, the subcommittee considers not only proper but necessary units of school taxation. Such districts are the concentrations, large or small, of population and wealth; they are the industrial and social centers of the country. We have already seen that, in 1893-94, $69,886,413 was expended for school purposes in the 443 cities of the Union. In Massachusetts $7,088,000 was expended in cities; in New York, $12,723,000; in Pennsylvania, $7,745,000; in Ohio, $5,097,000; in Illinois, $8,110,000. If we had the figures for the smaller cities and the incorporated towns, the aggregate would be much increased. Now, not only do the cities, taken together, raise by taxation nearly all of the school money that is expended in them, but, as will be shown in another place, many of them contribute largely to the support of rural schools. Again, they must in the future, collectively as before, contribute still more largely to this end. Special districts, then, are essential as taxing units, care being taken to secure approximately a fair distribution of the public burdens. As a rule, dwellers in cities are much better able to pay heavy taxes than dwellers in the country, but there is great reason to fear that they do not always do so.

The school district, in the commonly accepted sense of that term, is not a desirable taxing unit, but the contrary. It is now such a unit in a majority of states, and the subcommittee is decidedly of the opinion that it should either be made much less prominent than it is or be abolished altogether. As a rule, the second course is to be preferred (except in special districts already mentioned). The town or township is the smallest area that should be employed for this purpose. Even this may be overweighted, as can easily be shown. The unanswerable objections to district taxation are the inequality in burdens that results, and the inability of many districts to carry the load that good schools would necessarily impose upon them. A few statistics will make both propositions perfectly clear.

In 1871 Superintendent Fallows, of Wisconsin, published a table showing the amount of property assessed per scholar, in the school districts of a certain township, which he believed to be a type of the state of things generally existing throughout that state. The maximum was $2,860; the minimum, $784; the average, $1,378. In 1878 Superintendent Graham, of the same state, published a table for the whole state, showing that the valuation of property per district varied from $2,300 to $1,979,708. Districts with less than $3,000 and districts with $40,000 were found in the same township. But the poor districts were required by law to maintain a school six months in the year, just as the rich ones were. The ratio of district taxation ranged from half a mill to fifty-five mills on the dollar. Superintendent Wells, of Wisconsin, published similar facts in 1893 for a number of states. He showed that in Rhode Island some districts were taxed fourteen times as heavily as others, and in Connecticut a similar disproportion existed. In New York the ratio of tax raised in two counties varied from .0012 per cent. in one district to .0431 in another. One township presented the extremes .0009 and .0070, and still another one .0048 and .0371. Two districts in one township paid respectively $5.66 and $58.11 per capita; two in another one, $5.43 and $60.37; two in a third, $11.25 and $181.85. "That is to say," says Mr. Wells, "the rate of taxation is seven times as great in one district as in another in the same town, and the per-capita cost of educating a child is eleven times as great."[1] But the first of these New York comparisons presents a ratio of almost forty to one.

Statistics such as these could be collected almost without limit. The most instructive way to study the subject is, so to speak, on the ground. If a man unfamiliar with it, who lives under the independent district system, will only take the trouble to collect the facts relating to his own county he may easily be astonished at the result. And yet, as a rule, the law lays upon the districts, rich and poor alike, the same burdens in respect to school maintenance. It is hard to see how or why the people have so long borne such inequalities—inequalities so contrary to the cherished American principle that the property of the state should educate the youth of the state; or, rather, it would be hard to see why they have borne them, if we did not know the extent of the public ignorance on the subject, and the strength of conservative habit, and did not see also how the district as a taxing unit is bound up in men's minds with the district as a unit of administration. But the two are not inseparable. The legislature of Ohio abolished the district as a taxing unit twenty-five years or more before it abolished the district as an administrative unit. In Connecticut, too, town taxes and district management are both met with in the same towns.

Before dismissing units of school taxation, a single point calls for closer attention. This is raised by the question, What is the advantage of looking to large units for supply rather than small ones?

The answer to this question rests upon the fundamental assumption

[1] "Township System of School Government." Madison, Wis., 1894.

that public education is a state function, and that the whole state is responsible for the education of all the youth of the state. Now, if the cost of public education bore the same ratio to the ability of the people to bear this cost in all the communities of the state, or, what is nearly the same thing, if the wealth per capita of all the communities were equal, then, as a matter of course, it would make no difference whether the school tax were levied upon large areas or small ones. But this is far from being the case. The cities are indeed concentrations of both absolute population and school population, as well as of wealth; but their wealth tends to increase much more rapidly than either the absolute or the school population. The fortunes of the country are either made in the cities or else tend to flow into the cities. The last report of the Census Office shows the per-capita wealth of the Union, of the states severally, and of the five groups of states, but it does not show the per-capita wealth of the cities and of the rural districts separately. The nearest approach to it is the tables showing the per-capita value of real estate with improvements, by states and counties. These averages throw important light upon the subject, and some examples will be given.

Illinois: state average, $860.88; highest county average, $1,311.90; lowest county average, $164.64.

Massachusetts: state average, $848.01; highest county average, $1,564.10; lowest county average, $466.65.

New York: state average, $969.66; highest county average, $1,733.35; lowest county average, $305.80.

Ohio: state average, $689.01; highest county average, $1,562.56; lowest county average, $265.99.

Pennsylvania: state average, $719.13; highest county average, $1,049.88; lowest county average, $187.26.

If personal property were included, the extremes per capita would be still more widely separated than they are at present. Formal argument is not needed to show that the rich counties are much more able to contribute to the expense of government, education included, than the poor ones, and the proposition that a due proportion of such expense should be thrown upon these units rests upon this fact. The tendency would be to remove inequalities in bearing the common burden. Levying the local school tax upon the township instead of the districts that compose it, or upon the county instead of the townships, would work in this direction. It is very true that townships are unequal in per-capita wealth as well as districts, and counties as well as townships; still the fact remains that large units are less unequal than small ones. Every step towards the highest taxing unit tends to distribute the burden more equally. In fact, the argument for removing a portion of the burden from the small taxing units to the large ones is the same that justifies us in calling upon society to educate individuals or families that are too poor to provide for their own education. Why do we impose a public tax for educational purposes at all? Simply because education is a common interest, while some individuals or families are unable to educate themselves.

It may be said that the line of reasoning which has been followed would lead to placing the whole burden of state education at the door of the state treasury. Why should not the state defray the cost of the common schools, just as it defrays the cost of the reform schools for boys and girls, and of the asylums and hospitals? It must be confessed that this would be strict logic. However, we are to remember that governments are never carried on according to strict logic, and cannot be from the very nature of the case. What is more, there are the best of reasons, as shown above, for making education, to a reasonable degree, a local charge — reasons that do not apply to some other public services. The people are more likely to be vitally interested in the schools if a portion of their cost is derived from local taxes. In no country of the world, so far as the subcommittee is aware, is elementary education made an exclusive general charge. It is not desirable that it should be. The present contention is for a reasonable distribution among the several taxing units. At the same time, it may be worth observing that in some countries there is a strong tendency, as in England and France, to rely more than formerly upon general rather than local supply.

The appropriations for schools that states make from the common treasury differ greatly in form as well as in amount. Massachusetts levies no state school tax, but the legislature nevertheless votes various specific appropriations, as for the salaries and expenses of state agents, aid to pupils of normal schools, compensation of local superintendents, the payment of high-school tuition for pupils living in towns whose valuation of property does not exceed $500,000 and that do not maintain a high school. Connecticut raises annually a state school tax equal in amount to $1.50 multiplied by the number of persons in the state between the ages of four and sixteen, as enumerated annually. Rhode Island, while not levying a state school tax, so-called, votes enough money out of the state treasury, each year, to make, with the income of the permanent fund, a total of $120,000. New York raises annually, by taxation based on the real and personal property of the state, such sum for the support of schools as the legislature shall determine. New Jersey assesses and collects a total state tax amounting to $5 for each person in the state between the ages of five and eighteen years. It is this tax that places New Jersey at the head of the column of northern states in respect to the per cent. of school revenue derived from a state tax. The constitution of Pennsylvania provides that the state legislature shall appropriate every year $1,000,000 from the state treasury for the use of schools, but the present appropriation is $5,500,000. Ohio levies a tax of one mill on the dollar of the grand tax duplicate of the state. Indiana raises eleven cents, and Kentucky twenty-two cents, on each $100 of taxable property. The Michigan law directs the supervisor of every township to levy a school tax of one mill on the dollar for schools within the township, but as the proceeds are kept within the districts where they are raised, this is only a compulsory local tax; still it stimulates further local taxation for the grand object. The legislature of Michigan also levies a specific tax on certain corporations, as railroads, etc., which is first applied to the payment of the interest on the various educational funds that the state has borrowed, as the university, agricultural college, and common-school funds, and then to the support of the common schools. Nebraska makes an annual levy and assessment not exceeding one and a half mills on each dollar's valuation on the grand list of taxable property. The California system of school finance will be mentioned under distribution and in an appendix. These are a few of the states; still others will be dealt with in connection with distribution.

The basis of school taxation, or the ultimate sources of school supply, is an important subject. Whether more money can be had for the schools often depends upon the manner in which it is proposed to levy the tax. In general, taxation for schools will conform more or less closely to the character of the state taxing system as a whole. While admitting the great importance of the subject, the subcommittee does not feel called upon to discuss it beyond offering brief remarks on two or three points.

Pennsylvania meets her annual state school appropriation, in whole or part. by laying a tax of four mills on the dollar on all moneys loaned by citizens of the state. Some states levy poll taxes, and some "occupation" taxes, for their schools. Quite miscellaneous sources of school revenue are met with in the state constitutions and laws. We find specific taxes on dogs, and on banks, railroads, and other corporations. Escheats and forfeitures are often, or commonly, devoted to the schools. The constitution of Nebraska prescribes that all fines, penalties, and licenses arising under the general laws of the state shall belong, and be paid over, to the counties where such fines, etc., may be levied or imposed; also that all fines, penalties, and licenses arising under the rules, by-laws, or ordinances of cities, villages, towns, precincts, or other municipal divisions less than a county, shall be paid over to the same respectively; and further, that all these moneys shall be appropriated exclusively to the use and support of common schools in the respective divisions where the same may accrue. Nor is Nebraska peculiar in so dedicating such funds. It has been suggested to the subcommittee that an inheritance tax would prove a popular, as well as an abundant, source of school supply.

DISTRIBUTION.

The subject of distribution is only less important than that of income. It is easy so to distribute school funds as, first, either to defeat, in whole or part, the very end sought in taxing the larger units for the benefit of the small ones; or, secondly, materially to weaken local enterprise and liberality, or wholly to destroy it. The subject will be considered under both these aspects.

1. The assistance that the large political and social units render to the small ones, as the state to counties, townships, and districts; or the county to townships and districts; or the township to districts, should be made contingent, in part at least, upon what the small units do for themselves. No community, it is believed, is so poor that it cannot do something towards educating its youth. Again, a state educational system should be so organized and administered as to stimulate, and not repress, local spirit and effort. It is a great mistake to remove the burdens of public education so far from the people that they forget, or tend to forget, their existence. The principle here involved is a vital one. History shows conclusively that popular education has flourished most in those states of our Union where government is most democratic.

It is difficult, or rather impossible, to lay down a general rule that shall govern the division of taxation between the state and the local communities. Two things are to be considered. One is the political institutions that exist in the state. If government is largely centralized at state capitals and county seats—*that* is one thing; if it is largely decentralized, as where the principle of local self-government is fully developed—*that* is quite another. For example, it would be idle to expect that the same results would obtain in the southern states that are found in New England, or even in that great group of states where the mixed system of local government prevails. The governmental machinery and the traditions of the people *will* assert themselves in such matters. The other factors to be considered are social, and particularly economical conditions. As remarked early in this report, where wealth is abundant and its distribution general and somewhat equal in different communities. school burdens may be thrown, and should be thrown, much more heavily upon localities than where the opposite conditions prevail. Density of population, relation of urban to rural population, average wealth per capita, ratio of wealth-producing population to the population of legal school age, the expenditure for education per pupil and per capita, and the per cent. of school revenue derived from state taxes and local taxes in the different states—are peculiarly interesting when studied together

(*Appendix A*). North Carolina shows the largest per cent. of state school tax (that is, of the whole tax) of any state in the Union, while the average population per square mile and the average wealth per capita are also small. Maine surpasses all the other New England states in these particulars. The proportionally high ratio of state taxation in the South is due to the two facts stated—political institutions and economical conditions. But there can be no manner of doubt that, as the cities of the South grow, towns multiply, and concentrations of population increase in number and in the value of property, local school taxation will materially increase. Legislatures could hardly prevent it if they should try, and it would be most unwise for them to try to do so.

2. Funds raised by the large taxing units should be distributed in such a manner as to bring the support of the rich and strong to the poor and weak. The only reason for taxing these units at all for general purposes is to secure this end. On no other principle can a state school tax, or even a county or township tax, be defended, unless indeed the county or township is a single school district. The practical question is, How shall such funds be distributed so as not to defeat the end in view? A historical account of the leading methods actually pursued will help on the inquiry.

The public-land states may be divided into two classes. From the admission of Ohio to that of Arkansas (1803–36) Congress gave to the congressional townships of such states, severally, 640 acres of land each for the perpetual use of schools, and vested the title in the state legislatures. Accordingly, in these states every township has its own independent permanent school fund,[1] which is sometimes managed by local authorities and is sometimes in the keeping of the state. Generally speaking, the sum of the township funds makes the so-called state school fund, so far as it is derived from public lands. If the township-unit system prevails, the ultimate distribution of income has been made in advance; if the district system, then the township distributes to the districts. From the admission of Michigan to that of Utah (1837–95) Congress gave the common-school lands to the states as units rather than to townships, which resulted in the establishment of consolidated state school funds. The annual income from these funds, so far as the subcommittee is informed, is uniformly distributed to the local school organizations on the basis of the youth of legal school age as enumerated every year. The ages vary, but the principle does not change. It should be added that since the admission of California, 1850, 1,280 acres of common-school lands have been given to every congressional township.

The rule of apportionment just explained is followed far more generally than any other. Thus, Maine distributes her state funds, from whatever

[1] Ohio and possibly other states offer some minor exceptions.

source derived, to the towns according to the number of children between the ages of four and twenty-one. Connecticut distributes the annual income of her permanent fund, and the proceeds of the tax of $1.50 for every child between the ages of four and sixteen, according to the number of children between those ages. Pennsylvania apportions her state tax of $5,500,000 annually, Ohio the proceeds of her one-mill tax, Michigan so much of her specific tax as goes to schools, and Indiana and Kentucky the proceeds of their state school taxes, according to the same general rule.

But other rules are followed. Vermont apportions her state tax to the towns, cities, and unorganized districts according to the number of legal schools maintained during the preceding school year. New Hampshire distributes her state funds to the towns according to the number of pupils returned as attending school not less than two weeks in the year. So much of the Massachusetts permanent fund as goes directly to the schools is apportioned to the towns of the state that have a property valuation of less than $3,000,000, towns ranking above that line receiving nothing. Furthermore, the scale is so adjusted that the poorer the town the larger the amount that it receives. Towns whose valuation does not exceed $500,000 receive $275 each; those exceeding $500,000 and not exceeding $1,000,000 receive $200; those exceeding $1,000,000 and not exceeding $2,000,000, $100, and those above the last amount and not above $3,000,000, $50. Again, a portion of the state fund is divided among the towns that are eligible on the basis of the ratio that the town's school tax bears to the whole town tax; the larger the ratio the more help it receives. Rhode Island distributes her annual state contribution of $120,000 as follows: first, $100 is assigned to every school, not exceeding fifteen in number, in a township; then the remainder is distributed to the towns proportionally to the number of children from five to fifteen years of age inclusive.

The state school moneys of New York are apportioned in a complicated manner. The state superintendent first sets aside the annual salaries of the school commissioners (district superintendents). Next he sets apart to every city, incorporated village having a population of 5,000 and upwards, and every union free-school district having a like population, which employ a competent superintendent of schools, $800; and to cities having more than one member of assembly in the state legislature, $500 for each additional member, to be expended according to law for the support of the public schools. He then sets apart any money that may have been appropriated by the legislature for library purposes, and $6,000 for a contingent fund. Next he sets aside to the Indians on reservations, for their schools, a sum equal to their proportion of the state school money, on the basis of distribution established by law. These sums set aside, the remainder of the state moneys is divided into two equal parts. The super intendent now apportions to every district in the state $100 (called a "distributive portion" or "district quota"), provided it has maintained a school, taught by a single qualified teacher or succession of such teachers for the legal term of the preceding school year; and the same sum for every additional qualified teacher or succession of such teachers, not counting monitors. The school year is 160 days, not including holidays that occur during the time, or Saturdays. This apportionment made, the superintendent divides the remainder of the school moneys among the counties according to their respective population as determined by the last preceding United States census, excluding Indians on reservations. But cities that have special school laws receive their due share separate and apart from the remainder of the counties in which they are situated.

The New Jersey state school tax, equal to $5 for each child in the state between the ages of five and eighteen, is raised by the several counties according to their amounts of taxable property respectively, as shown by the tax rolls of the townships and wards of the counties. Ten per cent. of this tax, when it is paid into the treasury, is known as a *reserve fund*, and is apportioned among the counties by the state board of education "equitably and justly, according to their own discretion." The 90 per cent. remaining is then divided among the counties in the proportion that they have contributed to the tax. When the state school moneys reach the counties they, together with all other school funds in the custody of the county, are distributed to the townships and cities on the following basis: (1) $200 for each teacher employed in the public schools for the full term for which the schools are maintained during the year next preceding (nine months); (2) the remainder according to the last published school census (children from five to eighteen years of age), *provided:* that no district shall receive less than $275, and that districts with fifty-five children or more shall not receive less than $375. If these funds are not sufficient to maintain a free school nine months in the year, then the inhabitants may raise by a district tax such additional amount as is needed for that purpose.

The local one-mill tax levied by Minnesota is expended within the districts where it is raised. It is, therefore, only a compulsory district tax, the same as in Michigan. The current school fund of the same state, which includes the income of the permanent fund, is distributed on the basis of the number of pupils who have attended school forty days or more in districts that have had school for five months or more during the year. In addition to the above apportionment, graded schools having not less than three departments, which come up to certain requirements, receive aid from the state to the amount of $200 each. Besides, there are eighty-five high schools that receive state aid to the amount of $400 each. The grants to these graded schools and high schools are paid from permanent appropriations that are met by general taxation, and are apportioned by the state high-school board, on evidence that the schools are complying with the requirements. Minnesota also gives the sum of $500 annually to state high schools providing elementary normal instruction of a kind that satisfies the high-school board. Wisconsin also has an approved high-school list, one-half the cost of maintaining these schools being paid from the state treasury. Moreover, Wisconsin pays $250 each to certain approved high schools in which manual training is taught.

The California system of school finance is a unique system. The state superintendent apportions to the counties the state school fund according to their respective numbers of school-census children (from five to seventeen, certain classes being excluded). Each county superintendent first ascertains the number of teachers every district in the county is entitled to on the basis of one teacher for every seventy school-census children, or fraction thereof not less than twenty, as shown by the next preceding school census, and then the number to which the county is entitled by adding these district numbers together. He then calculates the amount of money to be raised at the legal rate of $500 a teacher. From this amount he deducts the quota of the state fund assigned to the county, and the remainder is the minimum amount of the county school fund to be raised by taxation for the ensuing year, *provided:* that the minimum of such fund shall not be less than $6 for every census child. The county fund thus made up is then distributed to the districts in accordance with this rule, *viz.*, $500 for every teacher, except (1) that to districts having less than twenty census children only $400 is assigned, and (2) that to districts having more than seventy census children $20 additional for every such child less than twenty in number shall be allowed. All school moneys remaining in the treasury after this apportionment has been made are then divided among the districts of the county in proportion to the average daily attendance upon each district during the preceding school year. District taxes may also be raised, subject to certain legal conditions (*Appendix C*).

The subcommittee does not feel called upon to deal with all the states, or even with all the peculiar modes of distributing school moneys. It believes that the enumeration of particulars now made is ample for the present purpose. Some remarks upon the leading rules or methods of distribution are, however, called for.

1. Distribution according to the school census or enumeration is open to a serious objection, *viz.*, it does not carry the money where it is most needed. For example, two districts lie side by side, one having twenty and the other forty youths of school age; the second district draws twice as much money as the other, but the cost of keeping up the two schools is practically the same. The same would be true of two township units,

unless the schools were consolidated. The result is that the district or township that needs the most help receives the least. The rule is simple and easily worked, but it tends partially to defeat the end of state or county aid.

2. The same objection holds against rules based on the school enrollment or on attendance, only with somewhat diminished force. Again, if the enrollment is followed, or attendance for a brief time, there is danger that some children will go to school long enough to be counted, and then drop out. Besides, such rules of distribution work in favor of the graded schools and against the rural schools, on account of their larger enrollment and more regular attendance.

3. Taking everything into account, the subcommittee is inclined to think that a fixed sum or sums, based on an arbitrary unit or units, is most equitable. Examples of such rules are furnished by the states of Massachusetts, Rhode Island, New York, New Jersey, and California. The most serious objection to such rules is that they are necessarily complicated; some of those given above are quite complicated. Then, if the fixed sum is so much a teacher, as in New York, or so much a district, as in Rhode Island and New Jersey, there is a temptation to the undue multiplication of schools or teachers. But this point can be safeguarded by fixing statutory limitations, as in California. No rule can be devised that will not be open to objection. The subcommittee does not believe it possible to invent any rule of distribution that will well accomplish the purpose of taxing large units for the benefit of small ones, unless it rests on the school or the teacher as a unit, with the necessary qualifications. The Massachusetts rule is open to the objection that the school needs of towns cannot always be measured by low valuations of property assessed for taxation, as the number of pupils to be educated is also a factor. If the method of distribution now recommended is objected to as an exclusive one, then it may be supplemented by basing a part of the appropriation on the school census, enrollment, or attendance. The resort to the United States census is most objectionable, as great changes of population occur in the course of ten years.

The difference in the working of the school-census method and the fixed-sum method of distribution is well shown by comparing the statistics of two states. For the fiscal year ending November 15, 1895, the mill tax of Ohio produced $1,720,922. Of the eighty-eight counties forty paid more into the fund than they received from it, while forty-eight paid less than they received. Some of the major counties of the state received more from the fund than they paid into it, while minor counties paid more than they received. For the year 1896 the city of Cleveland actually received $2,616.67 more from the state than it paid to the state. Assuredly, a rule that makes the agricultural counties of Ohio, or many of them, contribute to the education of Cleveland, the most populous city in the state, is a travesty of common sense. But the same year Cincinnati paid in round numbers $70,000 more than it received. This is hardly better than repealing the mill tax outright, and letting the burden of education fall directly upon the cities and townships. On the other hand, the state of New York, in 1896, paid a total general school tax of $4,062,903, of which $3,500,000 was immediately distributed to the counties again. Fifty-four of the sixty counties received more from this tax than they contributed to it; only six counties paid more than they received. Erie county paid $241,597 and received $185,460; while the corresponding figures for Kings and New York counties were $503,603 and $387,879, and $1,884,584 and $636,133, respectively. The New York rule *does* bring the strong to the help of the weak.

A question arises in respect to separate funds for buildings, the payment of teachers, and incidental expenses. In the opinion of the subcommittee such division is desirable. The need of providing new buildings is often made an excuse by boards of education for keeping down the salaries of teachers. The triple fund would not indeed prevent such injustice, which makes teachers as such contribute to buildings, but it would *tend* in that direction. It is often stipulated in school laws that state funds apportioned to communities shall be wholly applied to the payment of teachers. This is a wholesome regulation. The cost of grounds, buildings, and incidental expenses should be met by local taxes or other local funds. Touching the division of the cost of public education, State Superintendent Stetson of Maine, in a private communication, thus defines the prospective policy of that state: "Local communities shall provide school lots and school buildings, and keep the same in repair. Two-thirds of the money raised for maintaining schools shall come from the state, and one-third from the local communities. The apportionment of the money to the several municipalities shall be upon the basis of average attendance. We shall also try to get a law prohibiting towns from receiving state aid, if they maintain schools having less than a certain average attendance." Such a law as this would serve to prevent the undue multiplication of districts, and would even work a certain measure of consolidation.

The distribution of taxes levied on railroads, telegraphs, long-distance telephone lines, express companies, and the like, is an important question. In some states, as New York, Texas, and Ohio, school taxes levied on railroads inure to the exclusive benefit of the districts or townships through which the tracks run, excluding any state tax that may be levied on such property. This rule the subcommittee regards as unjust. The location of railroads is determined largely by physical conditions, and the mere fact that a line happens to run through its territory, where probably not a dollar of the stock or bonds is owned, is no reason why a district or township should profit thereby to the exclusion of other and less fortunate districts or townships. In Pennsylvania the taxes on railroads are paid into the state treasury and are distributed by the legislature along with other revenues, the public schools, normal schools, and colleges being included among the objects of the appropriation. California has a similar provision. The mode of distributing the Michigan specific tax has already been described. It is believed that such revenues as the foregoing should inure to the common benefit of the state; but what is here said, let it be remarked, in no way relates to pending controversies about the taxation of railroads or other similar property.

The Nebraska law contains one excellent feature that is worthy of mention. All public high schools in the state that, as determined by the State Department of Education, have a proper equipment of teachers, appliances, and course of study, are open to attendance by any person of school age residing outside the district who is a resident of the state and whose education cannot be profitably carried on in the public school of the district of his residence. Such pupil must have a certificate signed by the county superintendent that he has completed the common-school course prescribed by the state department for work below the high school. He must attend at the high school nearest to his residence or at a high school of approved grade in the county of his residence. Any school board that furnishes high-school instruction to such pupil is authorized to charge fifty cents a week for the time that he has been in attendance, and it is made the duty of the county board to pay all such bills out of the county school fund. Massachusetts and Ohio, and perhaps other states also, provide for educating qualified pupils in high schools in other places than those where they reside, provided there are no home schools for them to attend, and this without cost to themselves. As Massachusetts is the only state that makes the provision of high schools compulsory under any circumstances, it may be well to mention the principal features of the state law in regard to that subject. Every town having a population of 4,000 persons or 500 families is obliged to maintain a high school, the grade of the school depending somewhat upon the fact whether it has the larger or the smaller population. Pupils living in towns that are not required to maintain a high school can attend any neighboring high school that will receive them. In such cases the state pays the tuition of the pupil, provided the valuation of the town in which he resides does not exceed $500,000; if the valuation does exceed that amount the town pays the tuition. High-school tuition is, therefore, wholly free to every qualified pupil in the state.

ORGANIZATION.

The subcommittee is not here interested in the subject of school organization further than it relates to school maintenance. Its relations to teaching, supervision, and studies are topics belonging to other divisions of the general report. The statement and enforcement of two propositions will answer the present purpose.

I. The first proposition is that the township-unit system is far superior to the district system, and should be substituted, if practicable, for that system wherever it exists. The superiority of the town or township as an administrative unit is as great as its superiority as a taxing unit. The principal advantages are the following:

1. If the schools of a township are under a single board elected from the township at large, schoolhouses will far more likely be built where they are needed than under the other system.

2. Equality of school provision will be much more fully secured in respect to schoolhouses and grounds, length of school terms, and the ability and character of teachers.

3. The tendency will not be to multiply schools unduly, but to restrict their number, bringing together more scholars, and thus making better classification, grading, and teaching possible, and increasing the interest and enthusiasm of the pupils.

4. Better supervision can be secured. The county superintendent can deal more effectively and easily with one board in a township than with six, ten, or twelve; while township and township-union supervision will be greatly promoted.

5. Simplicity and economy of administration will be facilitated, and the sense of official responsibility be enhanced.

6. The tendency will be to employ teachers for longer terms, and thereby to restrict, in a considerable degree, the evils that flow from frequent changes. On this point the statistics of Mr. Gass, presented in this report, may be mentioned.

7. The strifes and contentions between districts that are now not infrequent will be prevented.

8. Transfers of pupils from school to school will be made more easy.

9. The reason last to be mentioned is perhaps the strongest of all. The relations of the township-unit system to school consolidation have already been suggested. The township system does not necessitate such consolidation, although it is likely to work that way; but consolidation is almost wholly dependent upon that system: schools *will not* be consolidated in great numbers if a plurality of district school boards have to do the work.

The subcommittee has stated that the adoption of the township-unit system *will be* followed by the reforms that have been mentioned. It is not, indeed, meant that such will be the unvarying result; there will be exceptions — perhaps many exceptions — when the whole country is considered, but the tendency *will be* strong in the directions named, or such *will be* the general character of the result. Not only is this the suggestion of common sense, but it is the teaching of experience as well (*Appendix E*).

The town-unit school system was the ancient system of New England. The classic school law enacted by the General Court of Massachusetts in 1648 ordered that the towns should found schools on their reaching a certain number of householders, the teachers to be paid either by the parents of such children as resorted to them for instruction or by the inhabitants in general by way of supply, as those who ordered the prudentials of the town should appoint. The word "township" is also used in the law. Connecticut followed the example of Massachusetts. The original New England town, which was a small concentration of population, was well adapted to this system. But "as the population of each little nucleus of settlement spread itself out from the center of the original 'plantation,' it early became convenient, in Massachusetts and Connecticut at least, to allow neighboring families at a distance from the local concentration, or nucleus, to form themselves into a school district." The original church parishes were divided in the same way. If these districts had been founded merely for the purpose of school supply, or to regulate attendance, there would have been, under the conditions existing, no objection to their formation, but the contrary. Unfortunately, however, these new districts also became units of school maintenance, bodies corporate and politic. These districts appear at first to have existed by sufferance merely, but the celebrated school law of 1789 legalized them, thus paving the way for the general introduction of the new system. Horace Mann declared in his Tenth Annual Report: "I consider the law of 1789 . . . . authorizing towns to divide themselves into districts the most unfortunate law on the subject of common schools ever enacted in the state." Still this "act was not repealed until manufacturing had restored those concentrations of population which in the early colonies had invited township control of school affairs." This was finally done. Mr. Mann in the same report (p. 37) bore this testimony to the superiority of the town system:

"As a general fact, the schools of undistricted towns are greatly superior to those in districted towns — and for obvious reasons. The first class of towns — the undistricted — provide all the schoolhouses, and, through the agency of the school committee, employ all the teachers. If one good schoolhouse is provided for any section of the town, all the other sections, having contributed their respective portions of the expense to erect the good house, will demand one equally good for themselves; and the equity of such a demand is so obvious that it cannot be resisted. If, on the other hand, each section were a separate district, and bound for the whole expense of a new house if it should erect one, it would be tempted to continue an old house long after it had ceased to be comfortable, and, indeed, as experience has too often sadly proved, long after it has ceased to be tenantable. So, too, in undistricted towns we never see the painful, anti-republican contrast of one school, in one section, kept all the year round by a teacher who receives $100 a month, while, in another section of the same town, the school is kept on the minimum principle, both as to time and price, and, of course, yielding only a minimum amount of benefit—to say nothing of probable and irremediable evils that it may inflict. In regard to supervision, also, if the school committee is responsible for the condition of all the schools, it is constrained to visit all alike, to care for all alike, and, as far as possible, to aim in all at the production of equal results; because any partiality or favoritism will be rebuked at the ballot box. In undistricted towns, therefore, three grand conditions of a prosperous school, *viz.*, a good house, a good teacher, and vigilant superintendence, are secured by motives which do not operate, or operate to a very limited extent, in districted towns. Under the non-districting system it is obvious that each section of a town will demand at least an equal degree of accommodation in the house, of talent in the teacher, and of attention in the committee; and should any selfish feelings be indulged it is some consolation to reflect that they, too, will be harnessed to the car of improvement."

The district system was at one time universal, and it exists in some form in a great majority of the states today. In Maine, New Hampshire, Massachusetts, and New Jersey it has been wholly swept away. In Connecticut and Rhode Island the town system is permissive, and exists side by side with the district system. The township system exists in Pennsylvania, Ohio, and Indiana. It is permissive in the upper peninsula of Michigan, in Wisconsin, and in Minnesota, and doubtless in other states. It varies somewhat in the organization of the local authority. The Massachusetts school committee consists of three members or a multiple of three, elected from the town at large. In New Jersey the board consists of three, five, or nine members, as the town may elect. The Ohio board consists of delegates or representatives elected by the subdistricts, one each. A single trustee elected by the people manages the schools of a township in Indiana, except that he is assisted by a director in each attendance district who looks after incidental local matters.

Considering the great superiority of the township system over the district system, it is not a little strange that its introduction in the room of its competitor should have been so steadily resisted as it has been. This opposition is due in part to the power of conservative habit, in part to the belief that the district system is more democratic, and in part to the popular fondness for office holding, all conjoined with much misconception and ignorance in respect to the merits of the two systems. It has also been urged in favor of the district, by politicians, that it is the best unit for canvassing the states for political purposes. Certainly it cannot be objected to the township system, in its pure form, that it is not sufficiently democratic. In 1875 there were 15,087 teachers employed in teaching the common schools of Ohio, and there were in the state at the same time more than 35,000 school directors and members of boards of education charged with the administration of the schools. This, assuredly, is an excess of democracy.

The "community" system is much worse than the district system, and fortunately it is confined to a single state. The Texas law permits parents, guardians, or other persons having control of children of scholastic age, residing in any one of the so-called "community" counties (thirty-five in number out of a total of 250), to unite and organize themselves into a free-school community entitled to the benefits of the available school fund belonging to the county, upon complying with certain prescribed conditions. The persons so uniting and organizing first address a petition to the county judge, who is *ex-officio* county superintendent of schools, duly signed by the petitioners, setting forth that the community is white or black, as the case may be, giving an alphabetical list of the names of children of scholastic age within the limits proposed, describing the capacity of the schoolhouse and the character of the other conveniences that the petitioners have to offer, naming persons to act as trustees, etc. The matter then passes into the hands of the judge, who has no discretionary power in the premises. He may not even throw aside such a petition either because it is signed by few persons or because the alphabetical list carries few names. The law does not fix any minimum number in either case. If the people of a neighborhood desire a school, no matter how few they may be, a school the judge must grant them. The "community" is a voluntary district in the strict sense of the term, having legal existence for one year only, and having no authority to levy a local school tax, and the evils that attend it are far greater than those that call so loudly for the abolition of the district system wherever that is practicable. The people of Texas can, however, congratulate themselves that the "community" school, which plainly originated in pioneer society, has lost ground in later years.

In the South, and in those western states that have the county system of local government, the only practical alternative to the district system of school organization is a county system. It must be remembered that in these states the town or township does not exist. Fortunately, such a system is not altogether unknown. In a few counties of Georgia it has been in successful operation for a number of years. These are the principal features of the system as it exists in Richmond county, in which the city of Augusta is situated:

The county is the unit area of organization, and the rural parts and the urban parts of the county district, as far as practicable, are treated just alike. A board of education, composed of representatives elected by the people of the county for the term of three years, one-third retiring each year, manages all the schools. The school tax is levied at a uniform rate upon all the property of the county, without revision by any other authority and without any limit as to rate or amount. The county and state funds are distributed to the schools according to the number of children to be educated. There is no district tax. The same qualifications are required for country and for city teachers. The teachers are treated as nearly alike as the conditions admit, and they are paid about the same salaries. The schools are in session the same length of time in a year, nine calendar months. The country schoolhouses, on the average, are situated four miles apart, and no child is out of walking distance of a school open nine months in the year, and taught by a good teacher. One superintendent has charge of all the schools. Augusta has nine-tenths of the taxable property of the county, but only three-fourths of the school population. In other words, the rural parts of the county pay one-tenth of the school tax and receive the benefit of one-fourth of it. For the most part, these are excellent provisions. The county would seem to be the natural area unit for popular schools under the county system of local government. The subcommittee confidently believes that this mode of school organization has a great future before it in the United States (*Appendix D*).

II. In those parts of the country where existing physical and social conditions render it practicable there should be such a consolidation of rural schools as will diminish the existing number of schools, schoolhouses, and teachers, and bring together, at advantageous points, the pupils who are now divided and scattered among the isolated schools of the township or other similar district. This step should be taken in the interest of good education as well as of public economy. To make this reform possible the children, as far as may be necessary or practicable, must be conveyed to and from the schoolhouses at public expense.

How absolutely fatal to good schools the existing conditions are in many parts of the country statistics show most conclusively. State Superintendent Wells of Wisconsin reported in 1894 that his state had 183 districts whose average attendance the previous year was not more than five each; that 858 others were not above ten each; while 2,481 more did not exceed twenty each. "In other words," he said, "3,522 country districts, about three-fifths of the total number, have an average attendance not exceeding twenty, and about two-fifths above that average, with the great majority near the lower margin."[1] Mr. H. R. Gass, of Michigan, citing the state report for his authority, states in a published paper that in 1886 the country schools of Calhoun county in that state required 158 teachers, and that they employed 342 different ones in the course of the year. The average length of the school in the district was 8.4 months, while the average term for which the teachers were employed was but 3.8 months. He cites a second county that presents like statistics, and then observes: "The ratio of the number [of teachers] required to the number employed is about the same as this throughout the state, the tenure being longer in the newer than in the older counties." This state of things Mr. Gass attributes to the prevalence of the district system. He refers to Massachusetts and Indiana, where changes of teachers are much less frequent and teachers' tenures much longer than in Michigan. While two teachers on an average were employed in Michigan for a school every year, but few schools in the other states employed more than one. In the same state, at the present time, there are over 1,000 districts that enumerate less than twenty-five children of school age each, while seventy counties contain 468 districts that enumerate less than fifteen each. The statistics at hand do not show the actual size of the schools. Nor are the small schools found in the newer and poorer parts of the state only; the oldest and richest counties have their fair share of them. In fact, the newer parts of a state often have the largest and best schools. Not only so, the oldest and most densely populated states frequently make a very poor showing. In 1894–95 there were 7,529 school districts in New York, in each of which the average attendance upon school during the year varied from one to twenty pupils, while the average daily attendance in each of 2,983 districts was less than ten pupils (*Appendix I*). In 1893 Vermont had 153 schools of six pupils or less each. In 1892 State Superintendent Luce of Maine reported that the average enrollment in the schools of that state for the previous year was less than twenty-five pupils to a school, and that the number of districts having less than twenty-five was larger than the number having more. He declared that there were probably between 1,000 and 1,200 existing schools in the state whose enrollment was twelve or less, and that 600 or 800 schools then existing could be abolished without detriment.[2] Twenty-five years ago a large number of schools on the Western Reserve, Ohio, long famed for schools, had dwindled to the most insignificant size. Still other statistics of similar import will be found in the report of the Subcommittee on Instruction and Discipline. Attention is drawn particularly to those relating to Rhode Island and Massachusetts.

[1] "The Township System of School Government." Madison, 1894.

[2] Quoted by Mr. Gass. See "Transactions of the Michigan State Teachers' Association, 1887."

But it is needless to multiply statistics, or to insist at length that thousands of rural schools furnish their pupils with a miserable preparation for the duties of life. When we consider the various elements that enter into good education, and especially training for social activities, it is not too much to say that a very small school is almost necessarily a very poor school. The facts are notorious. Hitherto it has been supposed that, although the cities and towns surpassed the rural districts in higher education, the rural districts contained a smaller proportion of illiterate persons. This has been the prevailing view in the northern states, and probably it was once in accord with the facts. The cities have been considered the great hives of illiteracy. But there is now grave reason to question whether the fact is not often the other way. Certainly it is so in the only state where, so far as the subcommittee is informed, the subject has been statistically investigated.[1] But however this may be, a remedy for the unsatisfactory state of the rural schools is one of the pressing needs of the day. What can be done? One thing that can be done is to consolidate many of the small schools by carrying back and forth such pupils as need to be carried, and thus, by one stroke, create several of the conditions of good schools. The interest that this subject is beginning to awaken is one of the hopeful signs of the times.

It was Massachusetts that led the way in developing the district system, and it is Massachusetts that is leading the way in consolidation. An act that dates from 1869 authorizes any town in the commonwealth to raise money by taxation to enable the school committee, in its discretion, to provide for the conveyance of pupils to and from the public schools at public cost. The towns were already empowered to build schoolhouses wherever they were really needed. Availing themselves of these powers,

[1] The state referred to is Michigan. According to the state census of 1894 the ratios of the foreign-born persons in the cities of the state, ten years of age or more, unable to read and write, and in the state at large, were practically the same, eighty-four in 1,000. But the ratios of the native-born in the cities, in the state at large, and therefore in the country districts, were quite different. In the cities it was fourteen in 1,000; in the state at large, twenty-one in 1,000; in the country, twenty-four in 1,000. For every fourteen persons ten years of age or upwards in the cities unable to read and write there were twenty-four in the country; that is, the ratio in the country is 70 per cent. greater than that in the cities. If the country rate of illiteracy could be reduced to the city rate, the number of illiterates of the native-born population ten years of age and upwards unable to read and write would be reduced about 8,000. Several facts, no doubt, enter into the explanation of the greater illiteracy of the country districts, but the most important of them is the inferiority of the country schools. It does not explain matters to say that Michigan is comparatively a new state, that much of it is thinly settled, that it contains large lumbering and mining districts, etc. The fact is that in the oldest and wealthiest parts of Michigan the cities, as a rule, surpass the counties in which they are situated in respect to popular intelligence. The city of Detroit ranks distinctly higher than Wayne county, and the same may be said of the cities of Grand Rapids and Ann Arbor as compared with Kent and Washtenaw counties. The counties named contain the cities mentioned.

many towns have entered upon the work of consolidating their schools. How the work goes on is shown by the following table exhibiting the sums of money paid for public-school transportation for a series of years.

Year	Amount	Year	Amount
1888, 1889	$22,118.38	1892, 1893	$50,590.41
1889, 1890	24,145.12	1893, 1894	63,617.68
1890, 1891	30,648.68	1894, 1895	76,608.29
1891, 1892	38,726.07	1895, 1896	91,136.11

The movement has extended beyond Massachusetts and reached every one of the New England states. In these states many hundreds of schools have been consolidated, and with the most gratifying results. Occasionally an unsuccessful experiment is reported, but the great stream of testimony runs strongly the other way. Longer school terms, better teachers, better grading, better instruction, more interest in the pupils, greater physical comfort on the part of the children, better supervision—these are the claims that are made for the new departure (*Appendices E* and *F*). Other things being equal, the new way is never more expensive than the old one, and often it is less expensive.

The movement has spread beyond New England. In 1894 a law was enacted in New Jersey providing for the transportation of pupils at public expense in order that rural schools might be consolidated with city ones. A most interesting experiment in consolidation is being tried in northeastern Ohio, where some schools had already died out, and many more were lingering on the verge of death. Permissive legislation has been obtained in several counties, and already many townships are working the plan successfully, while many others are looking on expectantly and are apparently on the point of making the new departure. The newspapers are quick to note the innovation, and it is already attracting attention beyond the borders of the state (*Appendix F*).

The distinct pedagogical advantages of consolidation are much more fully set forth in the reports on supply of teachers and instruction and discipline than here. In this report the topic is dealt with mainly as it is related to organization and administration. The fact is, however, the several aspects of consolidation are inseparably connected. As a rule, whatever promotes simplicity and ease of administration promotes good instruction, and *vice versa*. No one of the subcommittees that handle the subject for a moment supposes that there is any charm in the word "consolidation" to cast all the evil spirits out of the rural school, but they all believe, after giving the subject mature consideration, that great possibilities of improvement lie in that direction. It is perfectly true that the consolidation remedy cannot be universally applied, because physical and social conditions often forbid. The fact is, that a large proportion of the children of the land will be schooled in little schools—rural schools, ungraded schools—or they will not be schooled at all. Suggestions looking to the improvement of these schools will be found in the reports of all the subcommittees; but insistence is here placed upon the fact that the consolidation remedy can be applied on a grand scale, with the largest promise of success. In most states some new legislation will be necessary to that end, but not in all. Wherever the township-unit system exists, the first step, and the long step, has already been taken. In such states it should not be difficult to secure the needed legislation in relation to transportation. State Superintendent Emery of Wisconsin has already notified the people of his state that the laws contain all the provisions that are necessary to enable them to move at once in the direction of school consolidation.

It is important that the consolidation reform shall not be misunderstood. It does not necessarily mean that there shall be only one school in a town or township. It does not mean either that parts of different townships or counties shall not be comprised in one school. These questions are merely matters of detail, and their adjustment will depend upon such factors as the size of townships, the distribution of villages or other local centers, the direction and condition of roads, streams, and bridges, the distribution of population, and the physical configuration of the township and the adjacent parts of the country.

It is noteworthy how the different phases of educational reform all tend to hold together. In the northern states the cause of school consolidation depends intimately upon the adoption of the township-unit system. A certain amount of consolidation can be effected by the abolition of small districts; it may be possible, also, for several independent districts to merge their schools into one, for the time at least, and still preserve their independence; but it is manifest that the first plan will not prove effectual, and that the second one will be infrequent and precarious. The subcommittee believes confidently, therefore, that the fortune of effectual consolidation is closely bound up with the fortune of the township-unit system.

It is also noteworthy, let it be remarked again, how different social elements tend to attract one another and so to coalesce. School consolidation, especially its practicability, turns largely upon means of cheap, safe, and easy communication throughout the school area. Here we touch a question intimately relating to social progress that has been receiving increasing attention the last few years. Reference is made to the improvement of roads. Those who have been promoting this movement have not probably regarded it as a measure of educational reform; but such it is. Perhaps there is no rural interest of a social nature that would be more decidedly enhanced by good roads than the educational interest. The people of some of the towns of Ohio, where the new plan is being tried, claim this as a decided advantage, that the drivers of the omnibuses serve as carriers for the mails between the farmhouses and the post offices, thus promoting the diffusion of intelligence in still another way.

Only a single point remains to be pressed, but it must be pressed strongly. This is the necessity of lengthening materially the time that the country schools, on the average, are in session each year, and the securing of a more regular attendance of the pupils. The legal years now vary widely in different states, and the practical, or real, years still more widely. Some communities always surpass the legal minimum of time, others as regularly fall below it. In the thickly settled states of the East the rural schools are in session eight, nine, or ten months in the year; but often in the South, and sometimes in the West, one-half the shortest of these terms is not reached. The legal year is frequently absurdly short. Until two years ago the Michigan year was but three months, and now it is but five months. It is quite unnecessary to argue that short schools are, even relatively, poor schools. In order to have a good school, it is necessary not only to bring pupils together in considerable numbers, but also to hold them to the work a certain number of hours each day, and a certain number of days each year. There must be a concentration of effort as of pupils. It is as wasteful a method of education to send children to school seventy or eighty days in the year as it is to send them two or three hours in the day. Persons interested in popular education, and particularly in rural education, should not rest, therefore, in their efforts until they have made the legal school year in every state at least 160 or 180 days.

But it will not be enough for the state simply to fix a minimum school year: it must see to the enforcement of the law. The law should hold communities to a rigid accountability in respect to maintaining schools of legal grade for the full legal period, to employing none but certificated teachers, and making all the required reports to the state educational department. Most school laws contain such provisions as these, but it is feared that they are not always enforced. The only practicable mode of enforcement is absolutely to withhold from the local organizations all aid from the superior taxing units, as the state, until they first observe the law.

And again, it will not suffice for the state to see that the prescribed quality of instruction is actually furnished. It might, perhaps, be thought that if the state only provided local schools, and made them free, the people would be only too glad to avail themselves of them to the full; but sad experience shows that this is not always the case. The indifference, ignorance, and selfishness of some parents come between their children and the schools. In communities where the school attendance is compulsory some parents are in an almost constant battle with the authorities, to keep their children out of the school as much as possible. It is possible that such extreme indifference or selfishness as this is more common in cities than in the country; and yet it is true, as a rule, that the country child's labor, especially the farm boy's labor, has a greater money value than the city child's labor, and that the farmer is, therefore, under a special temptation to keep his boys out of school. On the whole, there is quite as much need of an efficient compulsory attendance law in the country as in the city, and perhaps more.

The subcommittee has not taken space to discuss, in general, the common education that the American states are now furnishing the American people. That is a large subject, and for the most part lies outside the field of the present inquiry. It will suffice to say on this large question that the people had better pay what they do pay for what they get than to go without it, or even twice, thrice, or four times the sum; but, at the same time, they might receive, and should receive, a great deal more for their money than at present. This is particularly true of the rural schools. No doubt there are many excellent schools in the country; but, on the whole, it may well be doubted whether any money that is expended in the people's interest is expended more wastefully than what goes to the country schools. No doubt the country school has points of advantage over the city school, as the freer communion with nature, but on the whole it is inferior. The typical "little red schoolhouse," so invested with sentiment, is a costly and unsatisfactory institution of education. Owing to social changes, in many parts of the country it is much less efficient and useful, at least relatively, than once it was, and a new organization is imperatively called for. Something should be done to stop the wasteful expenditure of the public money. State Superintendent Stetson, speaking for his state, puts the case thus in a communication to the subcommittee:

"I have devoted quite a number of pages in my report [1895] to showing the people of Maine that we are wasting an enormous sum of money in this state because of the unbusinesslike methods which are used in the expenditure of its school funds. This waste is made in every direction in which money is spent. We pay more than we need to for school lots, the erection of school buildings, the furnishing of school appliances, text-books, fuel, making repairs, etc., etc. The waste along these lines aggregates more than one-third of a million of dollars each year. I have shown in the report that the money which we spend for common schools is sufficient to maintain schools taught by professionally trained teachers, and superintended by competent superintendents; that, in addition to doing these two important things, we would have money enough left to supply them with the appliances necessary for a successful school, and also furnish the needed apparatus, library books, and make all the needed repairs and additions. I feel that I have demonstrated this point so that there will be no further question about it in the state of Maine. The whole matter turns upon the simple point that we are alarmingly wasteful in our expenditure of school money.

"Personally I am in favor of local communities being responsible for providing school buildings. I think two-thirds of the funds required for the maintenance of the common schools should be furnished by the state, and that the other third should be raised by local taxation; that the state should examine all teachers and issue all licenses to teach; that towns thus receiving state aid must employ teachers who hold such certificates. The state should inspect the school accounts of the towns receiving state aid."

The subcommittee deems it advisable, now that the whole ground has been covered, to restate the fundamental propositions that have been urged in this report. These all start from the one central postulate that a provision of funds sufficient for their adequate support is essential to the existence and life of good schools. The three-fold division of the subject will be preserved in the summary.

I. REVENUE.

1. The great resource of the public schools is, ***and must continue to be,*** some form or forms of public taxation.

2. Such areas or units of taxation should be created, or continued if already in existence, as will fully develop the sound American principle that the whole wealth of the state shall be made available for educating all the youth of the state.

3. To accomplish this end, resort must be had to the larger units of taxation, especially where population is sparse and wealth meager. The following recommendations must be specifically urged: (1) a liberal provision of funds from the state treasury; (2) a county tax in at least all the county-system states; (3) a town or township tax in the states where this civil division exists; (4) taxes in special districts, that is, in cities and villages. The school district, in the commonly accepted sense of that term, is not a desirable taxing unit, but quite the contrary, and should be abolished as such unit.

II. DISTRIBUTION.

1. Funds raised by the large political or social units for general school purposes should be distributed in such a way as to bring the rich and the strong to the help of the poor and the weak.

2. Such rules of distribution should be adopted as will accomplish

this end. In order to do this, distribution must be based, to a certain extent at least, upon fixed or arbitrary units; that is, so much money must be given to the school or to the teacher.

3. The large taxing units should render assistance to the small ones only upon the condition that the small ones first do something for themselves.

III. ORGANIZATION.

1. In the states where the town or mixed system of local government exists, the town- or township-school system should, as far as practicable, be substituted for the district system; in the county-system states the county-school system is the natural alternative to the district system.

2. In those parts of the country where existing physical and social conditions render it practicable, there should be such a consolidation of rural schools as will diminish the existing number of schools, schoolhouses, and teachers, and bring together, at advantageous points, the pupils who are now divided and scattered among the isolated schools of the township or other similar districts.

3. There is urgent need of lengthening materially the time that the country schools, on the average, are in session each year. The ideal should be a minimum school year in every state of at least 160 or 180 days.

The subcommittee does not expect to see, and does not desire to see, the school systems of the country all brought to one uniform pattern. It is too well aware of the great diversity of conditions that exist to think such a thing is possible. Even more, a certain variety, and so conflict, of systems is conducive to life, activity, and improvement. Neither is the subcommittee under any illusions as to what is possible, or probable, in a field of education so vast as that offered by the United States, with the great number of authorities, state and local. At the same time there are certain general laws governing successful school systems and schools that cannot be ignored. Some of the principal of these laws have been set forth above; and it is believed that their general recognition will be followed by a marked improvement of the common schools, and so of the popular education, of the country.

Some persons may ask, "How shall the principles laid down in this report be made practical?" "How shall they be established in communities or states where they do not exist, or exist only in part?" To these questions only a general answer is needed. The state legislature, the law-making authority, is the only source of power in relation to education, as well as in relation to all other branches of the state government. Accordingly, if the school law is defective and weak, the legislature must be called upon to repair and strengthen it. No progress can be made without an efficient law and efficient school authorities. But how shall the legislature be induced to act in the premises? In precisely the same way that it is induced to act in other matters. Facts, arguments, persuasion, must be addressed to the members of the legislature. Above all it is important that the public mind shall be informed as fully as possible upon all branches of the subject. If the people generally knew how much better schools they *might* have than those that they *do* now have, and for no more cost, it is impossible to believe that they would not bestir themselves to effect reforms. The subcommittee marks out what it believes to be broad lines of educational progress. It enforces its views, as far as possible, with appropriate arguments. But it must necessarily leave the application of these views and arguments to the exigencies existing in particular communities or states to such persons, belonging to these communities or states, as are interested in the subject and are familiar with all the local facts and conditions.

B. A. HINSDALE, *Chairman*,
W. S. SUTTON,
S. T. BLACK.

REPORT OF THE SUBCOMMITTEE ON SUPERVISION.

The Subcommittee on Supervision of Rural Schools has taken into careful consideration the various topics submitted for investigation. Its inquiries have extended into all the states and territories except Indian Territory and Alaska, and the facts are based on returns more or less full from all parts of the country.

Professional supervision is today regarded as an essential factor in our school system. It has been observed that the schools that are closely supervised by men who thoroughly know their business at once respond to the influence of this supervision. Expert supervision has resulted in systematic, orderly, and well-directed instruction. It is a matter of remark that the most competent superintendents have the best schools, and that cities noted for their excellence in school work have attained this pre-eminence through the medium of intelligent supervision. This is also true of those counties which have come under the same influence.

"There is no other agency in our school system that has done so much for the improvement of our schools in organization, and in methods of instruction and discipline, as the superintendency."

The attention of the profession, however, has been mainly directed toward expert supervision in city schools, and but little heed has been paid to the demand for such work in rural districts. It is quite time that our inquiries should be directed toward the character of the supervision demanded by the country school. If supervision through a competent superintendent is a good thing for city schools, there is every reason why it would be a good thing for rural schools.

STATE SUPERINTENDENT.

Although the state superintendent stands at the head of the public-school system of the state, his work is more closely related to rural than to city schools. As this report has reference only to the conditions of rural schools, your subcommittee will consider the duties of this officer as bearing upon that part alone of the general school system. No officer connected with the administration of state affairs requires higher or more essential qualifications than that of superintendent of public instruction. He should be a man of high moral character, well acquainted with approved methods and with the history and condition of education in his state. He should be in close touch with the educational spirit of the times, and should be one whom the profession regards as authority in all that constitutes excellence in school matters. It is also agreed that he should be an experienced teacher, of broad and thorough scholarship, and a good public speaker. With these qualifications there should be combined a large share of good common sense, and sufficient executive ability to manage the details of his office.

The legal term of office in Massachusetts and Rhode Island is one year. In Connecticut it is at the pleasure of the state board. In twenty states the term of office is two years; in four states, three years; in seventeen states, four years; but in no state does it exceed four years. The average length of term of the state superintendent is two years and ten months. The lowest salary paid is $1,000 and the highest $5,000 per year. The average salary is $2,475 per year. In answer to the question as to how much time the state superintendent devotes to supervision of schools, we had definite answers from thirty-seven states, in which we find that nineteen of these superintendents devote more than half of their time to visiting schools and traveling in the interest of education, and eighteen devote less than half their time. Quite a number of the state superintendents report that they divide their time equally between the office work and supervision. In only a few of the states does the state superintendent exercise no supervision, and in several the supervision is carried on through deputies or agents.

The state superintendent under present arrangements has but little time for personal inspection of school work. The superintendents in fourteen states visit each county once a year and in eight states once every two years. From the other states no definite information could be obtained. Many superintendents say, as often as practicable; in some instances, not at all. Our information is to the effect that most of the state superintendents devote as much time to supervision as they can spare, but that it is generally considered secondary to work of a clerical nature. There are undoubtedly in some states sections which have never been visited by the state superintendent or his deputy.

By some means the influence of the state superintendent should be extended until it reaches every rural school in the state. In all possible ways the office should be made useful to the teachers and school officers. The rural schools need this stimulating, helpful influence more even than those of the city. While in most states the office has but little more than advisory powers, yet, through lectures at associations and through the inspection of institutes, the state superintendent ought to be able to convince the teachers of rural schools that he is in close sympathy with their work.

The work of the state superintendent ought to be made more effective by so increasing his clerical force as to enable him to spend more time in direct contact with the schools and school officials of the state. The careful compilation of statistics is very important, but it can be intrusted to a skillful statistician, while much of the routine work of the office can be well done by clerks. The higher and by far the more important work of directing educational movements, of instructing the people, and of creating public opinion and arousing public interest devolves upon the state superintendent. There is a general demand for more assistance in his office, longer tenure of service, and more liberal financial support. His work should be so related to that of the superintendents in the various subdivisions of the state for school purposes that the whole may be properly articulated, and the county or town superintendents be under his direction and control. He should come in frequent contact with them by conventions held for the purpose of instructing them in their particular duties, and should send them such circulars and letters as may be necessary to aid and direct them in their work.

The state superintendent should have the power to withhold the state appropriation from all counties or school districts not complying with the law in every particular, because he would then hold the key to the situation and could enforce his orders.

The main duties of the state superintendent are not only to organize and direct educational influence and laws already existing, but also to go among the people in the spirit of Horace Mann, and, by public addresses, by the liberal use of the press, and by securing the assistance of the leading men of the state, to arouse and keep alive an interest in the cause of popular education. In connection with the rural schools especially the state superintendent not only has great possibilities for a wise supervisory influence, but also great opportunities to arouse and instruct the people.

In a majority of the states the most needful legislation is that which bears upon the organization and maintenance of rural schools, and a supply of competent teachers for the same. The state superintendent, therefore, should be a man able to secure the co-operation of the legislature for the enactment of proper statutes. This can be done only by one who sees clearly the great needs of the school system, and who is able to go before the people and the legislature and unite all influences to obtain the necessary legislation. While putting into this high office any person solely through his political affiliations is to be deprecated, the state superintendent should be a man who knows how to approach the leaders of all parties and convince them of the justice and soundness of his plans, viewed from the high vantage ground of the general good.

COUNTY, TOWNSHIP, OR DISTRICT, SUPERINTENDENT.

A still more important question opened for discussion is the character and degree of supervision below that of the state superintendent.[1] Thirty-eight states, mainly in the South and West, have county superintendents, whose duty it is to visit the schools and exercise the duties usually belonging to their office. The New England states generally have what is known as township or district supervision, which arises in large part from their political organization. In New England the town is the dominant political unit, while in the South and West it is the county. The simplicity and effectiveness of supervision is promoted when the units of political organization and of school administration are identical. This condition has its limitations, however, in the amount of territory to be covered and in the density of population, which is a varying quantity. The main point is to bring every rural school of the country as far as possible under the watchful care of a competent supervising officer. Responsibility is a strong stimulant. It is one of the weak points in our present system that too often the rural school-teacher is responsible to no one.

In regard to the operation of the two principal methods of supervision there is no reason why any section should abandon the practice which has been found best adapted to its peculiar conditions. It must be conceded, however, that a single township, containing on an average ten or twelve schools, is too small a territory to engage profitably the entire attention of one person. In such a case one of two things must necessarily happen: either the schools are supervised to the point of interference, or the supervision becomes uncertain, feeble, and unsatisfactory. In a general way, the rural township is too small a supervisory unit. Wherever it has been tried the supervisor has generally had some other busi-

[1] In this report the term supervisor is used to include also county superintendent, commissioner, or any other term by which the supervising officer of a county or supervisory district is usually designated.

ness to attend to, and thus his work has been found wanting in those results which are most desirable. In order that the work of overseeing and directing may be effective, it must engage the entire time and the best thought of the supervisory officer.

A proper remedy for this is the combination of towns for supervisory purposes. Three, four, or five towns could be united in one supervisory district, until a sufficient number of schools have been secured to engage the entire attention of one good man. The burden of his salary could be borne by these towns in the proportion of the number of schools they contribute to his work. This plan is in operation in Massachusetts, and has been satisfactory. A complete exposition of the Massachusetts plan of supervision of township schools is found in A. W. Edson's monograph, "Supervision of Schools in Massachusetts" (Boston, 1895).

In that state 253 of the towns are supervised by 155 supervisors. While some of the large towns can alone support a supervisor, several of the smaller ones must unite to secure the services of an efficient officer. In addition to what the towns do for themselves the state grants to those of low valuation, when they combine into a supervisory district, the sum of $750 to pay for a supervisor. These towns, however, are required to raise an additional sum equal to that furnished by the state, thus insuring a sufficient sum for the employment of an expert school man. By these means 93 per cent. of the children of Massachusetts have been brought under close supervision. The salary paid to a supervisor is at least $1,500 a year, and he is enabled to devote all his time to the work and to inspect each school once a month. It is true that there are still about 100 towns in Massachusetts without supervision, yet the feasibility of co-operative supervision with aid from the state is proven beyond all doubt.

"The state aid to a district amounts at present to $1,250—$750 towards the superintendent's salary and $500 towards the salaries of the teachers. The remainder of the superintendent's salary, $750, must be raised by the towns of the district. They are at liberty, of course, to raise more than $750 for the purpose, if they desire to do so" (Massachusetts State Report, 1895).

What has been said regarding the combination of towns for supervisory purposes can be repeated with equal emphasis as to other small divisions of territory termed "school districts." The same principle applies here as elsewhere, that the interests of the schools included in a given territory should be sufficient to warrant the employment of a thoroughly competent person, at such a salary as would justify devoting his entire time to his work. After all has been done, there will still be vast sections of country, especially in the West and Southwest, without any means of efficient supervision. No present remedy can be devised to aid them. It can be safely left for the several states, as population increases, to look after the interests of the schools in the light of the experience of older communities about them.

The worth of the county superintendency is acknowledged, but in many cases the county is too large an area and contains too many teachers for one man to properly supervise. The county is as much too large a unit for supervisory purposes as the township is too small. This remark, however, does not apply to every county nor to any one state. In counties where the number of teachers is too large for one man to supervise, the county superintendent should have one or more assistants or deputies to aid him in his work. They should be directly responsible to him for the kind and character of their work, and should be charged solely with supervisory duties. The importance of having one superintendent for the county or district to whom other supervisors are responsible must be emphasized, as it would be an error and a fruitful source of strife if in any territory there should be two or more supervisors having concurrent jurisdiction.

THE COUNTY UNIT.

Since this report is a symposium of suggestions for supervising rural schools, it may not be amiss to discuss a plan of supervisory organization that has found favor in some few counties that contain large cities as well as a rural population. We mention it here because it has valuable features for supervising the rural schools. There is but one school board for the entire county. One set of men legislates for the whole area, and it is their duty to relate the urban and suburban and rural schools into a sympathetic system. This is based upon the idea that every city is bound to respect the people that immediately environ it. It is to the interest of a large city to have good roads leading to it, good crops in the fields around it, and good schools to which the farmers may send their children.

With this as a foundation principle there is but one school fund for the entire county, raised by taxation upon all property in the county, whether it be in or out of the city. This makes the general school fund, which is distributed upon the basis of school population and according to the needs of the city wards and the rural communities. The same qualification for teachers is required whether they teach in a city graded school or in a country ungraded school, and the same salary is paid to them and in the same way, and for just as long a term. In this system one superintendent is in charge of the whole area. He looks after a city graded school one day and the next day may be twenty miles away inspecting a country school. Expert supervision by a superintendent and his assistants is thus extended into the rural districts, and both city and country school receive the benefit of what there may be in each that is of real value.

Upon this plan, as a matter of course, a large portion of the school fund raised by taxation on city property is annually distributed to the country schools. The city is really made to assist in supporting the rural schools around it. And who shall say it is not a good thing for the city to do, especially in agricultural sections, in which the education, liberal and special, of the farmer's child is the probable salvation of the farming interests of the country. We should not lose sight of the truth that the farmer's child is to be made a useful citizen, not only content to stay in the home in which he was born and reared, if that is best, but fitted to fill honorably any station in life to which he may be called. To do this he must have all the opportunities of education and culture that the city affords. This can be brought about in no other way than at the city's expense, for wealth is massed in our populous centers. The expert supervision, the well-trained teacher, the long term, the modern text-book, the good schoolhouse, can be placed at the farmer's door by the agencies of the neighboring city, that owes him this and much more (*Appendix D*).

TRAINED TEACHERS NEEDED IN COUNTRY SCHOOLS.

Supervision is one of the vital needs of the rural schools, since most of their teachers are inexperienced. The number of normal-school graduates in rural schools is lamentably small. The reason is that the normal-school graduate can obtain a better salary by teaching in a larger field. The demand for this class of teachers makes their salaries so high that the country schools cannot afford to employ them. As soon as teachers become proficient by reason of experience acquired in rural schools, the probabilities are that they will be induced to seek better positions in cities where their experience and abilities will command higher salaries.

Add to this the other fact that many young men begin to teach as a stepping stone to some other profession, and while they are teaching a country school are studying law or medicine, and their hearts are with that rather than with teaching; and also add that many young girls teach until they marry, or as long as they are compelled to teach, and no longer, that they have no real love for their work and no wish to stay in it, and we see how the problems multiply.

Rural schools suffer from lack of trained teachers. In them, as a general thing, are young graduates from the village high school, or some favorite among neighborhood families, or a type of ancient teacher whose placid life is not disturbed by the vexing problems of his profession. This raw material must be developed, made shapely, orderly, and systematic, if time is to be saved to the children, and schools properly supported. A bright and live supervisor will bring order out of confusion, harmony out of discord, and will give life and beauty to that which before was inert and ungainly.

Teaching is a great art, based on a profound science. The supervisor is the expert who has given this art and science his careful attention, and whose business it is both to know how to teach, and to show others the way of teaching. He can in some measure compensate for the lack of skilled work in the school by closely supervising and guiding inexperienced teachers and showing them what to do. An expert is one who possesses skill gained by practice. A supervisor who claims to be an expert should have experimental knowledge of "the how to teach." He is supposed to have given careful attention to those things which characterize a good school. Not only must he know how to teach, but he must know how to instruct others in the art and science of teaching. He must be a skilled teacher of teachers. Without this directing spirit, schools must necessarily suffer until teachers happen upon some better way. It is a great misfortune for schools to wait for wisdom in teaching until the many mistakes of teachers have pointed out better methods. The presence of skilled supervision has been the salvation of many schools.

It is one province of supervision in the country school to bring teachers into contact with each other, to illustrate better ways of teaching, to break up the isolation and monotony of rural school life, and to take to the doors and homes of people and teachers alike the life and freshness which have been the result of research and study on the part of the best minds in the profession. The province of supervision in rural schools falls far short of its legitimate purposes when it begins and ends in the schoolroom.

This point is not sufficiently well appreciated by those who have the oversight and care of schools scattered over a large tract of territory. Country schools have an environment of their own which should neither be forgotten nor ignored. The best supervisory work is that which brings into the rural school everything in farm and rural life which is strong and pure and wholesome. It is possible for the supervising officer so to exert his influence as to give grace and dignity to each individual school, and make it the rallying point for every good influence, a blessing to the entire community in which it is situated.

Attention is here called to the fact that in general but little care is taken in the selection of officers chosen to look after the interests of the rural schools. In the majority of states the county superintendents are elected by the people of the county without any regard to the preparation or qualifications they may have for the work. Very few states require the superintendents to have any special qualifications, and in many instances supervisors are put in charge of teachers who know more about teaching than they do, and are required to hold examinations that they themselves could not pass. Add to this the fact that the superintendents are generally paid very small salaries (average $828 for the whole country) or a meager *per diem*, and that many engage in other business and regard supervision of schools as an incidental matter, and it becomes apparent that professional supervision is too often the exception rather than the rule.

WORK OF SUPERVISORS.

We need everywhere trained superintendents of schools. "Supervision of schools should rank next in importance to the instruction in schools; indeed, so necessary to successful instruction is competent supervision that the two should receive together the watchful oversight of the state" (New Jersey State Report, 1894). Supervisors should know as much of teaching as the teachers under them, and should be able instinctively to distinguish good teachers by their manners, dress, speech, disposition, and character. The best work of a supervisor is his skill in selecting teachers. Not by the results of examination alone, for some learned people make poor instructors; not by yielding to the pressure of family or political influence, for this will ruin any system of schools; not by selecting his own friends or favorites, for this is unworthy of his office; but by following the knowledge that comes to him through study, by long experience, by careful observation, and by conscientious conviction, which enables him to know a teacher when he meets one, though he may not be able to tell why.

Teaching is a matter of both disposition and knowledge. The former cannot be examined, but it ought to be recognized; careful supervision will aid in developing it. Skill in doing this is an essential characteristic of a good supervising officer, especially in connection with rural schools. If the cry is raised (and it is) that there is not enough money to pay for professional supervision, the reply is that it would be wiser to have fewer teachers in order that those employed might be better qualified. A supervisor who is an expert can so arrange and organize the system that a less number of teachers can do the work and do it better, because each one is thoroughly competent. "A good superintendent earns many times his salary; a poor superintendent is too dear at any price. The work of supervision may be unsatisfactory either because the number of schools is too large for the oversight of one person, or because the supervising officer lacks the talent for moulding, inspiring, and directing the work of others" (Pennsylvania State Report, 1895). Underpaid supervision is often unskilled and inefficient, and against this we raise our decided protest. Such supervision is of no value whatever to the schools—a penny-wise policy that economizes in the wrong place. A supervisor should have no other business than to care for the schools. He should not be a merchant, nor a lawyer, nor a farmer, nor an active teacher. His business should be to supervise the schools of his county, or township, or district, or whatever his area be called.

With a given sum of money for school purposes, to devote a part of it to skilled supervision will bring more children under enrollment, better teachers in the community, better instruction in the schools, and more satisfaction to the people, than if all the money were spent in paying the salaries of teachers.

In twenty-eight states the supervisors are required by law to visit each school twice a year, in the other states they are allowed to visit the schools as often as practicable. In one or two states the supervisors visit the schools very seldom. The length of time the supervisor spends in each school varies from fifteen minutes to one-half day. The time seems to depend very largely upon circumstances, the number of pupils, the character of the teacher, the efficiency and the pay of the supervisor. A skilled supervisor inspecting an intelligent teacher can do more service in fifteen minutes than an unskilled supervisor visiting a poor teacher can do in a whole day. The average time spent in the ordinary rural school by the school supervisor is about one hour every year.

In twelve states the supervisors devote all their time to the work. In these states the average salary is $1,002 a year. In fourteen states the supervisors devote only a part of their time to supervision, with an average annual salary of $408. Sixteen states report that in some counties the supervisors devote all their time to supervision, while in other counties the supervisors devote but a small part of their time to that work. In these states the salaries paid supervisors vary from $100 to $2,000 or $3,000 a year. Where good salaries are paid they devote all their time to supervision. Where small salaries are paid they devote but little time to this special work. All states have some supervision, though it varies greatly in amount and in efficiency.

In many sections of the country a supervisor not capable of suggesting to teachers better methods of teaching and not able to detect false methods pays only a perfunctory visit to the schools. He merely sees whether the building is clean, whether the children look bright and interesting, whether the enrollment is good, such facts as would be noticed by any person of ordinary common sense. Too often the contact of the average supervisor and the teacher of the rural schools is nothing more than a mechanical business performance, with such elements of aid and encouragement as any intelligent visitor may give the school. Although this is not without advantage, it falls far below the standard of professional supervision.

How many teachers a supervisor can direct cannot be discussed except in a general way. Schools are more widely separated in some localities than in others, roads are better, teachers are better, and supervisors vary greatly in the rapidity with which they work. As a general rule, however, every rural school ought to be visited at least once in two months. Supervision cannot be called close that does any less than that, and it would be better if the schools could be visited once every month.

No accurate information can be gained concerning the conditions of the school, nor can the proper influence be exerted over teacher and pupils, unless the supervisor has time at his disposal to make a reasonably thorough examination of the school and its surroundings. Sometimes, with an inexperienced teacher, he may find it necessary to spend the entire day in the school, while in other cases he may be able to visit two or more schools in one day. The point is that he must not feel compelled to shorten his visit, or to leave his work half done, in order to meet other engagements. To make his visits effective in the highest degree requires time and patience. The length of his visit must depend upon the necessities of the school, and of these he must be his own judge. An ideal system of supervision would give one supervisor from fifty to seventy-five teachers to supervise. Where the number of teachers is greater some will be neglected, for a supervisor generally has many interruptions in his work, such as rainy days, holidays, and the demand upon his time for office work, board meetings, committee meetings, public addresses, etc., so that it is impossible to put in every day in supervision. Allowance must be made for other important duties.

Attention is also called to the power which the supervisor can exert through rightly conducted teachers' meetings, institutes, associations, and round tables. Here he may meet the teachers under his direction, and make use of the information which he has gathered in visiting their schools. From free and open discussions by the teachers he will get an insight into their habits of thought and their methods of expression. Such meetings help break up the unsocial character of rural teachers by bringing them into contact, so that each learns something from the experience of all the others. In this way teachers and supervisors become better acquainted, gather fresh courage and new inspiration, and go home feeling that they have much in common, and that, if they will, they can in many ways be mutually helpful. The most deadening influence about the country school is its isolation. Nothing is more potent in overcoming this than frequent gatherings in which teachers, school officers, and parents freely discuss matters of common interest. To encourage such meetings is one of the duties incumbent upon the supervisor. Without being too prominent, he may still be the inspiring spirit, guiding, directing, and stimulating the tone and energies of all who participate in the proceedings (*Appendix F*).

LEGAL REQUIREMENTS AND QUALIFICATIONS.

The necessity of establishing some qualifications to be required of those who are to occupy the position of supervising officer is emphatically insisted upon.

"If it is desirable to insist upon a certain degree of qualification for a school-teacher in the humblest district of the state (this proposition has passed beyond the realm of discussion), it would seem that there is no question that the superior officer clothed by statute with such extended powers as a school commissioner ought to be a person possessing some fixed qualification for the performance of the duties of his office. The schools of the state will never reach that degree of efficiency which the state has a right to demand, and which is expected from the generous provision made for their support by the people, until this evil is corrected. Some standard of qualification should be insisted upon, and the power of removal in case of the election of a person not possessing these qualifications should be vested in the state superintendent" (New York State Report, 1895).

In only seventeen states are there any qualifications, beyond that of being a resident and a voter. In some states a first-grade license is required, in others a normal or university course, and again in others he must be an experienced teacher. In a majority of the states, however, the electors are allowed to choose any person without regard to educational qualifications.

In answer to circulars of inquiry the following information was obtained regarding supervisors:

Wisconsin — By the law of 1895, must hold a university, normal, state, or special superintendent certificate.

New York — No standard of qualification.

Pennsylvania — Must hold a college diploma, or a state or local certificate; must have at least three years' experience in teaching.

Michigan — Must be a graduate of a reputable college, university, or state normal college, or must hold a state or first-grade certificate.

Mississippi — Must hold a first-grade certificate.

Texas — Must be a person of educational attainments and hold a first-grade teacher's certificate.

Tennessee — Can be appointed only from applicants who pass an examination on questions sent out by state board.

Georgia — Must pass a satisfactory examination.

Louisiana — Must have a common-school education.

Montana — Must hold a first-grade certificate and have one year's experience as teacher.

South Carolina — Must be able to conduct a teachers' institute.

Kentucky — Must be able to obtain a first-class teacher's certificate, hold a state diploma, or state certificate.

Arkansas — Must have a first-grade certificate.

Maryland — The county school board may require applicants to be examined by the state superintendent.

Utah — Must have a valid certificate not lower than the grammar grade.

West Virginia — Must be skilled in the art of teaching.

Iowa — First-class certificate, good for two years, a state certificate, or a life diploma.

It is unquestionably true that a supervisor should be as well and as highly educated as the better teachers he supervises. He should be a man of broad and generous culture, a lover of good books, versed in the best literature of the day, one whose presence is an influence for good, and whose words are an inspiration. To require him to be in every case a graduate of some higher school would be unreasonable, perhaps, but he should be a friend of higher education in every sense of the word. He must for a long time continue to be one from whom will come the influence which will lead the pupils in the rural district to strive for the highest education possible under the circumstances. His influence should be given to the establishment of rural or township high schools wherever the population will permit it. These schools should include in their courses whatever is required on the one hand for entrance to the school of the next higher grade, or, on the other, those studies, a knowledge of which can be made so to change life on the farm, in its various forms, that it will become more attractive and more profitable. In the establishment and conduct of such schools the influence of the supervisor should be a very prominent factor.

A supervisor should have a thorough knowledge of school work. He should know what a teacher ought to do in managing a class of pupils of any age on any subject. This is one of the things he is paid to know. He should be an expert to whom teachers may go for advice and direction. If the advice is good and the direction wise, teachers will have confidence in the administration of the schools, and rely more and more upon the supervisor. The system is thus reduced to uniformity and becomes a source of strength. The supervisor should be able to direct teachers in their professional reading, and select wisely a library of teachers' books, and place them where they are most needed. He should know about school periodicals and be able to form his teachers into reading clubs and circles, and direct their studies. He should be able to arrange teachers' meetings so that time will not be wasted, and that teachers will come with pleasure and stay with profit. He ought to be able to aid in selecting a library suited to the wants and tastes of an agricultural community (*Appendix L*). In school extension he should be a leader, for he can thus make his influence felt in every part of his territory. In directing the home reading of the pupils and the people he may, if he will, find an immense field of usefulness. He can thus create and foster an interest in the welfare of the farm and the home as adjuncts to the rural schools.

He can understand and sympathize with teachers better if he has an experimental knowledge of their work. No supervisor is so good as he who climbed from the lowest rounds and knows all the steps. That this is indispensable we are not prepared to state. There are some very excellent supervisors who have but little experience in teaching, but who have seen enough and studied enough to know how it ought to be done. Experience would have been helpful, however, in understanding the limitations of their work.

First and foremost a supervisor should be able to instruct his teachers in the methods of organization and management of schools. This is particularly the case in rural schools where so few teachers have acquired skill in teaching. But instruction with a teacher is like instruction with a child. There must be an awakening, an arousing, a hungering after instruction. The conditions of "being filled" are that we must "hunger and thirst." The supervisor must inspire his teachers with a desire for better things. He should lead them to see that time is precious, and that the children in school this year may be on the farms next year and no more in school forever. They must know what to do and do it. The supervisor should be a source of inspiration. His corps of teachers must be alive, and eager, and studious. The thing most to be abhorred in school work is the teacher dead to advancement in professional studies. The supervisor must rouse teachers to work out for themselves plans and methods for building up their schools, and must set forth the principles which should control them in their work.

The county superintendent, or the supervisor of schools in any rural community, should have had recent experience in the schools which he is to supervise. In cases where this is not possible he should make a careful study of the peculiar surroundings of the schools of which he is to take charge. If the new departure which seems to be at hand in rural school education is to be a success, it must be carefully conducted in reference to those environments which are peculiar to each section. The supervisor who is to have a controlling influence in choice of text-books, in courses of study, in the selection and use of libraries, should be thoroughly conversant with the physical characteristics of his district, with the interests of the people, with their sources of wealth and living, and with the home life of the children (*Appendix O*). Whether it be a mining or a grazing region, whether agriculture or horticulture predominates as an interest, he should make himself at home in that domain of science or knowledge which will increase his usefulness as a school officer.

THE HOME AND THE SCHOOL.

The parents of children need instruction as well as the children themselves. The home influence and the school influence should be harmonious, or confusion and uncertainty will arise in the child's mind as to what he should do. The people must be reminded that the school is an integral part of the community, and not a separate affair which the law compels them to support, and which takes their children away when their assistance on the farm is most valuable (*Appendix O*).

In establishing the true relations between the home and the school, between the necessities of physical and those of intellectual education, the supervisor of rural schools finds an unlimited field of usefulness. In rural districts parents are often ignorant of the advancement education has made since the days when they went to school, and they are often too ready to criticise anything new. The supervisor must gain their confidence, so that they will yield their ideas to his, and allow the teacher in their school to follow his directions without any hindrance from them.

The supervisor can exert a wonderful influence in bringing the fireside to the support of the teacher. To do this he must be able to educate the people concerning their relation to the school, as to sending the children regularly, as to providing necessary material, such as books, etc., as to allowing every teacher to pursue those methods of teaching which his skill and experience suggest as best suited to the wants of the school. At meetings of agricultural clubs, at town rallies, at educational "barbecues," at commencements, at spring festivals, at farmers' institutes, he should embrace every opportunity of saying a word for the schools, in order to arouse the people and interest them in the whole system of education. The columns of the country paper afford the supervisor a very ready means of reaching the people. Almost every farmer takes the county paper that comes weekly to his fireside, which gives the news of the outside world and the doings of his neighbors. School news is an important item and should never be omitted. Every week the paper should contain something of educational interest from the pen of the supervisor, though not always over his signature—suggestions for improvement, statistics of enrollment and attendance, new and better ways of teaching, plans for schoolhouse construction and decoration. The press is valuable to every teacher and helpful to the system of education by bringing farmers into sympathy with the great educational movements of the world. The press gives a larger audience, though it enforces a shorter address. But a little every week, full of variety and interest, will eventually build up a healthy sentiment in the county and educate parents as well as children.

The supervisor should have a direct or indirect control of the selection of teachers. The crisis in the history of schools is when teachers are to be chosen. No one is so well qualified to choose them wisely as a faithful supervisor, and no one is more likely to do so conscientiously, since he knows the value of efficient teachers. This control can be given him directly or indirectly. If he does not wish to have the direct choice in individual instances, the same may be accomplished by giving him the power to examine and license teachers for his supervisory district. No one, then, can be selected by the board of directors except such as are approved by him. He prepares an eligible list to which the board is limited in making its choice. If the superintendent is conscientious and courageous in the preparation of this list, he can safely leave the responsibility of the individual appointments to the board.

In many cases the questions for such examination are prepared at the state office. In some instances the county board conducts the examinations, and in a few the answer papers are sent to the state office for final examination and approval or rejection.

The supervisor should be slow to condemn a teacher who is honestly striving to succeed, but if, after faithful and earnest effort, teachers clearly prove that school teaching is not their vocation, or, after repeated warnings, teachers will not try to do the right kind of work, it is clearly the duty of the supervisor to report the facts to the directors, and his report should be given great weight by them. The power to revoke the certificate is usually in the hands of the supervisory officer. It should be exercised with great caution and deliberation, but fearlessly whenever there is sufficient reason for it.

Since the supervisor is responsible for school methods and for results in teaching, the arrangement of the course of study and the selecting of the text-books should be largely, if not entirely, left to his direction. It is his particular business to know books as well as to know teachers. It is not to be expected that the men who constitute the ordinary "committee on text-books" and whose daily business has no relation whatever to school texts and their use, can decide what book is best for use in the schoolroom. It is very well to have a committee on text-books composed of the members of the board, to prevent possible abuse, but the advice of the supervisor should have much influence in determining the character of the books used in the schools.

SCHOOL DIRECTORS.

It is important that the relations between the supervisor and the school officers should be clearly defined. The directors[1] stand much nearer the people and have an immediate interest in the welfare of the schools. They contract with the teachers, care for the financial affairs of

[1] Director includes whatever term is used to designate the local school officers in any state — as director, commissioner, school committee, trustee, etc.

the district, purchase supplies, and are charged with the general business management. The success of the school depends very largely upon the kind of men who are elected to that office. In the rural districts especially the duties of the director are mainly of a supervisory nature. He should inspect frequently the schoolhouse and school premises; he should see to it that everything is provided which is necessary for the comfort and convenience of both teacher and pupils, that the outbuildings are in a decent condition, and that the supplies are used with due regard to a wise economy. In the discipline of the school he should give a strong moral support to the teacher, and his influence should at all times be on the side of order and obedience. The board of directors should make such rules and regulations for all the schools under its control as it deems necessary for the preservation of school property, for securing punctuality and regularity, and for the general welfare of all concerned, and it should support the teachers in their rigid enforcement. It should be in constant correspondence with the supervisor, so as to keep him informed respecting the progress of the school, and in case a teacher is derelict in his duties, or if for any reason the school needs a special visitation, it should inform him at once. On the other hand it should be the aim of the supervisor to establish the most cordial and intimate relations with the local directors. The supervisor should magnify the office of the director. Whenever he visits the school he should, if possible, induce the director to go with him. If at such visits they inspect the condition of the outbuildings and the premises, the supervisor can often propose plans for the improvement of the buildings which the director will more readily appreciate and approve.

The inspection of a school by a competent supervisor is an object lesson of importance to the director. He is able to see at what points the supervisor is aiming, and he learns something of his ideas and plans. He will thus be better able to counsel and advise the teacher in the frequent visits which he makes to the school, and make more intelligent and specific reports to the supervisor. The practice on the part of the supervisor of calling the directors together at stated times for mutual conference is very commendable. These officers are often ignorant of their duties, but in a large majority of cases they are willing and anxious to learn. There is no more effective way of improving the rural schools than that of instructing and informing the men who have them in their immediate charge. No doubt large sums are lost to the various funds through carelessness on the part of treasurers and secretaries in the rural districts in keeping their accounts. The supervisor should make it his duty to audit these books at least once each year, with a view to accuracy of statistics and economy in expenditures, and this should be one of his duties under the law.

THE VISITATION OF SCHOOLS.

The supervisor's method of visiting schools may be considered briefly. First, he visits schools to see how and what the teachers teach, whether their manner is composed, their method clear and concise, their style interesting; whether they are teaching valuable facts, or wasting time on trifles; whether they are teaching what is right or what is wrong. Second, he goes to find out what the pupils know. This is a test of the past work of teachers, which is shown by the general manner of recitation, the promptness with which pupils reply, the amount of information they have, the degree of skill they manifest, or the power of original thinking they have developed. Third, he inspects the physical conditions of the school building and grounds. He should note the conditions of the outbuildings, and if he finds them unsuitable in any respect, he should say so frankly to teachers and directors, and insist upon a change at once. The supervisor must know whether good light, good seats, proper temperature and ventilation, and thorough drainage are secured. The supervisor should carefully observe the moral atmosphere which surrounds the school, whether it is on the side of order and obedience, of modesty, and of all those virtues which make the character of the typical American citizen. All these are demanded in order that good teaching may be made possible, and good health and public morals may be preserved.

Such being the purpose of the visit, the supervisor should put himself in easy and cordial relations with the teacher and the pupils, that he may have a true understanding of what each can do. The teacher may conduct one or more recitations in the various subjects of study, in order that the supervisor may see the usual methods of instruction. The supervisor can then suggest improvements if needed, and can even take the class in hand and demonstrate them. That he should ask for a class in any particular study and give the pupils a rigid oral or even written review, while the teacher may be attending to some other duty, is proper, for by this means he can find out how much instruction has been given since his last visit and how thoroughly the course of study is being adhered to. It is, however, often best to allow the teacher to pursue the usual routine of exercises, in order that the supervisor may see the school at its everyday work.

An inspection of the teacher's register should not be forgotten. Such a register in every rural school should show the name and age of each pupil, the studies pursued, where each class commenced and its progress during the term, so that a new teacher can at a glance understand at what point the study of each branch to be taught is to be taken up. The supervisor should insist that such a register be carefully kept by every teacher under his control.

A private record of his own, in which names, dates, classes heard, conditions of rooms and premises, material needed, and general observations, are kept, will aid the supervisor. He can by this means trace the development of any one school and can more readily observe whether it progresses or retrogrades.

SCHOOLHOUSES AND FURNITURE.

Before closing, your subcommittee desires to emphasize the proposition that the supervisor should have a controlling voice in the erection of the rural schoolhouse, as respects all its sanitary conditions. Before the contract for a new building can be legally let, the written approval of the supervisor should be necessary, certifying that as concerns heating, lighting, ventilation, and everything which conduces to the health and physical growth of the pupils, the requirements of hygienic rules and sanitary science have been carefully and fully complied with. The rural schoolhouse should be built in accordance with the laws of sanitation and modern civilization (*Appendix M*). It never will be until the state, speaking through the supervisor, compels it as a prerequisite for receiving a share of the public funds.

The supervisor should not be blind to the small things which minister to the comforts of the pupils. Often the rural school-teacher has received no instruction upon these points. If the supervisor finds pupils facing a strong light, he should call attention to the evils likely to ensue, and suggest a remedy. The same is true as regards unsuitable desks or seats. The necessity of proper ventilation and proper temperature should be constantly dwelt upon. Without a thermometer, with no means of ventilation except the door and windows, the rural school-teacher needs and appreciates all the suggestions an intelligent supervisor may make.

Akin to this is the suggestion that the supervisor should insist that the schoolroom be kept clean and neat for sanitary reasons. The floors should be scoured as often as they are soiled; the wood, trash, and ashes should be carefully kept away from around the stove. The walls should be swept free of dust, the chalk racks kept clean, and the window panes polished. Pupils also should be required to keep their desks in order and their books clean. It is stimulating to the little ones and helpful to teachers for the supervisor to have them show their books, and to take occasion to comment on the care or on the untidiness with which they are kept.

No better educational influence can surround the children than a well-arranged schoolroom whose floors and windows are clean, whose walls are free from dust and decorated with pictures, whose school grounds are well-ordered and shaded by trees and adorned with flowers, and the school presided over by a qualified teacher who is the personification of neatness and good cheer. Under such conditions the child is self-restrained and respects himself because his surroundings are respectable. The child naturally puts himself in harmony with his environment. If the teacher is neat and the schoolhouse is in proper order, the pupil will copy the example. Day by day beautiful, comfortable, and clean surroundings will have their ethical influence upon his development, until he comes in time to abhor anything that is not beautiful, well-ordered, and clean. This point is too often overlooked in plans for supervision. The reverse of this feature is also true. The rural schoolhouse, generally speaking, in its character and surroundings is depressing and degrading. There is nothing about it calculated to cultivate a taste for the beautiful in art or nature. If, under the influence of intelligent supervision, this can be changed, it will be a work over which coming generations will rejoice.

"There is scarcely a sounder principle in pedagogy than that care begets care; order, order; cleanliness, cleanliness; and beauty, beauty. Things conspicuously good command the respect of children, invite their imitation, and in ways real, though obscure, sink into their souls and mould their being. The power of good example in men and women no one disputes, but there is power akin to it in things, provided they embody the better thoughts of men and women — a power of which more should be made in school management than is made at present" (Massachusetts State Report, 1895).

If children are daily surrounded by those influences that elevate them, that make them clean and well-ordered, that make them love flowers, and pictures, and proper decorations, they at last reach that degree of culture where nothing else will please them. When they grow up and have homes of their own, they must have them clean, neat, bright with pictures, and fringed with shade trees and flowers, for they have been brought up to be happy in no other environment. The true test of our civilization and culture is the kind of home we are content to live in, and the influences of our schools should help to form a disposition for those things that make home life happy and healthy. If the farmer's boy can be taught to love books when he is at school, he will have a library in his home when he becomes a man; if the farmer's girl can be taught decoration at school, she will want pictures and flowers and embroidery when she becomes a woman.

We appeal also for the influence of classical art in our schools. If we have pictures, why not have reprints of those that have moved the hearts of men? Why not have the best looking down from our school walls? They are within the reach of any purse. One reprint from the great masters is an uplifting influence for all time. Cheap and gaudy advertisements, glaring and painful chromos, depress the true spirit of art and perpetuate the crudeness we seek to overcome.

The same can be said of music. If we are to sing songs, why not sing the songs of masters? They have sung many for children, beautiful far beyond the rude compositions that fret our ears everywhere. Also with literature. Why not read the simple classics written for the little ones, and the greater classics for the older ones? Why not in all things get the noblest and best that the world has given, and use them to help our children onward and upward?

The silent influence of clean surroundings, of cheerful teachings, of classical pictures and music and literature, the presence of flowers and their care, the planting of shade trees and studies of their growth, will be a supervision so constant and so searching that no child can escape it. Under its potent warmth, like the steady, quiet shining of the sun, the child plant grows into all the marvelous possibility of flower and fruit.

SUMMARY.

1. As to the character of the supervisor who is brought in contact with the rural school-teacher in the discharge of his official duties:

(1) He should be selected with special regard to his peculiar fitness for that office. Whether his office is elective or appointive, his qualifications, in order that he may be eligible, should be such as to enable him to challenge the respect of those whose work he is required to supervise.

(2) In regard to his scholarship, it should breathe that essential spirit of learning necessary to making good, strong schools. The position of supervisor should be made professional with a view of meeting the demand for the best education which the rural school can possibly afford. This requires a scholarship which is above that of the ordinary man. The tendency to put persons in the supervisory position who have no mental attainments worthy of mention is earnestly deprecated.

(3) In regard to moral character, the supervisor should be a living, inspiring example of such a life as alone is worthy the Christian civilization of our times. He should carry with him a spirit of sincerity in his work, so that people, teachers, and pupils may look to him with hearty respect, and with entire confidence in the integrity of his purposes.

(4) In regard to his professional spirit, he should be in touch with the best educational thought of the times, carrying with him to the country school-teacher, and to the people of a rural community, the freshness and life which come from reading and studying whatever bears upon the questions he is called upon to aid in solving. He should be a leader, endowed by nature with strong native sense, and at the same time able to impart enthusiasm and energy to all with whom he comes in contact.

2. As to the purposes of rural school supervision:

(1) It should serve to inspire and stimulate the rural school-teacher. If the supervisor is alive to his opportunities, every teacher within the sphere of his influence will be quickened and lifted up to higher efforts for the good of the school. The teachers should learn to look upon him as a friend, and not as a critic; as a wise counsellor, and not as a mere fault-finder.

(2) It should be the means of awakening and stimulating the pupils as well as the teacher. They should look for the visits of the supervisor with pleasure, and profit by his talks and advice. By instituting a system of central examinations for the rural schools, he may quicken and encourage the brighter pupils to obtain the best education within their means. The influence of a scholarly supervisor over the pupils is a very desirable thing in the rural school.

(3) The improved condition of the rural schoolhouse is a sure index of the work of a competent supervisor. The present lamentable condition of these buildings is due largely to ignorance and neglect. Competent supervision in skillful hands can work a marvelous change. The cultivation of a spirit of order and neatness which leads to the ornamentation of the school grounds and to a watchful care over all the environments of the schoolhouse, is one of the purposes of supervision.

(4) Supervision does not accomplish its legitimate purpose when it fails to cultivate a strong, healthy public opinion in favor of everything which tends to make a good school. Hence, the supervisor who contents himself with a perfunctory visit to the school only is not a supervisor in the broad sense of that word. A large share of the work of the supervisor is away from the school and among the people.

3. As to the results to be expected from intelligent supervision:

(1) In regard to the school, it unites teachers for a common purpose, and, by teachers' meetings and by the visitations of the supervisor, it breaks up the monotony and isolation of the country school. Under its influence better teachers find their way into the schools, better methods of instruction prevail, and the tone and spirit of the school are greatly improved.

(2) In regard to the community at large, supervision is just beginning to do its legitimate work. In the establishment of school libraries, in the relation of the supervisor to the directors, in an improved school architecture in which due regard is had to sanitary conditions, in the ornamentation and care of the school grounds, in school extension, in the introductidn of studies which will add to the attractiveness and profit of life on the farm, in the consolidation of small districts into larger and stronger schools, in awakening a public interest in rural education, there is a field large enough to occupy the time and thought of the most progressive and most intelligent supervisor. It is here we are to look in the

near future for the best results of supervision as concerns the rural schools of the country.

LAWTON B. EVANS, *Chairman*,
CHARLES R. SKINNER,
HENRY SABIN.

REPORT OF THE SUBCOMMITTEE ON SUPPLY OF TEACHERS.

The Subcommittee on Supply of Teachers has distributed a large number of circular letters of inquiry, designed to elicit information in regard to the agencies now existing for the preparation of teachers for rural schools, and for the improvement of teachers already in the service, and also in regard to certain conditions, as to the manner of certificating, employing, and paying teachers, which affect the supply. In connection with this inquiry the attempt has been made to gather information as to the defects and excellencies of existing systems, together with suggestions for improvement. To these a sufficient number of replies has been received to justify the belief that they give a fair average statement of the conditions which this report has to meet. Without attempting to summarize the returns, your committee would state the results of the inquiry upon the problem presented, and mark out the lines which must be followed, and to what end, in order that the child in the country school may receive the education which is his due. In some state systems progress along these lines is much more advanced than in others, and in some individual cases the desired end has been attained; but this is true, as regards the entire country, in so small a degree that it is unnecessary, even if it were possible, to particularize. With but few exceptions the recommendations made could be justified by reference to various states or communities in our own country, and there are none which do not rest upon successful experiences at home or abroad. It will be found quite impossible to treat the rural school in any of its aspects without touching in some degree upon ground common to all classes of schools, and this is especially true as regards that branch of the problem assigned to this subcommittee.

Certain conditions now very general must be changed in order that the rural school may be supplied with better teachers.

TEACHERS.

There must be in rural communities a clearer appreciation of the qualities essential to a good teacher. It is too often the case that no distinction is made between a teacher of superior scholarship, of proved ability in instruction and discipline, of long experience, and one far inferior in all the qualities essential to success.

The teacher must be engaged for the school year. In many cases the engagement is from term to term, and these frequent changes are without exception classed among the most potent causes of failure in the rural school. It is widely true that the school is in session less than half the year; it is often true that in this short school year two teachers are employed, and seldom does a teacher remain a second year. Engagements should be for a longer term than one year, or continuous, and terminated only for cause, as is the case in many cities.

One of the most important points to be considered in a system of schools is that of the authorities employing teachers and assigning them to their work. In cases in which the county or township is the unit of school administration, the problem is solved; in case the district system prevails, the district containing one school, it is evident that the employment and assignment of teachers should be transferred to the authorities of the larger school unit, in order that in the assignment advantage may be taken of peculiar abilities and aptitudes.

The authority which examines should not employ.

Closely allied to this question is one of great interest in the southern states, namely, that of assignment of teachers to negro schools. For a full treatment of this subject see *Appendix J.*

SCHOOL YEAR.

The school year must be lengthened to a full school year of nine or ten months. In many states a minimum length is prescribed by statute, but in few cases is this sufficient. Whatever efforts may be made for the improvement of the rural school, until there can be offered a "year's work and a year's wage," it will be difficult and often impossible to retain accomplished teachers for continuous service; with this, many such teachers would choose this service, from family and social connections, and from a natural preference for rural life.

In countries in which people are accustomed to the action of centralized authority, prescription settles the matter, as in France, where the school year is more than forty weeks; in England, where, as conditions of receiving the government grant, the principal teacher at least must hold the government certificate of qualification, the school premises must be in good sanitary condition, the staff, furniture, and apparatus must be sufficient, and *the school must have met 400 times (200 days) in the year.*

In countries like our own, in which popular initiative in political matters has been the rule, success must usually come by other methods, and in this respect we have much to learn from our neighbors. In Canada the schools have been lengthened to a full school year mainly under the stimulus given by the mode of distributing the government grants.

Letters and reports have been received from the different provinces. By these it appears that the average length of the school year was in Ontario 212 days; in New Brunswick, 216 days; in Nova Scotia, 198.7 days, the full school year being 216 days, and some schools exceeding this limit. A report from Regina, in the province of Assiniboia, states that the full school year is considered to be twelve months less the holidays, amounting to seven weeks, but this limit cannot be attained where the sparseness of the population obliges the pupils to travel long distances, on account of the severity of the winters.[1]

Adding to our plan of requiring a minimum school year the Canadian plan, already in a degree recognized in some recent school legislation, of making the amount of government grant depend in a large degree upon the length of the school year and the average attendance, consolidating schools wherever practicable, and giving from the larger units of school administration to aid the smaller and weaker, the obstacle of the short term and insufficient compensation can be removed.

SUPERVISION.

Incompetent supervision forms one obstacle to a supply of better teachers. This obstacle may be removed by securing professional supervision, as is provided by the plan of district supervision so successfully applied in Massachusetts, and just enacted in Maine. The subcommittee on supervision treats this subject fully.

It is necessary that more definite tests of professional fitness for the work of supervision be instituted. The extension of pedagogical instruction in colleges and universities in recent years is gradually elevating the work of supervision to a higher pedagogical plane, yet the point has not been reached of demanding professional preparation as an essential condition. For examples of the requirements of more definite tests of fitness see Ontario and France (*Appendix N*).

It is not unreasonable to hope that in the not distant future the popular standard of education may be so raised that on all educational boards of control, from the state board down to the county or township school board, so much of pedagogical fitness, from the professional point of view, may be demanded as to insure the intelligent consideration of such questions pertaining to the profession as may come before them.

[1] The subcommittee is under obligation to more than it can name, throughout the United States, for information. For aid in its inquiries received from the provincial school authorities of Nova Scotia, New Brunswick, Quebec, Ontario, and Manitoba, and from Mrs. Etta F. Grover, of Regina, Assiniboia, and Mr. Chisholm, Principal of the high school in Regina, it would here express its thanks.

There are various recognized agencies for the improvement of teachers.

ASSOCIATIONS.

The state associations are mainly in the control of teachers representing systems of schools; in but few states are rural school-teachers much in evidence at these meetings. The fact that in some states the opposite condition holds shows that the state association may be made a powerful means of uplifting for the rural schools.

In many of the states vigorous county associations are found, although this is by no means universal. In these the rural school receives more recognition, but not often all which is its due. When the county association holds frequent sessions, and makes the interests of the rural schools prominent, it proves one of the most efficient agencies.

Some of the states report local associations of rural school-teachers which are very efficient. Generally the success of these is largely dependent upon the spirit of the local or county superintendent. With good professional supervision in township and county, the wants of rural schools and their teachers can find due consideration in local and county associations; and by proper organization of rural school sections in the state associations there may be secured such an affiliation of state, county, and local associations as will insure in time a full recognition of the peculiar needs of the rural schools.

It is desirable that the affiliation between these associations be such as to secure in part the working together, along the same lines of thought, during the same years, by the local, county, and state associations, under the inspiration of the State Department of Education.

SUMMER SCHOOLS OF SEVERAL WEEKS' DURATION.

In some cases summer schools are apparently conducted for the purpose of enabling those attending to pass examinations for certain certificates. The tendency is necessarily toward cramming for the examinations, and so far they cease to be educative in any proper sense of that term.

There is another class of summer schools, often held in connection with colleges and universities, conducted by able teachers, specialists in their departments, for the purpose of advancing education along true lines. Among these, the Agassiz School at Penekese many years ago, was a revelation and an inspiration to the teachers of the United States. These schools have multiplied in number and enlarged in scope throughout the land, and have proved of great advantage to thousands, not only by increasing their knowledge, but also and much more by bringing them under the personal influence of leaders of thought and masters in teaching.

A third class, with professional courses in psychology, pedagogy, and methods, often combining the character of the second class, preceding, offers great advantages for professional improvement. There should be in every county one of these for the especial benefit of teachers of the common schools; they should be free of tuition, organized and conducted under the supervision of the State Department of Education, continuing from four to ten weeks. There should be provision for practice teaching, and the instructors should be familiar with rural schools, their condition and needs.

INSTITUTES.

The normal institutes, so-called, organized in some states, especially in the West, are essentially the same as the third class of summer schools, described above.

County institutes of one week or more, held during the school year, may exert a great influence in the improvement of teachers. When they are conducted under efficient supervision, with a body of instructors capable of increasing the range of thought of teachers, and are organized under such laws as will secure the attendance of the teachers of the county, they prove a powerful means of educational advance.

For the description of such an organization of institutes and results see *Appendix P*.

Teachers' conventions or institutes of one day, as conferences between teachers, or with superintendents, will prove effective to a greater or less degree according to the purpose, plan, and mode of conducting. In order to secure the best results, they should be held at intervals so frequent that the effect may be continuous.

READING CIRCLES.

The success of the Chautauqua movement, of various organizations for home study, and of teachers' reading circles, in some cases, proves that these may be made generally efficient. There will be no lack of interest on the part of the teachers, if the organization and direction be wise.

The problem is apparently not a difficult one in the larger places, with systems of schools, where numbers of members are readily brought together, but the case is quite different in the case of rural schools. The results reported clearly indicate certain elements essential to success. To secure the advantage of organization there must be a central board of control. This may be a state board with auxiliary boards in counties and towns. Not only are books for reading to be selected, but a plan of work should be carefully drawn up and widely circulated among teachers. The central board should keep in touch with the members of the circles, papers based upon the books read should be written and carefully examined, and the results attained should in some way be passed to the teacher's credit; thus, for a certain number of certificates indicating the completion of a course, a diploma may be granted.

The plan of organization is perhaps best formed by the teachers of the state acting through their associations, and the courses of reading can best be made out by committees chosen by the teachers for this purpose; the work may be directed by a committee, but, from comparison of results reported, the varying degrees of success, and the many failures, your committee believes it desirable that there should be in the state department of education a bureau of teachers' reading circles, with sufficient force to keep in touch with the local circles, to conduct and encourage correspondence with them, and in every way to promote their interest and efficiency.

Effective study demands the use of books for consultation and reference. Hence the reading circles should be conducted in conjunction with the lending libraries hereafter mentioned.

The reading circles must be considered as a means of improvement, especially for teachers already in the service. No other agency can really take the place of personal instruction in the original preparation of a teacher for his work. (See *Appendix Q.*)

LIBRARIES.

The country town has suffered, and still suffers, from the lack of books. In many states there is now a movement toward the extension of free library privileges, and wherever there is a town library every school should be made a branch. This system of library extension, becoming universal in cities, can be extended to country as well. By frequent exchange of books, under the immediate direction of the teacher as branch librarian, every teacher and pupil will have the use of a larger library in addition to the special library which should be found in every school. Some books should be added to the library for the special benefit of teachers.

The library belonging to the school is a necessity. Books lent for a time serve their purpose, but a love for good books and the ability to use them aright come most surely from daily companionship. From the library center, the school can be carried into the home. A more valuable work can hardly be done by the rural school-teacher than this, of developing a love for good reading.

In addition to these there should be established in the county, or the state, or both, a professional library for the use of teachers. This might well be a state library with county branches, and the management of it might well be under the bureau of reading circles which has been mentioned. Such a state school library has been established in New York (*Appendix L*).

TEACHERS' TRAINING CLASSES.

The agencies thus far treated tend to the improvement of teachers already in the service, none of them furnish a first supply for rural schools, and there is a lack of special agencies designed for that end. The investigations of your subcommittee show that the existing normal schools in general do comparatively little in this direction, except by the teaching of their undergraduates. Although originally established for the benefit of the common school, they have naturally tended to keep step with the development of systems of schools in cities and large villages; the majority of rural teachers, often a vast majority, are now without any professional preparation whatever. The tendency is strikingly shown in returns from the Oswego, N. Y., Normal School: "Nine-tenths of our pupils come from the country; not one-tenth ever teach in rural schools." In one of the older states, after many years' existence of normal schools, of more than 12,000 teachers in the public schools of all classes less than 5,000 have ever attended normal schools, less than 4,000 have graduated from normal schools. Over 1,500 vacancies occur annually in the schools of the state; the normal schools of the state graduate about 300 annually, nearly all of whom become teachers in graded schools.

One of the leading states of the Union, with a well-organized school system and a grand equipment of normal schools aiming directly to train teachers for the rural schools, reports that a majority of its teachers have had professional training. Many other states report a much smaller proportion of trained teachers; one, 8 per cent.; another, with one of the best school systems, 30 per cent. As a contrast, an answer to the inquiry of your committee, from Manitoba, states: "Sixty-six per cent. of the teachers employed in the province in 1895 were trained. After this year *all will have training*." (See *Appendix N*.)

The cause for such a contrast appears later in this report.

The normal-school system was first devised especially for the benefit of the rural schools, and in obedience to a tendency which had become increasingly strong for some years previous to the time of their establishment. Some brief passages of educational history bearing upon this subject are here cited:

In 1823 Samuel Reed Hall opened a normal school in Concord, Vt., a school for the academic and professional education of common-school teachers, with a school for practice in teaching. Here Mr. Hall's lectures on school keeping were delivered to his class. These were afterwards published. The character of his work led to his being called to the principalship of the English department of Phillips Academy at Andover,

Mass. He was afterwards invited to take charge of Holmes' Academy, Plymouth, N. H., and consented on condition that the school should be called a teachers' seminary. He opened this teachers' seminary in 1837 and continued it two years. In this school there was a classical department and no practice school, but the course, as printed in *Appendix K*, shows the pedagogical character of the institution and the provision made for its students to gain experience in teaching.

In 1829 a training school for teachers of the common schools was opened in the town of Effingham, N. H., by Hon. J. W. Bradbury, ex-United States Senator from Maine, now living, at more than ninety years of age, in Augusta, Me. By request, Hon. W. W. Stetson, State Superintendent of Maine, recently visited him to ascertain the facts in regard to this school, and the interview is annexed to this report as *Appendix K*.

The sole purpose of Horace Mann in the establishment of the first state normal school in Massachusetts, a purpose zealously carried out by the principal, Cyrus Peirce, was to elevate the common schools of the country. The course of study of the normal school was for one year. In the first year of the school a model school was organized, in which normal school students had daily practice in teaching. Mr. Peirce himself taught in the model school, as he felt that upon its success the success of the normal school very largely depended. Almost all the pupils at first came from country towns, almost all returned to teach in country schools. There was not then the difference between the rural school and the city school which now exists. In 1847 John D. Philbrick began the experiment of modern grading in Boston, and, with the full development of this system, later, the contrast between the school of the country and the school of the town became more and more marked, and the rural school problem appeared. The normal-school course, at first simple and adapted to the conditions it was designed to meet, developed to keep pace with the developing school system, and gradually drew away from the rural schools.

The normal school is often removed still further from those who would teach in rural schools by the tendency to raise the standard of admission to the requirements of a high-school course. The fact that most of the towns of the state have a high school is no proof that all those who will teach rural schools can go through a high-school course of three or four years, and then a normal-school course of two or three years. Great care should be taken that the normal school does not get too far from those whom it was especially set to serve. There is needed a more careful determination of the qualities and attainments requisite for entrance upon the work of preparation. for teaching. These are sometimes given in larger measure by the experiences and responsibilities of country life than by the graded city high school, and with these every added step in education is great gain. So far as raising the standard of admission is in response to a claim that all academic studies should be taken out of the normal-school course, it may be said that the claim is not universally recognized as valid by those who have had most experience of work at home, and can find but little warrant abroad. In the normal schools of Prussia, Austria, Switzerland, and France, for example, a larger proportion of time is given to academic studies than in many of the normal schools of the United States,[1] but with directions, certainly in France, that in all the course the professional aim shall be constantly kept in view.

It is evident that for the fitting preparation of teachers for the rural school some agency is needed intermediate between the brief convention or institute and the normal school, with its two or four-years' course, so far beyond the reach of the majority of rural school-teachers. What shall it be?

Several facts must be kept in mind in the solution of the problem: (1) A large proportion of the teachers of rural schools cannot afford the time and expense of a two-years' course in a normal school. (2) The receipts from employment in the rural school under present conditions do not remunerate one for the expense of a normal-school course. This is a simple matter of business, and sentiment will not change the facts. (3) Other conditions remaining the same, attendance at a school is in an inverse ratio to the distance between school and home. This is especially true for a short course.

To meet these conditions there is needed a normal training school with a short course of study. The place—a village which will give over its schools to this normal training school for practice schools. These practice schools, organized as primary schools in one room and as grammar schools in another, will show what can be done with schools in the simplest form of gradation. For a part of the course all the grades should be brought together to illustrate the work of the one-teacher school, such work as should be done in the ungraded school. A faculty of five or six good teachers, including practice-school teachers, would suffice for such a school.

This the general organization—what the work? Treatment of matter essential to good teaching would be grounded on simple fundamental principles. Deficiencies in education would be supplemented by sound teaching; principles of teaching and of school management would be taught and illustrated. Many might learn to do well what they had never done at all; most would learn to do better what they had done poorly.

[1] See Report of Committee on Normal Education, Proceedings of National Council of Education, 1892.

From these schools would come many students for fuller courses of training and a still wider usefulness.

This plan in its development would give a system of district training schools, analogous to the county model schools of Ontario, and the training schools of Quebec and Manitoba, with a course of study and training of one year, the first half of which should be mainly academic, for those who need this preparation, the second half mainly professional, the work so planned that those of more advanced scholarship need take only the course of the second half year. Of these schools there should be at least one in every county of the state (*Appendix N*).

The practice in teaching should be thoroughly organized. Every teacher in the school should be, in a certain sense, a training teacher; he should be responsible for the methods of teaching in his own subjects, and should direct lessons given by members of his classes to children from the model training schools. Besides such lessons, illustrative of methods of teaching, the pupil-teacher should be trained in conducting school work in the schoolrooms, under conditions similar to those which she will find in her own school. While teaching in the practice school under the direction of a teacher in charge, she should be left more and more to her own judgment; she should be held responsible for the control and direction of the school, and for the teaching of a class, not merely of a group.

The membership of the class for training should be limited to such numbers as will give the full advantage of the training course, or, with a practice school of the size presupposed, to about twenty-five. A large class necessitates the teaching of groups, not of full classes with the control of a school. The French law limits the number of students in each normal school to three classes of twenty-five each.

The practice schools should be under the exclusive instruction and control of their regular teachers a sufficient proportion of the time to keep them up to the standard of veritable model schools as well.

The completion of this course should give a teachers' certificate of elementary grade, which would also give admission to the state normal school with due credit on the normal-school course for work already accomplished.

There should be a summer term for rural school-teachers in every normal school in the United States. The plant of the normal school has cost thousands, in some cases hundreds of thousands of dollars, and for two or three months in the summer this investment remains entirely unproductive. The success of the summer term in The University of Chicago is significant, and the Winona plan, adopted this year in all the state normal schools of Minnesota, sets the example for the nation (*Appendix S*). In normal schools the work of the first year—*or the first part* of the course—should be so planned as to have a unity in itself as a preparation for rural school-teachers, and the results accomplished in the summer term should count on this course, so as to encourage subsequent attendance at the normal school. The summer term should not be an institute nor a summer school, in the usual sense, but should combine the elements of the other terms of the year; the attendance of children in the training school could be secured easily for two or three hours a day.

There should be organized in all states a system of normal-school extension analogous to the university extension. Wherever a class of sufficient size can be formed, a teacher should be provided. The work should be so organized and conducted as to lead to definite results which can be credited to the members of the class.

There are two possible agencies in the preparation of teachers for rural schools that have not been mentioned:

1. *City Training Schools.*—In large cities it is not to be expected that the city training school will prepare teachers for rural schools; all their graduates usually find employment at home. But cities in this country with a population of more than 50,000 are comparatively very few, and it is reasonable to suppose that training schools in cities of less than 50,000 will prepare more teachers than can be provided with employment in those cities. The surplus will naturally seek positions in the village and country schools.

Birmingham, Ala., a city of about 50,000, has had a training school for eight years. During that time 25 per cent. of the graduates of this school have found employment in the ungraded schools of the county and state. If the training school is encouraged, it can be made an important factor in the preparation of teachers for rural schools. A part of the course in these schools should, therefore, deal with the conditions of the ungraded schools of the county, and the instruction should be specifically adapted to meet those conditions.

2. *Agricultural Colleges.*—Many pupils in agricultural schools and colleges teach during their course. In some cases the agricultural college is brought nearer the people by the establishment of branches. Thus in Alabama there has been established in each congressional district a branch agricultural school, closely related to the agricultural and mechanical college of the state. Cannot such schools accomplish much in the specific preparation of teachers for the work of the rural schools?

3. *High Schools.*—An effective auxiliary in the training of elementary teachers may be found in high schools. In 1894–95 there were in New York 247 such classes, with 2,482 students. The regulations prescribe the professional qualifications of the teachers who are to instruct these classes, and the equipment and the opportunities for observation and

practice to be furnished. The course of study, extending through one year, covers the ground of common-school studies, including with subject-matter the treatment of methods of teaching, the history of education, school management, and school law. The school is to furnish each day the opportunity for the class, or some members of it, to observe methods of teaching in the several grades of common-school work, and, when practicable, the opportunity to teach in such grades under proper criticism and direction.

A system similar to this is in operation in the province of Quebec.

Although these training classes cannot take the place nor do the work of special training schools, yet they offer a ready means for effecting some immediate improvement in the teaching force of the state, and for the selection of those who have such fitness for teaching as will justify their pursuing a special professional course. The teachers of such classes must themselves have received thorough pedagogical instruction, else the result must be a failure; hence the necessity is apparent for pedagogical courses in all colleges.

According to the generalizations of the superintendent of the last census, over an area of our country of 1,688,827 square miles, containing a population of two to forty-five to the square mile, the occupation of the people is mainly agriculture; of this territory 1,096,790 square miles are occupied by a people mainly engaged in systematic agriculture, leaving about 260,000 square miles, with a population of forty-five and upwards to the square mile, in which the leading interests are commerce and manufactures, and in which professional and personal service are in large demand. The numbers engaged in the principal occupations in the United States, according to the latest United States census, were as follows:

Farm and garden,	8,375,979
All the professions,	944,323
Domestic and personal service,	4,360,506
Trade and transportation,	3,325,962
Manufacturing and mechanical industries,	5,091,669

In behalf of all these occupations, except the professions and agriculture, the claim has been made and has been allowed that special instruction in their interests be made an important part of the school curriculum—in commercial courses; in cooking; in manual training, on which such vast sums have been expended. Indeed, for many of the professions much of the school instruction is a direct preparation.

Much is said of the necessity for considering the environment of the child; for bringing into his school life the thoughts and interests of his home life, that the school may not prove to him a thing remote and foreign; of making the school a recognition of his past and a preparation for his future. Little sign of this can be found in the ordinary rural school.

The courses of study in normal schools of all grades should recognize more fully than they do the environment and probable future life of the children in the schools, or rather, they should recognize the lines along which lives of most probable future happiness would lie. As has been shown, much the largest class of the workers of this country is engaged in agriculture. The environments of their children are rural. The rural school should aim especially to make country life more attractive and beautiful, and should pay more attention to rural industries. Every normal school should have as a means of instruction a school garden, planned and conducted not merely to teach the pure science of botany, but also the simple principles of the applied science of agriculture and gardening; and every rural school should also have its garden, through which the training of the normal school may reach the home. This element of industrial training should be especially emphasized in the colored normal schools and rural schools of the South.

Other countries lead us. A *farm* has been set apart for this line of instruction at the Provincial Normal School at Truro, Nova Scotia. The school garden is common in the countries of Europe most advanced in popular education. The school garden and the nursery of fruit trees are a feature of the normal schools of France; there is a course of agriculture in the normal schools for men, of horticulture in the normal schools for women.

The course in agriculture treats of preparation of the soil, special culture of trees and shrubs, of fruit trees, grafting, and the vegetable garden.

The course in horticulture in the normal schools for women treats of the garden in its general arrangements—the fruit garden, the vegetable garden, the flower garden.

Each garden has a space reserved as a botanic garden for instruction in the science of botany.

The instruction received in the normal school is applied in the school garden of the rural school.[1]

[1] The school garden in the New Hampshire State Normal and Training School has proved a source of interest and of instruction to pupils of all grades in the training schools and in the normal schools, such as nothing else can replace. In this garden all the grains and vegetables grown in the region were cultivated, together with a great variety of flowers. Each class in school had assigned to it a plot, for which it was responsible. In the George Putnam School, in Boston, a part of the school yard was turned into a garden, which has received several prizes from the Massachusetts Horticultural Society. On certain days the Jardin des Plantes in Paris is used as a place for botanical study by the school children. I found once on the roof of a London schoolhouse, which was used as the girls' play ground, a large and beautiful collection of plants. And yet

A French report says that the French farmer is at first opposed to book farming; but when he sees that the products of the teacher's garden are superior to his own, he is glad to learn.

M. Boutan, an inspector general of public instruction, says in a report: "We can cite several departments in which, thanks to the initiative of the teachers, the wealth of the country has increased from year to year, and from which the exportation of fine fruit has become the source of considerable profit."

There can be no doubt that great improvements in agriculture might result from the general diffusion of such instruction through school gardens, under the direction of qualified teachers. Is there any other means for such improvement in sight of this generation? And a still higher good for the country life might come from thus blending its utilities and its beauties in the thought of the child.

Your subcommittee would also emphasize the importance of two other lines of work already developed in the graded schools, and of a third, which must be made prominent in all schools—language, elements of science or nature study, and morals. Whatever goes into the common school must go into the normal school. Hence, even in the brief course of normal-school training, the instruction in the English language, instruction in the essential elements of its beauty and strength, instruction leading toward such command of its best forms as will tend to make it a transparent medium for the expression of thought, must be held of fundamental importance. There must be such training in elementary science and in manipulation as will give the teacher essential knowledge and skill in this line of teaching, and there must be such instruction in elementary psychology and ethics as is necessary for the comprehension of general principles of method, and of the scope and methods of instruction in morals; and as the result of all the preparation which can be given there should be a clear comprehension of the essential aims of education. Would that all our teachers could have constantly in mind and at hand such a statement as is found on the desks of the common-school teachers of France (*Appendix R*).

EXAMINATION AND CERTIFICATION OF TEACHERS.

Were teaching a profession in the sense in which law and medicine are professions, teachers themselves would formulate the terms of professional recognition; but evidently the time for that is not yet. What the public school is immediately to aim for is uniformity in state examinations, and we have to consider the agencies, the standards, the methods for these

the rural school almost utterly ignores its only possible laboratory, the out-of-doors, the garden laboratory, right at hand. Here lies a duty, not a choice merely, for the normal school.—C. C. ROUNDS.]

examinations. The agency may be the state superintendent of public instruction, a special examining board, or a state board of education when such board exists. Times and places for examination should be announced frequent enough and numerous enough to meet all reasonable demand. The scope and character of the examinations should be announced long enough beforehand to enable candidates to consider the matter deliberately, as is now done in regard to examinations for admission to college and for the civil service. Information as to books for use and as to modes of preparation should be given. Each examination should be conducted by an expert, and the papers should be critically examined.

Certificates granted should be graded as to the range of the examination, not as to length of validity, unless the certificate be a provisional one. A one-year's physician would receive little credit; why should a one-year's teacher receive more?

Examinations should cover the range of work required of the teacher, and should be written, oral, and practical. The written examinations should be planned not merely to test the candidate's range of acquirement, but rather his accuracy, his general style of thought and expression. The oral examination should test the range of attainment, the personality of the candidate, and his readiness in resource. These two are generally combined in one—the written form, but there are great advantages in the separation whenever it is practicable.

The examination for the elementary certificate should cover the ground of common-school studies, with so much of the elements of natural science as is demanded for the intelligent teaching of the nature lessons in the common school course. The questions should be few, but comprehensive, and such as will fairly test the reflective power of the candidate.

The professional examination for the elementary grade of certificate should not be severe, but should require clear general statements regarding methods of conducting recitations and the organization and management of a school.

The practical examination, or the test of skill, for the elementary grade of certificate, should include some test of the candidate's ability to plan a lesson and an examination paper in some common-school subject, and to conduct a recitation. If the candidate has been a member of a class in training, a record of this practical work might be brought over from the work in that class.

So much ability as is implied by this examination is necessary to the good teaching of any school. Wherever this ability cannot be secured now for the rural school, a clear public appreciation of the need will lead to a supply of the means.

The examination for the advanced certificate should in general cover the ground of an English high-school course of at least three years, or fair equivalents for such a course. A special certificate might be given for a foreign language. This examination should include psychology and ethics, drawing, and the elements of vocal music.

The professional examination for the advanced certificate should include history of education, methods of teaching, general principles of pedagogy, and the organization and management of schools.

The practical examination should include the preparation of plans of lessons and of examinations; judging the character of a lesson and a written paper; teaching, including an oral lesson on some subject in nature study, elements of science, language, or morals.

As in the examination for the elementary certificate, if the candidate is a member of any training class, the practical examination can be taken in that class.

Formulating the preceding statements, teachers' certificates should be graded in two general classes—elementary and advanced—and in each class three grades.

ELEMENTARY.

(1) Elementary scholastic certificate, Grade 3.
(2) Elementary professional certificate, Grade 2.
(3) Elementary certificate of skill, Grade 1.

ADVANCED.

(1) Advanced scholastic certificate, Grade 3.
(2) Advanced professional certificate, Grade 2.
(3) Advanced certificate of skill, Grade 1.

A life certificate of either class and honorable recognition in the profession should be granted after a certain period of successful teaching to those holding the first-grade certificate of that class.

In each class the higher certificate presupposes the lower; thus Grade 1 cannot be obtained without 3 and 2.

Many, if not most, of the examinations of teachers for rural schools in the United States today do not go beyond the range of the elementary certificate, Grade 3, as here given; the elementary certificate, Grade 2, could be obtained by attendance upon a teachers' training class in a high school. A course in a district training school organized as described in this report, or a partial course of one year in a state normal school, should give the complete elementary certificate. In many cases thoughtful and successful teachers in the rural school, by their own study and the help afforded by a well-conducted reading circle and a normal extension course, could rise from the elementary certificate, Grade 3, to the complete elementary certificate. A high-school course would give advanced certificate, Grade 3, and, with the course in a high-school teachers' training class, might give advanced certificate, Grade 2. The complete advanced certificate could be obtained by a two-years' course in a normal school.

This gradation of examinations and certificates will utilize to the utmost the existing educational agencies, will point out to teachers a way in which they may rise step by step, and will thus encourage their advance, and will secure to the rural school the benefit of their improvement.

A question will arise as to the interval between the elementary and the advanced certificate. (For a wider interval established in Manitoba see *Appendix N.*) In many cases it may be best to lower the standard of the advanced certificate and make it intermediate between the elementary certificate and the normal-school diploma attesting the completion of a two-years' course. On this question your subcommittee pronounces no opinion. It would point out a way by which the teachers of the rural school as it now is may be taken as they are and induced to enter upon a course of advanced study, and by which the school may derive all possible benefit from the advance; and your subcommittee believes that, by such a course, standards will gradually be raised all along the line.

Your Subcommittee on the Supply of Teachers for Rural Schools, in closing its report, would call attention to some of the main points in this discussion.

It appears that there are numerous agencies which may be made available for the improvement of rural school-teachers already in the service. With these the only question is that of more perfect organization.

Although there is in general an increase in interest in educational questions, and an elevation of standards of teaching, yet the large majority of rural school-teachers now enter upon their work with no professional preparation; the improvement in the character of rural schools, where there has been any improvement, has been slow; large sections of the country report no advance, some report a decline.

The causes for this condition, and the changes needed, are not far to seek:

1. The school year must be lengthened to a full school year of nine or ten months, in order that skilled teachers may be retained. This result can be secured, as it has been secured elsewhere when its absolute necessity has been recognized. The state, among other conditions for payment from the school fund, may prescribe a full school year, which is done in England, as logically as six, or seven, or eight months, now done in some of our states, or it may secure this result, as it has been secured in Canada, by making the length of the school so prominent a condition in the distribution of the school fund as to insure the co-operation of the county and the town to this end.

2. The existing agencies for the supply of teachers for rural schools

do not suffice. There must be modifications in these, and the provision of others.

3. There must be some definite standard for the certification of teachers, coming within reach of the teacher of the rural school, and encouraging advance to such higher degrees of attainment and skill as will give full professional recognition. And your committee believes that some provision should be made to secure inter-state recognition.

The question of finance does not lie within the province of this subcommittee, but it does not believe that the financial difficulty need prevent the necessary reform. When there is once full recognition by the state of its final responsibility for the education of every child within its borders, there will be possible such an adjustment of expenses between it and the lower educational units as will be burdensome to none and just to all.

Your subcommittee has sought to ascertain accurately what the rural school now is; in all its suggestions it has had in view the rural school as it ought to be. It believes that this nation can have such a system of schools for all its people as may challenge comparison with any other, and that it will have such a system when it clearly perceives the injustice and the peril of the present condition, and the way in which safety lies.

CHARLES C. ROUNDS, *Chairman*,
DAVID L. KIEHLE,
JOHN H. PHILLIPS,

REPORT OF THE SUBCOMMITTEE ON INSTRUCTION AND DISCIPLINE.

Your Subcommittee on Course of Study, Methods of Instruction, and Discipline in Rural Schools begs leave to report herewith that it has carefully considered the conditions which prevail in thinly settled districts with the intent to discover the evils that exist in the schools as a consequence of those conditions, such, for example, as (1) the want of classification and (2) the impossibility of thorough instruction on the part of the teacher, as well as (3) the lack of that stimulus which comes to the pupil from working at reasonable tasks in company with his equals. Your committee has hereinafter described and discussed various remedies, which it believes will have useful results in practice.

About one half of all the teachers in the United States teach what are called ungraded schools. They receive in one room pupils of all ages and all degrees of advancement, from ABC's upward, sometimes even to algebra and Latin. In extreme cases each pupil is a class by himself in all branches, except perhaps reading, writing, and spelling. It quite often happens that there is no uniformity of text-books, each pupil having a different edition or different author; the teacher is often obliged to borrow the pupil's book when he hears him recite.

According to Mr. Hinsdale's studies of the United States census (see *Appendix A*) the sparsely settled region of the country includes, first, one-third of the whole domain entirely uninhabited or containing fewer than two inhabitants per square mile; secondly, an area of 1,688,827 miles with from two to forty-five inhabitants per square mile, leaving only 260,000 square miles containing more than forty-five to the square mile, and the 443 cities with an aggregate of nearly 19,000,000 people.

It happens that ungraded rural schools with a very small attendance are to be found even in the most thickly peopled states and often in proximity to cities. Rhode Island in 1895 reports 158 out of its 263 schools as ungraded and sixty-four of them as containing fewer than ten pupils each; three towns have in the aggregate thirty-nine schools averaging fewer than ten pupils. Vermont in 1893 reported 153 schools with six pupils or less each. Massachusetts in 1893–94 reported sixteen towns with an aggregate of nearly 100 schools with an average of eleven pupils. New York in 1894–95 reported 2,983 schools with fewer than ten pupils each and 7,529 with less than twenty. Other examples are mentioned in the report of the Subcommittee on Maintenance.

A school with ten pupils of ages from five to fifteen years, of different degrees of advancement, some beginning to learn their letters, others advanced from one to eight or nine years in the course of study, cannot be graded or classified to advantage, but must for the most part be taught individually. The beginner who does not yet know a letter should not be placed in a class with another who began last year and can now read lessons in the middle of the primer. It will not do to place in the same class a boy beginning numeration and another one who has already mastered the multiplication table. The beginner in grammar has not yet learned the technique, and is confused and discouraged by the instruction given to another pupil in his class who has already learned the declensions and conjugations.

Any attempt, in short, to instruct two or more pupils in a class, when there is a difference of a year's work in their advancement, results in humiliating and discouraging the less advanced and in making the maturer pupils conceited. Higher learning in the possession of a fellow-man seems to an illiterate person as something magical, or bordering on the miraculous: he can make combinations of thought which surprise those who are unused to them. The case is worse with the child in school. To him the elevation given by a year's study seems an endowment of nature and not a result of industry. Permanent injury to the pupils is very often occasioned by wrong classification. For not only does the lower suffer from discouragement, but the higher pupil is necessarily injured by not being held to his best. The teacher is perforce obliged to adapt the lesson to the average of the class. This does not give enough work for the advanced pupil, although it gives too much for those below the average. There is not enough demand upon the first to continue the increase of his powers; he becomes indolent and stops growing.

For these reasons classification as above described ought not to be expected in the rural school; it must remain ungraded, and as a result the teacher must resort to individual instruction wherever there are intervals of a year or more in degrees of advancement between pupils, and this is the actual practice in perhaps the majority of such schools. The older pupils at least should have separate grammar, history, and arithmetic lessons.

It is understood by your subcommittee, as a matter of course, that even in a small school of six to ten pupils there may be two or more pupils of sufficiently near stages of progress to form one class—for example, two beginners in arithmetic, grammar, geography, or history. It may be that a dull pupil has already been studying arithmetic, grammar, or history for a quarter or a half year, and that a bright pupil just commencing the study would be able to keep up with him on a review from the beginning of the book; but it would not do to place a dull pupil commencing a study with a bright one who had already a half year's start in it. It often happens that pupils placed in the same class at the beginning of the year separate widely in power to learn new lessons before the middle of the year. In such cases a class should be broken up to prevent the twofold injury, namely, to the bright pupil by assigning him too short lessons, and to the dull pupil by assigning him more than he can well accomplish.

The teacher, even after forming classes in writing, reading, and spelling, has twelve to fifteen lessons to hear in a forenoon and nearly as many more for the afternoon. There is an average of less than ten minutes for each recitation. The ideal of the recitation or class exercise is that the teacher probe to the bottom the pupil's preparation of his lesson, and correct bad habits of study. If the pupil fails to master by sufficient industry the details—the facts and external items—the teacher counsels and reproves, requiring more work on the same lesson. If he finds that the details are mastered the teacher next tests the combinations, the thoughts that the pupil has used in connecting one fact with another and in seeing relations. Facts are connected so as to form a science when each one is made to throw light on every other fact, and all explain each. So a lesson is learned properly when the pupil can place each item in its systematic relation to the whole. He must understand the bearings of all; he must think out the interrelations.

Hence it happens that the good teacher is not satisfied with a memoriter recitation of the details of the lesson—still less with a word-for-word rendition of the text-book. Not the mere words of the book, nor even the disconnected facts or details which the words indicate, but to bring out the thought which unites these details and explains them, is the main object of the good recitation. But such a recitation requires time. The teacher cannot probe the pupil's knowledge in five minutes and correct his bad habits of study—nor in ten minutes. In the necessarily brief recitation of the ungraded school there is barely time to test the pupil's mastery of the external details of the lesson, the mere facts and technical words. It is for this reason more especially that the rural school has been the parent of poor methods of instruction—of parrot memorizing and of learning words instead of things.

At the beginning of this century only one-thirtieth of the inhabitants of the United States lived in towns of 8,000 people or upwards, and more than 90 per cent. of all the public schools were ungraded schools. The question has often been asked how it is that so many able men who became scholars and statesmen and professional men of eminence could have come from schools as poor as the rural school is said to be. Such eminent men as were produced in those times came from the rural school; there were few graduates from graded schools to compete with them. Of the men now living, past the middle age of life, nearly all received their early education in the rural ungraded school, because even as late as 1850 at least 80 per cent. of all the public schools were ungraded, there being only 12½ per cent. of the population resident in cities. The rural school threw on the pupil the burden of his education. He was obliged to get his knowledge from books, such books as he could come to possess. Bright pupils do pretty well by themselves if given good books and taught how to read and to understand the technique used in the elementary books of mathematics, grammar, and the other liberal arts. Any country boy who acquires a love for books, who has access to the best ones, and studies them with energy, will by middle age become a learned man.

In the ideal classified school the teacher has two classes of pupils, each class containing within it pupils substantially at the same stage of advancement. The pupils of a given class recite together in all the branches, and the teacher has a half hour for a lesson and can go into the dynamics or causal relations of the facts and events treated.

Each pupil in a class learns as much from his fellow pupils as from the teacher direct; for the teacher draws out of the class its store of observations and reflections on the topic of the lesson. He shows up the one-sidedness of the preparation of the individual pupil; some have neglected this point and some that other point. Each has probably neglected something. But, on the other hand, each of the diligent ones has brought forward something new that is valuable to his fellows. Each pupil finds through the recitation of the others that they have seen some things that had escaped his notice, although he supposed that he understood thoroughly the book presentation of the subject. His teacher suggests many new ideas and criticises the one-sidedness of the views of the pupils and also, it may be, of the text-book. All the statements of the book are brought to the test of verification—either through the child's experience or through other authorities. The child thus learns the method of study.

The ideal classified school can teach and does teach proper methods of study; the rural school cannot do this effectively in its five- or ten-minute recitations. It is because of this that wise directors of education have desired the consolidation of small schools into large schools wherever practicable. Two schools of ten each furnish on an average one-half as many recitations if united as they do when separate, owing to the possibility of pairing or classifying pupils of the same degree of advancement. Ten such schools united into one will give 100 pupils, with a possibility of classes of ten each, which can be more efficiently taught than before, because the pupil can learn more in a class than by himself. The class in the hands of a good teacher is a potent instrument for reaching all sides of the pupil's observation and reflection. Again, it is evident that five teachers can teach the 100 pupils united in one school far better than the ten teachers were able to teach them in the ten separate schools. If still further consolidation were possible and 400 pupils were united in one school, the classification might be improved to such a degree that a teacher could easily take the charge of two classes of twenty pupils, and ten teachers could do far better work for each pupil than was done by the forty teachers in the forty small rural schools before consolidation. Hence, economy becomes a great item in what are called "Union Schools."

Your subcommittee, in this discussion of the advantages of classifying and the corresponding disadvantages of the want of classifying, has assumed that as good teachers are supplied to the rural schools as to the schools of villages and cities—teachers of experience and skill, teachers of thorough academic and professional training in normal schools. It is assumed that states have made provision for good salaries in these ungraded schools, and that the license to teach requires professional training.

It is admitted as a fact, however, that the average rural school-teacher receives a small salary—not more than one-half that of the teacher in the city or large village. It is true, as reported by the Subcommittee on Maintenance of Schools, that some states, notably California, New Jersey,

Massachusetts, Rhode Island, and others to a greater or less degree, are providing, by a wise distribution of school money, to secure skillful teachers for these small, ungraded schools. But the evils above described as appertaining to instruction in ungraded schools are of such a character as not to yield to ordinary remedies.

Your subcommittee would call special attention at this point to the evil results that come from the attempt to remedy the defects of the rural school by forcing on it the system of classification found in cities. It is assumed that some of the benefits of the close grading possible in cities will be gained for the rural schools if they can roughly group the whole school into three or four classes. A rural school of thirty pupils comprising children from six to sixteen years of age, and covering different degrees of progress from beginners up to those of eight or nine years of schooling, are grouped, let us suppose, into four classes or grades—thus leaving intervals of two or more years of school work between a given group and the next one above it.

Your subcommittee has already pointed out the evils of classifying pupils in such a way as to bring together pupils differing in degree of advancement by intervals of two years. In fact, it has been found in city schools that one year's interval between classes is too much. The greatest danger of the graded school system in cities comes from holding back bright pupils for the sake of the slower and duller pupils. Next to this is the evil to the dull ones who are dragged forward at an unnatural rate of progress to keep up to the average rate of the class. The best pupils are engaged in "marking time," while the slowest are constantly spurred forward by teachers and parents to keep with their class, and their school years rendered miserable. Their self-respect is undermined by a false standard, that of mere speed in learning. The "marking time" injures the bright pupil by developing lax habits of study, while the forced marches of the slow pupil tend to destroy his poise of character. It has been found desirable, therefore, in city schools to make the intervals between classes as small as possible, so as to favor frequent transfers, namely, on the one hand, of bright pupils who are becoming capable of a greater amount of work into a higher class, and, if necessary, of those who are falling behind the average of the class into the next one below. Intervals of a half year are, therefore, adopted in a majority of the progressive city school systems, and many prefer intervals of a quarter of a year where it is practicable to make them, that is, where a large number of pupils makes possible the assignment of a requisite quota for each class. At the request of the subcommittee, Dr. E. E. White, an eminent authority on all that relates to school management, has furnished a statement of his views of classification in the rural school, illustrating them by a programme, which allows twenty-five minutes for each recitation. But the intervals between the classes amount to two years' work, and inasmuch as he expressly provides for capable pupils, letting them "work ahead of their classes," he leaves the question where it is left by the subcommittee, unless the pupils are supposed to do their "advance work" without the teacher's supervision (*Appendix I*).

Your subcommittee would respectfully call attention to the danger of attempting to classify the rural school in imitation of the city school as peculiarly liable to happen in those schools where professionally educated teachers are employed.

The state and city normal schools have very properly laid stress on grading and classification, and on the methods of instruction by classes, and have ignored individual instruction. Their graduates have mostly sought and obtained places in the graded schools of cities and villages. In fact, the graded schools have outbid the rural schools for teachers having professional training. But, with the new movement to secure better teachers for rural schools by larger appropriations from the state, it has happened that many experiments of classification are attempted which result disastrously in the manner described, namely, by demoralizing, or destroying the courage and ambition of the exceptionally bright and the exceptionally dull pupils. The charge has been made that such rural schools as adopt a partial grading system are apt to become stiflers of talent by placing a premium on the average scholars, and holding back the promising youth of the district.

It is obvious from this that where state normal schools furnish teachers for the rural districts there should be conducted a special inquiry into the influence of the size of the school in determining the uses and the dangers of grading and classifying pupils.

There is no doubt, moreover, that the abuse of classification is the crying evil of the schools of villages and small cities. For the average pupil these village graded schools are uniformly good, but they often work injury to the exceptional pupils and are in this respect sometimes inferior to the ungraded schoolsin sparsely settled districts.

Your subcommittee would here explain that the technical terms "grading" and "classification" are often used, as above, to signify the same thing, namely, the dividing of the pupils of a school into groups or classes, each containing children of the same, or substantially the same, degree of advancement. But another meaning is often given to one of these terms. The work of the year, more or less, is also called the work of a grade, and the work of the elementary school, consisting of the first eight years' work, is divided into eight grades. It will be readily understood in this second use of the word "grade" as covering a year's work that a school may be graded, that is to say, its work may be arranged upon a programme of eight grades, each one of which requires a certain modicum of reading, writing, arithmetic, geography, grammar, etc., for a year's work, and yet have only ten or twenty pupils, and perhaps these representing only three or four of the eight grades. By a graded school, as applied to such a state of things, is meant simply a school whose programme requires a regular sequence of studies and a full quota of studies for each pupil. If a pupil is at a certain degree of advancement in his arithmetic the programme of the graded system would place him also in a class correspondingly advanced in geography, history, reading, or other studies. But the small rural school has been called "ungraded" because it contains or may contain pupils of all grades, from the lowest to the highest, and consequently obliges the teacher to scatter his teaching force over a wide range of topics. The large school permits specializing by dividing the school in such a way that the pupils of one grade, or perhaps two grades, are taught by one teacher, the next one or two grades by another teacher, etc., permitting each teacher to specialize his work by giving him fewer topics to teach, and consequently insuring longer recitation periods and constant improvement in skill.

It is to be supposed that all schools will be graded in the sense that they will have a course of study, and that pupils will take up their branches of study in due order, and that these studies will be associated, so that a given degree of advancement in one study implies a given degree of advancement in another. What is properly called the correlation of studies presupposes that a certain degree of advancement in arithmetic corresponds to a certain degree of advancement in geography, reading, grammar, and other studies, all of these being determined within limits by the pupil's age. The word "grading," as a synonym for classification, is freely used by your subcommittee in this report, but it has discussed the topic indicated in the other and less frequent use of the word "grading" in that part of its report which follows, relating to the course of study.

THE COURSE OF STUDY.

Your subcommittee has assumed that the course of study in the rural schools should be substantially the same as that of the city schools. The differences should concern only minor details. It would, therefore, refer here to the report of the Committee of Fifteen for fuller details, and for the discussion of the grounds for selecting the several branches of the course of study. The course of study of the elementary school, whether urban or rural, should contain those branches which give the child an insight into the physical world and the means of conquering it for human uses, and also an insight into human nature and the motives that control the actions of men. The child should above all be taught how to combine with his fellows to secure reasonable ends. The windows of the soul are to be opened by the five branches of the course of study, thus enabling the youth to see (1) the conditions of inorganic nature by arithmetic and the elements of physics and chemistry; (2) the conditions of organic nature by studying plants and animals, the land, water, and air, and, besides these, the means that man invents and uses to connect each place with the rest of the world—these things belonging to geography. These two "windows" look out upon nature. The three others enable us to see man; (3) literature and art as revealing human nature, arousing pure and high aspirations in the youth, and freeing him from narrow and mean views of life; (4) the study of the structure of language, as found in the several subdivisions of grammar and rhetoric; (5) history, which treats of the greater self—of man as a social whole.

These five branches belong to all schools, for they relate to the substance of humanity and are necessary for entrance upon civilization. Besides arithmetic, geography, literature, grammar, and history, there are collateral branches that each school should include—some of them information studies, such as oral courses in the sciences, in history, and in the arts—others of the nature of disciplines, or arts of skill, such as vocal music, gymnastics, manual training, the art of cooking, and some special attention to the elementary principles of the useful arts practiced in the neighborhood of the school, namely, farming, horticulture, grazing, mining, manufacturing, or the like (*Appendices G* and *H*).

In general these collateral branches should relate to the pupil's environment and help him understand the natural features of that environment, as well as the occupations of his fellow-men in the neighborhood. There are two things to understand in this matter of the geography of the environment. First, what it is and how it came to be—its land and water, its mountains and river valleys, its climate and soil, its productions, mineral, vegetable, and animal, and their peculiarities, how they differ from the productions of the rest of the world. Second, the means by which man procures from nature what is useful for himself and others, manufactures it and uses it, or exchanges it with his fellow-men so as to share in the productions of all climes and places, no matter how far distant. If a comparison must be made, this second topic of elementary geography is more important than the study of the natural features of the environment, because it is more immediately useful to the pupil and to the community in which he lives.

Let the pupil beginning the subject of geography commence with what is nearest to his personal and social interests, namely, with the products of the industries of his section. Let his studies go out from these products in two directions: first, to the natural conditions which make these products possible and which furnish in general the raw material, secondly, in the direction of the purpose of this, the uses made of it, the things produced, the needs and wants of his fellow-men near and far;

and the productions of the other parts of the world which are needed in his section to complete the supply of articles for food, clothing, shelter, protection, and culture. These items, including natural production and the human occupations of manufacture and exchange, may be said to be the chief theme of geography as it should be taught in the elementary schools. But the home environment is also to be kept in mind by the teacher throughout the entire course. Arithmetic should gain concreteness of application by its use in dealing with home problems. Literature should be pointed and applied, so far as may be without becoming provincial, to the pupil's environment; and so the other branches—history, and even grammar—should be brought home to the pupil's knowledge or experience in the same way. The pupil should have prepared for his study a list of the chief provincialisms of speech to which his section is addicted, and to the peculiarities of pronunciation in which his neighborhood departs from the national or international standard of usage.

The Committee of Fifteen has already advanced the opinion that the industrial and commercial idea is the central idea in the study of geography in the elementary schools. It leads directly to the natural elements of difference in climate, soil, productions, races of men, religion, political status, and occupation of the inhabitants, and it explains how these differences have arisen in some measure through cosmic and geological influences. It should be the teacher's object to make the pupil understand, just as early as his growing capacity admits, the peculiarities of his habitat, leading him to study the land and water formations in his neighborhood, and giving him power to recognize in the visible landscape about him the invisible forces that worked in the past, and still are at work in the present, moulding these shapes and forms. On the basis of this knowledge of the elements of difference produced by nature in soil, climate, and configuration of the landscape, he should explain the grounds and reasons for the counter process of civilization which struggles to overcome these differences by bridging the rivers and tunneling the mountains—by using steamboat and railroad so as to unite each particular habitat with the rest of the world. He should see how man adapts to his needs the climate of each place by creating for himself a comfortable temperature, using for this purpose clothing and shelter, as well as fuels of wood and coal or derived from oils and gases, to protect from cold, and on the other hand utilizing ice or power fans, and creating easy access to summer dwellings on the heights of mountains, or at the seashore, to mitigate the heat. He turns the soil into a laboratory, correcting its lacks and deficiencies by adding what is necessary to produce the crop which he desires. He naturalizes the useful plants and animals of all climes in his own habitat. It is evident that the details of the process by which differences of soil, climate, and production arise, important as these are, should not be allowed to occupy so much of the pupil's time that he neglects to study the counter-process of industry and commerce by which man unites all parts of the earth to his habitat, and progressively overcomes the obstacles to civilization by making climate and soil to suit himself wherever he wishes.

To restate this important point in a word, it is true that the deeper inquiry into the process of continent formation, the physical struggle between the process of the upheaving or upbuilding of continents, and that of their obliteration by air and water; the explanation of the mountains, valleys and plains, islands, volcanic action, the winds, the rain distribution, is indispensable to a comprehension of the physical environment. But the study of the cities, their location, the purposes they serve as collecting, manufacturing, and distributing centers, leads most directly to the immediate purpose of geography in the elementary school, for it is the study of that civilization in which the pupil lives and moves and has his being.

Keeping this human standpoint in view all the time as a permanent interest, the inquiry into causes and conditions should proceed concentrically from the pupil's use of food and clothing to the sources of the raw materials, the methods of their production, and the climatic, geologic, and other reasons that explain their location and their growth. It is important in this as in all matters of school instruction to avoid one-sidedness. Although the human factor should receive the most emphasis, special care should be exercised lest the nature factor should be neglected.

Your subcommittee would refer to the discussion of this subject under the head of "Geography" in the report of the Committee of Fifteen for further illustration.

There is not much use in requiring instruction in branches not yet reduced to pedagogic form. It is necessary that matters taught should be so systematized for school use as to admit of arrangement in a progressive series of lessons, the first of which alone would be useful if no second lesson followed, and the subsequent lessons each useful if the pupil studied none of the following.

Each lesson when arranged in a pedagogic form leads up to the following lesson and makes it easy to grasp, just as each stair makes the next one easy to climb. For example, the first lesson in cookery is an exercise in accurate measurement by spoonfuls and cupfuls, etc., and calculated not only to aid in the next lesson and make it possible, but also to be of use through life in the kitchen. Concerted efforts are being made in agricultural colleges to reduce to pedagogic form the arts of the farm, the garden, and the forest.

THE PROGRAMME OF STUDIES.

Your subcommittee deems it important to call attention again in this place to the prevalence of a misconception in regard to the relation of the course of study to the system of grading and classification. Every school, whether ungraded or graded, should have a course of study minutely arranged so as to show the average or reasonable rate of progress of the pupil of a given age and advancement in the work of the school; but, as has already been shown, it is not required that the school shall contain classes in each and all of these grades, nor indeed classes at any given stage of progress in the course of study as laid down for any particular quarter or term of the year. Above all it must be understood that in laying down the quarters or other divisions of a grade or year's work it is not to be expected or desired that the pupils entering school at the beginning of the school year in the fall should commence at the beginning of any grade's work. If a class consisting of two or more individuals (or of one individual only) left off the previous year in the third quarter's work of the fourth grade, it should begin its work after vacation at the point where it left off, unless there are special reasons which require a review of some portions of the work.

The course of study is the measuring rod or scale which is used to determine at what point in the eight years' work of the elementary course a pupil has arrived. It should not be used as the Procrustean bed on which to stretch the work of the school in order to give it uniformity. It has happened not infrequently in the past that upon the first adoption of the graded system the superintendent of city schools held annual examinations on the completion of the work of the grade, and for this purpose insisted upon the unreasonable requirement that all of the pupils in the school should have begun the work of a grade on the first day of the year and should be expected to finish the grade work in the fourth quarter of the year. This was said to be for convenience of promotion—all pupils leaving the work of one grade and passing to the next were said to be promoted. This fiction has effected serious injuries in city schools. The apparent reason for such a system was the convenience of the superintendent who desired to make only one set of questions for each grade, and hold his examinations all at one time. If he had adopted a plan of preparing an examination for any class of pupils at the time when they should have completed the work of the grade (whether in the first, second, third, or fourth quarter), such a system need not have existed. The false idea of promotion has also been the source of great evils. When a pupil has finished the work laid down in the course of study for any grade, he should begin the work of the succeeding grade at once, and it is not necessary to have any special examination. The class teacher is supposed to examine her pupils from day to day, for each recitation is [illegible] should be made gradually [illegible] the end of the year [illegible] be a matter of at least weekly [illegible] a review character rather than [illegible]

[illegible] the elementary school will cover eight years' work [illegible] annual, or other [illegible] expected that the rural school [illegible] have each and every grade represented. [illegible] in the first grade, two in the [illegible] in the fourth grade, two [illegible] and seventh, and two in the eighth grade.

[illegible] that the discipline of the rural school [illegible] that of the city school. The [illegible] of regularity, punctuality, and industry are [illegible] a training of the will which [illegible] great importance in producing the future good citizen. It must not be [illegible] small, therefore the discipline is of less importance. The formation of habits of order, and of respect for the rights of [illegible] necessary for the good citizen, whether of country or town.

REMEDIES FOR THE EVILS OF THE RURAL SCHOOL.

Your Subcommittee would here point out that some of the evils of the rural school are due to its non-social character, its inability to furnish to each of its pupils that educative influence that comes from association with numbers of the same age and the same degree of advancement. The rural school furnishes only a few companions to the youth, and those either above him or below him in grade of progress in studies. The remedy for the evils of the ungraded school are suggested by this very feature or characteristic. Radical remedies in this case must all contain some device to bring together pupils of different districts and bring into wholesome competition with one another the pupils of the same grade of advancement.

Transportation to Central Schools.—The collection of pupils into larger units than the district school furnishes may be accomplished under favorable circumstances by transporting at state or local expense all the pupils of the small rural districts to a central graded school and abolishing the small ungraded school. This is the radical and effective measure which is to do great good in many sections of each state. As shown already by the Subcommittee on the Maintenance of Schools, Massachusetts, in which the plan began under the town superintendent of Concord, Mr. John B. Tileston (about the year 1878 in Concord, or even earlier in the town of Quincy, see *Appendix F*), paid in 1894–95 the sum of $76,608 for the transportation of children from small rural schools to central graded schools—213 towns out of a total of 353 towns and cities using this plan to a greater or less extent, and securing the two-fold result of economy in money and the substitution of graded for ungraded schools. The spread of this plan to Maine, Vermont, New Hampshire, Connecticut, Rhode Island, New Jersey, Ohio, and some other states (see Report of Bureau of Education for 1894–95, pp. 1469–82) demonstrates its practicability. Experiments with this plan have already suggested improvements, as in the Kingsville experiment in Ohio, where the transportation reached in all cases the homes of the pupils and yet reduced the cost of tuition from $22.75 to $12.25 a year for each of the fifty pupils brought to the central school from the outlying districts.

Improvement of Roads.—Wherever this plan of abolishing the small ungraded school is practicable it is by far the best remedy to be applied.

But there will remain large numbers of small ungraded rural schools in which the plan of transportation is not feasible by reason of great distances and poor roads. The Agricultural Department is seconding the efforts of many states to improve roads in rural districts. In many places road improvement is a necessary condition previous to the betterment of rural schools.

Special Appropriations for Small Rural Schools.—The device of securing skilled and professionally trained teachers by providing, as in California, a sufficient salary for each district, no matter how few its pupils (see *Appendix C*), has already been described by another subcommittee (that of matriculation. [illegible] a wise measure provided it does not hinder the consolidation of schools through the adoption of the Massachusetts plan. [illegible] to preserve the small ungraded school in places where consolidation is feasible, it will in the end be an injury to the cause of rural schools. Your subcommittee therefore ventures to call attention to the importance of adopting such laws as are operative in California, New Jersey, Massachusetts and New York for the better remuneration of rural school teachers and with a proviso that makes it a pecuniary advantage to a town to abolish its outlying ungraded schools and provide transportation to a central school.

Concentration of the Higher Grades of Pupils.—Where transportation of the whole school is not feasible it sometimes happens that the teaching may be very much improved by the transfer of two or three of the pupils of the higher grades who consume very much of the teacher's time. By transportation of these two or three pupils to the central school the teacher thus relieved may find time for much better instruction of the pupils in the lower grades who remain under his charge.

School Exercises at the Town or County Centers.—For the small ungraded schools that cannot be abolished, perhaps one-third of all the schools in the United States at the present time, your subcommittee suggests the provision of occasional meetings at town centers or county centers, perhaps twice a year or oftener, under the direction of township, union township or county superintendents, as the case may be. The meeting should have as its primary purpose the bringing together of advanced pupils—say sixth to ninth years' work for examination and comparison, the examinations to be chiefly written. Certificates should be given to those who complete the elementary course of eight years as a whole or in any one of its branches, permitting a pupil who passes in one branch this year, say in grammar or history, to pass in another branch at a subsequent examination whenever he presents himself. These examinations have been in operation in several counties of New Jersey for nearly twenty years.

This plan has an interesting and profitable illustration of many of its features in the operation of the Boxwell law in Ohio. (State School Commissioner Corson, Report 1895-96.) It was also carried out years ago in many particulars by Superintendent Wade in West Virginia.

The Proper Use of Competitive Examinations.—It is understood by your subcommittee that the prejudice against competitive examinations is well grounded. It often happens that schools are subjected to mere mechanical drill in order to secure a higher per cent. in this sort of examination. High per cents. cannot be obtained by entire classes upon work which requires not only a knowledge of details, but a knowledge of the causal relations underlying them. Your subcommittee desires to say that it does not recommend indiscriminate competitive examinations, but that it recommends written work and examinations which test the thinking ability of the pupil and lead him to considerate inquiries and accurate statements. High per cents. on anything except mechanical work, such as spelling, the multiplication table, the tables of weights and measures, and paradigms, are not desirable.

The plan of township and county union exercises of rural schools above described obviously includes the good feature of social interconnection, each pupil of the remote districts working consciously in combination with many others towards a common end, and all the pupils stimulated both in school and out of it by this social motive.

Promotion of Home Reading.--The excellence of the Chautauquan plan for the promotion of home study lies in the same feature. Each reader is stimulated and encouraged by the consciousness that he is working on a task common to the endeavors of a vast multitude. The task is dignified and ennobled by such social participation. The youth in the rural district is by this plan to be made a home student, and his education is thus to be extended beyond the school. He may have obtained his first recognition in the township examination while he was a member of a rural school. He is an object of semi-annual inquiry on the part of the township or county superintendent for years afterwards. Each new teacher that comes to the rural school is charged by the superintendent with the duty of looking up the young men and young women who made a record in the central examinations, and inquiry is made after their continued reading and study. This in itself will be a powerful influence to cause young people to continue self-culture by studying a prescribed series of books in years subsequent to the school period. It will add dignity and self-respect to the rural school-teacher who is charged with the work of making friendly inquiry into this school extension, and of offering help in case of application from any of the parties interested.

Reviewing Studies.—The rural school with its five-minute or ten-minute recitations cannot do much in the way of reviewing previous lessons. The good teacher in a graded school carries on from day to day a review of previous lessons. He gathers up and connects with the lesson of the day all the essential threads that bind it to what has gone before. It is this work of reviewing that will be assisted by the occasional examinations at the township center.

Moreover, the old evil of the rural school, that of having all pupils begin at the beginning of the book at the commencement of each annual term, will be removed. For the superintendent will have a record of the standing of the advanced pupils and will require a report from the new teacher as to their programme of study.

This plan also points to the utility of more written work in the rural school. A set of questions prepared beforehand and given to a pupil at the close of the week, as above recommended, will test not only his knowledge of the superficial details of his week's work, but also of his understanding of their deeper connections and principles, as no oral recitation could be made to do.

School Extension.—In this connection another branch of what is called "school extension" or "university extension" is practicable. Home reading can be managed from the same center, namely, the rural school. Everything that adds social importance to the rural teacher may be of service. It is evident that those pupils who have graduated from the public school and have entered upon the business of life may profitably carry on useful courses of reading in the various departments of literature and art, science, and history. The township or union township superintendent, in conjunction with the county superintendent or state superintendent, should set into operation as far as possible courses of home reading, employing the aid of the rural school-teachers to carry this into effect. A record containing the names of the persons who have undertaken home reading, the names of the books completed, and the dates of such completion, will form an interesting record. This home reading, moreover, should have its social gatherings in which there are discussions of the contents of particular books that are read. For this purpose the township superintendent or the county superintendent may select specially well-fitted persons who shall present analyses of the books and discussions of their contents. It is desirable that the course of home reading shall not be one-sided, but shall move in each of the three directions: literature, including poetry and prose; science, looking towards the organic and inorganic kingdoms of nature, the plant, the animal, and the details of matter and force; and towards archæology, ethnology, and sociology, and politics, history, biography, and art. One must not be altogether dissatisfied if it is found that the novel is the chief book in demand, especially in the first five years of the home reading circle. In our day the novel discusses every question of history, politics, sociology, and natural science. The old-fashioned novel which describes manners has its great use, too, in the fact that it gives to the people of whom we are speaking, the people of the rural districts, a ready knowledge of manners and customs of polite society. In this respect it is sometimes more useful than books of science and history.

Lancasterian or Monitorial Plan.—The topic of written work suggests a further topic of great importance in the rural schools, namely that of the occasional employment of older pupils in the work of supervising the exercises of less advanced pupils—a committee of two or three pupils to examine and mark the papers written by those studying geography; a monitor assigned for some hour in the day to inquire into the work of a backward or dull pupil who has reached a difficult place in arithmetic; a similar assignment of a pupil to help another in a grammar lesson or a history lesson; these are cases where the monitorial or Lancasterian system may have greater or less utility. It cultivates directive power and self-respect in a pupil to be called to the aid of the teacher. But the dangers of it are well known. No weak disciplinarian should try the monitorial system. On the other hand, every strong disciplinarian in the ungraded school can use some features of it to advantage.

The bane of the Lancasterian system was its use to furnish cheap assistant teachers in graded schools. It resulted in bringing into the schools a class of so-called "pupil-teachers," educational novices in the place of experienced and professionally trained teachers who ought to be everywhere employed in graded schools. Limited entirely to ungraded schools and to teachers with disciplinary power, the older pupils may profitably be employed to help in the work of the school. But they should not take up any work continuously—it should all be occasional, inasmuch as every thread of the school work must come under the eye of the schoolmaster frequently—daily, or nearly as often. If he has asked an older pupil to explain a point in arithmetic to a dull pupil the latter will show the degree of efficiency of that help, in the first recitation after it.

Another rule for the guidance of the teacher is: never to employ a monitor unless such assignment of work is useful both to the pupils taught and to the pupil-teacher.

A teacher may gain time needed for assistance of the advanced pupils in some important study by requiring in advance the assistance of these pupils in some of the following forms:

(1) Marking examination papers.

(2) Helping pupils over some difficulty in arithmetic, grammar, or other branch having strict logical sequence in its topics.

(3) In explaining the thought of a reading lesson to a backward pupil.

The effort of one pupil to explain to another a difficult passage of literature is one of the most profitable of all school exercises. There will undoubtedly be crudities in the explanation, but this will all come out under the teacher's subsequent tests, and the exercises will increase in profit through the final explanation given by the teacher.

(4) In assisting to test mere memory work on the part of a pupil, as in the case of the spelling of difficult words, the learning of paradigms in grammar, the learning of the required tables of weights and measures, the multiplication table, etc., or in any other necessary data that have to be fixed in the memory. In general, what is nearest to mechanical work may be supervised at times by monitors, and monitors may be useful in assisting in the preparation of thought lessons that are to come later

before the schoolmaster, as, in the example given, the getting out of the thought of a reading lesson — or even of a history lesson.

In conclusion your subcommittee would lay chief stress on the function of school extension, above sketched in outline, as the most profitable line of work for the improvement of the rural school — both pupils and teachers.

WILLIAM T. HARRIS, *Chairman*,
ADDISON B. POLAND,
LLOYD E. WOLFE.

Mr. Poland, while concurring in most particulars, desires to add the following statement:

While I concur most heartily in nearly all of the recommendations made by the Subcommittee on Course of Study, etc., I feel compelled to state that, in my opinion, the report somewhat exaggerates the difficulties and dangers of attempting to classify pupils in rural schools. It fails to discriminate between rural schools of ten pupils each and schools of a larger number, say thirty to sixty pupils each.

The general argument is based upon conditions that exist in a "school with ten pupils of ages from five to fifteen years;" and the conclusion drawn is that "for these reasons, classification as above described ought not to be expected in the (any) rural schools."

The conclusion, it seems to me, is altogether too general. My own observation of rural schools in the states of Massachusetts, New York, and New Jersey has led me to believe that their efficiency as a rule is in direct ratio to their wise and careful gradation; that, in fact, the best-graded schools are the most efficient. I am speaking, of course, of rural schools containing twenty-five pupils and upwards, where partial grading, at least, is generally believed to be practicable. Grant all the cases of individual hardship that the report truly affirms of misgraded pupils, yet the total loss of efficiency is immeasurably less than where no grading is attempted. Economy of teacher's time, longer recitation period, class emulation, etc., more than offset the disadvantage, often only theoretic, of a pupil's working in advance of his point of "maximum efficiency."

I am not, therefore, in full harmony with the report, in so far as it may have the effect to discourage teachers from attempting to classify pupils, whenever and wherever practicable.

A. B. POLAND.

Mr. Wolfe, while agreeing in many points with Mr. Harris, desires to make the following statement:

Perhaps my opinion may be characterized as explanatory or supplementary rather than dissenting. Believing with Dr. Harris that the chief aim of the report of the Committee of Twelve is to provoke thought, I make this contribution to that end. Complete unanimity no more exists among the members of this committee than among the great army of teachers for whom the report is prepared; nor is such unanimity desirable. The subject will be treated under the following heads:

1, *The present condition and trend of rural school grading and classification in the states of the Union;* 2, *Dr. Harris' plea for individual instruction rather than the instruction (in the same class) of pupils who are more than one year apart in their advancement;* 3, *The underlying pedagogic principles that seem to justify Dr. Harris in opposing the doctrine of his report to a body of opinion on classification and grading which is gathering volume and momentum with each decade;* 4, *Objections to the doctrine of the report.*

1. Recent decades have witnessed a strong movement in many of the states of the Union to model the rural school course of study, grading, and classification after the ideal of the city graded school. Several states prepare, publish, and distribute state courses of study for rural schools, and send out, at stated times, uniform examination questions prepared with reference to the course of study and the system of grading and classification set forth therein. In other states, the county school authorities issue the rural school course of study. In still other states, the school journals and associations hold up the grading and classification of rural schools as an ideal to be obtained in the near future.

2. The burden of Dr. Harris' report is: "Be ye not unequally yoked together." Just here a word of explanation of the expression "the ideal of the city graded school." This ideal is a course of study divided into at least eight yearly divisions, or grades of work, the pupils of the school being divided into eight corresponding divisions, or grades. A school is graded when the pupils of a certain year, or grade, are pursuing the work of a corresponding year, or grade, in all the branches. It is, therefore, evident that the word "grade" has two meanings — a grade of work and a grade of pupils. All pupils who are graded are classified, unless there be but one pupil to the grade. But all pupils who are classified are not necessarily graded. A pupil without classmates is graded when he pursues all the work of the corresponding grade, and yet he cannot be said to be classified. Pupils may be grouped in classes, and thus be classified, and yet not be graded, because they may be pursuing work of different grades. Dr. Harris is not opposed to a course of study for rural schools, nor to dividing that course of study into eight divisions, or grades of work, nor yet to grouping pupils into classes, or grades, provided classmates are not more than a year apart in their advancement. But most rural school courses of study necessitate the grouping of the pupils of the fifth and sixth years of advancement into one grade; also, the grouping of the pupils of the seventh and eighth years into another grade. It thus happens that

not only are pupils two years apart in their advancement yoked together in the same class and grade, but that, on alternate years, they are obliged to study the sixth year's work before the fifth, and the eighth before the seventh. It will thus readily be seen that the main thought of Dr. Harris' report is a standing protest against the grading and classification of pupils in the rural school as now practiced in many of the states.

3. We are now to inquire what pedagogic principles can be invoked to justify Dr. Harris in throwing the whole weight of his influence against the evolution of the ungraded country school into the graded school. And first, we must bear in mind that the subject of the report of Dr. Harris is "Instruction and Discipline in the Rural Schools." First, *efficient instruction must be adapted to the capacity of the learner, otherwise it cannot be grasped and assimilated.* Second, *other things being equal, instruction is more efficient when given to pupils associated in classes than when given to individual pupils.* Not only does a pupil gain much information from his classmates during a recitation, but the recitation gives him an insight into the individual capacities and peculiarities of those among whom he is to succeed or fail in professional or business life. Third, *efficient instruction requires a reasonable length of time for a class exercise.* In a city graded school, with at least one teacher for each grade of work, the three principles—adaptation of instruction to the capacity of the learner, grouping of pupils into classes, and a reasonable time for recitation—can be conserved. But, in a rural school with one teacher, to maintain one of these principles is to sacrifice another. The principle of the adaptation of instruction to capacity can be adhered to by dividing the pupils into eight grades of advancement; but such division gives a minimum time for recitation and a minimum association of pupils. If, however, pupils of the third and fourth, fifth and sixth, seventh and eighth years of advancement be grouped into three corresponding grades, we secure a longer time for recitation and a larger measure of association, but we violate the principle of adaptation of instruction to capacity, thus associating, in the same grade and class, pupils two years apart in their advancement. It thus appears that the problem of the most efficient instruction in a rural school with one teacher is one of maxima and minima. The principle of adaptation of instruction to capacity forever antagonizes the other two. A maximum adherence to it means a minimum adherence to the other two, and *vice versa*. Perfect adaptation of instruction to capacity would necessitate a grade for each pupil. Dr. Harris' report shows that he feels that, when pupils one year apart in advancement have been grouped in the same grade, this great principle of adaptation of instruction to capacity has been strained to its utmost limit, and that any sacrifice thereafter must come from other antagonistic and minor principles. His

report throughout shows that he considers adaptation of intruction to capacity the paramount and controlling principle; and the fact that he has made this the burden of his report shows with what trained acumen he has brushed aside the trivial and subsidiary, and has laid grasp upon the vital and fundamental. A still more universal principle underlies this valuable report. It is this: that the success of an institution of any kind — political, religious, economic, educational — depends upon its adaptation to its environment. A republic is, no doubt, abstractly the best form of government; but equally true is it that, under certain environment, an aristocracy or a monarchy is better than a republic. I take it, then, that Dr. Harris has been a spectator of this evolution of the rural school, with its peculiar environment, into the city graded school, with a very different environment, till he has said to himself: "This is a forced and artificial evolution." Having arrived at the conviction that the rural school with one teacher cannot, without injury, be metamorphosed into a graded school, Dr. Harris addresses himself to the problem of changing the present rural school conditions, (1) through transportation of pupils and (2) through pupil-teachers. Now this goes to the very heart of the question. For, through the transportation of pupils to central schools, the rural school conditions are transformed into city school conditions, and instruction can then proceed in harmony with the three principles above discussed. Or, if pupil-teachers are employed, or if the pupils of the higher grades — fifth, sixth, seventh, and eighth, or seventh and eighth only — be transported, the rural school condition will be in a measure removed, and instruction can proceed more in harmony with these principles. It is true that transportation of pupils now seems practicable only in a small portion of the territory of the United States, and that pupil-teaching meets with but little favor among rural school-teachers and pupils; but a careful study of the report of Dr. Harris will, no doubt, lead to a larger use of pupil-teachers and a much wider extension of pupil transportation, especially in the upper grammar grades. During the last few decades there has been in operation in many of the western states a strong evolutionary force, which has eliminated most of the high-school branches from the majority of the country schools. In such cases, the pupils who have completed the eight years' work of the country school are expected to find high-school instruction elsewhere at their own expense of tuition and transportation. May not this same evolutionary force, in its own due time, similarly eliminate from the rural schools the work of Grades 7 and 8? Whether such rejected pupils will be transported or not will depend upon the sentiment of the community. In favor of the ultimate transportation of not only Grades 7 and 8, but of higher grades, is that great socialistic force that has given birth to our free-school system, our postalsy stem, and our asylums for physical, moral, and mental delinquents. Having addressed himself to the modification of rural school environment through pupil transportation and pupil-teachers, the Doctor finds himself face to face with a great body of rural school conditions which are unmodified and at present unmodifiable. It is here that he makes his plea for individual instruction rather than the instruction, in the same class, of pupils who are more than a year apart in their advancement.

4. The branches of the eight years' course of the rural school are: writing, drawing, music; physiology, grammar, civil government; spelling, language, geography, history; reading; arithmetic. We shall be able to get a better understanding of the subject if we suppose a city school of eight grades, four rooms, and four teachers to be suddenly reduced to one-fourth its former number of pupils, rooms, and teachers. There will then remain one teacher, one room, eight grades of pupils and eight grades of work, and, say, forty pupils; that is substantially rural school conditions. This one teacher now finds that, while he has no more pupils to instruct than he had before, these pupils are scattered among the eight grades. If he adheres strictly to the former graded structure of the school, keeping each grade of pupils distinct in all the branches (allowing six recitations a day to each grade), he will have eight times six, or forty-eight, classes. This gives him an average of about five minutes for a recitation period. The inadequacy of this time for the development of a subject needs no comment. He must group these scattered pupils into classes, largely ignoring grades, and many of these classes will contain pupils from different grades. By almost unanimous consent it is agreed that the pupils of the eight grades can be grouped, for general exercises, in writing, drawing, and music, requiring but one recitation period for each branch. One recitation period will answer for each branch in grammar, physiology, and civil government; two recitation periods each in spelling, language, geography, and history; four in reading; five in elementary numbers and arithmetic. This gives twenty-three recitations, ranging from ten minutes in the lowest grades to twenty in the highest. It will be observed that I state above that many of these classes will contain pupils from different grades. Here appears the significance of my definitions of *class* and *grade* in the beginning of this discussion — definitions on which the teachers of this country are far from being a unit. The fundamental principle underlying *grading* is symmetrical development; the fundamental principle underlying *classifying* is harmonious development. Symmetrical development aims to advance the pupil with equal pace in all the branches; harmonious development aims to advance him in harmony with his individual capabilities. Many of the pupils of our best graded schools are classified in violation

of the principle ot harmonious development. This statement takes no note of mistakes in grading, by which pupils are assigned to the wrong grades. The grading of schools in accordance with the principle of symmetrical development necessitates a violation of the principle of harmonious development. I have reference to those pupils who are assigned to the right grade in a majority of the branches they pursue, but who, in one or more branches, belong to grades above or below the one to which they are assigned. It, therefore, follows that the reorganization consequent upon transforming the four-teacher school into the one-teacher school would bring some pupils into classes better suited to their abilities than the classes to which the graded system had assigned them, thus bringing about a classification more in harmony with the principle of adaptation of instruction to the capacity of the learner. Classification and its correlative principle of harmonious development are the corner stone of the rural school; grading and its correlative principle of symmetrical development are equally fundamental to the city school. In a graded school the pupil is assigned to classes belonging to one grade only; in the country school he is assigned to classes adapted to his capacity, regardless of the number of grades represented by these classes. I institute no comparison here as to the relative merits of the principles—harmonious development and symmetrical development—but simply state the fact of their relations respectively to the city and rural schools.

If practical adaptation of instruction to the capacity of the pupil were really attainable in the graded school, I should hesitate to recommend a classification that would group, in one class, pupils more than a year apart in their advancement. But such adaptation is largely ideal and theoretical. However well the school be graded, the strongest pupils and the weakest are separated by a long distance in the character, or grade, of their work. Whether in the primary, the grammar, the high school, the college, or the university, a certain per cent. of the students do most of the highest order of work. These strongest pupils discover and develop the deepest relations. The weaker pupils soon learn to repeat the stereotyped expressions of these relations, and to store them away in their memories to be fished forth at stated intervals by the written test. The apostle Paul, that he might not offend his brother, would eat no more flesh while the world stood; but a large per cent. of the students of all grades, not from fear of offending their brother, but from their very mental constitutions, abstain, with equal fidelity, from the strongest mental diet. I can select, at random, one-half the pupils from Grades 6 and 7 of a city school, and put them to studying, indifferently, North America, South America, Europe, or Asia, and the former leaders in Grades 6 and 7 respectively will still lead. What is true of geography is true of history, civil government, physiology, spelling and reading, and, in a measure, of grammar and arithmetic. Certain pupils are mentally built for accuracy, clearness, depth, and power; others, for relative inaccuracy, obscurity, shallowness, and weakness. A rule requiring, as a condition of promotion, that all pupils, of any certain grade, should do as high an order of work as is being done by some of the pupils of that grade, would virtually stop the wheels of promotion. Many of the pupils would never reach a higher grade; many others would do so only after repeated attempts and failures.

The gist of Dr. Harris' objection to grouping pupils who are more than a year apart in their advancement is that the more advanced pupils will be kept marking time, while the less advanced will be dragged along at an unnatural rate. My answer is that the stronger pupils will do the higher order of thinking, just as they always do, while the weaker pupils will do the lower order of thinking, as they always do, getting some knowledge from the books, some from the teacher, and some from their stronger classmates. The rural school has the advantage over the city school in that its pupils learn much from the recitation of classes to which they do not belong. In a graded school, the walls of the schoolroom shut pupils out from what is being recited in other grades. In a rural school, the pupil can listen to the recitation of any grade. You tell me that this is absorption, that the pupil gets this outside knowledge at the expense of the preparation of his own lessons, and that the practice of listening to other recitations militates against the principle that a great aim in education is to learn to master the printed page; but it is nevertheless the testimony of many of our greatest educators that the knowledge thus obtained by them in the country school was invaluable. The mind has strange and subtle methods of threading its way to knowledge, not always in harmony with the pedagogue's theory. What teacher in arithmetic (who has had the courage, temporarily at least, to lay aside his cut-and-dried solution-formulæ) has not been surprised and delighted at the ingenious methods different pupils have of solving problems? What master of the topical method in history, civil government, or literature has not marveled at the rich relations revealed by pupils when left free to take their own initiative? A nation does not postpone its entrance upon a career of republican government till all its members are ready for self-government. The members of a church are not of equal intellectual or spiritual caliber, nor are the members of a family; yet they are associated in one class—the state, the church, the family. In actual life, persons of all degrees of advancement behold alike the same procession of the heavens, the same succession of seasons, the same world-happenings; but all do not get the same kind and amount of information from the marshaling of the constellations, the budding and fruiting of spring and summer, and the drama of events daily unfolding. I grant that the examples above given are not identical with the thing to be exemplified; but they present important elements of similarity. Finally, I am fully convinced that the rural school conditions necessitate a departure from the doctrine so ably laid down by Dr. Harris, and I believe principles can be found to justify such departure. Whether or not I have found these principles and set them forth in this supplementary report is another question.

L. E. WOLFE.

APPENDICES.

CONTENTS.

		PAGE.
Appendix A.	Some Sociological Factors in Rural Education, - - - - -	123
Appendix B.	Permanent School Funds and Receipts of School Moneys, - -	126
Appendix C.	California System of School Maintenance, - - - - - -	130
Appendix D.	The County as the Unit of School Organization, - - -	132
Appendix E.	Comparative Cost of Township and District Systems, - -	133
Appendix F.	Transportation of Pupils and Extract from Quincy, Mass., Report	135
Appendix G.	Enrichment of Rural School Courses and Remarks on a Course of Study for Rural Schools, - - - - - - - - - - -	142
Appendix H.	The Farm as the Center of Interest, - - - - - - -	152
Appendix I.	The Country-School Problem, with Course of Instruction for Rural Schools, - - - - - - - - - - - - -	161
Appendix J.	Negro Teachers for Negro Schools, - - - - - - -	185
Appendix K.	Work of Hon. J. W. Bradbury and Teachers' Seminary at Plymouth, N. H., - - - - - - - - - - -	188
Appendix L.	New York State School Library, with a List of Books for Rural Schools and Communities, - - - - - - - - -	189
Appendix M.	Hygiene and Health in Public Schools with Schoolhouse Plans,	193
Appendix N.	School Systems of Ontario; New Brunswick; Manitoba; France; and Norway, - - - - - - - - - - - - -	198
Appendix O.	Extension Work in Rural Schools, - - - - - - -	202
Appendix P.	Institutes in Pennsylvania, - - - - - - - - - -	204
Appendix Q.	Thomas Arnold. A Study, - - - - - - - -	205
Appendix R.	Intellectual and Moral Education, - - - - - - -	206
Appendix S.	Continuous Sessions in Normal Schools, - - - - - -	207

APPENDIX A.

SOME SOCIOLOGICAL FACTORS IN RURAL EDUCATION.

[From a paper read before the Department of Superintendence of the N. E. A., at Jacksonville, Fla., February, 1896, by B. A. Hinsdale, Professor of the Science and the Art of Teaching in the University of Michigan. (See "Journal of Proceedings and Addresses of the Thirty-fifth Annual Meeting, held at Buffalo, July, 1896," pp. 261–9.) A discussion on the same lines, but much fuller, will be found in Dr. Hinsdale's work, entitled "Studies in Education," pp. 313–38.]

First we will give our attention to density of population. The importance of this element in the rural school problem becomes obvious at a glance. In populous districts fewer schools and districts relatively are called for, while, at the same time, owing to the larger numbers and the more varied attainments of the pupils, the system can be more fully developed. The school and the home, under the present system, cannot be far apart; otherwise children will attend the school with difficulty, or not at all. Once more, the interest and enthusiasm of pupils and teachers depend directly upon the number and the ability of the pupils present. For the majority of children individual instruction, or anything closely approaching it, is not to be commended. Aristotle condemned such instruction on political grounds. It may also be condemned on pedagogical grounds Children need the inspiration of numbers. Besides, numbers contain ethical value. As a rule, you can no more make a good school out of a half dozen pupils than you can make a powerful galvanic battery with one or two pairs of plates. Then, again, the question of cost is directly involved. Where pupils are scattered and the schools are small education is necessarily very expensive, provided it is at the same time good. Generally, however, it is bad.

To illustrate: Some twenty years ago I investigated one of the old townships in northern Ohio with respect to its school condition, and with these results: Schools, 7 in number; youth of school age enumerated, 191; pupils enrolled in schools, 103; average daily attendance, 71; average size of schools, 10 pupils; largest enumeration in any district, 85; smallest, 12; largest enrollment, 37; smallest, 3; largest daily attendance, 25; smallest, 3; largest cost per pupil in any district, $42.60; smallest, $18.56. The average cost per pupil the same year in the state was $13.36. Argument is not needed to show that this was an inefficient and wasteful township system of education. How much better it would have been if the seven schools could have been consolidated, thus putting all the pupils under two or three teachers. I remember a school in Ohio, within sight of my own home, that was kept in session a whole summer with but two pupils in attendance, and those two were all there were in the district. My father, who was a man of close observation, was in the habit of remarking in my boyhood that a farm of 1,000 acres situated all in one school district would, as a rule, spoil the school, by reducing the number of children, and I have often seen confirmation of his statement.

The Census Office at Washington considers those parts of the country that have a population of less than two to the square mile unsettled. These parts amount to a little more than one-third of the whole, not including Alaska. Once more, in constructing its tables and maps to show density of population, the Census Office excludes the cities, or those centers of population containing 8,000 persons or more. In 1890 the second of the two rules excluded 443 centers of population, containing an aggregate of 18,835,670 inhabitants, or 29.12 per cent. of the whole.

The whole country, less the parts excluded by the first rule, the Census Office has divided with reference to certain *maxima* and *minima* of population, as follows:

2 to 6 to a square mile,	592,037	square miles.
6 to 18 " "	394,943	"
18 to 45 " "	701,847	"
45 to 90 " "	235,148	"
90 and above "	24,312	"
Total,	1,947,287	"

The Superintendent of the Census makes some interesting remarks upon the economical significations of these statistics, as follows:

"These limits define in a general way the extent and prevalence of various classes of industries. The first group, two to six to a square mile, indicates a population mainly occupied with the grazing industry, or a widely scattered farming population. The second group, six to eighteen, indicates a farming population with systematic cultivation of the soil, but this either in an early stage of settlement or upon more or less rugged soil. The third group, eighteen to forty-five to a square mile, almost invariably indicates a highly successful agriculture, while in some localities the beginnings of manufactures have raised into this group a difficult farming region. Speaking generally, agriculture in this country is not carried on with such care and refinement as yet to afford employment and support to a population in excess of forty-five to a square mile. Consequently the last two groups, forty-five to ninety and ninety and above to a square mile, appear only as commerce and manufactures arise, and personal and professional services are in demand."

He might have introduced education with equal propriety. The statistics given throw a direct light upon school material, and an indirect one upon school resources. Much the same may be said of churches and the intellectual and moral instruments of society generally. There is, therefore, cause for deep regret that such large areas of country are falling off in population. From 1880 to 1890 more than 400 counties, or about five times as many as there are in the state of Ohio, suffered in this way.

But, secondly, the character of the population must be considered as well as its number. It is evident that a certain homogeneity is very conducive to public education. The children of such a community can be educated together, and hence more cheaply and more effectively. One system of schools suffices for all classes. But if the children must be segregated in different schools according to non-educational tests, one of two things will certainly happen: either public education will become expensive, or it will become inferior in quality. Looking at the subject from this point of view merely, it is unfortunate that in large portions of the United States popular education should be embarrassed by the race question. In 1890 the per cents. of white and colored population, respectively, were distributed in the five great divisions that the Census Office recognizes in the following manner:

North Atlantic States,	98.4	1.6
South " "	63.2	36.8
North Central States,	98.0	2.0
South " "	68.3	31.7
Western States,	94.8	5.2

If per cents. for the states severally were given the contrasts would be still more striking. The per cent. of colored people in New Hampshire, for example, was .18, while in South Carolina it was 59.87. Now there is little probability that the educational value of such statistics as these will be exaggerated. The presence of a large colored population in any state or other community tends to affect popular education unfavorably in three ways: to increase its cost, to make its quality inferior, and to lower both the intellectual and moral level of society and its money-earning capacity.

In one respect the rural parts of the country are better off, upon the whole, than the cities. Religious differences do not disturb popular education to the same extent. Relatively, parochial schools are much fewer in number.

In the third place, the wealth of society is a very important factor in education, and particularly in rural education. Naturally the per-capita wealth of the several divisions of the country varies greatly. In 1890 these were the averages:

North Atlantic States,	$1,132 per capita.
South Atlantic States,	579 "
North Central States,	1,129 "
South Central States,	583 "
Western States,	2,250 "

In the North Atlantic states the maximum was in Rhode Island, $1,459 per capita; the minimum in Maine, $740. In the South Atlantic states the maximum was in Maryland (excluding the Federal District), $1,043 per capita; the minimum in South Carolina, $348.

Now it is perfectly well understood that a good modern system of state education can be supported only at great public cost. Still more, the cost is all the time increasing. Our total expenditures for this purpose the last twenty years have been mounting upward by leaps and bounds. At present the money expended by the states together is $175,-000,000 annually, which is more than twice the cost of supporting the national government before the Civil War. Education has come to be a great item in the budget of every highly civilized country in the world.

Fourthly, the character of the population in respect to its money-earning power must be taken into the account. The size of the average family and the relative number of taxpayers, or the adult males, and their productiveness as economical agents, all become educational factors of much importance. If families are large, the number of children to be schooled is proportionally great; which, under some conditions, would add to the efficiency of the schools, and under other conditions would increase their cost. Then the larger the relative number of adult males, and the greater their producing power, the higher their intelligence and educational needs, and the greater their ability to provide the sinews for educational warfare. We need not enter into the correlation of the size of the family and its material condition. It still remains true, however, as in the time of Solomon, that the destruction of the poor is their poverty. In respect to educational possibilities there is the greatest difference between a community having a high ratio of adult male population of large wealth-producing power and a community having a small ratio of such population with small wealth-producing power. The country taken together in 1890–91 showed surprising variations in this respect. There were 91.4 taxpayers for each 100 children six to eighteen years of age; but in different sections the ratio varied from 65.9 to 100 in the South Central states to 156.7 to 100 in the western states. In South Carolina there were but fifty-five adult males to earn the money with which to school 100 children, thirty-two of whom were colored men. Comparing the taxpayer factor with the per-capita tax for education, some very striking results are obtained. Dr. Harris has shown[1] that in Montana a contribution of $5.85 per taxpayer furnished in 1890–91 $16.02 for each child of school age, while in Texas a contribution of $6.55 per taxpayer produced a result of only $4.48 for each child. Mississippi, after raising per taxpayer about half what Nevada raised, had only about one-eighth as much as the latter state for each child of school age. The causes that affect the ratio of school children to the adult population are beside the present inquiry. But it is perfectly obvious that this is an educational factor of much value.

Little logical acumen is required to see either the educational value or the social congruence of such factors as the wealth per capita of the country or of any state in it,

[1] Report of the Commissioner of Education, 1890–91, p. 24.

the expenditure per capita for public education, the expenditure for the same purpose per pupil in the schools, and the per cent. of illiteracy, taking the population ten years old and more into the account. These items are shown in the following table:

North Atlantic States,	$1,132	$2.06	$23.65	6.2
South Atlantic States,	579	.96	8.25	40.1
North Central States,	1,129	2.81	19.96	6.7
South Central States,	583	.98	7.59	39.5
Western States,	2,250	3.55	34.03	11.6

It must be remembered, however, that these statistics are, in part, now several years old.

Perhaps I should observe that statistics may be taken too seriously. We need not now examine the arguments by which Mr. Buckle and others like him have sought to show that man has no free agency, but that society is governed in all its movements by laws as fixed as those of material nature. It answers the present purpose to say that the highest state of education is not always found in the most populous, the richest, or the most homogeneous states. France is much richer than Germany, but she is inferior in education. England is far richer than Scotland, and has been behind her in schools of popular education since the time of John Knox. Relatively, Rhode Island is the richest and most populous of the American states, but she has never led the American common-school column. There are other factors than those that are distinctly social which enter into the problem. Educational traditions and ideas, public spirit, and force of character all tell. At the same time it would be the sheerest folly to exclude or belittle the material factors that enter into public education and all similar social interests.

APPENDIX B.

PERMANENT SCHOOL FUNDS.

I. CONNECTICUT.

It began to be noticed as early as 1824 that the Connecticut common-school fund was not working altogether as it had been expected to work. (See James G. Carter's "Letters to the Honorable William Prescott, LL.D., on the Free Schools of New England, with Remarks upon the Principles of Instruction," Boston, 1824.) Connecticut, however, made the fatal mistake of distributing the income of the fund to the towns and districts without requiring them to raise by taxation an equal amount, or, indeed, any certain amount, for the support of their schools. In 1853 Connecticut was expending on her schools only one-third as much per pupil as the neighboring states were expending, while she was raising by taxation only one-tenth or one-twentieth part as much as they were raising per pupil. Dr. Henry Barnard says: "Taxation for school purposes had not only ceased to be a cheerful habit of the people, but was regarded as something foreign and anti-democratic. The supervision of the schools had become in most societies a mere formality, and the whole system seemed struck with paralysis." And yet the governor of the state had sounded the alarm as early as 1826, while prominent citizens had counseled other states not to repeat the mistake that Connecticut had made. (See a valuable article on the Connecticut School Report, subhead, "The School Fund and Its Effects," in *The American Journal of Education and School Review*, edited by Absalom Peters and Henry Barnard, Vol. I. (1856), pp. 590-9.)

II. TEXAS.

Mr. C. Lombardi, member of the school board of Houston, Tex., contributed to *The Business Record* of that city, November, 1896, the following article, entitled "Our School Fund":

First of all comes the question of revenues. While we have been boasting of our princely educational fund, consisting of millions of acres of land, we have forgotten to inquire into the location, character, and value of this land. It was long taken for granted that any kind of wild land would increase in value as time passes. It was argued that as the amount of land in any country is a fixed quantity, and as population tends to increase steadily, land could not but increase in value as population increases. But a rude shock awaited these plausible theories when suddenly land values began to decline, not only here, but everywhere, in other states as well as in Texas, in Europe as well as in America, along with the depreciation of agricultural products. Many circumstances led to this result, chief of which is the long interval of peace among civilized nations, thus liberating and increasing an immense productive force, formerly largely devoted to the destruction of both life and the means of life; the facilities and cheapness of transportation, and the opening up of immense tracts of land in other portions of the world, made accessible to cheap labor. It was found that the most abundant commodity in the universe is raw, untilled land.

Then as to the character of the land set aside for our school fund. Time was when any kind of land was supposed to have some value, if only for pasturage or mining purposes. Here again a revolution has taken place, making wild grazing lands almost valueless, and mining lands in this state quite so. The demand for range cattle has been transferred to the domestic-fed cattle raised on small farms, and our great cattle industry of the past has practically passed away.

As for mining lands containing iron, copper, and coal, the great abundance of all these found nearer to market and closer to lines of transportation, together with the greater facilities for working old mines afforded by modern invention, and the agitation for a lower tariff policy throughout the South, has put a quietus to any thought of developments or investments in Texas for some time to come.

Hence, while our school fund derived from the sale and lease of land has not increased in value, the scholastic population has largely increased, and the financial demands for public education are increasing every day. They are increasing not only by reason of the natural increase of the scholastic population, but also by reason of the very progress achieved in educational methods and the higher ideal attained. Not only has this higher ideal induced more people to send children to school, but it is demanding a higher standard of ability and character in the teachers, and this costs more money.

What is the remedy? Obviously special taxation as a supplement to our revenue from the school fund. Either that or a curtailing of our school facilities, and this last is not to be thought of. But here again we labor under a singular disadvantage from the fact that we have a school fund, that we have exaggerated its importance and value, and indulged in extravagant boasts about it. Our people have become too much accustomed to rely on this great school fund, and will be unwilling to entertain the idea of raising a school revenue by taxation. Had we never had a school fund, or never talked about it, our people would probably not hesitate to tax themselves heavily for the benefit of the schools, as do the people of Colorado, for example. But it will be difficult to reconcile the glory of our great school fund, which has been dinned into the taxpayer's ears, with the necessity of going deep into his pockets to supply the educational deficit.

It is just as well that we should begin to consider this matter and bring it before the people. It is bound to become an issue sooner or later, and the sooner the better. We must not wait until we are confronted with a deficit so great as to paralyze our schools and destroy their efficiency. Other things demand the attention of the friends of popular education, but this is fundamental.

APPENDIX C.

THE CALIFORNIA SYSTEM OF SCHOOL MAINTENANCE.

Every portion of this state is embraced in the 3,243 school districts into which California is at present (1896) divided. Under our law every city and incorporated town constitutes a separate school district, unless subdivided by the legislative authority thereof. Only two cities of the state are subdivided into separate school districts.

SOURCES OF REVENUE.

STATE—

(1) *Permanent Fund.*—The permanent school fund of the state consists of the receipts from the sales of school lands (sections 16 and 36 of each township), and now amounts to $4,000,000. The interest on this fund, together with the interest on school land, yields an annual income amounting to $260,000, or more.

(2) *Poll Tax.*—There is a state school poll tax of $2 levied on each male inhabitant, between the ages of twenty-one and sixty years. From this source the state school fund receives nearly $370,000 annually.

(3) *Collateral Inheritance Tax.*—There is a tax of 5 per cent. on collateral inheritances, which is paid into the school fund of the state. The amount received from this source, of course, varies from year to year.

(4) *State School Tax.*—The statutes require that there be levied on all property in the state an ad-valorem tax sufficient to raise the sum of $7 yearly for each census child. On account of the allowance made in levying the tax for possible delinquencies, the actual sum realized is somewhat in excess of $7 per child.

The revenue derived from these four sources for the fiscal year ending June 30, 1896, was:

(1) From Permanent School Fund,	$264,429.00
(2) From State Poll Tax,	362,794.12
(3) From Collateral Inheritance Tax, etc.,	102,688.45
(4) From State School Tax (ad valorem),	2,320,270.08
Total State Moneys,	$3,050,181.65

The school census for the year was 323,130. The average, therefore, per census child from all state sources was $9.43.

COUNTY—

Each county is required by law to levy a county school tax, the maximum rate of which shall not exceed 50 cents on each $100 of taxable property, nor the minimum rate be less than sufficient to raise $6 for each census child in the county.

DISTRICT—

The charters of cities having boards of education provide for the levying of school taxes within the corporate limits, in addition to the state and county school taxes.

School districts governed by boards of school trustees may, by vote of the people, levy additional taxes for school purposes, the maximum rate being fixed at 30 cents on each $100 of taxable property. They may also, in any year, levy a tax of 70 cents per $100 for building purposes.

BONDS—

Any school district in the state may, by a two-thirds vote, bond itself for the purchase of lots, erection of buildings, etc.

The constitution and law of the state require that all property shall be assessed at its "full cash value." The word "property," as defined in the constitution, includes "moneys, credits, bonds, stocks, dues, franchises, and all other matters and things real, personal, and mixed, capable of private ownership."

DISTRIBUTION OF SCHOOL FUNDS.

For the purpose of fixing a primary base for the distribution of school funds, there is taken, during the month of April, each year, a census of all the children in the state between the ages of five and seventeen years. The term "census children" must not be confounded with the term "children of school age," as the latter embraces all children between the ages of six and twenty-one years.

The method of distribution is unique, combining, as it does, the enumeration and average daily attendance methods. Its strong point is the marked recognition it gives to the principle that the state, as a whole, is interested in the education of all its citizens. To that end the rich and populous centers are made to contribute to the poor and sparsely settled districts. At the same time the local and county taxes imposed are a constant reminder that each locality must share with the state the responsibility of educating its youth.

All state school moneys are apportioned by the superintendent of public instruction to the several counties in proportion to the number of school-census children, as shown by the returns of the school-census marshals of the preceding school year, and the moneys so apportioned are distributed to the several county treasurers by the state treasurer, on the order of the state superintendent.

The county school funds are collected by the county tax collector, and turned over by him through the county auditor to the county treasurer, who is the custodian of all school funds. It is the duty of each county auditor to notify the county superintendent of schools of all school moneys received — both state and county. The entire revenue is distributed by the county superintendent of schools to the various school districts (including cities) on the basis of the number of teachers to which each district is entitled. This number is determined by calculating one teacher for every seventy census children, or fraction thereof of not less than twenty census children, in the district. He then apportions to each district $500 for every teacher assigned to it. Should a district have less than twenty and more than nine census children, he must apportion to it only $400. Districts having less than ten census children lapse, unless supported by voluntary contribution. Such districts usually lapse, their territory being absorbed by adjoining districts. This provision of the law is not intended to govern the number of teachers actually employed by a district; it simply furnishes a basis for determining the amount of money to which a school district is annually entitled from the public funds.

All school money remaining on hand after distributing $500 (or $400, as the case may be) per teacher is apportioned to the several districts in proportion to the average daily attendance in each district during the preceding school year. The amount varies in the different counties, ranging from $2 or $3 per child in average daily attendance in a few sparsely settled counties to $10 or $12 in the more densely populated. The average for the entire state is not far from $8 for every child in average daily attendance.

In distributing the school money the county superintendent considers each city in the county, no matter how large, simply as a school district, which it is under the law; and for this purpose each city superintendent must report school statistics to the county superintendent, just as does the teacher in the most insignificant district in the county.

As an illustration of the method of distribution, suppose district "A" has a census roll of 1,000 children, and an average daily attendance of 600 for the preceding school year. The county superintendent discovers from the school statistics in his office, after apportioning $500 for each teacher in the county, that the amount per child in average daily attendance is $8. Dividing 1,000 by 70, we find that "A" is a "fifteen-teacher district." Five hundred dollars multiplied by 15, plus $8 multiplied by 600, equals $12,300, the amount that "A" receives in a year from the state and county school funds.

As before remarked, the treasurer of each county is the custodian of all school funds; all orders on said funds drawn by the local district or city authorities must pass through the hands of, and be approved by, the county superintendent before they can be paid by the treasurer.

It might be urged that such a system, while it guards the educational rights of children in the poorer districts, may overstimulate a desire for the creation of new school districts. It has that tendency, but the state has thrown some safeguards around it (although perhaps not yet sufficient) by imposing certain restrictions upon the creation of new districts in the way of distance from the nearest schoolhouse and the minimum number of census children required. Under the law the schools of the state are enabled to maintain an average of eight and seven-tenths months per year.

SAMUEL T. BLACK.

Sacramento, Cal.

APPENDIX D.

THE COUNTY AS THE UNIT OF SCHOOL ORGANIZATION.

The following paragraphs are from an article by Mr. Lawton B. Evans, Superintendent of Schools for Richmond county, Ga. (See the *Educational Review*, April, 1896.)

I believe very firmly that the county or township is the proper unit of educational organization. If one system of schools can be made to extend over a whole county, including the city and villages, the organization will be upon a basis of territory. By this means the entire country can after awhile be brought under a uniform organization. So long as the organization is by cities we merely organize by locality, which can never be uniform or entire. It will always remain a one-sided development. A proper policy is to induce the people hereafter to organize by area rather than by spots. The effect of this will be to give to the rural child the same school advantages as to the city child, and there is every reason in equity and good sense why these advantages should be the same.

I come from an illustration of this kind of organization, and it may not be amiss to tell something of the schools of Richmond county, Ga., in which county is situated the thriving city of Augusta. Here for the past twenty-five years has been in operation what is known as the county system.

One board of education, composed of representatives elected by the people for a term of three years, one-third of the membership expiring every year, has charge of the entire school interests of the city of Augusta and of the county of Richmond. This board of education has the unique power of levying a school tax directly upon the people of the county, without revision by any other authority and without any limit as to rate or amount. The school tax is levied and collected as a uniform rate upon all property of the county, whether it is in the city or out of it. This forms the general school fund of the county, supplemented by the state appropriation.

When it comes to the distribution of this fund no regard is paid to the amount raised by any ward of the city or any district of the county, but the fund is distributed according to the necessities of each ward and district, determined by the number of children to be educated. The school fund of the whole county is raised by a tax on all the property of the county, and is distributed upon the basis of the school population of each community. Thus it happens that a community rich in naught else but children will get a flourishing school paid for by its wealthier but less fortunate neighbors.

As a matter of fact, a large part of the money paid by the city is annually spent in the rural districts, for the city has nine-tenths of the taxable property, but only three-fourths of the school population. So it happens that the rural schools pay one-tenth of the school tax and receive the benefit of one-fourth of it. Augusta has spent in the past twenty years the sum of $200,000 in building schoolhouses and paying school-teachers for the children who live in the country districts around her. Augusta has shown her faith in the proposition that every city needs to be environed by an intelligent, industrious, and contented population.

When it comes to the teachers the same qualifications are demanded for rural schools as for city schools. Upon the regular examination terms, and upon issuing of licenses to teach, an applicant does not know whether he will teach in the city or out of it, and to many it is a matter of indifference. And I know whereof I speak when I say that there are young women graduates of normal colleges doing high-grade work in country schools ten miles beyond the limits of the city, and doing it happily and cheerfully. We believe firmly in the further proposition that a country school is entitled to as good a teacher as a city school, and that those who live in the fields are as deserving of education as those who dwell beside the asphalt. Carlyle must have had a country child in his mind when he said: "This I consider a great tragedy: that one soul should remain in ignorance that had capacity for higher things."

The teachers are treated as nearly alike as can be. City and country teachers are paid about the same salary. They get it at the end of every month and on the same day. The certainty and the regularity of a fixed compensation create a sense of security, safety, and comfort for a teacher, and accordingly increase his efficiency. No teacher can do his best work when he works at starvation rates, is paid once every three or four months, and often in scrip that he must discount. There is much philosophy and also economy in the maxim that advises us to pay a public servant well and watch him closely. So we draw no distinction of locality. First-class work is worth as much twenty miles from town as it is in the heart of the city.

The schools of the county all run nine calendar months. They all begin at the same time and close at the same time. During the last year every child of the county, regardless of where he lived, was offered nine months of actual tuition.

So far as schoolhouses are concerned, these are located in rural districts so as to be on an average of four miles apart. No child is out of walking distance of a school open nine months in the year and taught by a good teacher. These houses are owned by the board of education and cost from $300 to $2,500 each, according to size and equipment.

One superintendent has charge of all the teachers in the county. The same degree of efficiency that should attend the supervision of city schools is likewise extended to the country schools. An expert teacher for all is the theory, and, so far as human effort can avail, it is carried out in practice. The same course of study is prescribed for the pupils, and the same course of professional reading is required of the teachers. The teachers of the city schools meet for instruction once a week, the teachers of the country schools meet once a month, and in addition have a two-months' institute in the summer months.

APPENDIX E.

COMPARATIVE COST OF THE TOWNSHIP AND DISTRICT SYSTEMS.

The subcommittee has made diligent inquiry as to the relative cost of the township-unit and independent-district systems of carrying on common schools. Naturally, it is a difficult thing to come at, as the elements entering into the problem are so fluctuating. Some testimony is presented below from three well-known state-school executives, all given in response to the inquiries of the committee.

I. FRANK A. HILL, Secretary of the Massachusetts State Board of Education:

I do not think it will be possible without a great deal of special investigation to furnish figures or statistics to show that the town plan is either cheaper or more expensive than the district plan. The expenditures for schools in Massachusetts have been gradually increasing, because of better buildings, better sanitation, better equipment, better teachers, and better salaries. I have a strong conviction, however, that the same amount of money may be made to go much further under town management than under district in the way of securing greater efficiency in the schools.

We are consolidating our scattered and thinly attended schools quite extensively in our rural towns, and transporting the children. In this way towns frequently save a little money, while providing better accommodations and securing better teachers. But the argument we use in favor of such consolidation is not the economical one; it is the educational one, rather, that the school efficiency is thus increased.

II. CHARLES D. HINE, Secretary of the Connecticut State Board of Education:

It is hardly right to say that the district system [in Connecticut] is an independent system. The town still remains the unit of financial management. All money from the state treasury goes to the town, is added to the town tax, and then is distributed by the town board of apportionment to the several districts. In only 138 of the 1,400 districts is a tax laid. These districts have the power to tax themselves, but you will see that they seldom exercise it. A few districts, probably not more than twenty-five, support their schools in part by district tax. The remainder of the districts mentioned have taxed themselves for occasional expenses, like insurance, repairs, or perhaps for building a schoolhouse.

As to the cost of the two systems, ... it must always be said, and I impress that upon those to whom I speak, that the two cannot be justly compared, except by going over a period of years. When towns enter upon the town system, they are likely to increase expenses, if their previous expenses have been stingy and inadequate. On the contrary, if under the district system they have been liberal, the economy which the town system permits will enable them to reduce their expenses. It follows, then, that you would have to know the policy under the district system before you could judge whether the town system had made a difference in the case. The tendency in the large districts in this state is to become practically independent, and to support the schools liberally under the district system. There are advantages of directness, power to borrow money, etc., which make it possible to secure liberal appropriations in large districts. The tendency in small districts is to diminish the cost because there are few children.

As a result, taking the average district, the town system shows in this state very much better schools, so far as instruction is concerned, as well as more efficient administration. It would be impossible, of course, to illustrate this by numerous examples. We have not been able to secure legislation compelling all towns to accept the town system. We are, however, advancing slowly toward that result by popular vote. In the last year eleven towns voted to adopt the town system, and now, out of 168, fifty-four are under town systems. It comes slowly, but it is coming as a result of a change of heart and of an endeavor to make better schools.

III. W. W. STETSON, State Superintendent of Schools, Maine:

There is some justice in the claim that the district system is, in one sense, cheaper than the township system. Under the district system the schools were maintained for a much less number of weeks than under the town system, especially in small districts.

When we were running under the district system, patrons of the schools were willing to bid off the board for less than a dollar a week; sometimes they boarded the teacher without expense to the district, and also furnished wood, repaired the schoolhouse, and kept it in proper condition generally. It was possible to have longer terms, because of these contributions.

Under the township system the town pays for the teacher's wages and board, and has to provide the wood, make the repairs, furnish a janitor, and provide for keeping the house clean. Shorter terms and donations made the old district school cheap in the sense of using but a small amount of money. It was also cheap in another sense. It was usually taught by some indigent relative of the agent. But in Maine we are not entirely free from this curse, even under the township system. We have discovered that 872 of the 4,600 teachers of Maine are related to or connected with the members of the superintending school committees in such a way as to have an unsafe influence in securing their appointments. There can be no question but that for an equal length of terms, if all the services rendered and materials furnished are paid for, the township system is much more economical than the district system. It is also true that when the conditions prevail that are indicated above, in the matter of money, the district system may be cheaper.

APPENDIX F.

TRANSPORTATION OF PUPILS.

The declining population of many towns and counties, and even larger districts affects the rural schools very unfavorably. (See *Appendix A.*)

I. Hon. C. R. Skinner, State Superintendent of Public Instruction of the State of New York, thus forcibly urges the need of consolidation in the schools of that state:

"In 1860 the school population of the state outside of its cities was 894,432. At the close of the school year of 1895 the school population of the state outside of its cities and villages containing upwards of 10,000 people was 609,146, a decrease of 285,286, or upwards of 31 per cent., while the number of school districts in 1860 was 11,358. While the number of school children has decreased during that time nearly one-third, there has been substantially no decrease in the number of rural districts. It needs no argument to show that the antiquated school-district system, which served the people so well in 1860, has outgrown its usefulness, and that, if the state of New York desires to keep pace with adjoining states in the advancement of her educational interests, some new system must be devised.

"The township system, or some unit larger than the present system, in my judgment, is the only solution of the difficulty, and until the state shall have adopted that system its rural schools will continue to decline in efficiency. There is, in my opinion, no better school in America than the union free school and village school of our state, but the results there obtained cannot possibly be achieved in the weak rural districts, where the average attendance is less than twenty pupils, and, as shown above, in nearly 3,000 districts less than ten. The ambitions and rivalries of the students—incentives to greater exertion on the part of the pupils—which prevailed thirty-five years ago in these country districts no longer exist. The school is lifeless, cannot be graded, there is little enthusiasm among the students, and that activity and earnestness which come from numbers are entirely lacking." (Report for 1894–95, pp. x, xi.)

II. The arguments for the reform have been luminously stated by Mr. A. W. Edson, one of the Massachusetts state agents, as follows (Fifty-eighth Annual Report of the Massachusetts Board of Education, 1893–94, pp. 215–17):

Consolidation and Transportation.—There is a decided tendency on the part of intelligent and progressive communities to close the small schools in remote districts and to transport children to the graded schools of the villages, where better classification, better grading, and better teaching are the rule. This is done not so much from an economic standpoint as because of the firm conviction that the children receive greater educational advantages there than in the small, ungraded schools.

The number of children in the back districts is small, and growing less every year. With few children and small classes there can be but little enthusiasm and progress.

The leading arguments in favor of the movement are:

1. It permits a better grading of the schools and classification of pupils. Consolidation allows pupils to be placed where they can work to the best advantage; the various subjects of study to be wisely selected and correlated, and more time to be given to recitation.

2. It affords an opportunity for thorough work in special branches, such as drawing, music, and nature study. It also allows an enrichment in other lines.

3. It opens the doors to more weeks of schooling and to schools of a higher grade. The people in villages almost invariably lengthen the school year and support a high school for advanced pupils.

4. It insures the employment and retention of better teachers. Teachers in small, ungraded schools are usually of limited education, training, or experience, or are past the age of competition. The salaries paid in cities and villages allow a wide range in the selection of teachers.

5. It makes the work of the specialist and supervisor far more effective. Their plans and efforts can all be concentrated into something tangible.

6. It adds the stimulating influences of large classes, with the resulting enthusiasm and generous rivalry. The discipline and training obtained are invaluable.

7. It affords the broader companionship and culture that come from association.

8. It results in a better attendance of pupils, as proved by experience in towns where the plan has been thoroughly tried.

9. It leads to better school buildings, better equipment, a larger supply of books, charts, maps, and apparatus. All these naturally follow a concentration of people, wealth, and effort, and aid in making good schools. The large expenditure implied in these better appointments is wise economy, for the cost per pupil is really much less than the cost in small and widely separated schools.

10. And, again, it quickens public interest in the schools. Pride in the quality of the work done secures a greater sympathy and better fellowship throughout the town.

Mr. Edson reports that the following objections have been made in Massachusetts:

1. Depreciation of property; decreased valuation of farms in districts where schools are closed.

2. Dislike to send young children to school far from home, away from the oversight of parents; and to provide a cold lunch for them rather than a warm dinner.

3. Danger to health and morals; children obliged to travel too far in cold and stormy weather; obliged to walk a portion of the way to meet the team, and then to ride to school in damp clothing and with wet feet; unsuitable conveyance and uncertain driver; association with so many children of all classes and conditions; lack of proper oversight during the noon hour.

4. Insufficient and unsuitable clothing; expense to parents of properly clothing their children.

5. Difficulty of securing a proper conveyance on reasonable terms, or, if the parent is allowed compensation, of agreeing upon terms satisfactory to both parties, parents and town officials.

6. Local jealousy; an acknowledgment that some other section of the town has greater advantages and is outstripping any other locality.

7. Natural proneness of some people to object to the removal of any ancient land-

mark or to any innovation, however worthy the measure or however well received elsewhere.

To these objections Mr. Edson, who is one of the most competent of authorities, replies:

The first one is more imaginary than real, for any level-headed man with children to be educated will place a higher value on the quality of the schools and the school spirit in the community than upon the number and accessibility of the schools. Experience has demonstrated the fact that property in towns committed to this plan has appreciated rather than depreciated in value.

The second and third objections are the most serious. It behooves school authorities to see that the danger is reduced to a minimum. Suitable conveyances, covered, should be provided, and competent, careful drivers selected. No risks should be taken. During the noon hour some teacher should remain with the children who carry luncheon.

The fourth, fifth, and sixth objections have no great weight. The last one has great influence with those people who choose to live, move, and die as did their ancestors, on the theory that this is the last generation, and that any special efforts at improvement are just so much more than is wise or necessary.

III. The experiment in consolidation now in progress in northeastern Ohio is of such interest and promise as to warrant extracts from the annual reports for 1895–96 of the two superintendents who have been most prominent in the work. This recent movement may have an interest for some minds that earlier movements would not possess.

1. Extracts from the report of Mr. F. E. Morrison, Superintendent of Kingsville, Ashtabula county:

The new school system, which is known as the Kingsville system of education, has been formulated and introduced with marked success.

By this system the pupils of the subdistricts are given the same advantages for obtaining an education as the village pupils, and this result has been obtained without working any disadvantage to the village pupils, for we have been enabled to open a new room and supply another teacher in the village schools, thus reducing the number of grades in each room and giving all the pupils better school advantages. We have sufficient room yet for several more pupils without crowding the rooms.

The pupils of the subdistricts have not only been given the advantage of more extended associations and larger classes with which to recite, but they have also the advantages of a school where the teacher has fewer recitations and can give more time and attention to each recitation; thus the pupil's progress is much more rapid than is possible in a school where there are three times as many classes and one-sixth the number of pupils. It is a fact that the work of the teacher depends more upon the number of classes to recite than the number of pupils in attendance. It is a pleasure indeed to note that the attendance in the subdistricts that have availed themselves of the new system has increased from 50 to 150 per cent. in some cases, and a larger increase in all cases; the daily attendance in the same subdistricts has increased from 50 or 60 per cent. to 90 or 95 per cent., thus increasing greatly the returns from the school fund invested. This has been accomplished at a saving of more than one thousand dollars to the taxpayers in the three years.

The Board of Education and citizens of Kingsville are to be congratulated for their progressive and energetic spirit in being pioneers in formulating and placing in operation a system of education superior to any in the state of Ohio, and which is to be the system of the future. The Board of Education has been enabled, under the new school law, to conduct its financial matters by better business methods, buying its supplies in quantities and letting its contracts on competitive bids, and by centralizing the schools, thus saving many needless expenses.

Since the schools were centralized the incidental expenses have decreased from $800 to $1,100 per year, to from $400 to $600 per year. All other expenses have also decreased, which may be seen from the following table compiled from the clerk's records:

EXPENDITURES OF THE BOARD OF EDUCATION OF KINGSVILLE, O.

1889-90,	$3,248.05
1890-91,	3,716.23
1891-92,	3,183.54
Total for three years,	$10,147.82
1892-93,	$3,153.44
1893-94,	3,072.73
1894-95	2,831.20
Total for three years,	$9,057.37

In giving these figures we have deducted the $600 with interest which was borrowed in 1889, and has been paid during the past three years.

It should be mentioned also that the permanent improvements made by the Board of Education during the past three years are nearly double the amount made during the preceding three years.

2. Extracts from the report of Mr. J. R. Adams, Superintendent of Madison Township, Lake county.

In my report to the board one year ago I called attention to the very low average attendance in some of our schools, the great expense per capita of educating the pupils in those small schools, and to the fact that, on account of the lack of interest and enthusiasm therein, good results could not be obtained, and suggested the plan of consolidation as the proper solution to the difficulties.

Acting upon my suggestion, the board, having in view only the best interest of the children for whom our schools exist, voted to consolidate three subdistricts at North Madison, No. 16 and No. 3 with No. 12, and also three at Unionville, No. 10 and No. 11 with No. 4, arrangements being made with the school board of Harpersfield township whereby the pupils of Subdistrict No. 1, of said township, might attend the school at Unionville upon payment by the Board of Education of Harpersfield to the Board of Education of Madison township the sum of $140 tuition.

Our school opened with two teachers and with an attendance of ninety-three pupils. This was certainly more than the number for which we had planned, and was a great surprise to me, for from No. 10, in which subdistrict there had been the previous year an attendance of only ten pupils, there came eighteen; from No. 11, in which there had been an attendance of only eight pupils, there came eighteen, and from the Harpersfield district, in which there had been an attendance of fourteen pupils, there came twenty-three. The number of pupils enrolled in this school was 107, with an average attendance of seventy-three.

Having tried the new plan for a year, it is no longer an experiment, but an experience with us; therefore, let us now candidly look at the results. First, I wish you to know what the patrons of the consolidated school think of the plan, and then to give you, as briefly as I can, some of my own observations. All the patrons in the school of Subdistrict No. 10 of Madison, and in Subdistrict No. 1 of Harpersfield, have signed a paper stating that they are well pleased with the plan and its results, and asking their respective boards to continue the plan another year. While there has been no canvass at Unionville, Subdistrict No. 4, to ascertain what the people there think of the plan, yet, from what I have heard, I am confident that they are unanimous in its support. The foregoing represents the opinion of patrons who send eighty-nine of the 107 pupils to this school. A large majority of the patrons in Subdistrict No. 11, who send eighteen of the 107 pupils to the school in question, have publicly expressed themselves as being dissatisfied with the plan, and that under it their children have not received the educational advantages which they ought to have received. Further comment is unnecessary.

Following are some of the good results which have come under my personal observation:

1. A much larger per cent. of enumerated pupils enrolled.

2. No tardiness among the transported pupils.

3. Irregular attendance reduced, the per cent. of attendance of transported pupils from two subdistricts being each ninety-four per cent., the highest in the township.

4. Pupils can be better classified and graded.

5. No wet feet or clothing, nor colds resulting therefrom.

6. No quarreling, improper language, or improper conduct on the way to and from school.

7. Pupils under the care of responsible persons from the time they leave home in the morning until they return at night.

8. Pupils can have the advantage of better schoolrooms, better heated, better ventilated and better supplied with apparatus, etc.

9. Pupils have the advantage of that interest, enthusiasm, and confidence which large classes always bring.

10. Better teachers can be employed, hence better schools.

11. The plan insures more thorough and complete supervision.

12. It is more economical. Under the new plan the cost of tuition per pupil on the basis of total enrollment has been reduced from $16 to $10.48; on the basis of average daily attendance, from $26.66 to $16.07. This statement is for the pupils in said Subdistricts Nos. 10 and 11.

13. A trial of this plan of consolidating our schools has satisfied me that it is a step in the direction toward whatever advantages a well-graded and well-classified school of three or four teachers has over a school of one teacher with five to eight grades, and with about as much time for each recitation as is needed to properly assign the next lesson.

I am now more thoroughly convinced than ever before that consolidation, or centralization, as it is sometimes called, is the true solution to the country-school problem.

In a private letter, of recent date, Mr. Adams says, since his report was made, consolidated schools have been established at two other points in Madison, at one place four schools, at the other three, each with two teachers. This makes five in the township (which is a very large one, owing to the "gore" on the lake). Five teams are employed to transport pupils, at a cost of about $1 a day for a team. Every conveyance carries about eighteen pupils. There is no trouble in transporting the pupils, even the youngest, three and a half miles, which is the greatest distance. In 1895 there were eighteen schools in Madison, with an average attendance of 217; in 1896 the number was fourteen, with an average of 260; this year there are ten schools, with an average that will reach over 300. The total expense will be about the same in this township as under the old plan, but the cost per pupil will be much less. Mr. Adams adds that the new plan is rapidly growing in the neighborhood, and the belief is spreading that the new system is sure to prevail generally in northeastern Ohio.

3. The following advertisement well illustrates the care that is taken in Madison township to secure suitable transportation for school children:

NOTICE TO BIDDERS

FOR TRANSPORTATION OF PUPILS OF THE TOWNSHIP SCHOOLS.

Bids for the transportation of pupils of the Madison township schools over the following routes will be received at the office of the Township Clerk until Friday, July 24 at 12 M.:

Route A. Beginning at County Line on the North Ridge road and running west on said road to schoolhouse in Dist. No. 12.

Route B. Beginning at Perry Line on the North Ridge road and running east to schoolhouse in Dist. No. 12.

Route C. Beginning on Middle Ridge road at residence of N. Badger, running thence west on said road to the residence of Rev. J. Sandford, thence north to schoolhouse in Dist. No. 12.

Route D. Beginning at Perry Line on River road, and running thence east on said road to schoolhouse in Dist. No. 6.

Route E. Beginning at the Hartman farm, thence by Bennett road to Chapel road, thence east to A. R. Monroe's, thence west on Chapel road to schoolhouse in Dist. No. 13.

Route F. Beginning at residence of J. H. Clark and running east on Chapel road to schoolhouse in Dist. No. 13.

All whose bids are accepted will be required to sign a contract by which they agree:

1. To furnish a suitable vehicle with sufficient seating capacity to convey all the pupils properly belonging to their route, and acceptable to the Committee on Transportation.

2. To furnish all necessary robes, blankets, etc., to keep the children comfortable; and in severe weather the conveyance must be properly heated by oil stoves or soap stones.

3. To provide a good and reliable team of horses, and a driver who is trustworthy, and who shall have control of all the pupils while under his charge, and shall be responsible for their conduct. Said driver and team to be acceptable to the said Committee on Transportation.

4. To deliver the pupils at their respective stations not earlier than 8:30 A. M. nor later than 8:50 A. M., and to leave at 4:05 P. M. (sun time).

Each contractor shall give bond for the faithful discharge of his contract in the sum of $100, with sureties approved by the president and clerk of the board.

The committee reserves the right to reject any and all bids.

By order of the committee. C. G. ENSIGN, *Clerk.*

4. Hon. T. J. Clapp, an active business man of Geauga county, who has also done good service in the legislature, makes a very flattering report of this work, in private letters to the chairman of the subcommittee. He says the centralization movement is spreading rapidly; many townships are using it, and all are delighted with the result. The feeling is becoming common that the old district school does not "measure up" to the demands of the time, and that centralization is the only hope of giving to all the children the educational advantages which they need to keep pace with the city and town schools The higher educational advantages are placed within the reach of all the children. The pupils riding three and four miles to reach school come to the schoolhouse in better condition than those who walk only half a mile. Mr. Clapp remarks that in his township the old wooden schoolhouses have been abandoned, and a new brick schoolhouse has been built at the center of the town, at a cost of $6,000, large enough to hold the single township school.

IV. The following reports the first transportation experiment in this country:

Wm. T. Harris, Commissioner of Education.

MY DEAR DR. HARRIS: I received the draft of your report for rural schools; also the pamphlet in regard to carrying pupils, etc. I thank you for them very much.

I looked up the matter of carrying pupils, and send you a copy of the report from the town of Quincy for the years 1874 and 1875, signed by J. Q. Adams, Asa Wellington, C. L. Badger, C. F. Adams, Jr., Wm. B. Duggan, and Jas. H. Slade. I have no doubt but that this is the first movement in the direction of carrying pupils in Massachusetts. You will notice that this is one year before my superintendency in Quincy. From the report of 1875 and 1876, my first report, are the following items, page 139:

Lappan Bros., conveying children, - - -	$129.00
Joseph T. French, " " - - - - -	392.50

FRANCIS W. PARKER.

CHICAGO, ILL., December 22, 1896.

EXTRACT FROM SCHOOL REPORT, QUINCY, MASS., 1874-75.

CRANE SCHOOL.

A reference to former reports of the school committee of the town will show that for many years the condition of the little school at Germantown has been steadily unsatisfactory. Isolated and small, classification was impossible, emulation unfelt, and enthusiasm absent. Ten pupils ranged from the primer to the proper studies of a high school. The most conscientious teacher soon lost hope and energy in such surroundings. For years committee after committee has striven in vain to afford a remedy. During the past summer, the teacher, who has been laboring there for a considerable period, declared her intention of resigning in despair. The committee, profoundly dissatisfied with the backwardness and lethargy of the school, was unable to assign the fault either to the teacher or to the pupils. At the same time, it became evident that the school building was unfit for occupation during another winter without extensive repairs. It was indeed shamefully dilapidated, decayed, and dirty. Competent mechanics, after careful survey, estimated the expense of necessary repairs to be at least five hundred dollars. Besides this extraordinary outlay, the regular expense in salary, care of house and fuel, incurred to maintain this school of ten scholars, was $560 a year. And yet this large expense availed those ten scholars but little or nothing. The committee, therefore, determined to try by experiment whether or not at one and the same time in this department the outlay might be reduced and the returns increased. It ascertained that it could contract for the transportation of all the school children in that school district to the Coddington school for about $420 yearly, and it thought it probable that when there they would be aroused and stimulated by the transfer to a large and graded school. The result has fully justified its anticipations. The whole number upon the register of the old Crane school was twelve, and of these the average number of attendance was never more than ten. Now seventeen are daily transported to the Coddington school from the same territory; and so great has been their interest that the attendance among them has been almost absolutely perfect. Meanwhile, both from the reports of teachers and from personal observation, the committee is thoroughly satisfied that they are making a progress in their studies which they never had approached at Germantown. For these reasons the committee thinks it decidedly for the interest of the town, and clearly beneficial for the pupils concerned, that the present experiment should be prolonged for at least a year more. It is persuaded that this policy will approve its wisdom to those who are now most doubtful if it can be fairly tried. The day of small, ungraded, remote, and isolated schools in a town like Quincy has passed away. Only absolute necessity can now justify it. Even if the plan we recommend was as much more costly as it is really less costly than the old one, we should not hesitate to urge its acceptance as decidedly the cheaper and better.

APPENDIX G.

ENRICHMENT OF RURAL SCHOOL COURSES.

At the Chicago meeting of the Committee on Rural Schools the undersigned were appointed a subcommittee to report, in the form of an appendix, a scheme for the enrichment and vitalization of the work of the rural schools by means of subjects drawn from rural life and surroundings. We do not deem it our province to discuss the theory of the rural school programme, much less the broader problems of the country school. It may, however, conduce to a better appreciation of what we suggest if we frankly state at the outset the assumptions on which we have proceeded.

We take it for granted that the work of every school, rural or otherwise, should embrace subjects drawn from its environment and from the life of its pupils. We assume that it should do this —

Because children should be taught to gather culture, knowledge, and inspiration from everything with which they come in contact;

Because children should acquire the habit of bringing to bear their knowledge and their mental powers upon every subject of thought that falls within their experience;

Because the study of the environment is especially effective in discipline and inspiration, since it is tangible, vivid, and impressive, and awakens strong and clear concepts, and produces deep and lasting educational effects;

Because mental acquisitions thus associated with the environment will be constantly revived by recurrent contact with it, and will thus be refreshed and kept alive and effective;

Because the basis for a successful study of the unseen and the intangible is best laid in clear and strong impressions of things seen and realized;

Because the school work is thereby made directly serviceable to the work of life, the value of immediate and practical utility being added to the superior disciplinary and inspirational values;

Because it puts life and soul into the work;

Because it serves as a bond of sympathy between the out-of-school life and the in-school life;

Because, in time (perhaps not at once, while inherited prejudices last), it will become a bond of sympathy between the patrons of the school and the work of the school.

We assume that a rural school, to be a true *rural* school, must take tone and color from rural surroundings, and must contribute directly to the enrichment and inspiration of rural life. We believe that this will aid in giving meaning and attractiveness to life in the country.

The following suggestions are offered in the hope that they may be helpful to teachers in making use of rural surroundings to enrich the work of country schools and to give vividness to the various formal studies. Our space being severely limited, it has seemed best to develop a few topics with some little fullness and let these suggest the treatment which others may receive. Those which we have been forced to neglect are quite as important and as rich in good material as the ones more favored. All are treated too scantily. What is really needed is a series of primers or a manual carefully worked out, embracing information as well as suggestions. But perfected tools come only with a perfected trade. The pioneer work must be done with poor implements. The progress of the work will bring better facilities.

We shall certainly be met with the criticism that the suggested work is impracticable, that the teachers cannot carry it out. This is far too true, but not wholly true. A success here and there will be a center of education, and from such beginnings, even though they may be small and scattered, the good work may grow. It must start somewhere and somehow, or must have many little starts in many places and in many forms. This little appendix does not hope to be anything but a passing contribution to an evolution that must be long and doubtless slow. The gravest difficulty lies in the defective education of our teachers. To remove this we would urge every normal school to give elaborate courses in the lines here suggested, and to recognize in other ways that the rural school furnishes a distinct problem that must be solved in its own way. It may be that the establishment of rural normal schools is the mode of solution. We would urge agricultural colleges to give short courses on rural science for the special benefit of country teachers, and to educate the people, through their institutes and by other means, to appreciate and to require the adaptation of the rural schools to rural needs. We would urge upon the agricultural colleges the adaptation and publication of matter on rural science and rural economy suitable for educational uses.

We begin our suggestions with the surface features, partly because a study of them is a natural foundation for that of the remaining environment, and partly because it is directly tributary to one of the leading formal studies.

I. STUDIES UPON THE SURROUNDING LANDSCAPE.

These should be found helpful (1) as a foundation for geography; (2) as a basis for imagining the aspects of other regions which must be studied through maps, descriptions, etc.; (3) as good material for oral and written descriptions, and hence as a basis for language work; (4) as a means for the culture of the sense of the beautiful, thus furnishing a rational basis for modeling, painting, and drawing; (5) as a mode of teaching the significance of things usually regarded as meaningless; (6) as an unconscious introduction to geological processes, and (7) as an aid to understanding many matters of agricultural interest.

1. *Surface Features, their Nature, Origin, and Meaning.*—Let there be a general study of the landscape of the neighborhood and a series of talks upon it for the purpose of gaining a true conception of what a landscape really is, and of laying the ground-work for comparisons with other parts of the face of the earth. The children should gain a vivid and definite idea of the nature of their own landscape as a type; if it be plain, whether it be very plain or but partially so; if undulatory, whether it be gently or strongly undulatory; if hilly, whether gently or roughly hilly; if mountainous, whether of the rounded, the rugged, or the grand type.

From the general survey of the landscape descend to its larger elements.

Note and plot[1] the hills and valleys of the neighborhood, first taking up those near and then reaching out farther and farther, so that there shall be a gradual passage from those that are familiar to those that are only occasionally or distantly seen. From these it will be a relatively easy step to those which must be wholly imagined. Thus the child is led out easily and naturally from his own environment to the general geography of the earth. In carrying this out, walks and occasionally more considerable excursions will introduce the idea of travel and of the methods by which geography is made, and, if verbal and written descriptions, sketches and maps are required, the children are started right in their geographical work by being made young geographers themselves in a limited

[1] It will be understood throughout that the work indicated should be done as largely as practicable and advisable by the children themselves, but the teacher will do well at times to lead them by example as well as instruction. The special mode of carrying out these suggestions must be left to the discretion and resources of the teacher. Our effort is only to point out certain main lines which, of course, need not be followed closely. The teacher will often find a different way preferable for himself, and will always find much to be filled in, and perhaps more or less to be left out as not adapted to the particular school or to its surroundings.

vated and uncultivated soil, of hard soil and mellow soil; and so lead on to the utility of the culture in permitting air and moisture to go in, etc.

Starting again with decay of rocks, lead the children to see that some parts of the rocks do not decay readily, and hence bits are left, and that these are washed about and form grains of sand or pebbles. Let them observe these and see that some are well-rounded and some are angular, according to the amount of wear, and thus the origin and meaning of sand or pebbles will become evident. The rolling action of brooks and rivers and of lake and seashores will be manifest. With a thermometer interesting experiments on the temperature of soils when wet and dry, when hard and when mellow, when stirred and unstirred, etc., can be made.

References:

"The Soil," by F. H. King. The Macmillan Co.

"Rock-Weathering and Soils," by George Merrill. The Macmillan Co.

"The Formation of Vegetable Mold," by Charles Darwin.

See also *Appendix L.*

II. APPLICATIONS OF LANDSCAPE STUDIES.

The study of the features of the landscape may be followed by a study of their influence on human affairs, and on the distribution of plants and animals. The following are some of the lines along which this may be carried out:

1. *The Location of Homes.*— Relative merits of different situations, such as summits, slopes, valleys, etc.; of different exposures, as southerly, northerly, etc.; of different relations to woods, openings, outlooks, etc.; of relations to springs, streams, and other bodies of water; of access to highways or to the several parts of the farm, and the bearing of the surface features on such communications. Do the sites of the later dwellings differ from the earlier? Are there discernible reasons for change? What determined the selection of the material of the first generation of houses? Does the material change with successive generations, and, if so, why?

2. *The Location of Roads.*— How far are they influenced by surface features? How far by other considerations? Distinguish wise and unwise locations. What is the effect of wash, drainage, etc.? What changes of location or of method of maintenance may be recommended?

3. *The Location of Adjacent Towns and Villages.*— Study the reasons for their particular situations. What bearing had natural means of transportation, roadway crossings, river fords or bridges, special agricultural or mineral resources, mill sites and like features upon their location? Do the dates of their founding, the rates of their growth and other features of their history show wisdom or unwisdom in their location? Note the bearings of their location on the interests of the surrounding country.

4. *Development of the Region as Affected by its Environment.*— Study the nature of adjacent manufactories and the reason for their location. What class was first developed, what later, what changes have taken place? Has there been increase or decline, and what is its meaning? What is their importance and the value of their products? How do they affect the rural interests? What sources of power are used and what remain still unused? Note the favorable and unfavorable features in the physical environment, the presence of mines, quarries, the facilities for transportation by railways, streams, canals, highways, etc., and their bearing upon the development of the region.

5. *Social and Civic Life of the Home as Affected by Surrounding Physical Features.*— Are the physical surroundings favorable to social gatherings and social life? Do the surface features lead to sparseness of dwellings, mountainous and difficult roads, or the opposite? Do they make the earning of a living easy and give time for social intercourse, for education, etc.? How do they affect the character of the people, etc.?

6. *The Distribution of Vegetation as Influenced by Surface Features.*— Sketch the timbered, prairie, marsh, and "bottom" areas. Note the effects of slopes, drainage, soils, etc., upon these. How do the physical conditions affect the roots, stems, leaves, and general forms of plants? Note the adaptation of different areas to different crops; also the adaptation of the region to different kinds of industry, *e. g.*, grazing, grain raising, etc. Note the changes in vegetation and compare the original with the present vegetation. Discuss the removal of forests. Where was timber first removed, and what timber? Where is it now reserved and why? Note the earlier and the later uses of timber supply, and the variation of prices and of uses of timber.

III. THE STUDY OF ATMOSPHERIC PHENOMENA.

In a manner analogous to the foregoing all the features of the air and sky *within the observation of the children* may be treated with interest and profit; the air itself, the winds, the clouds, rain, snow, hail, thunder, lightning, heat, cold, dew, evaporation, etc. The keynote should be observation, followed by inquiry, reading, reasoning, forecast, etc. The systematic prediction of tomorrow's weather at the close of each day will greatly stimulate acute observation of delicate features of cloud, wind, etc., and will build up that judgment of weather which is so important to the farmer.

It is urged that teachers secure from the nearest weather bureau station copies of the daily weather maps, and copies of the monthly summaries of the weather and crop conditions of the United States. A careful study of these maps and summaries, *supplementing the pupils' own daily observations*, will form a good basis for other geographic study. The data furnished by the Weather Bureau are particularly valuable for several reasons: (1) They are collected by trained observers; (2) the stations are so distributed as to fairly represent the whole country; (3) observations are uniformly and regularly made every day at all stations; (4) the various meteorological conditions are automatically recorded by instruments of precision, insuring great accuracy of detail; (5) the various data are appropriately represented daily upon one map which, thus, day by day presents a clear picture of the climatic and crop conditions of the whole country.

By these means the pupils will be much interested in working out the relative amounts of rainfall, cloudiness, and sunshine; also the average and the extremes of temperature found in the areas and belts devoted to the great crops, as wheat, corn, oats, tobacco, cotton, and sugar cane. The relative amounts of rain, cloudiness, and sunshine for the seasons may be readily determined. The incidents of the season in the localities where the pupils live frequently afford excellent opportunity for forming a picture of other localities far removed from their own. Thus a study of the character of the rain and the clouds in winter gives a basis for picturing arctic regions, and the same study in summer an equally sound basis for picturing tropical regions. For example, in June, 1892, there was a fall of nearly eleven inches of rain at Chicago; with the summer temperature, an almost tropical verdure was the result. In September and October in Chicago, in 1891, the rainfall was about two-thirds of an inch; this closely approximated the average precipitation in Arizona, and, when considered in connection with the unusually high temperature of the year, it became an easy matter for the pupils to picture desert conditions and modes of desert formation. By similar means the study is capable of almost indefinite expansion.

IV. THE STUDY OF PLANT LIFE.

In like manner, the plants of the region may be treated. The purpose here, as before, is not so much to learn *about* plants as to come into *actual intellectual contact* with them by observation, interest, sympathy, and appreciation. Not only should the plants be observed in all their parts and functions, but their history, mode of propagation, preferences for soil, topographic situations, exposures, etc., should be studied. The association of plants with one another--"plant societies"—are especially interesting and profitable for study. The cultivated as well as the native plants should be included, and the reasons for cultivating some plants and neglecting or warring against others afford large possibilities of interest. As farming is essentially plant culture, the vital relations of such studies are evident, if carried out on the right lines. The old-fashioned botany, the grinding out of the Latin names by an "Analytical Key," is not at all the thing here urged, but direct inquiry into the nature, life, habits, functions, associations, and services of plants.

To give a more concrete idea of what we have in mind, the following is offered as an illustration. It is not set up as a model. There are many ways of reaching like results.

1. *Growth from the Seed.*—With several seeds (beans, for example) in the hands of each pupil, invite a careful inspection of their surfaces, as a first step. Write upon the board a list of things observed, *e. g.*, (1) stem scar (hilum), (2) small dot on one side of hilum where pollen tube entered to fertilize the seed (micropyle), (3) ridge on side of hilum opposite from micropyle (radicle), (4) one end of bean has different slope from the other, (5) a light line or ridge extending longitudinally around the seed, etc. Request pupils to bring other varieties of beans, and see how many of the observed points are common to them all. As a training in the *exact* use of words in oral expression require the pupils to describe precisely what has been observed. As a training in written language require the pupils to write out what has been seen. This will react to *intensify* the seeing.

To introduce the quantitative element, let a pint cup, or a straight-sided bottle, or a glass be exactly half-filled with beans, and mark the surface of the beans with a string or rubber band. Now fill the vessel with water and put in a warm place for twenty-four hours. Set some pupil to watch the first stages of change, and charge him to be able to state the next day just what they were. On the next day measure the amount of change in volume. What has caused this change? If the water put in was first accurately measured or weighed (and every country school should have means of measuring and weighing), pour out what remains and measure it. Compute the difference. Compare the loss of the water with the increase of the beans. What has become of the water? By what means have the beans grown? Here are the first steps of growth.

Distribute the swollen beans among the pupils, and let them again look for the points observed in the dry bean. Have any disappeared? Have others appeared? Have any changed in character? Let the skin be removed. What features previously noted are removed with it? Do you now see an explanation of any features noted on the outside? Carefully note the two seed leaves (cotyledons), the radicle, and the now very evident first two leaves. Study the pea, pumpkin seed, and corn in the same manner.

As a next step, fit two layers of thick cloth to the inside of a round pie tin. Wet these pieces of cloth and place between them some of the seeds which have been studied, and turn the two pie tins together to prevent evaporation (which introduced a slight error in the experiment above). Place these in a warm place to germinate, noting the temperature. Encourage some pupil to repeat the experiment in a place where the temperature is between 32° and 45°, recording the temperature from time to time. Urge another to try the experiment, using cloths wrung out very dry. Compare results to find out the effects of heat and moisture. Try different seeds to see what differences of conditions they require. These are capital experiments which fix the foundation principles of moisture and temperature in plant growth.

When these tests have sufficiently advanced, urge the boys and girls to request permission to test the germinatory power of the seeds which their parents expect to plant in the spring. (This seed study is best done from February to April.) Place 100 seeds of a given kind under the conditions described, and note how many sprout in three, four, five, etc., days. All seeds should be tested before planting, and this is practical work which, if rightly done, will be appreciated by parents as being immediately useful as well as instructive and disciplinary.

2. *Growth from Buds.*—When vegetation begins to start in the spring, make an excursion at noon or after school to gather specimens of large buds. Clip sprigs of the Balm of Gilead, cottonwood, or hickory, set them in water and study in the manner of the bean, and so reach the fundamental idea that the bud and the seed are in nature much the same. Pick off the scales one by one until the leaves are reached, inquiring what the scales are for; what the cotton; what the varnish. Count the number of true leaves, and then go a little later to the trees again and see how many leaves the shoots from similar buds then have. Are they the same in number as in the buds? Or have new ones formed? When were these buds formed? Why were they formed the year before? Let the children ponder over these questions.

Study the arrangement of buds and of leaves on the stems. Lead the children to discover the law that buds and leaves are placed as far apart on the stem as possible, and in a symmetrical order. Lead them to discover that this order places the leaves where there is the least shading, where the movements of sap up and down feed all leaves and branches quite equally, so that the stem will be equally loaded on all sides. Let them learn to distinguish fruit buds from leaf buds. Have them explore the gardens and orchards to see if there is an abundance of fruit buds. Teach them to distinguish between live and dead buds, particularly in regard to fruit-trees. All this should be done with a definite educational purpose, in which the utility of the knowledge has also a clear recognition.

References:

"Principles of Plant Culture," Professor C. S. Goff. Published by the author, Madison, Wis.

"Flowers in Relation to Insects." The Macmillan Co.

Gray's Botany.

Bessey's Botany.

See also list in *Appendix L.*

V. THE STUDY OF ANIMAL LIFE.

Along essentially the same lines the animal life may be treated. Here a new and important factor enters, conscious life, and this affords a most fruitful field for educating the sympathies and moral sentiments of the children. Nothing so contributes to a real and vital (not merely sentimental) sympathy with living things other than ourselves as a careful study of their lives and habits. The child comes to see the world as they see it, and to appreciate and sympathize with them in their efforts to work out the purposes of their lives. And even if these purposes strike across human interests, the sympathy will not be entirely absent, and cruelty will grow more and more rare as sympathetic education progresses. The education of the sympathies finds little space in the formal school programme, and hence the special value of utilizing the opportunity here afforded.

There are several other topics which may be treated in like manner, as mensuration in its application to land measurements, etc., various phases of economics as applied to rural affairs, the social and civic aspect of country life, etc.

We respectfully submit the foregoing suggestions, fully conscious of their limitations, in the hope that some little helpfulness may be found in them.

T. C. CHAMBERLIN,
W. S. JACKMAN,
F. H. KING,
Committee.

A COURSE OF STUDY FOR RURAL SCHOOLS.

A course of study for country school children should be framed with direct reference to the actual conditions that prevail in country life and, in large measure, determine it. Among the most important points to be kept in mind are the following:

1. *There is a general lack of appreciation of the immediate surroundings.*

This is not peculiar to country people; it is simply a fact in the country, as it is in the city. Education can confer no greater boon than that of showing how the real pleasures of life may be derived from one's own immediate surroundings, and from the work he is called upon to perform.

2. *There is an almost total lack of scientific skill in farm work.*

The prejudice against farm machinery has been extremely strong. Farmers have been forced into using it because other vocations have drawn away the help that formerly was depended upon for hand labor. The treatment of the soil is, in the extreme, unscientific. The American farmer, in this respect, is scarcely ahead of the Chinese; his unscientific methods have made him the target of every caricaturist. In this, and in a score of other ways, the farmer pays the penalty of his ignorance.

3. *In the country there is great dearth of social life.*

This, more than hard work, deprives the country of its strength. Bad roads are largely responsible for the present social condition. In many places farmers, and especially the wives and daughters, live in dreary isolation for more than half the year, because no means of travel yet invented will master the mud of country roads. To properly recognize the foregoing conditions, therefore, it would seem that a course of study should contemplate three lines of interest:

1. *In the earlier years, especially, great attention should be given to the picturesqueness and natural beauty of the surroundings.*

Without trained and careful effort in this direction, the intensely practical character of their contact with the various things about them will close the eyes of the children to many beautiful things that should be a source of joy and pleasure throughout life. Much out-door study should, therefore, be encouraged. The children should be familiar with every brook, and waterfall; with every cliff, wooded copse, and ravine. The hills, cloud-capped, basking in sunshine or glistening with snow, should be permitted to work their silent influences into the children's lives. The country pupils are not naturally insensible towards these scenes; but the usual tendency of school life is to belittle and destroy all kinship that the children may originally feel for the beautiful. As an adjunct in this phase of study, drawing, painting, and modeling should hold at least equal place with reading, in these early years.

2. *To supply the demand for scientific skill a good deal of attention should be given to—*

(1) *Mechanics.*—Pupils should be taught enough of practical mechanics to enable them to ward off the legion of fakirs that beset the farmer with their labor-saving (?) devices.

(2) *Manual Training.*—Scarcely a day in a farmer's life passes when there is not some demand made for skilled hand work with tools. The "stitch in time" on the farm is frequently fatally delayed when it involves a trip to a neighboring mechanic.

(3) *Mathematics.*—The farmer suffers more loss today from his ignorance in this subject than any other. Bookkeeping, as applied to farm accounts, should be carefully taught. Taking the amount of money at stake on the farm into account, no other business in the world tries to get along with so little bookkeeping. As a natural result, there is infinite waste in a hundred ways that are unnoticed. The time has come when the farmer must learn the lesson that the merchant already knows, that, if he is to gather a competence, or even earn a livelihood, it must be done by a careful saving of *small* margins of profits

upon all the things with which he may work, instead of by large gains upon a few things. Few farmers, simply because no accounts are kept, realize that badly stacked hay and grain, poorly fed stock and illy cultivated fields result in actual cash loss, just as surely as though the money were spent at the gaming table. The arithmetic of the farm account would be of incalculable value to the farm boy if he learned nothing else. The study of form and elementary geometry should be made very prominent. Every farm boy should be taught the elements of trigonometry and surveying. He should know how to "run a line," and how to lay off fields so that the same may be worked to the greatest advantage. He should be taught how to lay out roadways at proper grade, and how to make them. Nothing would hasten the era of good roads more than to show the farmer how much loss in actual cash may be charged to bad ones, through loss in harness, vehicles, horseshoes, horses, and time.

(4) *Biology.*—To show the splendid opportunity before every farmer of intelligence for study in this field, it is only necessary to cite the fact that it was by a close study of domesticated animals and plants that Darwin was able to probe the mysteries of life more profoundly than any before him. It is by no means necessary that the farm boy should study the sunshine only to find its value in pounds of beef; by the nature of the case he is, if intelligent, brought into closer touch with the great problems of life and energy than any other being. It would broaden, not diminish, the scope of this interest if from boyhood he were to learn everything possible about the care and scientific feeding of animals; if he were to learn exactly, for example, how to feed for beefsteak, and how to feed for butter, with the greatest economy. The study of plants would furnish an interesting analogy. The selection of seed; the cultivation of crops with due reference to roots and top; planting, care, and grafting of fruits; the relative value of forage, grain, and other crops, and many similar topics, are subjects for exhaustless study, every hour devoted to which would bring actual cash returns, and at the same time furnish a broad basis for an understanding of the plant world.

(5) *Meteorology and Physics of the Atmosphere.*—By a careful study of the maps and other materials supplied by the United States Weather Bureau, every farm boy should learn something of the nature of the great storms that are likely to visit his region. A careful study of the weather maps, supplemented by good collateral reading, would leave very little to be desired in his geography.

(6) *Mineralogy.*—The composition, the origin, and the treatment of soils, how their productiveness may be renewed and conserved. The relation of the soil to the underlying rock. The origin and relative value of the native rock. The geological history of the country.

(7) *Chemistry.*—A practical knowledge of the principal elements which enter into the soils, plants, and animals. The chemistry of foods.

These subjects should be presented not only from the economic, but also from the more strictly scientific or philosophic side. Because "Man shall not live by bread alone," he has always despised the science of bread for bread's sake. Country children, as well as all others, must be allowed to have an insight into the deeper and more general problems of creation if they are to be satisfied with their work. An intelligent study of nature from the economic standpoint inevitably involves a study from the scientific side also.

It would be a service of inestimable value to the rural schools, and, for that matter, to schools everywhere, if the many government publications bearing upon the studies of nature could be placed in libraries easily accessible to teachers and pupils. The best of these should be in every schoolhouse as books of reference. These works are worth a great deal more than many of the text-books that are far more pretentious.

3. If the country is ever to acquire that refinement which the human being feels it is his right to possess, it must grow it. There are those who believe that, sometime, the

great tide of youth that is now pouring in upon our cities will turn back upon itself, and thus carry to the country the culture that the soil could not of itself produce. It is not to be. Those who are once engulfed in the vortex of the city never go back; and if their children or children's children are by some chance cast out upon the country, they must begin life afresh, as did the primeval man.

Certain physical conditions that now prevail in the country must be improved, or social progress will be forever stayed. The chief of these obstructive conditions is the unspeakable system of roadmaking. Good roads, with their natural *sequelæ*, would practically solve the problem of country life. They would mean hours of social intercourse instead of hours of dreary, monotonous solitude. They would mean free delivery of goods from the stores in towns. They would mean free and daily delivery of mail. Better have three- or even four-cent postage, if necessary, with free delivery every day, than one-cent postage and the "catch-as-catch-can" delivery of the present time. Good roads would mean the rapid extension of the trolley-car system, which would reduce to the minimum the labor of exchange of commodities between one locality and another, and between country and town. As in the city the attention of children is being directed more and more to municipal affairs, so in the country let the children study practically all these conditions, which lie at the foundation of their physical, intellectual, and moral welfare.

Whatever else the course of study may do, let it breathe hope for the country boys and girls; not the hope of a life that, to be realized, must be lived in the city, but let it rouse the anticipations of a life that has its background in the sunsets, the hills, the woods, the orchards, and the waving grain fields of the country. A genuine life, intelligently lived, alone can bring culture. Whether the instrument of living is the plow or the pen, it matters but little; the furrow well turned, and the line well written, are both fundamental and absolutely uninterchangeable in human society.

Country life, not less than that in the city, may have its aspirations that are truly noble. The schools must not confuse or destroy these by trying to "citify" the country or by seeking to "countrify" the town.

The city and the country express the equation of life; a weakness in one member means the ruin of both. Each must supplement, but not destroy, the other, and both must be preserved.

WILBUR S. JACKMAN.

Chicago Normal School.

APPENDIX H.

THE FARM AS THE CENTER OF INTEREST.

Nowhere on earth has a child such advantages for elementary education as upon a good farm, where he is trained to love work and to put his brains into work. The best-taught school in a densely populated city can never equal in educative value the life upon a good farm, intelligently managed.

The child on the farm is made responsible for something, for some work, for some care-taking, and out of this responsibility grow trustworthiness, habits of work, and a feeling of personal power in all the essential elements of character, with the exception of those much-needed phases that spring from personal contact with society outside of home.

The surroundings of the child upon the farm in contrast with the complexity of city surroundings are comparatively simple; the same forms, colors, sounds are repeated in endless succession, presenting innumerable variations and at the same time complete harmony and unity. The trees, the shrubs, the foliage, the flowers, the fields, the hills, valleys, plains, and brooks create distinct, everlasting images in the child's mind; images impressed, concentrated, and expanded by countless sensations, by countless contrasts, that stream in through every avenue of the soul.

Then, too, everything appeals to the child as useful or non-useful. Farm work means the necessities of life, the comforts of home, the possibilities of an education. The reaction of the child upon his environment is the main thing, however; his power to conquer nature with his own hands and mind, together with continual lessons which bring home to him the inevitable action of and his dependence upon the laws of nature, as they assist, or as they baffle, his efforts.

The child enters school with senses keen, character in full tide of formation, and the impulse to act fully organized. He has, besides, acquired a comprehensive knowledge of his environment. This instinctive, spontaneous growth should go on and have full opportunities for complete development.

The statement of what a farm does for a boy in its general lines may easily be taken from the experience of a farm boy in New England, for instance. It is possible for me to give the story of such a one from actual experience — what he learned, what he studied, and what he acquired.

The scene is upon a rocky farm in New Hampshire; the boy an ordinary child, such as you may meet anywhere in this world of ours. As soon as he found himself upon the farm, at eight years of age, he began to study — to study in the best sense of that much-abused word. He began the study of geography — real geography. He observed with ever-increasing interest the hills, valleys, springs, swamps, and brooks upon the old farm. The topography of the land was clear and distinct; its divisions into fields, pastures, and forests were to him the commonest facts of experience. The image of the whole farm and all that it contained is one of the clearest and most distinct memories in his mind today.

The boy not only studied geography, but the foundations of geography, geology, and mineralogy. He knew in an elementary way the nature of the soils; why one field was better than another for a certain crop, and began to reason upon cause — sunshine, drainage, drought, and fertilization.

He studied botany. All the kinds of grasses he knew — timothy, clover, red top, silver grass, pigeon grass; how they were sown, how they came up, grew, were cut, cured, and fed to the cattle; what kind of hay was best for sheep, and what for oxen. He knew the different weeds, too — the rag weed, smart weed, pig weed; he had a practical knowledge of these from close contact, with the hoe and his bare hands. This knowledge of plants took in medicinal herbs — caraway, camomile, catnip, docks, worts, and mints, lobelia, pennyroyal, and g get. These practical lessons in herbs were doubly impressed, sometimes in a painful way, although they were intended to relieve pain.

The flowers that grew on the farm and surrounding farms, wild and cultivated, hollyhocks and lilacs in the garden, the golden-rod and violets of the pasture, and the sweetest flower that ever blossoms, lifting its delicate petals close by the snow banks in the early spring, the harbinger of the resurrection — the trailing arbutus, taught him lessons of beauty, trained his eye for color, deepened his reverence for God.

He knew the trees — the maple with its sweet burden of spring, the hemlock, and the straight pine which he used to climb for crows' nests. He noted the difference in woods, and their value. As soon as he could wield an axe he cut the trees for lumber, fences, and firewood. With all the shrubs he was acquainted; in fact, he got an elementary but very useful classification that has made the subject an interesting one throughout his life, and prepared him to appreciate the practical value of botany in the schools.

He studied zoölogy, too. The animal life of the farm was very close to him. The brutes were his early companions. The domesticated animals he knew — the frisking lambs, the knowing and antagonistic buck, the tricky mare. He helped to break steers, to kill hogs, to hunt for eggs, to feed the chickens. He knew the wild animals, the squirrels, the rabbits, the woodchucks; the insects, the grasshoppers, and ants; bugs that scurried away when he lifted a stone.

With the birds he was intimately acquainted — the wrens that built their nests in the barn and sheds, the robin redbreast, the shrieking blue-jay, the tiny warblers in the woods, the wise crow, and the timid partridge that would give her life in defense of her young.

He had a practical knowledge of meteorology. He could tell the time of noon upon the instant, by two infallible monitors, his stomach and his shadow. He could foretell storms with nearly as much wisdom as is exercised by the Weather Bureau. The coming of a shower was known to him — the hurry-scurry to get the hay into the barn. The long, steady breezes from the east brought on the storm, and a storm was a welcome thing to a boy on a New England farm! It meant a day of perfect delight on the dear old river. The ostensible purpose of the boy was to catch a few small fish — the real purpose, worship, alone by the rushing floods, the quiet pools, the pebbly beaches, and the silent woods.

In fact, every subject now known in the curriculum of the university this boy studied in an elementary way. He was really grounded in these studies. He observed, investigated, and drew inferences, perfectly unconscious, to be sure, of what he was learning, or how he was learning; but still, he learned, and he studied, and the best lesson of all was his personal reaction upon his environment. His plowing, hoeing, haying, digging, chopping, lumbering, his mending of sleds, and making of cider, sugar, lye, and soap were all so many practical lessons in life which exercised his body, stimulated his mind, and strengthened and developed his purpose in life.

He lived to become a school-teacher, and taught school earnestly and bunglingly for twenty years before he had even a suspicion of the value of his farm life and farm work.

How the work of the children upon the farm is to be brought into the school, concentrated and expanded; how this great, spontaneous, ever-increasing interest is to be made use of; how this organized energy is to be turned into the main life current, are questions of questions. It is the imperative duty of parents and teachers to determine how the farm life of the boy and the girl may be recognized by use in the schoolroom. Which of all the studies the boy has begun should be discontinued? Are they not all essential? Must they be held in abeyance until he reaches the door of a high school or a college? That the child begins them spontaneously and instinctively is argument enough for their continuance.

Without attempting a course of study, I may be allowed to make some suggestions. In these suggestions I present only the common and common-sense things needed in farm work and farm life, and endeavor to show why they form the substantial basis of all study.

GEOGRAPHY, GEOLOGY, MINERALOGY.

The child's knowledge of geography may be made the basis of all his further study of that subject. He brings into school geographical images of the farm and the surrounding landscape. He is tolerably well acquainted with the topography of his district and, it may be, of the town. First, find out how much the pupils really know of these subjects. Get them to describe the farm or any part of it. How many fields are there? Where are the pastures? The woods? What are you raising in each field? How many cattle have you? Describe them. Tell about the sheep, the horses, the hens. Get pupils to sketch the farm on the blackboard, paper, or slates.

A pile of sand in the yard might be used for modeling the farm, showing hills and valleys, plains and brook basins. In winter rough boards with raised edges might be used for sand modeling. Later, chalk modeling should be used to indicate the relief of the land.

The beginning of political geography by the divisions of the farm into fields and pastures may be made. The lay of the land, the relative positions of these, form good lessons in the points of the compass. Pupils would compare one farm with another, so that in time they could model and draw the whole district, including the roads.

If there is a stream in the neighborhood, it may be used as a study of the brook basin, the wearing of water — a good introduction for geology. The examination of the soil after rains, especially loosened soil, may be studied to show the effect of storms in erosion. The dip and formation of the surface, division into hills or plains, bottom lands, and bluffs, may be related to the working of the stream.

The study of mineralogy may begin with the study of soils, the kind of soils, and the forms of the grains. Specimens of gravel, sand, loam, vegetable mold, clay, and rock should be brought by pupils to school and studied. How is vegetable mold formed? What in the soil is useful for plant life? How does the soil change through vegetation and under cultivation, and also under the action of heat, water, frost? It is easily seen that all these are elementary studies in weathering — dynamical geology.

If there are rocks on the farm, they may be studied; the archaic rocks, the secondary rocks, the strata, and the dip of the rocks — all so many points of introduction to geology. Boys on the farm will know something of the mineral on different parts of the farm, in different fields. In general the bottom land is the richest, and the question might easily be asked, Why? In this relation uses of the different kinds of soil may be studied. Questions of why one crop will grow in one portion of the farm, and not in another, and why crops should change or rotate from year to year, should all be brought in.

Housekeeping, butter and cheese-making, cooking, gardening, and affairs pertaining to home economy should be taken into the school. Draw and describe your garden. Divide it into beds. Locate the flowers, the vegetables. Sketch your hens, the turkeys. How do you make bread?

METEOROLOGY.

Elementary studies in distribution of heat would come through the changes of the seasons. The shadow stick may be used, showing the changes in the sun's position relative to the earth. A sun dial on the schoolhouse should be made. The daily changes in the sunlight coming through the different windows may be measured through shadows on the wall. It is a very easy matter to get the daily weather reports and examine them. Every country school should have a thermometer, barometer, anemometer, and rain gauge, to measure the force of heat, the weight of the air, the velocity of the wind, and the depth of the rainfall. Pupils should make weather reports day by day and compare them with the printed weather reports. The elementary study of air and its composition should be made; its weight, direction, and velocity. The study of evaporation of water, followed by the forms of water in the air — fog, mist, and cloud, should be made. Pupils may be called upon to make daily prophesies of the weather, and give their reasons for the same. Every change of the atmosphere, shower, rain, hail, snow, or wind may be taken advantage of for this purpose.

The uses of water may be discussed, especially the uses of water for vegetable life; the drainage of the land, especially on farms where the land has to be tiled, or where irrigation is necessary. Questions like these may be subjects of investigation: How far does the water go down into the earth? What stops it? The cause of a spring? A brook, creek, rivulet, or river? The saturation of different kinds of soil and rock by water.

Depth of the wells and changes in the water level. Into this discussion would come the question of floods and flood plains, and of silt brought down by the water, how and where deposited, that is to say, if there is a creek or a river on or near the farm.

These are some of the innumerable points in regard to meteorology that impinge on the child from all sides, and lead to higher and more difficult questions and investigations.

PLANT LIFE.

I should place first in this study the crops upon the farm; the study of the corn; its history; its nature; different kinds of corn; the uses of corn. The same may be said of wheat, oats, rye, and barley. How land should be fertilized for different crops. Study of the food of plants, nutrition, etc. The grasses may be studied; different kinds of grasses brought into the schoolroom.

In the spring germination of seeds may be especially noted. Seeds should be planted in boxes in the schoolroom. It would be an excellent plan to have a half-acre garden near the school, in which the experiments could be performed, and in which the farmers of the district would take a deep interest. The garden could be made of value, and should include everything that is raised on the farm. There should be a preliminary study of plants, especially flowers, in regard to function. Little or no attempt, at first, should be made to close analysis, or to classification. The guide in the elementary study of all subjects should be function.

Forests; different kinds of trees on the farm; leaves, and bark of the trees; deciduous and non-deciduous trees; the uses of wood for heat, shelter, and household furniture.

ZOÖLOGY.

The study of domestic animals and their functions; cows, and different kinds of cows; milk, and how milk is changed to butter and cheese. The history, for instance, of butter and cheese-making, from the old-fashioned churn to the creamery. Study of horses, and sheep; use of wools; meat of different animals. Study of wild animals, birds. Get each pupil to make a list of all the birds he sees upon the farm during the year; when they come, how long they stay, when they depart. This would bring observations in regard to migration. Name the birds staying upon the farm all summer. Where do they build their nests? How do they raise their young? What do they eat? What birds are injurious to the farm? What birds are useful? The pupils could learn many a profitable lesson: would find that most of the old ideas about birds are totally wrong; that many, if not all, of the birds that have been counted mischievous are really helpful; that birds are needed on the farm to kill destructive insects; that the little damage which crows, for instance, bring about is comparatively nothing to the good they do; that the birds are really "nature's militia" to destroy the enemies that menace the life of vegetable, plant, and tree.

Another study is that of destructive insects; the wood-borers, the cankerworms, the weevil; a very practical study. Then there are the bees, wasps, butterflies, and their uses in efflorescence. The wonders of honey-making. The earthworms and the effect they have upon the soil. The boy will be sure not to leave out the woodchuck, the fox, the coon, or the muskrat. He may even learn that the unpleasant little skunk has a use and a place in the world.

PHYSICS AND CHEMISTRY.

Wherever forces are seen, felt, or handled, an inquiry into the nature of such forces is the study of physics. Meteorology is one of the great departments of physics. Distribution of sunshine, the working and nature of heat, the force and wearing of water, measurements of air, of the wind, are all close to the child, who needs only good teaching to lead him to close and closer investigation.

Practical uses of force suggest many problems: force of running water; running mills; force of wind is turning windmills; the economical application of force in farm machinery from the apple-parer to the reaper; the mystery of the lever revealed by wedge and crowbar; the turning of the grindstone; and the use of the jackscrew in raising buildings.

Chemical changes are taking place in earth, air, and water, and are continually applied in the household affairs. The teacher has an excellent opportunity to call attention to the chemistry of cooking; to yeast; to milk in its transmutation to butter and cheese; the making of lye and soap; the oxidation of metals. The composition and nature of different soils are a fruitful study; the effect of sunlight upon foliage in the production of leaf green; the transpiration of water through vegetable tissues, bearing nutrition from cell to cell. The burning of wood and its change into ashes.

The children upon a farm are called upon to apply daily the laws of chemistry and physics. It is the province of the teacher to lead them to apply these laws more and more intelligently, to the end that a deep interest is aroused and they are made earnest and everlasting students of these subjects.

MATHEMATICS.

There can be no work properly done upon the farm without measuring. Most of this measuring is done by what is called "rule of thumb," or so-called practical judgment. The farmer estimates weight of cattle, hogs, or sheep by sight. He can tell how much cord wood or timber a certain area of forest will produce. In fact, measuring in everything he does is absolutely essential. There is no better way for the teacher to study the processes of measuring, or arithmetic, than to inquire into the everyday demands of farm work, and no better way to teach arithmetic than to bring the measuring necessary for farm work into the schoolroom. The elementary work, and the work that ought to be continued throughout the course, should be largely estimation with eye and hand, of length, of distance, area, volume, bulk, force, and weight; the estimates to be verified by actual measurements. That which a farmer is called upon at every turn to do should be begun with the children. And here the parent can supplement the teacher at every step.

When developing the mode of judgment, the pupil should be trained to use the chain in measuring areas, the yard-stick in measuring cord wood, forceps in lumber, dry measure for grain, scales for weights, liquid measure for milk, vinegar, or molasses.

The outcome of all raising of crops is commercial value. There should be a system of farm bookkeeping, in which writing and arithmetic play a prominent part. Children could be easily trained to keep books for their parents, and the work of the farm be made to present all the problems and conditions for a complete mastery of all essentials in arithmetic.

READING AND LITERATURE.

The suggestions already given are for the elementary study of subjects. Interest in all these subjects will lead directly to a great desire to know more of the observations and investigations of others. Here reading and the study of text-books have their great place. The first steps in reading may be short stories of the farm, of the crops, of the animal and plant life, written in simple sentences upon the blackboard. The reading lessons should be closely related, and from beginning to end bear directly upon the subjects the child studies.

Nor is there wanting a great and extensive literature on geography, geology, mineralogy, and botany. Books like "The Soil," written by F. H. King, University of Wisconsin, and "The Great World's Farm," by Salina Gaye, would arouse an intense interest if the subjects here named were really used for the education of the child. Poetry may be brought in at every step — the poetry of the farm, the clouds, the air, the winds, the flowers, the fields. The pupil will find that the poet and the artist have embalmed in deathless prose or poetry the commonest things of earth, air, and water by which he is surrounded. Thin, vapid, sensational, injurious reading would have no place in his life if all reading were carefully selected in the direction of his aroused, sustained, and educative interests.

The process of learning to read is a very simple one if the free, spontaneous action of the mind is not obstructed by abnormal methods. When the proper stage of development, which manifests itself in an intense desire to gain knowledge through the printed page is reached, the child will learn to read as easily as he has already learned to hear language. All reading should come close to the child, should enter into his personal experience; should be about something he feels the need of knowing — facts about his pets, about things he loves to do — words that re-image familiar scenes. This would make reading and the selection of good literature a habit for life.

WRITING, GRAMMAR, SPELLING.

Writing is one of the modes of thought expression. The fundamental necessity is *to have something to express*, some image to control and steady the hand, some earnest desire to communicate with others by means of writing. Skill in writing takes care of itself if the teacher writes rapidly and well. Technical skill is nine-tenths imitation. The main thing is the impulse which the teacher discerns, seizes upon, guides, and controls. The farm is rich with interesting subjects, rich for the novice of six, or the pupil of sixteen. Descriptions of animals, plants, forests, fields, pastures, hills, valleys, soils, the germination of seeds, the gardening, the shower, the clouds, the rainstorm, hailstorm, snowstorm, the cyclone, the raising of crops, the cutting and curing of hay, the harvest, the market — these are among the innumerable subjects that may be made of intense interest to the children of the country. The little ones may write a word, a line, or a paragraph; the older ones, pages.

And in such work comes the one sensible method of teaching spelling and grammar. Writing is spelling and punctuation, just as speech is fundamentally pronunciation. Using correct language is grammar, and where can pupils use correct language to better advantage than by writing under the direct impulse of thought?

MANUAL TRAINING, ART.

One central and invaluable thing gained on the farm is the necessity for and habit of work. All work on the farm should be honored in the schoolroom by expanding and concentrating it. The school should send back the children to the farm filled with the dignity of labor.

The work of the farm, in a broad sense, is manual training, but most farm boys get a coarse way of doing manual training. They do not learn to use their hands expertly as they should. On all farms there should be workshops for the mending of tools, construction of materials and apparatus for farm work, and in the country school there should also be a small manual training department in which pupils may be trained to use their hands skillfully in making things needed for the farm and the home.

No argument is here made for manual training; I would, however, enter an earnest plea for its adoption in the school on the score that it would make labor both honorable and interesting, and that its value as a potent factor in the development of the brain would be recognized and appreciated by both parents and teachers.

Apparatus for experiment could be made with a small outfit, a bench, a few tools, lumber, and metals. Much of the lumber could be brought by the pupils from the farm. They could cut the wood. If it needed sawing, it could be sawed at the mill. Wood manual training is one of the best ways to learn the uses of woods. There should be a small forge, and some work in iron and other metals as well. Every boy and girl should have a work bench at home and wood-carving materials, to develop the instinctive habit of whittling into something useful and ornamental. Long winter evenings could be profitably utilized in manual training and the exercise of the arts.

The objects of art are countless, the modeling, painting, and drawing of land surfaces in geography, and illustrations in geology and mineralogy. Landscape and plant life furnish a great number of subjects for painting. Children have a perfect passion for drawing, until it is crushed by over-attempts at accuracy, or by the drawing of flat copies. With a good blackboard, which is the best piece of educational apparatus ever invented for school or home, children could show the different kinds of crops; draw cornstalks, grasses, flowers, and trees. Of course, these drawings would be crude, but at the same time they would be satisfactory to the child, and justly, for they would correspond with his images; the drawing, in turn, would stimulate observation, and the result would be clearer insight. Exact drawing could be introduced in measuring, or arithmetic, and in making projection drawings or manual training. Experience has shown that children take great delight in such work, and that is in the highest degree educative.

Art study leads to the cultivation of taste, and many farmhouses, many cold and desolate sitting-rooms could be made beautiful by the art of the children; and their comfort enhanced by the manual training. Every effort should be made to project the work of the school into the life of the child. Invention may be stimulated by asking pupils to plan a hen house, wood shed, barn, farmhouse, and the selection of trees and shrubs to beautify yard, garden, and landscape.

INDUSTRIES AND COMMERCE.

The study of the commercial side of farm products should have its place in the school The cost, the selection, the use of crops, and their value in selling. Here arithmetic and bookkeeping would come in. Transportation of crops would have its place, the team, the railroads. Where farm products are consumed. The subject of farm tools, instruments of work, may be studied. How crops are prepared for the market; the question of mills; the preservation of foods; barns; winter protection of cattle; ensilage Transportation, beasts of burden, wagons, railroads, steamboats, in our own and foreign countries. The beginning of history, how others live and have lived, is involved in this idea of commerce.

The geographical distribution of soil may be considered, as well as the distribution of air, moisture, heat, and plant life, and through the careful and thoughtful study of the farm the whole earth, in time, may be brought to the child.

HISTORY.

The elements of history are everywhere present on the farm. The history of farming tools, from the sickle to the reaper; from the crude plow of the poet to the steam plow of today; from the hoe to the cultivator. The history of butter-making, from the old-fashioned churn to the model creamery. The story of the mill; the history of the potato; of maize; of the tomato. How beets are now competing with sugar cane. If there is an experimental station in the neighborhood, it should be used as an auxiliary to the school, where the history and present status of agriculture may be studied.

Most towns in the eastern states, and some in the West, have interesting local histories. There are generally stories of the Indians, of settlements, of colonization, of noted men and women, of the part taken by the citizens in the Civil War. A strong love for history can be induced and fostered by beginning this study close to the home.

The breakfast and dinner table furnishes excellent starting points in the study of history. How much does the farm in itself furnish of the food of the family? What is obtained outside, and where is it obtained? History of the making of cloth, the story of the spinning wheel and the spinning jenny; the hand loom and the power loom. The study of the inventions used on the farm will lead directly to the biographies of their inventors and the relation of machinery to human progress. The history of roads and road making, back to the time of the Romans. There should be lessons in every school upon the necessity and practicability of good roads, and the best methods and material for making them.

CONCLUSION.

The tremendous advantage of a rational course of work in country schools is that it would make a strong, binding union of the home and the school, the farm methods and the school methods. It would bring the farm into the school, and project the school into the farm. It would give parent and teacher one motive, in the carrying out of which both could heartily join. The parent would appreciate and judge fairly the work of the school, the teacher would honor, dignify, and elevate the work of the farm. Farmer and housewife would be ready to discuss the methods of the farm and housekeeping in the school. Children, parents, and teachers could meet at stated periods and hold discussions in the direction of their highest interests. One of the best meetings I ever attended was a union of grangers and teachers in Oceana county, Mich. One hour was devoted to a discussion of how to raise potatoes, and the next was given to the education of children.

The farmers would become deeply interested in having libraries in the schools, carefully selected. Long winter evenings could be spent around the fireside in mutual study; parents helping children, and the children, in turn, arousing and stimulating parents.

Country life too often fails in the proper social conditions. It tends to isolation. A common purpose of education would obviate this. The farmer would often invite the school to visit his farm, and to study it. Pleasant and profitable social meetings would be the order of the day. The teacher with clear ideas of what education ought to be would bring the people of a district together to discuss the welfare of their children. Exhibits of pupils' work, of manual training and the arts would naturally follow and greatly increase the interest.

It is an indisputable fact that cities draw largely upon the country for men of action and affairs. There are, no doubt, some notable exceptions to this rule, but in the main, the leaders, both men and women, successful manufacturers, bankers, doctors, lawyers, ministers, statesmen, have received their early education upon the farm or in the workshop.

Education deserves to be regarded in a broader and more rational light. Real education should be read in terms of character — character translated into action. Sound judgment, common sense, wisdom acquired by observation and tempered by experience, with genius to help one's self, and power to plan and execute, entitle a man to a diploma from the world at large, if not from a university. Education which is worthy the name generates the power that penetrates life and makes it better.

No method, no system of schools, no enrichment of courses of study, not even the most successful of teachers, can ever take the place in fundamental education of the farm and the workshop. No matter how good the city schools may be, or may be made; no matter how good the state of society may be, the vital reinforcements of city life that lead to progress and prosperity, so far as we can see, must always come from the sturdy stock of the farm. This fact, upon which most educators agree, puts upon the country school an immense responsibility. It is no small office to train the men and women who are to lead and guide the future of the republic.

The country schools have every advantage, so far as material means are concerned; their environment is rich in organic and inorganic forms; but in one thing they are lacking — the teacher who can utilize that which offers itself in such abundance. This is a want which every thoughtful person deplores, a want that will be met when the farmers themselves realize what a powerful influence for good their schools may be made.

When skill, expertness, and insight control the methods of country schools; when excellent teachers remain in the same schools year after year, the already powerful influence of country life upon the destinies of the nation will be mightily enhanced.

A large majority of boys and girls upon the farm entertain mistaken notions of life in cities, and early form a desire to enter into the seemingly greater advantages to be found in such centers. This leads to the congestion of cities, and disturbs the social balance. School education alone can cope with this disease of the body politic, and this by fostering an interest in farm life and farm work.

Boys must be led to see something more in farm life than patient, continuous work of planting, sowing, care-taking, and reaping. Many a young man leaves the farm to become a mere counter-jumper in the city, who, if he had the right education, would make himself an influential and successful farmer.

My plea, then, is that the country school should make farm labor and all labor honorable; should dignify it; should show that the environment of the country furnishes inexhaustible resources for intellectual life; should see to it that the æsthetic side of child nature be assiduously cultivated; that the child bring a loving heart to nature, have an appreciative eye for beautiful things; that he be led to see the possibilities in the landscape of the farm — the necessity of making excellent roads, well lined with shade trees; that the so-called practical things of life, hard and severe labor, should have their highest outcome in the cultivation of the love of the beautiful in life — that love which leads the soul to profound reverence for all things of earth, because they are loving gifts of an infinite God.

FRANCIS W. PARKER.

Chicago Normal School.

APPENDIX I.

THE COUNTRY-SCHOOL PROBLEM.

[A paper read before the National Council of Education, July 10, 1894, by Emerson E. White, LL.D.]

It is not my purpose to deny or obscure the real difficulties involved in what is called "The Country-School Problem." This is not a question of nomenclature, but a problem of school organization under special conditions.

The problem may thus be stated:

Given a school of twenty to forty pupils from five and six to, say, sixteen years of age, accommodated in one room and taught by one teacher.

To find the best possible organization and administration that the conditions will permit.

The facts that enter into the problem are (1) that the pupils possess very unequal ability and attainments, and those who at a given time are nearly equal in attainment make unequal and varying progress; (2) that the pupils need instruction and training adapted to their ability and needs each successive term, and hence this instruction must have *sequence*, thus permitting progress; and (3) that the health and physical endurance of teacher and pupils limit the daily school session to about six hours. It is also to be kept in mind that the problem involves the providing of the best possible instruction and training not in one branch, not merely in "the three R's," but in all the essential elementary branches.

I. NON-CLASSIFICATION SOLUTION.

The first solution proposed makes no provision for the classification of the pupils, but each pupil is taught by himself in all branches of study. It is seen that this plan gives as a minimum as many separate teaching exercises as there are pupils in the school, provided each pupil has only one daily lesson. If only "the three R's" are taught, and each separately, there will be three times as many teaching exercises as there are pupils, and, if the three exercises for each pupil are combined in one, the length of time devoted to each exercise must be increased. But the modern programme of school instruction includes from five to seven school arts, and, in case of the more advanced pupils, several additional branches of study, as geography, English grammar, history, and physiology.

It is unnecessary to take time to show that it is not possible for one teacher to instruct twenty or more pupils, each by himself, in the essential elementary branches. The number of exercises thus required reduces the length of each to so short a time that no efficient instruction is possible; and hence the non-classification solution proposed for the country school may be dismissed as *impracticable*. The plan of individual instruction is only feasible in a school composed of very few pupils.

We sometimes hear of the old-time country school in which there were no classes, each pupil being taught by himself, if taught at all; but I am satisfied that this school exists in the imagination, and not in history. If it ever had an existence it certainly preceded the organization of the common school, if it did not precede any school composed of more than ten pupils. Even ten pupils under one teacher necessitate some classification to permit any efficient instruction or drill.

My father was a pupil in one of the early common schools in New England, and I was a pupil in a still more primitive school in the then backwoods of Ohio, but neither my father nor myself ever saw the wholly unclassified country school of which the present generation of teachers is hearing. In at least two of the three *common* branches—*i. e.*, branches common to all—the pupils in the old-time school were classified. It is true that little attempt at classification was made in teaching the ABC's or the *a-b-abs*, but necessity forced an early classification in both reading and spelling—imperfect, it is true, but necessary and helpful. I now see in my mind's eye the row of big boys and girls that sat on the back seats and read together in the old English reader, and I also see the rows of boys and girls, who constituted the successive classes in spelling, standing on the floor and "toeing the mark."

No attempt was made in the first schools which I attended at classification in arithmetic, and later the attempt was first confined to the multiplication table, which few pupils perfectly mastered, and so common drills were feasible. As a rule, each pupil "ciphered" by himself, at his own gait, going to the teacher or some pupil for assistance, when needed. The fact that most of the pupils never reached fractions, and fewer ever acquired much skill in integer processes, is evidence of the weakness of individual work even in such a study as arithmetic.

A few clever pupils who needed only opportunity for study made good progress without instruction, sometimes remarkable progress, and this was not only true in arithmetic, but also in geography and English grammar, when these branches were reached. The lack of classification in these studies was doubtless an advantage to these few exceptional pupils, but no one who actually knows the old-time country school can commend the progress made by nine-tenths of its pupils. It is not too much to claim that its helpfulness to the great majority of its pupils was increased by improved and wider classification. I well remember the first introduction of classification in arithmetic in the rural schools of my native state. I now see the little blackboard that was first nailed to the wall of that primitive schoolhouse, for, though scarcely in my teens, I was installed as teacher for the first class formed in arithmetic.

When I passed from the dignity of a pupil-teacher to the honors of a teacher, my best work for the country school was in the introduction of improved classification—not only in reading and spelling, but in all the branches taught. Nearly all of the pupils fell into groups or classes with positive advantage. Those who could work ahead with incidental assistance were permitted and encouraged to do so.

II. THE GRADED-SCHOOL SOLUTION.

Another solution proposed is the adoption of a graded course of study with term sections—the annual school session being divided into, say, two terms—the plan of grading adopted in most cities. In other words, the solution proposed is the grading of country schools with one teacher on the plan of the graded schools in cities.

It is seen that this organization divides an elementary course of study into at least sixteen sections, each including sections of the several branches, and it separates the pupils into sixteen or more corresponding grades, if there be a term interval between the grades.[1] The fact that the pupils in each grade study several branches necessitates as many class exercises as there are branches of study. It is thus seen that an average of three class exercises in each grade gives at least forty-eight daily exercises.

It is true that in practice there may be no pupils in several of these term grades, but the reduction in the number of classes thus occasioned will be fully offset by the fact that the pupils in several upper grades study more than three branches, and thus require more than three class exercises to each grade. It seems unnecessary to add that such a classification of the one-teacher school is wholly impracticable. I know of no successful attempt to grade the country school with a *term interval* between the grades.

The more common mode of grading the country school is the nominal adoption of the *year* or session interval between the grades. When this plan of grading is strictly adhered to, and there are pupils in all the grades, there are as many separate class exercises as there are year sections in the course of study multiplied by the average number of branches therein. This gives from thirty to forty class exercises—too many for satisfactory class instruction and drill. But in a school of thirty to forty pupils there are necessarily very few pupils in the upper grades, and none in some grades. These breaks are occasioned by the attendance of pupils only a part of the school session, by the failure of pupils to do the work assigned them, and other causes. It thus often happens that country schools may not *at any one time* actually contain more than five or six grades of pupils, even when they are following a graded course of study with eight or nine-year sections; but the reduction in the number of class exercises thus occasioned does not make a strict adherence to this city plan of grading feasible. Hence in practice various modifications are made; and some of these are easily made if the school be not dominated by, and sacrificed to, the fetich called the "graded system." Several of these feasible modifications may be worthy of consideration.

1. Since the several classes are all taught by the same teacher it is feasible to permit pupils to recite in different grades, strict grading being sacrificed to the best possible classification *in each branch*. Thus a pupil may recite in the fifth grade in arithmetic, the fourth in geography, and so on.

This modification of the graded system is practicable only to a limited extent in cities, since the several grades of pupils occupy, as a rule, separate rooms and are taught by different teachers, and they are thus required to keep a common step in *all* the branches of the course.

2. Since the upper classes in a country school often contain not more than two or

[1] N. B.—The term "grades" is used in this paper to denote those formal divisions of pupils which correspond to the more permanent divisions in the course of study, which are separated by transitional or promotion lines. The pupils in a given grade may be taught in one or more classes in all the branches, or they may be taught in one class in some branches, and in several classes in other branches; and these classes may be changed from time to time, and without reference to grade divisions or intervals. It is thus seen that the terms gradation and classification are not used as synonymous.

three pupils, it is feasible for a bright pupil to work ahead of his class while he continues to recite in it. Thus a pupil may be studying decimal fractions or denominate numbers while reciting with advantage in common fractions; for, while these daily reviews in common fractions may give him little new knowledge, they will increase his skill in fractional processes—and skill in numerical processes is the chief end of elementary training in arithmetic. Indeed, skill of some sort is the chief end of more than half of the exercises in the elementary school, and this requires *repeated action*. Experience shows that it is entirely feasible for capable pupils to work ahead of their classes in such studies as arithmetic, geography, history, etc., and that this is often successfully done with very little assistance. It is thus seen that the one-teacher school permits a happy combination of class instruction and individual work, especially in the case of bright pupils.

3. Another modification may be made in certain art studies, as writing, language, drawing, and singing. For the purpose of drill in these branches, a country school may readily be divided into three classes, and these, except in music, may be taught *simultaneously*, as will be more fully shown later. This arrangement not only reduces the number of classes, but it greatly increases the class practice of the pupils. Nor is it found a serious objection that the classes in these branches are, at any given time, two or more years apart. These arts have phases that correspond respectively to the three psychical phases through which elementary pupils pass as they advance in the course; and the wise teacher can readily so adapt class instruction and drill to the common needs of the pupils in each phase of progress as to afford to all valuable practice. This is successfully done in many country schools.

The feasibility of these and other modifications have saved the country school in many instances from the Procrustean evils that have so often characterized the graded system in cities. The defects of the graded system in cities does not necessarily inhere in the system as it may be practically administered in one-teacher schools in the country. The year interval between grades in cities well-nigh necessitates the "lock-step" advance of the pupils. The classes are too large (or are supposed to be) to permit the teacher to give needed assistance to the strong pupils who may be capable of working ahead in any or all of the studies of a grade, and, at the same time, the interval between the classes is too wide to permit the pupils, with very *few* exceptions, "to jump over" to the next higher grade. We have seen many city classes in which the pupils in the upper third of the class were in ability one year in advance of those in the lower third, and yet these pupils were chained together for one year, and then the only mode of relief was the non-promotion of the lower-third pupils, thus necessitating their going over again an entire year's work. Thoughtful teachers know what this means. The pregnant fact is that the year interval between the classes in elementary schools in cities is incompatible with a flexible classification of pupils. It is everywhere attended with a serious sacrifice of time and opportunity.

In the one-teacher school these evils of the graded system may be somewhat lessened, but, after all feasible modifications have been made, the system, with even a nominal year interval between the grades, is not a satisfactory organization of the country school. The modifications permitted relate chiefly to the classification and advancement of the pupils, but the course of study must be followed. *The essential thing in the graded system is the graded course of study.* To abandon the prescribed sequence and co-ordination of the topics and exercises in the course of study is to give up the system *as such*. But experience shows that it is not practicable to prescribe an "invariable order" of topics and exercises for a one-teacher school. The limitations and conditions of such a school necessitate variations from the prescribed course in order to reduce the number of class exercises, and hence the course of study as well as the grading of pupils must be flexible. System and order must often be sacrificed to the needs of the pupils and the limitations of the teacher. The adoption of well-adjusted courses of study for country schools has unquestionably resulted in great good, but the blind following of such courses in time and order has often resulted in loss. Much of the difficulty that has attended the graded system in country schools has been thus occasioned. What the one-teacher school imperatively demands is not only a flexible and adjustable classification of pupils, but *a flexible course of study*—that is, a course of study which permits changes in the order of topics whenever such changes will result in fewer class exercises with a positive gain in better instruction.

This leads to the consideration of a third solution of the problem before us, and this may be called —

III. THE THREE-GRADE SOLUTION.

The three-grade organization of the country school, or, if preferred, the three-department organization, is based on the psychical transitions which appear in an elementary course of training.

The first of these psychical periods includes the kindergarten and the lower primary classes, with pupils from four or five to eight years of age. This is pre-eminently the objective period of training in which primary knowledge is taught objectively, and primary skill in reading, writing, number, language, etc., is acquired by doing, largely by imitation. The reader is the only book needed by the pupils.

This is followed by, say, three years that may be called the transitional or middle period of elementary training. In this period pupils pass increasingly from concrete facts to their simpler generalizations, from processes to rules, and from the known to the related unknown by either imagination or thought; and skill in the several school arts is increased by practice under guidance, increasingly under ideals. The only text books needed are in reading, arithmetic (first book), and, later, geography (elementary), and these, both in matter and method, should be intelligently adapted to the psychical conditions and needs of young pupils. This is pre-eminently the *fact and skill period* of elementary training.

The next three or four years constitute what may be called the advanced or grammar period. The pupils have now sufficient skill in interpreting written or printed language and sufficient thought power to study, with proper instruction, a complete arithmetic, a school geography, and later (seventh and eighth school years) English grammar, United States history, physiology, and the elements of natural science.

It is seen that the grading of the elementary school on this psychical basis is about the same as that secured by its division into three departments when the number of pupils is sufficient to employ three teachers—one for the lower or primary classes, another for the secondary or middle classes, and a third for the more advanced pupils

This is a natural and simple grading for a country school with one teacher. The distinction in the work of the three grades or divisions is sufficiently marked to permit a definite statement of the knowledge and skill to be acquired in each; and, at the same time, the pupils in each grade can, from term to term, be reclassified, thus keeping the number of classes as few as possible and at the same time putting each pupil where he can make the most progress.

The number of classes in the two upper grades need not exceed two each in any branch, and not more than three separate classes will be needed in any branch in the primary grade—making not more than six or seven different classes in any branch, with an average of not more than four classes in the principal branches. The exercises in writing, language, drawing, and other arts can each be given *in one period*—a very important consideration, since it greatly reduces the number of exercises and, at the same time, secures needed instruction and desired progress.

The course of study can readily be arranged on the same basis. The studies and exercises of each grade may be grouped, thus dividing the course into three well-defined sections—primary, middle, and advanced—and the attainments required for promotion from one grade to the next higher can be definitely prescribed. It is not necessary to divide the course into year and term sections with a prescribed order of subjects and parts of subjects for each term, as is often done in graded courses for cities. There should be a division of the course into three sections, with a general order or sequence of topics in each, but the teacher should be left free to form classes with varying intervals between them, and the progress of each class should not be fixed by a time schedule—as is sometimes done in city schools with many teachers. To reduce the number of classes in a given grade it may be necessary to take up parts of subjects in a different order from that laid down in the course of study, and no two classes may make equal progress.

The essential provision is that the work provided for each grade be completed *as a condition of promotion to the next higher grade.* This will establish a clear distinction between the several grades, and, at the same time, it will allow that flexibility of classification *between* grade lines which is essential in a one teacher school.

It is not meant that pupils shall be stopped at the line that separates two grades until they have reached the standard in *all* branches of the lower grade, as is generally required when a school is divided into three departments, each under a separate teacher and occupying a separate room. In a one-teacher school pupils may and should be permitted to pass a grade line in any branch when they are prepared to do the work of the next higher grade. In practice it will be found that most pupils can, with advantage, cross the grade line in all branches at the same time, but this result should not be forced.

THREE-GRADE PROGRAMME.

A course of study on these three psychical grades of work and attainment makes a three-grade programme of class exercises and seat work both feasible and desirable.

I have elsewhere[1] presented such a programme with a full statement of its uses and advantages in a one-teacher school. It must suffice to insert the programme here, with a brief explanation.

This programme indicates not only the class exercises, but also the study or seat work, the class exercises being denoted by bold-face type and the study or seat work by common type. The day session of the school is divided into periods of twenty, twenty-five, and thirty minutes each, the spelling drills in the two upper grades being considered one period; and the teacher's time is divided equitably among the three grades of pupils. The A-grade pupils have eight exercises each day, the B-grade pupils six exercises, and the C-grade pupils five; but, as is seen, the A-grade pupils have two more studies than the B-grade, and the B-grade pupils have one more study than the C-grade. The extra time required to prepare and direct the seat work in Grade C will make the time devoted by the teacher to this grade nearly, if not quite, equal to that devoted to the B-grade.

A rural school of some thirty pupils will probably have two classes in several branches in the A-grade, two classes in one or more branches in the B-grade, and possibly three classes in the C-grade; making in all some seven different classes of pupils. The time allotted to any branch (as arithmetic) in a given grade must be divided between the several classes (if there be more than one class in the grade), but not equally from day to day, the time devoted to each class depending on the nature of the lessons. One day the upper class in Grade A in arithmetic, for example, may have only ten minutes, and the lower class fifteen minutes, and the next day this may be reversed. What the programme requires is that the several exercises do not together exceed the time assigned to the grade. Writing, language, and drawing in all three grades are to be taught simultaneously in the same

[1] White's "School Management," pp. 86–94.

THREE-GRADE PROGRAMME.*

Closing Time	Minutes	Primary (C)	Secondary (B)	Advanced (A)
9.10	10	OPENING EXERCISES		
9.35	25	Seat Work †	Arithmetic	**Arithmetic**
10.00	25	Number On slate or with objects	**Arithmetic**	Geography
10.25	25	**Number**	Geography	Geography
10.45	20	Form Work Paper folding, stick laying, etc	Geography	**Geography**
10.55	10	RECESS		
11.15	20	Silent Reading	**Geography**	Grammar
11.35	20	**Reading and Spelling**	Form Work Map draw'g, sand molding, etc	Grammar
12.00	25	Excused from School	Reading	**Grammar**
		NOON INTERMISSION		
1.10	10	†	†	†
1.30	20	Form Work Clay model'g, paper cutt'g, etc	**Reading**	Reading
1.50	20	Silent Reading	Seat Work †	**Reading**
2.10	20	**Reading and Spelling**	Animal or Plant Study	U. S. History or Physiology
2.40	30	**Writing[2] or Language[3]**	**Writing[2] or Language[3]**	**Writing[2] or Language[3]**
2.50	10	RECESS		
3.10	20	Number On slate or with objects	Spelling	**U. S. History or Physiology**
3.35	25	**Drawing,[2] Singing,[2] or Moral Instruction[1]**	**Drawing,[2] Singing,[2] or Moral Instruction[1]**	**Drawing,[2] Singing,[2] or Moral Instruction[1]**
3.50	15	Excused from School	**Spelling**	Spelling
4.00	10		Arithmetic	**Spelling**

† As may be provided for by the teacher.

NOTES: The small figures at right indicate the number of lessons a week.

United States history may be taught the first half of the session, and physiology the second half; or each branch may have two lessons a week.

On Friday the last twenty-five minutes may be devoted to instruction in hygiene, temperance, physics, natural history, etc.

period. The inexperienced teacher may not see how this can be successfully done, but the apparent difficulty has been solved in hundreds of schools.

The most hopeful improvement of the country school lies in the adoption of a simpler grading than that of the city school, a more flexible classification, with opportunity for individual study and progress, and a workable daily programme. It needs system, but not rigidity — an elastic system adapted to its conditions and limitations. The danger is that the rural school may be sacrificed to rigid grading, as has been true in so many cities. What the country school needs is not a Procrustean system of grading and promotions, but such an organization as will permit its single-handed teacher and diverse pupils to make the best possible use of time and strength.

It is idle to talk of abandoning all attempts to improve the classification of country schools. Attempts at classification in reading and spelling are as old as the school itself, and classification in other branches has attended, if it has not made possible, most improvements that have been made. The disappointments have usually been due to unwise attempts to introduce into rural schools the rigid graded system as developed in the cities. Such attempts ignore conditions and limitations.

It seems wise to add here that the one-teacher school will not permit a perfect organization. It has necessary limitations, and, after the best possible has been done, it will still have its imperfections. It is, however, my belief that the teacher of a country school, if competent, has some advantage over the teacher of the "highly organized" city school. It is certainly possible to make the one-teacher school a most valuable agency for the elementary education of children.

REMARKS.

It seems important to call attention to the fact that the term "grade" in this paper is used in the sense of section or department, and not as synonymous with class. The term grade is applied to the three divisions of the pupils of a school, which correspond respectively to the three recognized psychical periods through which pupils pass as they advance from the kindergarten to the secondary school. It would possibly have been better if the term *section* had been used instead of grade, and, perhaps, still better if the word *group* had been employed, the term used by the Subcommittee in its report. Indeed, the reader can substitute the terms *group* or *groups* for *grade* or *grades*, as the case may be, throughout the paper, without materially changing its meaning. The sense in which the term grade is used is explained in the footnote on page 163, and it is also made clear in the paper. The term applies not only to the three groups of pupils, but also to the corresponding divisions in the course of study.

The division of the course of study into three sections or groups has important practical advantages. Among these advantages are:

1. Needed freedom of classification and instruction in each section. This advantage can be fully appreciated only by those who have actually used the plan in rural schools. The fact that the subjects and disciplines in each of these sections are closely related facilitates reclassifications and sometimes a temporary union of classes.

2. A standard and an evidence of progress. The promotion of pupils from one section to the next higher is stimulating evidence of progress, and, as a result, the advancement of pupils from section to section affords a wholesome incentive throughout the entire course. The fact that pupils are known as primary, or secondary, or advanced (Group I., or Group II., or Group III.), affords both satisfaction and stimulus.

3. A needed reduction of class exercises in writing, drawing, language, and other school arts in which skill is the chief end. Reference to the programme on page 167 will show that instruction and drill in writing and language are provided for in only *one period* each day, and the same is true of drawing, singing, and moral instruction. This is not accomplished by making each of these subjects a general exercise for the entire school,

but the pupils in each section (group) have a lesson adapted to their ability and attainments, thus securing desired progress from year to year. It is found entirely feasible to teach the pupils of a rural school in each of the school arts in three sections (groups), and, what is very important, the three section exercises can be taught *in one period*, as shown in the programme. The manner in which this is done in practice is shown in the writer's "School Management," p. 92, and the feasibility of the plan is attested by its successful use by hundreds of teachers. In teaching the several school arts, skill is the chief end, and this can only be attained by guided practice. The needed preparatory instruction in any elementary art lesson can be given within five minutes, and hence in less than fifteen minutes the pupils in three sections, beginning with the highest, can be prepared for fruitful practice; and then the remaining part of the period can be devoted to an inspection of the pupils' work in each section, the giving of needed instruction, etc. It is true that physical exercises and even singing, as usually taught, can be made a general exercise, but it would be a great gain if the pupils in the primary section, at least, were given separate instruction in music. No school art in which progress from year to year is desirable should be taught in a rural school as a *general* exercise. The three-section plan affords time for instruction and practice, and secures desired progress.

4. A workable programme, one that regulates class exercises *and seat work*. I am confident that no rural teacher who uses a section (group) programme long enough to become skillful will ever go back to a class programme with its numerous and unequal divisions of time. The regulation of the seat work of pupils is an important element in school administration.

The great desideratum of the rural school is a practical reduction in the number of daily class exercises. The three-section plan reduces the number of exercises in teaching the several school arts to a minimum, and it also facilitates a reduction in the number of exercises in arithmetic, geography, history, and other branches which require previous preparation by the pupil. The manner in which this is accomplished is pointed out in the paper. It is true that the very best that can be done in this direction still leaves the rural school with too many class exercises and, as a consequence, too little time in each for satisfactory instruction. The brevity of class exercises is, however, in part offset by the fact that the classes are *small*, and also by the further fact that the section programme permits a variation in the time given to exercises, the time depending *on the nature of the lesson*, the essential condition being that the time devoted to the classes in a given branch shall not exceed the time allotted to the section.

It seems unnecessary to guard the reader against the inference that the pupils in each of the three sections are to be taught as one class in each branch, thus giving an interval of two or more years between successive classes. This is only true of *skill exercises in art studies* — exercises that do not require previous preparation by pupils. In these art studies there may be an apparent interval of at least two years between the sections or classes, but this is not a serious difficulty in actual practice. In the other branches the pupils in a section may be subdivided into classes, with a varying interval between them. This interval need not be *common* to all the branches, as in graded schools in cities, but each branch may have its own interval, and this be unequal and varying. The interval between two successive classes in arithmetic in a section may not exceed one term, while the interval between the corresponding classes in English grammar may be a year. It is not only true that a uniform class interval of one year is incompatible with a workable classification of rural schools, but any *fixed* interval between classes results in rigidity and loss.

Nor is it desirable in a rural school to keep the classes in the several branches abreast as they advance in the course, as is the practice in graded schools. It is wholly unnecessary to keep a class in arithmetic, for example, "marking time" while the pupils are bringing up belated work in grammar or history. In a one-teacher school there is no serious loss or inconvenience if the pupils do not maintain the same rate of progress in all the branches of the course. What is needed is a free movement forward, not only of individual pupils, but of the several classes.

There is, in my judgment, no serious difficulty in teaching the pupils in a rural school in most instances in classes. This can readily be done in all art or skill branches, and in the other branches *most* of the pupils can be classified with advantage. When a pupil can not profitably keep step with a class, he should be permitted and encouraged to work by himself. It may be that in a term or so he will reach a class in which he can recite, at least for a time; and, while he is working by himself in one branch, he may be in classes in other branches.

The rural school must make provision for individual progress, but individual study and instruction should not prevent needed classification and a regulating system. A graded course of study, with its sequence of topics and exercises, and its division into natural sections, makes a return to the unclassified condition of tne old-time country school impossible, as well as undesirable.

A hint of my ideal of a one-teacher rural school is given below by means of a graphic illustration. I take a school of thirty (30) pupils, and suppose twelve of these pupils to fall in Group I. (using the terminology of the subcommittee), ten in Group II., and eight in Group III. The pupils are designated by numbers, those in the first group by the exponent 1; those in the second group by the exponent 2; and those in the third group by the exponent 3.

	Group I. (C)	Group II. (B)	Group III. (A)
Reading and Spelling	$1^1\ 2^1\ 6^1\ 9^1\ 11^1$ $3^1\ 4^1\ 7^1\ 10^1\ 12^1$ $5^2\ 8^1$	$13^2\ 16^2\ 18^2\ 20^2$ $14^2\ 17^2\ 19^2\ 21^2$ 15^2	$22^2\ 25^3\ 28^3$ $23^3\ 26^3\ 29^3$ $24^3\ 27^3\ 30^3$
Arithmetic ...... Oral in Group I.	$1^1\ 2^1\ 7^1\ 8^1$ $3^1\ 4^1\ 9^1\ 10^1$ $5^1\ 6^1\ 11^1$	$12^1\ 13^2\ 19^2$ $14^2\ 15^2\ 18^2\ 20^2\ 21^2$ $16^2\ 17^2\ 22^2\ 23^3$	$24^3\ 30^3$ $25^3\ 27^3\ 28^3\ 29^3$ 26^3
Geography....... Oral in Group I.	$1^1\ 4^1\ 8^1\ 11^1$ $2^1\ 5^1\ 7^1\ 9^1\ 12^1$ $3^1\ 6^1\ 10^1$	$13^2\ 16^2\ 18^2\ 21^2$ $14^2\ 17^2\ 19^2\ 22^2$ $15^2\ 20^2$	$23^3\ 26^3$ $24^3\ 27^3\ 28^3\ 29^3\ 30^3$ 25^3
English Grammar.	For synthetic lan	guage exercises, see below	$23^3\ 26^3\ 28^3$ $24^3\ 29^3$ $25^3\ 27^3\ 30^3$
History and Physiology			$22^3\ 28^3$ $24^3\ 26^3\ 29^3$ $25^3\ 27^3\ 30^3$
Writing and Language.........	$1^1\ 5^1\ 9^1$ $2^1\ 6^1\ 10^1$ $3^1\ 7^1\ 11^1$ $4^1\ 8^1\ 12^1$	$13^2\ 16^2\ 19^2$ $14^2\ 17^2\ 20^2$ $15^2\ 18^2\ 21^2$ 22^2	$23^3\ 27^3$ $24^3\ 28^3$ $25^3\ 29^3$ $26^3\ 30^3$
Drawing, Singing, etc............	$1^1\ 5^1\ 9^1$ $2^1\ 6^1\ 10^1$ $3^1\ 7^1\ 11^1$ $4^1\ 8^1\ 12^1$	$13^2\ 17^2$ $14^2\ 18^2\ 21^2$ $15^2\ 19^2\ 22^2$ $16^2\ 20^2$	$23^3\ 27^3$ $24^3\ 28^3$ $25^3\ 29^3$ $26^3\ 30^3$

Supposing the pupils to have a lesson daily in each branch or group of branches (as indicated), the above scheme gives only fifteen daily class exercises, not including those in Group I. in reading and spelling, number, and geography. Weekly exercises are not represented. It is possible for a teacher to do good work with this number of exercises with small classes. The largest amount of individual work is found in Group III. In practice there would doubtless be more irregularities in classification than can well be shown in the illustration.

Columbus, O. EMERSON E. WHITE.

COURSE OF INSTRUCTION FOR RURAL SCHOOLS.

Prepared in accordance with the directions of the Committee of Twelve at its meeting in Chicago, November 18, 1896.

SUGGESTIONS.

[This course of study is arranged in four groups, partly with the thought that whenever the schools of a township are gathered at one or more central points the first two may constitute the basis of work for the lower, and the last two for the higher room. Whether the three-group system explained by Dr. White be used, or the four-group, as indicated in this course, must depend very largely upon the size and advancement of the school. The principles are the same in either case.—HENRY SABIN.]

"*The course of study is the measuring rod or scale which is used to determine at what point in the eight years' work in the elementary course a pupil's work has arrived. It should not be used as the Procrustean bed on which to stretch the work of the school in order to give uniformity.*" (Report of Subcommittee on Instruction and Discipline.)

It is the aim in this course of instruction to present the most essential topics in orderly sequence, without any prescription of methods of teaching. It can be begun at any age from five to seven; it can be continued, often with profit, to a later age than is here stated. It is believed that this course offers every facility for combinations of classes, for transfers of pupils, and for any system of alternation.

This course recognizes the essential elements entering into accepted courses of instruction. Each of the four groups comprises about two years' work. In these groups there will be divisions into sections—as (*a*), (*b*)—only when absolutely necessary. Experience has shown that, within the age limits of the several groups, the work as laid down can be done. Whenever a pupil is able to do the work of the succeeding group he should pass to it. In small schools there will be much individual instruction, and in these will seldom be found pupils representing all these grades of work. In large schools, with one teacher, a skilful teacher can to a considerable extent secure assistance from the more advanced pupils in certain work with the younger, to the mutual advantage of teacher and taught, as well as to the school as a whole. This has been done in this country, and is done throughout England today under the pupil-teacher system.

Whenever several schools working on such a course are consolidated so as to employ two teachers, if one teacher take Groups I. and II., and the other Groups III. and IV., the school is at once graded into a primary and a grammar school, and the next step in gradation will give one group to each teacher. In this gradation the work of each group will be expanded as circumstances allow. If, in the course as here laid down, a line of work —as elements of science—must be omitted, the time can be added to other subjects; if in some subjects—as elements of science and morals—but few lessons can be given, even these lessons, carefully prepared and well taught, will tend to make the teacher a better teacher, the pupil a more thoughtful pupil, and to raise the standard of the school.

To carry out such a plan of work as is here outlined, the pupil as he advances must do more and more for himself under the guidance of the teacher, very much to the advantage of the pupil. Thus, in arithmetic, there is provision for but two formal recitations per week in Group III.; for but one in Group IV. For the rest the pupil learns to do by doing.

The studies are grouped, each group comprising about two years' work:

	GROUP I. (5-7 years.)	GROUP II. (7-9 years.)
Reading.	(*a*) First exercises in reading; from blackboard and chart; Primer and First Reader; and appropriate literature. (*b*) First and Second Readers, and other reading of similar grade. Children should be taught carefully such selections as will awaken interest and lead to a desire to read for themselves. In all grades children should memorize choice selections appropriate to their age.	(*a*) Second Reader and literature of similar grade. Fables and folk stories, etc. (*b*) Third Reader or books of similar grade. Literature as supplementary readings. (See general directions in I.)
Spelling.	Taught chiefly in connection with reading. Oral and written.	Taught chiefly in connection with reading and other studies of group. Chiefly written.
Writing.	In this section the child should learn to write legibly and neatly, and should form the habit of writing with correct position of paper, body, and hand. Use the pen early.	Use simplest forms of letters; train to uniformity in spacing between letters and words, and in size and height of letters; in short, in all the qualities which constitute a neat and legible written page. Insist upon careful penmanship in all written work.

GROUP III. (9-11 years.)	GROUP IV. (11-13 years.)	
Fourth Reader at discretion of teacher for drill; the reading should be largely of literature, as supplementary reading. The drill should be mainly in the reader, and the choice of literature as supplementary reading should be such as the pupil can read with such ease as to give pleasure and thus develop a desire to read good literature. Take great care to cultivate a taste for good reading. Train pupils in proper use of the library.	The reading of good literature, as much as can be carefully read. Memorizing of choice selections should receive careful attention. Encourage home reading. III. and IV. should constitute one class each, and the reading lesson drill need not be a daily exercise. From the first give careful attention to the cultivation of the speaking voice.	**Reading.**
Words to be selected chiefly from reading and other studies of group. Chiefly written.	Words to be selected from studies of group, or spelling-book. To be taught chiefly in connection with written work.	**Spelling.**
See Group II. Much practice to give ease and rapidity, never sacrificing legibility and neatness. Much writing, to form the habit of easily expressing thought with the pen.	See Group III. Writing in this group should be chiefly in composition, in written lessons, and reviews, in practice in business forms, and in correspondence.	**Writing.**

Language.

GROUP I. (5-7 years.)

(*a*) Conversational lessons on familiar experiences and familiar things. Reproduction of stories told by the teacher; invention of stories suggested by pictures, etc. All this will be training in observation and thinking as well as in expression. Great care is necessary as to choice of words and tones of voice.

(*b*) Similar to (*a*), adding written to oral expression; instruction in correctness of the written forms, as the form of the sentences, the use of capitals and punctuation. Memorizing of choice selections.

GROUP II. (7-9 years.)

(*a*) See (*b*), Group I. Combination of oral and written work. Seek variety in subjects. Base lessons on nature lessons, readings, etc. Careful attention to form and use of complete sentences in recitation and conversation, to purity of tone, clearness of enunciation, correctness of pronunciation in speaking, to legibility and neatness in writing.

(*b*) Work of previous years continued and expanded; oral narration, invention (from pictures, etc.), description, with written sentences from the same; letter writing, with special attention to the general form of the letter; careful attention to the vocabulary of the child. Memorizing of choice selections.

In much of this work all the group can be taught as one class, but pupils of very unequal advancement should not be classed together.

History.

GROUP I.

Short stories, such as will interest the child, drawn from biography, history, and travels. Explanation of historical pictures.

The teacher must have at hand appropriate books for the readings by herself or by the pupils, hence the necessity for a school library.

GROUP II.

See Group I. Conversations on current events within the knowledge or easy comprehension of the child. Conversations, stories, and readings on the lives of eminent historical characters, and on the memorable in historical events, such as can be easily imagined and comprehended by the child. National manners and customs and modes of life, such as can be fully illustrated. All this instruction must be made clear and interesting by stories, descriptions, and illustration.

Language.

GROUP III. (9-11 years.)

See Group II. Much written work in connection with and based upon the school work in its various departments. The sentence and its parts; general classification of words into parts of speech according to their use in the sentence, not teaching definitions nor treating of subdivisions. Careful teaching of the construction of the paragraph. Letter writing, with special reference to correct forms of social and business letters. Readings in literature by teacher and by pupil in school and home. Memorizing of choice selections long enough to have unity in themselves.

Some text-book of language lessons must be used in the rural schools, in order that a course of teaching may be carried out effectually.

GROUP IV. (11-13 years.)

(*a*) Letter writing, with special reference to subject-matter, to form and expression.

Much writing in connection with school work, and from outlines wrought out by teacher and pupils. Throughout the course careful attention should be paid to the correction and enlargement of the pupil's vocabulary.

(*b*) A course in grammar by rational use of a text-book. Preparation of plans for themes by the pupil, and writing from them.

(*c*) Readings in literature by pupils in school and home. Memorizing of choice selections long enough to have unity in them selves.

All written lessons and examinations should be so planned that they will be lessons in composition as well.

By this course of instruction the pupil should now be able to express his own thoughts clearly, in correct form, and in well-chosen words.

History.

GROUP III.

See Group II. Extension of course of Group II., with wider range, and with more and more readings by the pupil.

Special attention to biography, with oral and written reproduction.

Readings in United States history. See IV.

In III. and IV. the course is by readings or text-book study by the pupil.

GROUP IV.

(*a*) Selected epochs of general history, with study of leading historical characters; a course of readings and of conversations. Main object to develop a love for historical reading.

(*b*) A course of study in United States history.

Geography.

GROUP I. (5-7 years.)

Familiar conversations and simple preparatory exercises, serving to excite a spirit of observation in the child by leading him to observe the most common phenomena of earth and sky. Lessons on relative positions of objects, and distances.

Points of compass learned from position of the sun, and applied. Oral lessons to teach terms of geographical description from the child's own observation. Modeling in sand. Stories of travel. Object lessons on products, domestic and foreign.

These lessons in I. and II. are of necessity mainly oral until the pupil can read fairly well; then geographical readers and primary geographies will give much assistance.

GROUP II. (7-9 years.)

See Group I.

Home geography: Observations of phenomena of earth and sky; of the seasons; of contour, surface, mountain, valley, plain, brook, river, pond, soils, vegetation; in short, of whatever elements of geographical study can be brought under the observation of the child, that his knowledge of his environment may serve as a basis for his future studies of the world.

Modeling in sand. Notion of map. Extension of study to immediately related regions. Notion of form of the earth; the globe. Illustrated lessons on races of men, and on the picturesque and curious in their customs and manner of life.

Arithmetic.

GROUP I.

(*a*) Instruction at first entirely objective; objects gradually discarded as the facts are learned. Numbers and the combinations which form them up to 9. Throughout the course the child must learn through his own perceptions and self-activity.

(*b*) Combinations represented by the digits in pairs up to 9 and 9. The fundamental operations or computations taught, so far as possible, while teaching the combinations; thus $3 + 1 = 4$, $2 + 2 = 4$; 3 and 1 are how many? (addition); 3 and how many are 4? (subtraction); two 2's are how many? (multiplication); how many 2's in 4? (division); etc. Fractions ½, ¼, ⅛. Grouping by tens, to give the fundamental idea of the decimal system. (The course in combinations (*a*) and (*b*) follows the grouping of the decimal system.) Reading and writing of numbers to 100. Constant application to concrete problems.

Number lessons in Group I. are mainly oral.

Simple problems involving addition, subtraction, multiplication, and division, using numbers of not more than three places.

GROUP II.

See Group I. (*a*) Reading and writing three and four place numbers. All the fundamental operations with numbers to 1,000. Values and relations of coins in United States money. Exercises with fractions ½, ¼, ⅛, ⅓, ⅙. Many concrete problems with much objective illustration. Establish connection between arithmetic and the experiences and businesses of farm life by simple, interesting, varied problems. Treat one difficulty at a time.

(*b*) Writing decimals to one, two, three places; addition and subtraction of the same. Common fractions with one digit for denominator. The units of measures and weights objectively taught; simple exercises involving compound numbers. Rapid calculations with small numbers and easy problems. Objects for counting and combinations in the first steps, and weights and measures illustrating all the tables taught, are necessary. The child should weigh and measure for himself before he is questioned in relative values.

GROUP III. (9-11 years.)	GROUP IV. (11-13 years.)	
See Group II. Continents and great land and water masses. North America and United States, with incidental treatment of other parts of the world, in connection with history and with current events. In all the study of geography note its correlations with other subjects, especially with history, literature, language.	(*a*) See Group III. Study of foreign countries, apportioning the time devoted to them, according to their relative interest and importance. (*b*) Work of this group to be divided if necessary. The use of modeling, map drawing, and the various means of illustration is presupposed throughout the course in geography, and also the treatment of physical, mathematical, industrial, and commercial geography, in due order and degree. As the subject will usually be taught in the rural school with the aid of text-books in which these topics are developed, it is deemed unnecessary to enter into details in this statement.	**Geography.**
(*a*) See Group II. Compound numbers and common fractions, simply treated.	(*a*) See Group III. Percentage with applications to business.	**Arithmetic.**
(*b*) Decimal fractions and percentage, with common business applications in easy problems.	(*b*) Ratio and proportion; simple treatment of square and cube root. Simple geometrical facts and constructions, with mensuration of plane figures. Business forms and simple bookkeeping. Throughout the course mental arithmetic should receive careful attention.	

Drawing.

GROUP I. (5-7 years.)

Drawing very simple familiar and nature-forms of beauty and interest. It is well, also, for the child to represent simple colored objects, as apple, lemon, orange, and natural objects at hand, according to the season, in solid color, as he sees them.

Illustrative drawing, by the children, may be frequently introduced as a means of interest; in all these exercises great freedom should be allowed.

Free paper cutting, as exercise in memory of proportions, may be an occasional exercise.

Practice on lines of various kinds as combined in symmetrical and pleasing figures, so conducted as constantly to exercise the invention and taste of the child.

Symmetrical arrangement of forms (tablets, seeds, etc.), by repetition in a line (borders) and around a center (rosettes); by selecting objects of different colors this may be made an exercise in color as well as form; occasional use of ruler in drawing lines and figures.

Color. — The spectrum colors, from the prism, should be taught, and colors in flowers and other objects should be carefully observed.

GROUP II. (7-9 years.)

During this period of two years, from large models, mainly by the visual appearance and not as form studies in the usual sense of that term, study the sphere, cube, cylinder; spheroid, prolate and oblate; square and triangular prism; pyramid, cone, ovoid; comparing with each other and with objects related to them, noting resemblances and differences.

(Some exercise in drawing these, using soft pencil — black, brown, or blue — and shading a little, avoiding pure outline in picturing solids. This work can be postponed to the next group.)

Paper cutting to the line of drawings and construction may be used as elementary manual training.

Draw circle, ellipse, oval, and other good forms with curved outline; draw leaves, fruits, nuts, and familiar objects of beauty and interest; drill on division of lines, bisection, trisection, quadrisection; judgment of length of lines; proportions of lines one to another; proportions of figures; accurate measurement of lines and distances; drawing and estimation of angles of various kinds; cultivate neatness and accuracy in work; symmetrical arrangements of tablets and other forms, as borders, rosettes, and other ornaments, and drawing the same; a part of each lesson should be given to free-arm movements and to exercises in drawing adapted to give freedom and accuracy in drawing outlines, right-lined or curved.

Exercise in picturing in color, with water color, or colored crayon, the various natural objects studied in this group.

Illustrative drawing.

Color.— Spectrum colors, hues, tints, and *shades.*

Drawing.

GROUP III. (9-11 years.)

Free-hand drawing of plane figures, right-lined or curved in outline; pictures of geometric solids and of natural and artificial objects, choosing objects good in proportion and outline; interest will be increased by drawing groups of objects. Once a week draw from geometric solids and simple objects in light and shade, drawing the shadows very simply. In autumn and spring, especially, study plant growth, and draw sprays of leaves and flowers; draw vegetables and fruits; construction of forms of regular solids by drawing, with instruments, cutting, folding, and pasting paper and cardboard; studies in design from natural plant forms, using colored crayon or water color if possible. Neatness and accuracy required in all work.

Drill as in II. in free arm movements and in exercises in drawing: practicing especially on circles, spirals, ellipses, ovals, reversed curves; judgment of proportions of lines and figures.

Commence collection and study of pictures.

Color.—Mixing colors; harmony of colors.

GROUP IV. (11-13 years.)

(*a*) Draw pictures of geometric solids and of natural and artificial objects in groups, choosing objects good in proportion and outline, giving special attention to arrangement of groups.

(*b*) Study foreshortening of horizontal and vertical surfaces; draw pictures of rectangular solids in different positions relative to the eye, singly and in groups; draw books, foliage, vases, etc.; draw in light and shade with simple background, using charcoal, pencil, or brush, and paper of size suited to the object; large paper, nine by twelve inches, is desirable for much of this work.

(*a b*) Exercises in drawing shapes of faces of objects — top and front — and working drawings with figured dimension lines, with drawing instruments, using pencil, or pen and ink. (Some of this work may be done in Group III.)

Free hand drill on curves, shade (or tint) lines, and judgment of proportions; drawing of original designs, using color; practice in use of drawing instruments; graphic solution of simple problems in geometry.

Color.—See Group III. Add complementary colors. Study color in vegetables, flowers, leaves, etc.

NOTE.—In drawing, as in the other subjects of this course, the aim has been to construct a course which will be helpful to teachers in the average rural school under fairly favorable conditions. The order of treatment of subjects in each group, and the amount of work done, must depend upon the conditions; in some cases more can be done than is here laid down, in many cases not so much. So far as the child learns to see clearly and to draw truthfully and well what he sees, and as he sees it, good work has been done. He should be encouraged to draw much, aside from his lessons and school exercises, from whatever is of interest to him.

(*See Remarks on Drawing on page 184.*)

Elements of Science, or Nature Study.

GROUP I. (5–7 years.)

In the work in nature study only so much should be attempted as can be well done.

The course in science furnishes an excellent basis for written work.

Simple object lessons, if possible with the object under the eye and in the hand of the pupil; conversational lessons on familiar things and on the phenomena of nature, designed to lead him to give attention, to observe, to compare, to question, to remember. Familiar talks on the human body and the care of it; on common animals known to the child, their distinguishing characteristics and habits; on common flowers and plants, especially food plants and plants of use in the arts, as corn, cotton, etc.; on stones and metals in common use which the child can learn to recognize. As early as possible he should have some care of plants in the schoolhouse or the school garden.

Correlations, especially with language and drawing, with geography and literature, should be kept in mind.

In nature study the development of appreciation of and love for the beautiful should be made prominent.

GROUP II. (7–9 years.)

See Group I. A graduated course of nature study following a systematic order of development, but observing the child's standpoint as determined by his experience and interests, studying things, phenomena, processes, properties, and classification of things, as animal, vegetable, mineral. Conversational lessons on the human body, its principal parts, their movements and their uses; on common animals, so conducted as to arouse interest in animal and bird life, especially treating of the uses of birds to the farmer, and the necessity for their protection, to stimulate observation regarding their habits, and to cultivate a sentiment of kindness in the treatment of them; on plants and the care of them, their parts, as roots, stems, flowers, fruits, seeds, and their growth; on some common minerals and their uses. Lessons on transformations of material in manufactured articles of common use.

Elements of Science, or Nature Study.

GROUP III. (9-11 years.)

Preceding course so expanded and taught as to give clearly some of the more important notions of natural science: the human body and the principal functions of life; distinguishing characteristics of animals taught from the study of types; useful and noxious animals, especially birds and insects; the study, in typical specimens, of the principal organs of the plant; plant growth, its order and conditions; some typical trees, and their characteristics, value and uses of their wood; fruit trees best adapted to the region; lessons on soils.

Every rural school should have a plot of ground prepared as a school garden, in which every pupil may cultivate and study plants. In this case the instruction in Groups III and IV would be extended to include the preparation of soils for cultivation, the action of fertilizers, the simpler agricultural operations, and the use of garden tools.

GROUP IV. (11-13 years.)

Revision and extension of the course in Group III., giving more of completeness and of scientific arrangement and form to the instruction. Cabinets should be collected for the school.

Physiology. General review by use of a text-book, giving special attention to hygiene and to the effects of stimulants and narcotics. Sanitation of school and home.

Zoölogy. Observation of the habits of animals throughout the year; study of available types; general classifications; geographical distribution.

Botany. Essential parts of the plant; order and conditions of growth; principal groups; geographical distribution of plants; uses of plants; study of trees.

Mineralogy. General treatment of the structure of the crust of the earth; soils, rocks, fossils, with illustrations from the neighborhood.

Excursions and collections by the pupil.

Physics and Chemistry. The elementary facts and principles of these sciences should be taught by simple experiments. The course will vary according to the qualifications of the teacher and the means of instruction. Various courses for this instruction have been prepared, giving methods in detail.

Only such selections from the above as can be well done.

Morals and Civics.

GROUP I. (5-7 years.)

Conversations with the children in all the school exercises, in which the teacher shall aim to secure the confidence and familiar participation of the children, and thus to learn their characters so as to guide their tendencies of thought and action. Special care regarding children in whom the teacher notices any moral defect or vicious tendency. Careful attention to propriety of conduct and good manners.

GROUP II. (7-9 years.)

Familiar conversations and kind individual counsel when needed. Simple stories, parables, fables, treated with reference to ideas of right and wrong. (Never make a class lesson from cases involving the conduct of the pupil; these should be treated by private admonition.) Practical exercises tending to arouse the moral sense of the class, by methods of school discipline, by often making the pupil the judge of his own conduct, by training the pupil to draw the appropriate lessons from facts observed by himself.

Morals and Civics.

GROUP III. (9-11 years.)

Continue course of Group II., with somewhat more of method. Conversations so conducted as to interest the pupil and induce the freest participation. Passages from history and literature treated from the point of view of right and wrong. All lessons and readings so arranged as to omit no important point of the following course: duties to parents, duties to brothers and sisters, duties toward employers, duties toward servants and employés, duties of the child in school, duties toward the native land and society, duties toward one's self, as cleanliness, temperance, economy, self-respect, modesty, the Golden Rule; duties toward God, not a course of religious instruction, but emphasizing especially two points: cultivating the feeling and habit of reverence, and a disposition of obedience to the laws of God.

Throughout the whole course kindness to animals should be most carefully taught.

Some work in civics should be taken up in III. as well as IV.

GROUP IV. (11-13 years.)

Instruction along the lines of the preceding course, expanding the instruction especially in regard to social morality and duties to the native land, treating under this last title the organization and principles of our form of government (civics).

As a preparation the teacher should carefully read some systematic treatises on ethics and civics, and the immediate test of success will be the fact that the pupils are heartily interested in the subject.

Morals and civics furnish an excellent basis for training in speaking and writing.

This course in morals, in its general classification and arrangement of topics, is in accordance with the course of moral instruction in the schools of France, and has been tested for several years in a training school in this country.

There is here given a scheme for distribution of time, the numbers representing the lessons per week:

	I.	II.	III.	IV.
Reading,	8	8=16	3	2=5
Language,	4	4= 8	4	4=8
Arithmetic,	8	8=16	2	1=3
Writing,	4	4= 8	2	0=2
Drawing,	3	3= 6		2=4
History and Geography,	4	4= 8		4=8
Morals,	1	1= 2		1=2
Elements of Science,	1	1= 2	2	3=5
Totals in I. and II.,		66	Totals in III. and IV.,	37

Giving to lessons in I. and II. an average of ten minutes each, and to those in III. and IV. an average of twenty minutes each, the total time will be 1,400 minutes for the week. If the daily session be six hours, and one hour per day be given to recesses and general school business, there remains a surplus of 100 minutes per week at the disposal of the teacher, which can be devoted to more instruction wherever needed.

This table is given merely as suggestive of possibilities, and not by any means as an ideal adjustment of ratios. In many schools much more time can justly be given to subjects here left with but little.

In all the work of this course it must be borne in mind that in the average rural school the complete course will never be in working at one time; that there must be much individual instruction; that in every good rural school there must be very much encouragement of the pupil to work by himself under the general guidance and direction of the teacher.

REMARKS ON DRAWING.

Object of the Course.—To develop correct notions of form as it appears and to represent these notions truthfully by drawing, and to cultivate appreciation of beauty of form.

Materials.—Geometrical solids large enough to be seen from any part of the room. These can be found in common objects or made from stiff paper or cardboard and tablets showing geometrical figures. A prism for teaching color; sticks one to five inches long for laying forms; paper for cutting and folding; good drawing pencils, soft and medium in hardness; drawing paper with surface to take pencil well; a good blackboard, and clear, soft crayons, with a few colored crayons; some colored pencils for pupils' use; water colors; some charcoal for more advanced work; an ample supply of common objects, leaves, flowers, fruits, etc., renewed from day to day from the neighborhood.

The statements of this course are necessarily brief and general; it is supposed that teachers will be aided in matters of detail by some of the published courses in drawing.

In teaching drawing as a truthful representation of the visual appearance of form there is not necessarily the strict sequence in the use of geometric models which there would be in a course of form lessons. For lessons in representation of the facts of forms as a basis for construction in connection with working drawings, see Group IV.

Some prefer in the early stages to drill only on planes and lines, postponing solids to a later period. In the French course in drawing the solid does not appear before our Group III., and then at first the drawing is a carefully graded course from low relief.

Those who prefer to work at first entirely from nature can select in order such exercises as are in accordance with this theory and mass the technique in the later stages of the course.

Historic ornament is left to the discretion of the teacher, as in most cases limitations of time would exclude it from the rural school. Teachers should themselves gain such knowledge of historic ornament and of the history of art as is possible. Excellent books treating of these subjects can be easily obtained, and the knowledge thus gained will enable them to add much of interest and value to their instruction.

For the complete treatment of this course it is desirable that the teacher should have had some special preparation for teaching drawing. In the rural school selections will often have to be made according to circumstances and the ability of the teacher. There should be at least three lessons a week, of twenty minutes each, in Groups I. and II., and longer lessons in Groups III. and IV. Exercises included in parentheses are left to the discretion of the teacher.

In all parts of the course in drawing care should be taken to cultivate an appreciation of the simple elements of beauty, and to develop a love for the beauties of nature and art; and the schoolroom should be furnished with some classic examples of art for study as well as for ornament. In this regard note the analogy between the study of art and the study of literature.

APPENDIX J.

NEGRO TEACHERS FOR NEGRO SCHOOLS.

The answer to the question "Should white teachers be employed in negro schools?" requires some knowledge of the past conditions of the negro, as well as an intelligent and sympathetic appreciation of his present status. I propose then to consider the question in the light of certain broad, fundamental principles which involve, essentially, the welfare and progress of the negro race.

Thirty years have passed since the emancipation of the negro became an accomplished fact. For thirty years he has been the subject of much contention and the object of much solicitude. During this period new nations have been born to civilization. Japan, for instance, whose birth was almost coincident with negro emancipation, has established herself "Queen of the Orient," and has demonstrated her right to a place of honor among the great nations of the earth. While much progress has been made by the negro race in the South, it must be admitted that this progress has been due too little to himself, and too largely to the external influences of the civilization under which he has lived. While marvelous development may be found in individual instances, the condition of the masses of the race is but little improved; the solution of the vexed negro question is as problematical as ever; the education of the race is still in an empirical stage. Unlike other races that have attained to civilization, the negro, with a few individual exceptions, has been content to be merely a passive spectator of the processes that have affected him. Incapable of initiative and executive power, and wanting in genius for organization, he has never been an active agent in the work of race redemption. He has never been accustomed to voluntary activity; he is here not of his own choice; a docile slave, he wrought on southern plantations until, without an effort of his own, he was made an American citizen. Having received his political elevation by legislation, he naturally expected to obtain a commercial, intellectual, and moral status in some such mysterious way. The progress of the negro race, remarkable though it may be, is not the result of social and political self-evolution, but an effect produced by extraneous causes.

If the education of the negro is to be anything more than a veneer, the race must obey that great law of human development which makes voluntary energy the source of power and progress. The intellectual power developed must be energized by proper incentives into self-activity; it must be made reproductive within the race itself. It is not enough that the race shall be environed with all the accessories of civilization. Its consciousness must be aroused, its powers energized, its sense of responsibility quickened. It must be taught to work out its own salvation, if its progress is to be real and enduring. The gospel must be preached by its own preachers; its schools must be taught by its own teachers. It must consciously realize its own responsibility for the effective use of the means at its command in the work of race development.

The position of the negro as a race has heretofore been one of dependence. Lacking the virtues of thrift, foresight, and economy, he is still very largely supplied from the white man's table; and in time of trouble, confidently appeals, and seldom in vain, to his former master for aid and relief. The negro wears his master's religion, and sometimes his politics, very much as he does his old clothes, as something entirely foreign and external to himself. By perpetuating this dependence, intellectual and moral, we acquiesce in a species of spiritual bondage that is almost as unfavorable to race progress as slavery itself. "Our real friends," says Emerson, "are those who make us do what we can." Judicious aid to a dependent people is necessary and praiseworthy, but, in my judgment, it should stop short of doing all their intellectual work for them.

To cultivate in the negro the sense of intellectual and moral independence, such avenues of service as will enable him to effect the uplifting of the race should not be closed against him. He requires these as worthy incentives to arouse his ambition and to stimulate his sense of responsibility. To be the teacher of his race is the one position of honor, dignity, and responsibility to which he may legitimately aspire. To throttle his energies and to close against him this avenue of activity and usefulness would be an unwarranted assumption of responsibility by the white race and an injustice to the negro.

But a further and more potent reason for employing negro teachers to teach negro schools is the fact that race identity is an important factor in educational work. The teacher and the taught must possess a common consciousness, a mutual affinity, as a condition of proper intellectual and moral growth. The teacher must embody in his personality the historic race epochs and processes of development represented in the pupil, in order that the intellectual powers of the child may be invested with that atmosphere of sympathy and appreciation necessary to their healthy activity. The historic consciousness of teacher and pupil must possess certain intuitive elements in common, as the result of common race processes, if the teaching is to be efficient and the development natural.

Again, it is a fact that cannot well be called in question that white teachers in negro schools can never realize, even approximately, the ideal relation that should exist between teacher and pupil. This is forcibly true in elementary schools. That relation requires love, not philanthropy; affection, not charity; sympathy, not pity. Occupying planes so widely separated, spheres of activity so diverse; without common blood or social ties, common history or common interests, common origin or common destiny, a white teacher and a negro class will never realize the ideal school. In such a case the teacher cannot appeal to the inner life of the pupil, and the craving consciousness of the child finds no responsive chord in the teacher. They must meet, if they meet at all, upon the cold, abstract plane of reason. The instinct of race identity, as strong in one race as in the other, as strong in the pupil as in the teacher, intervenes as an insuperable barrier. Between teacher and pupil must ever remain this chasm of race difference, as deep as human consciousness itself. Call it prejudice if you will, but it exists as a God-implanted instinct of which the teacher can never divest himself—out of which the pupil can never be educated. Although it be tempered by philanthropy, sweetened by religion, or even smothered by fanaticism, it still exists, and will continue to exist as long as humanity.

The principles here emphasized are not restricted in their application to the negro race; like all natural laws they are universal, and are modified in their operation only by the variation of the conditions involved. They are true in their application to the American Indian and to the Mongolian, to the Fiji Islanders and to the Kaffirs of South Africa.

Experience in the missionary field has demonstrated the fact that the successful propagation of the gospel requires the preparation of native teachers and native preachers as a primary condition. The foreign missionary may direct and supervise, aid and inspire, but he remains a foreigner still — a being apart and something different from the people. The native teachers and preachers of our missionary fields are the hope of heathendom, because they alone can fulfill the requirements of the law of race identity.

Nor is this principle confined to race relations; in a lesser degree it operates between different families of the Caucasian race, and indeed between any two people differing in nationality and language. School men of wide experience will testify to the fact that few teachers of English or American birth can successfully manage a school of Irish, German, or Swedish children; on the other hand, a native French or German teacher, be he ever so proficient in scholarship, or fertile in resources, finds much difficulty in the discipline of American children, and years of striving are usually required to bridge the chasm of difference.

In elementary and secondary education I regard this law of race identity as vital and imperative, but in the province of higher education its authority, under certain conditions, may possibly be relaxed without serious consequences. Institute instruction, however, and the guidance and supervision of negro teachers by the whites must still be continued as a matter of duty and as an administrative necessity.

The important principle involved here is primarily that of co-ordination — not of text-books and curricula — but the vital co-ordination of the teacher with the child. When we impose upon the child a relation so incongruous, physically, intellectually, and morally, we violate a primary law of nature as well as an established pedagogical principle. The fact that the vast majority of negro teachers are deplorably incompetent no one will deny. But the remedy is to be sought in the improvement of these teachers, and not in the substitution of white teachers. Novel as the statement may appear, I confidently hold that no white teacher is competent to teach negro children. We must remember that for the teacher there are conditions and qualifications antecedent to scholarship, and tests more important than the uniform state examination.

Other considerations in the same line might be adduced, such as the necessity for modifying our courses of study and adapting our methods of teaching to the wants of negro schools. It remains to be seen whether the instruction of an infant race can proceed along the same lines and by the same methods as that of a race whose culture is based upon centuries of struggle and self-effort, without involving the violation of all sound economic and pedagogic doctrine. But the consideration of these lines would carry me beyond the limits and the object of this discussion.

In conclusion let me briefly summarize the argument for employing negro teachers in negro schools:

1. The educational development of the negro must be from within, and by the race itself, and not solely through extraneous agencies.

2. The intellectual and moral dependence of the race should not be perpetuated. The negro needs to be stimulated to independent activity.

3. As a teacher of his race the negro occupies a position of trust and honor, which he needs to quicken his sense of responsibility, and to furnish him the incentives and the means for race elevation.

4. The teacher and the pupil must possess a common consciousness, whose historic processes have common elements, resulting in common intuitions. The teacher must embody in his character the race epochs and processes represented in the child.

5. The instinct of race identity renders impossible the realization of an ideal relation between the white teacher and the negro pupil. The teacher and the child must be co-ordinated.

J. H. Phillips.

Birmingham, Ala.

APPENDIX K.

J. W. BRADBURY.

Hon. J. W. Bradbury, United States Senator from Maine 1847-53, was a teacher for ten years, commencing at the age of seventeen. He had among his pupils Hawthorne, Longfellow, Abbott, Cheever, Cilley.

He had completed his studies for admission to the bar in 1829, but it would be some months before the court could make provision for his examination.

He had learned in visiting schools that teachers were ignorant of proper methods of instruction, and, hoping to assist them to some definite ideas of what studies should be taught in the common school, the order in which they should be taken, and the methods which should be used in teaching them, he gave notice in August, 1829, that a training school for teachers would be opened in Effingham, N. H. The school was in session during September, October, and November. About sixty teachers were in attendance. Instruction was given in the subjects taught in the public schools and in the methods that should be used in teaching them, and the ability of his pupils to comprehend the instruction in methods was tested by *requiring them to teach the subject to the class under his criticism.*

At this time he had not heard of the existence of such a training school in this country.

In the winter of 1829-30 Mr. Bradbury was a member of the school committee of Parsonsfield, Me. The methods which he had taught in his Effingham training school were adopted in Parsonsfield. By improved methods of examination of teachers better teachers were secured, the quantity and quality of work done in school were raised, and the schools of Parsonsfield were placed on a higher plane. It is some evidence of the character of this movement that more than 600 women have gone out from this small country town and become good teachers.

TEACHERS' SEMINARY AT PLYMOUTH, N. H.

[Extracts from catalogue, 1839, in which year the school was closed from failure in appropriation.]

"This seminary has been founded with the hope of improving popular education, by elevating the character of teachers. . . . . The trustees have three prominent objects in view: (1) to educate teachers for common and other schools; (2) to fit students for college; (3) to furnish the means for a thorough English education. . . . .

"The school embraces a department for males and one for females. . . . . The course of study in the Teachers' Seminary requires four years in the male department and three in the female department, with the exception of one term each year, during which the members may be absent to teach school."

In the course of study were taken English language, history of the United States and of England, physics and chemistry, with experimental lectures; mathematics, including trigonometry and conic sections; political economy, intellectual and moral philosophy, logic, natural theology, lectures on the history of education and the art of teaching, in addition to the common-school studies

Studies were suspended in the winter terms of the last three years of the course in the male department to allow students to teach, and in the summer terms of the same years in the female department for the same purpose.

Although the students in the classical department far outnumbered those in the teachers' department — eighty-seven to twenty-eight — yet all the statements show that the teachers' department was the leading one in the interest of the principal, and scholarships, of which there were several, were founded only in this department.

APPENDIX L.

NEW YORK STATE SCHOOL LIBRARY.

The New York legislature of 1895, in an act entitled "An Act for the Encouragement of Common Schools and Public Libraries," authorized the State Superintendent of Public Instruction to establish a state school library for the benefit and free use of the teachers of the state. . . . . The books selected embrace those bearing directly on the profession of teaching, with others relating to studies in psychology and the training of children, together with those referring to special studies in school. Particular attention has been given to the selection of works on civil government, political economy, and social and moral questions, as discussed by teachers with the children. Volumes on the natural sciences have been provided for popular use rather than for technical or professional reading. Care has been taken to provide, to a limited extent, books relating to history, general literature, and art.

Any teacher may have the use of the books of this library free of expense, except for postage and express, and he may purchase books from the list at a fixed price. (From Report of State Superintendent of Public Instruction, New York, 1896.)

LIST OF BOOKS FOR RURAL SCHOOLS AND COMMUNITIES.

The committee has endeavored to make out a list of books for study and reading for parents, teachers, and pupils in the country schools. It wishes to acknowledge the assistance of President F. W. Parker, of Professor L. H. Bailey, of Cornell University; Professor F. H. King, University of Wisconsin, and Professor D. L. Kiehle, of Minnesota.

Colonel Parker makes this suggestion: "The mere reading or study of these books, without copious illustrations direct from nature, would be like reading any other books without experience back of them. My suggestion is this: that the books be read in connection with the study of nature. The teachers can easily make the right selections; for instance, the study of soils in the time of plowing, the study of plants in the time of growth, etc. Specimens may be brought into the schoolroom, or better, the pupils may go to the specimens by field excursions.

"I am quite sure there are many other books, but I have not had sufficient time to get hold of them.

"I wish to call the attention of the teachers to a fact that should be well known, that the United States government publishes some of the best books on farming and nature known. I have appended a very brief list here, but the trustees of schools and principals of schools can very easily get all of these valuable documents from their representative in Congress."

AGRICULTURE.

The Soil. Franklin H. King (Rural Science Ser.) The Macmillan Co. Reading and study for school and home; excellent for study of upper grades, and farmers meetings.

The Fertility of the Land, J. P. Roberts. The Macmillan Co. Reading and study for home and school. Excellent.

First Principles of Agriculture, Edward B. Voorhees. Silver, Burdett & Co. Reference.

Irrigation Farming, Lute Wilcox. Orange Judd Co. Reference.

Farm Drainage, C. G. Elliot. United States Department of Agriculture (Farmers' Bulletin No. 40). Reference.

Tillage and Implements, W. J. Malden. G. Bell & Sons. Reference.

Our Farming, T. B. Terry. The Farmer Co., Philadelphia. Reference.

Yearbook of the United States Department of Agriculture. Reference.

Farmers' Bulletins, United States Department of Agriculture. Reference.

Relation of Soil to Climate, E. W. Hilgard. Bulletin No. 3, United States Weather Bureau Department.

Some Physical Properties of Soil in their Relation to Moisture and Crop Distribution, Milton W. Whitney. Bulletin No. 4, United States Weather Bureau Department.

Fluctuations of Ground Water, Franklin H. King. Bulletin No. 5, United States Weather Bureau Department.

Laws of Rainfall, Gustavus Hinrichs. United States Department of Agriculture.

Forest Influence upon Climate, Water Supply, and Health, B. E. Fernow. Bulletin No 7, Division of Forestry.

HORTICULTURE.

The Principles of Fruit-Growing, L. H. Bailey. The Macmillan Co. Reading and study for home and school.

American Fruit Culturist, J. J. Thomas. Orange Judd Co. Reference.

Landscape Gardening, Edward Kemp. Orange Judd Co. Reference.

How to Make the Garden Pay, T. Greiner. Orange Judd Co. Reference.

Principles of Plant Culture, E. S. Goff, Madison, Wis. Reference.

Plant-Breeding, L. H. Bailey. The Macmillan Co. Reference.

Nursery-Book, L. H. Bailey (Garden Craft Ser.). The Macmillan Co. Reference.

Horticulturist's Rule-Book, L. H. Bailey. The Macmillan Co. Reference.

BOTANY.

How Crops Grow, S. W. Johnson. Orange Judd Co. Reference.

How Crops Feed, S. W. Johnson. Orange Judd Co. Reference.

Familiar Trees and their Leaves, F. S. Mathews. D. Appleton & Co.

Familiar Flowers of Field and Garden, F. S. Mathews. D. Appleton & Co. Excellent for reference. May be profitably studied with the flowers and plants throughout the year.

The Garden's Story, G. H. Ellwanger. D. Appleton & Co. Reference.

How Plants Grow, Gray. American Book Co. Reference.

Botany for Public Schools, Abbie G. Hall. Geo. Sherwood & Co. Reference.

Botany for Young People, Gray. American Book Co. To be read with specimens by intermediate grades.

From Seed to Leaf, J. H. Newell. Ginn & Co. Reader.

Talks Afield, L. H. Bailey. Houghton, Mifflin & Co. For teachers. Good for field excursions.

Chapters on Plant Life, S. B. Herrick. Harper & Bros. To be studied with specimens and microscope by intermediate grades.

How to Know the Wild Flowers, Mrs. Wm. S. Dana. Chas. Scribner's Sons.

Plants and their Children, Mrs. Wm. S. Dana. American BookCo.

SCIENCE.

Sunshine, Amy Johnson. The Macmillan Co. Reading book for grammar grades.

Forms of Water, Tyndall. D. Appleton & Co. Eighth grade.

Weather, Ralph Abercromby. D. Appleton & Co.

Natural History of Selborne, Gilbert White. Ginn & Co. Eighth grade.

The Great World's Farm, Selina Gaye. The Macmillan Co. Charming, and very profitable for grammar grades and home study.

Elementary Meteorology, W. M. Davis. Ginn & Co. Teachers and parents, and for reference.

A Popular Treatise on the Winds, W. Ferrel. John Wiley & Sons. Teachers' study and reference.

Elementary Text-Book of Physical Geography, R. S. Tarr. The Macmillan Co Excellent for study and reference.

The Geological Story Briefly Told, J. D. Dana. American Book Co. Excellent for reading and reference.

First Book in Geology, N. S. Shaler. D. C. Heath & Co. Unexcelled reading book for seventh and eighth grades.

The Story of the Hills, H. N. Hutchinson. The Macmillan Co. Reading book for eighth grade.

Monographs on Physical Geography. American Book Co. Excellent for teachers' study.

Round the Year, L. C. Miall. The Macmillan Co. Teachers.

Autumn, Winter, Spring. Three small volumes. Ginn & Co. Reading for third and fourth grades.

Science Readers, Vincent T. Murche. The Macmillan Co.

Systematic Science Teaching, E. G. Howe. D. Appleton & Co.

ANIMAL LIFE.

Honey Bee, L. L. Langstroth. J. B. Lippincott Co. A practical treatise. Reference.

Manual for the Study of Insects, J. H. Comstock. Comstock Publishing Co., Ithaca, N. Y. Reference.

Half Hours with Insects, A. S. Packard. Estes & Lauriatt. Reference.

Buz; or the Life and Adventures of a Honey Bee, Maurice Noel. Henry Holt & Co. Reading, eighth grade.

Boys and Girls in Biology, S. H. Stevenson. D. Appleton & Co.

Ants, Bees, and Wasps, Lubbock. D. Appleton & Co. Reference.

The Population of an Old Pear Tree, E. van Bruyssel. The Macmillan Co. Grammar grades.

My Saturday Bird Class, Olive Thorne Miller. D. C. Heath & Co. Fourth grade.

Little Brothers of the Air, Olive Thorne Miller. Houghton, Mifflin & Co.

In Bird Land, L. S. Keyser. A. C. McClurg & Co.

Tenants of an Old Farm, H. C. McCook. Fords, Howard & Hulbert. Habits of insects.

Domesticated Animals, N. S. Shaler. A. C. McClurg & Co.

Life Histories of American Insects, Clarence M. Weed. The Macmillan Co. Entertaining and instructive.

NATURE STUDY.

Nature Study and Related Subjects, Wilbur S. Jackman, Chicago Normal School.

Tommy-Anne and the Three Hearts, Mabel Osgood Wright. The Macmillan Co. A good reading book for intermediate grades.

The Beauties of Nature, Lubbock. The Macmillan Co. Home reading.
Man and Nature, G. P. Marsh. Chas. Scribner's Sons. Reference and reading.
Forest Trees, Wild Apples, and Sounds, H. D. Thoreau. Houghton, Mifflin & Co.
John Burroughs' Works. Houghton, Mifflin & Co.

- Winter Sunshine. Parents and teachers. For pupils, The Apple.
- Riverby. Parents and teachers. Selections for home reading.
- Wake-Robin. Parents and teachers. Selections for older pupils.
- Pepacton. Parents and teachers. Selections for pupils: Springs, Idyl of the Honey-Bee, etc.
- Locusts and Wild Honey. Home reading. Selections for pupils: Sharp Eyes, Strawberries, Is it Going to Rain, Bed of Boughs, etc.
- Signs and Seasons. Home reading. Selections for pupils: The Tragedies of the Nests, A River View, Bird Enemies, Phases of Farm Life.
- Birds and Poets. Home reading.

Bass's Nature Stories for Young Readers. D. C. Heath & Co. Excellent for third and fourth grades.

MISCELLANEOUS.

Art of Beautifying Suburban Home Grounds, F. J. Scott. D. Appleton & Co.
A Text-Book on Roads and Pavements, F. P. Spalding. John Wiley & Sons.
United States Government Reports.
Water and Land, Jacob Abbott. Harper & Bros.
What Darwin saw in his voyage round world in Ship "Beagle." Harper & Bros.
Brooks and Brook Basins, Alex. Frye. Ginn & Co.
The Story of a Stone, in Science Sketches, David Starr Jordan. A. C. McClurg & Co
The Earth and its Story, Angelo Heilprin. Silver, Burdett & Co.
Formation of Vegetable Mold, Darwin. D. Appleton & Co.
Science Primer of Physical Geography, A. Geikie. American Book Co.
Up and Down Brooks, Mary E. Bamford. Houghton, Mifflin & Co.
Every-Day Occupations, H. W. Clifford. Boston School Supply Co.
Modern Industries and Commerce, Robt. Lewis. Boston School Supply Co.
Camps in Rockies, Wm. Grohman. Chas. Scribner's Sons.
Coal and Coal Mines, H. K. Greene. Houghton, Mifflin & Co.
The Sea and its Wonders, Mary and Elizabeth Kirby. T. Nelson & Sons.
Canoemates, Kirk Munroe. Harper & Bros.
Campmates, Kirk Munroe. Harper & Bros.
Talking Leaves, W. O. Stoddard. Harper & Bros.
An Iceland Fisherman, Pierre Loti. A. C. McClurg & Co.
Hunter Cats of Connorloa, H. H. Roberts Bros.
John Brent, Theo. Winthrop. Henry Holt & Co.
The Electrical Boy, J. T. Trowbridge. Roberts Bros.
How to Study Geography, F. W. Parker. D. Appleton & Co.
Methods and Aids in Geography, C. F. King. Lee & Shepard.
The Story of the Plants, Grant Allen. D. Appleton & Co.
Wonders of Plant Life, S. B. Herrick. G. P. Putnam's Sons.
Intelligence of Animals, Ernest Menault. Chas. Scribner's Sons.
Elementary Meteorology, F. Waldo. American Book Co.
The Food of Plants, A. P. Laurie. The Macmillan Co.
Agriculture, R. H. Wallace. J. B. Lippincott Co.
Garden Craft Series. The Macmillan Co.
Rural Science Series. The Macmillan Co.
The Story of our Continent, N. S. Shaler. Ginn & Co.

Glimpses at the Plant World, F. D. Bergen. Ginn & Co.
Animal Memoirs, Parts I.-II., S. Lockwood. American Book Co.
The Survival of the Unlike, L. H. Bailey (Garden Craft Ser.). The Macmillan Co.
Elements of Geology, LeConte. D. Appleton & Co.
Town Geology, C. Kingsley. The Macmillan Co.

APPENDIX M.

HYGIENE AND HEALTH IN PUBLIC SCHOOLS.

Dr. G. Stanley Hall has said: "What shall it profit a man if he gain the whole world of knowledge and lose his health?" In our public schools, especially in the high schools, many a promising young life has been sacrificed by over-study. The system of marks and medals, now happily disappearing from many of our best schools, has driven many an ambitious boy and girl to an early grave at the point of a pencil, because that system stimulates those very pupils who need no spur and whom the spur injures. More frequently the health of pupils is injured by ignorance of the most obvious laws of health, or by criminal neglect of those laws, and by the impure air of schoolrooms. Unsuitable furniture which cramps and distorts the growing bodies of children, and poor light which impairs the sight, have also a long account to settle with children thus ruined for life.

The evils of unsanitary schoolhouses have attracted most attention in the crowded schoolrooms of cities, but these evils are not confined to densely populated places. They appear equally in the rural districts, and they are less known only because the cases of injury are scattered, and the statistics are less easily obtained.

The vigorous country boy and girl may for a time resist the evils of a schoolroom, alternately too hot and too cold; of drafts of cold air in winter through cracks in the floor and poorly-built walls; of outhouses too filthy for use and sources of moral defilement; of seats and desks, built for cheapness and not for comfort, and more racks for torture than like a proper resting place for the growing bodies of little boys and girls. But however much the injury may be concealed, the deadly work goes on in many a country school. Take a single instance. Many a man has suffered for years from hemorrhoids brought on by ignorance or neglect in childhood; neglect, because proper accommodations were not provided or not properly cared for at the schoolhouse; ignorance, because the school gave no instructions in hygiene- not the technical hygiene suitable for physicians, but the obvious, ordinary hygiene that relates to clothing, proper bathing, eating, and the excretions.

Physiology is now required by law to be taught in the schools of nearly all the states. As too frequently taught, it concerns itself about the chemical effects of certain substances upon various parts or processes of the body. Such a treatment of the subject is too abstruse for children in the schools, it goes beyond their knowledge and their experience. They need to be taught the effect of green apples upon the stomach before they are taught the effect of alcohol upon the brain. We ought to learn wisdom from the concrete teaching of nature about eating green apples in her monitory pains. People mean well when they teach the evil effect of alcohol to little boys and girls who do not know what alcohol is. It would be better to teach these children the good effect of wholesome food and drink, and especially to teach them that the whole alimentary canal should be kept in healthy, regular, and daily movement throughout, and to teach this and all that relates to the necessary bodily functions with delicacy and propriety, and without any squeamishness. Is any teacher too delicate, cultured, and refined a lady or gentleman to give this instruction concerning the bodies of the children? Then let them be relegated to the land of spirits, to teach where the mortal coil has been shuffled off. It is high time to inaugurate a campaign of hygiene, and not the least important branch of child study is the study of their bodies, and how those bodies may be made in school to grow strong, robust, healthy, natural, at ease—"the temple of the living God."

In making the many advancements in education in recent years the pedagogical literature of the past three hundred years or more has been ransacked, and the educational philosophy of many eminent and venerable teachers has been exploited to constitute the new education—Comenius, Pestalozzi, Froebel, Herbart, and the rest; it is worth while now to bring to the front the maxim, "Mens sana in corpore sano," and to found an educational philosophy on that. Already we have physiological psychology which seeks to trace mental phenomena through a study of the brain, and missionaries are now learning to convert the heathen by making their bodies comfortable without their eating the missionary. Benevolence now seeks to raise humanity, both intellectually and morally, by first improving men physically. Let the schools follow the lead of philosophy and of religion in this regard.

It is well known that no child can learn well or grow mentally when in bodily discomfort. Dullness, uneasiness, and consequent disorder in a school, are directly traceable to vitiated air. If the body is numb with cold, if the feet are damp and chilled, the mind becomes stupid; and the sweltering heat of a badly ventilated schoolroom, the uneasiness of an over-loaded stomach, of constipation, and of uncomfortable clothing, will produce the same result. Moreover, an abnormal condition of the body is often the source of immorality. We blame the first Adam too much; the real Adam is nearer home, and of this generation and every generation that neglects the laws of health. The outbuildings of ill-governed schools with ill-taught children sometimes give evidence of fearful demoralization, and the demoralization is contagious, like a plague.

An important part of school hygiene, then, relates to the lavatories or water-closets. This is not the only, nor perhaps the most important, part of school hygiene, but it needs emphasis most at present, because it is nearly always neglected. In rural districts the outhouse is generally located in a remote part of the grounds, where its offensiveness may not interfere with the school, and it is the prey of tramps and bad boys who delight in defiling it. The closet should adjoin the schoolhouse, and be accessible through the house only. This location would compel its being kept inoffensive, and make it easy to do so. It should then be used by every child with the same freedom as at home in a well-regulated family. And the child should be taught in school to respect his body in every part and in all its functions—that nothing about it is defiling unless he himself makes it so; and that, while we are animals, we should be rational animals, and not brutes. Such teaching should not be indelicate nor obtrusive; but it is important, because respect for the body is at the foundation of self-respect and true manliness. This special teaching of hygiene has often been neglected through a false modesty which is highly indelicate, and which is itself the evidence of an impure mind.

For health, for comfort, and for intellectual and moral well-being, the schoolhouse should be well-constructed and suited to its use. It should stand in the middle of the grounds, high, well-drained, and ornamented with trees and shrubs. The well should be so located as to supply pure water. The architecture should be simple and show a refined taste, for the schoolhouse is an educator. It should be as convenient and as well-built as the best homes, in order that the children of the well to-do may not despise it, and in order that the children of the poor may see how the best people live. The schoolhouse will thus become an inspirer in the young to higher living, for education is more than learning from books. It is a training also in how to live.

Churches are built as an example of noble architecture, to be an object lesson leading upward to a higher life. They are usually grander than the houses of the worshipers, and the poorest man in the congregation has an ownership in them. Municipal and state buildings often display, or are meant to display, the community's ideal of a home for itself. And so the schoolhouse should exhibit the taste and to some extent the aspiration of the neighborhood. It should be a little better than the best dwelling house.

Below is an attempt to show the least that should be tolerated in any community where the Americans of the future are to be educated. The ideal room may be repeated in a single building to any number below sixteen or twenty.

THE IDEAL
RURAL SCHOOL HOUSE

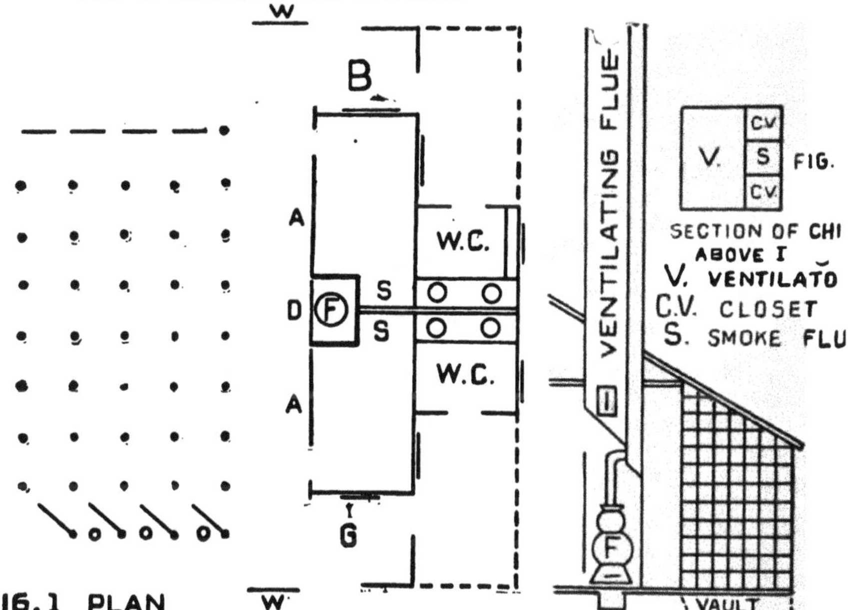

FIG. 1 PLAN

FIG. 2 ELEVATION.

This plan provides for forty-eight pupils—one desk and chair in each of the squares, 3 ft. by 3 ft., indicated by the dots. The desks at the front are at right angles to the wall, and each succeeding desk toward the back is at a greater angle than the last, till about 45 degrees is reached at the last. The teacher's desk is at T in the left front. The surface of the floor is 720 sq. ft., or 15 sq. ft. each for forty-eight pupils, which is the least allowable. If the room is 13½ ft. high its contents are 9,720 cu. ft., or 200 cu. ft. each the regulation number), and only 120 cu. ft. for the teacher when all the pupils are present.

Fig. 1. This represents a schoolroom 24 ft. by 30 ft., with (B) boys' entry and (G) girls' entry. The entire south side has a series of windows as near each other as the construction will permit, and extending to within three or four feet of the corners of the room. These windows should be three or four feet from the floor, and they should extend entirely to the ceiling of the room. Only the two outer ones need to be built so as to open. In cold climates all the windows should be double.

Near the entry door, both on the boys' and on the girls' side, another door leads into the cloakroom, which is 11 ft. by 6 ft. in size, and each cloakroom is provided with a sink (S) and two windows, five feet from the floor, one looking into the entry opposite a corresponding one above the outside door, and the other looking into the back piazza. The last of these windows must be stationary, the one looking into the entry may be open in summer, but never in winter, for a reason that will appear later.

From the entry on each side of the house another door opens backward upon a piazza accessible in no other way, and enclosed with heavy lattice-work (shown in Fig. 2) or stout wire screens, and from this piazza a door leads into the closet, which is provided with a single window protected by heavy screens.

Each vault must be built as nearly air-tight as possible (preferably of brick), must be connected closely with the under side of the floors, and must have a ventilating pipe of galvanized iron leading from the end of the seat at the top and entering a separate flue in the chimney next to the smoke flue, as seen in Fig. 2.

The furnace, F (Fig. 1 and Fig. 2), has a large stove, with 10-inch fire-pot (if for coal) enclosed in a brick chamber, some 3 ft. by 3 ft., from which a door opens into the schoolroom. This door is six or seven feet high and three feet wide, and is very carefully protected on the inside with tin, or better, it may be made of tin or sheet-iron. Above this door is a transom, three feet wide and two feet high, either open entirely or filled with a screen of light wire and large mesh, and from the top of this transom and within the chamber or furnace a sheet-iron partition or diaphragm slopes backward, at an angle of about 45 degrees, to back side of the furnace.

Below the stove and in the bottom of the furnace is an opening 2 ft. by 2 ft. connecting with a fresh-air duct of the same size that extends beneath the floor to the outer walls beneath the outside steps, where it must be covered with a wire screen and be protected from the dust.

The tin door of the furnace being closed and the stove heated, the air becomes rarefied, rises to the top, is deflected by the slanting partition or diaphragm, and enters the schoolroom through the transom. At the same time the fresh air is supplied to the bottom of the furnace through the duct described above. This duct should be supplied with a valve by which it may be closed if necessary. The smoke flue of the stove is shown in Fig. 2, and behind it is the flue for ventilating the vaults.

But the warm air will not enter the room unless a corresponding volume of air is withdrawn at the same time; and this exhaust should be from near the floor, and on the same side of the room on which the fresh air enters near the top of the room. For the purpose of exhausting the vitiated air of the schoolroom, the furnace flue is extended upward through the roof; and it should be contracted near the top. This flue is represented in Fig. 2 (the large flue); and it will be heated by both the smoke flue on one side of it (which may be of metal) and by the diaphragm or slanting partition at the bottom. This diaphragm will be heated by the hot air impinging against its under side.

The vitiated air from the schoolroom reaches this ventilating flue as follows: The partition between the schoolroom and the cloakroom is raised 2 inches or 3 inches from the floor; on each side of the flue and above the diaphragm there is an opening of 18 inches by 24 inches, through which the air is exhausted from the top of each cloakroom, and as the doors and windows of this room are always closed (as said above) in cold weather, the vitiated air is withdrawn from the schoolroom into the cloakroom, where the clothing is thus warmed and ventilated.

In order to secure warmth and perfect ventilation, it will be perceived that the floor of the schoolroom and the cloakrooms must be perfectly tight, and the walls should be lined with brick, or otherwise made tight, at least three feet from the floor, and all the entry doors must shut very close. In other words, good construction is indispensable to comfort—both warmth and ventilation. It is for this reason that double windows are requisite in cold climates. All the warm air within which strikes the cold glass of a window is at once chilled, falls to the floor, and creates a draft. Moreover, the best-lighted part of the room is close to the window; and the first row of seats may be placed near the windows, as shown in Fig. 1, if the window is double.

At night and before the children arrive in the morning the cold air duct and the ventilating flues (I) leading from the cloakrooms may be closed. In that case, the door (D) of the furnace being open, the air within the schoolroom will come into direct contact with the stove, rise through the transom, and thus rotate throughout the schoolroom and warm all parts of it; and children may one by one warm their feet at the stove. But when the room is filled with children, the door (D) would be closed, and the fresh-air duct and the ventilating flues (I) must be open, in order that the stove may constantly heat the fresh air and ventilate as well as warm the room.

In summer the diaphragm above the furnace may be raised to a vertical position; if then the door (D) be closed, the warm air of the schoolroom may pass upward through the transom and the ventilating flue, while the fresh air is supplied through the entry doors and windows, at W W (for this purpose and not for light), and through the two windows that may be raised in the front. In mild weather or on damp days a fire in the enclosed stove will help to produce the upward draft without heating the room.

A pailful of dry earth must be thrown into each vault every day, and the contents of the vault must be removed every week. This can be done by sliding outward a water-tight trough made for the purpose and fitted into each vault. These troughs should then be replaced, and each door through which the trough is drawn should be securely locked.

The house should have a dry, clean, and warm cellar; but where this cannot be afforded the house should stand on a sufficient number of posts two or three feet high and boarded around to the ground. These posts, and especially the foundation of the chimney and of the vaults, must be absolutely secure from frost, and the floors might be boarded below the joists and plastered between; and there must be felt or thick layers of paper between the floors. A cold floor is costly and dangerous; and the cold schoolhouse costs more in the end, in health and in fuel, than it costs to build a tight, warm house at first.

As to the light. The best light for the pupil comes from the left, with no cross lights; but if the whole left side of the room is one continuous window, then the pupils in the back part of the room will face the light, though the window is at the left. To obviate this difficulty the first rows of desks might be placed with the axis at right angles to the window. After the first two rows, each desk is placed with its axis at a greater angle than the last, till the last row is at an angle of 45 degrees. Such an arrangement is novel, but upon reflection there seems to be no necessity for the prevailing rectangular placement of school desks, with the teacher at the middle front. In this plan the teacher is at the left front of the pupils at T, and the oblique situation of the desks is shown. This position requires chairs and not shelves for seats — the only rational seat; and there is no excuse for any but adjustable seats and desks.

The best light is from the top of the window. A window properly lights the room only at a distance of one and a half times its height. The south light is the best. The north light is too cold in winter and lacks the effect of the sun's rays in the room — chemical and hygienic effects not explained, but known to exist. The east and the west window admit the slanting rays in the morning or afternoon. In summer, though the rays are hot, they are nearly vertical at noon and do not shine directly in at the windows of the south exposure. But there should be very light shades to roll from the top and temper the light when it is too bright, and dark shades to roll from the bottom to shut out the light sometimes — to shut it out from the bottom because, as said above, the light from the top of the window shines across the room. An awning of white cotton cloth on a rectangular frame outside the window would be inexpensive and worth many times the cost in a single summer.

Any intelligent carpenter could build a house like the one described, and if some architect would build into it only a little good taste and chaste beauty, the house as well as the teacher would be an educator and a public benefactor.

A. P. MARBLE.

New York City.

APPENDIX N.

SCHOOL SYSTEMS.

ONTARIO.

[From Ontario School Regulations, Arts. 93-6.]

The system of public education in Ontario requires that every position be filled by a trained teacher, and no teacher receives a permanent certificate who does not possess the requisite qualifications as to (1) scholarship, (2) a knowledge of pedagogical principles, and (3) success in teaching as shown by actual experience.

The institutions for the preparation of teachers are, first, the county model schools, which one must attend for a session in order to be eligible for examination for a third-class certificate, without which no one can begin teaching in any public school in Ontario; the normal schools, of which there are two, one at Toronto and one at Ottawa, and which one must attend in order to obtain a second-class certificate and a permanent license; and the School of Pedagogy at Hamilton, in which are trained the first-class public-school teachers, the assistant and principals of high schools and collegiate institutes, and the public-school inspectors. Only first-class teachers can be appointed principals of county model schools or members of county boards of examiners. The board of examiners for any county may, with the approval of the education department, set apart any public school to be a county model school for the professional training of teachers.

There are sixty county model schools in Ontario, averaging about thirty pupils in attendance. Pupils may be admitted on a high-school primary certificate, which is granted to those who complete the first two years of a high-school course, although the pupils have often completed three or four years of the course. The course of study and training continues from the first of September for four months; it comprises school organization and management, methods of instruction, school law and regulations, music, and physical exercises; the course in training comprises observation of the work of the regular teachers, practice in teaching, criticism of work, and discussion of methods.

The minister of education may prescribe a course of reading for teachers of public schools. The course shall extend over three years, comprising three books each year. Any teacher who desires a certificate of having taken the public school teachers' reading course shall make a synopsis of not less than ten nor more than fifteen pages of each book read, and transmit the same to the inspector of his district. The managing committee of each teachers' institute shall appoint two persons who, with the inspector, shall form a committee, to determine whether the synopsis made by the teacher indicates that the books have been intelligently read, and for each book so read the inspector shall issue a certificate, and any teacher submitting a certificate for nine of the books prescribed shall receive a diploma certifying to the completion of one full reading course of three years.

In Ontario the law requires that the inspectors of schools shall hold first-class certificates, certifying to completion of the course of professional study of the School of Pedagogy at Hamilton, and shall have had three years' experience in teaching.

NEW BRUNSWICK.

The salaries of teachers shall be provided for from the three following sources, *viz.*: firstly, the provincial treasury; secondly, the county school fund; thirdly, district assessment. All other items of fixed or current expenditure shall be provided for by district or local assessment. In the distribution of the provincial and county school fund the number of days of school session and the average attendance are made factors of such importance as to encourage a long school year (average for the province, 215 days in 1895) and regularity of attendance.

The amount of provincial and county money to be received in any district in aid of schools will depend almost exclusively on the direct efforts made by the inhabitants of each district in maintaining their own schools . . . . and every such effort will be duly supplemented by funds from the county and province. ("Manual of School Law of New Brunswick," Arts. 12-23, and Remarks, p. 56.)

MANITOBA.

In reply to inquiries contained in the circular of the National Council of Education, forwarded by your correspondent at Regina, I beg to say that there is one normal school for the province for the training of first and second-class teachers, and four training schools for professional instruction of teachers holding third-class certificates. No academic work is done in either the normal or training school. The normal school course is five months in length, that of the training school three months. These institutions are public, and supported by the province and controlled by the educational department. The training schools are conducted by the inspectors, who spend eight months of the year in the rural schools and are thoroughly conversant with the requirements of rural districts.

No one is admitted to either normal or training school until he has a non-professional certificate of the grade for which the school affords professional training. The examination for third class certificates covers the ordinary subjects of the public-school course, with physics, botany, algebra to the end of simple equations, and one book of Euclid, with deductions. Certificates of this grade are good for three years, subject to a limitation to be hereafter mentioned.

The second-class non-professional certificate covers ground corresponding in the main with the requirements for matriculation into Harvard, and the first class corresponds with the first year of university work, omitting in each case all languages except English. About one-third of the time of the above courses is given to practice in teaching. In the schools of the towns where the normal and training schools are situated practice is given in each of the grades, but the time spent in the first four grades is about three times that spent in the second four. Practice in teaching and a written examination on history of education, psychology, management, methods, etc., count equally in determining a candidate's fitness to receive a certificate. The certificate issued is good for one year. If, after this year of probation, the inspector so recommends, a third-class certificate good for three years, or a second or first (according to the grade of non-professional certificate held) good for life or good conduct, is issued. Otherwise the certificate lapses.

Heretofore the holder of a non-professional certificate was allowed to teach without training for one year. Hereafter, however, no teacher will be allowed to teach in any public school who has not at least the professional training above outlined for third-class certificates.

About 75 per cent. of the graduates are from rural districts and country towns. Sixty-six per cent. of the teachers employed in the province in 1895 were trained. After this year all teachers will have training.

Institutes are held by the inspectors and normal-school instructors at points chosen by the Department of Education. They last from two to three days. Eighty per cent.

of the teachers attend. The aim of these institutes is to stimulate to professional study. They are a valuable means of stimulating teachers and arousing interest.

Circulars are sent to teachers and secretaries of school districts, giving notice of place of meeting and programme. Provincial grant is payable to districts whose teachers attend the institutes, as if the school were open.

Upwards of 80 per cent. of the teachers of the province are organized into voluntary associations. The aim and scope of the work are much the same as those of the institutes, but the work is done by the teachers themselves instead of by the normal instructors and inspectors. Several associations sometimes combine to secure the services of a prominent educationalist from outside of the province. The only qualification for membership is that of being a teacher actively engaged in teaching.

Reading circles have been organized only to a limited extent, and the data for reply cannot be obtained. All teachers take one or more teachers' journals. The desirability of doing so is kept before teachers by the inspectors. Certificates to teach are granted only by the Department of Education for the province, so that the provincial or state certificate is the only one valid here.

Teachers are chosen by the school boards of the various districts. Teachers in rural schools are engaged from year to year as a rule. In towns and cities the engagement is continued without re-election. It is impossible to say to what extent anything besides merit operates to determine the choice of teachers in rural districts. In towns appointments are made largely on advice of the supervising officer.

The maximum salary is $1,400 in towns and $720 in rural schools, with an average of $428 for the province and $368 for rural districts. In ten years the average salary has fallen about $90 per annum, owing in part to general depression and in part to competition of large numbers of young teachers using the profession as a stepping stone to some other line of work.

All improvement in educational work, and in status of teacher, must come through better education of the teachers. It is only where our class-rooms are filled with cultured and earnest men and women that teaching will become a profession, and take rank in public estimation in accordance with the importance of the interests committed to the schools.

Winnipeg. DANIEL McINTYRE.

FRANCE.

In France, which has made so great an effort in late years to advance popular education, the law requires that the candidate for the office of inspector of schools shall be at least twenty-five years of age, shall have had several years' experience in teaching, and shall hold certificates indicating a high grade of scholarship. In his written examination he is required to write a paper on some subject in pedagogy, and one on some subject in school administration; then follows an oral examination covering a wide range of psychology, ethics, pedagogy, and school administration; and then a practical examination, which consists of the inspection of a school, followed immediately by a verbal report.

In view of the increasing importance of inspection it is recommended that the standard be raised so as to require a certificate of qualification for a professorship in a normal school.

NORWAY.

The main obstacle in the way of perfecting the rural schools of Norway is of a geographical kind. Mountain peaks and ranges, valleys and woods, rivers and rapids, are so many barriers to human intercourse of any sort. There are few clusters of farms or cottages sufficient to form villages, so that children very often have to go miles to and from school without other means of transport than sleds, skis, or skates.

In spite of these natural hindrances, Norway is well known to have a more enlightened rural populace than most other countries. Every Norwegian peasant under fifty can read, write, and figure; all can read.

Some, or rather many, years ago the country districts of Norway had itinerant teachers, perambulating from farm to farm, gathering about them the nearest children where they came. Teaching of this kind was necessarily very defective, and often the teachers knew so little that it was a case of the blind leading the blind. Norway has changed all that. For twenty-five years or more the teaching force has been uniformly good, trained in the state-endowed seminaries or normal schools. A great majority of these rural teachers are sprung from the people amongst whom they work; they have the advantage of knowing their pupils' condition, peculiarities, and points of view.

Most inhabitants of the city above the laboring classes send their children to higher schools (Borgerskoler and Middelskoler), if they in any way can afford the school fees. In the country it is different. There even well-to-do farmers send their children to the public schools; they have no choice, unless, indeed, they go to the trouble and expense of employing private tutors, which some do.

As a rule, the school children are divided into two classes or grades, attending alternately every other day; each child, in this way, getting about fourteen to eighteen hours' schooling a week, or say 500 to 550 hours a year, the summer vacation lasting only one month.

The branches taught are reading, writing, arithmetic, singing, history, political geography, grammar and composition, religion, and, sometimes, drawing. Norway has an established church (the Lutheran), and all its public schools, therefore, have something of a parochial stamp. Biblical history and the catechism have their hour or even two daily — a serious drawback, admitted to be such both by religious persons and those more latitudinarian. Dissenters' children are, however, exempted from religious instruction, if their parents so desire.

To an American these school hours may seem few; but then the Norwegian children have an advantage over the American: above the primary grade no time is wasted on spelling, it being taken for granted that any child who has arrived at a tolerable command of the mother tongue knows how to spell. To be sure, the Norwegian language has fewer difficulties of pronunciation and spelling than the English.

Quite a prominent factor in the educational system of Norway are the authorized readers. Beginning with short rhyme and moral stories, they carry the child through the country's great past by means of selections from the sagas; contain chapters on botany, zoölogy, physics, and physiology, besides selections from the poets; but the best thing about these readers is their valuable information on almost all topics of vital national interest, from the Lofoden fisheries to the mining industries; they give, in short, a complete picture in miniature of the whole country.

Of late these readers are being discarded for one that promises to be still better, especially in a linguistic respect. As far as language is concerned, Norway is in a somewhat unsettled condition, chiefly in the rural districts. It has an heirloom of old Norse; its various dialects are direct descendants of the language still spoken on Iceland; but its official language is Danish. Of late a fusion of the two has been effected, there is an imperceptible but real change going on, new words are constantly being imported from the dialects into the literary language. Now the chief purpose of the new reader, quite extensive in matter, is to get the actually spoken language as near as possible, the objections to the old readers being that they are too old fashioned, "bookish."

As to the teachers of the rural districts, they are generally very able men (women teachers are employed in the cities only). They are not men of the world, to be sure; but, looked down on by their urban brethren, living on a pittance, they are, perhaps, truer "servants of the idea" (to use an old Norwegian expression) than many more favored and respected men. I have often thought that the branches formally taught in a Norwegian country school are of little significance in comparison with the loftiness of intellectual and moral aim often imparted by the teachers to their scholars.

The country schooling is nominally ended at the confirmation age, say fourteen. But in many places the education is continued in the half-free night schools, where the common-school branches are taught as before, special stress being laid on composition, history, and national literature. Under an able teacher these popular evening schools are very delightful, the teacher often being more of an older and wiser friend than a formal instructor.

A few words must be given to the so-called people's high schools (Folkehøjskoler), institutions patronized by young men and women generally better off. These institutions were founded by the Danish clergyman and educator, Grundtvig. They have always been of more importance in the land of their origin, Denmark, than in Norway. The principals of these schools are generally university-trained, high minded men, and many of the leaders in Norwegian public life and literature have been connected with them. Of these schools it might be said what Emerson said of books, they are there mainly to inspire. They might also be styled rural counterparts of the university extension and Chautauquan movements. Much of the best in Norwegian national life can be traced directly back to these schools. They are, however, high schools only by courtesy.

Norway is a democratic country. For that reason forces are always at work in the direction of lifting the lower strata up into the daylight of culture and knowledge. Conventions of teachers and educators for the purpose of furthering this aim are very common. All the while self education is going on. But a few nights ago I read the following letter addressed to a Christiania editor:

"We have an association of young men here, and a library of about 2,000 volumes. We meet once a week, and have readings and lectures. Last week we had a lecture on Schiller's "Wilhelm Tell." With Goethe and Schiller I am fairly well acquainted, but, as Dante is to me an honored name only, please recommend me a good translation of his works."

This letter from a young farmer voices a yearning for light and culture quite common in the rural districts of Norway.

OSCAR GUNDERSEN.

Chicago, Ill.

APPENDIX O.

EXTENSION WORK IN RURAL SCHOOLS.

The following extracts are from a report upon Extension Work in Agriculture, by Professor L. H. Bailey, of Cornell University, Ithaca, N. Y.:

The plan of effort in this teaching was to visit two schools during the day, one in the forenoon and one in the afternoon. The arrangements were made in advance with the school commissioner or the trustees, and the fact that the speakers were to be at the schoolhouse was ordinarily announced some days in advance, so that parents and friends could visit the school at that time if they chose. The teacher was in every case willing to omit the regular exercises for an hour or two, in order that our instructors might take up the work of object teaching with the children. The motive in this work was to find out just how the pupils could be reached by means of object-lesson teaching, and just how much interest they would be likely to manifest in agricultural matters in case it were ever found to be desirable to introduce such teaching as a part of the district school work. The instructor would first explain the reason for his coming, and give the school to understand that no new text-books were for sale and that no new classes were to be required at the hands of the teacher. He then ordinarily took up some simple object lesson. It might be, in one place, a stalk of corn which he had in his hand, and the process of growth of which he would explain from seed to harvest; it might be, in another case, the germination of a bean or a pumpkin seed; it might be, in another case, the habits or structure of a potato bug or some other insect; it might be, again, the reasons why there were knots and knot holes in the woodwork in the schoolhouse; it might be a very elementary talk upon the different plant foods which are in the soil; it might be, in other cases, a very brief sketch, with charts, of some fungus; and so on. These exercises were uniformly well received by both the pupils and the teachers, and this work has, I think, awakened more inspiration in the minds of our instructors than any other attempt which we have yet made to reach the people. The teachers in the schools have without exception expressed themselves as willing and desirous of taking up some such simple exercises as a rest for the pupils two or three times a week, if only they themselves could be instructed in the proper methods of carrying on the work. In order to afford this instruction to the teachers, we are now proposing to issue a series of experimental leaflets on object lessons and place these in the hands of the teachers.

There is no doubt of the necessity for work of this kind with the children. The love or antipathy of the farm is engendered at a very early age in the minds of the young. This has been demonstrated in these October meetings, when we have asked those children who live on farms and who still desire to do so to raise their hands, and we almost uniformly find that the number who desire to live on farms is far less than those who actually do live on them. With these children, ranging trom six to fifteen years of age, the question of pecuniary profits upon the farm has appealed very little, but they are influenced directly by the environments under which they are living. These environments must be improved; and if they are, there is every reason to expect that children will love the country better than the city. We have thought, therefore, that it is eminently worth the while to instill the love of nature and the knowledge of a multitude of living things in the minds of the children. An important question here arises: What is to be the future of our rural schools and of the agriculture of the state if the present generation, as seems so clearly indicated, is not satisfied with rural life and feels no interest in maintaining or contributing to the agricultural and educational interests of the state? While many more rural schoolhouses must become deserted, there are thousands of children already in our cities who are deprived of school advantages because adequate room does not exist for them to get into the schools of the city. The further problem also arises of the difficult economic questions to be met in our cities as the result of congestion of population. The standard of teaching had been much improved in New York state. It had been gratifying to meet so universally teachers who are not only well qualified, but who are doing excellent work in their schools, and who have the true teaching spirit. Our educational forces are thoroughly efficient and well equipped, but there is a need of different application of our school work in rural districts. The life of the district needs to be changed, and it can in no way be so effectively done as through our schools. The best work cannot be done in schools with an attendance of only half a dozen children. School districts will be forced to even greater consolidation in the future, and it would be desirable if families could also be consolidated, for it is the lack of social opportunity that is felt. It is the isolation of the farm home that the boy and girl dislike in these days of close communication and contact with the world which are brought about by steam and electricity. School grounds could be enlarged. They should furnish the opportunity for planting trees and shrubs; for the planting of seeds and growing of flowers; for having a nicely kept lawn, and, in time, these things, with their influences, would extend to the homes of children who do not have them and bring with them those attractions and interest that make a home what it ought to be, pleasant and inviting in its surroundings.

All this work, as I have said, has been experimental — an attempt to discover the best method of teaching the people in agriculture. We believe that the most efficient means of elevating the ideals and practice of the rural communities are as follows, in approximately the order of fundamental importance: (1) The establishment of nature study or object lesson study, combined with field walks and incidental instruction in the principles of farm practice in the rural schools; (2) the establishment of correspondence instruction in connection with reading courses, binding together the university, the rural schools, and all rural literary or social societies; (3) itinerant or local experiment and investigation, made chiefly as object-lessons to farmers and not for the purpose, primarily, of discovering scientific facts; (4) the publication of reading bulletins which shall inspire a quickened appreciation of rural life, and which may be used as texts in rural societies and in the reading courses, and which shall prepare the way for the reading of the more extended literature in books; (5) the sending out of special agents as lecturers or teachers, or as investigators of special local difficulties, or as itinerant instructors in the normal schools and before the training classes of the teachers' institutes; (6) the itinerant agricultural school, somewhat after the plan of our horticultural schools, which shall be equipped with the very best teachers, and which shall be given as rewards to the most intelligent and energetic communities.

All these agencies, to be most efficient, should be under the direction of a single bureau wholly removed from partisan political influence and intimately associated with investigational work in agriculture. Such a bureau should also have most intimate relations with the Department of Public Instruction, for not only must the public schools be reached, but teachers must be trained. The teachers in our public schools are now of a high grade, and they will quickly seize opportunities to prepare themselves to teach the elements of rural science. There should be facilities placed at the disposal of every normal school in the state, whereby it may receive courses of lectures upon rural subjects from teachers of recognized ability, and teaching-helps, in the way of expository leaflets should be placed in the hands of every teacher who desires them. All this work of carrying the modern university extension impulse to the country is too important and too fundamental to be confined to any one particular agricultural interest or to any one district of the state; and it is a work, too, which should be treated as a teaching extension and not as an experiment-station extension.

In conclusion, I must say that the farmers, as a whole, are willing and anxious for education. They are difficult to reach because they have not been well taught, not because they are unwilling to learn. It is astonishing, as one thinks of it, how scant and poor has been the teaching which has even a remote relation to the tilling of the soil; and many of our rural books seem not to have been born of any real sympathy with the farmer or any just appreciation of his environments. Just as soon as our educational methods are adapted to the farmer's needs, and are born of a love of farm life and are inspired with patriotism, will the rural districts begin to rise in irresistible power.

APPENDIX P.

INSTITUTES IN PENNSYLVANIA.

1. Every county holds an institute annually for a week. Towns, cities, and boroughs hold separate ones for a day or two, or for a week. The course of instruction and the corps of instructors in county institutes are entirely determined by the county superintendent, who is always an experienced teacher.

The considerations that secure attendance are: (1) Continuance of salary for the week, if the time be spent at the institute; (2) closing the schools by law during the institute week; (3) the knowledge that the county superintendent will discriminate against teachers not in attendance, and that directors will do likewise; (4) an institute programme that attracts, that wins outsiders interested in education.

Only sickness keeps teachers away as a rule. It is unusual for more than one in a hundred to be absent. Often every teacher is present. The effect of the institutes upon the schools is most potent. The professional spirit of the teachers is intensified, the quality of the teaching is improved, and the interest of the public in education is aroused. It is a great revival period, covering the state, the audiences being limited generally by the capacity of the largest halls available.

2. Local institutes are held at different dates in different sections of almost every county, conducted by the teachers of the neighborhood, and are attended by teachers and pupils from adjoining sections. There is generally but one local institute a year in each section. It continues for one day. The subjects all relate to work in rural schools.

Pennsylvania. D. J. WALLER, JR.

APPENDIX Q.

THOMAS ARNOLD (1795–1842).

A STUDY FOR RURAL TEACHERS.

We are to study this month the contributions of Thomas Arnold to educational doctrine and practice. One of the great biographies in English literature is Dean Stanley's "Life of Thomas Arnold." An American educator says that to become familiar with this biography marks an era in the life of a teacher. For material concerning Dr. Arnold's pedagogical work consult Oscar Browning's "Arnold and Arnoldism" (*Foundations*, of February, 1897), Payne's "Lectures on Arnold" (pp. 129 and 261, Vol. IV., *Foundations*), "Tom Brown at Rugby," and Carlisle's abridgment of Stanley's "Life of Arnold."

The discussions to take place at the institute session, to be held on the 13th proximo, will be founded upon the following questions:

1. Give a brief biographical sketch of Arnold, calling especial attention to events having formative influence upon his character.
2. Describe the school at Rugby.
3. How did Arnold contribute toward dignifying the profession of teaching?
4. What was his theory with respect to teaching morality?
5. Compare Arnold's views concerning school management with the views advocated respectively by Locke and Herbert Spencer.
6. Prove: Arnold hated shams.
7. Discuss two excellent characteristics of his instruction.
8. What practical lesson with respect to self-government should the teacher learn from the study of Arnold?
9. Of what feature of the modern English school would Arnold have entirely disapproved, and upon what grounds?
10. To what one thing, above everything else, do you attribute Arnold's success?
11. Give in parallel columns a comparative view of the contributions made to educational history by Ascham, Locke, Spencer, and Arnold.

Each of the following paragraphs has bearing, direct or indirect, upon this month's esson:

1. "A schoolmaster's influence is with the young, the strong, and the happy; and he cannot get on with them unless in animal spirits he can sympathize with them, and show them that his thoughtfulness is not connected with selfishness and weakness."—Arnold.

2. "What I want is a man who is a Christian and a gentleman, and one who has common sense and understands boys. I do not so much care about scholarship, as he will have immediately under him the lowest forms in the school; but yet, on second thought, I do care about it very much, because his pupils may be in the highest forms; and, besides, I think that even the elements are best taught by a man who has a thorough knowledge of the matter. However, if one must give way, I prefer activity of mind and an interest in his work to high scholarship; for the one may be acquired far more easily than the other." —From one of Arnold's inquiries for a master.

3. "A master should have sufficient vigor of mind and thirst for knowledge to persist in adding to his own stores without neglecting the full improvement of those he is teaching."—From a letter of Arnold to a newly appointed master.

4. "The lapse of years has only served to deepen me in the conviction that no gift can be more valuable than the recollection and inspiration of a great character working on our own."—Dean Stanley, referring to Arnold.

5. "There is no short or royal road to good teaching other than the king's highway of good living. He who wishes to teach well must, first of all, try to live well. He who wishes to do something in his chosen life-work, must aim to be something. He who wishes to have a good influence, must first be a good influence."—James H. Carlisle, of South Carolina.

6. "Not the most eloquent exhortations to the erring and disobedient, though they be in the tongues of men or angels, can move mightily upon your scholars' resolutions till the nameless, unconscious, but infallible presence of a consecrated, earnest heart lifts its holy light into your eyes, hallows your temper, breathes its pleading benedictions into your tones, and authenticates your entire being with its open seal."—From Huntington's "Unconscious Tuition."

7. "The glory of the children is unity with nature; the glory of the teacher is unity with childhood."—G. Stanley Hall.

W. S. SUTTON.

Houston, Tex.

APPENDIX R.

INTELLECTUAL AND MORAL EDUCATION.

[From Les Nouveaux Programmes des Écoles Primaires, a handbook containing the course of study, time tables, directions and explanations for the guidance of the teacher.]

INTELLECTUAL EDUCATION.

The aim of intellectual education in the common school is not to give an exhaustive course of instruction, but to secure to the child the practical knowledge along many lines which he will need in life, so taught as to exercise his faculties, cultivate and enlarge his mind, and thus constitute a true education.

To attain the end of true education it is demanded that there be a continual interaction of the minds of teacher and pupil. The teacher must lead the pupil from the known to the unknown, from the easy to the difficult, from the study of concrete realities to the abstract idea, thus developing the power to compare, to generalize, to reason, without the aid of material examples. The teacher must respect the pupil's intuitive power of grasping, not all truths, but the simplest and most fundamental, and must take care not to waste time in idle discussion, nor in the acquisition of useless knowledge. He must follow the guidance of nature, developing the judgment of the pupil by leading him to judge, the power of observation by making him observe much, the power of reasoning by aiding him to reason for himself.

MORAL EDUCATION.

Moral education is designed to complete, to elevate, and ennoble all the other instruction of the school. While the other studies develop skill and cultivate intelligence in certain special lines, moral instruction tends to develop the essential character of man himself. The power of moral education depends less on the precision and the logical connection of the truths taught than on strength of feeling, liveliness of impression, warmth of conviction. It moves the will. It does not undertake to analyze all the reasons for moral action, but it aims, before all else, to produce and to repeat the act; to form a habit of thought which will govern the life. It is not to be considered a science so much as the art of inclining the will toward the good.

In moral instruction the teacher represents society. He is to organize, and to make clear and definite, the fundamental moral ideas which the child brings to school; to strengthen these ideas; to make them a motive power in the habitual conduct of life, and thereby to train the child for the varied duties of citizenship.

The moral lesson must be kept distinct in character and form from other lessons. It is not enough to give the pupil correct ideas and to furnish him with wise maxims: he must be led to feel the majesty of the moral law. The teacher must keep clearly in mind that it is for him to develop, to render acute, to correct, to strengthen the moral sense by exercising often, but with extreme care, the conscience of the child. The instruction should be limited, especially in the earlier years, to the essential elementary points, to those which are clear, simple, yet imperative; avoiding the finer developments of ethics which are appropriate only at a more advanced age, it should aim to lead the child to a moral life by such an accumulation of beautiful examples, of good impressions, of wholesome ideas, of salutary habits, and of noble aspirations, that he may carry from school with his acquisitions of elementary knowledge that which is far more precious — a good conscience.

Success in this instruction demands that the teacher be an example of what is taught; that he avoid a mechanical method; that he feel, himself, the true character or force of every lesson, and that he watch the moral development of his pupils with the same solicitude as he watches their progress in scholarship; that he have as much care for the development of character as for that of intellect. This alone can give to the teacher the title of educator, and to elementary instruction the name of liberal education.

APPENDIX S.

CONTINUOUS SESSIONS IN NORMAL SCHOOLS.

[Inserted at the request of the Chairman of the Subcommittee on Supply of Teachers, as a suggestion worthy of careful consideration.]

A plan for continuous sessions in normal schools has been devised by President Shepard of the State Normal School at Winona, Minn., which, by virtue of a recent act of the legislature, will be entered upon July 1, 1897. It provides for continuous sessions in the schools at Winona and Mankato of four quarters annually of twelve weeks each. The quarters will open respectively July 1, October 1, January 1, and April 1. This arrangement of quarters is designedly in the interest of the rural school-teachers. New classes in all subjects will be commenced each quarter, and classes will graduate each quarter. Any rural school-teacher will be able to attend at least one full quarter each year. The work of each quarter will constitute a unit of credit on the regular courses of the school. The subjects and methods of introduction in the earlier quarters of the several courses will be those which are especially suited to the needs of teachers of rural schools.

A special summer-term course of six weeks, from July 1 to August 15, is provided for those whose schools begin before the close of the regular summer quarter (October 1). The work of this term will also apply on the regular courses as a minor unit of credit.

The advantages of this plan are apparent. The valuable and extensive equipments of the state normal schools will be made available throughout the year instead of standing idle, as now, many weeks during that part of the year when teachers, especially rural school-teachers, are most at liberty to attend school.

Teachers in rural school service may take up and pursue regular normal-school courses without withdrawing from teaching service. This will be a distinct gain, both to the teaching supply and to the self-supporting teacher who must alternately teach and attend school. It is well known that this constitutes the most valuable and most progressive class of rural school-teachers.

The beginning of new classes each quarter enables teachers to attend school with equal advantage any quarter when at liberty. The present practice of normal schools in graduating classes but once a year and at the close of the graded school year is greatly to the disadvantage of the rural schools. These graduates are largely absorbed by the graded schools, which just at that time of the year are organizing their teaching corps for the following year. When the rural school officers later in the year apply for graduate teachers there are usually none to be had. Under the "Winona" plan at least three classes will be graduated at times during the year when the graded-school situations are not open and just when the rural-school situations are open. This will tend to direct a large and valuable supply of normal-school graduates into rural-school service.

INDEX.

Adams, J. R. Ohio, report on consolidation and transportation, 138.

Administrative Machinery, topic of inquiry, 9.

Advertisement, notice to bidders for transportation of pupils to township schools, 139

Agassiz School at Penekese, an inspiration to teachers, 80.

Agricultural Environments, committee to prepare a paper on, 11.

Agricultural Schools, efforts made to reduce to pedagogic form the arts of farm, garden, and forest, 104; having pupils teach during their course in, 87; in each congressional district in Alabama, 87.

Agriculture, course in, should be provided in normal schools, 89; of what it should treat, 89; instruction in, prescribed by law in some states, 89; extension work in, 202; list of books in, 189.

Alabama, agricultural schools in each congressional district, 87; J. H. Phillips of, paper on negro schools by, 185; training school at Birmingham, an important factor, 87; salaries paid teachers in, 15.

Animal Life, chemicals entering into, 151; list of books on the subject, 191; the study of, 149.

Appendix A. Sociological factors in rural education, 123; children and teachers need the inspiration of numbers, 123; school conditions in Ohio twenty years ago, 123; population per square mile in the United States, 124; character of population considered, 124; education supported only at great cost, 125; character of population in respect to money-earning power, 125; expenditure per capita, per cent. of illiteracy, 126.

Appendix B. Permanent school funds and receipts of school moneys, 126; working of common school fund in Connecticut, 126; Texas school-fund lands, 126; grazing and mining lands, 127; remedy for evils of depreciation, 127; receipts of school moneys in United States, 128.

Appendix C. California system of school maintenance, 130; sources of revenue, 130; the permanent fund, 130; poll tax, 130; collateral inheritance tax, 130; state school tax, 130; districts may vote a school tax, 130; assessment of property, 130; distribution of school funds, 131; moneys remaining on hand, 131.

Appendix D. The county as the unit of organization, 132; the system in Richmond county, Ga., 132; large amount of money paid by cities spent in rural districts, 132; qualifications of teachers, 133; treatment of teachers, 133; schools operated nine calendar months, 133; in regard to schoolhouses, 133; superintendent has charge of all schools, 133.

Appendix E. Comparative cost of the township and district systems, 133; system discussed by F. A. Hill, 134; by C. D. Hine, 134; by W. W. Stetson, 134.

Appendix F. Transportation of pupils, 135; school population in New York outside cities, compared, 135; township system the probable solution, 135; arguments by A. W. Edson in favor of consolidation and transportation, 135; leading arguments in favor of consolidation and transportation, 136; experiments in progress in Ohio, 137; report by F. E. Morrison, 137; report by J. R. Adams, 138; good results of workings of the transportation system, 138; notice to bidders for transportation of pupils, 139; report by T. J. Clapp, 140; cost of transportation, 140; result in Crane School, Quincy, Mass., 141.

Appendix G. Enrichment of the work of the rural schools, 142; introduction by the subcommittee, 142; suggestions offered, 143; studies upon the surrounding landscape, 143; surface features, nature, origin, and meaning, 143; reference books, 144; the study of streams, 144; study of soils, 145; books of reference, 146; application of landscape studies, 146; location of homes, 146; of roads, 146; of towns and villages, 146; development of the region as affected by environments,

146; social life of the people as affected by surrounding physical features, 146; distribution of vegetation as influenced by surface features, 147; the study of atmospheric phenomena, 147; maps should be secured from Weather Bureau, 147; the study of plant life, 147; growth from seed, 148; growth from buds, 149; books of reference, 149; the study of animal life, 149; course of study for the rural schools, 149; lack of appreciation of immediate surroundings, 150; lack of scientific skill in farm work, 150; dearth of social life in the country, 150; attention should be given to the picturesqueness and natural beauty of surroundings, 150; scientific skill, mechanics, manual training, etc., 150; mathematics, 151; biology, 151; meteorology, 151; mineralogy, 151; chemistry, 151; government publications a help in schools, 151; social physical conditions must be improved, 152.

APPENDIX H. The farm as the center of interest, 152; child studies from nature, 152; work of the child upon the farm should be brought into the schoolroom, 154; geology, geography, mineralogy, how taught, 154; meteorology, study of, would come through the seasons, 155; plant life, 156; zoölogy, 156; chemistry and physics, 156; mathematics as applied to farm life, 157; suggestions relating to reading and literature, 157; as to teaching reading, writing, and spelling, 158; manual training and art, 158; industries and commerce, 159; history, 159; conclusions, 160; libraries should belong to schools, 160; farmer boys have mistaken ideas of city life, 161; advantages of country schools for an appreciation of nature, and in resources for intellectual life, 161.

APPENDIX I. The country-school problem, 161; facts that enter into the problem, 161; non-classification solution, 161; the graded-school solution, 163; common method of grading the country schools, 163; feasible modifications, 164; evils in the one-teacher school, 164; the three-grade solution, 165; course of study, 165; three-grade programme, 166; hopeful improvement lies in simpler grading, 168; advantages of dividing course of study into three groups, 168; needed freedom of classification and instruction in each section, 168; a standard and an evidence of progress, 168; a needed reduction of class exercises, 168; a workable programme, 169; provision made for individual progress, 170; graphic illustration of an ideal one-teacher rural school, 170; course of instruction for rural schools, 171; suggestion and description of the plan, 171; scheme for distribution of time, 177; the plan illustrated, 184; course in arithmetic, 176; in drawing, 178; in elements of science, 180; in geography, 176; in history, 174; in language, 174; in morals and civics, 182; in reading, 172; in spelling, 172; in writing, 172; objects of the course, materials, 184; advantages of a rational course, 160.

APPENDIX J. Negro teachers for negro schools, 185; review of progress made, 185; the negro as a dependent, 186; white teachers cannot realize the ideal relation between teacher and negro pupil, 186; potent reason for employing negro teachers for negro schools, 186; co-ordination of teacher and child, 187; summary of arguments for employment of negro teachers for negro schools, 187.

APPENDIX K. Paper relating to J. W. Bradbury, 188; was United States senator from Maine, 188; opened training school for teachers in Effingham, N. H., 188; remarks regarding success of the school, 188; Teachers' Seminary at Plymouth, N. H., extracts from an early catalogue, 188.

APPENDIX L. New York state school library, 189; character of books selected, 189; list of books for rural schools and communities, 189; in agriculture, 189; horticulture, 190; botany, 190; science, 191; animal life, 191; nature study, 191; miscellaneous books, 192.

APPENDIX M. Hygiene and health in public schools, 193; impure air, bad light, and unsuitable furniture, 193; evils of unsanitary schoolrooms, 193; physiology as now taught, 193; lavatories or water-closets, relation to school, 194; how a school house should be made, 194; architecture of churches and schoolhouses compared, 194; plan and details of an ideal schoolhouse, 195.

APPENDIX N. County model schools, 198; review of systems, Ontario, 198; New Brunswick, 199; Manitoba, 199; France, 200; Norway, 200; supervisors must hold first-class certificates in Ontario, 198; admission to normal or training schools in Manitoba, 199; salaries in New Brunswick, 199; salaries in Manitoba, 199; how teachers are chosen in Manitoba, 199; review of school work in France, 200; review of school work in Norway, 200; branches taught in Norway, 201; high schools in Norway, 202; libraries in Norway, 202.

Appendix O. Extension work in rural schools, 202; simple object-lesson teaching, 202; home surroundings must be improved, 203; love of nature fostered, 203; school grounds beautified, 203; extension work a means of elevating rural communities, 204; normal schools should have facilities to aid, 204; leaflets should be issued, 204; benefits of such instruction to the rural districts, 204.

Appendix P. Institutes in Pennsylvania, 204; county superintendent in charge, 204; considerations that secure attendance, 205; professional spirit of teachers intensified, 205; quality of teaching improved, 205; interest of the public aroused, 205; local neighborhood institutes, 205; subjects relating to rural school work, 205.

Appendix Q. Life and work of Thomas Arnold, 205; influence of the schoolmaster with the young, 205; should be a Christian, 206; should have vigor of mind, 206; no other royal road to good teaching than good living, 206.

Appendix R. Intellectual and moral education, 206; aim of intellectual education, 206; end of true education, how attained, 206; guidance of nature must be followed, 206; pupil must be led to observe, judge, and reason for himself, 206; design of moral education, 207; special work of the teacher, 207; moral sense and conscience of the child must be developed and strengthened, 207; instruction confined to essential points, 207; the teacher should be an example of what is taught, 207; should have as much care for development of character as of intellect, 207.

Appendix S. Continuous sessions in normal schools, 207; plan at Winona, Minn., 207; special provisions for rural teachers, 207; such work should apply on regular courses, 208; extensive normal-school equipments thus utilized to full extent, 208; a teacher may attend any quarter, 208; the tendency will be to direct a supply of graduates into rural-school work, 208.

Arithmetic, plans of a course of study in, 167, 170, 176, 177, 184.

Arkansas, Congress gave public lands to, for school use on admission to Union, 35; qualifications required of superintendents in, 67; salaries paid teachers in, 55.

Arnold, Thomas, paper on life and work of, 205.

Atmospheric Phenomena, study of, 147; teachers should secure weather maps from Weather Bureau, 147.

Bailey, L. H., New York, assistance rendered committee in selecting list of books, 189; extracts from paper by, on agricultural extension work, 202.

Barnes, Earl, California, report from special committee to investigate rural-school problem, 7.

Bidders, notice to, for transportation of pupils, 139.

Biology, course of study in rural schools, 151; demand for scientific skill requires study of, 150.

Birmingham, Ala., training school at, an important factor, 87.

Black, S. T., California, made member committee to investigate rural-school problem, 7, 8; member Subcommittee on School Maintenance, 8; reports from committee to investigate rural-school problem, 5; reports from Subcommittee on School Maintenance, 20; paper by, on California school maintenance, 130.

Books of Reference, agricultural, 146; animal life, 101; biographical, 205; botanical, 149; educational, 123, 166; geographical, 144; on government, 30, 47; on horticulture, 190; on nature study, 191; on science, 191; miscellaneous, 192.

Botany, list of books on the subject, 149, 190.

Boutan, M., France, wealth of country increased through school-garden system, 90.

Bradbury, J. W., New Hampshire, opened training school at Effingham, 84; remarks regarding success of the school, 188.

Brown, G. P., Illinois, reports from special committee on plan to investigate rural-school problem, 7.

California, system of school maintenance, 130; sources of revenue, 130; the permanent fund, 130; poll tax, 130; collateral inheritance tax, 130; state school tax, 130; districts may vote a school tax, 130; assessment of property, 130; distribution of school funds, 131; moneys remaining on hand, 131; salaries paid teachers in, 15; law for better remuneration of rural teachers, 108; secures skilled teachers by wise use of money, 98; method of distributing school tax, commended by subcommittee, 38.

CANADA, length of school year in, 79; longer school year secured, 93.

CHAMBERLIN, T. C., Illinois, requested to prepare a paper on agricultural environments, 11; reports from special committee on enrichment of rural-school courses, 142.

CHAUTAUQUAN PLAN, for promotion of home study commended, 109.

CHEMISTRY, demands for scientific skill requires study of, 150; course of study in, in rural schools, 151; suggestions on study of, 156.

CHICAGO UNIVERSITY, success of summer term is significant, 86.

CHISHOLM, MRS., Assiniboia, subcommittee returns thanks for information, 79.

CITIES, are hives of illiteracy, 47; ratio of foreign-born and illiteracy in, in Michigan, 48; concentration of population and wealth in, 31; training schools in, surplus teachers will seek employment in rural schools, 87; country schools have points of advantage over those in, 52.

CLAPP, T. J., Ohio, report on centralization and transportation, 140.

CLASSIFICATION, in rural schools, 162; present condition and trend of rural schools, grading and classification in United States, 113; should not be expected in rural schools, reasons, 97; should not be expected when there is great difference in work, 92; ideal classification, 97; pupils in large numbers easily taught, 97; city system of, unwise in rural schools, 99, 100; of pupils in different degrees of advancement, 99; stress laid upon, by normal schools, 100; abuses of, in the village schools, 100; relation of course of study to, 105, 165; also term-grading used to signify the same thing, words defined, 100; all schools understood in a certain sense to be graded, 106; the solution of the country-school problem, 163; common methods of, in country schools, 163; feasible modifications of, 164; evils of, in the one-teacher school, 164; the three-grade solution, 165; three-grade programme, 166; hopeful improvement in simpler, 168; certificates of examination in two-grade, 92; one-half the teachers in United States teach in ungraded schools, 94; small ungraded schools should often meet in town centers, 108; large proportion of all children is in ungraded schools, 50; best done through consolidation of schools, 49; evils of grading as applied to city and rural schools alike, 17.

COLORADO, salaries paid teachers in, 15.

COMMITTEE ON RURAL SCHOOLS reports, 7; of Nine appointed on rural-school problem, 7; increased to twelve, 8; report, 5; report by chairman, 7; special of three appointed to formulate plan of work, 8; plan formulated, 8; Subcommittee on School Maintenance appointed, 8; its report, 20; Subcommittee on Supervision appointed, 9; its report, 55; Subcommittee on Supply of Teachers appointed, 9; its report, 77; Subcommittee on Instruction and Discipline appointed, 10; its report, 94.

COMMUNITY SYSTEM, law of Texas relating to, defined, 45.

COMPETITIVE EXAMINATION, referred to by subcommittee, 83.

COMPULSORY ATTENDANCE, selfishness of parents, 52; difficulties attending enforcement, 52; in relation to high-school education in Ohio, 41.

CONCORD, MASS., consolidation of schools commenced at, 107.

CONCORD, VT., normal school opened at, by S. R. Hall, 83.

CONNECTICUT, early order that towns should found schools, 43; legal term of office of state superintendent in, 56; adopts plan of collecting pupils into larger units, 307; the town and district systems exist in, 44; cost of town and district systems discussed by C. D. Hine, 134; districts not equally taxed, 30; how state school income is distributed, 36; working of common-school-fund system in, 126; as a non-public land state, 24; salaries paid teachers in, 15.

CONSOLIDATION, reasons for, 46; promise of success through, 50; dependent upon contingencies, 50; good roads a helpful element, 51; number of schools, schoolhouses, and teachers diminished by, 54; how suggestions of subcommittee relating to may be made practicable, 54; discussed by subcommittee, 12; bids fair to prove of great benefit, 18; great possibilities of improvement through, 49; the reform should not be misunderstood, 50; arguments of A. W. Edson and others in favor of, 135; experiments in progress in Ohio, 137; report on, by F. E. Morrison, 137; report on, by J. R. Adams, 138.

CONTENTS REPORT OF COMMITTEE OF TWELVE ON RURAL SCHOOLS, 5.

CONTINUOUS SESSIONS IN NORMAL SCHOOLS, paper on, 207; Winona plan, 207; special provisions for rural teachers, 207; teachers may attend at any quarter, 208; tendency of, to supply rural schools with trained teachers, 208.

CONVEYANCE OF PUPILS, laws of Massachusetts relating to, 48; money paid for, for several years, 49; paper on, 135; arguments in favor of, 135; experiments in progress in Ohio, 137; good workings of the system, 138; notice to bidders for transportation of pupils, 139; cost of, 140; result in Crane school, Massachusetts, 141.

COUNTRY-SCHOOL PROBLEM, paper by E. E. White, 161; facts that enter into the problem, 161; non-classification solution, 161; the graded-school solution, 163; common method of grading the country schools, 163; feasible modifications, 164; evils in the one-teacher school, 164; the three-grade solution, 165; course of study, 165; three grade programme, 166; hopeful improvement lies in simpler grading, 168; advantages of dividing course of study into three groups, 168; needed freedom of classification and instruction in each section, 168; a standard and an evidence of progress, 168; a needed reduction of class exercises, 168; a workable programme, 169; provision made for individual progress, 170; graphic illustration of an ideal one-teacher rural school, 170.

COUNTY MODEL SCHOOLS, review of systems, Ontario, 198; Manitoba, 199; New Brunswick, 199; France, 200; supervisors must hold first-class certificates in Ontario, 198; admission to, in Manitoba, 199.

COURSE OF STUDY FOR RURAL SCHOOLS, paper by W. S. Jackman, 150; lack of appreciation of immediate surroundings, 150; lack of scientific skill in farm work, 150; dearth of social life in the country, 150; attention should be given to picturesqueness and natural beauty of surroundings, 150; scientific skill, mechanics, manual training, 150; mathematics, biology, meteorology, mineralogy, chemistry, 151; government publications a help in schools, 151; should be substantially the same in rural as in city schools, 101; what the child should be taught, 101; geography of the environments, 102; means by which that which is useful is procured from nature, 102; instruction in branches not yet reduced to pedagogic form, not desirable, 104; relation of course of study to grading and classification, 105; promotion defined, 105; there should be much written work provided for in, 106; divisions of, 106; programme in country schools, 167; hopeful improvements in simpler grading, 168; advantages of a division of, into three groups, 168; a graphic illustration of an ideal one-teacher rural school, 170; course of study for one year, 16; remarks on, by subcommittee, 16, 18; paper on, 171; suggestions and description of plan, 171; advantages of a national, 160.

CRANE SCHOOL, Quincy, Mass., result of consolidation and transportion, 143.

DELAWARE, salaries paid teachers in, 15.

DIRECTORS, board of, relation between school officers and supervisor should be well defined, 70; cordial relations must exist with supervisor, 71; inspection of the school of importance to, 71; should meet the supervisor at stated times for consultation, 71.

DISTRICT, subject of supervision in, 13; supervisor must be acquainted with conditions in, 14; supervisor must have controlling influence in, 14; the term district as used in school legislation, 21; the town-district or unit system, 22; term as applied often misleading, 22; history of the Ohio law, 22; district system defined, 23; incorporated villages, towns, and cities, as units of taxation, 29; rate of taxation greater in one than another, 30; as a taxing unit, abolished in Ohio, 30; levying school tax upon township instead of district, 31; the assistance large units render to smaller ones, 34; distribution of school tax in, 36; comment of subcommittee on rules governing distribution of school moneys, 37; of tax received from telegraphs, telephones, and railroads, 40; substitution of township unit for district system, 42; strife between districts prevented, 42; new districts became units at an early date, 43; schools of undistricted towns superior, 43; districted and undistricted towns compared, 44; district system at one time universal, 44; one trustee manages the schools of a township in Indiana, 44; district system in many states, 44; superiority of the township system, 44; the community system of Texas, 45; the county system in the South and West, 45; the county system in Georgia, 45; number of small schools not confined to poorer districts, 47; money paid for transportation of pupils for several years, 49; better attainments through consolidation of schools, 49; that which promotes ease of administration promotes good instruction,

49; promise of success through consolidation, 50; consolidation must accord with local contingencies, 50; consolidation in the North depends upon the township-unit system 50; good roads an element of consolidation, 50; "little red school house" a costly affair, 52; the district not a desirable taxing unit, 53; when town or township system should be substituted for district system, 54; number of schools, schoolhouses, and teachers, diminished by consolidation, 54; states having township or district supervision, 58; operation of the two methods of supervision, 58; combination of towns for supervisory purposes, 59; combination applicable to small districts, 59; a county too large for one superintendent, 60; county superintendents should have deputies, 60; plan of superintendency in counties containing cities, 61; one school fund raised by entire county, 60; superintendent looks after city and rural schools in county, 60; taxes raised on city property distributed to rural schools also, 61; money spent for good supervisors is well spent, 64; employment of teachers in the district by the supervisor, 69; distribution of income to towns and districts in Connecticut, 126; may vote a tax in California, 130; opinions regarding district system, 134.

DRAWING, course of study in, 178; programme relating to, 167, 170; remarks on, 184.

EDSON, A. W., Massachusetts, arguments by, favoring consolidation and transportation, 135.

EFFINGHAM, New Hampshire, early training school opened at, 84, 188.

ELEMENTS OF SCIENCE, plan of study in, 167, 184.

EMERY, J. Q., Wisconsin, says laws contain necessary elements to enable consolidation, 50.

ENDOWMENTS, schools have outgrown, 25; sometimes harmful, 24; gifts should be encouraged, 25; apportionment of public lands in admission of states, 35.

ENGLAND, to secure government grant, school must have met four hundred times during the year, 78; richer than Scotland, but behind in schools, 126.

ENRICHMENT of the work of the rural schools, paper on, 142.

EVANS, L. B., Georgia, made member Committee on Rural Schools, 8; chairman Subcommittee on School Supervision, 8; reports from Committee on Rural Schools, 5; reports from Subcommittee on School Supervision, 55; paper by, on the county as the unit of school organization, 132.

EXAMINATION AND CERTIFICATION OF TEACHERS, scope and character of, 90; certificates should be graded as to range of examination, 90; should cover the range of work required, 91; examination for elementary certificates, 92; certificates graded into elementary and advanced classes, 92; a life certificate should be granted, 92; examinations of today reviewed, 92; proper use of competitive examinations, 108.

EXPENDITURES, topic of in uiry, 8; of school moneys in California, 131; under county-unit system, 132; cost of township and district systems discussed, 133; school moneys, how distributed in New Brunswick, 198; revenue from public lands, how apportioned, 35; plan of, discussed, 34; comments of subcommittee on methods governing, 35; comparative statements of receipts and disbursements, 36; of money received from telegraphs, telephones, and railroads, 40; under county system, 46; of money paid for transportation of pupils, 46; money wastefully expended, 52; should be disbursed in such manner that the strong will help the weak, 53; such an amount of money must be given to the schools, 54; taxes raised in cities often distributed to rural schools, 61; in certain cities, 29; towns should not receive state aid, 40.

EXPRESS COMPANIES, distribution of tax levied upon, 40.

EXTENSION WORK, in rural schools, 202; simple object-lesson teaching, 202; home surroundings must be improved, 203; love of nature fostered, 203; school grounds beautified, 203; extension work a means of elevating rural communities, 204; normal schools should have facilities to aid, 204; leaflets should be issued, 204; benefits of this work to the rural teacher, 204.

FALLOWS, SAMUEL, Wisconsin, statement as to amount of property assessed per scholar, 29.

FARM, as the center of interest, paper on, 152.

FRANCE, school year in, is more than forty weeks, 79; farmers in, opposed to book farming, 79; law in, limits number of students in each normal school, 86; much richer than Germany, but inferior in education, 126; review of school systems in, 200.

FUNDS, permanent school, and receipts of school moneys, 126; working of common school fund in Connect cut, 126; Texas school-fund lands, 126; grazing and mining lands, 127; remedy for evils of depreciation, 127; receipts of school moneys in United States, 128.

GASS, H. R., Michigan, ratio of teachers required to number employed, 47.

GEOGRAPHY, the child should be taught from surroundings, 154; plan of a course of study in, 176; programme, 167, 170, 184.

GEOLOGY, the child should be taught from surroundings, 154.

GEORGIA, the county system of supervision in, 45; qualifications required of school superintendents in, 66; operation of county system in Richmond county, 132.

GERMANY, not so rich as France, but superior in education, 126.

GIFTS, to popular education, should be encouraged, 25; apportionment of public lands at admission of states, 35.

GOOD ROADS, a helpful element in consolidation and transportation, 50.

GRADING, the solution of the country-school problem, 163; common methods of, in country schools, 163; feasible modifications, 164; evils of, in the one-teacher school, 164; the three-grade solution, 165; arrangement of course of study, 105, 165; three-grade programme, 166; hopeful improvement in simpler, 168; certificates of examinations in two grades, 92; one-half the teachers in the United States teach ungraded schools, 94; small ungraded schools should often meet at town centers, 103; large proportion of children is in ungraded schools, 50; best done through consolidation of schools, 49; stress laid upon, by normal schools, 100; evils of, as applied to city and rural schools alike, 17; classification used to signify the same thing, words defined, 100; classification in early schools, 162; present condition and trend of rural schools, grading and classification in United States, 113; should not be expected in rural schools, reasons, 97; ideal classification, 97; pupils in large numbers easily taught, 97; city system of, unwise in rural schools, 99, 100; as to pupils in different degrees of advancement, 99; abuses of, in the village school, 100.

GRAHAM, ROBERT, Wisconsin, as to amount of property assessed per scholar, 30.

GRAMMAR, suggestions relating to teaching, 158, 167, 170, 174, 184.

GROVER, MRS. ETTA F., Assiniboia, subcommittee returns thanks to, for information, 79.

GUNDERSEN, OSCAR, Illinois, paper by, relating to school system in Norway, 200.

HALL, S. R., Vermont, normal school opened by, in Concord, Vt., 83.

HARRIS, W. T., U. S. Commissoner of Education, made member committee to investigate rural-school problem, 8; chairman Subcommittee on Instruction and Discipline, 10; reports from Subcommittee on Instruction and Discipline, 94; reports from committee to investigate rural school problem, 5.

HILL, F. A., Massachusetts, discusses cost of town and district plan, 134.

HINE, C. D., Connecticut, discusses cost of town and district system, 134.

HINSDALE, B. A., Michigan, moves appointment of committee of five to submit plan for investigating rural-school problem, 7; report of committee, 7; made member of committee to investigate rural school problem, 7; moves increase in number of the committee, 8; made member committee to formulate plan of work, 8; plan adopted, 8; chairman Subcommittee on School Maintenance, 8; report of subcommittee, 20; reports from committee on rural-school problem, 7; paper by, on sociological factors in rural education, ordered printed in appendix, 11; the paper, 123.

HISTORY, elements for teaching the history of farm implements, everywhere present on the farm, 159; programme for teaching, 167, 170; plan of a course of study in, 174, 184.

HOME AND SCHOOL, they should be harmonious, 69; parents too willing to criticise anything new, 69; the county newspaper should contain items from pen of supervisor, 69.

HOME READING, comments on, 18; promotion of, recommended, 109.

HORTICULTURE, list of books on the subject, 190.

HYGIENE, impure air, bad light, and unsuitable furniture, 193; evils of unsanitary schoolrooms, 193; physiology as now taught, 193; lavatories or water-closets, relation to school, 194; how a schoolhouse should be constructed, 194; plan and details of an ideal schoolhouse, 195.

ILLINOIS, per-capita value of real estate, state and county, 31; amount expended for school purposes in cities, 29; salaries paid teachers in, 15.

INDIANA, levies a tax for school purposes, 33; local authority called township trustee, 22; the township system exists in, 44; one trustee manages a township in, 44; teacher's tenure longer than in Michigan, 47; salaries paid teachers in, 15.

INDIANS, money set aside for schools for, in New York, 36.

INDUSTRIES AND COMMERCE, study of the commercial side of farm life, 159.

INSTITUTES, assistance rendered rural schools by, a topic of inquiry, 9; not forgotten in the investigation, 17; in Manitoba, 199; normal, as organized in the West, 81; exert an influence for good, 81; when of one-day duration, 81; in Pennsylvania, 204; county superintendent in charge, 204; considerations that secure attendance, 205; professional spirit of teachers intensified, 205; quality of teaching improved, 205; interest of the public aroused, 205; local neighborhood institutes, 205; subjects relating to rural-school work, 205.

INSTRUCTION AND DISCIPLINE, subcommittee appointed to consider subject, 10; line of inquiry to be pursued, 10; order in which to appear in report, 11; report embraces important suggestions, 17; report of Subcommittee on, 94; one-half the teachers in United States teach ungraded schools, 94; small attendance in ungraded schools, 95; attempts to instruct where there is a year's difference in advancement, 95; classification, should not be expected in rural schools, 96; eminent men have come from rural schools, 97; the ideal classified school, 97; skilled teachers secured through wise use of money, 98; classification of pupils in different degrees of advancement, 99; the terms grading and classification defined, 100; all schools understood to be graded in a certain sense, 101; course of study should be substantially the same in rural as in city schools, 101; what the child should be taught, 101; geography of the environments, 102; means by which that which is useful is procured from nature, 102; manner of study, 102, 103; relation of course of study to grading and classification, 105; promotion defined, 105; there should be much written work in school, 106; divisions of the course of study, 106; discipline should be strict in rural schools, 106; many evils of the rural schools due to nonsocial character, 106; transportation to central schools, 107; collection of pupils into larger units than the district schools, 107; transportation of pupils often not feasible by reason of poor roads, 107; special appropriations to secure skilled teachers, 107; concentration of higher grades of pupils, 107; small ungraded schools should often meet at town centers, 108; competitive examinations, 108; promotion of home reading recommended, 108; reviewing studies, 108; school extension, 110; Lancasterian or monitorial plan reviewed, 110; Chautauquan plan, excellence of, 109; assistance rendered teacher by advanced pupils, 110; supplemental statement by A. B. Poland, 112; believes report exaggerates difficulties of classification, 112; conclusions of entire report too general, 112; teachers should not be discouraged from attempting classification where practicable, 112; supplemental statement by L. E. Wolfe, 112; present condition and trend of rural-school grading and classification, 113; instruction in the same class, of pupils who are more than one year apart in advancement, 113; underlying pedagogic principles, 114; objections to the doctrine of the report, 116.

INTELLECTUAL AND MORAL EDUCATION, 206; aim, attainment, and end of, 206; pupil must be led to observe, judge, and reason for himself, 206; designs of moral education, 207; special work of teachers in, 207; moral sense and conscience must be strengthened, 207; teachers should be examples of what they teach, 207; should have as much care for development of character as of intellect, 207.

IOWA, qualifications required of school superintendents in, 67; salaries paid teachers in, 15.

ISOLATION OF RURAL SCHOOLS, conclusions by subcommittee, 19.

JACKMAN, W. S., Illinois, requested to prepare a paper on agricultural environments, 11; reports from special committee on enrichment of rural-school courses, 142.

KANSAS, salaries paid teachers in, 15.

KENTUCKY, levies a tax for school purposes, 33; how state school fund is distributed, 36; qualifications required of school superintendents in, 67; salaries paid teachers in, 15.

KIEHLE, D. L., Minnesota, made member committee to investigate rural-school problem, 7; made member committee to formulate plan of work, 8; made member Subcommittee on Supply of Teachers, 9; reports from committee to investigate rural-school problem, 5; reports from Subcommittee on Supply of Teachers, 77; assistance rendered committee in selecting books, 189.

KING, F. H., Wisconsin, requested to prepare a paper on agricultural environments, 11; reports from special committee on enrichment of rural school courses, 142; assistance rendered committee in selecting books, 189.

KINGSVILLE, Ohio, experiment at, in transportation to central districts, 107, 137.

LANCASTERIAN, or monitorial plan, comments on by subcommittee, 110.

LANDSCAPE, studies upon the surrounding, 143; nature, origin, and meaning of surface features, 143; books of reference, 144, 146; the study of streams, 144; the study of soils, 145; application of landscape studies, 146; location of homes, 146; of roads, 146; of towns and villages, 146; development of the region, as affected by environments, 146; social and civil life of the people, as affected by surrounding physical features, 146; distribution of vegetation as influenced by surface features, 147.

LANGUAGE, plan of a course of study in, 174; programme of study, 167, 170, 184.

LIBRARIES, improvement of teachers by, topic of inquiry, 9; supervisor should be able to select, 67; a boy taught to love, will possess library when a man, 74; are established through intelligent supervision, 61; comments on establishment of, 20; in country towns, 82; teacher and school helped by, 82; as property of the school, a necessity, 82; professional, for use of teachers, 82; farmers should be interested in schools having, 169; New York state school, 189; character of books selected, 189; list of books for rural schools and communities, 189; in agriculture, 189; horticulture, 190; botany, 190; science, 191; animal life, 191; nature study, 191; miscellaneous books, 192; in Norway, 202.

LOUISIANA, salaries paid teachers in, 15.

LUCE, N. A., Maine, average state enrollment, 47.

MAINE, law creating county superintendency enacted, 21; raises half its school money by state taxation, 27; prospective policy as to school money, 40; manner of distributing income from public-land endowment, 35; cost of town and district system discussed by W. W. Stetson, 134; salaries paid teachers in, 15; money is wasted through unbusinesslike methods, 53; average population per square mile, 35; the district system has been swept away, 44; average daily attendance of pupils in, 47; adopts plan of collecting pupils in large units, 107; paper relating to J. W. Bradbury, 188; early training schools for teachers opened in, 188.

MANITOBA, model-school system, institutes, 199; subcommittee acknowledges aid from 79; review of school systems in, 199.

MANN, HORACE, Massachusetts, purpose of, in first normal school, 84.

MANUAL TRAINING, advantages of, on the farm, 158; demand for scientific skill requires study of, 150.

MARBLE, A. P., New York, paper on hygiene and health in public schools, 193.

MARYLAND, qualifications required of school superintendents in, 67; salaries paid teachers in, 15.

MASSACHUSETTS, adds to the school fund by taxation, 25; old plan of taxation for support of schools, 26; per cent. derived from local school taxes, 28; levies no state school tax, 32; manner of apportioning school fund, 36; manner of apportioning school money in, commended by subcommittee, 39; amount expended for school purposes in cities, 29; led the way in developing district system, 48; raises money by local taxation for transportation of pupils, 48; sum paid by Quincy for transportation of pupils, 107; salaries paid teachers in, 15; law for better remuneration of rural teachers, 108; secures skilled teachers by wise use of money, 199; value of real estate, by state and counties, 31; local authorities called school committees in, 22; school committee consists of three, or a multiple of three, 44; old district system has been swept away, 44; combination of towns into supervisor districts, 61; town and district plan discussed by F. A. Hill, 134; pupils may attend high school in places other than their residence, 41; population governs maintenance of high schools, 41; superior school law enacted by general court, 43; tenure of teachers in, longer than in Michigan, 47; report as to ungraded schools and attendance, 95; purpose of Horace Mann in opening first normal school, 84; early graded schools opened by J. D. Philbrick, 84; school garden in George Putnam School, awarded prizes, 89; arguments by A. W. Edson in favor of consolidation, 135; consolidation of schools at Concord, 107; report from Crane school, Quincy, as to transportation, 143.

MATHEMATICS, demand for scientific skill requires study of, 150; as applied to farm life, 157; course of study in, 177; programme, 167, 170, 184; its study in rural schools, 150.

McINTYRE, DANIEL, Manitoba, paper on county model schools, 198.

MECHANICS, demand for scientific skill requires study of, 150.

METEOROLOGY, course of study in rural schools, 151; study of, would come through the seasons, 155.

MICHIGAN, levies a one-mill tax for school purposes in townships, 33; distribution of school tax, 37; how state fund is distributed, 36; salaries paid teachers in, 15; H. R. Gass reports ratio of teachers required as to number employed, 47; Congress gave public lands for school purposes, 35; township system permissible in, 44; ratio of illiteracy considered, 48; tenure of teachers shorter than in Massachusetts, 47; length of school term in, 51; qualifications required of school superintendents in, 66.

MINERALOGY, child should be taught from surroundings, 152; as a branch of study in rural schools, 151; demand for scientific skill requires study of, 150.

MINNESOTA, salaries paid teachers in, 15; distribution of local one-mill school tax, 37; township system permissible in, 44; Winona normal-school plan, continuous sessions, 207.

MISSISSIPPI, qualifications required of school superintendents in, 66; contribution per taxpayer, 125.

MISSOURI, salaries paid teachers in, 15.

MONITORIAL SYSTEM, reviewed by subcommittee, 110.

MONTANA, contribution per taxpayer, amount of, 125; qualifications required of school superintendents in, 66; salaries paid teachers in, 15.

MORALS AND CIVICS, plan of course of study in, 182.

MORAL INSTRUCTION, comments on, 19; programme, 167, 184.

MORRISON, F. E., Ohio, extracts from report of, on consolidation and transportation, 137.

NATIONAL COUNCIL OF EDUCATION, meetings of, 7; report to, on rural-school problem, by Henry Sabin, 7; C. C. Rounds, President, urged immediate action, 7; B. A. Hinsdale moved a committee of five to submit plan for further investigation, 7; committee reported, 7; Committee of Nine appointed, 7; committee empowered to enlarge its number to twelve and to fill vacancies, 8; directors of general association authorized appropriations for use of committee, 8; committee makes final report to, 5.

NATURE STUDY, love of, fostered, 203; list of books adapted to, 191.

NEBRASKA, excellent features in law governing distribution of school money, 41; raises a school fund through fines and penalties, 33; salaries paid teachers in, 15.

NEGRO TEACHERS AND SCHOOLS, paper by J. H. Phillips, 185; review of progress made, 185; the negro as a dependent, 186; white teachers cannot realize the ideal relation between teacher and negro pupil, 180; potent reason for employing negro teachers to teach negro schools, 186; co-ordination of teacher with the child, 187; summary of reasons for employment of negro teachers for negro schools, 187.

NEVADA, salaries paid teachers in, 15.

NEW BRUNSWICK, school year in, 216 days, 79; review of school system in, 199; subcommittee acknowledges aid from, 79.

NEW HAMPSHIRE, law creating county superintendency enacted, 21; manner of apportioning state-tax income, 36; training school for teachers opened at Effingham, 84; Teachers' Seminary, extracts from early catalogue of, 188; per cent. of colored population, 123; adopts plan of collecting pupils into larger units, 107; district system swept away, 44; school gardens in state normal and training schools a success, 89; salaries paid teachers in, 15.

NEW JERSEY, adds to school revenue through income from certain riparian rights, 25; extract from report on supervision of schools, 63; school boards consist of three, five, or nine members, 44; district system has been swept away, 44; certain examinations in use twenty years, 108; secures skilled teachers by wise use of money, 98; manner of raising state school tax, 32; law for better remuneration of rural teachers, 108; adopts plan of collecting pupils into larger units, 107.

NEW YORK, raises state school tax annually, 32; manner of apportioning school-tax income, 10, 36; amount of general school tax paid annually, 40; tax levy upon railroads in, 40; derives small revenue from permanent school fund, 25; per-capita value of real estate in, state and by counties, 31; expenditure of revenue, 1894–95, 24; amount expended for school purposes in cities, 29; manner of distributing school money in, commended, 38; taxes in districts vary, 30; number of teachers' training classes in, 87; salaries paid teachers in, 15; law for better remuneration of rural teachers in, 108; report as to ungraded schools and attendance, 95; average daily attendance of pupils, 47; few teachers in the rural schools are from normal schools, 83; need of consolidation urged by C. R. Skinner, 135; extracts from paper by L. H. Bailey, on agricultural extension work, 202.

NEW YORK SCHOOL LIBRARY, act creating, 189; character of books selected, 189.

NORMAL INSTITUTES, assistance rendered rural schools by, a topic of inquiry, 9; not forgotten in the investigation, 17; in Manitoba, 199; normal, as organized in the West, 81; exert an influence for good, 81; when of one-day duration, 81; in Pennsylvania, 204; county superintendent in charge, 204; considerations that secure attendance, 205; professional spirit of teachers intensified, 205; quality of teaching improved, 205; interest of the public aroused, 205; local neighborhood institutes, 205; subjects relating to rural-school work, taught in, 205.

NORMAL SCHOOLS, as a topic of iniquiry, 9; assistance rendered rural schools, 9; teachers from, number lamentably small in rural schools, 61; farm set apart for, in Truro, Nova Scotia, 89; school garden in New Hampshire Training School, a success, 89; do not fully prepare teachers for rural schools, 83; result at Oswego, N. Y., 83; rural teachers are seldom from normal schools, 83; proportion of trained teachers in rural schools, 83; normal schools were first devised for rural teachers, 83; a normal school was opened by S. R. Hall, 83; other early training schools, 84; purpose of Horace Mann in opening first normal school in Massachusetts, 84, standard often too far removed from teachers in rural schools, 84; an intermediate agency desirable, 85; rural teachers often cannot afford time and expense of extended normal course, 85; distance between normal school and home, a factor, 85; subcommittee's idea of a needed normal school, 85; practice in teaching should be provided for, 86; membership of the training classes should be limited, 86; French law limits number of students to each school, 86; certificate of elementary grade, from county normal, 86; a summer term for rural teachers, suggested, 86; cost of a normal school plant, 86; a normal-school extension should be organized in every state, 87; city and training schools, 87; normal schools cannot be supplanted by training classes, 88; what the course of study in, should recognize, 88; courses in agriculture and horticulture recommended, 89; details of each course in, 89; whatever goes into the common schools should be taught in the normal schools, 90; instruction in normal schools, 90; stress laid upon classification and grading by, 100; institutions in Ontario for teachers, 198; admission to, in Manitoba, 199; paper by Irwin Shepard on continuous sessions in, 207; the Winona plan, 207; advantages of the plan, 208; new classes begin each quarter, 208; extensive normal-school equipments thus utilized to full extent, 208; the tendency will be to direct a supply of graduates into rural-school work, 208.

NORTH ATLANTIC STATES, per cents. of moneys raised by state and local taxation, 27.

NORTH CAROLINA, state and local tax, per cent. of, for schools, 27; shows largest percentage of school tax, 35.

NORTH CENTRAL STATES, per cents. of moneys raised by state and local taxation, 27.

NORWAY, review of school work in, 200; branches taught in schools, 201; high schools in, 202; paper on school system in, by Oscar Gundersen, 200.

NOVA SCOTIA, a farm has been set apart for instruction at Truro Normal School, 89; length of school year in Nova Scotia, 79; subcommittee acknowleges aid from, 79; land set apart for school garden in, 89.

OCCUPATIONS, number of persons engaged in the principal, in the United States, 88.

OHIO, constitution empowers legislature to provide taxation for school purposes, 27; levies a tax for school purposes, 33; derives but small revenue from permanent school fund, 25; distribution of tax levied upon telephones, telegraphs, and railways in, 40; receipts from the one-mill tax, 39; how one-mill tax is apportioned, 36; Congress gave public land to, for school use, on admission to Union, 35; amount expended for school purposes in cities in, 29; adopts plan of collecting pupils into larger units, 107; experiments in consolidation in 137; report by F. E. Morrison on consolidation and transportation, 137; report by J. R. Adams on consolidation and transportation, 138; report by T. J. Clapp on consolidation and transportation, 140; operation of the Boxwell law in, 108; drivers of transportation omnibusses, carry the mail, 51; number of teachers and school directors in, 45; average size of schools, twenty years ago, 123; salaries paid teachers in, 15; schools in Western Reserve dwindled to insignificant size, 48; school boards consist of members elected by subdistricts, 44; local authority called a board of education in, 22; high schools compulsory in, 41; pupils may attend high schools in places other than their residence, 41; the subdistrict and its history, 22; the township system exists, 44; paper by E. E. White of, on the country-school problem, 161.

ONTARIO, school year in, is 212 days, 79; review of school systems in, 198; district training schools analogous to model schools of, 86.

ORGANIZATION AND ADMINISTRATION, included in index under subject of school maintenance.

OSWEGO, New York, returns from, show nine-tenths of pupils from the country, not one tenth teach in rural schools, 83.

PARKER, F. W., Illinois, paper by, ordered printed in appendix, 11; paper by, the farm the center of interest, 152; assistance rendered committee in selecting list of books, 189.

PENNSYLVANIA, raises school appropriation by tax on money loaned by citizens, 33; legislative appropriation for use of schools, 32; derives no revenue from permanent school fund, 25; how state school fund is distributed, 36; distribution of railroad tax, 48; amount expended for school purposes in cities, 29; per-capita value of real estate, state and by counties, 31; salaries paid teachers in, 15; the township system exists in, 44; qualifications required of school superintendents in, 66; institutes in, 204; county superintendent in charge of institute, 204; considerations that secure attendance at institute, 205; professional spirit of teachers intensified, 205; quality of teaching improved, 205; interest of the public aroused, 205; local neighborhood institutes, 205; subjects relating to rural-school work taught at institutes in, 205.

PERMANENT SCHOOL FUNDS, and receipts of school moneys, 126; working of common-school fund in Connecticut, 126; Texas school-fund lands, 126; grazing and mining lands, 127; remedy for evils of depreciaton, 127; receipts of school money in, United States, 128.

PHILLIPS, J. H., Alabama, made member committee to investigate rural-school problem 8; made member Subcommittee on Supply of Teachers, 9; reports from Subcommittee on Supply of Teachers, 77; reports from committee to investigate rural-school problem, 5; paper by, on negro schools and negro teachers, 185.

PHYSIOLOGY, as now taught in schools, 183; programme for teaching, 167, 170.

PLANT LIFE, study of chemical elements entering into, 151; study of, 147, 156; growth from the seed, 147; growth from the bud 148; books of reference on, 149.

POLAND, A. B., New Jersey, made member committee to investigate rural-school problem, 7, 8; member Subcommittee on Instruction and Discipline, 10; reports from Subcommittee on Instruction and Discipline, 94; reports from committee on rural-school problem, 5; makes additional statement to report on instruction and discipline, 112; believes report of subcommittee exaggerates difficulties of classification, 112; conclusions of the report too general, 112; teachers should not be discouraged from attempting classification where practicable, 112.

POWERS OF GOVERNMENT, as related to education, considered, 20.

PRESTON, J. R., Mississippi, reports from committee on plan to investigate rural-school problem, 7.

Programme, three-grade, for school work, 167, 170, 184.

Public Instruction, any system of, involves sociological factors, 20.

Qualifications, required of school supervisors in different states, 67.

Quebec, teachers' training class in, 88; district training classes analogous to training schools in, 86.

Railroads, distribution of taxes levied upon, 40.

Reading, plan of a course of study in, 172; suggestions regarding, 157; programme, 167, 170, 184.

Receipts of School Money, statistics of, by states, 42.

Reports of Committees, on state school systems, 7; on plan for improving condition of rural schools, 7; on investigation of rural-school problem, 5; special, on plan of work, 8; Subcommittee on School Maintenance, 20; on School Supervision, 55; on Supply of Teachers, 77; on Instruction and Discipline, 94.

Revenue, schools included in index under subject of school maintenance.

Rhode Island, legal term of office of state superintendent in, 56; levies no state school tax direct, 32; manner of distributing school-tax income, 37; comments on by subcommittee, 39; reports as to ungraded schools and attendance, 95; the town and district systems exist in, 44; some districts pay heavier taxes than others, 30; secures skilled teachers through wise use of money, 94; richest and most populous state relatively, yet never led in common schools, 126; adopts plan of collecting pupils into larger units, 107; salaries paid teachers in, 15.

Roads, a helpful element of consolidation, 51, 107.

Rounds, C. C., New Hampshire, President of the Council, 7; made member committee to investigate the rural-school problem, 7, 8; made member Subcommittee on Supply of Teachers, 9; reports from Subcommittee on Supply of Teachers, 77; reports from committee to investigate rural school problem, 5.

Rural Schools, committee on rural-school problem appointed by National Council, submits report, 7; appointment of committee on rural-school problem recommended, 7; names of committee appointed, 7, 8; appropriation to pay expense of investigation, urged, 8; committee to report in two years, 8; power to enlarge or fill vacancies, 8; held its first meeting, 8; number members increased to twelve, 8; names of members added, 8; committee as finally constituted, 8; special committee to formulate plan of work, 8; meeting of special committee, 8; plan of work adopted, 8; meeting at Jacksonville, 10; Buffalo meeting, 10; experts invited to meet with committee, 10; Chicago meeting, 10; names of distinguished visitors, 10; preliminary reports of subcommittees considered, 11; printing intrusted to chairman, 11; date of publication fixed, 12; members to send out typewritten copies of report, 12; order in which reports are to be printed, 11; conditions make slight difference in systems necessary, 12; review by chairman of reports of subcommittee as to consolidation of schools, 13; as to transportation of pupils to school, 13; as to revenues, 13, 19; as to school supervision, 13; as to relation of school, home, and farm, 14; as to supply of teachers, 14; as to qualifications of teachers, 15; as to course of study for one year, 16; as to instruction and discipline, 17; as to competitive examinations, 18; as to home reading, 18; conclusion of introduction by chairman, 19; summary of introduction by chairman, 19; revenues for, 23; distribution of revenues for, 34; organization of, 42; supervision of, 55; trained teachers needed in, 61; work of supervision in, 63; home in connection with, 69; visitation and inspection of, 72; schoolhouses and furniture for, 73; teachers for, 77; school year in, 78; libraries in, 82; instruction and discipline in, 94; course of study in, 101; remedies for the evils of, 107; extension work in, 202; plan of visitation, 202; love of or antipathy for farm, engendered at an early day, 203; future of rural schools and agriculture, 203; best work cannot be done where the attendance is small, 203; an attempt to discover best method of teaching agriculture in, 203.

Sabin, Henry, Iowa, makes report to National Council of Education on the rural-school problem, 7; made member committee on investigation of the rural-school problem, 7; made chairman of committee, 8; member Subcommittee on School Supervision, 9; reports from Subcommittee on School Supervision, 55; reports with committee on rural-school problem, 5; as chairman of committee, makes introduction to and summary of reports, 7.

SALARIES, new buildings often an excuse for low salaries, 40; state fund often applied to payment of, 40; table of, paid teachers by states, 15; paid state superintendents, 56; paid county superintendents, 65; a good superintendent earns more than his salary, 65; do not remunerate for expense of instruction in normal school, 85; teachers in rural schools receive small, 98.

SCIENCE, elements of, course of study in, 180; list of books on subjects of, 191.

SCHOOL EXTENSION, comments on, 110.

SCHOOL GARDENS, are common in Europe, 89; in New Hampshire, a source of interest, 89; in George Putnam School, awarded prizes, 89; land set apart for, at Truro Normal School, Nova Scotia, 89; other countries lead us in taking advantage of, 89.

SCHOOLHOUSES, relation of supervisor to, 9; new ones often an excuse for low salaries, 40; when likely to be built, 42; undistricted towns provide all schoolhouses from a common fund, 43; a good house in an undistricted town creates a demand for other good buildings, 43; poor houses often continue in use long after ceasing to be tenantable, 44; under county system, sometimes four miles apart, 46; number of, could be diminished by consolidation, 47, 54; towns empowered to build in Massachusetts, 48; local communities should provide, 53; supervisor should have controlling voice in planning, 73; comfort of pupils should be observed, 73; cleanliness should be promoted, 73; advantages of, when well arranged, 73; beautiful environments should be created, 74; an appeal for classical art and music in the schoolroom, 73, 74, 75; as to character and purpose of the rural schools, supervision is to improve the condition of, 75; better houses a result of intelligent supervision, 76; location of, in Georgia, 132; impure air, bad light, and unsuitable furniture in, 193; evils of unsanitary schoolrooms, 193; relation of water-closets or lavatories to, 194; how water-closets or lavatories should be constructed, 194; the architecture of churches and schoolhouses compared, 194; plan and details of an ideal schoolhouse, 195.

SCHOOL MAINTENANCE, subcommittee appointed to consider subject of, 8; line of inquiry to be pursued, 8; unit system discussed, 12; consolidation of schools, 12; report of Subcommittée on, 20; town- and township-unit system, 22; district system explained, 23; revenue for, raised and distributed, 13; revenue the first essential to improvement, 23; endowments for, 24; wild-lands endowment, 24; endowments sometimes harmful, 24; schools have outgrown endowments, 25; Texas, great possibilities from lands, 25; gifts to popular education, 25; New York and Ohio derive small income from permanent fund, 25; Connecticut a non public land state, 24; interest in creation of permanent school fund began a century ago, 24; great resource of public schools is some form of public taxation, 26; a liberal provision of funds from state treasury is indispensable, 26; per cent. of school money raised by state and local taxes in the United States, 27; in states where the county is the sole unit of taxation, 28; special districts, villages, towns, and cities, as units of taxation, 29; property assessed per scholar, 29; result if personal property was included, 31; distribution of school funds, 34; assistance that large political units render to smaller ones, 34; distribution of funds raised by large taxing units, 35; other rules follow, 36; distribution of funds according to school census, 38; relation of organization and administration to, [illegible]; township-unit system a substitute for district system, 42; when schoolhouses are likely to be built, 42; equality of provision for schools more fully secured, 42; simplicity of administration facilitated, 42; tendency to employ teacher for longer term, 42; strife prevented, 42; transfer of pupils made easy, 42; the town-unit system, early history, 43; schools in undistricted towns superior, 43; districted and undistricted towns compared, 43; district system at one time universal, 44; in Indiana, one trustee manages the schools of the township, 44; the district system in many states, 44; superiority of the township system, 44; the community system of Texas, 45; the county system in the South and West, 45; the county the unit area of organization, 46; the county as a unit of organization has a great future, 46; rural schools should be consolidated, 46; teachers changed too frequently under the district system, 47; number of small schools not confined to poor districts, 47; a small school usually a poor one, 48; cities are considered great hives of illiteracy, 48; better teachers, better schools, through consolidation, 49; that which promotes ease of administration promotes good instruction, 49; great possibilities of improvement attained through consolidation, 50; consolidation should not be misunderstood, 50; consolidation in the North depends upon the township-unit system, 50; good roads an element of consolidation, 50; elements essential to a good school, 51; reports should by law be made to state educational department, 51; how to enforce such law, 51; difficulty with parents when school attendance is compulsory, 52; temptation of farmer to keep his boys out of school, 52; waste of money through unbusinesslike methods, 52; local communities should be responsible for providing school buildings, 53; as to revenue and taxation, 53; as to distribution of revenue, 53; where town or township system should be substituted for the district system, 54; number of schools, schoolhouses, and teachers, diminished by consolidation, 54; time that rural schools are in session each year should be lengthened, 54; general laws governing, which cannot be ignored, 54; how suggestions of subcommittee may be made practicable, 54; the county as the unit of organization, 132; the system in Richmond county, Ga., 132; large amount of money paid by cities spent in rural districts, 132; qualifications of teachers, 133; treatment of teachers, 133; schools operated nine calendar months, 133; in regard to schoolhouses, 133; superintendent has charge of all schools, 133.

SCHOOL SYSTEMS, review of, Ontario, 198; New Brunswick, 199; Manitoba, 199; France, 200; Norway, 200; supervisors must hold first-class certificates in Ontario, 198; admission to normal or training schools in Manitoba, 199; salaries in New Brunswick, 199; salaries in Manitoba, 199; how teachers are chosen in Manitoba, 199; review of school work in France, 200; review of school work in Norway, 200; branches taught in Norway, 201; high schools in Norway, 202; libraries in Norway, 202.

SCHOOL TERM, average length of, materially lengthened, 51; length of, in East and West, 51.

SCOTLAND, not so rich as England, but superior in education, 126.

SHEPARD, IRWIN, Minnesota, paper by, on continuous sessions in normal schools, 207.

SKINNER, C. R., New York, member committee to investigate rural-school problem, 8; made member Subcommittee on Supervision, 9; reports from committee to investigate rural school problem, 5; reports from Subcommittee on Supervision, 55; urges need of consultation of schools, 135.

SOCIOLOGICAL FACTORS IN RURAL EDUCATION, paper on, 123.

SOILS, study of, 145; chemical elements entering into, 151.

SOUTH ATLANTIC STATES, moneys raised by state and local taxation, 27.

SOUTH CAROLINA, salaries paid teachers in, 15; qualifications required of school superintendents in, 66; per cent. of colored population, 123.

SOUTH DAKOTA, salaries paid teachers in, 15.

SPELLING, suggestions relating to teaching, 158; plan of course of study in, 172; programme, 167, 170, 184.

STATISTICS, of salaries paid teachers, by states, 15; of expenditures for schools in United States, 23; enrollment of children in cities, 24; ratio of cost of schooling children in city and country 24; income from endowments, 24; ratio of revenue derived from taxes and permanent fund, 26; per cents. of school moneys raised by state and local taxation, 27; expenditure for school purposes in cities, 29; amount of assessed property per scholar, 29; per-capita value of real estate, state and county, 29; state tax for school purposes in several states, 22; distribution of school money in several states, 30; comparative statement of receipts and disbursements, 38; population governing compulsory maintenance of high schools in Massachusetts, 41; number of teachers in common schools of Ohio, 45; as to scholars attending in isolated or detached schools, 46; average daily attendance in New York, Vermont, Maine, 47; ratio of illiteracy in Michigan considered, 48; money paid for transportation for several years, 49; salaries paid state superintendents, 56; time put in by state superintendents, 56; supervisors and towns in Massachusetts, 59; state aid to districts in Massachusetts, 59; supervisor's salary in many states, 64; length of school year in several localities, 78; comparatively few rural teachers are from normal schools, 83; percentage of trained teachers, 83; of teachers' training classes in New York, 87; area occupied by people interested in grazing, 88; number engaged in the principal occupations in United States, 88; inhabitants per square miles, 98; ungraded rural schools and attendance, 95; as to people living in towns at beginning of century, 97; sums paid for transportation of pupils, and towns using the plan, 107; cost of tuition reduced by consolidation system, 107; average size of schools and enrollment in Ohio twenty years ago, 123; maximum and minimum of population, 123; per cent. of white and colored population in United States, 124; per-capita wealth of population in United States, 125; amount of contribution per taxpayer, 125; expenditure per pupil, and per cent. of illiteracy, 126; receipts of school moneys in the United States, 128; revenue from various funds in California, 130; school census and facts, California, 130; school population in New York, 135; expenditures in Kingsville, O., 138; cost of transportation of pupils to township school, 140.

STETSON, W. W., Maine, defines prospective policy as to school money raised, 40; says money is wasted through unbusinesslike methods, 53; discusses cost of town and district systems, 134.

STREAMS, the study of, 134.

SUBCOMMITTEES, Subcommittee on School Maintenance appointed, 8; its report, 20; Subcommittee on Supervision appointed, 9; its report, 55; Subcommittee on Supply of Teachers appointed, 9; its report, 77; Subcommittee on Instruction and Discipline appointed, 10; its report, 94.

SUMMER SCHOOL, purpose of, 80; when held in connection with colleges, 80; should be one in every county, 80; sometimes called institutes, 81.

SUPERINTENDENTS, manner of electing, and qualifications for, state, a topic of inquiry, 9; relation to school officers, 9; distribution of school tax by, in California, 38; salaries paid to, 56; time devoted by state superintendents, 56; influence of, 57; work of, should be more effective, 57; work in his office, 57; his relation to superintendents of subdivisions, 57; should have power to withhold state appropriations, 57; main duties of, 57; he should be able to control legislation, 58; should not be put into office through political affiliations, 58; manner of electing, and qualifications for, county and district superintendents, a topic of inquiry, 9; relation to school officers and the public, 9; relation to school building, 9; may deal easily with township boards, 42; is in charge of institutes in Pennsylvania, 204; most competent, have best schools, 55; have done much for improvement of school system, 55; qualifications essential for, 56; word supervisor defined, 58; operation of the two methods of supervisor, 58; combination of towns for supervisory purposes, 59; combination applicable to small districts, 59; worth of county superintendent ackowledged, 60; the county too large for one supervisor, 60; county superintendents should have deputies, 60; plan where county contains large city, 60; where one looks after both city and rural schools, 60; supervision a vital need of rural schools, 61; a capable supervisor will bring order out of chaos, 61; a supervisor should be an expert, 62; the term defined, 62; what should be expected of a supervisor, 62; he should bring teachers into contact for exchange of thought, 62; sufficient care not usually given to his selection, 62; an expert supervisor will instinctively distinguish good teachers, 6[illegible]; a good superintendent earns his salary, 63; money spent for good supervision is well spent, 63; visit of superintendent to schools, 64; salary of, in many states, 64; an unqualified supervisor pays only perfunctory visits to schools, 64; supervisor must have time at his disposal, 64; relation of supervisor to teachers' meetings and institutes, 66; a standard of qualification should be established for supervisors, 64; a supervisor should be as well educated as the better teachers, 67; qualifications recommended by committee, 67; he should be familiar with the physical characteristics of his district, 68; must gain the confidence of parents, 69; can exert an influence in support of teacher by parents, 69; the county newspaper should contain items from his pen, 69; he should have control in the selection of teachers, 69; should be slow to condemn a teacher, 70; selection of text-books should be left to, 70; relation existing between school officers and supervisor should be well defined, 70; should meet the directors at certain times for consultation, 71; supervisor's method of visiting schools considered, 72; moral atmosphere of school to be observed, 72; supervisor should keep private register, 73; should have a controlling voice in erection of schoolhouses, 73; should be observant of comfort of pupils, 73; should regard the condition of surroundings, 73; conclusions of committee as to character of supervisor, selection, scholarship, morals, professional spirit, 75; results expected of intelligent supervision, such as better teachers, better methods, establishment of libraries, 76; authority which examines should not employ teachers, 78; small ungraded school should meet often at town centers under direction of, 108; supervisor will have a record of advanced pupils, 109; should encourage school extension, 110; has charge of all the schools in a county in Georgia, 132.

SUPERVISION, subject of inquiry, 9; subcommittee to investigate, 9; subject discussed, 13; report of Subcommittee on, 55; territory investigated, 55; professional supervision regarded an essential factor, 55; result of expert supervision, 55; superintendency has done much for the school system, 55; qualifications essential for state superintendent, 56; salaries paid state superintendents, 56; time devoted by state superintendents, 56; influence of state superintendents, 57; work of state superintendents should be more effective, 57; should have power to withhold state appropriation, 57; his main duties, 57; he should be able to control legislation, 58; states having county superintendents, also township or district supervision, 58; operation of the two methods of supervision, 58; combination of towns for supervisory purposes, 59; combination applicable to small districts, 59; a county too large for one superintendent, 60; county superintendents should have deputies, 60; plan of supervision in counties containing large cities, 60; one school fund raised by entire county, 60; superintendent looks after city and rural teachers, 60; taxes raised on city property distributed to rural schools, 61; supervision a vital need of rural schools, 61; number of normal-school graduates lamentably small, 61; rural schools suffer for want of trained teachers, 61; skilled supervision necessary, 62; money spent for good supervision is well spent, 62; standard of qualification for supervisor in seventeen states, 66; qualifications recommended by the subcommittee, 67; home and schools should be harmonious, 69; county newspaper should contain items from pen of supervisor, 69; he should control the selection of teachers, 70; selection of text-books should be left largely with supervisor, 70; close relation should exist between supervisor and directors, 71; directors and supervisors should meet for consultation, 71; methods of supervisor considered, 72; moral atmosphere of school should be observed, 72; teacher's register should be inspected, 72; supervisor should have controlling voice in the erection of schoolhouses, 73; teacher and supervisor should be observant of comfort of pupils, 73; cleanliness should be promoted, 73; advantages of a well-arranged schoolhouse, 73; beautiful environments should be created, 73; appeal for classical art and music in the schools, 74; as to purpose of rural-school supervision, inspires the teacher, stimulates the pupils, and improves the condition of the schoolhouse, 75; teacher should be engaged by the year, 78; school year lengthened to a full year, 78; school year in several localities, 79; obstacles set by incompetent supervision in employment of teachers, 79; more definite tests of fitness for supervision required, 79; associations in most of the states, 80; local associations of rural teachers, 80; summer schools, 80; what they should be, 80; institutes as organized in the West, 81; county institutes exert an influence for good, 81; reading circles may be made very efficient, 81; libraries in country towns, 82; belonging to the school a necessity, 82; professional libraries for use of teachers recommended, 82; normal schools do not fully prepare teachers for rural schools, 83; proportion of trained teachers in rural schools, 83; early normal schools, 83; the subcommittee's idea of needed normal schools, 85; teachers' training classes cannot take the place of training schools, 88; school-garden system fully explained, 89; scope and character of examination of teachers discussed, 90; school year must be lengthened, 93; existing agencies for supply of rural teachers do not suffice, 93.

SUPPLY OF TEACHERS, subcommittee to consider subject, 9; line of inquiry to be pursued, 9; subject discussed, 11; report of subcommittee, 77; that schools may be supplied with better teachers, conditions must change, 77; distinction between teachers is seldom made, 77; must be engaged for school year, 78; obstacles set in way of employment by supervision, 79; recognized agencies for improvement of, 80; reading circles, their object, 81; teachers helped by libraries, 82; the normal school was first devised by rural teachers, 83; the normal-school standard is often too far removed from rural teachers, 84; an intermediate agency desirable, 85; rural teachers often cannot afford time and expense of extended normal course, 85; a summer normal term suggested for rural teachers, 86; two possible agencies in preparation of rural teachers, 87; training classes an effective auxiliary, 87; cannot take the place of training schools, 88; teachers of rural schools are largely without professional preparation, 93; one-half the teachers in the United States teach in the ungraded school, 94.

SUTTON, W. S., Texas, made member committee to submit plan for investigating the rural-school problem, 7; member of committee to investigate rural-school problem, 7; member Subcommittee on School Maintenance, 8; reports from Subcommittee on

School Maintenance, 20; reports from committee on rural-school problem, 5; paper by, on work of Thomas Arnold, 205.

TAXATION, Massachusetts adds to school fund by, 25; New Jersey adds by income from certain riparian rights, 25; schools must depend on some form of, 26; percentage derived from, compared with permanent fund, 26; funds from state treasury indispensable, 26; old plan in Massachusetts, 26; local units are often too poor to carry the burdens, 27; legislature in Ohio may make provision for, 27; country divided between two or more units, 27; percentage raised by local, 27; political and economical conditions often govern, 27; per cents. raised by state and local, by divisions of states, 27; large per cent. of total revenue comes from local, 28; grounds and buildings should be purchased by local, 28; where towns and townships are a large taxing unit, 27; local taxes in New England, 27; incorporated villages, towns, and cities are units of, 29; special districts as a taxing unit, 29; dwellers in cities better able to pay than those in the country, 29; varies in many states, 30; state tax for school purposes in several states, 32; division of, between state and local communities, 34; how distributed in several states, 35; distribution of railroad, telephone, and telegraph tax, 40; superiority of town or township tax as a taxing unit, 42; one-third of money should be by local, 52; a county tax in all the county systems, 53; a town or township tax, 53; larger units must help smaller ones, 54; taxes raised on city property distributed among rural schools, 61; a supplemental aid, 127; poll tax in California applied to school revenue, 130.

TEACHERS, electing, employing, paying, and improvement of, through meetings, topics of inquiry, 9; supply for rural schools discussed, 14; essential qualities, 15; table of salaries by states, 15; ability and characte ishould be secured, conditions governing, 43; tendency to employ for longer term, 42; employment of, in undistricted towns, 43; number in common schools of Ohio, 44; are treated and paid alike under county system, 46; number of, would be diminished by consolidation of schools, 46; ratio of the number required to number employed, 47; changes frequent under district system, 47; better teachers attained through consolidation of schools, 49; towns receiving aid should employ teachers holding state certificates, 53; needed legislation as to supply of, 54; where the number is too large for one supervisor, 59; demand for normal graduates makes high salaries, 61; rural schools suffer through want of trained teachers, 61; teaching an art, 62; duty of the expert supervisor, 62; teaching defined, 63; fewer teachers and better qualifications, 63; relation of supervisor to, 65; meeting of teachers should be arranged for, 67; supervisor can exert an influence in support of teacher by parents, 69; as to questions for examination, 70; directors contract with, 70; teacher should observe the comfort of pupils, 73; good teacher is not satisfied with a memoriter recitation, 97; five teachers can teach one hundred pupils in a union school, 98; receive small salaries in rural schools, 98; what the teacher should have the pupil understand as to his habitat, 103; special appropriation to secure skilled teachers, 107; should seldom employ a monitor, 111; assistance rendered by advanced pupils, 111; teachers and children need the inspiration of numbers, 123; same qualification demanded for rural as city schools, 133; suggestions to rural teachers on enrichment of course of study, 142; should secure from Weather Bureau copy of weather maps, 147; negro teachers for negro schools, 185; institutions for preparation of, in Ontario, 198; 66 per cent. are trained in Manitoba, 199; teachers in Norway, 201; qualities of improved, 205; benefits derived through agricultural extension, 204; special provisions for, in continuous sessions of normal schools, 207; special work in moral training, 207; should be an example of what he is to teach, 207; should have as much care for development of character as of the intellect, 207.

TELEGRAPHS, distribution of taxes levied upon, 40.

TELEPHONES, distribution of taxes levied upon, 40.

TENNESSEE, qualifications required of school superintendents in, 66.

TEXAS, magnificent possibilities of permanent fund, 25; distribution of tax levied upon telephones, telegraphs, and railroads, 40; the community system defined, 45; qualifications required of school superintendents in, 66; working of school-fund system, 126.

TOWN- OR TOWNSHIP-UNIT SYSTEM, defined and explained, 22; Ohio law historical, 22; comparative relations, 22; when a large taxing unit, 27; congressional endowment of public lands, 35; superiority of, as a taxing unit, with reasons, 42; relation of township-unit system to consolidation, 42; adoption of the unit system followed by other reforms, 42; town-unit system an early idea, 43; benefits resulting from an undistricted town, 43; one trustee manages the schools of a township in Indiana, 44; superiority of township system, 44; great possibilities for improvement through consolidation in, 49; first step taken in consolidation where township-unit system exists, 50; there should be only one school in a township or town, 50; consolidation must depend upon local factors, 50; consolidation depends upon township-unit system in the North, 50; good roads a helpful element of consolidation, 50; a town or township tax urged, 53; system in use in New England, 58; operation of the two methods of supervision, 58; combination of towns for supervisory purposes, 59; township or county the proper unit of organization, 132; comparative cost of township and district systems, 133; arguments for consolidation and transportation considered, 135.

TRAINING CLASSES, an effective auxiliary in preparing teachers, 87; details relating to, 88; cannot take the place of training schools, 88.

TRANSPORTATION OF PUPILS, discussed, 13, 19; where rural schools are consolidated, 46; the reform should not be misunderstood, 50; to central districts, 108; collection of pupils into larger units than the district school, 108; contentration of higher grades of pupils, 108; township system the probable solution, 135; arguments by A. W. Edson in favor of consolidation and transportation, 135; arguments in favor of, 136; good results of the transportation system, 136; notice to bidders for transportation of pupils, 139; cost of transportation, 140; results in Crane School, Quincy, Mass., 141.

UNION SCHOOLS, none better than, 135.

UNIT OF ORGANIZATION, remarks on, 12; terms town and township explained, 22; Ohio law historical, 22; superiority of township system, 44; when town or township system should be substituted for district system, 54.

UTAH, salaries paid teachers in, 15; qualifications required of school superintendents in, 17; Congress gave public lands for school fund, 35.

VERMONT, normal school opened at Concord, by S. R. Hall, 83; adopts plan of collecting pupils into larger units, 107; law enacted creating county superintendents, 21; average daily attendance of pupils in, 47; report as to ungraded school attendance in, 95; manner of apportioning school-tax income, 36; salaries paid teachers in, 15.

VIRGINIA, salaries paid teachers in, 15; visitation of schools, supervisor's methods considered, 72; moral atmosphere should be observed, 72; teacher's register should be inspected, 72; teacher should pursue usual routine, 72; private register should be kept by supervisor, 72; inspection of school by supervisor, 73.

WAGES, tables of, paid rural teachers, by states, 15.

WELLS, O. E., Wisconsin, as to amount of property assessed for schools, 30; reports small attendance in isolated and detached schools, 46.

WESTERN STATES, per cents. of moneys raised by state and local taxation, 27.

WEST VIRGINIA, salaries paid teachers in, 15; qualifications required of school superintendents in, 67.

WHITE, E. E., Ohio, views of classification, 99; facts that enter into the problem, 161; common method of grading the country schools, 163; feasible modifications, 164; the three-grade solution, 165; course of study, 165; three-grade programme, 166; hopeful improvement lies in simpler grading, 168; advantages of dividing course of study into three groups, 168; a needed reduction of class exercises, 168; a workable programme, 160; provision made for individual progress, 170; graphic illustration of an ideal one-teacher school, 170.

WINONA, plan of continuous sessions of normal school, 207.

WISCONSIN, salaries paid teachers in, 15; statement as to amount of property assessed per scholar, 29; township system permissible in, 44; laws contain all that is necessary to enable consolidation, 50; qualifications required of school superintendents in, 66.

WOLFE, L. E., Missouri, made member committee to investigate rural-school problem, 7, 8; member Subcommittee on Instruction and Discipline, 10; reports from Subcommittee on Instruction and Discipline, 94; statement by, supplementary to report, 113; present condition and trend of rural-school grading and classification in the United States, 113; instruction in the same class of pupils more than one year apart in advancement, 113; objection to doctrine of the report, 116; reports from committee to investigate rural-school problem, 5.

WRITING, suggestions relating to teaching, 158; programme for, 167, 170, 184; plan of a course of study in, 172; there should be much written work provided for the rural schools, 106.

WYOMING, salaries paid teachers in, 15.

ZOÖLOGY, study of domestic animals, 156.

INDEX TO REPORT

PAGE

ABSTRACTS,
of statistical reports of school commissioners and city superintendents........................8-22, 34-35
of financial reports of school commissioners and city superintendents.............................. 23-33

ALBANY,
report of Charles W. Cole, city superintendent..... 431

ALBANY NORMAL COLLEGE,
report of executive committee.................... 133

ALLEGANY AND CATTARAUGUS RESERVATION,
report of William K. Harrison, superintendent..... 551

AMERICAN MUSEUM OF NATURAL HISTORY,
report of Prof. A. S. Bickmore.................. 223

AMSTERDAM,
report of Charles S. Davis, city superintendent..... 438

APPEALS,
table of decisions in........................... 67
decisions in.................................... 77

APPENDIX,
exhibit No. 1, views of normal school buildings.... 974-975
exhibit No. 2, council of school superintendents.... 977
exhibit No. 3, New York state association of school commissioners and superintendents............. 1073
exhibit No. 4, State teachers' association.......... 1129
exhibit No. 5, patriotic instruction in the public schools....................................... 1277
exhibit No. 6, report of the committee of twelve.... 1307

APPORTIONMENT OF SCHOOL MONEYS, PAGE
table 5
statistics concerning 56

ARBOR DAY xxxvii
1. Law establishing arbor day 957
2. Letter of State Superintendent to teachers 959
3. Letter of State Superintendent to children 960
4. Arbor day in Spain 962
5. How to plant trees 962
6. Suggestions for programs 963
7. Specimen programs 964
8. Selections appropriate for arbor day programs 965

ASSOCIATION OF SCHOOL COMMISSIONERS AND SUPERINTENDENTS,
proceedings of 1073

ATTENDANCE,
statistics of 45

AUBURN,
report of B. B. Snow, city superintendent 439

BINGHAMTON,
report of R. H. Halsey, city superintendent 440

BLIND, INSTITUTION FOR,
report of superintendent W. B. Wait 577

BROCKPORT NORMAL AND TRAINING SCHOOL,
report of local board 147

BROOKLYN,
report of Wm. H. Maxwell, city superintendent 443

BUFFALO,
report of Henry P. Emerson, city superintendent 444

BUFFALO NORMAL AND TRAINING SCHOOL,
report of local board 156

CENSUS,
biennial xv
the law and its enforcement 935
specimen blanks used 941

CENSUS—*Continued* PAGE
tabulation of attendance........................ 944
tabulation of special statistics.................... 948

CENTRAL NEW YORK INSTITUTION FOR DEAF-MUTES,
report of principal.............................. 565

CERTIFICATES,
commissioners', uniform examinations for......... 579
state.. 733
tabulated statement of.......................... 750
to whom issued in 1897......................... 751
program of examination, 1898.................... 752
statistical table................................ 752
college graduates'.............................. 773

CHARTS, GRAPHIC,
on school statistics............................. 64–65

CHILDREN,
statistics concerning........................... 45

CHILD STUDY,
report of Anna K. Eggleston..................... 873
New York society for............................ 882

CITY SUPERINTENDENTS OF SCHOOLS,
statistical reports, abstract of................... 11
list of... 429
written reports of............................... 431
state council of, proceedings................... 977

CITY TRAINING SCHOOLS xxv

COHOES,
report of Geo. E. Dixon, city superintendent....... 448

COLLEGE GRADUATES' CERTIFICATES,
1. Law of 1888, as amended, authorizing.......... 775
2. List of certificates issued, 1897................. 778
3. List of normal diplomas indorsed, 1897......... 780
4. List of state certificates indorsed, 1897......... 780

COMPULSORY EDUCATION.......................... xiii
reports of inspectors under compulsory education law........................ 917

COMMISSIONERS, PAGE
course of study.............................. xxv
list of.............................. 263
districts.............................. 265
written reports.............................. 272

CORNELL UNIVERSITY,
state scholarships in.............................. 757
law and rules governing.............................. 759
examination questions for scholarships.............................. 765
list of state scholars.............................. 769

CORNING,
report of Leigh R. Hunt, city superintendent....... 449

CORTLAND NORMAL AND TRAINING SCHOOL,
report of local board.............................. 162

COUNCIL OF SCHOOL SUPERINTENDENTS............ 977

COURSE OF STUDY FOR COMMON SCHOOLS xxv
questions for examinations, 1896-97............... 707

CURFEW, THE.............................. xxxviii

DEAF AND DUMB, INSTITUTIONS FOR,
1. List of superintendents.............................. 558
2. Reports of superintendents:
New York Institution for the Instruction of Deaf and Dumb.............................. 559
Institution for the Improved Instruction of Deaf-Mutes, New York.................. 562
St. Joseph's Institute for the Improved Instruction of Deaf-Mutes...................... 564
Central New York Institution for Deaf-Mutes. 564
Western New York Institution for Deaf-Mutes. 566
Le Couteulx St. Mary's Institution for the Improved Instruction of Deaf-Mutes.......... 571
Northern New York Institution for Deaf-Mutes. 572
Albany Home School for the Deaf........... 575
3. Statistical table.............................. 576

	PAGE
DECISIONS IN APPEAL CASES,	
table of	67
by State Superintendent	77
DEFECTIVE SCHOOLS	xxix
DISTRICT QUOTA,	
statistics concerning	55
DISTRICTS,	
statistics concerning school	43
commissioner, list of	265
DUNKIRK,	
report of J. W. Babcock, city superintendent	450
EGGLESTON, ANNA K.,	
child study	873
ELMIRA,	
report of E. J. Beardsley, city superintendent	451
EDUCATIONAL ASSOCIATIONS	xxxix
EVIL LITERATURE	xxxvii
EXAMINATIONS,	
licensing of teachers	xvii
uniform	579
state	733
Cornell	757
EXHIBITS,	
1. Statistical tables, 1897	1
2. General school statistics	41
3. Decisions of State Superintendent in appeal cases	65
4. Normal schools	129
5. American Museum of Natural History	221
6. School commissioners	261
7. City superintendents of schools	427
8. Village superintendents of schools	503
9. Indian schools	548
10. Institutions for defectives	557
11. Uniform examinations for commissioners' certificates	579

EXHIBITS—*Continued* PAGE

12. State certificates.............................. 733
13. State scholarships in Cornell university......... 757
14. College graduates' certificates—indorsement of normal diplomas and state certificates issued in other states.............................. 773
15. Teachers' institutes.......................... 781
16. Teachers' training classes...................... 815
17. Child study.................................. 871
18. Compulsory education 914
19. Second biennial school census................. 933
20. Arbor day.................................... 953

APPENDIX

1. Views of normal school buildings............... 974–975
2. State council of school superintendents......... 975
3. State association of school commissioners and superintendents.............................. 1071
4. State teachers' association.................... 1129
5. Patriotic instruction in the public schools....... 1277
6. Report of the committee of twelve.............. 1307

EXPENDITURES 61

FLAGS ON SCHOOLHOUSES........................... xxxv

FINANCIAL ABSTRACTS,
of commissioners.............................. 23, 28
of superintendents............................. 26, 31

FREDONIA NORMAL AND TRAINING SCHOOL,
report of local board........................... 167

FREE SCHOOL FUND,
statistics concerning 60

GENERAL SCHOOL STATISTICS 41

GENESEO NORMAL AND TRAINING SCHOOL,
report of local board........................... 171

GENEVA,
report of W. H. Truesdale, city superintendent..... 452

PAGE

GLOVERSVILLE,
report of James A. Estee, city superintendent...... 454

HEALTH AND DECENCY,
act.. 411
report of school commissioners relative to......... 413

HORNELLSVILLE,
report of W. R. Prentice, city superintendent...... 456

HUDSON,
report of F. J. Sagendorph, city superintendent.... 458

INDIAN SCHOOLS,
1. Names and addresses of superintendents....... 551
2. Reports of superintendents:
William K. Harrison, Allegany and Cattaraugus reservation 551
W. W. Newman, Onondaga reservation....... 552
Calvin O. Harvey, St. Regis reservation....... 553
J. S. Raynor, Shinnecock and Poospatuck reservation............................... 553
Charles C. Parker, Tonawanda reservation.... 554
William P. Mentz, Tuscarora reservation..... 555
3. Statistical table............................ 555

INSTITUTES................................... xxi
report of supervisor.......................... 783
reports of conductors......................... 797

INSTITUTION FOR THE BLIND 577

INSTITUTIONS FOR THE IMPROVED INSTRUCTION OF DEAF-MUTES 562

INSTITUTIONS FOR THE DEAF AND DUMB........... 559

ITHACA,
report of H. W. Foster, city superintendent....... 461

JAMAICA NORMAL AND TRAINING SCHOOL,
statement concerning.......................... 176

JAMESTOWN,
report of Rovillus R. Rogers, city superintendent... 464

JOHNSTOWN,
report of W. S. Snyder, city superintendent........ 465

EXHIBITS—*Continued* PAGE

12. State certificates.............................. 733
13. State scholarships in Cornell university......... 757
14. College graduates' certificates—indorsement of normal diplomas and state certificates issued in other states............................ 773
15. Teachers' institutes........................... 781
16. Teachers' training classes..................... 815
17. Child study.................................... 871
18. Compulsory education 914
19. Second biennial school census.................. 933
20. Arbor day...................................... 953

APPENDIX

1. Views of normal school buildings............... 974–975
2. State council of school superintendents......... 975
3. State association of school commissioners and superintendents.............................. 1071
4. State teachers' association.................... 1129
5. Patriotic instruction in the public schools....... 1277
6. Report of the committee of twelve.............. 1307

EXPENDITURES 61

FLAGS ON SCHOOLHOUSES.......................... xxxv

FINANCIAL ABSTRACTS,
of commissioners.............................. 23, 28
of superintendents............................ 26, 31

FREDONIA NORMAL AND TRAINING SCHOOL,
report of local board.......................... 167

FREE SCHOOL FUND,
statistics concerning 60

GENERAL SCHOOL STATISTICS 41

GENESEO NORMAL AND TRAINING SCHOOL,
report of local board.......................... 171

GENEVA,
report of W. H. Truesdale, city superintendent...... 452

GLOVERSVILLE,	PAGE
report of James A. Estee, city superintendent	454
HEALTH AND DECENCY,	
act	411
report of school commissioners relative to	413
HORNELLSVILLE,	
report of W. R. Prentice, city superintendent	456
HUDSON,	
report of F. J. Sagendorph, city superintendent	458
INDIAN SCHOOLS,	
1. Names and addresses of superintendents	551
2. Reports of superintendents:	
William K. Harrison, Allegany and Cattaraugus reservation	551
W. W. Newman, Onondaga reservation	552
Calvin O. Harvey, St. Regis reservation	553
J. S. Raynor, Shinnecock and Poospatuck reservation	553
Charles C. Parker, Tonawanda reservation	554
William P. Mentz, Tuscarora reservation	555
3. Statistical table	555
INSTITUTES	xxi
report of supervisor	783
reports of conductors	797
INSTITUTION FOR THE BLIND	577
INSTITUTIONS FOR THE IMPROVED INSTRUCTION OF DEAF-MUTES	562
INSTITUTIONS FOR THE DEAF AND DUMB	559
ITHACA,	
report of H. W. Foster, city superintendent	461
JAMAICA NORMAL AND TRAINING SCHOOL,	
statement concerning	176
JAMESTOWN,	
report of Rovillus R. Rogers, city superintendent	464
JOHNSTOWN,	
report of W. S. Snyder, city superintendent	465

	PAGE
KINGSTON,	
report of Charles M. Ryon, city superintendent....	467
LE COUTEULX ST. MARY'S INSTITUTION FOR IMPROVED INSTRUCTION OF DEAF-MUTES,	
report of principal...........................	571
LIBRARIES.	
school..	xxvi
statistics of.................................	63
teachers' state...............................	xxviii
LICENSES, TEACHERS',......................	xvii
statistics concerning.........................	54
LITTLE FALLS,	
report of Thomas A. Caswell, city superintendent..	469
LOCKPORT,	
report of Emmet Belknap, city superintendent.....	470
LONG ISLAND CITY,	
report of John E. Shull, city superintendent........	471
MIDDLETOWN,	
report of J. F. Tuthill, city superintendent.........	472
MT. VERNON,	
report of C. E. Nichols, city superintendent.......	474
NEWBURGH,	
report of R. V. K. Montfort, city superintendent...	475
NEW PALTZ NORMAL AND TRAINING SCHOOL,	
report of local board.........................	177
NEW YORK,	
report of John Jasper, city superintendent........	476
NEW YORK CITY SCHOOLS......................	xxix
NEW YORK INSTITUTION FOR THE INSTRUCTION OF DEAF AND DUMB,	
report of principal...........................	559
NEW YORK STATE ASSOCIATION OF SCHOOL COMMISSIONERS AND SUPERINTENDENTS................	1071
NIAGARA FALLS,	
report of N. L. Benham, city superintendent.......	479

NORTH TONAWANDA, PAGE
report of Clinton S. Marsh, city superintendent.... 480

NORMAL SCHOOLS.............................. xvi
1. List of schools, principals and officers of local boards.............................. 131
2. Reports of local boards:
Albany.............................. 133
Brockport.............................. 147
Buffalo.............................. 156
Cortland.............................. 162
Fredonia.............................. 167
Geneseo.............................. 171
Jamaica.............................. 176
New Paltz.............................. 177
Oneonta.............................. 183
Oswego.............................. 187
Plattsburgh.............................. 195
Potsdam.............................. 198
3. Regulations concerning admission.............. 206
4. Statistical tables.............................. 210
5. Meetings of normal school principals; secretary's report.............................. 215

NORMAL SCHOOL BUILDINGS,
views of.............................. 974–975

NORMAL SCHOOL DIPLOMAS,
issued in other states, list of diplomas indorsed..... 780

NORTHERN NEW YORK INSTITUTION FOR DEAF-MUTES,
report of superintendent.............................. 572

OGDENSBURGH,
report of Barney Whitney, city superintendent.... 482

OLEAN,
report of Fox Holden, city superintendent......... 483

ONEONTA NORMAL AND TRAINING SCHOOL,
report of local board.............................. 183

OSWEGO, PAGE
report of Geo. E. Bullis, city superintendent....... 484

OSWEGO NORMAL AND TRAINING SCHOOL,
report of local board........................... 187

PARIS EXPOSITION xxxvi

PATRIOTIC INSTRUCTION xxxiii
to promote study in public schools................ 1277

PHYSIOLOGY AND HYGIENE xxxvii

PLATTSBURGH NORMAL AND TRAINING SCHOOL,
report of local board........................... 195

POUGHKEEPSIE,
report of Edward Burgess, city superintendent..... 486

POTSDAM NORMAL AND TRAINING SCHOOL,
report of local board........................... 198

PUBLIC MONEYS,
received and apportioned, statistics concerning.... 56
receipts and payments common school fund........ 57
receipts and payments free school fund........... 60

QUOTAS, DISTRICT,
statistics concerning............................ 55

RETIREMENT OF TEACHERS xxxii

REGISTRATION,
number of pupils registered...................... 53

RENSSELAER,
report of R. W. Wickham, city superintendent..... 487

REPORTS,
of school commissioners, statistical abstracts...... 8
of school commissioners, financial abstracts........ 23
of school commissioners, written................. 272
of local boards of normal schools................. 133
of city superintendents, statistical................ 16, 21
of city superintendents, financial................. 26, 31
of city superintendents, written.................. 431
of village superintendents, written................ 507
of American Museum of Natural History.......... 223

REPORTS—*Continued* PAGE
of institute conductors.......................... 797
of superintendents of Indian schools.............. 551
of superintendents of institutions for defectives.... 559
of teachers' institutes.......................... 783
of teachers' training classes.................... 817
of inspectors under compulsory education law...... 917

ROCHESTER,
report of Milton Noyes, city superintendent....... 488

ROME,
report of Harrison T. Morrow, city superintendent.. 489

RURAL SCHOOL PROBLEM.......................... xi

SALARIES OF TEACHERS.......................... ix

SCHENECTADY,
report of S. B. Howe, city superintendent......... 490

SCHOOL A STATE, NOT A LOCAL INSTITUTION........ xii

SCHOOL ARCHITECTURE........................... xxxv

SCHOOL BUILDINGS,
views of normal.............................. 974-975

SCHOOL COMMISSIONERS,
statistical reports of, abstract from............ 8
financial reports of, abstract from.............. 22
names and post-office addresses of............... 263
school commissioner districts.................... 265
written reports of............................... 272
act relating to health and decency............... 411
reports of school commissioners relative to the health and decency act....................... 413

SCHOOL COMMISSIONER DISTRICTS,
towns composing.................................. 265

SCHOOL DISTRICTS.............................. x
statistics concerning............................ 43

SCHOOL LIBRARIES.............................. xxvi
statistics concerning............................ 63

ST. REGIS RESERVATION, PAGE
report of Calvin O. Harvey, superintendent........ 553

STATISTICS,
graphic.................................64–65, 214–215
comparative.............................. 38, 39
general.................................. 41
tables................................... xl

SUMMER INSTITUTES........................ xxii
Chautauqua............................... 787
Thousand Island park..................... 791
Glens Falls.............................. 794

SUPERINTENDENTS OF CITY SCHOOLS,
list of.................................. 429

SUPERINTENDENTS AND PRINCIPALS OF GRADED SCHOOLS,
list of.................................. 415

SUPERINTENDENTS OF VILLAGE SCHOOLS,
list of.................................. 505

SYRACUSE,
report of A. B. Blodgett, city superintendent....... 492

TAX,
state, levied for common schools................. 3

TEACHERS,
licensing of............................. xvii
salaries of.............................. ix
statistics concerning.................... 53

TEACHERS' INSTITUTES...................... xxi
Names and addresses of institute conductors....... 783
1. Report of supervisor A. S. Downing............ 783
2. Reports of institute conductors and instructors:
Henry R. Sanford......................... 797
Isaac H. Stout........................... 798
Welland Hendrick......................... 799
Archibald C. McLachlan................... 800
Percy I. Bugbee.......................... 802

TEACHERS' INSTITUTES—*Continued*

3. Reports of drawing and primary work: PAGE
   - Gratia L. Rice.............................. 802
   - Florence B. Himes.......................... 806
   - Anna K. Eggleston.......................... 806
   - Summer (see summer institutes)............. 786
4. Law regulating attendance and closing of schools. 808
5. Statistical tables:
   - List of institutes held from August 31, 1896, to May 31,1897, showing attendance........ 812
   - Comparative summary for fifteen years....... 786
   - Statement concerning, by State Superintendent................................ xxi

TEACHERS' TRAINING CLASSES.................... xxii

1. Report of Supervisor A. S. Downing........... 817
2. Reports of inspectors:
   - S. W. Maxson............................... 823
   - F. H. Wood................................. 824
   - Willis D. Graves........................... 826
   - Wayland E. Stearns......................... 827
3. Regulations and course of study for........... 828
4. Statistical tables relating to................. 862

TEACHERS' LICENSES,

- comment on xvii
- statistics concerning 54

TEACHERS' SALARIES,

- comment on...................................... ix
- statistics concerning 54

TONAWANDA RESERVATION,

- report of Charles C. Parker, superintendent........ 554

TROY,

- report of John H. Willetts, city superintendent.... 494

TUSCARORA RESERVATION,

- report of William P. Mentz, superintendent........ 555

UNIFORM EXAMINATIONS FOR COMMISSIONERS' CERTIFICATES, PAGE
1. Regulations governing uniform examinations.... 581
2. Questions submitted at examinations from July 31, 1896, to July 31, 1897.................... 589
3. Statistical table showing results by commissioner districts.................................. 686
4. List of first grade certificates granted by school commissioners from July 31, 1896, to July 31, 1897...................................... 689
5. List of first grade certificates renewed by school commissioners from July 31, 1896, to July 31, 1897...................................... 698
6. Holders of vocal music certificates............. 705
7. Holders of kindergarten certificates............ 706
8. Holders of special drawing certificates.......... 706

UTICA,
report of George Griffith, city superintendent...... 495

VIEWS OF NORMAL SCHOOL BUILDINGS............. 974–975

VILLAGE SUPERINTENDENTS OF SCHOOLS,
1. List of.................................... 505
2. Written reports of.......................... 507

WATERTOWN,
report of William G. Williams, city superintendent. 500

WATERVLIET,
report of A. M. Wright, acting city superintendent.. 501

WESTERN NEW YORK INSTITUTION FOR DEAF-MUTES,
report of superintendent........................ 566

YONKERS,
report of C. E. Gorton, city superintendent........ 501

Lightning Source UK Ltd.
Milton Keynes UK
UKHW012135180219
337529UK00012B/1369/P

9 781527 995130